The **Rough Guide** to

# Kerala

written and researched by

## David Abram

www.roughguides.com

# Contents

**Playing gods** colour section following p.112

**Elephant madness** colour section following p.240

◄◄ Backwaters near Alappuzha ◄ Mural, Aranmula

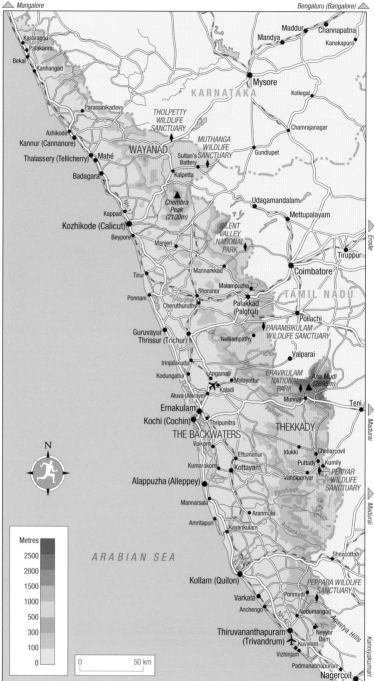

# Introduction to
# Kerala

**Green and gold are the defining colours of Kerala: green for the tropical lushness that bursts from every patch of ground in the state; gold for the prosperity that has for many thousands of years been a consequence of this abundance. You see the two in combination everywhere, in the borders of the white cotton *mundu* worn by Keralan men, in the ceremonial umbrellas hoisted over temple deities as they're processed on elephant back during festivals, and in the make-up of the *kathakali* hero, framed by his trademark jewel-encrusted headdress.**

Gold and green will also dominate your first impressions of Kerala if, like most travellers, you arrive by plane from the Arabian Sea. Landing at Thiruvananthapuram (Trivandrum) or Kochi (Cochin), a flash of vivid golden sand brings the ocean to an abrupt end, giving way to a carpet of vegetation: bands of shaggy coconut palms interwoven by tangled rivers, canals, lagoons and water-logged rice paddy that stretch to a horizon bounded by forested mountains.

The lower slopes of the Western Ghats, less than 100km inland, are the source of the **spices** that drew traders from across the world to the shore known for centuries as the Malabar Coast. Ships from ancient Rome, China, the Arabian peninsula, Portugal, Holland and Great Britain sailed to India's southwestern seaboard to fill their holds with pepper, as well as cinnamon, cardamom and ginger. They brought with them a cornucopia of new ideas, technologies, foodstuffs and religions, which the Keralans embraced and made their own.

Scan the skyline of any town in the state today and you'll see, rising from the red-tiled rooftops alongside mosque minarets and the brass finials of Hindu temples, whitewashed church gables whose congregations claim descent from converts evangelized by Saint Thomas in the first century AD. In Fort Cochin, the region's pre-eminent colonial trading post, cantilevered fishing

5

∎

## Fact file

• Edged by 580km of coastline, Kerala is 130km wide at its broadest point and covers a total surface area of 38,863 square kilometres; it takes around twelve hours to ride from one end to the other by train.

• In March 2001 (the date of the last census) the population of Kerala stood at 31.8 million, of whom 56 percent were Hindu, 25 percent Muslim and 19 percent Christian.

• Both the literacy rate (91 percent) and life expectancy (73 years) are the highest in India. GDP weighs in at Rs37,500 (£545/$845) per capita, bolstered by remittances sent from overseas (one in six Keralans work abroad).

• Malayalam is the official language of the state and the mother tongue of nearly all Keralans (also known as "Malayalis"). English is most people's second language, and is widely spoken in large towns, resorts and in businesses across the state.

• Keralans consume more alcohol per head of population than any other Indian state, with sales in excess of $1.2 billion annually – a major source of tax revenue for the government.

nets introduced by Chinese immigrants hang like giant predators along a waterfront dotted with Portuguese *palacios*, Dutch merchants' mansions, British warehouses and Jewish synagogues.

Adaptability and openness to the outside world continue to be central to the Keralan character. When recession started to bite in the 1970s, many **Malayalis** (a name derived from the official state language, Malayalam) left to work in the Persian Gulf. Now remittance cheques sent home by them account for 25 percent of GDP. Behind the state's economic success story lies its long-standing policy of **universal education**. Thanks to enthusiastic patronage from the region's ruling maharajas and, after Independence, successive communist governments, Kerala enjoys the highest literacy rates of any Indian region and has led the field when it comes to gender equality and family planning.

Yet while innovation has always been central to Kerala's prosperity, Malayalis remain

◄ Tea plantation

staunchly **conservative**. Traditional dress is the norm, even in the cities, while the old hierarchy of caste, in spite of decades of social reform, continues to dominate political life. From the visitor's point of view, this can have its downsides – not least the fact that most temples remain off-limits to non-Hindus. But it also accounts for the survival of

▲ Houseboat on the backwaters

Kerala's extraordinary **traditional arts scene**. A wealth of Malayali music, dance and ritual drama forms continue to be widely performed and enjoyed across the state, in precisely the same contexts as they have for centuries. One of the world's most elaborate systems of holistic medicine, **ayurveda**, has also been kept alive for thousands of years in Kerala, where it now enjoys a new lease of life as a spa therapy.

Moreover, thanks to Kerala's go-ahead tourism industry, you can enjoy these unique cultural phenomena from the comfort of some truly wonderful **accommodation**. Whether an ancestral *tharavadu* mansion made of teak or a converted *kettu vallam* rice barge in the backwaters, a British tea planter's bungalow high in the Cardamom Hills or a royal hunting lodge lost in the jungle, heritage hotels and homestays run by local families offer plenty of excuses to get off the beaten track and will deepen your experience of a region that, for all its paradoxes and contradictions, never fails to astonish.

# Where to go

Kerala's largest city and administrative capital is **Thiruvananthapuram** (Trivandrum), in the far south of the state, but its principal tourist hub, where the majority of travellers first alight, is the former colonial trading port of **Kochi**, 220km further north. Facing the modern metropolis of **Ernakulam** from across the harbour, the time-worn backstreets of **Fort Cochin**, lined by old Portuguese, Dutch and British houses, provide the main focus for visitors, with a broad choice of homestays and heritage hotels, and atmospheric little restaurants, cafés and art galleries. Fronted by a channel that's still busy night and day with maritime traffic, Fort Cochin's iconic Chinese fishing nets are the defining feature of the waterfront, but

you'll see dozens more of these quirky contraptions dangling from riverbanks in the **backwaters** to the south. Boats and punted canoes ferry sightseers out of Fort Cochin each morning to typical lagoon- and river-side villages where life, dominated by inshore fishing, crab farming and coir production, seems little affected by the presence up the highway of a major city.

For trips deeper into the famous **Kuttanad** backwaters, however, the market town of **Alappuzha**, a couple of hours' drive south of Kochi, is the best springboard, particularly if, like tens of thousands of visitors each year, you want to explore the region in a converted rice barge. A fleet of nearly 500 handsome old *kettu vallam*, capped with elegant coir canopies, waits on the outskirts to whisk passengers over the glassy expanse of Vembanad Lake, or along the network of palm-fringed canals and rivers crisscrossing this densely populated rice-growing area. For a more hands-on experience, you can also jump on one of the clapped-out local ferries connecting Kuttanad's myriad settlements, or stay a few nights in one of the many heritage homestays occupying antique, gable-roofed *tharavadukal* houses.

The southern gateway to Kuttanad is the old spice port of **Kollam (Quilon)**, a popular stop for travellers en route to or from the nearby beach resort of **Varkala**, with its spectacular red cliffs and famous temple. Hindus have come to the village's sacred white-sand beach for many centuries to immerse the ashes of recently deceased loved ones in the sea. But pilgrims these days are far outnumbered but the ranks of sun-worshipping backpackers who congregate on the beach and clifftop cafés overlooking it.

The state's other main resort, **Kovalam**, further south, is looking a little jaded these days, but serves as a convenient base for day-trips into **Thiruvananthapuram**, where you can shop for traditional Keralan metalwork, admire the elegant lines of the old palace and temple, or browse some of the region's best museums. Rising alluringly inland, the forested hills around the reservoir at nearby **Neyyar Dam** offer an easy retreat when the heat becomes too much.

Running in a virtually unbroken line along the length of Kerala, the mighty **Western Ghats** encompass a region that's radically different from the coastal plains, with vast tea gardens and coffee plantations wrapped around the flanks of jagged, grass-topped mountain peaks. Wild elephant, tigers and rare lion-tailed macaques, to name but three of the seventy or more species of mammals to be found in the Ghats, inhabit more remote tracts of forest. A former royal hunting reserve centred on a man-made lake, the **Periyar Wildlife Sanctuary** has long been the first stop of visiting wildlife enthusiasts, but its burgeoning popularity has lately encouraged more discerning travellers to explore forest zones further north in the range, around the spectacularly situated tea station of **Munnar**, or the hidden valley of the **Parambikulam Wildlife Sanctuary**.

To reach Parambikulam you'll have to cross the lush paddy fields of the Nila region, dominated by the holy **Bharatapuzha River**. This is the heartland of the state's traditional culture, where the martial-art-influenced **kathakali** dance-drama, and its ancient Sanskrit predecessor, **kudiyattam**, originated, along with the female classical dance form, **mohiniyattam**. Performances of all of these are a regular feature of life in **Thrissur**, seat of the former ruling dynasty, although this prosperous town is better known for its annual **Puram** festival in May, when ranks of sumptuously decorated elephants lead processions of massed drum orchestras, backed by extravagant firework displays. Thrissur also celebrates Kerala's colourful **Onam** festival (Aug/Sept) in style, with the astonishing **Pulikali**, or **tiger dance**, in which thousands of masked, painted men descend on the streets in a raucous celebration.

▲ Fishermen, Kollam

Insulated from the tourist enclaves of the south by an eight- to twelve-hour train ride, **northern Kerala** and its capital **Kozhikode (Calicut)** see comparatively few visitors. But the region holds enormous potential for independent travel, with its own distinctive, Muslim-influenced atmosphere and some superb heritage homestays and ayurvedic spas. For most foreign travellers, however, the main incentives to venture up north are the extraordinary Hindu spirit-possession rituals known as **theyyem**, held in villages throughout the winter around the coastal town of **Kannur (Cannanore)**. While you're in the region, other destinations worth extending your trip to reach include the wonderfully unspoilt **Valiyaparamba backwaters**, and the exquisite **Wayanad** hill tract, which holds some of southern India's finest rainforest and mountain scenery, and some superbly situated eco-resorts.

# When to go

The **best time to visit** Kerala is between late December and February, when the skies are clear and humidity at its least debilitating. From March onwards, the heat and stickiness become increasingly uncomfortable in the pre-monsoon build-up. After a month of intense sunshine alleviated by short showers, the rains erupt in earnest in the first week of June, with a massive storm that sweeps off the Arabian Sea. This is considered the auspicious time to begin a course in ayurvedic treatment, but a beach holiday is out as the sand often disappears under the high tides and crashing waves. The second annual monsoon – known as the "retreating" monsoon because its prevailing winds are from the northeast – lasts from October to December. Although lighter than its predecessor, it leaves the skies frequently overcast and is accompanied by high humidity levels.

## Average temperatures and rainfall

| | Jan | Feb | Mar | Apr | May | Jun | Jul | Aug | Sep | Oct | Nov | Dec |
|---|---|---|---|---|---|---|---|---|---|---|---|---|
| **Kochi (Cochin)** | | | | | | | | | | | | |
| Av daily max (°C) | 31 | 31 | 31 | 31 | 31 | 29 | 28 | 28 | 28 | 29 | 30 | 30 |
| Rainfall (mm) | 23 | 20 | 51 | 126 | 297 | 723 | 592 | 353 | 195 | 340 | 178 | 41 |
| **Thiruvananthapuram (Trivandrum)** | | | | | | | | | | | | |
| Av daily max (°C) | 30 | 31 | 32 | 31 | 31 | 29 | 28 | 28 | 28 | 29 | 29 | 30 |
| Rainfall (mm) | 20 | 20 | 43 | 122 | 249 | 331 | 215 | 164 | 123 | 271 | 207 | 73 |

# things not to miss

*It's not possible to see everything that Kerala has to offer in one trip – and we don't suggest you try. What follows, in no particular order, is a selective taste of the region's highlights: idyllic beaches, outstanding monuments, spectacular festivals and great places to stay. They're arranged in five colour-coded categories, which you can browse through to find the very best things to see and experience. All highlights have a page reference to take you straight into the Guide, where you can find out more.*

**01** **Snake boat races** Page **133** • With prows shaped like rearing cobras, traditional Keralan longboats are raced at various locations during the early monsoon.

**02 Fort Cochin** Page **176** • The cosmopolitan history of Kerala's colonial trade is evocatively preserved in the backstreets of Fort Cochin, along with the famous Chinese fishing nets.

**04 Malabari cuisine** Page **231** • Bearing traces of northern Kerala's enduring Arab influence, the cuisine of the Malabar region is elaborate, fragrant and packed with exotic flavours. Sample some of the best of it in the city of Kozhikode (Calicut).

**03 Wayanad** Page **235** • Experience some of south India's most spectacular mountains and forest from the comfort of a luxury homestay, plantation retreat or treehouse eco-hideaway.

**05** **Papanasam beach, Varkala** Page **115** • Varkala's amazing red cliffs provide the perfect backdrop for bodysurfing and sunset yoga sessions.

**06** **Kalarippayat** Page **89** • Kerala's acrobatic martial art has ancient roots, but enjoys a passionate following in special gyms across the state.

**08** **Kathakali** Page **296** & *Playing gods* **colour section** • The extraordinary make-up and costumes of Kerala's trademark ritual theatre generate an unforgettable atmosphere.

**07** **Puram, Thrissur** Page **196** • The biggest and most thrilling of all Kerala's temple *utsavams*, centred on a huge elephant procession; smaller events are staged across the state between November and February.

**09** **Munnar** Page **213** • The high peaks, forests and wildlife sanctuaries around the tea-growing town of Munnar boast superb hiking and superb accommodation – British-era tea planters' bungalows, occupying magnificent natural balconies high in the hills.

**10** **Backwater cruises, Kuttanad** Page **128** • Explore the famous Kuttanad backwater region in a converted rice barge or (more eco-friendly) punted canoe.

**12** **Ayurveda** Page **104** • Pamper yourself with a full-body massage or follow a more elaborate course of holistic herbal treatment in traditional, Keralan-style spas.

**13** **Parambikulam** Page **211** • There's no better organized park in Kerala than this gem of a wildlife sanctuary, tucked away in a hidden valley above Palakkad, where you can see wild elephants, bison and flying squirrels, among others.

**11** **Padmanabhapuram Palace** Page **107** • The high-watermark of traditional Keralan architecture.

**14 Sadya** Page **37** • The ultimate Keralan banana-leaf feast, served during the annual harvest festival of Onam, and in simpler versions at everyday "meals" joints.

**15 Kuttanadi homestays**
Page **34** • Experience the distinctive elegance of traditional backwater architecture from the inside by staying in one of the region's exquisite little homestays.

**16 Keralan murals** Page **152** • Some of Kerala's finest medieval murals line the gateway of the Mahadeva temple in Ettumanur.

**17 Theyyem** Page **299** & *Playing gods* colour section • Gods possess the bodies of dancers dressed in outlandish, elaborate masks and costumes during rituals held in small village temples around Kannur (Cannanore).

# Basics

# Basics

# Getting there

Most visitors to Kerala fly into either Kochi (Cochin) or Thiruvananthapuram (Trivandrum), though the northern city of Kozhikode (Calicut) also has an international airport. From the UK, getting there by air will mean at least one change of plane – normally in the Gulf. Travellers from North America can expect an additional stopover in London – though there are direct flights from the US and Canada to the Gulf, and to Mumbai in India. Flying from Australia or New Zealand requires a minimum of one change, usually in Southeast Asia or Hong Kong, and often another in Chennai or Mumbai. There are no direct charter flights to Kerala, but the state remains a key destination for package tours from the US and the UK.

**Airfares** always depend on the **season**, with the highest being from roughly November to March, when the weather in Kerala is best; fares drop during the shoulder seasons – April to May and August to early October – and you'll get the best prices at the height of the monsoons, in June and July. Fares also peak in early to mid-September, around Onam (the harvest festival) as Keralan emigrants travelling home create a surge in demand, and – most of all – over Christmas and New Year.

A wide range of **operators** run **package holidays** to Kerala, which include the cost of the flight, hotels and transport around the state by car. Some also offer special-interest tours on subjects ranging from textiles to religion, food and wildlife. In addition, many companies will arrange tailor-made tours, and can help you plan your own itinerary. For a list of operators running tours to Kerala, see p.21.

## Flights from the UK and Ireland

There are no direct flights from the **UK** to Kerala. The most convenient route is to fly scheduled **via Colombo** with SriLankan Airlines (from around £450–550), or through one of the **Gulf States** with a carrier such as Qatar Airways, Emirates, Etihad or Gulf Air. Either way, you're looking at a total flying time of between eleven and twelve hours, plus the stopover.

Routing passengers through their hub cities, Dubai and Doha respectively, Gulf and Qatar offer the most consistently competitive fares, starting at around £400. Both have daily onward departures to all three airports in Kerala. Transit times are typically 3–4hr with Gulf; or 1–2hr with Qatar – handy if your outbound flight leaves on time, but a major drawback if it doesn't, as missed connections can mean a frustrating day killing time in Doha. Indian carriers offering flights to Kerala from the UK via the Gulf include Air India and Jet.

An alternative route, which can save you money but increases travelling time, is to fly **via Mumbai** and pick up a domestic connection there. Carriers with direct daily flights to Mumbai from London include British Airways (who offer good-value deals from around £425), the pricier Air India and Jet. For the onward leg to Kerala, you can either opt for one of the scheduled domestic companies – Air India or Jet – or their low-cost competitors: Paramount, Kingfisher, GoAir, IndiGo, SpiceJet and Air India Express. Of the bunch, Jet is the most dependable and flexible, but also the most expensive, with fares to Kochi/Thiruvananthapuram starting at £70 one-way. You can book tickets through agents in the UK and Ireland, or via the Jet website (see p.21). Air India's fares are comparable with those of Jet, but the nation's domestic carrier is notoriously unreliable, with frequent delays and poor service; their online booking is also more hit and miss.

There are no direct flights to anywhere in south India from **Ireland**. Your best bet is to link up with a scheduled or charter departure from London.

## Flights from the US and Canada

Whether you fly to Kerala from the **US** and **Canada** via Europe (from the East Coast) or over the Pacific (from the West Coast), it's a long haul, involving one or more intermediate stops. Air India and Jet both fly to Mumbai direct from New York, but you'll arrive fresher and less jet-lagged if you stop over for a few days somewhere en route. Agents will often break the journey into two sections anyway, which allows a wider choice of carriers for the transatlantic (or transpacific) leg.

From the **east coast**, you'll stop over somewhere in Europe (most often London), the Gulf, or both. Figure on at least eighteen hours' total travel time. Prices are most competitive out of New York, where the cheapest low-season consolidated fares to Thiruvananthapuram/Kochi hover around US$1200–1400 (rising to US$1650–1800 in high season). From Washington or Miami, figure on US$1200–1400 in low season, US$2000 in high season; from Chicago, US$1800/2200; and from Dallas/Fort Worth, US$2000/3000. From the **west coast**, it works out slightly quicker to fly west rather than east – a minimum of 22 hours' total travel time – and there may not be much difference in price.

From **Canada**, typical discounted low- and high-season fares to Kochi from Montreal, Toronto and Vancouver are Can$2300/2800.

## Flights from Australia, New Zealand and South Africa

There are no nonstop flights to India from either **Australia** or **New Zealand**; you have to make at least one change of plane in a Southeast Asian hub city. The choice of routes and airlines is bewildering, and most agents will offer you a combination of two or more carriers to get the best price. **Flying west**, the main, and cheapest, Indian gateway city tends to be Chennai (Madras), with Mumbai not far behind. As a rule of thumb, the best-value tickets from

---

## Six steps to a better kind of travel

At Rough Guides we are passionately committed to travel. We feel strongly that only through travelling do we truly come to understand the world we live in and the people we share it with – plus tourism has brought a great deal of **benefit** to developing economies around the world over the last few decades. But the extraordinary growth in tourism has also damaged some places irreparably, and of course **climate change** is exacerbated by most forms of transport, especially flying. This means that now more than ever it's important to **travel thoughtfully** and **responsibly**, with respect for the cultures you're visiting – not only to derive the most benefit from your trip but also to preserve the best bits of the planet for everyone to enjoy. At Rough Guides we feel there are six main areas in which you can make a difference:

- Consider what you're contributing to the **local economy**, and how much the services you use do the same, whether it's through employing local workers and guides or sourcing locally grown produce and local services.
- Consider the **environment** on holiday as well as at home. Water is scarce in many developing destinations, and the biodiversity of local flora and fauna can be adversely affected by tourism. Try to patronize businesses that take account of this.
- Travel with a purpose, not just to tick off experiences. Consider **spending longer** in a place, and getting to know it and its people.
- Give thought to how often you **fly**. Try to avoid short hops by air and more harmful night flights.
- Consider **alternatives to flying**, travelling instead by bus, train, boat and even by bike or on foot where possible.
- Make your trips "**climate neutral**" via a reputable carbon offset scheme. All Rough Guide flights are offset, and every year we donate money to a variety of charities devoted to combating the effects of climate change.

Australia are on departures from the east coast. Expect to pay around Aus$1800–2000 for flights from either Sydney or Melbourne to Mumbai.

From **New Zealand**, the cheapest fares to south India are in the NZ$2000–2250 range if you depart from Auckland; add on approximately NZ$150 for flights from Wellington or Christchurch. There are no direct flights, and most travellers change in one of the major Australian cities or in Hong Kong.

From **South Africa** you can fly direct to Mumbai from Johannesburg with South African Airlines from around ZAR4000–4250 (flying time 8hr 30min), and pick up an onward domestic flight to Kerala from there, or go indirect via the Gulf, which will be cheaper, but involves one more change.

## Airlines and agents

### International airlines

Aer Lingus Ⓦwww.aerlingus.com.
Air Canada Ⓦwww.aircanada.com.
Air France Ⓦwww.airfrance.com.
Air India Ⓦwww.airindia.com.
Air Pacific Ⓦwww.airpacific.com.
Alitalia Ⓦwww.alitalia.com.
American Airlines Ⓦwww.aa.com.
bmi Ⓦwww.flybmi.com.
British Airways Ⓦwww.ba.com.
Cathay Pacific Ⓦwww.cathaypacific.com.
Continental Airlines Ⓦwww.continental.com.
Delta Ⓦwww.delta.com.
EasyJet Ⓦwww.easyjet.com.
EgyptAir Ⓦwww.egyptair.com.eg.
Emirates Ⓦwww.emirates.com.
Etihad Airways Ⓦwww.etihadairways.com.
Gulf Air Ⓦwww.gulfair.com.
KLM (Royal Dutch Airlines) Ⓦwww.klm.com.
Kuwait Airways Ⓦwww.kuwait-airways.com.
Lufthansa Ⓦwww.lufthansa.com.
Malaysia Airlines Ⓦwww.malaysia-airlines.com.
Monarch Scheduled Ⓦwww.flymonarch.com.
Northwest/KLM Ⓦwww.nwa.com.
PIA (Pakistan International Airlines) Ⓦwww.piac.com.pk.
Qantas Airways Ⓦwww.qantas.com.
Qatar Airways Ⓦwww.qatarairways.com
Royal Jordanian Ⓦwww.rj.com.
Ryanair Ⓦwww.ryanair.com.
SAS (Scandinavian Airlines) Ⓦwww.flysas.com.
Singapore Airlines Ⓦwww.singaporeair.com.

SN Brussels Airlines Ⓦwww.flysn.com.
South African Airways Ⓦwww.flysaa.com.
SriLankan Airlines Ⓦwww.srilankan.lk.
Swiss Ⓦwww.swiss.com.
Syrian Airlines Ⓦwww.syrianairlines.co.uk.
Thai Airways Ⓦwww.thaiair.com.
United Airlines Ⓦwww.united.com.

### Domestic airlines

Air India Express Ⓦwww.airindiaexpress.in.
Go Air Ⓦwww.goair.in.
IndiGo Airlines Ⓦhttp://book.goindigo.in.
Jet Airways Ⓦwww.jetairways.com.
JetLite Ⓦwww.jetlite.com.
Kingfisher Airlines Ⓦwww.flykingfisher.com.
Paramount Airways Ⓦwww.paramountairways.com.
SpiceJet Ⓦwww.spicejet.com.

### Travel agents

**North South Travel** UK ☎01245/608 291, Ⓦwww.northsouthtravel.co.uk. Friendly, competitive travel agency, offering discounted fares worldwide. Profits are used to support projects in the developing world, especially the promotion of sustainable tourism.
**STA Travel** UK ☎0871/2300 040, US ☎1-800/781-4040, Australia ☎134 782, New Zealand ☎0800/474 400, South Africa ☎0861/781 781; Ⓦwww.statravel.co.uk. Worldwide specialists in independent travel; also student IDs, travel insurance, car rental, rail passes, and more. Good discounts for students and under-26s.
**Trailfinders** UK ☎0845/058 5858, Ireland ☎01/677 7888, Australia ☎1300/780 212; Ⓦwww.trailfinders.com. One of the best-informed and most efficient agents for independent travellers.
**Travel CUTS** Canada ☎1-866/246-9762, US ☎1-800/592-2887; Ⓦwww.travelcuts.com. Canadian youth and student travel firm.
**USIT** Ireland ☎01/602 1906, Northern Ireland ☎028/9032 7111; Ⓦwww.usit.ie. Ireland's main student and youth travel specialists.

## Tour operators

**Aadi Kerala** India ☎0484/266 4005, Ⓦkeralatravelagent.in. What this Ernakulam-based crew don't know about Kerala is not worth knowing. Particularly recommended for off-track village tours, kayaking on the backwaters, bicycle holidays, trekking and birdwatching, although they do tailor-made luxury tours as well, using the very best hotels and homestays.
**Abercrombie and Kent** UK ☎0845/070 0600, Ⓦwww.abercrombiekent.co.uk, Australia

①1300/851800, New Zealand ①0800/441638, ⓦwww.abercrombiekent.com.au. Upmarket two-week bespoke and set itineraries covering the main highlights, with stays in luxury hotels.

**Adventure Center** US ①1-800/228-8747, ⓦwww.adventurecenter.com. "Spice tour" of Kerala, featuring a backwater trip.

**Ampersand Travel** UK ①020/7289 6100, ⓦwww.ampersandtravel.com. The popular 17-day "Kerala Adventure" hops between the state's most famous upscale homestays and boutique hotels.

**Audley Travel** UK ①01869/276222, ⓦwww .audleytravel.com. Privately guided, tailor-made itineraries covering all the usual sights, plus a handful of off-track destinations.

**Butterfield & Robinson** US ①1-800/6781-1477 or 1-866/551-9090, ⓦwww.butterfield.com. Supported cycling tour of central Kerala.

**Cox & Kings** UK ①020/7873 5000, ⓦwww .coxandkings.com. Wide range of five- to nine-day tours.

**Exodus** UK ①0870/240 5550, ⓦwww .exodustravels.co.uk. Experienced specialists in small-group itineraries, offering a two-week cycling tour of Kerala, or a fortnight's trek that involves a superb stage across the top of the Western Ghats.

**High Places** UK ①0845 257 7500, ⓦwww .highplaces.co.uk. Biking, hiking and backwater boat rides around the state's lesser-known beauty spots.

**Insider Tours** UK ①01233/281 1771, ⓦwww .insider-tours.com. The most original "hands-on" and ethical itineraries on the market, taking you to some more obscure corners of the state, as well the backwaters, wildlife reserves and beaches.

**Kerala Bike Tours/HC Travel** UK ①01256/770775, ⓦwww.keralabiketours.com. Kerala's mountains and beaches on classic Enfield Bullet motorcycles.

**Kerala Connections** UK ①01892/722440, ⓦwww.keralaconnect.co.uk. Bona fide Kerala experts whose tailor-made trips cater for a range of budgets, reflecting their knowledge of the state's lesser-known nooks and crannies.

**Kerala Travel Centre** UK ①01376/310130, ⓦwww.keralatravelcentre.co.uk. A true Kerala specialist, with one of the longest and most thoroughly researched accommodation lists in the business – at very competitive prices.

**Live India** UK ⓦwww.liveindia.co.uk. Enfield motorcycle tours to remote and fascinating locations well off the regular tourist trail, with stays in characterful hotels. The trips are led by experts with more than twenty years' experience of biking around India.

**Pettitts India** UK ①01892/515966, ⓦwww .pettitts.co.uk. Their "Rural Images of Kerala" tour ventures further off the beaten track than most, with the emphasis on culture, and staying in some choice homestays and heritage hotels.

**SD Enterprises** UK ①020/8903 3411, ⓦwww .indiarail.co.uk. Run by Indian railway experts, SD Enterprises puts together budget packages to Kerala – the rates are rock-bottom but they don't always list the hotels they use.

**Steppes East Travel** UK ①01285/880980, ⓦwww.steppestravel.co.uk. Exclusively tailor-made tours, using only top-drawer accommodation.

**Trans Indus Travel** UK ①020/8566 3739, ⓦwww.transindus.co.uk. The only high-end operator with its own dedicated office in Kochi/Ernakulam, Trans Indus offers benchmark tours devised by experts – whether off-the-peg itineraries, or tailor-made trips – at competitive rates.

**The Ultimate Travel Company** UK ①020/7386 4646, ⓦwww.theultimatetravelcompany.co.uk. London-based travel agency specializing in upmarket holidays; their Kerala properties feature only the cream of the state's luxury addresses.

**Wilderness Travel** US ①1-800/368-2794, ⓦwww.wildernesstravel.com. Their seventeen-day "Treasures of south India" tour takes in the highlights of Tamil Nadu alongside those of central Kerala and its backwaters.

**Worldwide Quest Adventures** US ①1-800/387-1483, ⓦwww.worldwidequest.com. The whistlestop "Sandalwood and Spices" tour calls at Periyar and Cochin en route between Tamil Nadu and Goa.

# Getting around

With private car ownership still very much the preserve of India's moneyed classes, most Keralans get about on public transport, which means services are frequent and inexpensive (though perhaps not quite as comfortable as back home). Wherever you're travelling, you won't have to wait long for a train, bus or ferry to appear – as often as not, already crammed to bursting with passengers. For shorter journeys, auto-rickshaws and taxis are just as ubiquitous, while visitors with limited time may opt for a car and driver to whisk them around, or even catch a flight from one end of the state to the other.

## By train

If you're spending your holiday exclusively in Kerala and not aiming to venture further afield in south India, chances are you probably won't travel very much by **train**. Given the hassles and delays that invariably attend most rail journeys in the state, it's nearly always quicker to go by bus or taxi – at least for short hops between towns and cities. That said, time your journey well and start close to your train's original point of departure (before it's had time to get seriously delayed), and rail travel can be an enormously enjoyable way to experience Kerala. People from all walks of life use the railways, from crisp-shirted businessmen cocooned in **air-conditioned** compartments, to the hoi polloi, crushed into "unreserved" carriages, with their never-ending procession of hawkers, beggars, buskers, hustlers and chai-coffee vendors.

The **main line** runs the length of the state, connecting the major towns and cities of the coastal strip before heading north towards Goa and Mumbai. In addition, a couple of **branch lines** peel eastwards across the mountains into neighbouring Tamil Nadu, and there's a quiet back line cutting through Alappuzha and the Kuttanad region.

### Types of train

While planning your journey, the first thing you need to do is settle on a specific train. Each service has a name and number, and not all of them travel at the same speed or offer the same degrees of comfort. Running twice weekly from Thiruvananthapuram up to Goa, via Kochi and Kozhikode, the fastest is the special a/c **Rajdhani Express** – one of Indian Railways' flagship trains. **Daily intercity services**, called "**express**" or "**mail**", cover the same route but stop a lot more frequently, and vary greatly in the amount of time they take to travel between stations. They are, however, still much faster than local "**passenger**" trains, which seem to spend a lot less time moving than they do marooned in the middle of nowhere at invisible signals.

### Classes of train travel

Indian Railways distinguishes between no fewer than seven **classes of travel**, though they will not all be available on every train. Moreover, unless you're planning to cover a long journey (such as the nine-hour haul from Thiruvananthapuram to Kozhikode), it's unlikely you'll need to fathom the intricacies of overnight travel, for which berths have to be reserved well in advance.

Travelling during the day, the important distinction is between regular "**unreserved**" or **third** class – how most of the locals will be travelling – and pricier a/c **second** or **first** – where most tourists end up, and for which you pay between three and five times more. Which of these will suit you is a matter of personal taste, but be warned that although "unreserved" class may be more picturesque, it'll certainly be a lot more uncomfortable, hot and dirty, with hard wooden seats and nasty smells emanating from the toilets.

**Air-conditioned travel**, unavailable on slower "passenger trains", falls into five categories, but the one you're most likely to come across is second-class two-tier. The name refers to the number of upholstered sleeper bunks that swing down from the walls of the compartments. In the daytime, these are fixed to the walls; the seats below can then accommodate six people, with another two on the opposite side of the corridor. Daytime passengers not staying on the train through the night, when the berths are lowered and seating space is limited, may purchase two-tier a/c tickets an hour or so before departure if there's room. Easily distinguished by their sealed-in windows, a/c carriages are usually coupled to the front of the train, and are always staffed by uniformed ticket inspectors and pantry-car attendants.

**"Ladies-only"** compartments exist on many trains; they can be full of noisy kids, but offer single women some respite from the incessant staring of open general carriages. Some stations also have ladies-only waiting rooms.

## Timetables

**Timetables** for all mail, express and superfast trains are available online at ⓦ www.indianrail.gov.in, though the website is poorly designed and takes some getting used to. Indian Railways' exhaustively detailed timetable *Trains at a Glance* is available in printed form from most station kiosks and online at ⓦ www.indianrail.gov.in. For checking fares and **availability**, you're better off using ⓦ www.cleartrip.com, a privately run site which also offers fast reservation facilities (see below).

Rail **fares** are calculated according to the exact distance travelled. *Trains at a Glance* includes a chart of fares by kilometres, and also gives the distance in kilometres of stations along each route in the timetables, making it possible to calculate what the basic fare will be for any given journey.

## Advance booking and sleeper trains

For shorter journeys of up to a few hours on passenger, mail or express trains, you won't need to book a seat during the day – just turn up at the station thirty to sixty minutes before departure and join the scrum around

the ticket hatch on the station concourse. Where available, you can specify what class you'd like to travel in; if you don't state a preference, you'll be issued with the cheapest standard fare in "unreserved" (sometimes also referred to as "general") class. Note that it's possible to upgrade later by swapping carriages and paying the TC (Ticket Controller) the difference – technically, this isn't allowed, but rail staff tend to be sympathetic towards foreigners who unwittingly find themselves in unreserved carriages.

**Longer journeys** can last all night, in which case you'll need to reserve a berth. This is where the various classes really start to show. In "**unreserved**", you'll be lucky to find so much as a square foot of floor space. Unless desperate, even travellers on the tightest of budgets should reserve a bunk in **sleeper class** (also called "second-class non-a/c" or "second-class reserved"), which costs Rs57 per 100km and entitles you to a swing-down, slatted bunk in a three-tier compartment. Next up the scale is **second-class a/c**, which costs Rs221/378 per 100km, depending on whether it's two- or three-tier (ie with four or six bunks per compartment); this is by far the most common form of a/c sleeper travel, available on almost every express and mail train, and comes complete with fresh cotton sheets, pillows and optional meals freshly cooked in an attached "pantry car". Finally, there's a separate class of super-fast luxury trains, such as the Kerala–Goa *Rajdhani Express*, which costs Rs438–555 per 100km (including meals), depending on which of the three categories of a/c you choose.

## Buying tickets

The easiest way to buy a ticket **in advance** is to log on to the **Indian Railway Catering and Tourism Corporation** site (ⓦ www.irctc.co.in) – or, better still, through ⓦ **www.cleartrip.com** (which charges Rs100 per ticket to process). After setting up an account, you can access your personal travel record, check your reservations and, if need be, cancel them. Online bookings can generally be made up to 90 days ahead of departure (less for some inter-city services) and up to the time of **chart preparation** for the train, which is normally 4hr before the train is scheduled to leave from its originating station. For trains that start before noon, the chart is usually prepared the previous night. Late-availability Tatkal tickets (see below) can also be booked online; these are released on a quota 36 hours prior to the chart closing.

**Tickets** can also be booked in person at the station itself. In the big cities, huge computerized reservation halls process streams of passengers from 8am until 8pm, Monday to Saturday, and until 2pm on Sundays. Queues and waiting times tend to be long. First off, fill in the requisite paper form with your personal details and the number, name and date of the train you wish to catch (available online, from *Trains at a Glance*, or, if he or she is feeling uncommonly charitable, from the desk clerk when you reach the head of the queue). Once you've paid, check to make sure the dates and other details are correct, and that it is "confirmed" not "wait listed", in which case an ominous "W" will appear next to your berth number; whatever number is listed next to the "W" on your ticket will be your position in a waiting list for allocation of unclaimed berths.

Most station booking halls have **"ladies' queues"**; travelling in a mixed group or a couple, women will find it easier to get all the tickets if they queue up on their own.

As demand for all berths is high year-round, reservations should be made as far in advance as possible – ideally at least a couple of weeks before your intended departure date, or a minimum of 36 hours. To avoid having to trek out to the station again, travellers following tight itineraries tend to buy departure tickets from particular towns the moment they arrive. At most large stations, it's also possible to reserve tickets for journeys starting elsewhere in the state.

If there are no places available on the train you want, ask if any seats or berths have been set aside as a **"tourist quota"**. This special allocation, reserved for foreign passport holders, is available in advance, but usually only from major or originating stations.

## Indian Railways sales agents abroad

**Australia** Adventure World ℡ 02/9956 7766, Ⓦ www.adventureworld.com.au.
**UK** SD Enterprises ℡ 020/8903 3411, Ⓦ www.indiarail.co.uk.

## Cloakrooms

Most stations in Kerala have **cloakrooms** (sometimes called "parcel offices") for passengers to leave their baggage. These can be very handy if you want to go sightseeing in a town and move on the same day. In theory, you need a current train ticket or Indrail pass to deposit luggage, but they don't always ask; they may, however, refuse to take your bag if you can't lock it. Losing your reclaim ticket also causes problems. Make sure, when checking baggage in, that the cloakroom will be open when you need to pick it up. The standard charge is currently Rs10 for the first 24 hours, Rs12 for the next 24 hours and Rs15 per day thereafter.

## By air

Kerala has three civil **airports**. By far the most efficient is Kochi (Ⓦ www.cochin-airport.com). Thiruvananthapuram (Ⓦ www.trivandrum-airport.com) and Kozhikode (Ⓦ www.kozhikode-airport.com) are both shambolic by international standards. The vast majority of passengers using all these airports tend to be en route to or from the Gulf States, but there are also plenty of flights between the three cities. It takes only forty minutes to fly from the capital to Kochi

### Tatkal tickets

Indian Railways' late-availability reservation system, or **Tatkal**, can be a great help for foreign tourists. A quota of ten percent of places is reserved on most trains under this scheme, which are bookable at any computerized office, and online (see p.25). Tickets are released at 8am, two days before the train departs, and are available up to four hours prior to the scheduled departure time. For an extra charge (Rs75–150 in non-a/c sleeper class, Rs150–300 in seated a/c carriages, or Rs200–300 in a/c sleeper carriages) you can guarantee a place.

and fifty minutes to reach Kozhikode – the trip between Kochi and Kozhikode takes thirty minutes.

**Air India Express** (T0484/238 1885, W www.airindiaexpress.in) operates the largest number of flights within the state. Its sibling company, Air India, also runs the same route, but only once per week.

Fares fluctuate according to the time of year and availability, but can easily be checked online. **Tickets** are most easily booked online, or at the airlines' offices, addresses for which are listed in the relevant city accounts throughout the Guide.

## By bus

Although generally less comfortable than travelling by train, **buses** fill the gaps in the rail network, and can be quicker. They go almost everywhere, and more frequently than trains (though mostly in daylight hours).

Services vary somewhat in price and standard. Painted in distinctive red and cream, those run by the government bus company, **KSRTC** (the Kerala State Road Transport Company), tend to be the most ramshackle of all. Invariably jam-packed, they cover both short and very long distances; in the latter case, express services are run which have limited stops. In more widely travelled areas there are usually additional **private** buses offering more leg-room and generally going faster – not necessarily a plus point when you consider the dilapidated state of the vehicles.

Some clue as to comfort can be gained from the description given to the bus. "Ordinary" buses usually have minimally padded fixed upright seats. "Deluxe", "Luxury" and even "Super-deluxe" are fairly interchangeable terms and when applied to government buses may hardly differ from "ordinary". Usually they refer to private services, though, and should then guarantee a softer, sometimes reclining, individual seat. You can check this when booking, and it's also worth asking if your bus has a video or music system – if so, the deafening noise will prevent any chance of sleep. Always try to avoid the back seats – they accentuate bumpy roads, launching you into the air several times a minute. Try to sit in the middle of the bus for safety.

**Luggage** travels in the hatch on private buses, sometimes at a small extra charge. You can usually squeeze it into an unobtrusive corner inside state-run vehicles, although you may occasionally be requested to store it on the roof (passengers travelling on the roof is a rare event these days); check that it's well secured and not liable to get squashed. A small tip (see p.62) is in order for whoever puts it up there for you.

## Booking tickets

**Buying a bus ticket** is usually less of an ordeal than buying a train ticket, although at large city bus stations there may be twenty or so counters, each assigned to a different route. When you buy your ticket you'll be given the registration number of the bus and, sometimes, a seat number. As at railway stations, there is usually a separate, quicker, ladies' queue; it may not be signed in English but is easy enough to spot.

You can always get on ordinary state buses without a ticket, while at bus stands outside major cities it's usually possible to pay on board, though you have to be sharp to secure a seat. Prior booking is usually available and is recommended for express state buses and private services; it's worth checking the precise departure point with the agent. You can usually pay on board private buses, too, although that reduces your chances of a seat.

## By boat

Operated by the **State Water Transport Company** (W www.swtc.gov.in), **government ferries** are the aquatic equivalent of the beaten-up KSRTC buses you see lumbering along Kerala's roads. They're a prominent feature of life in the **backwater regions**, where they form essential links between disparate villages and market towns. Cheap and relatively frequent, they're also a great way for tourists to experience this unique part of the country – though they're not always as safe as they could be. A spate of recent disasters has led to the imposition of stricter rules, but ferries are still frequently overloaded, and the fleet as a whole remains deplorably run-down.

The place you're most likely to use an SWTC ferry is in **Kochi/Ernakulam**. Municipal ferries chug throughout the day and evening across the city's busy harbour, connecting the main jetty in Ernakulam with various islands and promontories, including Fort Cochin.

Full details of routes and fares appear along with useful travel hints in the relevant sections of the Guide. For an overview of backwater travel by **tourist boats** – including *kettu vallam* rice barges around Alappuzha and the Kuttanad region – see the box on p.128.

## By car

It's much more usual, given the chaos reigning on the roads, for tourists in Kerala to be driven than it is for them to drive. Car rental firms operate on the basis of supplying **vehicles with drivers**. You can arrange them through any tourist office or taxi firm, and local taxi drivers hanging around hotels and city ranks are also available for day hire. Cars will cost around Rs1500 per day, which should include a maximum of 200km, with additional kilometres charged at around Rs6–7/km. On longer trips, the driver sleeps in the car, for which his firm may charge an additional Rs150–200. You should generally tip the driver Rs15–175 per day too.

Most tourists succumb to the romance of that quintessentially Indian automobile, the **Hindustan Ambassador** Mark IV, based on the design of the old British Oxford Morris. Sadly, however, the car's appalling suspension and back-breaking seats make it among the most uncomfortable rides in the world. Older models, in particular, can make for some gruelling journeys, with dashboards that become burning-hot and suffocating fumes plaguing the front seats. All in all, you'll be much better off in a modern two- or four-door hatchback – ask your rental company for the options.

Air conditioning adds considerably to the rate, and with larger cars such as SUVs, the daily rate of Rs1500 tends only to cover the first 80km, after which stiff additional per-kilometre charges apply. See the box below for specific advice on arranging a taxi for tours.

None of the big international chains offers **self-drive** car hire in Kerala – a telling fact in itself. Unless you've had plenty of experience on the state's notoriously bad roads, we strongly recommend you leave the driving to an expert. If you're still determined to go it alone, try **Inspiration Kerala** (Ⓦinspiration kerala.org), though don't expect the same terms and conditions you may be used to abroad.

---

## Renting a car and driver: some tips

**Renting a car and driver** in Kerala can result in all manner of problems, most of them based on misunderstandings that could be avoided at the planning stage. The following pointers should help you negotiate a smoother trip.

- Always compare prices between companies (bearing in mind that Rs1500–1750 for 200km and Rs7/km thereafter is standard).
- You should fix your itinerary, the approximate mileage, travelling time, pick-up and drop-off locations – and, crucially, who is paying for fuel, road taxes and tolls, and the driver's overnight allowance – with the rental company in advance.
- Pin the details of any agreement down in a written contract.
- Should a deposit be required (one may be asked for, but you're entitled to refuse), it's a good idea to wait until the time of departure to pay it – otherwise a different car may turn up from the one you agreed to. The remaining balance should be settled on the last day of the trip. Whatever happens, never pay the full amount in advance and always insist on a receipt for any money you hand over.
- Never leave your passport or a credit card slip as security.
- Ideally, meet the driver (especially if it is for a long journey) ahead of departure, in order to ensure that his English is up to the task.
- Before leaving, check the vehicle (tyres, brakes, lights, indicators, steering), and if something is not safe, insist it is fixed before leaving, or get them to change the car.

Driving in Kerala is not for beginners. If you do drive yourself, expect the unexpected, and count on other drivers taking whatever liberties they can get away with. Traffic circulates on the left, but don't expect road regulations to be obeyed. In the city, it's heavy and particularly undisciplined: vehicles cut in and out without warning, and you have to cope with pedestrians, cyclists and cows wandering nonchalantly down the middle of the road as if you don't exist. In the country the roads are narrow, in terrible repair and hogged by overloaded Tata trucks that move aside for nobody. To overtake, sound your horn – the driver in front will signal if it is safe to do so; if not, he will wave his hand, palm downwards, up and down. The vast number of potholes doesn't make for a smooth ride either, and during the monsoon, roads can become flooded and dangerous; rivers burst their banks and bridges get washed away. Ask local people before you set off, and proceed with caution, sticking to main highways as much as possible. It is very dangerous to drive at night – not everyone uses lights, and bullock carts don't have any.

Officially, you need an **international driver's licence** (IDP, type #1949, available through post offices, the AA or RAC in the UK) to rent and ride anything, but in practice a standard licence will suffice if you're stopped and asked to produce your papers by the local police.

**Insurance** is compulsory, but not expensive. Car seat-belts are not compulsory but very strongly recommended. **Accident** rates are high, and you should be on your guard at all times. If you do have an accident, it might be an idea to leave the scene quickly and go straight to the police to report it; mobs can assemble fast, especially if pedestrians or cows are involved.

**Fuel** is reasonably cheap, at around Rs52 per litre for petrol (or Rs49/litre for diesel), but the state of the roads will take its toll, and mechanics are not always very reliable, so a knowledge of **vehicle maintenance** is a help, as is a check-over every so often to see what all those bone-shaking journeys are doing to your car. Luckily, if you get a flat tyre, puncture-wallahs can be found almost everywhere.

## By motorbike

It is hard to overstate the sense of freedom that breezing around the backroads of Kerala on a motorcycle can bring. On a **rented bike** you can reach the state's remote beaches and cover long distances with relative ease, and air temperatures are warm enough to mean you don't have to keep wrapping and unwrapping layers each time you stop and start.

The downside, of course, is that two-wheelers can be perilous. Kerala's roads rank among the most dangerous on the planet, and at least a half of all recorded traffic accidents in the state are motorcycle riders or their pillion passengers. Before driving away, therefore, ensure the lights and brakes are in good shape, and be especially vigilant at night: many roads are poor and unlit, and stray cows and carts can appear from nowhere. Also make sure to look out for is the **speedbreakers** that slow progress on all Keralan roads. These speedbumps, often of massive proportions, are rarely marked, and regularly cause accidents when riders hit them at speed.

Motorcycles are available for rent in the coastal resorts of Kovalam and Varkala. In theory you need an **international licence** (see above), although a regular one should suffice. **Helmets** are compulsory: you're unlikely to be stopped for not wearing one on backroads, or riding around the resorts, but out on the main highways the police may wave you over and spot-fine you if you're

## Motorcycle safety

When renting a motorcycle, always try for one that's less than a year old – Kerala's roads play havoc with suspension and brakes, and maintenance standards might not always be what you're used to at home. Take the bike out for a quick spin before you start to negotiate the price: test the brakes and lights and check the tyre treads. Its owner should also provide a helmet and insurance papers.

It's also a good idea to know in advance where the best **accident and emergency units** are located.

bare-headed. In any case, it makes sense to wear one given how dangerous the Keralan roads can be. The owner of your rented motorbike should be able to provide an Indian-made helmet, but it may not fit and isn't likely to be of the best quality; consider investing in a new one (they're available in Thiruvananthapuram's Chalai Bazaar area) or, better still, bring one from home which you know hasn't been cracked.

**Rates** for motorbikes vary according to season, duration of rental and vehicle; most owners also insist on a deposit and/or passport as security. The cheapest bike, a scooter-style Honda Activa 100cc, which has automatic gears, costs around Rs300–350 per day. These are reliable and fine for buzzing to the beach and back, but to travel further you need a bit more power. Other options include the perennially stylish Enfield Bullet 350cc, although these are heavy, unwieldy and – at upwards of Rs450–500 per day – the most expensive bike to rent.

Two-stroke **fuel** is sold at service stations (known locally as "petrol pumps") in the main towns and along the national highway. In out-of-the-way places, it's also sold in mineral water bottles at general stores or through backstreet suppliers. But you should avoid these whenever possible as some bulk out their petrol with low-grade kerosene or industrial solvent, which makes engines misfire and smoke badly.

As a rule of thumb, a newish 100cc scooter or geared bike should manage at least 35–40km per litre. Be warned, however, that **fuel gauges** rarely work, and those that do shouldn't be trusted. When riding in remote areas of the state where fuel stops may be few and far between, take a spare litre with you.

Most villages also have a **motorcycle-repair** specialist (or a "puncture–wallah"), although in theory the person you rented your machine from should foot the bill for routine maintenance (including punctures, blown bulbs and any mechanical failures). Damage to the bike incurred during a road traffic accident, of course, has to be paid for by you. It is important you agree on such details with the owner before driving away; you should also exchange mobile (cell) phone numbers.

Listings for firms running **motorcycle tours** in Kerala appear under "Tour operators" on p.21.

## Cycling

Indian-made, gearless **Hero bicycles** – ideal for a gentle jaunt along the shady backlanes of the coast but hard work over longer distances – may be rented in most towns and resorts. The going rate is around Rs100–150 per day, and you could be asked to leave a **deposit**, or even your passport, as security – though you should think twice about doing this, perhaps suggesting a photocopy instead. Up in Periyar, you can also rent modern, European-made **mountain bikes** for longer cycle rides through the Cardamom Hills – see p.158.

**Bringing a bike** from abroad requires no *carnet* or special paperwork, and most airlines allow you to take cycles at no extra cost – though they may insist on them being flat-packed in cardboard covers (available through good cycle shops). Spare parts and accessories may be of different sizes and standards in Kerala, though, and you may have to improvise. Bring basic spares and tools and a pump. Panniers are the obvious thing for carrying your gear, but fiendishly inconvenient when not attached to your bike, and you might consider sacrificing ideal load-bearing and streamlining technology for a backpack you can lash down on the rear carrier.

## City transport

City transport takes various forms, with **buses** the most obvious. These are usually single-decker, and can get unbelievably crowded.

If you're visiting a variety of places around town, consider hiring a **taxi** or **auto-rickshaw** for the day. Find a driver who speaks English reasonably well, and agree a price beforehand.

### Taxis

**Taxis** in Kerala are usually cream- or white-painted Ambassadors. Meters are few and far between: as a rule you should expect to haggle out a fare in advance. Naturally, it helps to have an idea of what that fare should be, though any figures quoted in this or any other book should be treated as being the broadest of guidelines only. Many railway stations, and certainly most airports, operate **prepaid taxi schemes** with set fares that you pay before departure.

## Auto-rickshaws

The **auto-rickshaw**, that most Indian of vehicles, is the front half of a motor-scooter with a double seat mounted on the back. Cheaper than taxis, better at nipping in and out of traffic, and theoretically metered, auto-rickshaws are a little unstable and their drivers often rather reckless, but that's all part of the fun. In Kerala, rickshaw-wallahs – recognizable by their official khaki shirts – are strictly unionized, which means they will normally use their meter without being prompted. At least, they nearly always do in larger towns and cities, but in more remote areas you may have to agree the fare in advance.

# Accommodation

In Kerala, perhaps more than anywhere else in India, getting your choice of accommodation right will make or break your holiday. While rarely less than acceptable, standards and styles in all categories differ enormously. The reason for this is the varying speeds with which local hotel and guesthouse owners have adapted to recent changes in the tourism market. Whereas a decade ago a basic room with running water was all that most visitors expected, nowadays prospective guests are looking for traditional architecture, period furniture and verandas with lovely views.

Whatever your budget, you can expect to stay in some memorable places, from old wooden *tharavadukal* homesteads surrounded by rice fields to ivy-fronted British bungalows on tea estates high in the hills; village huts in the backwaters; and beachside resorts offering sea views from their overflow pools.

**Prices**, particularly in tourist centres and at popular high-end homestays, are extremely high by Indian standards – although at the bottom of the market you can still find bargains, especially if the season is slack.

## Hotels and guesthouses

Kerala has a huge number of hotel beds to suit every budget, most of it at standards that compare well with more developed parts of the world. While supply struggles to keep up with demand in many towns and cities, where Indian visitors account for the bulk of the custom, in the coastal resorts and hill stations frequented by foreigners, vacancies are rarely hard to come by, other than over the peak Christmas–New Year period – and in a handful of exceptionally popular establishments, where you'll have to book well in advance whatever the time of year.

Not all hotels have **single rooms**, but most offer a reduced rate for **single occupancy**. It's also easy to find rooms with capacity for three or four people – Indians like to travel in groups and hotels always keep extra fold-away beds to hand, for which an additional tariff (usually 25–30 percent of the double rate) applies.

Officially, all establishments are obliged to provide a printed tariff list and most do. However, like most other things in India, the

## Luxury and service tax

**Luxury tax**, a levy imposed by state governments all across India, is slapped on top of all hotel bills. It varies from region to region, but in Kerala the rates are the highest in the south of the country, at 7.5 percent for non-a/c rooms and 12.5 percent for a/c. Note that this applies not to the actual price of your room (for which you may have haggled out a discount) but the amount stated on the hotel's printed tariff card or website – ie the offical rack rate. In addition, watch out for **service charges**, often slapped onto bills by high-end hotels for no apparent reason whatsoever. They're usually fixed at around 10 percent and apply not just to your room rate, but also extras and food.

price of a room may well be open to **negotiation**. If you think the rate is too high, or if all the hotels in town are empty, try haggling: you'll nearly always be offered a reduction. Note, however, that **luxury tax** (see above) will be applied not to the discounted rate you've agreed, but to the official rack rate.

### Inexpensive hotels

While accommodation prices in Kerala are generally on the up, there's still an abundance of **cheap hotels and lodges**, catering for less well-off Indians. Most charge Rs300–400 for a double room with en-suite bathroom; or Rs250–300 for one with shared facilities.

Budget accommodation tends to be cheaper the further you get off the beaten track; it's most expensive in the resorts of Kovalam and Varkala, where prices are double or triple those for equivalent accommodation in most other areas.

**Cold showers** or "bucket baths" are the order of the day – not really a problem in Kerala as the heat means that, except in the hills, you're unlikely to want hot water. Moreover, even cold water never comes out of the tap very cold, and by mid-afternoon can be positively warm if it's been sitting in a tank on the roof.

Even so, it's always wise to check out the state of the bathrooms and toilets before taking a room; most will be spotless, but you can never be sure. And not all will have Western "sit-down" loos.

### Mid-range hotels

You don't need to pay through the nose for creature comforts in Kerala. A large, clean double, with a freshly made bed, cable TV, laundered towel, and your own spotless bathroom with sit-down toilet and 24-hour hot running water can still cost under Rs750.

Generally speaking, different categories of rooms will be on offer in any one establishment, ranging from the most basic "standard" or "economy" option, to "deluxe", "super-deluxe" or even "executive deluxe". The thing that most affects tariffs in mid-scale hotels, however, is **air conditioning** (abbreviated in Kerala, and throughout this book, as a/c), which is likely to add Rs500–1000 to the rate. Many visitors consider a/c to be a necessity in Kerala, where the heat and humidity can be so oppressive as to preclude any chance of sleep for eight or nine months of the year. In

### Koder House - Heritage Boutique Hotel
### (Live the Legend)

FACILITIES:- There are FIVE 800 Sqft.(Deluxe) and ONE 600Sqft (Junior) sheer luxury suites, and each is grand with a huge bedroom, sitting room and bathroom with Jacuzzi. And services are equally select. The **MENORAH** Seafood Restaurant overlooks a Plunge Pool, and the only restaurant serving **Authentic Kerala and Jewish food**. Our 1000sqft.spectacular teakwood flooring WINE & BEER Lounge with a central balcony offers cocktails, Indian and imported wine 'n' beer, served with scrumptious snacks. Personal valet for each room. Plus of course, there is a Business Centre, Library, Bridge and services like Foreign exchange, Electronic safe, Internet data Port and Cable TV in each room, Doctor-on-call and Laundry.

Koder House, Tower Road, Fort Cochin,Cochin - 682 001, Kerala, India - Tel. +91 484 2218485/86/87/88 Fax 2217988

E-mail : koderhouse@gmail.com Web Site :-www.koderhouse.com

## Accommodation price codes

All **accommodation prices** in this book have been categorized according to the price **codes** below, which correspond to the cost of a double room in high season (Nov to mid-Dec and mid-Jan to Feb), all taxes included.

Rooms covered under codes ❶ and ❷ are usually very basic but often include en-suite ("attached") bathrooms and sometimes even a TV; some will have shared bathrooms. You can expect hotel rooms in codes ❸ and ❹ to be en suite, most likely with a TV, and have a better standard of decor and furnishing and maybe a balcony; some of the cheaper a/c rooms fall into this category or, if non-a/c, will have mosquito nets provided. Hotels in codes ❺ and ❻ are guaranteed to be smart, spacious, more tastefully furnished and more often than not a/c; breakfast may be included too. Hotels in codes ❼ and ❽ become positively luxurious, almost invariably with a/c, and boast far better facilities (such as swimming pools) and service; most top-end business hotels belong here. Code ❾ is the preserve of the five-stars run by companies such as the *Taj Group*, as well as upscale heritage homestays or boutique hotels pitched at well-heeled foreign tourists; these provide quality to match anywhere in the world.

In non-touristy parts of the region, and in most major towns and cities, accommodation prices will be the same throughout the year. But in the resorts along the coast, and in wildlife sanctuaries and hill stations, rates fluctuate wildly with demand, inflating two- or three-fold during peak season (mid-Dec to mid-Jan).

❶ Rs300 and under
❷ Rs301–500
❸ Rs501–700
❹ Rs701–1200
❺ Rs1201–2000
❻ Rs2001–3000
❼ Rs3001–4500
❽ Rs4501–7000
❾ Rs7001 and over

smarter hotels, it usually comes as standard, whether you use it or not.

The quality of the a/c itself varies: in cheaper places, rattling old "air-cooler" boxes fitted into windows may be the only option, whereas a recently renovated or newer place will have installed quieter and more effective "split a/c" units, or central air-conditioning systems. Either way, the bell boy ("room boy" in Kerala) should show you how to operate the unit when you check in.

### Upmarket hotels

Kerala has devised its own spin on the conventional five-star campus, relocating **antique wood houses** from villages to luxury resort enclaves on the coast and backwaters. And in the Western Ghats of inland Kerala, you'll find so-called **eco-resorts**, often consisting of tree houses or thatched, village-style mud huts equipped with low-impact comforts. British-era planters' bungalows on tea or coffee plantations are another atmospheric way to experience the High Ranges, while restored

royal palaces, Syrian-Christian mansions in the backwaters and luxury ayurveda spas provide other tempting possiblities.

**Modern** business-grade hotels, usually the best options in large towns and cities, tend to belong to chains. It's becoming more common for these places to quote tariffs in US dollars (or euros in the case of places south of Kovalam), starting at $100 and rising to a hefty $500 – sometimes even more for suites. Note that only the standard "rack rates" will be offered to you if you walk into a top hotel direct, though special reductions are available online.

### Hostels

**YMCAs** and **YWCAs** in Kerala are confined to big cities and offer exceptional value – which is why they're invariably fully booked. We list several in the Guide; if you're hoping to stay in one, book by telephone several weeks in advance.

### Homestays

Well-to-do Keralan families with beautiful old country mansions dominate the so-called heritage **homestay** market. With a few exceptions, these tend to be far less anonymous than hotels. You're welcomed as part of the family by your hosts, who'll chat with you at meal times and show you around their estate or local village – all of which can make for a very memorable and rewarding time, particularly if you have children in tow. The big surprise here, though, is the cost, which is astonishingly high by Indian standards. It's not unusual for the more reputed homestays, in particularly lovely properties and locations, to charge

£100–130/$150–200 per night for a double room. You are, of course, paying not merely for the accommodation, so much as the all-round experience of staying somewhere unique, often with original antiques and a traditional Keralan atmosphere, and for the time and attention of hosts.

There also exists a handful of more formal **heritage hotels** that offer rooms in historic buildings but without the family hospitality. They're normally run by upscale chains, and usually hold top-notch ayurveda spas.

# Food and drink

Food is one of the major highlights of any trip to Kerala. For anyone used to the heavy, over-spiced curries typically dished up in "Indian" restaurants abroad, the subtlety of south Indian cuisine will come as a revelation. Keralans bring the same ingenuity and wealth of deep-rooted traditions to food preparation that they've brought to bear on their sacred arts and festivals – with results that are no less sophisticated or surprising.

The fertile climate, soils, seas and inland waterways of the state have provided Keralan cooks with an uncommon variety of ingredients, augmented over the centuries by many others imported by traders and colonizers – not least the chilli, brought by the Portuguese. Keralans have always been quick to adapt to new culinary trends, and the recent tourism boom means a host of dishes familiar from home are also on offer in the resorts, often given a local twist.

By Western standards, eating out in Kerala is extremely **inexpensive**. Even in a smart five-star restaurant, you'll rarely pick up a bill of over Rs1000 (around £15/$22), while in a workaday local diner, a filling, delicious,

freshly cooked feast comprising a dozen or more different dishes can be had for a mere Rs50 or less.

## Keralan cuisine

**Kerala** boasts one of the richest and most varied cuisines in India – so much so, in fact, that it's misleading to talk of a single style of cooking. Over the centuries, each of the region's many castes, sub-castes, religious minorities, traders and colonial overlords adapted the wealth of produce available locally – whether bitter gourds, mangos, jackfruit, tapioca or plantain – and created their own distinctive culinary traditions. All of them, however, retain certain common traits,

In Kerala – perhaps even more so than elsewhere – **eating with your fingers** is *de rigueur*, and cutlery may not always be available. Wherever you eat, remember to use only your right hand (see p.60), and wash your hands before you start. Use the tips of your fingers to avoid getting food on the palm of your hand.

notably the prominence of locally grown spices (such as cumin, pepper, turmeric, cinnamon, cloves and curry leaves) in elaborate combinations with fresh coconut and chillis.

Refined in the kitchens of Keralan palaces and temples, the cooking of Namboodiri Brahmins, the highest Hindu caste, is one of the oldest styles. Strictly **vegetarian**, it's based on the ayurveda principle that flavours should promote a harmonious balance (*rasa*) of mind and body. Whereas Namboodiris prefer non-stimulant *satvic* foods (such as unpolished grains and pulses, nuts, fruit and fresh vegetables), lower castes make greater use of the innumerable **spices** that flourish in Kerala's moist, tropical climate, using them to enhance the strong tastes of meat and fish.

Freed of the dietary taboos imposed on higher-caste Hindus and Muslims, **Syrian-Christians** are resolutely "non-veg", relishing beef, pork and duck, as well as all manner of exotic river fish and seafood. In the far north, **Moppila Muslims** fused the recipes of their Arab forefathers with the indigenous cuisine of the Malabar coast to devise the delicious biriyanis and *pathiri* rice-flour breads still enjoyed in the homes and neighbourhood restaurants of Kozhikode. By contrast, the dishes once prepared by **Cochin**'s Jewish, Anglo-Indian and Indo-Portuguese house-holds have all but disappeared, preserved only in a handful of tourist restaurants.

## Rice

**Rice**, in various, often unrecognizable, forms, is the basic staple of every Keralan meal, eaten three or more times a day. For lunch, locals get through gigantic heaps of the stuff, usually the kind known in Malayalam as *puzhukkalari*. This local rice, a slightly reddish-streaked variety with plump, separate grains, has a much-enriched vitamin and mineral content – the result of it having been soaked and parboiled while still "raw", before being only partly milled. It's far more sustaining and tasty than the white, fluffy, fully milled *pachari* that the rest of India eats. In "meals" restaurants, you're always presented with a choice between the two.

As well as being prepared for lunch, rice may be coarsely pounded, blended into a batter and steamed in moulds as *puttu*, or finely ground and squeezed into a paste through small holes to create Keralan-style vermicelli, or *iddiappam*. *Appam*, steamed pancakes much loved by Syrian-Christians in particular, are also made from rice flour – after it's been made into batter and fermented overnight to give a subtle, yeasty flavour. *Appam* really come into their own in combination with rich, full-flavoured Christian *ishtews* (stews), such as those made from lamb for the traditional Easter meal.

Up in the northern Malabar region around Kozhikode (Calicut), local Moppila Muslims have their own type of flatbread made from

## Home cooking

Although typical Keralan breakfasts are widely available and local dishes feature in the south Indian thalis served at "meals" restaurants across the state, the best, most authentic food of all is that prepared in homes. Most Keralan women, even those with servants to help in the kitchen, are expert cooks, trained by generations of mothers, grandmothers, aunts and elder sisters. One of the great attractions of **homestay accommodation** (see p.34) is that it allows you to sample their skills, and even learn them yourself on cookery courses.

Another, more accessible, source of great Keralan food is the local *thattukada*, or hot meals stall. In towns and cities all over the state, these pop up from around 7pm on street corners, beachfronts and intersections to provide wholesome, freshly cooked local meals at low prices – mostly for men working away from home. From steaming vats and sizzling griddles, platefuls of delicious green-bean curry, dhal and egg masala are spooned piping hot onto fresh *appam*, *iddiappam* and *parottas*, which you eat on tin plates while seated on rough wooden benches. And the cost of this great food is negligible: you'd have to have the appetite of a sumo wrestler to spend more than Rs30 at a *thattukada*.

## Sadyas

Thiruvonam, the final day of the spring harvest festival, **Onam**, is when Keralans welcome the mythical King Mahabali into their homes, holding a sumptuous family banquet, for which everyone dresses up in their finest new Onam clothes, or *onakkodi*.

Served on glossy green plantain leaves, the meal – known as a *sadya*, or *onasadya* – is the culmination of ten days' festivities and takes a suitably elaborate form. As many as a couple of dozen different preparations may be included in the feast, all of them scrupulously vegetarian and cooked according to traditional recipes. An extraordinary array of tastes is encompassed – sour, tangy, hot, bitter and sweet – but each should, in principle, be balanced by another, promoting equilibrium and a sense of wellbeing in mind and body afterwards – as per the precepts of ayurveda.

The order and style of serving are conducted with a similarly rigid attention to detail. Starting on the tapered side of the leaf (always placed pointing to the left), the *upperi* (fried banana chips) come first – both plain, and plastered in sticky *jaggery* (raw sugar cane) as *sharkaravaratti* a delicacy, that used to be reserved for the highest castes only, but is nowadays enjoyed across the social spectrum. Next to them are spooned blobs of *nakkam* – an array of mango and lime pickles, and pungent ginger-based condiments called *inji thayyir* – followed by the *ozhikan*, runny dhals and *sambars* in little terracotta pots which will later be poured over the rice. Thicker vegetable *kootu* – including at least one kind of mild *avial* and watery pumpkin or cucumber *olan* (see "Vegetables and pulses", below) – go immediately to their right, but above the dividing spine of the leaf. When the *kootu* are in place, the guests are seated, the rice is served and the eating can begin – with the pouring of the *ozhikan* over the rice.

The final course, *maduram* (literally "sweet"), will consist of at least two, and possibly three or four, different *payasam* (see "Sweets and desserts", p.39). When that's finished, the diners fold their plantain leaves away from them and heave themselves over to the wash basin for a rinse off.

The *sadya* is an ancient Keralan tradition that's reinvented itself with the changing patterns of modern life, not least because it tends to unite family members living in different districts or countries. Traditionally, the job of preparing them kept the women folk in most Hindu households busy for days, but it's more common now for professional caterers to do most of the hard work.

rice flour, called *pathiri*. They're eaten in various forms: steam-cooked, flavoured with fish, shallow fried, dipped in egg or layered with coconut.

Finally, rice also forms the basis of the definitive Keralan dessert, *payasam* (see "Sweets and desserts", p.39).

### Vegetables and pulses

In Kerala, being a strict **vegetarian**, or even a vegan, is nothing like the privation it is often construed as in the West. On the contrary, vegetarian Malayali cooking is considered by many as the *haute cuisine* of south India – a testament to both the extraordinary wealth of fresh produce available in local markets and the ingenious techniques Keralans have devised over the centuries to enhance their flavour. Dishes tend to have two parts to their name: the main ingredient followed by the way it's prepared. There are literally hundreds of possibilities for both, but you'll find the same terms cropping up time and again.

Nearly all veg dishes will contain **coconut** in some form. For cooking, the flesh of the nut is scraped from the shell and mashed or ground (traditionally with a heavy stone mortar and pestle, but more often with an electric blender in modern kitchens). It adds richness, texture and substance – as well as protein – to dishes, and has a soothing effect on the piquancy produced by the pepper, fresh ginger and chopped green chillis that, along with curry (*karhi*) leaves and at least five spices, are added for flavour.

One of the most popular stock recipes for vegetables in Kerala is **avial**, in which lightly boiled or steamed hard vegetables, particularly okra ("ladies' fingers"), are dressed with a sauce made from roughly grated coconut and yogurt. Notable for not containing any oil, *avial* is said to have been invented by a sixteenth-century king after his kitchen ran out of cooking oil on the twenty-ninth day of a thirty-day feast.

**Thoran** is another light, oil-free concoction you'll see everywhere, in many different forms. After being poached in a wok, the main vegetable ingredients are overlaid with a paste made from fresh coconut and shallots. Spinach *thoran* is a Malayali favourite, often served with prawns sautéed in garlic and ginger. A dish very similar to it, and which is often served on Hindu feast days such as Onam, is **pachadi**, where the vegetables are finished with curry leaves and mustard seeds spluttered in hot oil. Bottle gourd (*kambalanga*) or cucumber (*vellarika*) and boiled lentils (*gram* or *urud dhal*) tend to be the main components of **olan**, a particularly wholesome stew that's closely associated with the Nair community. It too gets a final coating (*tarka*) of hot oil flavoured with whole mustard seeds and curry leaves.

Other distinctively Keralan vegetable dishes include **kadala**, a mixture of chickpeas and onions, and **kootu**, in which Bengali *gram* (maize flour) lentils (*kadala-parippu* in Malayalam) are cooked with plantain (*pachhakai*), elephant yam (*chena*) and snake gourd (*padavalanga*).

Another vegetable you may not recognize, either on market stalls or your plate, is **tapioca**, known in Malayalam as *kapad*. Produced from the root of the cassava plant, this rather bland, starchy staple is rich in carbohydrate, vitamins and minerals, and sometimes takes the place of rice to accompany fish. Although served in many village homes, it rarely appears on restaurant menus.

## Meat

Meat may be considered highly polluting among upper-caste Hindus, but it's central to the diets of Kerala's **Christian and Muslim** minorities. Syrian-Christians, in particular, have a reputation for being die-hard carnivores, enjoying both beef (strictly avoided by all caste Hindus) and pork (prohibited in Islam), as well as all kinds of poultry (hence the huge flocks of ducks you'll see waddling around the backwaters and paddy fields of central Kerala).

Eaten on festive occasions such as Easter and Christmas, **lamb stew** is the quintessential Syrian-Christian dish. To the uneducated eye it looks not unlike its Irish namesake, but the sauce is enriched with coconut and the aromas of cardamom, cinnamon, ginger and pepper, with heaps of green chillis for heat. It's nearly always mopped up with steaming-hot *appam*, as indeed is its drier cousin, **erachi olathu**, for which pieces of lamb are simmered in ground fennel seeds and other spices before the moisture is reduced, leaving a tasty, slightly crunchy coating on the meat. Duck curry (**thaararu kootu**) and country chicken curry (**kozhi kootu**) are two other Christian standards, though they're prepared differently by different sects, and from region to region: in Thrissur, for example, chicken curry is likely to be dark brown because of its base of fried, grated coconut, whereas in Kochi it'll come Goanstyle as a fiery, red and sour **vindaloo**, reflecting the city's former Portuguese influence.

Among the Moppila Muslims of the north, mutton (goat rather than sheep) is more often the meat of choice – consumed as kebabs or as mince, or packed into *pathiri* flatbreads. For wedding feasts, caterers still serve the classic Moppila delicacy, **aadu nirachathu** – lamb with a rich stuffing of chicken and egg.

## Fish

In spite of diminishing stocks, fish remains the principal source of protein for Kerala's poorer and low-caste communities – Hindu, Christian and Muslim alike – especially along the coast. **Mackerel** and **sardines** are eaten almost daily as part of the lunchtime rice plate, deep-fried in crunchy coats of millet or in dry *thorans* called *karimeen pollichathu*. When soured with *kodampuli* (a kind of tamarind), and simmered in a hot red curry sauce using an earthen pot (*chatti*), they're transformed into *meen vattichathu*.

Choice cuts from the catches landed by the deep-sea trawlers each day nearly all end up on the tables of Kerala's foreign tourists in resorts such as Varkala and Kovalam. Marlin, barracuda, kingfish, pomfret, shark, tuna and – tastiest of all – seer fish are available from November until March.

In Keralan homes, and traditional Malayali restaurants around the state, you're more likely to be served **river fish** caught in the lagoons and backwaters. Distinguished by its gold and green stripes, the flat *karimeen*, or "pearlspot", is the best-loved of all, occupying a comparable place in Keralan culture to fish and chips in Britain or salted cod in Portugal. It's caught at night using lights: the fish are attracted to the surface and snatched by hand from the water. It's most often eaten after being marinated in spices and steam-baked in a banana leaf as *karimeen pollichathu*.

The other typical Malayali fish dish you'll see on menus everywhere is **moillee** (or "moily"), a simple but delicious curry in which slices of fish (kingfish is best) are simmered in a typically Keralan mixture of coconut juice, green chillis, ginger and curry leaves. It's quick to cook and perfect with local red *puzhukkalari* rice.

## Chips: upperi

One of the most pervasive aromas of any Keralan market is the smell of frying plantain chips – **upperi** in Malayalam. They're made in a similar way to potato fries, only in vats of bubbling coconut oil, using thin slices of unripe, raw plantain, a kind of tough, savoury banana. In recent years, sweeter, ripe plantain has started to come into fashion, and you'll also occasionally see lumps of tapioca (*kapad*) and slender strips of jackfruit being deep-fried in the same way. *Upperi* are also an essential constituent of any Onam *sadya* feast (see p.37), when they may be coated in sticky sweet *jaggery*.

## Sweets and desserts

Malayalis have a fiendishly sweet tooth, especially when it comes to that most Keralan of delicacies, **halwa**. A speciality of the Kozhikode (Calicut) region of northern Kerala, *halwa* is a sticky brown sweet made from a base of rice flour (rather than wheat, favoured in similar preparations in other parts of India) and molasses or raw sugar cane (rather than refined white sugar). This mixture is then diluted with lots of coconut milk and slow-simmered and stirred for hours until it starts to thicken, when ghee (purified butter) or coconut oil and *gram* (maize flour) are poured in.

Over the years, the Arab-influenced confectioners of the Malabar region added various kinds of nuts and dried fruit (such as dates, pineapples and figs) and many garish colourings to the basic *halwa* recipe. Stroll through central Kozhikode and you'll be dazzled by brightly lit blocks in a vast range of colours.

A less dentally corrosive Keralan dessert, which you'll be served to round off any substantial Malayali meal, is **payasam** – a southern version of the north Indian *kheer* – closely resembling rice pudding, only much lighter, and delicately spiced with cardamom. Unlike its northern cousin, *payasam* is prepared with coconut instead of cow's milk. For centuries, brahmin priests at the Guruvayur temple have made huge vats of it each day to give as offerings to the Krishna deity, dispensing it afterwards to worshippers as *prasad*, or sacred "blessed".

*Payasam* also features prominently in Onam *sadyas* (see p.37), where it comes in two forms: white *paal payasam*, made with rice and sugar, and dark brown *parippu payasam*, enriched with mung beans and molasses. You might also come across a version made with bananas and pineapple (*pazham payasam*) and another, *ada pradhaman*, derived from cooked rice flakes, which has a different texture.

## Fruit

What **fruit** is available varies with region and season, but there's always a fine choice. Remember that it should always be peeled first. Roadside vendors often sell cut and peeled fruit that is sprinkled with salt and spices, but don't buy it if it looks like it's been hanging around for a while.

**Mangos** are usually on offer by late March, but not all are sweet enough to eat fresh – some are used for pickles or curries. Keralans are picky about their mangos, the ripeness of which they gauge by feel and smell before buying. Among the varieties appearing at different times in the season – from spring to summer – look out for Alphonso, which is grown in Goa, and Langra, which is grown all over the south. Oranges and tangerines are generally easy to come by, as are sweet melons and thirst-quenching watermelons, but Kerala is famous above all for its **bananas**, which are available year round. Try the delicious red bananas of Kovalam, or the Nanjangod variety, which are considered by many in the city as the best, and most extravagant (at Rs5 or so per fruit). While travelling on buses, bananas provide a good fallback in places where safe, nourishing and hygienic food might not otherwise be readily available and they're especially good for upset or sensitive stomachs. Note that certain types, however, such as the Nendrakai variety are used only for cooking.

Other **tropical fruits** available year-round include coconuts, papayas and pineapples; lychees and pomegranates are more seasonal. Among less familiar fruit, the *chikoo*, which looks like a kiwi and tastes a bit like a pear, is well worth trying, as is the watermelon-sized jackfruit (*chakkai*), whose spiny green exterior encloses sweet, slightly rubbery yellow segments each containing a seed. The custard apple, its knobbly green case housing a scented white pulp with large black seeds, is another interesting seasonal fruit, with a sweet, creamy texture that does indeed resemble custard.

## Veg vs non-veg

Many Hindu castes in Kerala abstain from eating meat and seafood, while some orthodox Namboodiri brahmins will not even eat onions or garlic, or any food cooked by anyone outside their household.

Eating places always state whether they are vegetarian or non-vegetarian – "**veg**" or "**non-veg**". Sometimes you will come across restaurants advertising both, indicating they have two separate kitchens and, often, two distinct parts to the restaurant so as not to contaminate or offend their vegetarian clientele. You'll also see "**pure veg**" advertised, which means that no eggs or alcohol are served.

Veganism as such is not common, however, so vegans need to be fairly vigilant and enquiring. Dairy products are present in most Keralan sweets, and in many restaurants and homes ghee (unclarified butter) is used for frying.

As a rule, **meat-eaters** should exercise caution in Kerala: even when meat is available, especially in the larger towns, its quality is not assured and you won't get much in a dish anyway. Note that what is called "mutton" is in fact goat. Hindus, of course, do not eat beef, and Muslims shun pork, but Christians throughout the state place both at the heart of their own brand of regional cooking.

**Fish** is popular throughout Kerala, particularly in the coastal towns, beach resorts and backwater areas, and whether served as steak or in curries is often phenomenally tasty.

## Where and when to eat

Finding somewhere decent to eat in Kerala is rarely a problem. In **towns** and **cities**, hygienic south Indian-style cafés and restaurants compete for custom on seemingly every street corner, open from dawn until late. In the **resorts**, prices in places oriented towards foreigners tend to be much higher, and the quality of cooking much patchier, but you'll be spoilt for choice, with everything from fresh local seafood to pizzas and pasta, cakes and healthy green salads.

As for authentic Keralan food, it's impossible to beat proper home cooking, which you'll be able to enjoy in homestays and small guesthouses all over the state. That said, the delicious, fresh and cheap fare served in **thattukada** hot meals stalls (see p.36) comes pretty close.

### Breakfast

Keralans are early risers, especially women in the villages, who invariably start the day in the pre-dawn darkness with a quick glass of chai before getting stuck into a couple of hours' grinding rice, coconut and spices for the day's meals. **Breakfast** proper gets under way when the kids are up, and consists of **puttu** – cylinders of roughly pounded rice and coconut steamed together in hollowed-out bamboos (or, more often these days, in aluminium tubes) – or **appam** – soft, slightly cupped rice pancakes that are deliciously spongy in the centre. **Iddiappams**, a kind of vermicelli, are another breakfast staple, made by squeezing runny rice dough through a special press and then steaming it. These are accompanied by the sweetest Keralan bananas, and maybe a cup of warm milk, or else with saucers of spicy **egg masala**, a rich, tasty gravy based on onions, or **kadala** curry, a spicy, dark-brown sauce made with chick peas and heaps of ginger and black pepper, which is poured over the *puttu*, *appam* or *iddiappam* and eaten with the fingers.

Washed down with cups of strong, milky chai or local filter coffee, versions of the standard Keralan breakfast are served in tea shacks (*chayakada*) and corner cafés all over the state – mostly to men, who use the opportunity to read the local paper and debate the latest political scandals.

In larger towns and cities, however, a more generic, **south Indian-style breakfast** prevails, based on dishes originally devised in the Karnatakan pilgrimage town of Udipi. These include scrumptious deep-fried savoury doughnuts made of chickpea flour called **vada**, and circular steamed rice cakes, or **iddlis**, which are broken up and soaked in **sambar** (a chilli-hot, sour, watery broth) or mushed together with **chatni** (a tangy paste, often made with ground coconut and finely chopped fresh green chillis). *Iddli-vada-sambar* breakfasts are dished up from dawn onwards, and around the clock in railway and bus stations. By 11am, however, most places will have switched to their lunchtime "meals" menu (see below).

Opening times are more erratic in the resorts of Kovalam and Varkala, where cafés serve a hotchpotch of travellers' standards such as banana pancakes, muesli, toast, omelettes, porridge (not always oatmeal), lassis and fruit shakes. Proper espresso is also widely available, along with freshly baked wholemeal bread, croissants (or a heavy, stodgy version of them) and copious fresh fruit salads with honey, grated coconut and yogurt (curd).

If you're staying in a smart hotel, **buffet breakfasts** are the norm, consisting of limp versions of Western food alongside much better renditions of generic north and south Indian standards and tasty Keralan specialities.

## Lunch: "Meals Ready"

**"Meals" restaurants** or **canteens** are among the best places to try genuine south Indian cuisine. Found all over Kerala, usually clustered around major bus stations and bazaars with a sign saying "Meals Ready" out front, they are a fast, cheap (around Rs35–50), informal and hygienic way to fill your stomach – and the food is usually terrific.

It's served either on a fresh plantain leaf or, more commonly these days, on large, round stainless steel trays (called by their north Indian name, thalis), with six to eight different preparations spooned by a succession of waiters into little bowls, along with blobs of pickle (*achar*) and sprinkles of salt. The conventional Keralan way to approach the meal is to break the **papadam** – the crisp-fried wafers that normally appear first – into the heap of **rice** that comes shortly after. On to this mound you pour whichever of the fiery red *sambar* or lentil-based **dhals** take your fancy. Mix them into a manageable sludge (with the fingers of your right hand only, of course; see p.60) and shovel into your mouth, without getting any on your face or shirt-front – not as easy as it may sound.

After the *ozhikan* (literally "to pour over") dishes, comes the *rasam*, a watery, hot soup soured with *kodampuli* (a kind of tamarind) or *kokum*, which is intended to aid digestion. Then you move on to the thicker vegetable dishes, known as "gravies", at least one of which in Kerala will be an **avial** – steamed root vegetables coated in roughly ground coconut and yogurt. Waiters continually patrol the dining hall, refilling any bowls that get emptied and loading more rice onto your banana leaf or tray (Keralans get through an unbelievable quantity of rice in the course of an average lunch and will find your apparent lack of appetite amusing).

Servings of vegetables, dhal, *rasam* and rice are "unlimited" (they'll keep coming until you can't manage any more), but you may have to pay a tiny bit extra if you want a second helping of yogurt, served in its pure form as "curd", which rounds every Keralan meal off: mix it into the last of your rice (Keralans will always accept a final spoonful for the purpose) – it'll help balance the heat of the spices. "Deluxe" meals will also include a small helping of sweet rice and mung bean pudding called **payasam**, deliciously spiced with cardamom and, in swankier places, saffron.

This is the generally accepted running order of dishes, but there are really no hard-and-fast rules. The only no-no that's guaranteed to attract the attention of the whole restaurant, and have your fellow diners chuckling into their lunches, is if you inadvertently mix up the *payasam* with the savoury curries. However well you manage, some good-natured curiosity is bound to attend the spectacle of a foreigner eating with his or her hands – though not as much as you'll attract by asking for a knife or fork. When you're done, head for the little tap in the corner to wash off the remnants.

As well as its main canteen or dining hall, most meals joints have a fancier a/c section (often upstairs and next door) where better-off middle-class diners, and women, can eat in greater comfort. The food's identical, but you'll pay Rs10–20 more for it.

Some places also have separate veg and non-veg sections (see p.40). In Kerala, non-veg "meals" are the same as "veg" ones, except they come with an additional chunk of fried fish or "mutton" curry.

### Snacks: udipi cooking

Most, but not all, "meals" restaurants serve menus of lighter, more generic south Indian snacks – though not usually at the same time. The so-called **udipi** menu – referring to a cuisine that was originally developed by brahmin priests of the famous Krishna temple at Udipi, coastal Karnataka, but which has since spread all over the country – starts early for breakfast (see p.40) but is generally suspended between 11am and 3pm for lunch meals.

In the afternoon, *iddli-vada-sambar-chatni* (see p.41) returns to the menu, along with the quintessential and most scrumptious of all *udipi* snacks, the **masala dosa**. Made from a batter of partly fermented rice and lentil flour, dosas are fried like French crepes on hot griddle irons until they're crunchy on the outside. Into the centre of the pancake is then spooned a blob of spicy potato masala, often packed with chunks of green vegetables, coconut, freshly chopped coriander and curry leaves. It's served while still hot with an accompaniment of *sambar* and *chatni*.

Many delicious versions of the basic dosa appear on *udipi* menus: a **rawa dosa** has semolina added to its batter, which is mixed with chopped onions and poured in sweeping, cross-hatched patterns on to the griddle to create an extra crunchy mesh. Order a "roast" or "**paper dosa**" and you could end up with a wafer-thin tube half a metre long.

**Uttappams** are another delicious *udipi* speciality – again, made from semi-fermented rice flour, but poured more thickly on the griddle, and served with a layer of green chillis, coriander, *sambar* and *chatni*. The tasty "cheese *uttappam*" offers a contemporary spin on the dish, featuring chopped tomatoes and finely grated cheese – south India's answer to the pizza.

### Hotel restaurants

Nearly every hotel or lodge in Kerala, no matter how small, has a restaurant attached to it. The smarter ones tend to be where the local middle classes dine, served by teams of brisk waiters wearing black ties and waistcoats. At lunchtime, fancy versions of the standard thali meal, featuring north Indian dishes and extra sweets and nibbles, are offered (for around Rs100–120) alongside the standard **multi-cuisine menu**. This is generally divided into four sections: north Indian, south Indian, Continental and Chinese.

Dishes can cost anywhere between Rs75 and Rs250, depending on how flash the hotel is, and vary greatly in quality. Stick to the Indian options and you won't go far wrong. "Chinese" can mean a whole range of culinary possibilities, few of which resemble anything authentically Chinese, but spicy and full of flavour nonetheless. Except in the top hotels, which employ internationally trained chefs, Continental (Western-style) dishes are the ones to avoid.

### Tourist restaurants

In the southern Keralan resorts of Kovalam and Varkala, the majority of café-restaurants lining the beachfront and clifftops bear little resemblance to the places where locals eat. Staffed by emigrant workers from Nepal or north India, most are seasonal bamboo and palm-thatch shacks that open for breakfast and stay open into the evening, serving a huge, catch-all menu of dishes tailored for the spice-sensitive Western palate.

After sunset, **seafood** takes centre stage, with the day's catch displayed on ice slabs out front. Seer fish, marlin, kingfish, barracuda, shark and swordfish are the star attractions, along with calamari (squid), fresh tiger or king prawns, crab and lobster (the latter imported and often previously frozen). You select your fish (or crustacean), and decide how you want it cooked (pan-fried with butter and garlic is best, but they'll also bake it dry in a tandoori oven with *tikka* spices on request); then settle down with a beer for a long wait.

Always ask the price before you order (anywhere between Rs200–300 is the norm), and check the size of the portion you'll get for that price.

## Drinks

Kerala is home to some of the world's premium **coffee**-growing areas and in many places coffee rivals tea in popularity. Filter coffee is drunk weak (by Western standards), milky and sweet. There's a whole ritual attached, with the hot coffee poured in flamboyant sweeping motions between tall glasses to cool it down. One of the best places to drink it is the *India Coffee House* cooperative chain, which has one or two branches in every town.

India's undisputed national drink, however, is **tea** (or **chai**) – grown on the border of Kerala and Tamil Nadu. The tea gardens of the Nilgiris produce fine, full-flavoured teas and often carry a high price tag to match the altitude. Tea is sold by chai-wallahs on just about every street corner, and is traditionally prepared with lots of milk and sugar (though if you're quick off the mark you can usually get them to hold the sugar – ask for "sugar separate"). Ginger, pepper and/or cardamoms may also be added to make a **masala chai**. English tea it isn't, but many travellers find it an irresistible brew. In tourist spots and upmarket hotels, you can get a pot of European-style "tray" tea, which generally consists of a tea bag in lukewarm water – you'd do better to stick to the pukka Indian variety, unless you are in a traditional tea-growing area.

Freshly made **fruit juices** are a real Keralan speciality. They are available everywhere from around Rs50, and are a wonderfully refreshing, healthy and heat-beating alternative to fizzy drinks. A couple of precautions apply though: firstly, make sure no ice is added (it won't have been made from purified water); and secondly, make sure the fruit is peeled to order and that your juice isn't made from something that's been hanging around for an hour or more, attracting flies.

Tender **coconut water** from green coconuts is delicious, very healthy (good if you have an upset stomach) and often the cheapest drink available. Green coconuts are common in coastal areas and are sold on the roadside by vendors who will hack off the top of the coconut with a machete and give you a straw to suck up the coconut water (you then scoop out the flesh and eat it).

India's greatest cold drink, **lassi** – originally from the north but now available throughout India – is made with beaten curd and drunk either salted, sweetened with sugar or mixed with fruit. It varies widely from smooth and delicious to insipid and watery, and is sold at virtually every café, restaurant and canteen in the state.

**Bottled water** is available everywhere. In some tourist places you can refill your own bottle with treated or boiled water, a popular initiative to help reduce street refuse. For more on bottled water, see p.45. **Fizzy drinks** are also widely available, with global brands like Coca Cola and Pepsi sold alongside locally produced alternatives – all contain a lot of sugar but little else.

## Alcohol

Keralans are officially the heaviest drinkers in India, with sales outstripping those of rice. A spiralling divorce rate and shocking rise in the number of drink-related road deaths are just two of the consequences. The only real beneficiary of the boom has been the state government itself, which strictly controls alcohol sales through its chain of **KSBC** (Kerala State Beverage Corporation) outlets. There are 337 of these liquor shops across Kerala (the long queues straggling outside them each evening are a feature of modern life in the state), and their income, together with licensing controls and alcohol tax, account for an amazing 40 percent of the government's total annual revenue.

### Beer and toddy

Licences for private bars are difficult to obtain as a result of the government monopoly, which is why in most of the tourist resorts, **beer** – though widely available – tends to be dispensed from Prohibition-style china teapots or with the bottles wrapped in napkins. Costing around Rs60–80 a bottle, Kingfisher is the leading brand, and the one containing the least glycerine, added as a preservative.

Kerala's home-grown alternative to beer is **toddy**, or *kallu* in Malayalam. Made by fermenting coconut sap, it comes in three varieties: *madhurakkallu* ("sweet toddy"), tapped in the cool hours of early morning and very mild; *andikkallu*, a slightly stronger version tapped in the evening; and *muttankallu*, which is left to brew for at least 24 hours and thus has a higher alcohol content. None, however, has a kick comparable to that of commercial beer, unless – as is often the case – it's been spiked with something. The sedative diazepam (Valium) – nicknamed *aana mayakki* (literally "elephant sedative") in Malayalam – is these days the drug of choice deployed by unscrupulous toddy-wallahs and is responsible for an upsurge of addiction across the state.

If you learn to read only one phrase in Malayalam, it will probably be the one for **toddy shops** (*kally shaap*), which appears on little signs wherever a shack is open for business. Because of the prevalence of adulteration, it's not a good idea to wander into any old one and order a glass; your hotel and guesthouse owners will know where the reputable places are, and a trip to one of these can be a memorable experience, not least because along with the toddy, they tend to serve great local food such as fried sardines and *karimeen*.

### Spirits and other liquor

**Spirits** usually take the form of "Indian Made Foreign Liquor" (IMFL), made to different recipes from their Western counterparts, although foreign spirits, such as various brands of Scotch whisky, Smirnoff vodka, Southern Comfort and Bacardi rum are increasingly gaining a foothold. Some types of Indian whisky aren't too bad, and are affordable in comparison. Indian gin and brandy can be pretty rough, though the rum is sweet and distinctive. Steer well clear of illegally distilled *arak*, which often contains methanol (wood alcohol) and other poisons. A look through the press, especially at festival times, will soon reveal numerous cases of blindness and death as a result of drinking bad hooch (or "spurious liquor" as it's called).

### Wine

In addition to spirits, India produces several varieties of **wine**, grown in the temperate uplands of neighbouring Maharashtra and Karnataka. The industry is still in its infancy, but with the help of technologies and expertise imported from overseas, standards are steadily improving. By Indian standards, even the cheapest brands, such as Vin Ballet and Riviera, are pricey (around Rs300 in the state-run "beverage shops"), and can easily double your restaurant bills. Still more expensive, and correspondingly easier drinking, are Grover's dry white, and Chantilly. At the top end of the market, (Rs700–850 in a resort restaurant) are Grover's La Reserve, Sula Chenin Blanc and wines from India's foremost winery, Chateau Indage. The latter, while the best on offer, are comparable with cheap South American or Bulgarian wines you'd expect to pick up for less than £5–6 in the UK. High-end restaurants also serve a selection of New World wines, at prices marginally higher than you'd expect to pay back home.

As for **sparkling wines**, you've a choice between Marquise de Pompadour (a crisp, refreshing champagne made from a blend of Chardonnay, Pinot Noir and Ugni Blanc grapes), or Joie-Cuve Clos (a better-structured sparkling wine with a fruit-filled bouquet, not unlike Cava).

# Health

The salubrious breezes of the Malabar make for a generally healthy climate, and if you are careful, you should be able to get through any holiday in the region with nothing worse than a mild dose of "Kerala belly". The important thing is to keep your resistance high by maintaining a balanced diet and getting plenty of sleep, and to be very aware of health risks such as poor hygiene, untreated water, mosquito bites and undressed open cuts.

## Medical resources for travellers

For up-to-the-minute information, make an appointment at a **travel clinic**. These clinics also sell travel accessories, including mosquito nets and first-aid kits.

### Travel clinics and resources

**International Society for Travel Medicine** ⓦwww.istm.org. A full list of clinics worldwide specializing in travel health.

### In the UK and Ireland

**Hospital for Tropical Diseases Travel Clinic** UK ☎020/7387 4411, ⓦwww.thehtd.org. **MASTA (Medical Advisory Service for Travellers Abroad)** UK ☎0870/606 2782, ⓦwww.masta-travel-health.com. Forty clinics across the UK.

**Nomad Pharmacy** UK ⓦwww.nomadtravel.co.uk. Clinics in London, Southampton and Bristol. **Tropical Medical Bureau** Republic of Ireland ☎1850/487674, ⓦwww.tmb.ie.

### In the US and Canada

**Canadian Society for International Health** Canada ⓦwww.csih.org. Extensive list of travel health centres in Canada. **CDC** US ☎1-877/394-8747, ⓦwww.cdc.gov. Official US government travel health site.

### In Australia, New Zealand and South Africa

**Netcare Travel Clinics** South Africa ⓦwww .travelclinic.co.za. Travel clinics in South Africa. **Travellers' Medical & Vaccination Centre** Aus ⓦwww.tmvc.com.au. Website listing travellers' medical and vaccination centres throughout Australia, New Zealand and South Africa.

## What about the water?

One of the chief concerns of many prospective visitors to Kerala is whether the water is safe to drink. To put it simply, it isn't, even though you might see locals drinking it freely. **Bottled water**, available in all but the most remote places, is a much safer bet, though it has a major drawback – namely the **plastic pollution** it causes. Visualize the size of the pile you'd leave behind you after getting through a couple of bottles per day, imagine that multiplied by millions and you have something along the lines of the amount of non-biodegradable landfill waste generated each year by tourists alone.

The best solution from the point of view of your health and the environment is to purify your own water. **Chemical sterilization** using **chlorine** is completely effective, fast and inexpensive, and you can remove the nasty taste it leaves with neutralizing tablets or lemon juice.

Alternatively, invest in some kind of **purifying filter** incorporating chemical sterilization to kill even the smallest viruses. An ever-increasing range of compact, lightweight products is available these days through outdoor shops and large pharmacies, but pregnant women or those with thyroid problems should check that iodine isn't used as the chemical sterilizer.

## Precautions

When it comes to **food**, be wary of dishes that appear to have been reheated. Anything boiled, fried or grilled (and thus sterilized) in your presence is usually all right, though seafood and meat can pose real risks if they're not fresh; anything that has been left out for any length of time, or stored in a fridge during a power cut, is best avoided. Raw unpeeled fruit and vegetables should always be viewed with suspicion, and you should steer clear of salads unless you know they have been washed in purified water. The fruit-seller on the beach may have handled the peeled fruit, so make sure you douse your slice of pineapple or melon with safe water before eating it.

Be vigilant about **personal hygiene**: wash your hands often, especially before eating. Keep all cuts clean, treat them with iodine or antiseptic (a liquid or dry spray is better in the heat) and cover them to prevent infection.

Advice on avoiding **mosquitoes** is offered on p.49. If you do get bites or itches, try not to scratch them: it's hard, but infection and tropical ulcers can result if you do. Tiger balm and even dried soap may relieve the itching.

Finally, especially if you are going on a long trip, have a **dental check-up** before you leave home. If you do go down with tooth trouble, however, don't despair. Kerala has plenty of international-standard dentists, many of them set up expressly for foreign custom. One that can be recommended in Kochi is the Emmanuel Dental Centre, Noble Square, Kadavanthara (☏0484/220 7544, ⓦwww.cosmeticdentalcentre.com).

## Vaccinations

No **inoculations** are legally required for entry into India, but diphtheria, typhoid and hepatitis A jabs are recommended for travellers to Kerala, and it's worth ensuring that you are up to date with tetanus, polio and other boosters. Vaccinations for hepatitis B, rabies, meningitis, Japanese encephalitis and TB are also advised if you're travelling further afield in India, or working in environments with an increased exposure to infectious diseases.

Transmitted through contaminated food and water, or through saliva, **hepatitis A** can lay a victim low for several months with exhaustion, fever and diarrhoea. Symptoms include yellowing of the whites of the eyes, general malaise, orange urine (though dehydration could also cause that) and light-coloured stools. If you think you have it, get a diagnosis as soon as possible, steer clear of alcohol, get lots of rest – and try to avoid passing it on. More serious is **hepatitis B**, transmitted like AIDS through blood or sexual contact.

**Typhoid fever** is also spread through contaminated food or water, but is rare in Kerala. It produces a persistent high temperature with malaise, headaches and abdominal pains, followed by diarrhoea.

**Cholera**, spread the same way as hepatitis A and typhoid, causes sudden attacks of watery diarrhoea with cramps and debilitation. Again, this disease rarely occurs in Kerala, breaking out in isolated epidemics; there is a vaccination but it offers very little protection. Most medical authorities now recommend immunization against meningo-coccal **meningitis (ACWY)** too. Spread by airborne bacteria (through coughs and sneezes for example), it is a very unpleasant disease that attacks the lining of the brain and can be fatal.

**Rabies** is widespread in Kerala, and the best advice is to give dogs and monkeys a wide berth – do not play with animals at all, no matter how cute they might look. A bite, a scratch or even a lick from an infected animal could spread the disease; if you're bitten or scratched and it breaks the skin, immediately wash the wound gently with soap or detergent, apply alcohol or iodine if possible, and go immediately to the nearest hospital for an anti-rabies jab.

## Heat trouble

The sun and the heat can cause a few problems. Many people get a bout of **prickly heat** rash before they've acclimatized – an infection of the sweat ducts caused by excessive perspiration that doesn't dry off. A cool shower, zinc oxide powder (sold in India) or talcum powder, and loose cotton clothes should help. **Dehydration** is another possible problem, so make sure you're drinking enough liquid, and drink rehydration salts when hot and/or tired. The main danger sign is irregular urination (only once a day, for instance). Dark urine probably means you should drink more. Prolonged dehydration can lead to unpleasant conditions such as kidney stones and gout.

Don't underestimate the power of the Keralan **sun**. A high-factor sunblock is vital on exposed skin, especially when you first arrive, and on areas newly exposed by haircuts or changes of clothes. A light hat is also a very good idea, especially if you're doing a lot of walking.

Finally, overheating can cause **heatstroke**, which is potentially fatal. Signs are a very high body temperature without a feeling of fever, headaches and disorientation. Lowering body temperature (a tepid shower for example) and resting in an air-conditioned room is the first step in treatment.

## Intestinal troubles

**Diarrhoea** is the most common bane of travellers. When mild and not accompanied by other major symptoms, it may just be your stomach reacting to unfamiliar food. But when accompanied by vomiting it's more likely to be food poisoning. In either case, the problem will probably pass of its own accord in 24–48 hours without treatment. In the meantime, it's essential to replace the fluids and salts you're losing, so take lots of water with oral **rehydration salts** (commonly referred to as ORS, or called Electrolyte in India). If you can't get ORS, use half a teaspoon of salt and eight of sugar in a litre of water. Travel clinics and pharmacies sell double-ended moulded plastic spoons with the exact ratio of sugar to salt. If you are too ill to drink, seek medical help immediately.

While you are suffering, it's a good idea to avoid greasy food, heavy spices, caffeine and most fruit and dairy products. Some say bananas and pawpaws are good, as are *kitchri* (a simple dhal and rice preparation), rice soup and coconut water. Curd or a soup made from Marmite or Vegemite (if you happen to have some with you) are forms of protein that can be easily absorbed by your body when you have the runs. Drugs like Lomotil or Imodium simply plug you up – undermining the body's efforts to rid itself of infection – though they can be useful if

you have to travel. If symptoms persist for more than a few days, a course of antibiotics may be necessary; this should be seen as a last resort, and only used following medical advice.

If your diarrhoea contains blood or mucus, the cause may be dysentery or giardia. With a fever, it could well be caused by **bacillic dysentery**, and may clear up without treatment. If you're sure you need it, a course of antibiotics such as tetracycline or doxycycline should sort you out, but they also destroy gut flora in your intestines, which help protect you (curd can replenish them to some extent) – and render your skin more sensitive to sunlight. If you start a course, be sure to finish it, even after the symptoms have gone; and stay out of the sun completely (or walk around under an umbrella and wear plenty of sunblock if not).

Similar symptoms, without fever, indicate **amoebic dysentery**, which is much more serious, and can damage your gut if untreated. The usual cure is a course of Metronidazole (Flagyl) or Fasigyn, both antibiotics which may themselves make you feel ill, and must not be taken with alcohol; avoid caffeine, too. Symptoms of **giardia** are similar – including frothy stools, nausea and constant fatigue – for which the treatment again is Metronidazole. If you suspect that you have any of these, seek medical help, and only start on the Metronidazole if there is blood in your diarrhoea and it is impossible to see a doctor.

Finally, bear in mind that oral drugs, such as malaria pills and the contraceptive pill, are likely to be largely ineffective if taken while suffering from diarrhoea.

## Bites and creepy-crawlies

Biting insects and similar animals other than mosquitoes may also aggravate you. The obvious ones are **bed bugs** – look for signs of squashed ones around cheap hotel beds. Other notorious culprits are **sandflies**, whose bites can become unbearably itchy. Head and body **lice** can also be a nuisance, but medicated soap and shampoo (foreign brands are normally more effective) usually see them off. Avoid scratching bites, which can lead to infection, sometimes in dangerous forms such as **septicemia** or **tropical ulcers**. Bites from ticks and lice can spread **typhus**, characterized by fever, muscle aches, headaches and, later, red eyes and a measles-like rash. If you think you have it, seek treatment.

**Worms** may enter your body through skin (especially the soles of your feet) or food. An itchy anus is a common symptom, and you may even see them in your stools. They are easy to treat: if you suspect you have them, get some worming tablets such as Mebendazole (Vermox) from any pharmacy.

**Snakes** are unlikely to bite unless accidentally disturbed, and most are harmless in any case. The best way to avoid them is to walk heavily, and never poke around holes or crevices in the ground. It's also a good idea to wear sturdy shoes rather than flip-flops at night. It's rare to get bitten, but if you do, try to identify the snake and seek immediate medical help: anti-venoms are available in most hospitals. A few **spiders** have venomous bites too, as do scorpions and some centipedes, but they hardly ever prove fatal. **Leeches** may attach themselves to you in jungle areas. Remove them with salt, a lighter, or a lit cigarette; never just pull them off.

## Malaria and other mosquito-borne diseases

The Keralan government recently declared that **malaria** had been eradicated from the state, but the truth is it hasn't entirely, and protection – from nets and proper repellent, if not full-blown prophylaxis – remains essential. The disease, caused by a parasite carried in the saliva of female Anopheles mosquitoes, is endemic everywhere in south India – although the WHO classes Kerala as a low-risk area. It has a variable incubation period of a few days to several weeks, so you can become ill long after being bitten. Programmes to eradicate the disease by spraying mosquito-infested areas and distributing free preventative tablets have proved ineffectual; the Anopheles mosquitoes quickly develop immunities to the insecticides, while the malaria parasite itself constantly mutates into drug-resistant strains, rendering the old cures ineffective.

### Prophylaxis

Some doctors and health clinics advise travellers to Kerala to take preventative tablets; some don't. But if you do end up taking them, keep to a strict **routine**, and cover the period before and after your trip. The most commonly used drug is **chloroquine** (trade names include Nivaquin, Avloclor and Resochin): you usually take two tablets weekly, but Kerala also has chloroquine-resistant strains, and you might need to supplement it with daily **proguanil** (Paludrine) or weekly **Maloprim**.

**Malarone** is the newest addition to the armoury against the deadlier *Plasmodium falciparum* strain, and is increasingly prescribed for people travelling to places where chloroquine- and other drug-resistant forms of malaria are present. Studies have claimed it to be 98 percent effective and to have relatively few side effects. The main drawback is that it's expensive and is only licensed for use for 28 days (although in practice it's probably safe for longer). Malarone is taken once daily with food or milk, starting two days before entering a malaria risk area and continuing daily until seven days after leaving the area. Children can also take it. **Mefloquine** (Lariam) is now seldom recommended by doctors owing to its harmful side effects.

**Side effects** of other anti-malarial drugs may include itching, rashes, hair-loss and sight problems. Chloroquine and quinine are safe during pregnancy, but most other antimalarials should be avoided. As the malaria parasite can incubate in your system without showing symptoms for more than a month, it is essential that you continue to take preventative tablets for at least four weeks after you return home: the most common way of catching malaria is by forgetting to do this.

### Symptoms

The first **signs of malaria** are remarkably similar to a severe flu – shivering, burning fever and headaches – and come in waves, usually beginning in the early evening. They may take months to appear but if you suspect anything, go to a hospital or clinic immediately for a blood test. Malaria is not infectious, but some strains are dangerous and can prove fatal when not treated promptly, such as the virulent choloquine-resistant strain, **cerebral malaria**.

## Preventing mosquito bites

The best way of avoiding malaria, of course, is to **avoid mosquito bites**. Sleep under a **mosquito net** if possible – one that can hang from a single point is best (you can usually find a way to tie a string across your room to hang it from). You can also burn mosquito **coils**, which are readily available in south India though not recommended for asthma suffers, or use plug-in **vapour mats or oil evaporators** – though none of these methods assures the same degree of protection as a net. If you find yourself having to rely on them, keep the air conditioning switched on all night (mosquitoes don't like cold air).

Although they are active from dusk till dawn, female Anopheles mosquitoes prefer to bite in the **evening**, so be especially careful at that time. Wear long sleeves, skirts or trousers, avoid dark colours, which attract mosquitoes, and make sure to smother yourself in **repellent**. An Indian brand, Odomos, is widely available, effective and much cheaper than comparable DEET-based sprays from home – although you might want higher-concentration solutions as a backup for times when you encounter lots of mosquitoes. People with sensitive skin, however, are advised to use the new wrist and ankle bands instead, as they are equally as effective as spray.

## Dengue fever, Japanese encephalitis and Chikungunya

Another illness spread by mosquito bites is **dengue fever**, whose symptoms are similar to those of malaria, with the additional symptom of aching bones. There is no vaccine available and the only treatment is complete rest, with drugs to assuage the fever. Occurrences are pretty rare but tend to come in mini-epidemics. It's also worth noting that while first infections of the disease are rarely fatal, it can be life-threatening if contracted a second time. Moreover, unlike malaria-carrying anopheles, the stripy "tiger" mosquitoes that carry dengue bite during the day.

**Japanese encephalitis**, yet another mosquito-borne viral infection causing fever, muscle pains and headaches, has been on the increase in recent years in rural rice-growing areas during and just after monsoon, though there have been no reports of travellers catching the disease and you shouldn't need the vaccine. The same is true of the African disease **Chikungunya**, a relatively rare form of viral fever that has afflicted most parts of south India over the past few years, notably Alappuzha (Alleppey) in southern Kerala, where it caused at least 125 deaths in 2006. The name is derived from the Makonde word meaning "to bend", referring to the doubled-up posture that's a common symptom of Chikungunya.

## HIV and AIDS

The increasing presence of **AIDS** has only recently been acknowledged by the Keralan government as a major problem. Should you need an injection or a transfusion while in the region, make sure that new, sterile equipment is used; any blood you receive should be from voluntary rather than commercial donor banks. Try to bring needles from home in your first-aid kit. If you have a shave from a barber, make sure he uses a clean blade, and don't submit to processes such as ear-piercing, acupuncture or tattooing unless you can be sure that the equipment is sterile.

## Getting medical help

**Pharmacies** can usually advise on minor medical problems, and most **doctors** in Kerala speak English. Many hotels also have a doctor on call. Basic medicaments are made to Indian Pharmacopoea (IP) standards, and most medicines are available without prescription – although always check the sell-by date.

**Hospitals** vary in standard; those in the big cities are generally world-class, and university and medical-school hospitals are best of all – though they're invariably much busier and more hectic than what you might be used to back home. One of the reasons for this is that Keralan hospitals as a rule operate a first-come-first-seen system: you turn up and wait in a queue to see the doctor or consultant, rather than book an appointment.

Private hospitals are often better than state-run ones, but generally require patients (even emergency cases) to pay for X-rays, scans, and blood and urine tests before procedures can be carried out. Costs are a fraction of private health care in the West, though be sure to keep all original documents and receipts to claim money back on insurance if need be. **Government hospitals** provide all surgical and aftercare services free of charge, and in most other state medical institutions, charges are usually so low that for minor treatment the expense may well be lower than the initial "excess" on your insurance. You will need a companion to stay, or you'll have to come to an arrangement with one of the hospital cleaners, to help you out in hospital – relatives are expected to wash, feed and generally take care of the patient.

**Addresses** of local clinics and hospitals can be found in the "Listings" sections for major towns in this book.

# The media

With literacy rates of around 88 percent for women and 91 percent for men, Kerala is by far the most media-oriented state in India, producing a string of regional dailies with readerships that outstrip most Western tabloids. Furthermore, with the advent of satellite and cable, dozens of new TV channels have sprung up, both in English and Malayalam. Radio has a similarly wide range of stations, though it tends to be more localized and there is less programming in English.

## Newspapers and magazines

Keralans have an insatiable appetite for news, views, information and gossip, and newsstands across the state groan under the weight of publications both in English and Malayalam. With a circulation close to 1.5 million and a readership of around nine million, the undisputed ruler of the region's **newspaper** roost is the mighty *Malayala Manorama*, the state's oldest daily. Like its main rival, *Mathrubhumi* (circulation one million), the *Manorama* comes in multiple editions from a string of different production centres covering all fourteen districts of the state. News coverage in all of them is irreverent and critical of the local and national government by Indian standards, with a fair measure of satirical sketches, cartoons and scandalmongering – in addition to all the usual movie and celeb tittle-tattle. An English version of the paper appears online at Ⓦ www.manoramaonline.com and is an excellent source of in-depth news on Kerala.

The most prominent national dailies are *The Hindu*, *The Hindustan Times*, *The Statesman*, the *Times of India*, *The Economic Times* and *The Indian Express*, all of which have regional pages and inserts and are widely read across south India; the *Deccan Herald* is a southern paper, though widely read all over India.

All **English-language** Indian newspapers are pretty dry, though written in a somewhat breathless style that's littered with quaintly dated expressions. Criminals are "miscreants" who get "nabbed" after being "swooped on" by the police, or else "abscond" from the crime scene. Rioters are "stone pelters" who "go berserk" before being "*lathi* charged" (broken up by police with sturdy bamboo canes).

All the major Indian newspapers have **websites**, with the *Times of India*, *The Hindu* and *The Hindustan Times* providing the most up-to-date and detailed news services.

A number of *Time/Newsweek*-style **news magazines** have hit the market over the past decade, with a strong emphasis on politics. Published by *Malayala Manorama*, the one with the best coverage of Keralan news is *The Week*. Others worth a browse are the top-selling *India Today*, published independently, *Frontline*, published by *The Hindu*, and *Outlook*, which covers the widest range of subjects. These often give a clearer picture of national politics than the dailies and also cover more international news. *Business India* is more financially oriented, and the *India Magazine* more cultural. Film fanzines and gossip mags are very popular; *Screen* and *Filmfare* are the best, though you'll have to be reasonably *au fait* with Indian movies to follow a lot of the coverage. Magazines and periodicals in English cover all sorts of popular and minority interests, and there are plenty of sports publications, especially on cricket.

As for **foreign publications**, large bookstores will stock slightly out-of-date copies of magazines like *Vogue* and *Cosmopolitan,* but not the major news dailies. For those you will have to head online.

### Television

With its diet of largely sober, edifying programmes on politics and traditional culture, the **government-run** national **TV** company, Doordarshan, has struggled to compete with the onslaught of mass access to cable and **satellite TV**. The main English-language cable network is Rupert Murdoch's **Star TV**, which incorporates BBC World and otherwise dominates the schedules. Zee TV (with Z News) presents a progressive blend of Hindi-oriented chat, film, news and music programmes. Star Sports and ESPN churn out a mind-boggling amount of cricket with occasional forays into other sports – both broadcast Premier and Champions League football, for example. Others include CNN, the Discovery Channel, National Geographic, MTV, the immensely popular Channel V, hosted by scantily clad Mumbai models and DJs, and an increasing number of channels showing Indian and Western films, like Star Movies, HBO, Zee Studio and AXN.

At the last count, no less than ten **regional TV channels** were transmitting out of Kerala: Doordarshan Kerala, Asianet and its network partner Asianet News, Surya and Kiran from the Sun Network, the Malayalam-language Kairali TV, India Vision, Jeevan TV, Amrita TV by the Mata Amritanandamayi Math (Amma Ashram), Manorama News (from the top-selling Malayalam daily, *Malayala Manorama*) and Shalom TV, a lurid evangelical Christian channel.

Most of these can be accessed through hotel television sets, depending on how many channels you receive in any given location.

# Festivals

Few places on the planet lavish as much time and creative energy on their festivals as Kerala. Every temple, mosque and church in the state stages its own annual celebration, featuring parades of elephants in gleaming golden headpieces, fireworks, feasting and performances of traditional arts such mohiniyattam dance and kathakali ritual drama.

Events vary in scale, but are always attended by huge crowds of locals, who respond to the old art forms with as much enthusiasm as their ancestors. Hundreds of thousands turn out for the largest events, like Thrissur's **Puram**, the mother of the state's Hindu temple festivals, and the famous **snake boat races**, held each monsoon in the backwaters, in which teams of over one hundred rowers and singers ride

## Principal Keralan festivals

The following list covers only Kerala's **main festivals**; scores more are held at other temples, mosques and churches year round; consult the nearest tourist office for details. As for **national public holidays**, India only has four: January 26 (Republic Day), August 15 (Independence Day), October 2 (Mahatma Gandhi's birthday) and December 25 (Christmas Day). Most businesses also close on the major holidays of their own religion.

The solar **Malayali calendar** months are given in brackets below, as most of the festivals listed are fixed according to it. Their equivalent dates in the Gregorian calendar vary from year to year, which is why you'll have to check online or at tourist offices if you want to find more precise timings. Just to confuse matters, some national festivals, such as Diwali and Dussehra, are dated according to the lunar Hindu calendar, which has different months (also named in brackets after the specific listing where relevant).

**Key**: **C**=Christian; **H**=Hindu; **M**=Muslim; **N**=non-religious.

### Jan–Feb (Makaram)

**(N) Malabar Mahotsavam** Kozhikode (Jan 13–15). Northern Kerala's premier cultural festival showcases the best of the region's music, dance, martial and ritual arts and cuisine on stages at the city's central maidan.

**(H) Pongala** The harvest festival, known elsewhere in India as "Makar Sankranti", is celebrated in Kerala with the building of small makeshift stoves in the street, on which lines of Malayali women dressed in their best saris prepare special *payasam* (see p.39) puddings.

**(H) Makara Vilakku** Sri Ayappan temple, Sabarimala (Jan 14). Culmination of the massive Ayappan pilgrimage, when the doors to the shrine are flung open to reveal the deity swathed in jewels, while a mysterious star, the "Makarajyothi", appears fleetingly on the horizon. See p.161.

**(H) Shiva Temple Festival** Ernakulam. *Kathakali* and classical music recitals accompany the nine-elephant parades around modern Ernakulam's busy Shiva temple.

**(H) Elephant Festival** Thiruvananthapuram. The capital's Shiva temple hosts a spectacular elephant procession.

**(N) Nishangandhi Festival** Thiruvananthapuram (mid-Jan). Top-drawer classical music and dance artists from all over the country perform on two open-air stages at the Kanakakannu Palace, alongside a popular food festival. See p.86.

**(C) Arthungal Perunnal** (Jan 20). Devotees crawl on their hands and knees from one of Kerala's oldest churches to the sea for the culmination of the Feast of St Sebastian.

**(N) Republic Day** (Jan 26). Military parades are held in Thiruvananthapuram.

### Feb–March (Kumbham)

**(H) Maha Shivratri** (the moonless night, usually early March). Anniversary of Shiva's *tandav* (creation) dance and his wedding anniversary, marked by strict fasting. A *Shivalingam* rises out of the sands of the Periyar River at Alua, near Kochi, attracting tens of thousands of pilgrims.

**(H) Holi** (usually early March). This crazy spring festival, in which coloured dyes and powders are thrown liberally around, is a much bigger deal in north India, but it's started to catch on in Kerala, where the paint bombs make life at street level hard-going and bonfires marking the defeat of the demon Holika are lit in parks.

**(H) Parippally Gajamela** (late Feb to early March), Paravur. Massive elephant procession, hosted by Kodimoottil Sri Bhagavathi (Badrakali) Temple between Kollam and Varkala, featuring more than fifty tuskers.

**(H) Puram** Guruvayur. Although the temple here is off-limits to non-Hindus, the big procession, featuring forty tuskers, and a spectacular elephant race, are well worth the visit.

**(H) Kakkoor Kalavayal** near Piravom, Ernakulam District. A specially decorated bullock cart known as the *rishabhavana* leads processions of caparisoned elephants, musicians and dancers around the temple, followed by dramatic bullock-cart races in newly harvested paddy fields.

**(H) Ettumanur Temple Festival**. The Mahadeva temple hosts the famous *ezhara ponnana* procession featuring "seven-and-a-half" statues of golden elephants. See p.152.

**(C) Maramon Convention** (Feb). Said to be the largest Christian gathering in South Asia, the ten-day Maramon Convention is held on the River Pamba at Kozhencherry.

**(H) Kuttikkol Thampuratty** near Erinhipuzha (around third week of Feb). One of north Kerala's most visually impressive *theyyem* festivals.

### March–April (Meenam)

**(H) Ramanavami** (9 of Hindu month of Chaitra). Birthday of Rama, the hero of the *Ramayana*, celebrated with readings of the epic and discourses on Rama's life and teachings.

**(C) Easter** (Good Friday). The big feast day for Kerala's Christians.

**(H) Bharani Festival** Kodungallur. Spirit possession trances, drinking and the singing of sexually explicit songs to the Goddess Bhagawati form the focus of this famous Tantric ritual. See p.203.

**(H) Arattu Festival** Thiruvananthapuram. Second of the year's biannual Arattu (see p.86).

**(M) Chandanakuda Mahotsavam** Beemapalli, near Thiruvananthapuram. Elephant processions, music, dance, traditional storytelling and swordplay mark the saint's day at the Beemapalli Dargah Shareef tomb – one of Kerala's main festivals.

### April–May (Medam)

**(H) Vishu** (April 14). Malayalis believe that fortunes over the coming year depend on the first object that's seen on Vishu, so displays of auspicious items (such as rice, metal mirrors, *uruli* bell-metal utensils and *nilavilakku* lamps) are arranged in most Hindu households.

**(H) Thrissur Puram Festival** Thrissur. Frenzied drumming and massive elephant parades, all in the blazing heat of early May. See p.196.

### June–July (Mithunam)

**(H) Champakulam Moolam Boat Race** Champakulam. To commemorate the installation of the local temple deity, this big snake boat race – said to be the oldest and most traditional in the state – is held at a lake near Alappuzha. See p.140.

### July–Aug (Karkatakam)

**(N) Independence Day** (15 Aug). India's largest secular celebration, on the anniversary of its Independence from Britain, is marked with parades and fireworks.

### Aug–Sept (Chaingam)

**(N) Nehru Trophy Snake Boat Race** Alappuzha (second Sat in Aug). The most spectacular of all Kerala's boat races, with longboats crewed by 150 rowers and singers. A grand procession precedes the start of the heats on Punnamada Lake. See p.133.

**(M) Ramadan** (first day). The start of a month during which Muslims may not eat, drink or smoke from sunrise to sunset, and should abstain from sex.

*(contd. overleaf)*

**(H) Guru Deva Jayanti** (Sept 3). Celebrations marking the birthday and *samadhi* of the spiritual leader and social reformer Sri Narayana Guru, staged at his former ashram on the outskirts of Varkala, and featuring processions of saffron-clad acolytes, cultural shows, community feasts and temple rituals. See p.116.

**(H) Onam** Lasting ten days, Kerala's harvest festival is the most important religious and social event of the Hindu calendar, reuniting families in much the same way that Christmas does in the west. *Pookalam* – geometric floral decorations – are laid out in the courtyards of houses; special Onam songs (*ona paattuu*) are sung; and everyone dons splendid new clothes (*onakkodi*) for the great Onam feast, *sadya* (see p.37), which brings the celebrations to a close.

**(H) Athachamayam** Thripunitra. Exponents of all Kerala's ritual and folk arts assemble to mark the start of Onam, with a colourful procession to the Royal Palace, accompanied by massive *chenda melam* drum orchestras.

**(H) Pulikali** Thrissur. Marking the fourth day of Onam, troupes of men cover their bodies in orange and black stripes, donning masks and belts of bells to perform surreal "tiger plays", accompanied by exuberant drumming – one of the state's more bizarre spectacles. See p.199.

**(N) Aranmula Snake Boat Race** Held on the Pamba River in central Kerala, this is among the more traditional of the state's famous rowing races. See p.153.

### Sept–Oct (Kanni)

**(H) Dussehra** (1–10 of Hindu month of Ashvina). Ten-day festival (usually two days' public holiday) associated with vanquishing demons, in particular Rama's victory over Ravana in the *Ramayana*, and Durga's over the buffalo-headed Mahishasura. Dussehra celebrations include performances of the *Ram Lila* (life of Rama).

**(M) Id ul-Fitr** Feast to celebrate the end of Ramadan.

**(N) Mahatma Gandhi's Birthday** (Oct 2). Rather solemn commemoration of Independent India's founding father.

**(H) Vidyarambham** (first week of Oct). In homes, temples, mosques and churches across the region, children between the ages of 3 and 5 are initiated into the world of learning – as many as 10,000 attend the ceremony in Kollam's Saravasti ("Goddess of Wisdom") temple.

**(H) Snake festival** Mannarsala. Over a week in Kanni, hundreds of cobra deities from the famous snake grove at Mannarsala are paraded and presented offerings, led by the senior female priest, Valliamma. See p.140.

### Oct–Nov (Thulam)

**(H) Diwali (Deepavali)** (15 of Hindu month of Kartika). Festival of lights, especially popular in northern India but increasingly celebrated in Kerala, to mark Rama and

exquisite wooden longboats along palm-fringed canals. The year is also marked by more intimate, family-oriented rituals in the home, the best-loved of them **Onam**, the annual harvest festival, when relatives gather from far and wide for elaborate *sadya* feasts (see p.37).

One of the most striking features of religious festivals in Kerala, both large and small, is the extent to which Hindu, Muslim and Christian celebrations resemble each other. Elephants handled by Hindu *mahouts*, dressed in traditional gold head ornaments (called *nettippattom* in Malayalam), feature both in Islamic celebrations and Hindu temple festivals (or *utsavam*), when the deities appear in processions outside the shrines, regaled by mass ranks of *chenda melam* drummers and trumpeters. Even some Syrian-Christian feast days feature elephant parades and *chenda* drums; almost every festival culminates in a massive, raucous firework display.

Sita's homecoming in the *Ramayana*. Festivities include the lighting of oil lamps and firecrackers, and the giving and receiving of sweets.

**(C) Feast of Mar Thoma** (Nov 21). A colourful procession of decorated carts leads to this ancient site where St Thomas first landed, at Kodungallur. See p.204.

**(H) Arattu** Thiruvananthapuram. Ten days of festivities inside the Padanabhaswamy temple culminate in a procession through the streets of the capital. Led by the maharaja of Travancore, the deity is carried to the sea for ritual immersion, accompanied by traditional drum orchestras, a 21-gun salute and huge crowds. See p.86.

### Nov–Dec (Virchikam)

**(H) Thiruvappana** Parassinikadavu, Kannur (Dec 1). The centrepiece of the Muthappam temple's annual festival is a spectacular *theyyem* performance representing the four phases in the life of the deity. See p.252.

**(M) Id ul-Zuha** Pilgrimage festival coinciding with the end of the *Haj* to commemorate Abraham's preparedness to sacrifice his son Ismail. Celebrated with the slaughtering and eating of sheep.

### Dec–Jan (Dhanu)

**(H) Kalpathy Ratholsavam** Kalpetta and Palakkad. Tamil Brahmins preside over these two famous processions, in which temple deities are dragged by devotees along the main streets of brahmin colonies on three huge, ornately carved and decorated *raths* (giant wheeled chariots).

**(C) Christmas** (Dec 25). Paper star lanterns and fairy lights decorate Christian homes, households exchange sweets, and families reunite with elaborate feasts.

**(N) Kochi Carnival** (final week of the year). A week of revelry in the streets of Fort Cochin, with costumed processions, masked dances and elephant processions.

**(N) Kerala Kalamandalam Festival** Cheruthuruthy. Annual festival of music and dance, featuring performances by graduates and staff of the renowned Kalamandalam Academy of Keralan performing arts. See p.206.

**(H) Thiruvathira**. Over the full moon of Dhanu, Keralan women keep all-night vigils for Lord Shiva, and dance around the family *nilavilakku* lamp, dressed in beautiful white saris (*kasavu mundu*) edged in gold.

**(M) Muharram** Commemorates the martyrdom of the (Shi'ite) Imam, the Prophet's grandson and popular saint Hussain.

**(N) Swathi Sangeetotsavam** Puttan Malika Palace, Thiruvananthapuram (usually first or second week of Jan). Carnatic and traditional Keralan music take centre stage for this dreamy annual festival in the grounds of the former Travancore royal palace, held in honour of "the Goddess" (Mahadevi). See p.88.

**Finding festivals** is often a matter of chance. You might follow the sound of drumming through the palm grove behind your hotel to discover a temple ritual in full swing, complete with dancers and a crowd of rapt onlookers, or pass a poster advertising a thirty-elephant parade happening that night near where you're staying. Notices of forthcoming events across the region are listed daily in the state's main daily, *Malayala Manorama*, although you'll need a helpful local to translate them for you. Wherever you are, check at local tourist offices to find out what's on and when. In Ernakulam, the Tourist Desk at the Main Boat Jetty (see p.170) hands out monthly events programmes and is a particularly good source of advice on festivals staged in more off-track areas. Kerala Tourism's website also hosts a detailed **"Events Calendar"**, with dates running twelve months in advance.

# Sports and outdoor activities

Kerala is not a place that most people associate with competitive sports. However, football has a huge fan base in the state, while cricket has started to claim a passionate following among young Keralans. The most popular adventure activities with foreign visitors are trekking, cycling and kayaking.

## Sports

While the rest of the country is cricket-crazy, Keralans have traditionally favoured **soccer** as the sport of choice – a status quo that the spread of cable TV is fast overturning.

### Football

Despite the passion that Keralans hold for football, not a single Keralan club is represented in India's premier division, the National Football League. While the state side has achieved some success in the prestigious Santosh Trophy, its top teams – Viva Kerala and FC Kochi (both based in Kochi's Jawaharlal Nehru Stadium) and State Bank of Travancore (based in Thiruvananthapuram's Chandrasekar Nair Stadium) – seem forever trapped in the Second Division. Lack of sponsorship is the reason most often advanced for the moribund state of Keralan football. With national attention focused on cricket, the region's utilities and most profitable companies prefer to have their logos emblazoned over the shirts of high-profile batsmen and bowlers.

Check the local press or ⓦwww.indianfootball.com for details of local fixtures; you can usually get in to see a match on the day, with the cheapest tickets going for around Rs75, and swankier seats costing up to Rs700.

### Cricket

**Cricket** is said to have been introduced to south India in the northern Keralan town of Thalassery (Tellicherry) by no less than Colonel Arthur Wellesley, the future Duke of Wellington. Since then, it's steadily grown in popularity and now looks to be overtaking soccer as the state's most popular game; you'll see it being played on open spaces all around the state – especially the beaches.

Coverage of the Indian team's matches dominates sports channels, though international matches are rarely hosted in Kerala. **Inter-state** cricket is, by contrast, easy to catch live. The most prestigious competition is the Ranji Trophy, whose games are usually held in the Municipal Cricket Ground at Thalassery (Tellicherry) Stadium; tickets can usually be bought on the day.

From 2011, Kochi will also host its own **Indian Premier League (IPL)** franchise – a move certain to raise the profile of Twenty20 cricket in the state. A consortium of industrial magnates and politicians bid $333 million for the new team, which will play in the brand-new, world-class stadium currently under construction in the city.

## Outdoor activities

Outdoor pursuits are only just starting to catch on in a state that's always been more into team sports. As yet, there is little in the way of infrastructure and facilities – which is all part of the appeal of regions such as the Western Ghat mountains, which offer some wonderful trekking possibilities. For information on Kerala's **wildlife sanctuaries** and **national parks**, see the box on p.307.

### Trekking

With Kerala's trekking scene still in its infancy, expect few qualified guides and no waymarked routes, let alone dependable maps. That said, some magnificent walks await the adventurous amid the hills of the interior, where the rainforests of the Western Ghats give way to exposed grassy uplands that, in places, exceed 2500m – the height of a respectable Pyrenean peak.

In the far south, **Neyyar Dam** and the adjacent **Peppara Wildlife Sanctuary** are springboards for several wonderful high-level walks. One of these – the day ascent of Kurisamala – is outlined on p.110, along with suggestions of where to stay and how to arrange the necessary paperwork and guides.

In central Kerala, **Munnar** is by far the best base to trek from, with a ring of superb mountain summits soaring above its picturesque tea gardens. A handful of local guides (see p.219) are on hand to accompany you, and they'll also help obtain permission from the Forest Department for longer routes.

The most obvious target for any would-be trekker in the north of the state is mighty Chembra Peak (2100m), whose slopes dominate the region of **Wayanad**. Full coverage on how to tackle the route, which can be completed in a strenuous day, appears on p.238. Also in Wayanad, some impressive mountain country immediately behind **Banasura Lake** offers some wonderful trekking possibilities (see p.241), as do the watershed peaks accessible from the remote **Fringe Ford** plantation bungalow (see p.243).

The best time for hill walking is between late December and the end of January, when humidity levels are at their lowest and visibility best. It isn't necessary to have any specialized gear, but you'll need a lightweight waterproof, fleece layers for added warmth (it can get surprisingly chilly above 2000m, even in Kerala), strong boots, a headtorch, sleeping bag, sunblock and, of course, bottles or platypus hoser bags with a minimum capacity of three litres.

## Cycling

Kerala's roads are too hectic, dangerous and potholed for long-distance **cycle touring** to be much fun for anyone but the most resilient and determined. But there are plenty of lesser frequented backroads – particularly in the mountain areas inland – which offer superb routes through magnificent forest and hill scenery, though a certain level of fitness is essential given the gradients. A handful of **firms** – notably Aadi Kerala (⊛keralatravel agent.in), Butterfield & Robinson (⊛www .butterfield.com), Exodus (⊛www.exodus travels.co.uk) and High Places (⊛www .highplaces.co.uk) – have devised itineraries for both small groups and individuals, with night stays in various kinds of accommodation along the way. They provide new, foreign-made mountain bikes or tourers, with a guide and van to carry your gear, tools and spare cycles. For day rides, some upmarket homestays and travel agents (such as Touromark in Periyar; see p.158) offer imported cycles for rent – they can also provide advice on the best routes in the area.

## Kayaking

**Kayaking** is a great way to explore the Keralan backwaters, and, increasingly, homestays and hotels in the region are offering it as an option for guests, along with trained guides to show you around. One base we can recommend in the heart of the Kuttanad backwaters is *Akkarikkulam Memoirs*, in Chennamkary near Alappuzha (⊛www.akkara kalammemoirs.com; see p.143), a heritage guesthouse which keeps its own small fleet of imported kayaks. On the River Periyar, inland from Kochi/Ernakulam, you can also canoe around the Thattekad Bird Sanctuary from the wonderful *Hornbill Camp* (⊛www.hornbill camp.com). Alternatively, contact Aadi Kerala (⊛keralatravelagent.in) and get them to arrange a bespoke kayaking trip around Kerala's best sites.

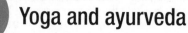

# Yoga and ayurveda

Yoga is taught all over Kerala, but particularly in the resorts of Kovalam and Varkala, and there are several internationally known centres where you can train to become a teacher. Kerala also hosts innumerable ashrams — communities where people work, live and study together, drawn by a common (usually spiritual) goal – the most famous and visited of them at Amritapuri in the backwaters, home of the "hugging Guru", Amma.

Details of teachers, courses and ashrams are provided throughout the Guide. Most places can enrol you at short notice, but some of the more popular ones listed on p.59 need to be booked well in advance.

## Yoga and meditation

The word "**yoga**" literally means "union", the aim of the discipline being to help the practitioner unite his or her individual consciousness with the divine. This is achieved by raising awareness of the true nature of self through spiritual, mental and physical discipline.

Many texts and manuscripts have been written describing the practice and philosophy of yoga, but probably the best known are the *Yoga Sutras of Patanjali*, written by the sage Maharishi Patanjali in either the second century BC or the second or third century AD. He believed the path to realization of the self consisted of eight spiritual practices which he called the "eight limbs": these were *yama* (moral codes); *niyama* (self-purification through study); *asana* (posture); *pranayama* (breath control); *pratyahara* (sense control); *dharana* (concentration); *dhyana* (contemplation); and *samadhi* (meditative absorption). Of these eight limbs the first four are "external" in nature while the last four are "internal".

Today it is **asanas**, or the physical postures, that are most commonly identified as yoga, but these are just one element of what to many practitioners is a complete transcendental philosophy.

### Types of yoga

A multitude of paths and practices exist to help the individual attain the ultimate goal of

union with the divine. **Hatha yoga** is the term most commonly used for the physical and spiritual practices described above, and there are innumerable approaches to teaching it. Broadly speaking, they all focus on a series of *asanas*, which stretch, relax and tone the muscular system of the body and also massage the internal organs. Each *asana* has a beneficial effect on a particular muscle group or organ, and although they vary widely in difficulty, consistent practice will lead to improved suppleness and health benefits.

**Iyengar yoga** is one of the most famous approaches studied today, named after its founder, B.K.S. Iyengar, a student of the great yoga teacher Sri Tirumalai Krishnamacharya. His style is based upon precise physical alignment during each posture. With much practice, and the aid of props such as blocks, straps and chairs, the student can attain perfect physical balance and, the theory goes, perfect balance of mind will follow. Iyengar yoga has a strong therapeutic element and has been used successfully for treating a wide variety of structural and internal problems.

**Ashtanga yoga** is an approach developed by Pattabhi Jois, who also studied under Krishnamacharya. Unlike Iyengar yoga, which centres on a collection of separate *asanas*, Ashtanga links various postures into a series of flowing moves called *vinyasa*, with the aim of developing strength and agility. The perfect synchronization of movement with breath is a key objective throughout these sequences. Although a powerful form, it can be frustrating for beginners as each move has to be perfected before moving on to the next one.

The son of Krishnamacharya, T.K.V. Desikachar, established a third major branch in the modern yoga tree, emphasizing a more versatile and adaptive approach to teaching, focused on the situation of the individual practitioner. This style became known as **Viniyoga**, although Desikachar has long tried to distance himself from the term. In the mid-1970s, he co-founded the Krishnamacharya Yoga Mandiram (KYM), now a flagship institute in Chennai, in neighbouring Tamil Nadu and, in 2006, an offshoot now steered by his son Kausthub, called the Krishnamacharya Healing and Yoga Foundation (KHYF).

The other most influential Indian yoga teacher of the modern era has been Swami Vishnu Devananda, an acolyte of the famous sage Swami Sivananda, who established the International Sivananda Yoga Vedanta Center, with more than twenty branches in India and abroad. **Sivananda**-style yoga tends to introduce elements in a different order from its counterparts – teaching practices regarded by others as advanced to relative beginners. This fast-forward approach has proved particularly popular with Westerners, who flock in their thousands to intensive introductory courses staged at centres all over India – the most renowned of which at Neyyar Dam, in the hills east of the Keralan capital, Thiruvananthapuram (see p.109).

## Ashrams

**Ashrams** – centres where followers of a particular guru or spiritual discipline may gather to study – are dotted all around south India, and Kerala is no exception. Foreigners tend to gravitate towards the state's two internationally famous institutions – Mata Amritanandamayi Math, three hours from Kollam (see p.140), and Sivananda Yoga Vedanta Dhanwantari Ashram, 28km east of Thiruvananthapuram (see p.109) – both are located in southern Kerala, within easy reach of its resorts and capital.

## Ayurveda

**Ayurveda**, a Sanskrit word meaning the "knowledge for prolonging life", is a five-thousand-year-old holistic medical system widely practised in India, but especially in Kerala. It stems from the same period of Vedic philosophy as yoga, and places great importance on the **harmony** of mind, body and spirit, acknowledging the psychosomatic causes behind many diseases. The skin is seen as a mirror of our inner health and the body manifests everything that happens internally. Unlike the allopathic medicines of the West, which depend on finding out what's ailing you and then killing it, ayurveda looks at the whole patient: disease is regarded as a symptom of imbalance, so it's the imbalance that's treated, not the disease.

Ayurveda theory holds that the body is controlled by three **doshas** (forces), themselves made up of the basic elements of space, fire, water, earth and air, which reflect the forces within the self. The three *doshas* are: *pitta*, the force of the sun, which is hot and rules the digestive processes and metabolism; *kapha*, likened to the moon, the creator of tides and rhythms, which has a cooling effect, and governs the body's organs and bone structure; and *vata*, wind, which relates to movement, circulation and the nervous system. People are classified according to which *dosha* or combination of them is predominant. The healthy body is one that has the three forces in the correct balance for its type.

To **diagnose** an imbalance, the ayurveda doctor not only goes into the physical complaint but also into family background, daily habits and emotional traits. Once a problem is diagnosed it is then treated with a combination of strict diets (vegetarianism is advised for long-term benefits), massage with essential oils, spiritual practice and ancient herbal medicine. In addition, the doctor may prescribe various forms of yogic cleansing to rid the body of waste substances. Popular **treatments** include *abhayanga* (full body massage), *shirodhara* (head and neck massage followed by a gentle stream of warm medicated oil dripping onto the forehead), *shiro abhayanga* (head massage) and *sarvanghadhara*, a full ayurveda oil massage followed by a selection of other treatments.

For more on ayurveda in Kerala, including a rundown of specific therapies and hospitals, see p.104. And for five ultimate "me-time" experiences, in high Keralan style, see Ayurveda Mana (p.207); Coconut Lagoon (p.151), Kalari Kovalikom (p.209), Neeleshwar Hermitage (p.254) and Somatheeram (p.106).

# Culture and etiquette

Cultural differences extend to all sorts of little things, and while allowances will usually be made for foreigners, visitors unacquainted with Keralan customs may need a little preparation to avoid causing offence or making fools of themselves. The list of dos and don'ts here is hardly exhaustive: when in doubt, watch what the locals around you are doing.

## Eating and the right-hand rule

The biggest minefield of potential faux pas has to do with **eating**. You can ask for a fork, but this is usually done with the fingers (outside tourist resorts and hotel restaurants), and requires practice to get absolutely right. Rule one is: eat with your **right hand only**. In Kerala, as right across Asia, the left hand is for unsavoury functions only, while the right hand is for eating, shaking hands, and so on. While you can hold a cup or utensil in your left hand, you shouldn't use it to pass food or wipe your mouth. The rule extends beyond food too: only accept things given to you with your right hand, for example.

The other rule to beware of when eating or drinking is that your lips should not touch other people's food. When drinking out of a cup or bottle to be shared with others, don't let it touch your lips, but rather pour it directly into your mouth. This custom also protects you from things like hepatitis. It is customary to **wash your hands** before and after eating.

## Temples and religion

Most **Hindu** temples in Kerala are closed to non-Hindus, but when visiting those that aren't you should dress (or more accurately *un*-dress) in the appropriate fashion, which for men means taking off your shirt and shoes, and wearing a white Keralan *mundu*. Women should also remove their footwear, but dress in full-length sari or skirt, covering their arms and legs.

When visiting **mosques**, men and women should both dress conservatively (long trousers for men; long dress with long sleeves for women), and cover heads with scarves. Dress codes for **churches** are the same as in the west, only you remove your shoes at the main doorway before entering.

Always ask someone official before taking **photos** in places of worship, whether Hindu, Muslim or Christian. And never photograph funerals or cremations.

## Dress

The most common cultural blunder committed by foreign visitors to Kerala concerns **dress**. People accustomed to the liberal ways of Western holiday resorts often assume it's fine to stroll around town in beachwear: it isn't, as the stares that follow tourists who walk through towns shirtless or in a bikini top demonstrate.

Ignoring local norms in this way will rarely cause offence, but you'll be regarded as very peculiar. This is particularly true for women (see "Women travellers", below), who should keep legs and breasts well covered in all public places. It's OK for men to wear shorts, but swimming togs are only for the beach, and you shouldn't strip off your shirt, no matter how hot it is. None of this applies to the beach, of course, except in the most remote coastal villages, where local people may not necessarily be used to Western sunbathing habits.

## Other possible gaffes

**Kissing** and **embracing** are regarded in Kerala as part of sex: do not indulge in public. In the larger, more cosmopolitan cities of Thiruvananthapuram and Kochi it is increasingly common to see young married couples holding hands, and if you do the same you shouldn't attract too much attention. In conservative Moppila districts of northern Kerala, however, avoid any physical contact with your partner. Be aware, too, of your feet: when entering a private home, you should normally remove your shoes (follow your host's example) and when sitting avoid pointing the soles of your feet at anyone. Accidental contact with someone's foot is always followed by an apology.

## Touts and beggars

Although there is nothing like the same amount of aggressive **touting** on the streets of Kerala as there is elsewhere in the country, you will undoubtedly find yourself being offered unwanted services or goods, from guides, rickshaws and rooms to garlands, toys and illegal substances, on a fairly regular basis. Then, of course, there are **beggars** and mendicants just asking for baksheesh (see p.62). The wisest approach is not to get dragged into a dispute and certainly not to display anger, which is often not understood and encourages people to bait you further. It is better to say a single, firm "No thanks", avoid eye contact and walk on briskly. Most touts will not follow you, but, if they do, ignore them by remaining silent; they will soon get bored and give up.

## Meeting people

Like most Indians, Malayalis tend to be very **gregarious** and enjoy getting to know their visitors, so expect to be quizzed about anything from world affairs to your family, job and monthly salary by people you come into contact with – especially taxi drivers, for whom such "chitchat" on long journeys provides a welcome distraction from the rigours of Keralan roads.

This same level of what might be regarded as nosiness back home does not, however, extend to **homestay** hosts, who are generally a lot more formal and old-fashioned when it comes to interacting with guests. Good manners, traditional courtesies and politeness are the order of the day if you stay with Syrian-Christian families in the backwaters, on plantations or tea estates in the hills, or at aristocratic heritage places. Always keep a clean outfit ready for dinner, especially if you'll be eating with the family.

Bear in mind, wherever you stay, that in the same way as Indian English can seem very formal, *your* English may seem rude to Keralans. In particular, **swearing** is taken rather seriously, and casual use of the F-word certain to shock.

## Women travellers

Compared with other regions of India, Kerala is an easy-going destination for **female travellers**: incidents of sexual harassment are relatively rare, and opportunities to meet local women frequent. At the same time, it is important to remember that significant cultural differences still exist, especially in those areas where tourism is a relatively recent phenomenon.

Problems, when they do occur, invariably stem from the fact that many travellers do a range of things that no self-respecting Keralan woman would consider: from drinking alcohol or smoking in a bar-restaurant, to sleeping in a room with a man to whom they are not married. Without compromising your freedom too greatly, though, there are a few common-sense steps you can take to accommodate local feelings.

The most important and obvious is **dress**. Western visitors who wear clothes that expose shoulders, legs or cleavage do neither themselves nor their fellow travellers

### Rape

**Rape** is probably less of a danger in Kerala than in most Western countries, but the number of sexual assaults on women travellers has seen a marked increase over the past decade. The few attacks on foreigners that have occurred have nearly all taken place at night.

It therefore makes sense to take the same precautions as you would at home: keep to the main roads when travelling on foot or by bicycle, avoid dirt tracks and unfrequented beaches unless you're in a group, and when you're in your hotel or guesthouse after dark, ensure that all windows and doors are locked.

any favours. Opt, therefore, for loose-fitting clothes that keep these areas covered. When travelling alone on public transport, it is also a good idea to sit with other women (most buses have separate "ladies' seats" at the front). If you're with a man, a wedding ring also confers immediate respectability.

Appropriate behaviour for **the beach** is a trickier issue. The very idea of a woman lying semi-naked in full view of male strangers is anathema to south Indians. However, local people in most of the coastal resorts have come to tolerate such bizarre behaviour over the past decade, and swimsuits and bikinis are no longer deemed indecent, especially if worn with a sarong – although in more conservative areas, particularly the far north, where most villagers are strict Muslims, you may have to take advice from your hotel staff about what to wear on the beach. Wherever you bathe, though, it's never OK to go **topless** – not even at established resorts such as Kovalam and Varkala, where men come expressly to ogle scantily clad Western women.

Not surprisingly, the beaches are where you're most likely to experience **sexual harassment.** Your **reaction** to harassment is down to you. Verbal hassle is probably best ignored, but if you get touched it's best to react: the usual English responses will be well enough understood. If you shout "don't touch me!" in a crowded area, you're likely to find people on your side, and your assailant shamed.

## Tipping and baksheesh

As a well-off visitor you'll be expected to be liberal with your **tips**. Low-paid workers in hotels and restaurants often accept lower pay than they should in the expectation of generous tips during the tourist season. **Ten percent** should be regarded as acceptable if you've received good service – more if the staff have really gone out of their way to be

helpful. Taxi and auto-rickshaw wallahs will not expect tips unless you've made unplanned diversions or stops. What to **tip your driver** at the end of long tours, however, is a trickier issue, especially if you've been paying Rs150–200 for their daily allowance, as well as paying for meals. The simple answer is to give what you think they deserve, and what you can afford. Drivers working for tour operators, even more than hotel staff and waiters, depend on tips to get through the off-season (many are paid only Rs200–300/day because their bosses know that foreign customers tend to tip well).

**Alms-giving** is less common in Kerala than other parts of the country, although people with disabilities and mutilations do tend to congregate in city centres, and popular resorts, particularly Kovalam, where they survive from begging. In such cases Rs5–10 should be sufficient. Kids demanding money, pens, sweets or the like are a different case: yielding to any request only encourages them to pester others.

## Public toilets

There are precious few **public toilets** in the cities other than in railway stations and bus stands, and those in the latter, especially, often leave much to be desired. If you get taken short, duck into a café, restaurant or hotel and ask to use their facilities – a request unlikely to be refused.

## Smoking

In 2003 Kerala became the first state in India to **ban smoking** from all public places, including streets, parks and beaches. Unlike such laws in the West, though, the ban doesn't extend to restaurants or bars, where it remains at the owner's discretion. There's a Rs200 on-the-spot fine for offenders, though the law seems to be more strictly enforced in larger cities than rural areas.

# Shopping

With Kerala enjoying a period of unparalleled economic prosperity, shopping has a major profile across the state. Gigantic hoardings tower over intersections, advertising the latest line in brocaded silk saris, sexily sequined tops, heavy gold jewellery and other expensive accoutrements for Malayali weddings. In the cities, brightly lit air-conditioned malls host international chain stores and brands. The old bazaars are packed with more traditional treasures, from the elegant bell-metal lamps you see at the entrance to most Keralan homes to the resplendently gilded, cotton-fringed nettippattom used to adorn festival elephants. As with most things in Kerala, prices are low by Western standards and affording this shopping bonanza will probably be less of a problem than getting all the stuff you buy home at the end of your trip.

## Where to shop

The backstreets of **Fort Cochin** and **Mattancherry**, in the city of Kochi, are traditionally where most visitors do their **souvenir shopping**. After Independence, departing Jewish and British families offloaded many of their heirlooms into antiques warehouses here, from where they were sold to visitors on cruise-liner stopovers or to wealthy Indians looking for "ethnic art" to decorate their penthouse apartments in uptown Mumbai. A couple of large emporia – notably Alberts Arts, Heritage Arts, Neroth John Chandy & Co and the Lawrence Art Gallery – in the area retain some genuine pieces from this era, but for the most part, the approaches to the Pardesi Synagogue and ground floors of the Fort's old Dutch mansions have been taken over by Kashmiri vendors selling generic Indian handicrafts made in the distant north – at exorbitant prices. The same range of carpets, Himalayan curios, Hindu icons and mirror-inlaid Rajasthani wall-hangings crops up in the boutiques around the entrances to luxury resorts across the state, and along the beachfronts in Kovalam and Varkala. The stuff they stock is often eye-catching, but to buy any of it for a reasonable price you'll have to allow for at least half an hour of hard bargaining.

Elsewhere, **markets** such as Chalai Bazaar in Thiruvananthapuram (see p.91), and the main streets in central Kollam and Alappuzha, where local people do most of their shopping, offer more authentically Keralan items at more authentically Keralan prices. Often overlooked, another great source of souvenirs is the busy modern centre of Ernakulam, whose MG Road is lined with trendy fashion stores, silk emporia and malls, with merchandise at more or less fixed prices. In most sizeable towns, the Keralan government also operates a chain of handicraft and cottage industries, promoting local wood- and metalwork.

## Bargaining

You will be expected to **haggle** over the price of almost all goods, with the exception of food, household items and cigarettes. Bargaining is very much a matter of personal style, but should always be light-hearted, never acrimonious. There are no hard and fast rules – it's really a question of how much something is worth to you. It's a good plan, however, to have an idea of how much you want, or ought, to pay. "Green" tourists are easily spotted, so try and look as if you know what you are up to, even on your first day, or put off purchases till later.

Don't take too much notice of initial prices. Some guidebooks suggest paying a third of the opening price, but it's a flexible guideline depending on the shop, the goods and the shopkeeper's impression of you. You may not be able to get the seller much below the first quote; on the other hand, you may end up paying as little as a tenth of it. If you bid too low, you may be hustled out of the shop for offering an "insulting" price, but this is all part of the game, and you'll no doubt be welcomed as an old friend if you return the next day.

Don't start haggling for something if you know you don't want it, and never let any figure pass your lips that you are not prepared to pay. It's like bidding at an auction. Having mentioned a price, you are obliged to pay it. If the seller asks you how much you would pay for something, and you don't want it, say so.

## What to buy

Kerala is a paradise for **souvenir shopping**, as well as a great place to pick up clothes and jewellery. **Things not to bring home** include ivory or anything else made from a rare or protected species, including snakeskin and turtle products. When it comes to **antiques** (more than 75 years old), if they really are genuine – and, frankly, that is unlikely – you'll need a licence to export them, which is virtually impossible to get.

### Metalware and jewellery

No household in Kerala is considered complete without the **coconut-oil lamp**, or **nilavilakku**. You'll also see these distinctive brass-coloured columns, which rise from cylindrical bases to wick saucers topped by spikes or bird-like figures, at *kathakali* recitals and in the foyers of most smart hotels. Other kinds hang from chains or shine from niches in the walls of temples. They're made from an alloy of copper and tin known as **bellmetal** (it gives a sonorous chime when struck) – as opposed to brass, which is a blend of copper and zinc.

Bellmetal is also used to make traditional Keralan cooking and puja utensils, including shallow bowls called *uruli* and water carriers with spouts known in Malayalm as *kindi*. Inferior, brass-coated steel versions are sold in bazaars across the state, but for the real thing you should travel to the village of **Nadavaramba** (see p.202), near Thrissur in central Kerala, where a family of traditional artisans maintains one of the last bell-metal workshops in the region.

Another dying craft is the manufacture of metal **mirrors**, or **valkannadi** – a Keralan speciality nowadays confined to the village

of **Aranmula**, in the south of the state (see p.153). To make them, an alloy of copper, silver, brass, white lead and bronze is cast in wax – the so-called "lost wax" technique – before being laboriously finished by hand. Few places, however, sell them: enthusiasts travel to Aranmula to buy them direct from the workshops.

These traditional alloys may be on the decline, but the popularity of **gold** has never been stronger in Kerala – largely due to the deluge of Gulf dollars pouring into the state, which poorer Malayali families tend to put into jewellery rather than a savings account. Gold emporia are often the largest and most glittering shops in Keralan cities. Try Bhima (Ⓦwww.bhimajewellery.com), who have showrooms in Kochi, Thiruvananthapuram and Alappuzha, the House of Alapatt (Ⓦwww .houseofalapatt.com), one of the major landmarks in Kochi, or Josco Fashion Jewellers (Ⓦwww.joscogroup.com), who have a dozen or so branches around the state.

In the resorts, **silver** tends to be more popular with visitors, though it varies in quality. Run mostly by Kashmiri vendors, boutiques stock a bewildering array of earrings, necklaces, pendants and bracelets, often encrusted with semiprecious stones such as turquoise, amber, labradorite, carnelian and lapis lazuli. They're sold by weight, regardless of how much work has gone into them or how large the stones are, though expect to have to haggle hard over the final price.

Last, but by no means least, the ultimate metalwork souvenir from Kerala has to be a **nettippattom** – the gloriously golden caparisons draped over the foreheads of elephants during religious festivals. You'll find them at top-drawer bell-metal shops in bazaars around the state. They're made in the village of Thiruvankulam, between Ernakulam and Thrissur in central Kerala.

### Woodwork and stone carving

Deep-red **rosewood**, inlaid with lighter-coloured teaks or shell to create geometric patterns, is used for carving elephants and heavy furniture, samples of which are to be found at most state-run emporia. Rosewood and teak are also used to make Keralan jewellery caskets, or **nettur petti**, which traditionally contained a woman's dowry goods and are embellished with ornate brass joints, clasps and corner pieces. Metal trunks have largely superseded them, but Keralan cabinet-makers still turn out reproductions for the tourist market.

**Sandalwood**, sourced in managed forests deep in the Western Ghat mountains, is an exquisite, but increasingly rare, material that Keralan carvers use to fashion figurines of Hindu deities – particularly the elephant-headed Ganesh (or Ganapati).

In the resorts you'll also see numerous figures sculpted from soapstone. These will have come from the village of Mamal-lapuram, just outside of Chennai in Tamil Nadu, renowned as India's **stone-carving** capital. Pieces range from larger-than-life-size icons for temples to pocket-size gods. Whatever their size, though, the figures are always precisely carved according to measurements meticulously set out in ancient canonical texts, which explains why little innovation has taken place over the centuries. The only development in Mamallapuram's output in recent decades has been in the design of chillums (pipes), and small pendants, bought wholesale for export to the summer festival hippy market back in Europe.

## Textiles and clothing

The homespun, handloom-woven, hand-printed cloth called **khadi** is sold all over Kerala in government shops called Khadi Gramodyog. Methods of dyeing and printing this and other textiles vary – in contrast to the tie-dyeing (*bandhini*) style of Rajasthan, in Kerala you are more likely to see the block printing and screen-printing of calico (from Kozhikode), cotton and silk.

**Saris** for everyday use are normally made of cotton, although **silk** is used more frequently in Kerala than in the rest of India. It takes years of practice to wear one properly, but they're usually a good buy, provided you're sure the textile is genuine. The classic Keralan sari – a **kasavu** – is made of light, raw, unbleached cotton with a border woven on handlooms from golden thread. Modern versions sometimes add colour to the edging, or layer cotton and gold thread over one another to create a shimmering effect. Also available in the same

traditional fabrics are shorter, narrower *mundu* – Keralan sarongs, worn by both men and women to weddings, festivals, naming ceremonies and other important events. Dependable Keralan *kasavu* specialists include Kasavukada in Kochi (@www .kasavukada.com) and Karalkada in Thiru-vananthapuram (@www.karalkada.com).

For women, **salwar kameez**, the elegant pyjama suits comprising a (usually long, loose) shirt (*kameez*) with baggy trousers that taper to a cuff (*salwar*), make good travel outfits, although in the sticky heat of Kerala you may find them too heavy. Long loose shirts – preferably made of *khadi* and known as **kurta pyjama** – are also practical. Tourist shops sell versions in various fabrics and colours. Block-printed bedsheets, as well as being useful, make good wall-hangings.

On top of this, with **tailoring** so cheap in India, you can choose the fabric you want and have it made into whatever you fancy. Kovalam and Varkala are packed with tiny hole-in-the-wall tailors holding shelves full of cheap cotton designed for the tourist market, though don't expect the garments to last all that long – the dye is particularly prone to leaching. Most tailors will also copy a piece of clothing you already have.

## Carpets and rugs

South India is less renowned for its **carpets** than the north, although the Tasara Creative Weaving Centre, near Kozhikode (Calicut), is a little-visited spot with a lively handloom and weaving industry. For everyday domestic use, **rag rugs**, made from recycled clothing, are good buys. Available just about everywhere, they cost little enough in Europe and North America, but in Kerala are fantastically cheap; many visitors buy large ones and post them home by surface mail.

Of course, you don't have to go all the way north to buy a **Kashmiri** rug or carpet. Any of the Kashmiris who have set up shop in the tourist centres will be delighted to sell you one, though it is best to learn something about what you are trying to buy before you lay out a lot of cash. A pukka Kashmiri carpet should have a label on the back stating that it is made in Kashmir, what it is made of (wool, silk or "silk touch", the latter being wool combined with a little cotton and silk to give it a sheen), its size, the density of knots per square inch (the more the better) and the name of the design.

## Keralan mural paintings

**Mural painting** is a traditional Keralan art developed between the fifteenth and nineteenth centuries, and is still widely studied and practised (see p.288). Rendered in rich, earthy reds, greens and yellows, mythological scenes – showing Vishnu reclining on the bed of serpents, or Krishna sporting with the *gopi* girls – are the most popular subject matter, and look superb when framed. Demand for large pieces to adorn the walls of temples and palaces having fallen off, mural artists these days turn out smaller works on paper for the tourist market. You can usually watch one or two at work in shops around Kovalam and Varkala. Prices vary according to the size and detail of the painting.

## Books and music

Of course, not everything typically Indian is old or traditional. **CDs and audio cassettes** of Malayalam, Hindustani classical, Carnatic, Bhangra, *filmi* and Western music are available in most major towns and cities for a fraction of what you'd pay back home. Sound of Melody and Music World (see p.189), both in Ernakulam, are Kerala's best-stocked CD stores.

**Books** are also excellent buys, whether by Indian writers or authors from the rest of the English-speaking world. Once again, they are usually much cheaper than at home, if not always so well printed or bound.

Worth looking out for in tourist areas and bookshops around Thiruvananthapuram and Ernakulam is a series of DVDs showcasing traditional Keralan arts such as *kudiyattam*, *kathakali*, *mohiniyattam* and *ottamthullal*. The series, published by Invis, captures some of the state's greatest performers in action, but at around Rs500 each, they're expensive by local standards.

Bamboo flutes are incredibly cheap, while other **musical instruments** such as tabla, sitar and *saroud* are sold in music shops in the larger cities. The quality is crucial; there's no point going home with a sitar that is virtually untuneable, even if it does look nice. A good place to start looking is Manuel Industries in Ernakulam (see p.189). For traditional Keralan drums, ask around the bazaar in Thripunitra, just outside Ernakulam (see p.190).

# Travelling with children

Keralans adore kids, and if you're travelling with any in tow, you can expect to have them constantly picked up and photographed – especially if they're fair-haired. This can, admittedly, get to be a bit wearing after a while, but it's generally done in the best of spirits. If you're staying in a small, family-run hotel or guest-house, meanwhile, contacts with other parents can be very rewarding.

The main problem with children, especially small ones, is their vulnerability. The most obvious thing to watch out for is the Keralan **sun**, which can roast young, sensitive skin at any time of the day or year. Come armed with sun hats and plenty of maximum-factor block, and keep skin covered as much as possible. Both Kovalam and Varkala beaches can be treacherous: always be wary of a strong **undertow**, which can arise at certain phases of the tide even in relatively shallow water.

Even more than their parents, children need protecting from unsafe drinking water, heat and unfamiliar food. All that chilli in particular may be a problem, even with older kids, if they're not used to it. Remember too, that **diarrhoea**, perhaps just a nuisance to you, could be dangerous for a child: rehydration salts (see p.47) are vital if your child goes down with it.

Make sure too, if possible, that your child is aware of the dangers of rabies; keep him or her away from **animals**, and consider a rabies jab. Bites and stings are, however, less of a problem than mosquitoes and the concomitant risk of malaria. Always ensure your children are well protected – at the very least with DEET-based repellent in the evenings, and that they're covered by a net at night. Special small nets for babies' cots are sold at local markets and may be available through your hotel or guesthouse.

**Formula milk** and jars of **baby food** are available at supermarkets in the main cities, but are not easy to get hold of elsewhere, and they will taste different from what your baby is used to. Therefore, dried baby food could be worth taking; mix it with hot (boiled) water – any café or guesthouse owner should be able to supply you with some. You'll find international brands of **nappies** such as Pampers and Huggies fairly widely available, but if you're getting off the beaten track you may want to consider going over to cotton ones – disposing of "disposables" can present major difficulties, even in the resorts, as there is no formal waste disposal provision in the state. A changing mat, bottle of Milton solution and sealable plastic containers for snacks are other necessities.

For touring, hiking or walking, **child-carrier backpacks** are ideal. If the child is small enough, a fold-up buggy is also well worth packing, especially if they will sleep in it (while you have a meal or a drink), although the pavements can be uneven. If you want to cut down on long journeys by flying, remember that under-2s travel for ten percent of the adult fare (or less in some cases), and under-12s for half price.

Most **hotels and guesthouses** will provide an extra bed for a small charge (usually less than 25 percent of the room rate). Bigger hotels may also be able to provide cots, but check first.

# Travel essentials

## Costs

Kerala is these days far from the cheap destination it was only a few years back, but if you're careful, a little currency can still go a long way. What you spend depends on where you stay, how you get around, what you eat and what you buy. In the **resorts** at the height of the tourist season, you'll be hard pushed to find a double room for much under Rs700, whereas in neighbouring towns, a night in a simple lodge can cost half that. Meals will rarely set you back more than Rs50 in a typical south Indian rice-plate restaurant, but in your average five-star can take a bite out of Rs1000.

Staying in one of the **beach-side enclaves**, such as Kovalam or Varkala, you should be able to manage quite comfortably on a budget of around Rs1500–2000 per day if you stay somewhere relatively basic, don't splurge on expensive seafood and wine every night, and get around by rented bicycle rather than taxi. Double that, and you can expect to stay somewhere with more space and a good-sized sea-facing balcony, eat well and get around by car. Anyone spending Rs5000–6000 per day, however, can really pamper themselves in a smart hotel with a pool, indulge in tiger prawn suppers and have ayurveda massages every day. To spend much more than that, you'd have to be staying in five-star or boutique hotels, and renting taxis for the duration of your holiday.

Throughout the Guide, in our accounts of attractions where **Indian visitors** are charged admission at a lower rate than other visitors, the lower price is shown in square parentheses.

## Crime and personal safety

**Crime** levels in Kerala are a long way below those of Western countries, and violent crime against tourists is extremely rare. Virtually none of the people who approach you on the street intends any harm: many want to sell you something, some want to practise their English, others (if you're a woman) to chat you up. As a tourist, however, you are an obvious target for the tiny number of thieves (who may include some of your fellow travellers), and it makes sense to take a few precautions.

Most tourists carry valuables in a **money belt**, though most hotels will also have a safe-deposit facility where you can store them. Budget travellers would do well to carry a **padlock**, useful both for securing the doors of cheap hotel rooms and for locking your bag to seats or racks in trains. The prime time for theft on buses and trains is just before you leave, so keep a particular eye on your gear then. Remember that routes popular with tourists tend to be popular with thieves too.

It's not a bad idea to keep a couple of hundred pounds or dollars separately from the rest of your money; it's also worth keeping a separate note of your travellers' cheque receipts, insurance policy number and phone number, and a photocopy of the pages in your passport containing personal data and your Indian visa. This will cover you in case you do lose all your valuables. When using your **credit card**, insist that the transaction is made in front of you, in order to prevent fraud.

If the worst happens and you get robbed, **report the theft** as soon as possible to the local police. They are very unlikely to recover your belongings, but you need a report from them in order to claim on your travel insurance. If you **lose your passport**, the police will issue you with the all-important

"complaint form" you'll need in order to travel around and check into hotels. Dress smartly and expect an uphill battle; city cops in particular tend to be jaded from too many insurance and travellers' cheque scams. Some even demand baksheesh to cooperate.

**Drugs** – even locally grown cannabis – are strictly illegal in Kerala, and you should avoid anyone using or selling them if you don't want to risk large fines or imprisonment.

## Electricity

**Voltage** is generally 220V/50Hz AC, though direct current supplies also exist, so check before plugging in. Most sockets are triple round-pin, but accept European-size double round-pin **plugs**. British, Irish and Australasian plugs will need an adaptor, preferably universal; American and Canadian appliances will need a transformer, too, unless they are multi-voltage. Power cuts and voltage variations are very common, so voltage stabilizers should be used to run sensitive appliances such as laptops (you can usually plug into one at internet cafés).

## Entry requirements

Almost everyone needs a **visa** before travelling to India. If you're going to Kerala to study or work, you'll need to apply for a special student or business visa; otherwise, a standard tourist visa will suffice. For details of other kinds of visas, check the websites on p.69.

### Tourist visas

**Tourist visas** are valid for six months from the date of issue (not of departure from your home country or entry into India), and usually cost £30/US$75. You're asked to specify whether you need a single-entry or a multiple-entry visa; as the same rates apply to both, it makes sense to ask for the latter just in case you decide to go back within six months. Note, however, that a ruling introduced in 2009 (in theory at least) prevents visitors on a tourist visa (or visas) from re-entering India within two months of their last visit except in exceptional circumstances, and with pre-arranged clearance from your local embassy or consulate – although, again, whether or not this ruling is likely to be strictly enforced remains unclear at the time of writing.

Visas in the UK, USA, Canada and Australia are no longer issued by Indian embassies themselves, but by various third-party companies (sub-contractors) – see below for details. The firms' websites give all the details you need to make your application. Read the small print carefully and always **make sure you've allowed plenty of time**. Applying in person, it's possible to obtain your visa by the following working day – but don't bank on it; three to four working days is more common. **Postal applications** take a minimum of ten working days plus time in transit, and often longer.

Elsewhere in the world, visas are still issued by the relevant local embassy or consulate, though the same caveats apply. Bear in mind too that Indian High Commissions, embassies and consulates observe Indian public holidays as well as local ones, so always check opening hours in advance.

## Visa agencies

In many countries it's possible to pay a visa agency (or "visa expediter" – see the list below to process the visa on your behalf, which typically costs £60–70/$100–120, plus the price of the visa. This is worth considering if you're not able to get to your nearest Indian High Commission, embassy or consulate yourself. Prices vary from company to company, as do turnaround times. Two weeks is about standard, but you can get a visa in as little as 24hr if you're prepared to pay premium rates. For a full rundown of services, check the company websites below, from where you can usually download visa application forms.

## Visa extensions

It is no longer possible to **extend a tourist visa** in India, though exceptions may be made in special circumstances. In addition, new rules introduced in late 2009 (see above) require that visitors travelling on a tourist visa must leave at least two months between visits to India. Thus, if your visa is about to elapse, it's no longer possible to pop over to a neighbouring country and then re-enter on a new visa a couple of days later.

## Indian embassies, high commissions, consulates and visa-processing centres abroad

**Australia** c/o VFS Global (🌐 www.vfs-in-au.net), which has offices in all states except Tasmania and NT; see website for contact details.

**Canada** c/o VFS Global (🌐 in.vfsglobal.ca), which has nine offices countrywide – see website for details.

**Ireland** Embassy: 6 Leeson Park, Dublin 6 ☎ 01/497 0843, 🌐 www.indianembassy.ie.

**Nepal** c/o Indian Visa Service Centre (IVSC), House no.296, Kapurdhara Marg, Kathmandu ☎ 01/400 1516, 🌐 www.indianembassy.org.np.

**New Zealand** High Commission: 180 Molesworth St, PO Box 4045, Wellington ☎ 04/473 6390, 🌐 www.hicomind.org.nz.

**South Africa** 852 Schoeman St (cnr of Eastwood St), PO Box 40216, Arcadia 0007, Pretoria ☎ 012/342 2593, 🌐 www.indiainsouthafrica.com; 1 Eton Rd, Parktown, PO Box 6805, Johannesburg 2000 ☎ 011/482 8484 to 9, 🌐 www.indconjoburg .co.za; The Old Station Building (4th floor), 160 Pine St, PO Box 3276, Durban 4001 ☎ 031/307-7020, 🌐 www.indcondurban.co.za.

**Sri Lanka** High Commission: 36–38 Galle Rd, Colombo 3 ☎ 011/232 7587, 🌐 www.hcicolombo .org. Consulate: 31 Rajapihilla Mawatha, PO Box 47, Kandy ☎ 081/222 4563.

**UK** c/o VFS Global (🌐 in.vfsglobal.co.uk), which has offices in London, Birmingham, Manchester, Cardiff, Edinburgh and Glasgow – see website for contact details.

**USA** c/o Travisa (🌐 indiavisa.travisaoutsourcing .com), which has offices in Washington, New York, San Francisco, Chicago and Houston – see website for contact details.

## Visa agencies

**CIBT** US ☎ 1-800/929-2428, 🌐 www.cibt.com. UK ☎ 0844/736 0211, 🌐 www.uk.cibt.com.

**India Visa Company** UK ☎ 020/8582 1117, 🌐 www.skylorduk.com/gle_visa.htm.

**India Visa Office** UK ☎ 0844/800 4018, 🌐 www .indiavisaheadoffice.co.uk.

**India Visa 24** ☎ 0800/084 5037, 🌐 www .indiavisa24.co.uk.

**Travel Document Systems** US; Washington ☎ 1-800/874-5100, New York ☎ 1-877/874-5104, San Francisco ☎ 1-888/874-5100, 🌐 www .traveldocs.com.

**Visa Connection** US & Canada ☎ 1-866/566-8472, 🌐 www.visaconnection.com.

**Visa Link** Australia ☎ 03/9673 1500, 🌐 www .visalink.com.au.

## Gay and lesbian travellers

**Homosexuality** is not generally accepted in Kerala, and gay sex was only recently decriminalized. It isn't surprising, therefore, that gay and lesbian life in the state is very low-key. The tourist scene is also straight-oriented, although one or other of the beach cafés in Varkala usually becomes a hangout for gay visitors during the season.

## Insurance

In the light of the potential health risks involved in a trip to Kerala – see pp.45–50 – **travel insurance** is too important to ignore. In addition to covering medical expenses and emergency flights, it also insures your money and belongings against loss or theft. Before paying for a new policy, however, it's worth checking to see whether you are already covered: some all-risks home insurance policies may cover your possessions when abroad, and many private medical schemes include overseas cover. In Canada, provincial health plans usually provide partial medical cover for mishaps overseas, while holders of official student/teacher/youth cards in Canada and the US are entitled to – albeit meagre – accident coverage and hospital in-patient benefits. Students will often find that their student health coverage includes vacations and one term beyond the date of last enrolment.

After exhausting the possibilities above, you might want to contact a specialist **travel insurance company**, or consider the travel insurance deal offered by Rough Guides (see box below). A typical travel insurance policy usually provides cover for the loss of baggage, tickets and – up to a certain limit – cash or cheques, as well as cancellation or curtailment of your journey. Most of them exclude so-called dangerous sports unless an extra premium is paid: in Kerala this can mean scuba diving, rafting, windsurfing and trekking with ropes, though probably not jeep safaris. Many policies can be chopped and changed to exclude coverage you don't need – for example, sickness and accident benefits can often be excluded or included at will. If you do take medical coverage, ascertain whether benefits will be paid as treatment proceeds or only after return home, and whether there is a 24-hour medical emergency number. When securing baggage cover, make sure that the per-article limit – typically under £500 – will cover your most valuable possession. If you need to make a claim, you should keep receipts for medicines and medical treatment, and in the event you have anything stolen, you must obtain an official statement from the police.

## Internet

All large cities and many tourist towns have places offering **wi-fi**, **internet** and **email** access – these are usually cybercafés, but also include many hotels and some STD (standard trunk dialling) booths. Charges are most commonly Rs30–40 for reading mail and browsing, and extra for printing; most cybercafés offer membership deals which can cut costs if you'll be around for a while. In the main cities and resorts faster ISDN/broadband connections are the norm. Most places with a decent broadband connection also have webcams and microphones, allowing for VoIP chats via systems such as

---

### Rough Guides travel insurance

Rough Guides has teamed up with WorldNomads.com to offer great **travel insurance** deals. Policies are available to residents of over 150 countries, with cover for a wide range of **adventure sports**, 24hr emergency assistance, high levels of medical and evacuation cover and a stream of **travel safety information**. Roughguides.com users can take advantage of their policies online 24/7, from anywhere in the world – even if you're already travelling. And since plans often change when you're on the road, you can extend your policy and even claim online. Roughguides.com users who buy travel insurance with WorldNomads.com can also leave a positive footprint and donate to a community development project. For more information go to ⑭ **www.roughguides.com/shop**.

Skype. Internet cafés listed in the Guide are marked on the relevant maps.

## Laundry

In India, no one goes to self-service laundries: if they don't do their own, they send it out to a **dhobi**. Wherever you are staying, there will either be an in-house *dhobi* or one very close by to call on. The *dhobi* will take your dirty washing to a *dhobi ghat*, a public clothes-washing area (the bank of a river, for example), where it is shown some old-fashioned discipline: separated, soaped and given a damn good thrashing to beat the dirt out of it. Then it's hung out to dry in the sun and, once dried, taken to the ironing sheds where every garment is endowed with razor-sharp creases and then matched to its rightful owner by hidden cryptic markings. Your clothes will come back from the *dhobi* absolutely spotless, though this kind of violent treatment does take it out of them: buttons get lost and eventually the cloth starts to fray.

## Mail

**Mail** can take anything from six days to three weeks to get to or from Kerala, depending on where you are and the country you are mailing to; ten days is about the norm. Most **post offices** are open Monday to Friday from 10am to 5pm and Saturday from 10am to noon, but town GPOs keep longer hours (usually Mon–Sat 9.30am–1pm & 2–5.30pm). **Stamps** are not expensive, but you'll have to stick them on yourself as they tend not to be self-adhesive (every post office keeps a pot of evil-smelling glue for this purpose). Aerogrammes and postcards cost the same to anywhere in the world.

**Sending a parcel** from Kerala can be a performance. First take it to a tailor to have it wrapped in cheap cotton cloth, stitched up and sealed with wax. Next, take it to the post office, fill in and attach the relevant customs forms, buy your stamps, see them franked and dispatch it. Surface mail is incredibly cheap, and takes an average of six months to arrive – it may take half, or four times, that, however. It's a good way to dump excess baggage and souvenirs, but don't send anything fragile this way.

## Maps

Even allowing for a bit of bias, we think you'll find the Rough Guide's **south India map** to be the most user-friendly on the market. Drawn at a scale of 1:1,200,000, it features clear modern mapping and up-to-date research, and is printed on plastic paper so it won't tear (and should even survive a dip in the Arabian Sea). It's also been tested and proofed on the road by the author of this guide. Another excellent map of south India is the Nelles India 4 (South) 1:1,500,000, which shows colour contours, road distances, inset city plans and all but the tiniest places. Ttk, a Chennai-based company, publishes basic **state maps**, which are widely available in Kerala and in some travel and map shops in the UK.

On the net, and much to the displeasure of the Indian government, **GoogleEarth**'s satellite coverage of Kerala at Ⓦmaps .google.com is impressive. Though its street mapping remains rudimentary, you can use the satellite images for superb bird's-eye explorations of backwaters and beaches not covered on most published maps.

## Money

India's unit of currency is the **rupee**, usually abbreviated "Rs" and divided into a hundred **paise** (pronounced *pi*-suh). Almost all money is paper, with notes of 10, 20, 50, 100, 500 and, more rarely, 1000 rupees; a few 5 rupee notes are still in circulation. There are 1, 2, 5 and 10 rupee coins; 25 and 50 paise coins, while still accepted, are increasingly rare.

Banknotes, especially lower denominations, can get into a terrible state. Don't accept **torn banknotes**, since no one else will be prepared to take them and you'll be left saddled with the things unless you can be bothered to change them at the Reserve Bank of India or large branches of other big banks. Don't pass them on to beggars; they can't use them either, so it amounts to an insult.

Large denominations can also be a problem, as **change** is usually in short supply. Many Indian people cannot afford to keep much lying around, and you shouldn't necessarily expect shopkeepers or rickshaw-wallahs to have it (and they may – as may you – try to hold onto it if they do).

Larger notes – like the Rs500 note – are good for travelling with and can be changed for smaller denominations at hotels and other suitable establishments.

It is worth noting that certain numbers are referred to differently in India and Pakistan to anywhere else in the world: a hundred thousand is a *lakh* (written 1,00,000); ten million is a *crore* (1,00,00,000). The words "million" and "billion" are not in common use, being replaced by ten *lakh* or a hundred *crore*, respectively.

## ATMs, cards and travellers' cheques

The easiest way to access your money is with **plastic**, though it's a good idea to also have some backup in the form of cash or travellers' cheques. You will find **ATMs** at main banks in all major towns, though your card issuer may well add a foreign transaction fee, and the Indian bank will also levy a small charge, generally around Rs25.

Your card issuer, and sometimes the ATM itself, imposes limits on the amount you may withdraw in a day – typically Rs10,000–20,000. Note, too, that unless you have advised your bank in advance that you will be using your card abroad, the first time you try to take money out after arriving in Kerala your request may be refused – a standard security procedure aimed at preventing fraud. If this happens, you will need to telephone your bank or credit card's 24-hour line for the block to be removed.

**Credit cards** are accepted for payment at major hotels, top restaurants, some shops and airline offices, but virtually nowhere else. American Express, MasterCard and Visa are the likeliest to be accepted. Beware of people making extra copies of the receipt, in order to fraudulently bill you later; always insist that the transaction is made before your eyes. One big downside of relying on plastic as your main access to cash, of course, is that cards can easily get lost or stolen, so take along a couple of alternatives if you can, keep an emergency stash of cash, and make a note of your home bank's phone number and website addresses for emergencies.

US dollars are the easiest **currency** to convert, with euros and pounds sterling not far behind. Major hard currencies can be

changed easily in tourist areas and big cities, less so elsewhere. If you enter the country with more than US$10,000 or the equivalent, you are supposed to fill in a currency declaration form.

In addition to cash and plastic (or as a generally less convenient alternative to the latter), consider carrying some **travellers' cheques**. You pay a small commission (usually one percent) to buy these with cash in the same currency, a little more to convert from a different currency, but they have the advantage over cash that, if lost or stolen, they can be replaced. Not all banks, however, accept them. Well-known brands such as Thomas Cook and American Express are your best bet, but in some places even American Express is only accepted in US dollars and not as pounds sterling. Visa and American Express offer **pre-paid cards** that you can load up with credit before you leave home and use in ATMs like a debit card – effectively travellers' cheques in plastic form.

It is illegal to carry **rupees into India**, and you won't get them at a particularly good rate in the West anyhow (though you might in Thailand, Malaysia or Singapore). It is also illegal to take them out of the country.

## Changing money

Changing money in regular **banks**, especially government-run banks such as the State Bank of India (SBI), can be a time-consuming business, involving lots of form-filling and queuing at different counters, so it's best to change substantial amounts at any one time. You'll have no such problems, however, with **private companies** such as Thomas Cook or American Express. Major cities and main tourist centres usually have several **licensed currency exchange bureaux**; rates usually aren't as good as at a bank, but transactions are generally a lot quicker and there's less paperwork to complete.

Outside **banking hours** (Mon–Fri 10am–2/4pm, Sat 10am–noon), large hotels may change money, probably at a lower rate, and exchange bureaux have longer opening hours. Banks at Mumbai and Chennai airports stay open 24 hours, but neither is very conveniently located.

Wherever you change money, hold on to **exchange receipts** ("encashment certificates"); you'll need them if you want to change back any excess rupees when you leave the country, and to buy air tickets and reserve train berths with rupees at special counters for foreigners. The State Bank of India now charges for tax clearance forms.

## Opening hours

Standard **shop** opening hours in India are Monday to Saturday from 9.30am to 6pm. Smaller shops vary from town to town, religion to religion and one to another, but usually keep longer hours. **India Tourism** offices are in principle open Monday to Friday 9.30am to 5pm, Saturday 9.30am to 1pm, though these may vary slightly; **state tourist offices** are likely to be open from Monday to Friday 10am to 5pm, but sometimes operate much longer hours – see p.74 for more on tourist offices.

For opening hours of post offices, see "Mail", p.71; for opening hours of banks, see "Changing money", p.72. For dates of **public holidays**, see the "Principal Keralan festivals" box, pp.52–55.

## Phones

Since the cellphone revolution, privately run phone **international direct-dialling** facilities – **STD/ISD** (Standard Trunk Dialling/International Subscriber Dialling) places – have become a rarity in Kerala – too few in number, in fact, to be relied upon. In addition, calling from them will cost more than dialling from a mobile if you have an Indian SIM card. Visitors therefore nearly all bring their own phones these days, and buy an Indian SIM card to cover their trip. This has traditionally been quick, cheap and relatively straightforward – involving taking a photocopy of your passport (photo and visa pages) to a cellphone shop or network outlet, filling in a form and paying a connection fee from Rs25–250 – though in the wake of the 2008 Mumbai terror attacks the government has threatened to clamp down on foreigners using SIM cards, which may well make the application process more complicated.

Coverage in Kerala is best with Vodafone, Airtel and Idea. Once your

### International dialling codes

| | From<br>India | To<br>India |
|---|---|---|
| UK | ☎ 00 44 | ☎ 00 91 |
| Irish Republic | ☎ 00 353 | ☎ 00 91 |
| US and |  |  |
| Canada | ☎ 00 1 | ☎ 011 91 |
| Australia | ☎ 00 61 | ☎ 0011 91 |
| New Zealand | ☎ 00 64 | ☎ 00 91 |
| South Africa | ☎ 00 27 | ☎ 09091 91 |

retailer has unlocked your phone, you pay for an initial charge card, which can be topped up ("re-charged" as it's known in Kerala) at any one of thousands of outlets around the state; denominations range from Rs10–1000, though only by paying certain figures (for example Rs222 with Vodafone) will you get the full amount in credits. Call charges to the UK and to the US from most Indian networks cost Rs2–3. Also get your card supplier to turn on the "Do Not Disturb" option, or you'll be plagued with spam calls and texts from the phone company.

**Indian mobile numbers** are ten-digit, starting with a 9 or an 8. However, if you are calling from outside the state where the mobile is based (but not from abroad), you need to add a zero in front of that.

Calling an Indian mobile from a UK landline, you can save a lot of money by dialling via a company such as Ratebuster (Ⓦwww.ratebuster.co.uk) or Best Minutes (Ⓦwww.bestminutes.co.uk). No sign-up is required; just check the firms' websites for their access number for India, wait for a connection, then key in the Indian number you want to reach.

## Photography

**Beware** of pointing your camera at anything that might be considered "strategic", including airports, anything military and even bridges, railway stations and main roads. Remember too that some people prefer not to be photographed, so it is wise to ask before you take a snapshot of them. On the other hand, you'll get people, especially kids, volunteering to pose.

Most photo shops can now transfer **digital** images onto a CD – useful in order to free up memory space. **Camera film,** sold at average Western prices, is widely available in Kerala (but check the date on the box, and note that false boxes containing outdated film are often sold). It's fairly easy to get films developed, though they don't always come out as well as they might at home. If you're after **slide film**, buy it in the big cities, and don't expect to find specialist brands.

## Time

Kerala, like the rest of India, is all in one **time zone**: GMT plus 5 hours 30 minutes. This makes it 5 hours 30 minutes ahead of London, 10 hours 30 minutes ahead of New York, 13 hours 30 minutes ahead of LA, 3 hours 30 minutes ahead of Johannesburg, 4 hours 30 minutes behind Sydney and 6 hours 30 minutes behind New Zealand; however, summer time in those places will vary the difference by an hour.

## Tourist information

The Indian government maintains a number of helpful **tourist offices** abroad. Other sources of information include the websites of Indian embassies and consulates, travel agents (though their advice may not always be totally unbiased), and the Indian Railways representatives listed on p.26.

Inside India, both national and the Kerala state government run **tourist information offices**, providing general travel advice and handing out an array of printed material, from city maps to glossy leaflets on specific destinations and activities. The Indian government's tourist department, India Tourism (ⓦwww.incredibleindia.org), has branches in most major Keralan cities. These, however, operate independently of the state-run Kerala Tourism's **information counters** (ⓦwww.keralatourism.org). Also run by the Keralan government is the Kerala State Tourist Development Corporation, better known by its acronym, KTDC (ⓦwww.ktdc.org), a commercial venture set up to promote the state-owned chain of hotels and tours.

## India Tourism offices overseas

**Australia** Glasshouse Shopping Complex, 135 King St, Sydney NSW 2000 ℡02/9555, ⓔinfo @indiatourism.com.au.
**Canada** 60 Bloor St (West), Suite 1003, Toronto, ON M4W 3B8 ℡1-416/962-3787 or 8, ⓔinfo @indiatourismcanada.ca.
**South Africa** PO Box 412542, Craighall 2024, Hyde Lane, Lancaster Gate, Johannesburg 2000 ℡011/325 0880, ⓔgoito@global.co.za.
**UK** 7 Cork St, London W1S 3LH ℡020/7437 3677, ⓔlondon5@indiatouristoffice.org.
**US** 1270 Ave of Americas, Suite 1808 (18th floor), New York, NY 10020 ℡1-212/586-4901, ⓔny @itonyc.com; 3550 Wilshire Blvd, Suite 204, Los Angeles, CA 90010-2485 ℡1-213/380-8855, ⓔindiatourismla@aol.com.

## Travellers with disabilities

For the **disabled traveller**, there is the advantage of social acceptance sometimes lacking in the West, as there are so many disabled Indians. On the other hand, you'll be lucky to see a state-of-the-art wheelchair or a loo for the disabled and the streets are full of all sorts of obstacles that would be hard for a blind or wheelchair-bound tourist to negotiate without help. Kerbs are often high, pavements uneven and littered, and ramps nonexistent. There are potholes all over the place, and open sewers. Some of the more expensive hotels have ramps for the movement of luggage and equipment, making them accessible to wheelchairs, though this is more by accident than design.

Then again, Indian people are likely to be very helpful if, for example, you need their help getting on and off buses or up stairs. Taxis and rickshaws are easily affordable and very adaptable; if you rent one for a day, the driver is certain to help you on and off, and perhaps even around the sites you visit. If you employ a guide, they may also be prepared to help you with steps and obstacles.

For more information about disability issues in Kerala, see the **Disability India Network** website at ⓦwww.disabilityindia.org.

# Guide

# Guide

# 1

# Southern Kerala

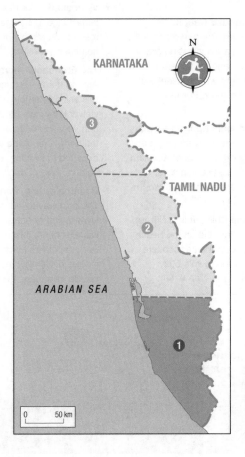

CHAPTER 1 # Highlights

✳ **Thiruvananthapuram** With its huge temple, royal palace, museums and traditional Keralan restaurants, the state capital makes an interesting day-trip from the nearby resorts. See p.82

✳ **Lighthouse Beach, Kovalam** The nerve centre of Kerala's busiest resort, where handnet fishermen rub shoulders with sunseekers from northern Europe. See p.98

✳ **Padmanabhapuram Palace** This elegant royal palace, an hour's drive south of Kovalam, is the finest specimen of regional architecture in south India. See p.107

✳ **Varkala** Chill out in a cliff-top café, sunbathe on the beach or soak up the atmosphere around the town's busy temple tank. See p.111

✳ **The backwaters** Explore the beautiful waterways of Kerala's densely populated Kuttanad region on a rice barge or punted canoe. See p.128

✳ **Vembanad Lake** Kerala's largest lagoon is ringed by resorts and atmospheric homestays. See p.137

✳ **The Ettumanur murals** Among the few examples of this ancient temple art form viewable by non-Hindus – and very fine ones at that, featuring a recumbent Vishnu depicted in swirling, earthy colours. See p.152

✳ **Bamboo rafting, Periyar** The best way to sidestep the crowds and get close to the wild elephants, bison and even rare tigers lurking in the jungles of Kerala's most visited wildlife sanctuary. See p.159

▲ Exploring the backwaters

# Southern Kerala

Kerala's intensely tropical south, stretching from the Tamil Nadu border to the Kuttanad backwaters, was formerly the heartland of the princely state of **Travancore**, the region's chief power in the eighteenth century. It was the Travancore rajas who, under sponsorship from the British East India Company, first developed **Thiruvananthapuram** as a capital, and whose patronage of education and the arts did much to shape Kerala's contemporary identity.

Traditional arts continue to thrive in the modern city, with two of south India's major music events – Nishagandi (mid-Jan) and the Swathi Sangeetotsavam (Oct/Nov) – staged in its open-air theatres each year, alongside regular performances of *kathakali* and *kudiyattam*. Thiruvananthapuram's principal sight, however, is indisputably the **Sri Padmanabhaswamy temple**, whose mighty gateway tower and red-tiled rooftops are reflected to superb effect in the waters of the adjacent bathing tank. The road leading to it, passing the royal palace of Puttan Malika, also serves as the venue for the city's largest **festivals**: Arattu (held biannually in March/April and Oct/Nov), and the harvest celebration of Onam (late Aug/Sept).

The arcane world of Keralan temple festivities couldn't be further removed from the holiday culture prevailing at nearby **Kovalam**, barely half-an-hour's drive south of the capital. The resort's quartet of sandy bays, interrupted by brown boulder headlands dotted with coconut trees, was where beach tourism in general, and the whole concept of **ayurveda-based holidays** in particular, first took root in Kerala. Foreign backpackers started coming here in serious numbers back in the early 1980s, staying in palm-leaf huts on the outskirts of the fishing village, but since then a low-rise concrete jungle has engulfed the groves behind the grandest of Kovalam's four bays, **Lighthouse Beach** – frequented by an incongruous mix of European ayurveda tourists and somewhat less healthy British sun-worshippers.

Once you are clear of neighbouring **Vizhinjam**, the area's busiest fishing harbour, you'll find idyllic sandy beaches fringing the entire coastline extending **south from Kovalam**. Backed by a lush curtain of coconut plantations, this stretch of coast is where you'll find the far south's most sophisticated spas, five-stars and boutique hideaways, nestling above hidden coves and amid the dense canopy of palm trees. The locals, however, still derive most of their income from coconut and rice cultivation, along with inshore **fishing** – the early-morning polyphonic songs of men hauling long handnets from the surf remain one of the area's defining features.

Aside from Thiruvananthapuram's museums, bazaars and great-value restaurants, possible targets for forays **inland from Kovalam** include the splendid former royal palace at **Padmanabhapuram**, an hour or so south. Another fine specimen of traditional Keralan architecture, **Koikkal Kottaram**, stands just outside the capital at Nedumangad, which can easily be slotted in to a trip to the **Agasthya Hills**, 25km

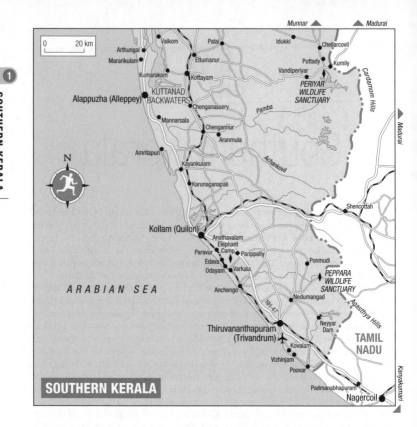

SOUTHERN KERALA

northeast. The hub of this beautiful hill region, and only an hour's drive away from the coast, is the lakeside settlement of **Neyyar Dam**, where Kerala's most popular yoga ashram, the Sivananda Yoga Vedanta Dhanwantari, attracts devotees from all over the world. With a couple of days to spare, you could press on deeper into the mountains to overnight at the hill resort of **Ponmudi**, set amid fragrant tea and cardamom plantations at an altitude of just over 1000m, or go for treks and jeep trips in the forests straddling the Tamil border.

North of Thiruvananthapuram, the Hindu pilgrimage village and tourist resort of **Varkala**, with its spectacular beach, is an essential stop on the well-trodden trail between the far south of the state and Kerala's famous **backwaters** region, **Kuttanad**. The gateway to this watery world, best explored on an old-style *kettu vallam* rice barge, is the market town of **Kollam** (Quilon) – a former dynastic capital and port. Heading north from there you might want to pause at **Amritapuri** for a hug from Kerala's world-renowned guru, Amma. Her ashram, a baby-pink pile of multistorey concrete towers, is one among several unique sights reachable from the backwaters' main hub, **Alappuzha**. Others include a Tantric snake-worship temple at **Mannarsala**, and the beautiful royal palaces at **Kayamkulam**.

A maze of canals and rivers unfolds from the southeast edge of Alappuzha – epicentre of the area's rice boat cruise scene. Because the boat operators tend to moor overnight on secluded riverbanks, few of their clients actually set foot on the myriad islands making up this fascinating micro-region, but the villages hold plenty of guesthouses and homestays – many of them in traditional gabled water-front houses where you can watch the world sail by from the comfort of a traditional pillared veranda.

Alappuzha also serves as the springboard for trips on to exquisite **Vembanad Lake**, the vast, shimmering lagoon to the north. You may not be able to make them out in the heat haze, but the lakeshore is dotted with luxury resort complexes, the main concentration of them around the **Kumarakom Bird Sanctuary** on Vembanad's eastern flank.

Unless you reach it by boat, access to Kumarakom tends to be via the town of **Kottayam**, capital of a prosperous rubber-growing region dominated by Kerala's wealthy Syrian-Christian community. Beyond a couple of ancient churches dating from the earliest days of Christianity in India, it offers little to detain travellers, although devotees of Arundhati Roy's *The God of Small Things* may wish to make a pilgrimage to the author's home village of **Aymenem**, on the outskirts of town, which inspired the novel's setting.

Kottayam also serves as a convenient pit stop on the long haul east from the coastal belt into the Western Ghat range. Chief among the attractions of the so-called "Cardamom Hills" is the **Periyar Wildlife Sanctuary**, a former royal hunting reserve whose impressive rainforest is centred on a reservoir where wild elephant and other animals still congregate. Safaris are conducted either on noisy diesel launches (which tend to scare any wildlife within earshot away) or on paddle-powered bamboo rafts – part of a groundbreaking eco-tourism initiative introduced by the local forest department.

## Some history

Travancore was the last in a long line of princely states stretching back to the second century BC, when the **Ay** dynasty were the dominant political power in the far southwest of India. For centuries, the Ays formed a buffer between the mighty Pandyan dynasty to the east, which ruled most of what is now Tamil country, and the **Cheras** to the north, whose gradual imperial expansion began in the first centuries of the Christian era, from their capital, the port city of Muziris (near modern-day Kochi).

Chera power was eroded by constant attacks from the south by the Pandyans and, after them, the powerful Cholas, but revived around 800 AD under an illustrious line of kings who would become known as the **Kulasekharas**. Under their enlightened rule, during the so-called **Second Chera Empire**, southern Kerala enjoyed three centuries of stability and prosperity. This was the region's classical golden age, when literature, the arts and commerce thrived, and when Malayalam began to take shape as a language distinct from Tamil. The capital, **Mahodayapuram**, grew famous all over the ancient world as a centre of learning and culture, boasting south India's only observatory.

However, in 999 AD, the region plunged into a century of tumult as war once again erupted with the Chola empire. Foreign trade declined, temples were neglected, centres of learning were converted into military academies, the capital was burned to the ground and the second Chera empire slowly began dissolving into smaller chiefdoms.

With the demise of the Kulasekharas, **Venad**, one of their former principalities, emerged as the most important *swaroopam*, or kingdom, in the south. On the back of brisk trade with China and Persia, Quilon (modern Kollam), its main port, became a glittering city of many temples and paved roads, described in glowing terms by Marco Polo. Over the coming four centuries, however, the rise of other regional dynasties gradually nibbled away at Venad's territory, pegging its kings back into a narrow belt between Thiruvananthapuram and the tip of India.

The modern history of Travancore as southern Kerala's major power begins with the accession in 1729 of **Raja Marthanda Varma**. By this time, what remained of Venad – now better known as "Thiruvitamkode" (later corrupted to Travancore) – was in rough shape: the priestly caste, in cahoots with the local nobility, controlled the workings of state; trade and taxation were dominated by competing European powers and the king's coffers were empty.

With support from, among others, the British East India Company, Marthanda Varma set about his policy of "blood and iron", crushing the power of the region's feudal lords and extending his territory northwards. In 1741, his campaign culminated in the dramatic defeat of the Dutch East India Company at the **Battle of Colachen** – the first time an Asian army succeeded in vanquishing a European power in open combat. Thereafter, Travancore controlled the local pepper trade, profits from which financed the move from the rajas' magnificent palace at Padmanabhapuram (now just across the Kerala–Tamil Nadu border, but included in this chapter) to the new capital at Thiruvananthapuram.

An invasion by Tipu Sultan, the legendary "Tiger of Mysore", was held at bay in the late eighteenth century, but only with more support from the British, an arrangement that ultimately led to Travancore becoming a Protectorate of the East India Company, with its own Resident and nineteen-gun salute. The peace dividend of Pax Britannica, however, enabled Travancore's rulers to fund the development of roads, schools, colleges, hospitals and artistic life in the region, whose population became one of the best educated in India. This widespread literacy is often regarded as having paved the way for the later **politicization** of the state's underclasses, not to mention its future economic prosperity.

For all its cultural advances, nineteenth-century Travancore remained under the grips of a particularly oppressive caste system. Agitation against the old social order coalesced around the **Vaikom Satyagrahya**, or "Movement Against Untouchability", led by such luminaries as the sage Sri Narayana Guru (see p.116). Not until the landmark "Temple Entry Proclamation" of 1936 were the doors of the Padmanambhapuram temple finally thrown open to Hindus of all castes.

These days the region, while retaining its unique ritual and art traditions, is at the forefront of innovation and commerce in Kerala. The prolific **Malayalam movie industry** is based on the outskirts of the capital, along with the **Vikram Sarabhai Space Centre** (VSSC), from where India's first satellite rocket was launched in 1963. Home to more than one hundred blue-chip companies, including the software giant Infosys, it also hosts the country's largest IT centre, **Technopark**, a giant, futuristic site on the northern outskirts with a workforce of more than 18,000 professionals. More than twenty percent of the region's income, however, comes from expatriate workers in the Gulf and beyond. As a result, fancy modern mansions appear on the outskirts of nearly every village in southern Kerala.

# Thiruvananthapuram (Trivandrum)

Kerala's capital, **THIRUVANANTHAPURAM** (still widely and more commonly known as **Trivandrum**), is set on seven low hills, only a couple of kilometres inland from the Arabian Sea. Despite its administrative importance – demonstrated by wide roads, multistorey office blocks and gleaming white colonial buildings – it's an easy-going state capital by Indian standards, with enclaves of traditional red-tiled gabled houses breaking up the bustle of its modern concrete centre, and a swathe of parkland spreading to the north.

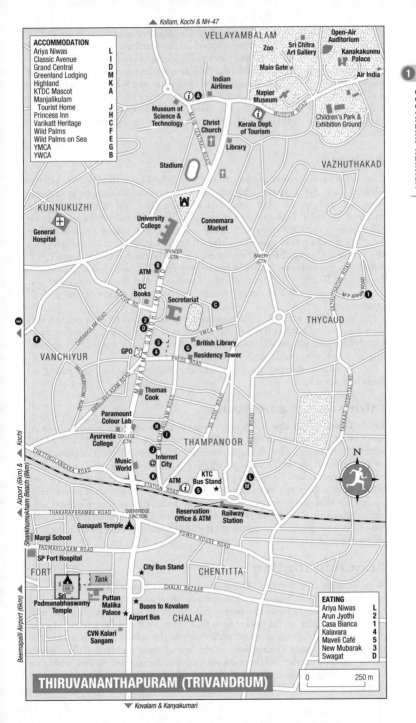

▲ *Kollam, Kochi & NH-47*

**ACCOMMODATION**
| | |
|---|---|
| Ariya Niwas | L |
| Classic Avenue | I |
| Grand Central | D |
| Greenland Lodging | M |
| Highland | K |
| KTDC Mascot | A |
| Manjalikulam Tourist Home | J |
| Princess Inn | H |
| Varikatt Heritage | C |
| Wild Palms | F |
| Wild Palms on Sea | E |
| YMCA | G |
| YWCA | B |

VELLAYAMBALAM

Open-Air Auditorium
Kanakakunnu Palace
Zoo
Sri Chitra Art Gallery
Main Gate
Napier Museum
Air India

Indian Airlines

Museum of Science & Technology
Christ Church
Kerala Dept. of Tourism
Children's Park & Exhibition Ground

Library

Stadium

VAZHUTHAKAD

KUNNUKUZHI
General Hospital

University College
Connemara Market

SPENCER JCTN.
BAKERY JCTN.

ATM
DC Books
Secretariat

MAHATMA GANDHI RD

CHIRAKULAM ROAD
STATUE RD

M P APPAN ROAD

THYCAUD

YMCA RD

GPO

British Library
Residency Tower
PRESS ROAD

VANCHIYUR

VAZHUTHACAUD ROAD

MANJALIKULAM ROAD

Thomas Cook

Paramount Colour Lab

Ayurveda College
COLLEGE JCTN.

S.S. COIL ROAD

THAMPANOOR

ARISTO ROAD

TAIKKAD HOSPITAL RD

Music World

Internet @ City

KTC Bus Stand

N

ATM

STATION ROAD

Railway Station

Reservation Office & ATM

OVERBRIDGE JUNCTION

THAKARAPARAMBU ROAD

Ganapati Temple

Margi School

SP Fort Hospital

PADMAVILASAM ROAD

City Bus Stand

CHENTITTA

POWER HOUSE ROAD

FORT

Sri Padmanabhaswamy Temple

Tank

Puttan Malika Palace

CHALAI BAZAAR

Buses to Kovalam
Airport Bus

CHALAI

CVN Kalari Sangam

**EATING**
| | |
|---|---|
| Ariya Niwas | L |
| Arun Jyothi | 2 |
| Casa Bianca | 1 |
| Kalavara | 4 |
| Maveli Café | 5 |
| New Mubarak | 3 |
| Swagat | D |

**THIRUVANANTHAPURAM (TRIVANDRUM)**

0          250 m

▼ *Kovalam & Kanyakumari*

◄ *Kochi*
◄ *Airport (6km) & Shankhumukham Beach (8km)*
◄ *Beemapalli Airport (6km)*

Although it has few monuments as such, Thiruvananthapuram holds enough of interest to fill a day away from the sands of nearby Kovalam. The oldest and most interesting part of town is the **Fort** area in the south, around the **Sri Padmanab-haswamy temple** and **Puttan Malika Palace**, with the traditional **Chalai bazaar** extending east. At the opposite side of the city centre, the **Sri Chitra Art Gallery** and **Napier Museum** showcase painting, crafts and sculpture in a leafy park. In addition, schools specializing in the martial art **kalarippayat** and the dance/theatre forms of **kathakali** and *kudiyattam* offer an insight into the Keralan obsession with physical training and skill.

## Arrival

Connected to most major Indian cities, as well as Sri Lanka, the Maldives and the Middle East, **Beemapalli airport** (ⓦ www.airportsindia.org.in/allAirports /thiru_general.jsp) lies 6km southwest of town. The best way to get to the centre is on the orange a/c airport bus (Rs15), which runs from the arrivals concourse to the City bus stand in East Fort, and from there on to Kovalam (much to the chagrin of local taxi-drivers). Auto-rickshaws can also get you into the centre for around Rs100 and there's a handy fixed-rate taxi service, for which you pay upfront: Rs200 to the railway station, and Rs400 for Kovalam's Lighthouse Beach. You'll find a Kerala Tourism information booth, ATM and Thomas Cook foreign exchange facility just before the exit of the arrivals concourse.

The long-distance KSRTC **Thampanoor bus stand** and **railway station** face each other across Station Road in the southeast of the city, a short walk east of Overbridge Junction on MG Road. There's a handy pre-paid auto-rickshaw stand directly outside the train station's main exit.

For details on **moving on** from Thiruvananthapuram, and on getting to **Kovalam**, see p.93.

## Information and tours

Kerala Tourism maintains information counters at the airport (theoretically 24hr) and KSRTC **Thampanoor bus stand** (Mon–Sat 10am–5pm; ⓣ 0471/232 7224), while KTDC hosts a visitor reception centre next to the *KTDC Chaithram* hotel on Station Road (ⓣ 0471/233 0031), where you can book accommodation in their hotel chain and tickets for various **guided tours**. Most of these, including the city tours (daily 7.30am–1pm & 1–7pm; Rs200), are far too rushed, but if you're really pushed for time and want to reach the tip of India, try the **Kanyakumari** tour (daily 8am–9pm; Rs500), which takes in Padmanabhapuram Palace (except Mon), Suchindram temple, and Kanyakumari, the southernmost spot in India, in the state of Tamil Nadu.

## Accommodation

With a couple of exceptions, Thiruvananthapuram's **hotels** and guesthouses are functional and bland. Visitors tend to avoid spending a night in the city unless they have to, preferring to travel in from the coast to see the sights, though tariffs in all categories are easier on the pocket here than at nearby Kovalam. Literally dozens of options lie within ten minutes' walk north of the railway and bus stations, in the district known as **Thampanoor** – the best of them up Manjalikulam Road, which runs due north from the main road outside the stations. As ever with state capitals and other large cities, it pays to book ahead, and reconfirm the day before checking in.

## Inexpensive

**Ariya Niwas** Aristo Rd, Thampanoor ☎0471/233
0789. Large, spotless, well-aired rooms with comfy
beds and great city views from its upper floors. The
best value in this bracket (Rs850–1000; plus
Rs700 for a/c) and only a 2min walk from the
railway station. A wonderful mural from Guruvayur
is on display in the lobby, and the best "meals"
restaurant in the state stands on the ground floor
(see "Eating", p.91). ❹

**Greenland Lodging** Aristo Rd, Thampanoor
☎0471/232 8114. Large and efficient lodge with
spotless en-suite rooms (some a/c) for Rs550. The
best low-cost option in the vicinity of the bus stand
and railway station. Book ahead or arrive before
noon. ❸–❹

**Highland** Manjalikulam Rd, Thampanoor
☎0471/233 3200, ⓦwww.highland-hotels.com.
The rooms in this lower mid-range option fail to
live up to the promise of the six-storey concrete
and tinted-glass facade, but it's well managed, only
a short walk from the stations, and easy to find.
The "economy" non-a/c options are dowdy, with
grim bathrooms; the a/c ones are worth the extra.
If it's full, try the *Highland Park* (☎0471/233 8800,
same website; ❹–❺), a little further up the same
street. ❸–❺

**Manjalikulam Tourist Home** Manjalikulam Rd,
Thampanoor ☎0471/233 0776. Don't be fooled by
the gleaming glass and marble ground floor –
above lurks a basic budget place offering variously
priced rooms, all of them clean and with good,
comfy mattresses. ❸

**Princess Inn** Manjalikulam Rd, Thampanoor
☎0471/233 9150, Ⓔprincess_inn@yahoo.com.
Well-scrubbed, respectable cheapie close to the
stations. One of the more welcoming and better-
value small hotels in this busy enclave, though it's
a bit more of a trudge up the lane from Station Rd
than some. ❷–❹

**YMCA** YMCA Rd, near the Secretariat
☎0471/233 0059, Ⓔymcatvm
@sancharnet.in. Neat, smartly furnished rooms at
bargain rates for the levels of comfort. The "luxury"
options (Rs500) are enormous and have high
ceilings, quiet fans, TVs and spacious bathrooms;
singles from Rs290; some a/c. Amazing value,
though you'll probably need to book at least two
weeks in advance. ❸–❹

**YWCA** Spencer Junction ☎0471/247 7308.
Spotless en-suite doubles (from Rs400) on the
fourth floor of a grubby, run-down office block.
Friendly, safe and central, with some non-a/c
rooms, but the place is locked at 10.30pm sharp.
Primarily for women, although couples and men
are welcome. ❷–❸

## Mid-range and luxury

**Classic Avenue** Manjalikulam Rd, Thampanoor
☎0471/233 35555, ⓦwww.classicavenue.net.
This *Best Western* affiliate – "a Sanctuary of
Reassure & Style" – offers formulaic four-star
comfort (including a rooftop pool, multi-cuisine
restaurant and hi-tech gym) in a tower block just
up the road from the train station. It offers three
grades of room – the only difference between them
being the size of their beds. The standard "classic"
ones are much the best value. ❽–❾

**Grand Central** Opposite the Secretariat, MG Rd
☎0471/247 1286, ⓦwww.grandcentral.in. Smart
business hotel in the city centre. The "standard"
rooms are on the small side for two, but cool and
quiet. The "executive" options on the top storey are
larger and more plush, with the best views. There's
also a quality a/c veg restaurant, *Swagat*, on site
(reviewed in "Eating"). ❻

**KTDC Mascot** Mascot Junction, near the Indian
Airlines office ☎0471/231 8990, ⓦwww.ktdc
.com. The city's only true five-star, at the north end
of town near the museums, is a state-run hotel,
patronized mainly by government flunkies while the
Kerala State Legislature is close by). Opening onto
long polished marble corridors lined with hardwood
panels, the fancier "executive" and "suite" rooms
occupy a wing built to house British officers in World
War I; the "standard" ones (from around Rs5000 per
double) are in a less attractive modern block. There's
an open-air pool, bar and a/c restaurant. ❽–❾

**Varikatt Heritage** Poonen Rd, near Cantonment Police Station, behind the Secretariat
(look for the brown gates) ☎0471/233 6057,
ⓦwww.varikattheritage.com. Trivandrum's
only heritage homestay – run by the affable
Col. K.K. Kuncheria (Gurkha Rifles, Rtd) – is a real
gem. It occupies a gorgeous 1830s Indo-Saracenic-
style bungalow originally built by a lovesick British
spinster, Miss Blanket, who followed a tea-planter out
to India after the two had met while holidaying in
Yorkshire. Romance bloomed, the couple married,
and eventually they returned to England. The house
was sold to a prominent local lawyer, in whose family
it has remained ever since. The three front-side
suites ($115), opening onto a high-ceilinged veranda
where you can enjoy a *chota peg* under the hunting
trophies after supper, retain their original rosewood
furniture – and more period atmosphere than the
much less appealing rear-side doubles ($90). ❾

**Wild Palms** Mathrubhoomi Rd ☎0471/247 1175,
ⓦwww.wildpalmsonsea.com. Cavernous
homestay-guesthouse in a modern, but rather
gloomy, suburban house, a 10min walk from MG
Rd. The place is large enough to afford a degree of
privacy, and the en-suite rooms are very spacious.

The same owners also run *Wild Palms on Sea* (see below). ⑤

**Wild Palms on Sea** 20km northwest of town (or 16km from airport) at Puthenthope ⑦0471/275 6781, ⑩www.wildpalmsonsea.com. This offshoot of *Wild Palms* comprises a compound of red-brick "cottages" next to a three-storey fusion building ranged around a curved pool – all set in a coconut grove next to the beach. The location's much more pleasant and peaceful than Kovalam, though not a great place for bathing. Half-board on request. ⑤–⑥

## Festivals of Thiruvananthapuram

The annual **Nishangandhi Dance and Music festival**, which hosts some of India's best-known artists, is held in the grounds of the Kanakakkunnu Palace, just to the east of the public gardens, in mid-January. Originally built as a cultural venue for the maharajas of Thiruvananthapuram, the large, open-air amphitheatre where the event is staged makes an ideal venue for evening performances of classical dances and music.

The **Arattu festival**, centred on the Sri Padmanabhaswamy temple, takes place biannually, in Meenam (March/April) and Thulam (Oct/Nov). Each time, ten days of festivities inside the temple (open to Hindus only) culminate in a procession through the streets of the city, taking the deity, Padmanabhaswamy, to the sea for ritual immersion. Five caparisoned elephants, armed guards and a *nagaswaram* (double-reed wind instrument) and *tavil* drum group are led by the maharaja of Travancore, in his symbolic role as the servant of the god. Instead of the richly dressed figure that might be expected, the maharaja (whose rank is no longer officially recognized) wears a simple white *dhoti*, his chest bare save for the sacred thread. Rather than riding, he walks the whole way, bearing a sword. To the accompaniment of a 21-gun salute and music, the procession sets off from the east gate of the temple at around 5pm, moving at a brisk pace to reach Shankhumukham Beach at sunset, about an hour later. After the seashore ceremonies, the cavalcade returns to the temple at about 9pm, to be greeted by an extremely loud fireworks display.

For ten days in March/April, Muslims celebrate **Chandanakuda Mahotsavam** at the Beemapalli Dargah Shareef tomb, 5km southwest of the city on the coastal road towards the airport. The Hindu-influenced festival commemorates the anniversary of the death of Bee Umma (aka "Beema Beevi"), a female descendant of the Prophet Mohammed revered for her piety and spiritual powers. On its first, most important, day, pilgrims converge on the mosque inside the complex carrying earthenware pots, or *chandana-kuddam*, covered in sandalwood paste and flowers, and containing money offerings. Activities such as traditional storytelling (*kathaprasangam*) and sword play (*daharamuttu*) take place inside the mosque, while the courtyard outside hosts dance and music recitals. In the early hours of the morning, a flag is brought out from Beema Beevi's tomb and taken on a procession, accompanied by a *panchavadyam* drum and horn orchestra and two caparisoned elephants, practices normally associated with Hindu festivals. Once more, the rest of the night is lit up with fireworks.

The great Keralan festival of **Onam** (late Aug or Sept) takes place during the late-monsoon harvest period, when Keralans remember the reign of King Mahabali, a legendary figure who, it is believed, achieved an ideal balance of harmony, wealth and justice during his tenure. Unfortunately, the gods became upset and envious at Mahabali's success and Vishnu packed him off to another world. However, once a year the king was allowed to return to his people for ten days, and Onam is a joyful celebration of the royal visit. Families display their wealth, feasts and boat races are held and, in Thiruvananthapuram, there's a week-long cultural festival of dance and music culminating in a colourful street carnival in which thousands of local women prepare *payasam* (Keralan rice pudding) in earthen pots in the street – the greatest gathering forms on the road leading to the Sri Padmanabhaswamy temple.

The precise **dates** of these events can be checked at Kerala Tourism's Festival Calendar (⑩www.keralatourism.org/festivalcalendar.php), and at any tourist information counter in the state.

## The City

Thiruvananthapuram's main sights – the **Padmanabhaswamy temple**, **Puttan Malika palace** and **Chalai Bazaar** – are clustered in the historic quarter of **Fort**, on the south side of the city. The district is compact enough to get around on foot, but you'll want to jump in an auto-rickshaw to reach the **museum** complex, on the opposite, northern, side of the centre. Connecting the two, **MG Road** is the city's main thoroughfare, lined by big banks, hotels and shopping malls. Traffic moves freely enough along it except during the evening rush hour, and when one of the frequent, but generally orderly, political demonstrations converges on the grand colonial **Secretariat** building halfway along.

### Sri Padmanabhaswamy temple

Padmanabha, the god Vishnu reclined on a coiled serpent with a lotus flower sprouting from his belly button, is the presiding deity of the Travancore house, as well as the principal idol within the **Sri Padmanabhaswamy temple**, a vast complex of interlocking walled courtyards, shrines and ceremonial walkways in the south of the city. Unusually for Kerala, the shrine was conceived in the Dravidian style more often associated with Tamil Nadu, featuring a tall, seven-tiered *gopura* gateway and high fortress-like walls. The image of this exotic skyline reflected in the waters of the temple's bathing tank has become iconic of the city. Non-Hindus are unfortunately not permitted inside – though no one will mind you admiring the exterior.

Most of Padmanabhaswamy's structures date from the eighteenth century, added by Raja Marthanda Varma (1729–58) to a much more ancient core within. According to legend, the temple was founded after Vishnu – disguised as a beautiful child – merged into a huge tree in the forest, which immediately crashed to the ground. There it transformed into a 13km-long image of the reclining Vishnu. Divakara, a sage who witnessed this, prayed for the god to assume a form

▲ Sri Padmanabhaswamy temple

that he could view in its entirety. Vishnu complied, morphing into the colossus that's now adored by millions of pilgrims annually.

Composed of 12,008 sacred stones, or *salagrams*, brought by elephant from the bed of the Gandhaki River in Nepal, the central **deity** is coated with a rare form of stucco known as *katusarkara yogam*, made according to an ancient ayurvedic recipe. To make offerings and perform *darshan*, or ritual viewing of the god, worshippers have to mount special stone platforms from which they can peer at different parts of the huge reclining Vishnu – feet, navel and face – through three openings in the floor, known as *vaayils*.

The main approach road to Sri Padmanabhaswamy is lined with stalls selling religious souvenirs such as shell necklaces, puja offerings, jasmine and marigolds. It's an atmospheric area for a stroll – particularly in the early morning and at dusk, when devotees make their way to and from prayers. As recently as the turn of the twentieth century, this was a "no-go" area for members of low-caste communities – possibly on pain of death.

## Puttan Malika Palace

The **Puttan Malika Palace** (Tues–Sun 8.30am–12.30pm & 3–5.30pm; Rs20, camera Rs15), immediately southeast of the temple, became the seat of the Travancore rajas after they left Padmanabhapuram at the end of the nineteenth century. It was commissioned by Raja Ravi Thirunal Varma, who died at the tender age of 30, only a year after the palace was completed. To generate funds for much-needed restoration, the royal family opened the palace to the public in the mid-1990s for the first time in more than two centuries. Although much of it remains off-limits, palace guides show you around some of the most impressive wings, which have been converted into a **museum**. The cool chambers, with highly polished plaster floors and delicately carved wooden screens, house a crop of dusty Travancore heirlooms. Among the array of portraits, royal regalia and weapons are some genuine treasures, such as a solid crystal throne – a gift from the Dutch – and some fine murals. The real highlight, however, is the elegant Keralan architecture itself. Beneath sloping red-tiled roofs, hundreds of wooden pillars, carved into the forms of rampant horses (*puttan malika* translates as "horse palace"), prop up the eaves, and airy verandas project onto the surrounding lawns.

The royal family have always been keen patrons of the arts, and the open-air **Swathi Sangeetotsavam festival**, held in the grounds during the festival of Navaratri (Oct/Nov), continues the tradition. Performers sit on the palace's raised porch, flanked by the main facade, with the spectators seated on the lawn. Songs composed by Raja Swathi Thirunal (1813–46), known as the "musician king", dominate the programme. For details, ask at the KTDC tourist counter.

## CVN Kalari Sangam

Kerala's most famous **kalarippayat** gymnasium, **CVN Kalari Sangam**, stands around 500m southeast of the Sri Padmanabhaswamy temple in East Fort. Housed in a modest red-brick building, it was founded in 1956 by C.V. Narayanan Nair, one of the legendary figures credited for the martial art's revival, and attracts students from across the world. From 6.30am to 8am (Mon–Sat) you can watch fighting exercises in the sunken *kalari* pit that forms the heart of the complex. Foreigners may attend courses, arranged through the head teacher, or *gurukkal*, although prior experience of martial arts and/or dance is a prerequisite. You can also join the queues of locals who come here for a traditional **kalari massage**, and to consult the gym's expert ayurveda doctors (Mon–Sat 10am–1pm & 5–7.30pm, Sun 10am–1pm).

## Kalarippayat

Practised in special earth-floored gyms and pits across the state, **kalarippayat** is Kerala's unique martial art – a distinctive brand of acrobatic combat drawing heavily on yoga and ancient Indian knowledge of the human body. Its techniques of hand-to-hand fighting, weapon skills and healing were first formalized in the twelfth century by the bodyguards of medieval warlords and chieftains, though plenty of evidence exists to suggest the form derives from practices two or more thousand years old. Under guidance from their gurus, young boys (and sometimes girls) would be trained for years as specialist fighters, who in time would be employed to wage duels and settle disputes on behalf of landowners and chiefs. In the eighteenth century, *kalarippayat* was banned by the British, but it has since made a strong comeback and now has numerous followers – Hindus, Christians and Muslims alike.

Two distinct **schools** survive – the southern and northern systems. Both, however, follow a similar progression. Once initiated, students are taught a complex set of strenuous exercises designed to render their bodies strong and flexible: kicks, jumps, animal postures, spins, step sequences and vigorous stretches, joined in increasingly long and complicated sequences. Sesame-oil massages, given with the feet and hands by teachers holding on to ropes suspended from the gym's rafters, are another essential part of the training. When the set moves have been mastered, students are eventually introduced to combat with weapons: the *udaval* (sword), *paricha* (shield), *kadaras* (dagger), *kuntham* (spear), *gadha* (mace) and *urumi* (a long flexible sword). The final stage, **verum kaythari**, focuses on barehanded combat against an armed enemy and is for advanced practitioners only.

Staged at gyms and tourist resorts across Kerala, *kalarippayat* **demonstrations** are never dull, and injuries, although rare, do happen. As part of their advanced training, masters, known as *gurukkal*, are initiated into a system of physical therapy combining oil massage and ayurvedic herbal medicine, which is why famous *kalarippayat* gyms, such as CVN Kalari in Thiruvananthapuram, double as traditional outpatient clinics.

For more places to **learn** *kalarippayat*, see p.183 & p.230.

## The Margi School

Thiruvananthapuram has for centuries been a major crucible for Keralan classical arts, and the **Margi Theatre School** (☎0471/247 8806, ⓦ www.margitheatre .org), at the western corner of the Fort area, keeps the flame of the region's oldest ritual theatre traditions burning brightly. **Kathakali** dance drama and the more rarely performed **kudiyattam** theatre form dominate the curriculum. By prior arrangement visitors can watch students being put through their paces; foreign students are also welcome to attend an introductory course. However, the reason most visitors venture out here is to watch one of the authentic *kathakali* or *kudiyattam* performances staged in its small theatre, details of which are posted on the school's website.

To reach Margi, head to the SP Fort hospital on the western edge of Fort, and then continue 200m north; the school is set back from the west side of the main road in a large red-tiled and tin-roofed building, behind the High School (the sign is in Malayalam).

## The Napier Museum

As well as serving as a welcome refuge from the noise and heat of the city, Thiruvananthapuram's **Public Gardens**, on the northern side of the centre, are the site of the **Napier Museum** (Tues–Sun 10am–5pm; Rs5). Named after the then British Governor of Madras, Lord Francis Napier, the flamboyant Raj-era building was commissioned in 1874 as part of the Travancore royal family's bid to bring arts and crafts to the "common man". Its architect, Robert Fellowes Chisolm (1840–1915), was an early proponent of the so-called "Indo-Saracenic" school, which sought to blend indigenous architectural features (in this case tiled, gabled roofs) with Islamic touches and typically colonial brickwork. The interior is no less extravagant, featuring stained-glass windows and striped walls that at times threaten to upstage the collection itself. Medieval Chola and Vijayanagar bronzes are the highlights of the exhibition, along with fifteenth-century Keralan woodcarvings, some minutely detailed ivory work and a temple chariot (*rath*).

## The Zoo

North of the Napier Museum, the spectacular rain trees of the former royal botanical gardens shade the city's famous **Zoo** (Tues–Sun 10am–5pm; Rs6). Its collection of animals, covering 75 species from the Subcontinent and beyond, are housed in a mixture of modern, open-style enclosures and an extraordinary campus of quirky Raj-era structures, little changed since they were built in the 1850s: Grecian friezes of gorillas adorn the ape area, the giraffes inhabit a Chinese pagoda and the barking deer shelter beneath a roof of Mangalorean tiles. Founded, like the museum, by the Maharaja of Travancore, the zoo must be one of the few in the world to have earned a place in literary history, as the place that novelist Yann Martel claimed inspired him to write his 2002 Booker-prize winning *Life of Pi* (the claim was later challenged after striking similarities were found between his book and Brazilian author Moacyr Scliar's *Max and the Cats*).

## Sri Chitra Art Gallery

You have to pass through the main ticket booth for the zoo to reach the **Sri Chitra Art Gallery** (Tues–Sun 10am–5pm; no photography; Rs10), which exhibits a handful of paintings from the Rajput, Mughal and Tanjore schools, along with pieces from China, Tibet and Japan. The meat of its collection, however, is made up of works by the celebrated Keralan painter, **Raja Ravi Varma** (1848–1906), a local aristocrat who started his career in the Travancore royal court before going on to achieve fame and fortune as a producer of Hindu mythological prints – forerunners of India's quirky calendar art. Varma's style was much criticized by later generations for its sentimentality and strong Western influence, but in his time he was regarded as the nation's greatest living artist. Reproductions of his portraits of beautiful, sari-clad Indian women, in particular, adorn walls all over India to this day. The one that crops up most often, however, is *Hamsa Damayanthi*, a portrait of Damayanthi listening to messages from her lover brought to her by a swan (a scene episode from the Hindu epic, the Mahabharata). The original hangs here, in the second room of the Sri Chitra gallery, along with images of some of Varma's former patrons and their wives. The real show stopper, though, is the painting of the Biblical heroine, *Judith*, on the wall to the right of the main doorway as you enter – a work considered too provocative for public exhibition in its day, and whose defiantly bare-breasted, sword-wielding subject still casts a powerful spell.

Also on view at the Sri Chitra, in rooms to the rear of the main building, are a couple of minor Tagores, and some striking, strongly coloured Himalayan landscapes by the Russian artist-philosopher and mystic, **Nicholas Roerich**, who resided in the Kullu Valley for two decades until his death in 1947.

## Shankhumukham beach

On Sunday evenings, half the city migrates to **Shankhumukham Beach**, 8km west of the centre, to stroll along the sand and watch the sun set. Fried-food stalls spring up on the roadside, and the *Indian Coffee House* does a roaring trade at its popular seafront branch. It occupies a building that once belonged to the royal family, where the Raja of Travancore used to preside over executions. A macabre painting displayed in the Puttan Malika Palace shows the cage of tigers used for this purpose: huge crowds would gather to gawp at the condemned criminals being torn limb from limb. These days, the main attraction, aside from the surf, is a huge sculpture in concrete of a curvaceous mermaid reclining on landscaped ground behind the *Indian Coffee House* – a work by the renowned Keralan artist Canai Kunuram. Shankhumukham draws the biggest crowds of all during the biannual **Arattu** festival, when the Padmanabhaswamy deity is brought, amid much pomp, from the temple to be ritually immersed in the sea here (see p.86).

### Markets and shopping

The **Gandhi Khadi Gramodyog**, between Pazhavangadi and Overbridge junctions, stocks high-quality handloom cotton and silk, as well as the usual range of metal and carved-wood souvenirs, replica dhows and so on. **Natesan's Antique Arts**, further up, is part of an upscale chain specializing in Thanjavur paintings, temple and church carvings, and traditional treasure boxes – all certified as exportable, but sold at premium prices. DC Books, on Statue Road, on the first floor of a building above Statue Junction, is the city's best **bookstore**, with a separate area devoted to Kerala.

The main source of fresh produce and everyday items is the 1km-long **Chalai Bazaar**, in East Fort. Lined with little shops selling flowers, incense, spices, bell-metal lamps and fireworks, it's a great area for aimless browsing. On your left (north side) as you enter the bazaar, look out for United Umbrella Mart, which sells brightly coloured temple parasols used in elephant processions. Further down on the opposite side of the road, the delightfully old-fashioned Ambal Coffee Works is another source of authentic Keralan souvenirs.

## Eating

Freshly cooked dosas, *iddli-vada-sambar*, biriyanis and other traditional snacks are available at streetside cafés throughout Thiruvananthapuram, including the perennially popular *Indian Coffee House* chain, which has several branches in the city centre – most famously the circular *Maveli Café* next to the KSRTC bus stand in Thampanoor. Out at **Shankhumukham**, they also manage a busy beachfront café that gets packed on Sunday evenings, when thousands of city folk descend for a sunset stroll. For proper Kerala-style thali "meals" and Malabari specialities, stick to the places below and you'll be in for a treat.

**Ariya Niwas** *Ariya Niwas* hotel, Aristo Rd, Thampanoor. Top-class south Indian vegetarian thalis dished up on banana leaves in a scrupulously clean non-a/c dining room on the hotel's ground floor, or in the pricier a/c dining hall on the first storey. Hugely popular with everyone from office workers to company directors and their families, and deservedly so: there's really nowhere better to eat in the city. The usual *udipi* menu, along with some north Indian and Chinese dishes, is served outside lunch hours (noon–3pm).

**Arun Jyothi** Opposite the Secretariat on MG Rd. A delightfully old-fashioned "meals" restaurant that does unlimited red- or white-rice Keralan thalis (Rs30) from noon to 3pm, including particularly delicious *avial*, an array of condiments, and *payasam* for desert. Dosas, *uttapams* and other *udipi* fare are served through the rest of the day.

**Casa Bianca** 96 MP Appan Rd. You couldn't make it up: a Swedish-run Italian restaurant in a middle-class district of Thiruvananthapuram – and a really fine one at that, serving scrumptious pizza, fresh pasta and crisp house salads, as well as a range of Continental mains, sandwiches and desserts. This has become one of the trendiest places to dine in the city, and the bakery on the ground floor does an equally brisk trade, not least in fresh cream cakes. Well worth an auto ride across town for.

**Kalavara** Press Rd. One of the city's most popular multi-cuisine restaurants, down a side street off MG Rd. You can eat in their dowdy first-floor dining room or, from 6.30pm onwards, on the more attractive rooftop terrace under a pitched-tile shelter. The furniture's plastic, but the food (mostly non-veg) is tasty and inexpensive: fish, beef, mutton and pork dominate the menu, and they do fish curry "meals" from 12.30pm to 2pm.

**Maveli Café** Next to the bus station on Station Rd, Thampanoor. Part of the *Indian Coffee House* chain, this bizarre red-brick, spiral-shaped café (designed by the renowned expatriate British architect, Laurie Baker) is a Thiruvananthapuram institution. Inside, waiters in the trademark *ICH pugris* serve dosas, *vadas*, greasy omelettes, mountainous biriyanis and china cups of the usual (weak and sugary) filter coffee. An obligatory pit stop, though a grubby one.

**New Mubarak** Off Press Rd. Great little no-frills backstreet joint that's famed for its spicy Malabari dishes, especially seafood. In addition to the usual masala-fry pomfret, kingfish, seer fish and pearlspot (*avioli*), you can order huge jumbo prawns, squid and crab, served with proper tapioca (*kappa*) curry and the famous house seafood pickle – at prices undreamed of in Kovalam (most mains Rs100–150). It's tricky to find: you have to squeeze down a narrow pedestrian alleyway off Press Rd (find your way to the *Residency Tower* hotel on Press Rd and ask there).

**Swagat** *Grand Central*, MG Rd. Fine vegetarian Indian food served by black-tie waiters in a blissfully cool a/c dining hall, with tinted windows and discreet Carnatic music in the background – just the ticket if you've had enough of the heat and humidity outside. Their Rs120 "Swagat Special" thali is one for monster appetites, featuring green plantain in coconut, ladies' finger masala and tangy *rasam*. They also do a full multi-cuisine veg menu, even at lunch. If you're in town on a Friday, don't miss their traditional banana-leaf *sadyas*.

## Listings

**Airlines** Website addresses for the following carriers are listed on p.21. Air India, Museum Rd, Vellayambalam Circle ☎ 0471/231 0310 (airport ☎ 0471/250 0585); Gulf Air, Ground Floor, Saran Chambers, Vellayambalam ☎ 0471/272 8003 (airport ☎ 0471/250 1205); Indian Airlines, Air Centre, Mascot Junction ☎ 0471/231 4781 (airport ☎ 0471/233 1063); Jet Airways, 1st Floor, Akshaya Towers, Sasthamangalam Junction ☎ 0471/272 8864 (airport ☎ 0471/250 0710); Kingfisher Airlines, Stargate Building, TC 9 / 888, Vellayambalam (☎ 1-800/209 3030); KLM/Northwest, c/o Spencer Travel Services, Spencer Junction, MG Rd ☎ 0471/246 3531; Paramount Airways (airport ☎ 9995 411664 or ☎ 9995 400002); Qatar Airways, Bela Vista, TC 30/1403, near SBT, Nalumukku, Pettah ☎ 0471/391 9091 (airport ☎ 0471/250 2548); SriLankan Airlines, 1st Floor, Spencer Building, Palayam, MG Rd ☎ 0471/247 1815 (airport ☎ 0471/250 1140).

**Banks and exchange** A string of big banks along MG Rd – including HDFC, the SBI, UTI and ICICI – have ATMs and change travellers' cheques and currency; there are additional ATMs next to the KTDC Tourist Reception Centre opposite the railway station, and immediately outside the station exit, next to the reservations hall. Thomas Cook maintains a foreign exchange counter at the airport and at its travel agency on the ground floor of the Soundarya Building (near the big Raymond's tailoring store), MG Rd (Mon–Sat 9.30am–6pm).

**Dentist** Kamala Dental Speciality Hospital, Sri Mulam Club Junction, Vazhuthacaud (☎ 0471/233 8420, ⌨ www.kamaladental.com).

**Hospitals** SP Fort Hospital (☎ 0471/245 0540), just down the road from the Margi School in West Fort, has a 24hr casualty and specialist orthopaedic unit; the private Cosmopolitan Hospital, in Pattom (☎ 0471/244 8182), is also recommended. The Government-run General Hospital, 600m east of Statue Circle on MG Rd, is one of the busiest in the state.

**Internet access** Internet City on Manhalikulam Rd charges Rs20/hr and is convenient if you're staying in Thampanoor. There's also a tiny, more cramped cybercafé to the rear of the *KTDC Hotel Chaithram*'s lobby, next to the bus stand (Rs30/hr).

**Photography and printing** The efficient Paramount Colour Lab on Ayurveda College Junction, MG Rd, has state-of-the-art digital printers, sells memory cards and will load data onto discs. In the bowels of the building below ground level there's also a counter specializing in business card printing (Rs2/card).

**Post office** The main post office is just south of the Secretariat on MG Rd.

Thiruvananthapuram is the main hub for traffic travelling along the coast. Towns within a couple of hours of the capital – such as Varkala, Kollam and Kanyakumari – can be reached by both bus and train; aim for limited-stop services rather than much slower "local" or "passenger" ones. For longer hauls, you're invariably better off on the **train**, as buses tend to hurtle along the coastal highway at terrifying speeds; they're also more crowded. The bus to **Kovalam** – just 10km away – generally takes 30–45 minutes; it's quicker and more convenient by **auto-rickshaw** (Rs100–125) or **taxi** (Rs400–500).

### By air
Construction of a new terminal building was well under way at the time of writing, but until it is finished, don't expect first-world efficiency of Thiruvananthapuram's **Beemapalli airport**, 6km southwest of the city, where departure formalities routinely take two hours (or more). Contact details for carriers with offices at the airport, and downtown, appear on "Listings" on p.92. For general advice on booking flights, see p.26.

As the roads to Beemapalli were recently upgraded, it's a comfortable enough journey by auto-rickshaw (around Rs100); taxis charge Rs200–250 from the railway station, and Rs400–500 from Kovalam's Lighthouse Beach.

### By bus
Buses to **Kovalam** – including the smart new a/c service connecting the resort with the airport – leave every 20 to 30min from the roadside in East Fort, just south of City bus stand. To reach anywhere else, you'll have to head for the grimy KSRTC **Thampanoor bus stand**. Services to **Varkala** leave from here at irregular intervals throughout the day from 7.25am – though it's worth noting that many of them are nail-bitingly slow, winding through dozens of villages and taking up to two-and-a-half hours instead of the one-and-a-half hours required by "super-fast" buses that follow the highway. For **Ponmudi**, there are departures at 5am and 8am. Heading **north** up the coast (to Kollam, Alappuzha, Ernakulam, Thrissur and Palakkad), the buses to aim for are the 6am or 5.30pm "super-deluxe a/c" specials, **tickets** for which – along with tickets for all other long-distance routes – may be purchased in advance at the reservations hatch on the main bus stand concourse (daily 6am–10pm). The Tamil Nadu bus company, TNSRTC, has its own counter on the same concourse. Numerous private bus companies also run inter-state services; many of the agents are on Aristo Road near the *Greenland Lodging*.

### By train
Reservations for long-haul train journeys – **to Kochi or points further north** – should be made as far in advance as possible from the efficient computerized booking office at the station (Mon–Sat 8am–2pm & 2.15–8pm, Sun 8am–2pm). Sleepers are sold throughout Kerala on a first-come, first-served basis, not on local stations' quotas. The following trains are recommended as the **fastest** and/or **most convenient** from Thiruvananthapuram.

### Recommended trains from Thiruvananthapuram

| Destination | Name | Number | Frequency | Departs | Total time |
|---|---|---|---|---|---|
| Alappuzha | Netravati Exp* | #6346 | daily | 10.00am | 2hr 50min |
| Ernakulam/ Kochi | Kerala Express | #2625 | daily | 11.15am | 4hr 15min |
| Kollam | Kerala Express | #2625 | daily | 11.15am | 1hr |
| Kottayam | Cape–Mumbai Express* | #6382 | daily | 8.05am | 3hr 25min |
| Kozhikode | Mangalore Exp* | #6347 | daily | 8.45pm | 10hr |

* via Kollam, Varkala, Ernakulam, Thrissur, Palakkad, Kozhikode, Kannur and Kasargode

# Kovalam

You have to envy the travellers who first discovered **KOVALAM** back in the 1970s. Before the appearance of the crowds and sunbeds that nowadays spill over the resort's quartet of beaches, not to mention the warren of hotels, shops and restaurants crammed into the palm groves behind them, this must have been a heavenly location. Four decades of unplanned development, however, have wrought havoc on the famous headland, with its golden sand bays and trademark boulder promontories. Virtually every conceivable patch of dry ground behind the most spectacular of them, **Lighthouse Beach**, has been buried under concrete, along with most of the area's Keralan character.

Kovalam's boom peaked in the mid-1990s, when European charter companies started sending planeloads of package tourists here. The backpackers promptly decamped north up the coast to Varkala, but the local businesses didn't really feel the pinch until the abrupt suspension in 2008 of charter flights from the UK. Now the resort depends on an unlikely mix of hedonistic British fifty-somethings on extended sun-and-booze breaks, and middle-aged German and Scandanavian ayurveda tourists who – forbidden by their doctors from lying in the sun – kill time drinking juices in the cafés.

The go-ahead Keralan government is hoping to reverse Kovalam's decline with the construction of an offshore **artificial reef** (see p.96) which, it claims, will generate perfect waves for big-spending surfers. But for the time being, the resort looks not a little down on its luck – a pale shadow of the beach paradise many come here expecting. For a holiday experience that lives up to the glamour of the brochures, you'll have to press further south down the coast, where a string of high-end resorts huddle in the coconut groves above a series of idyllic coves. A world away from the poor fishing villages just beyond their high walls, these places offer a seductive combination of traditional Keralan architecture, ayurveda masages and exclusive beach access – at eye-poppingly high prices.

## Arrival and information

**Buses** from Thiruvananthapuram (see p.93) loop through the top of the village before coming to a halt outside the gates of the *Leela*, on the promontory dividing

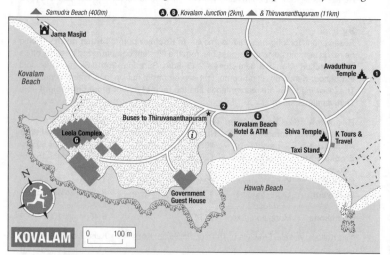

Hawah and Kovalam beaches. If you don't intend to stay at this northern end of the resort, or at Samudra beach, get off a couple of hundred metres earlier, just past the *Blue Sea* hotel where the road bends – then follow the lane branching to the left which drops steeply downhill towards the top of Hawah Beach.

Expect to be plagued by commission touts as you arrive; an approach via the back paths is a good way of avoiding them. The friendly **tourist office** (daily 10am–5pm, closed Sun in low season; ☏0471/248 0085, ⓦwww.keralatourism .org), just inside the *Leela*'s gates close to where the buses pull in, stocks the usual range of glossy leaflets on Kerala and can offer up-to-date advice about cultural events in the area.

## Accommodation

Kovalam is chock-full of **accommodation in all categories**. Little of it could be considered great value by Indian standards, but since the demise of charter tourism in the resort, rates have taken a bit of a tumble, particularly mid-range, and you can pick up some hefty last-minute discounts if the season is slack. Whatever your budget, it's worth trying to haggle down the quoted price, especially for stays of a week or more. As ever, ignore offers of rooms in the street – the tip that your hotel- or guesthouse-owner will be obliged to pay the tout will be added to your room tariff.

Unless otherwise stated, all the following hotels are marked on the **map** below.

### Budget

**Moon Valley Cottage** Behind Lighthouse Beach ☏9446 1029 1248, ⓔsknairkovalam@yahoo .com. This simple budget guesthouse stands right next to the footpath leading from the rear of Lighthouse Beach to the Avaduthura Devi temple. Its pleasantly decorated rooms are really big for the price, with mosquito nets and quality bedding. The best are hidden around the back of the building, which overlooks open fields rather than the busy path to the front. The same owner also

offers a couple of similarly well-priced two-bedroom apartments in another building nearby. ④

**Rockland (Kiki's)** Lighthouse Rd ☏0471/248 0588. *Rockland (Kiki's)* is one of a cluster of three co-run budget hotels, sandwiched together just off the lane above the south end of Lighthouse Beach. It has the edge over its neighbours because its six comfortable rooms – all en suite and with balconies – look straight through coconut palms to the sea. Reasonable rates, given the location. ④

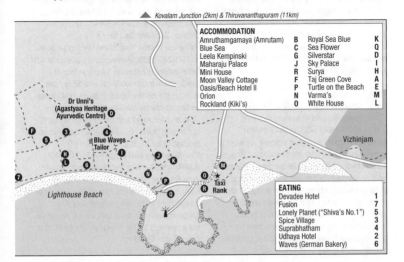

▲ *Kovalam Junction (2km) & Thiruvananthapuram (11km)*

**ACCOMMODATION**

| | | | |
|---|---|---|---|
| Amruthamgamaya (Amrutam) | B | Royal Sea Blue | K |
| Blue Sea | C | Sea Flower | Q |
| Leela Kempinski | G | Silverstar | D |
| Maharaju Palace | J | Sky Palace | I |
| Mini House | R | Surya | H |
| Moon Valley Cottage | F | Taj Green Cove | A |
| Oasis/Beach Hotel II | P | Turtle on the Beach | E |
| Orion | N | Varma's | M |
| Rockland (Kiki's) | O | White House | L |

Dr Unni's (Agastyaa Heritage Ayurvedic Centre)

Blue Waves Tailor

Vizhinjam

Lighthouse Beach

Taxi Rank

**EATING**

| | |
|---|---|
| Devadee Hotel | 1 |
| Fusion | 7 |
| Lonely Planet ("Shiva's No.1") | 5 |
| Spice Village | 3 |
| Suprabhatham | 4 |
| Udhaya Hotel | 2 |
| Waves (German Bakery) | 6 |

## Waves of change

The Boxing Day tsunamis which swept up the Keralan coast in 2004 caused far less damage and loss of life in Kovalam than they did in the fishing villages of neighbouring Tamil Nadu. But a new wave of change looks set to engulf Kerala's flagship beach resort in their wake.

To prevent any further erosion of the money-spinning sands lining **Lighthouse Beach**, the state government has embarked on construction of a spectacular 500-metre-long **artificial reef** across the bay – at a cost of Rs40 million (nearly US$900,000). A large slice of the bill will be covered by the TRP (Tsunami Rehabilitation Programme) – funds earmarked for rebuilding infrastructure and livelihoods destroyed by the 2004 disaster. However, opponents of the scheme claim that far from benefiting Kovalam's fishing communities by protecting the coast, the new reef may actually cause further destruction by diverting waves onto similarly fragile beaches nearby, which local people use for fishing.

The real impetus behind the scheme, they claim, is not coastal protection, but to transform Kovalam into India's number-one watersports destination. By limiting wave heights to around 1m, the reef, built of geo-textile bags filled with sand, will facilitate year-round surfing, as well as waterskiing and sports fishing – none of which is likely to improve the lot of poor folk in the area, except perhaps the lads who rent out surfboards on Lighthouse Beach.

**Sky Palace** Lighthouse Beach ℡ 0471/248 7906, ℡ 9745 841222. Basic but comfortable option two blocks back from the waterfront, just half a minute's walk from the beach. The en-suite rooms, opening on to a sociable common veranda, are very clean and a good size for the money, with gleaming floors and crisp white sheets. ❹

**Surya** Lighthouse Beach ℡ 0471/248 1012, Ⓔ kovsurya@yahoo.co.in. Professionally run budget travellers' guesthouse down a narrow lane from the seafront. It's secure and quiet, with pleasant rooms for the price (a/c and non-a/c); some of the verandas look straight onto adjacent buildings, but there's lots of space inside, with new beds and sound plumbing and electrics. One of the better budget options. If it's full, try the equally spruce *White House* (℡ 0471/248 3388; ❹) next door. ❷–❸

### Mid-range

**Amruthamgamaya (Amrutham)** Panagodu, near Venganoor (see map, p.101), ℡ 0471/645 5423, ℡ 9447 856461, Ⓦ www.amrutham.in. A great option if you want to base yourself away from the busy coastal strip, but within striking distance of the beaches. It's essentially an ayurveda centre, but with comfortable accommodation in beautiful, large octagonal rooms overlooking a terraced garden. Home-cooked vegetarian meals are served on a high rooftop overlooking a sea of palm trees, and there's a gorgeous pool to relax in. Superb value, but tricky to find: phone ahead for directions. ❻

**Blue Sea** 100m before junction to Hawah Beach ℡ 0471/248 1401, ℡ 9349 991992, Ⓦ www .hotelskerala.com/bluesea. Half-a-dozen quirky round buildings in the rear garden of a grand double-fronted colonial-era mansion overlooking the main road above Hawah Beach. Each contains three rooms, arranged on separate storeys around a (rather shabby) central pool; they're spacious, cool and good value, with plenty of outside balcony space. There are also a couple of older, more atmospheric rooms in the main house, furnished with antique carved wood beds and fronted by pillared verandas. An established favourite, with welcoming owner-managers – brothers Sabu and Saji. ❺–❻

**Maharaju Palace** 30m behind Lighthouse Beach ℡ 0471/248 5320, Ⓦ www.maharajupalace.nl. This Dutch-owned guesthouse, a block in from the beach, offers boutique style at affordable rates. Occupying a modern house in a well-kept tropical garden, its marble-lined rooms are impeccably clean and decorated with Indian handicrafts and comfy cane chairs on the verandas. Breakfast is included in the price. ❺

**Mini House** Lighthouse Rd ℡ 0471/248 0867, ℡ 9947 480969, Ⓔ seapearlkovalam@hotmail .com. Six large, simply furnished, sea-facing non-a/c rooms in a prime spot on the rocks above a small cove, just under the lighthouse. The balconies catch uninterrupted breezes, though you pay a premium for the fine views. Ask for #212 if it's available. ❺–❻

🏃 **Oasis/Beach Hotel II** Lighthouse Beach ☎0471/248 6575, Ⓦwww.thebeachhotel -kovalam.com. Stylish, German-run boutique hotel at the quiet end of Lighthouse Beach. Its ten rooms all have big, sea-facing balconies, and are light, spacious and airy, with terracotta-tiled floors, block-printed cotton bedspreads and earthy Madhubhani paintings on spotless white walls. The five pricier a/c options on the upper storey boast superior views of the bay; and there's private parking in the basement. Not to be confused with its sister concern, *Beach Hotel I*, below *Waves* restaurant, which isn't nearly as nice. ⑥–⑦

🏃 **Orion** Lighthouse Beach ☎9447 161436, Ⓦwww.orionbeacheresort.com.
If you're up for the full-on Lighthouse Beach experience, book a room at this friendly family-run place, which has dominated the seafront since it opened in the early 1980s. The rooms are simply furnished, and range widely in size, but all are well aired and great value considering the plum position. Some almost overhang the sands – perfect at sunset. Owners Mrs Leelamma Joseph and her son George run a tight ship and are always on hand to help. ⑤–⑦

**Royal Sea Blue** Behind Lighthouse Beach ☎0471/212 7857 or 248 4157, Ⓦwww.royal seablue.com. Three-storey block that's a bit of an eyesore, but in a peaceful location well off the road in the palm groves. Fronted by a large garden that's big enough for kids to run around in, the rooms are sparkling, with polished marble floors, TVs, fridges and separate a/c units (Rs500 extra). ④–⑥

**Sea Flower** South end of Lighthouse Beach ☎0471/248 0554, Ⓦwww.seaflowerkovalam .com. You can't get closer to the sea than the orange- and cream-painted *Sea Flower*, which rises straight from the sand. Facing the surf, its spacious, breezy and comfortable rooms are spread over two storeys – the upper ones cost Rs350 extra, but are worth it for the views and welcome breezes. ④–⑤

**Silverstar** Behind Lighthouse Beach ☎0471/248 2983, ☎9895 673443, Ⓦwww.silverstar-kovalam .com. Owned by a hospitable Swedish-Keralan couple, the *Silverstar* is hidden away in the palm groves a couple of hundred metres inland from the beach. Centred on a well-shaded, beaten-earth courtyard, the location is leafy and cool, and tranquil by Kovalam standards. The rooms are generous, with verandas or terraces out front, and new mozzie nets inside; there's a pool in the

garden and rooftop area for yoga. Rates include breakfast. ⑤–⑥

**Varma's** Lighthouse Rd ☎0471/248 0478, Ⓔvijayavarmasbeachresort@hotmail.com. One of the few places in Kovalam that's tried to incorporate traditional Keralan architecture into its design. The result is an attractive blend of modern comforts and old-style Malabari wood and brass decor. Rooms come in three categories, tastefully fitted with block-printed textiles, and opening onto secluded balconies. The "a/c deluxe" options on the top floor have stupendous views down the cliffs to Vizhijam; the "non-a/c deluxe" options at lobby level have no outlook whatsoever. ⑦–⑧

## Luxury

**Leela Kempinski** Hawah-Kovalam ☎0471/248 0101, Ⓦwww.theleela.com/kovalam. This "five-star-deluxe" resort, set in 44 acres of mature woodland, sweeps down the hillside to its own exclusive end of Kovalam Beach. Wonderful views extend out to sea and up the coast from a pair of dreamy infinity pools, overlooked by a stylish terrace bar. Rooms come in a range of categories, from around $300. ⑨

**Taj Green Cove** GV Raja Ratapara Rd, Samudra ☎0471/248 7733, Ⓦwww.tajhotels.com. *Taj Group*'s luxury resort is spread over a lush, wooded hillside 1km back from Samudra beach (over the headland from Hawah). Clad with local grey granite and elephant-grass thatch, its faux-rustique chalets are lined with polished teak and open onto lovely sea-facing verandas smothered in greenery. Golf buggies ("club cars") whisk guests from the lobby area, with its open-kitchen *Jasmine* restaurant, infinity pool and bar billiards table, to a private fishing lagoon and sunbathing area next to the sea. Rooms from $400 per night. ⑨

**Turtle on the Beach** ITDC Rd ☎0471/251 4000, Ⓦwww.turtleonthebeach.com. An über-hip boutique hotel with designer interiors fashioned from topical hardwoods and polished stone, pitched mainly at wealthy *desi* tourists from the big city – hence the ferocious a/c and giant plasma TVs. Service is snappy and the location much more inspiring than you'd imagine from the entrance side (though it's not actually on the beach, as the name implies). For a cool Rs13,500 (US$300) you can enjoy the stupendous panoramic views from the Presidential Sky Suite, which boasts its own exclusive rooftop party terrace, pergola and jacuzzi. Most doubles Rs7000–9500 (US$150–200). ⑨

# The beaches

Kovalam consists of four distinct coves, each with markedly different characters. The largest and most developed, known for obvious reasons as **Lighthouse Beach**, is where most foreign tourists congregate. It takes about five minutes to walk from one end of the bay to the other, either along the sand or on the paved esplanade which fronts a long arc of hotels, guesthouses, handicraft shops and restaurants. Lighthouse Beach came through the Boxing Day tsunami of 2004 more or less unscathed, but the beach itself was much reduced in size afterwards. A major sea defences project was in full swing at the time of writing to create an **artificial reef** roughly 100m offshore (see box, p.96).

The red-and-white-striped **lighthouse**, on the promontory at the southern end of the beach, opens each afternoon (daily 3–5pm; Rs25 [Rs10]; camera Rs20), when you can scale the 142 spiral steps and twelve ladder rungs to the observation platform. On clear days, views extend over the beach as far as Beemapalli mosque in one direction, and south to Poovar in the other. South of the lighthouse, a tiny white-sand cove opens into a much larger beach, overlooked by a scattering of upmarket hotels, accessed via the lane that peels off Lighthouse Road before *Varma's Beach Resort*. Many tourists mistakenly believe this is a private area, but it isn't.

Heading in the opposite direction (northwards) from Lighthouse Beach, you round a small rocky headland to reach **Hawah Beach** (aka **Eve's Beach**) – almost a mirror image of its busier neighbour, although backed for most of its length by empty palm groves. In the morning before the sun-worshippers arrive, it functions primarily as a base for local fishermen, who hand-haul their massive nets through the shallows, singing and chanting as they coil the endless piles of rope.

North of the next headland, **Kovalam Beach** is dominated by the angular chalets of the five-star *Leela* above it. Home to a small mosque, the little cove is dominated by coach-loads of excited Keralan day-trippers on weekends. To get there, follow the road downhill past the bus terminus. Only a short walk further north, **Samudra Beach** was until recently a European package tourist stronghold, though the large hotels clustered just beyond it, on the far side of a low, rocky headland, nowadays host mainly metropolitan Indian and Russian holidaymakers.

## Ayurveda centres

A significant proportion of the northern Europeans in Kovalam are here to receive treatment in one of the growing band of **ayurveda centres** that have opened around the resort. These range from grubby massage shacks in the palm grove behind Lighthouse Beach to fully accredited Olive Leaf clinics in the nearby five-stars – which function more as rejuvenation spas than proper clinics. When it comes to treatment for medical conditions, only a handful of places are worth considering. Foremost among them is **Amruthamgayam** (aka "Amrutham"; ☎0471/645 5423 or ☎9447 856461; ⊛www.amrutham.in), tucked away on the edge of Venganoor village, 4km inland from Kovalam (see p.96 for a review of their accommodation),

---

### Warning: swimming safety

Due to unpredictable rip currents and a strong undertow, especially during the monsoons, swimming from Kovalam's beaches is not always safe. The introduction of lifeguards has reduced the annual death toll, but at least four or five tourists still drown here each year, and many more get into difficulties. Follow the warnings of the safety flags at all times and keep a close eye on children. There's a first-aid post midway along Lighthouse Beach.

which is recommended both for the standard of its practitioners and overall ambience. Equipped with traditional palm-thatch, mud-walled huts, as well as an open-sided yoga hall where clients may attend free classes, it has a fully certified doctor and offers the full gamut of ayurveda treatments at much lower prices than the nearby resorts, in a tranquil location well away from the brouhaha of the beachside. The centre is marked on our map on p.101, but phone ahead for directions, as not even the local rickshaw-wallahs know how to find it.

In Kovalam itself, Dr Unni's **Agasthyaa Heritage Ayurveda Centre** (℡0471/248 0797, ⓦwww.unnidoc.com) enjoys a worldwide reputation, attracting patients, mainly from Sweden, to its ever-expanding premises in the palm groves behind Lighthouse Beach.

## Eating, drinking and nightlife

Lighthouse Beach is lined with identikit cafés and restaurants specializing in **seafood**: you pick from displays of fresh fish such as blue marlin, sea salmon, barracuda and delicious seer fish, as well as lobster, tiger prawns, crab and mussels. They are then weighed, grilled over a charcoal fire or cooked in a tandoor (traditional clay oven), and served with rice, salad or chips. Meals are **pricey** by Indian standards – typically around Rs300–500 per head for fresh fish, and double that for lobster or prawns – and service is often painfully slow, but the food is generally very good and the ambience of the beachfront terraces convivial.

For **breakfast** any number of cafés offer the usual brown bread, fruit salad and pancakes; you could also try a traditional Keralan breakfast at one of the local teashops near the bus stand. Freshly cooked, delicious Keralan rice-plate thali **"meals"** are served at the ramshackle *Devadee Hotel*, near the Avaduthura Devi temple behind Lighthouse Beach for only Rs40. It's a rough-and-ready place, and you'll have to squeeze onto narrow tables to eat, but the food is delicious and probably more hygienic than most of the stuff served on the beach.

**Nightlife** in Kovalam is sedate, revolving around the beachfront cafés. Beer and spirits are served in most places, albeit in discrete china teapots from under the table due to tight liquor restrictions.

**Fusion** Lighthouse Beach. Along with *Waves*, the funkiest place on Lighthouse Beach, with three innovative menus (Eastern, Western and fusion), served on a first-floor terrace overlooking the bay. Try the fish creole in orange vinaigrette with cumin potatoes, one of the Keralan seafood specialities, or home-made tagliatelle and chilli pesto. They also have a fine selection of drinks, a hefty sound system playing Indo-Western music, and a toilet that has to be seen to be believed. Most mains Rs180.

**Lonely Planet** ("Shiva's No.1") Behind Lighthouse Beach. Flanked by a pond that's alive with croaking frogs, the covered terrace of this large, family-run budget travellers' place is one of the most enduringly popular restaurants in the village, and a relaxed spot to while away an evening. Its menu of north and south Indian vegetarian standards is nothing to write home about, though inexpensive for Kovalam (most mains Rs50–80) and the food is well tempered for the sensitive Western palate. On Wed evenings they host a cultural show with

all-you-can-eat buffet (7.30–9pm; Rs150; book in advance).

**Spice Village** Behind Lighthouse Beach. In much the same mould as the nearby *Lonely Planet*, though smaller and run by a posse of local lads in snazzy shirts rather than a family, and it also serves cold Kingfishers.

**Suprabhatham** Near the *Silverstar*, next to a small Shiva temple. Simple, popular vegetarian café-restaurant in a well-shaded garden, where you can order inexpensive Indian breakfasts, fresh juices, lassis and shakes, as well as an extensive multi-cuisine menu: the "Bengali aubergine" and "chunky avocado salad" are popular specials. Evenings tend to end with the staff downing stiff whisky-and-soda slammers around 10.30pm, after which the service and cooking degenerate rapidly.

**Udhaya Hotel** Near the bus terminus. Hidden away behind a tiny general store, this local teashop serves the best Keralan breakfasts for miles, in a narrow, blue-walled cafeteria lined with Hindu, Muslim and Christian religious pictures.

▲ Fishing near Kovalam

Huge trays of steaming *iddiappam* (rice-flour vermicelli), *puttu* (rice rolls) and *appam* (steamed pancakes made from fermented rice flour) are brought at regular intervals down the stairs from the kitchen on banana leaves, and served with tin plates of egg masala, spicy *sambar* and more-ish chickpea *chana vada*. The chai's delicious too. You'll be hard pushed to spend more than Rs40 per head.

🏃 **Waves (German Bakery)** Lighthouse Beach. This rooftop terrace, shaded by a high tiled canopy, functions as a laidback café during the day, where you can order light meals, snacks, German cakes and delicious, freshly ground coffee. After sunset, its atmospheric designer lighting makes a great backdrop for more sophisticated cooking: the extravagantly outsized menus list Thai and Kerala seafood curries, lobster in vodka, fish steaks with sesame and coriander crust, or steamed prawns with lemon and chilli sauce. For dessert, go for the Malabar fruit flambée. Most mains Rs175–250.

## Listings

**Banks, exchange and ATMs** There's an ATM in the *Kovalam Beach Hotel*, on the road leading up from the southern end of Hawah Beach; otherwise, the nearest are up at Kovalam Junction, 3km inland on the national highway (roughly Rs100 return in an auto-rickshaw), where both ICICI and Canara Bank have small sub-branches. Pheroze Framroze, near the entrance to the *Leela* and bus stand, offers competitive rates for currency and travellers' cheques.

**Books** Kovalam doesn't have a major bookshop, but many of the tailors and clothes stalls supplement their trade by dealing in the usual hit-and-miss selection of secondhand books, and there's a decent selection on offer at a stall upstairs in *Waves (German Bakery)*.

**Internet access** Countless places in the lanes behind Lighthouse Beach offer web browsing for Rs40/hr, though connection speeds are slow by Keralan standards.

**Motorbike rental** K Tours & Travel, behind Hawah Beach opposite the Shiva temple, offer Honda Kinetic 100cc scooters for Rs300–350/day. You'll need to leave your driver's licence or passport as security.

**Tailors** Dozens of little tailor shops are crammed in to the alleyways behind Lighthouse Beach. You can have light cotton clothes made to measure, or get them to copy your favourite garment from home, using a wide choice of coloured calico. One that comes highly recommended is Mr George of *Blue Waves Tailor* (☎ 9388 676878), opposite *Seafood Corner* restaurant, who specializes in export-quality yoga clothing.

# North of Kovalam

NH-47, the hectic national highway connecting Kovalam and the capital, gives an unrepresentative impression of the belt running north of Samudra. Immediately west of the road, hidden from the traffic by dense palm groves, lies a string of typically Keralan fishing villages, opening on to undeveloped **Pozhikkara Beach**. The area can be easily reached on foot from Kovalam: head north from Samudra along near-deserted sands for forty to fifty minutes until they are broken by a salt-water lagoon at **PACHAL-LOOR**, a quiet hamlet sandwiched behind the sea and highway.

Overlooking the sand spit at the river mouth here are two secluded places to stay. The British-run *Lagoona Davina* (☎0471/238 0049, ⊛www.lagoon adavina.com; ⑨) is a small, exclusive boutique hotel patronized mainly by well-to-do Brits. Costing Rs4000–6500 per night in season, its rooms are individually styled, with carved-wood four-posters, pretty Indian textiles and animal paintings. Some (but not all) have lovely sea views, opening onto a terrace where staff wearing cummer-bunds and gold-edged saris serve a mixture of Keralan dishes and low-fat European cuisine (Rs840 for three courses plus glass of port).

The other guesthouse at Pachalloor, ⚑ *Beach and Lake Resort* (☎0471/238 2086, ⊛www.beachandlakeresort .com; ⑥–⑧), lies across the water from *Lagoona Davina*. It's a more down-to-earth affair, with less inspired interiors, but an even better location closer to the surf and fishing beach. Divided between a sand spit on the river mouth and a newer complex on the mainland, the rooms are spacious, with corre-spondingly large bathrooms. The more modern block, in earthy, Keralan-style exposed brickwork, holds the smartest "super-deluxe" air-conditioned rooms, which are huge and overlook the water, and there's a swimming pool across the lane. If you're on a budget,

AROUND KOVALAM

Trivandrum-Beemapalli Airport

KERALI ROAD
ANAYARA ROAD

BEEMAPALLI ROAD
TRIVANDRUM BYPASS ROAD
KOVALAM ROAD

Thiruvananthapuram

Karamana River

KANTAVANMARI ROAD

Beemapalli Dargah

Pozhikkara Beach

Ⓐ Pachalloor
Ⓑ

Vellayani Freshwater Lake

Vellayani Temple

NH-67

Ⓒ
Samudra
KOVALAM JUNCTION

See "Kovalam" map

Ⓓ
Kovalam

Vizhinjam

Nellinkunnu Ⓔ
Beach Ⓕ Nellinkunnu
Ⓖⓖ
Ⓗ Pulinkudi
Pulinkudi Ⓘ Ⓙ
Beach Ⓚ
Ⓛ
Chowara

Ⓜ

Karichal Lake

Chowara Beach
Marappalam

Pulluvilla

ARABIAN SEA

NH-67

Arulakam

N

0    2 km

Ⓝ
Ⓞ Poovar

### ACCOMMODATION

| | |
|---|---|
| Amruthamgamaya (Amrutam) | D |
| Beach and Lake Resort | B |
| Bethsaida Hermitage | I |
| Dr Franklin's | J |
| Friday's Place | N |
| Isola di Cocco | O |
| Karikkathi Beach House | F |
| Lagoona Davina | A |
| Nikki's Nest | K |
| Paradise Gardens | G |
| Somatheeram/ Manaltheeram | M |
| Surya Samudra | H |
| Taj Green Cove | C |
| Thapovan | E |
| Travancore Heritage | L |

ask if any of their twin-bedded economy rooms are vacant – they don't face the water, but are air-conditioned and nicely furnished.

Both of Pachalloor's guesthouses organize guided **backwater trips** and offer ayurveda massages and yoga classes. If you book in advance, drivers can be dispatched to meet you at Thiruvananthapuram airport; otherwise take a taxi 6km along the highway towards Kovalam, and bear right along the "bypass" where the road forks, just after the Thiruvallam bridge. After another 1km or so, signs on the right-hand side of the road point through the trees to the guesthouses.

# South of Kovalam

A tightly packed cluster of tiled fishers' huts, **VIZHINJAM** (pronounced "Virinyam"), on the opposite (south) side of the headland from Kovalam's Lighthouse Beach, was once the capital of the Ay kings, the earliest dynasty in south Kerala. During the ninth century the Pandyans fought to control it, and it was the scene of major Chola–Chera battles in the eleventh century. A number of simple small shrines survive from those times, and can be made the focus of a pleasant stroll through coconut groves, best approached from the centre of the village rather than the coast road – brace yourself for the sharp contrast between hedonistic tourist resort and workaday fishing village.

A strikingly modern pink **mosque** on the promontory overlooks the Muslim quarter, home to around 3000 fishermen; the Christian area, with a population of around 7000, lies on the opposite side of the bay, beneath a large church. Tension between the two has frequently erupted into riots, and the village remains something of a communal flashpoint, a situation not helped by ongoing disputes over proposals to upgrade Vizhinjam harbour into a massive container port. The plan was recently shelved in favour of a rival site in Tamil Nadu, but the recriminations rumble on.

On the far side of the fishing bay in the village centre, 50m down a road opposite the police station, a small unfinished eighth-century **rock shrine** features a carved figure of Shiva with a weapon. The **Tali Shiva** temple nearby, reached by a narrow path from behind the government primary school, may mark the original centre of Vizhinjam. The simple shrine is accompanied by a group of *naga* snake statues, a reminder of Kerala's continuing cult of snake worship, a survivor from pre-Brahminical times.

Toward the sea, ten minutes' walk from the village's main road along Hidyatnagara Road, the grove known as **Kovil Kadu** ("temple forest") holds a square Shiva shrine and a rectangular one dedicated to the goddess **Bhagavati**. Thought to date from the ninth century, these are probably the earliest structural temples in Kerala, although the Bhagavati shrine has been renovated.

## Nellinkunnu, Pulinkudi, Chowara and Poovar

Golden-sand beaches fringe the shore stretching **south from Vizhinjam**, interrupted only by the occasional rock outcrop and tidal estuary. This dramatic coastline, with its backdrop of thick coconut plantations, can appear peaceful compared with Kovalam, but it's actually one of the most densely populated – and intensely political – corners of the state. Fishing villages, dominated by outsized churches and garishly painted Hindu temples, line the entire 25km of road that

## The price of fish

From the comfort of a sunbed in Kovalam, it's easy to be lulled by official tourist office rhetoric about Kerala being a "land of plenty". But you only have to stroll around the headland to neighbouring Vizhinjam to realize that for the **traditional fishing communities** who live and work on this stretch of coast, life is far from a beach.

Kerala's fishermen rank among the region's poorest groups, suffering levels of income, literacy and life expectancy well below the state average. Their one-room mud-brick, plastic-walled shacks are little more than slums, often without running water. Child mortality rates are high, and alcoholism and domestic violence all too common.

The roots of this enduring poverty, which has proved impervious to Kerala's much-touted communist reforms and trickle-down from the ongoing economic boom, are many and complicated. Barred until the 1930s from temples, churches and schools, local fishermen have always been trapped on one of the lowest rungs of the social hierarchy. For centuries they were obliged to sell their fish at rock-bottom rates to socially superior dealers, who often doubled as money-lenders. With interest rates fixed at a crippling ten percent per day, anyone who borrowed to buy a new boat or net would soon find himself bogged down in spiralling debt.

The problem was only compounded by the arrival on India's southwest coast of the Roman Catholic Church. Francis (later "Saint Francis") Xavier and other Jesuit missionary priests who travelled here in the sixteenth century in search of converts found fertile pastures amid the disempowered, oppressed sub-castes of Malabar and Travancore. But the churches they left in their wake creamed a further ten percent off the income of their poor congregations – hence the large churches and tiny dwellings in many Christian quarters.

In the 1960s and 1970s, some progress was made when radicalized Marxist clergy, inspired by Latin-American-style **Liberation Theology**, attempted to unionize Kerala's fishing communities. **Cooperatives** were set up to buy and market the daily catch, enabling them to bypass middlemen and claim fairer prices for their fish, as well as access low-interest loans. However, the benefits of collective action were soon wiped out by a big government-led promotion of **mechanized trawler fishing** in the 1980s, which in the space of a few years decimated fish stocks and led to a fifty percent drop in yields for inshore fishers.

Among the consequences of the deepening poverty and resentment has been an upsurge in **communal tension**, as rival political parties seeking to exploit the discontent for short-term electoral gains stoke up hatred between opposing religious communities. In Vizhinjam, repeated – and often violent – clashes between Christians and Muslims have given rise to a bleak no-man's-land between the Muslim quarter, clustered around the large pink mosque on the north side of the harbour, and the larger Christian area, spread below the church on the opposite side of the bay. Communal divisions were further exacerbated by the **2004 Boxing Day tsunami**, or more particularly the TRP (Tsunami Rehabilitation Programme) aid which arrived in its wake: most of the money came not from the government, but NGOs with religious or caste affiliations, and was spent accordingly.

winds south along the shoreline. As in Vizhinjam, communal tensions often run high, and the sand remains primarily somewhere to defecate and work rather than swim from (the undertow can be treacherous) – not that this has in the least deterred the developers. In the last decade, virtually every metre of land backing the prettiest stretches of coast has been bought up and built on. Five kilometres south of Kovalam, at **Nellinkunnu** and neighbouring **Pulinkudi**, low, terraced cliffs enfold a sequence of beautiful palm-backed coves, each overlooked by its own luxury resort complex. Nearly all of them follow the same formula, focusing on

## Keralan ayurveda treatments

"Health tourism" is very much a buzz phrase in Kerala these days. International-standard hospitals and dental clinics have mushroomed around resorts such as Kovalam, catering for cost-conscious patients from abroad who've travelled here expressly for treatments, while no self-respecting luxury resort is without its own money-spinning "ayurvedic spa" or "wellness centre". Hippies who first came here to drop out are, three decades on, returning to detox and de-stress – and even for the odd hip replacement.

Synonymous with the boom in health travel is Kerala's close association with **ayurveda medicine**. Ayurveda, literally "science of life" (described in more detail on p.59), is an ancient system of herbal healing practised throughout India. Nowhere, however, are its Sanskrit roots so strictly adhered to as in the far southwest of the country, where the great sage **Agasthya** is said to have developed the *siddha* form of medicine from which modern ayurveda evolved. Legend also attributes the discovery of the sacred Agasthya Malai on the Tamil–Kerala border, famous as a source of medicinal herbs of unparalleled potency, to Agasthya. According to tradition, eighteen families were originally chosen by Lord Brahma to hold the secrets of ayurveda. Over time these dwindled to eight – known as the **Ashtavaidyas** – of whom only six still practise, mostly around the towns of Thrissur and Kozhikode.

The Keralan approach to ayurveda has two distinct elements: first, the body is cleansed of toxins generated by imbalances in lifestyle and diet; secondly, its equilibrium is restored using herbal medicines, mainly in the form of plant oils applied using a range of different massage techniques. A practitioner's first prescription will often be a course of **panchakarma** treatment – a five-phase therapy during which harmful impurities are purged through induced vomiting, enemas, and the application of medicinal oils poured through the nasal cavity. Other less onerous components, tailored for the individual patient, may include: *dhara*, where the oils are blended with ghee or milk and poured onto the forehead; *pizhichi*, in which a team of four masseurs apply different oils simultaneously; and, the weirdest looking of all, *sirovashti*, where the oils are poured into a tall, topless leather cap placed on the head.

Alongside these, patients are prescribed special balancing foods, and given vigorous full-body **massages**, or *abhayangam*, each day. Some practitioners may also offer **marma chikitsa** foot massage, a Keralan speciality where pressure is applied to the body with the soles of the feet; to control how much weight he or she brings to bear, the masseur grips a knotted rope suspended from the ceiling. The technique, which focuses on key connective energy "*marma*" points, was originally developed by masters of the martial art *kalarippayat*; part of every fighter's training routine involves a gruelling oily rubdown before dawn, as does the beginning of a typical *kathakali* student's day.

ayurvedic *panchakarma* treatments (see above), with accommodation provided in individual thatched, air-conditioned "cottages" or antique wooden houses relocated from Keralan villages.

It's worth renting a scooter and exploring the back lanes and secluded beaches of this distinctive area – a sometimes surreal mix of undeveloped Malayali fishing villages and sumptuous wellness retreats. One of the region's most memorable views can be enjoyed just north of **Chowara** village, 8km south of Kovalam, where an oddly proportioned kneeling Christ statue surveys the sands from atop a rocky bluff. Beyond it, an endless sandy beach yawns south to the horizon, scattered with hundreds of wooden boats.

### Where to go

Kerala's tourist resorts are full of places offering ayurveda cures for every conceivable ailment. Few of them, however, are staffed by fully qualified practitioners, despite what the certificates displayed on their walls may suggest. Standards of both treatment and hygiene vary greatly, as do the prices – a significant factor if you sign up for a minimum three-week stint, as most places advise. Women travellers also sometimes complain of sexual harassment at the hands of opportunistic male masseurs; cross-gender massage is forbidden in ayurveda, though the rule is routinely ignored in small, tourist-oriented centres. Note, too, that backstreet clinics might use dodgy oils that can cause skin problems.

The only way to guarantee bona fide treatment is to splash out on somewhere that's been approved by the government. Kerala Tourism's **accreditation scheme** divides centres into **Green Leaf** establishments – which apply the highest standards of hygiene, employ only pukka staff, never allow cross-gender massage, and use top-grade oils and medicines – and **Olive Leaf** ones, which offer equally dependable treatments, but in more traditionally Keralan surroundings, with massage tables carved from medicinal hardwoods, beautiful earth-walled practice rooms, yoga *shalas* and steam baths on site. This is the kind of place generally referred to as an **ayurvedic spa** and will nearly always be attached to a posh seaside hotel or heritage resort, offering packages that include gourmet vegetarian meals, yoga lessons and cultural programmes in the evenings. We've listed many such places in this chapter, but have – with a handful of tried and tested exceptions – steered clear of smaller, less expensive clinics, whose credentials may be harder to verify.

For all the claims many make, most outfits around Kovalam and Varkala – even the pricey ones – should be regarded primarily as places to seek **rejuvenation** rather than cures for **serious medical conditions**. If you've come to Kerala in search of treatment for a chronic illness of some kind, then you'd do better to explore the possibility of a spell at one of the old *Ashtavaidya* **ayurveda hospitals** listed below, which are famous all over India for the quality of their doctors and medicines, produced on their own organic estates and in-house labs. You'll need to set aside a minimum of four weeks, and book at least nine months in advance.

**Arya Vaidya Sala Kottakkal** near Malappuram in northern Kerala (26km from Kozhikode airport) ☏0483/274 2216, @www.aryavaidyasala.com.

**SNA Oushadhasala** near Jubilee Museum, Thrissur ☏0487/242 0948, @www .thaikatmooss.com.

**Vaidyaratnam Oushadhasala** Thaikkattussen, 8km from Thrissur ☏0487/235 3610, @www.vaidyaratnammooss.com.

Regardless of the kind of treatment you go for, and where you go for it, bear in mind the **optimal season for ayurveda** is said to be during the monsoons (June–Oct), when the air is free of dust and the humidity promotes detoxifying perspiration.

Chowara Beach peters out 12km further south at **Poovar**, where the Neyyar River flows into the sea. Before some cataclysmic event threw up a sandbar here, a harbour used to overlook the river mouth, which some historians claim may have been the port Orphyr – famous in the ancient world as a source of spices, slaves and gemstones. The backwaters behind the sandbar today shelter a cluster of luxury hideaways, only reachable by boat, and these make comfortable bases for forays beyond the tourist belt at the southern tip of Kerala. Non-guests may travel out to them, but will have to pay for the transfer (usually around Rs250).

# Accommodation south of Kovalam

The 20km stretch of coast between Kovalam and Poovar harbours more than thirty **luxury resorts** and **ayurveda spas**, in addition to a handful of more homely **guesthouses**. The following, divided into areas, are the pick of the crop. All are marked on the map on p.101.

## Nellinkunnu and Pulinkudi

**Bethsaida Hermitage** Pulinkudi ☎ 0471/226 7554, ⊛ www.bethsaida-c.org. An "eco-friendly ayurvedic beach resort" with a difference. The comforts – huge, well-furnished rooms in brick cottages or imposing modern blocks, with two huge pools, à la carte restaurant and prime location right next to a beautiful cove – are standard for the area. The profits, however, support a church-run orphanage for 2000 boys and girls – a great initiative that's been doing a fine job for more than a decade. At Rs6500–10,000 per night it's a notch cheaper than most of the competition. ❾

**Karikkathi Beach House** Pulinkudi ☎ 0471/240 0956, ⊛ www.karikkathibeach house.com. Simplicity is the essence of this exquisite little bolthole, nestled amid the palm trees above a quiet cove, just a stone's throw from the surf. You pay more for the location than luxury, though the two houses – encircled by a low wall, each with a pair of en-suite rooms opening onto a common, sea-facing veranda – have their own understated style: white walls, traditional terracotta tiles, wood furniture and window shutters set the tone. Staff are on hand to provide drinks and meals. One of the most desirable places to stay in south India, though such exclusivity comes at a price ($195 per double room, or $350 if you book a whole house – recommended for privacy). ❾

**Paradise Gardens** Pulinkudi ☎ 0471/226 8304, ⊛ www.paradise-gardens.com. Secluded beach villas accommodating two–four or two–six guests, exquisitely designed with terracotta mosaic floors, whitewashed walls and designer bathrooms, and set in abundant gardens very near this area's loveliest cove. $275–225 per double. ❾

**Surya Samudra** Pulinkudi ☎ 0471/248 0413, ⊛ www.suryasamudra.com. The dreamiest of all the "heritage resorts" on this strip, though of late, under new management desperate for more wealthy Indian guests, a more bling and corporate feel has begun to creep in. Still, it looks sumptuous: an army of Keralan woodworkers and stone-sculptors from Mamallapuram in Tamil Nadu was drafted in to reconstruct its antique, gabled villas, scattered across a 21-acre promontory between a pair of quiet beaches, and each room is individually styled with devotional statues and opulent textiles. The stone carvings, oiled rosewood and bowls of floating hibiscus and marigolds glow to magical effect in the evening light, and the pool has lovely sea views. $340–1050. ❾

**Thapovan** Nellinkunnu ☎ 0471/248 0453, ⊛ www .thapovan.com. This German-run heritage resort comprises two parts: one in a grove next to the seashore, and another higher up the hillside on a cliff. The latter's elevated position and views across the palm canopy to Vizhinjam give it the edge, and the traditional teak chalets, set amid well-tended gardens, are lovely. Regular Indian Classical concerts, plus the usual ayurveda and yoga facilities. Doubles Rs3600–6750. ❾

## Chowara

**Dr Franklin's** Chowara ☎ 0471/248 0870, ⊛ www.dr-franklin.com. Dr Franklin was among the first Keralan physicians to spot the tourism potential of ayurveda medicine, and though his resort may not be as easy on the eye as some in this area, the *panchakarma* treatments it provides are of the highest quality. Accommodation comes in the form of "special" or larger "deluxe" rooms with tiled floors and patios, thatched mud huts (fully en suite) and swish new Western-style rooms. ❼

**Nikki's Nest** Azhimala Shiva Temple Rd, Chowara ☎ 0471/226 8822, ⊛ www.nikkisnest.com. Set on a steep slope with direct access to a hidden cove below, this family-run resort of Keralan-style structures (gable-roofed, wooden houses, a/c rooms and semi-detached cottages) blends traditional architecture with modern amenities. The campus centres on a multi-cuisine restaurant and good-sized pool, with uninterrupted views of the sea and beach. $150–320. ❾

**Somatheeram** Chowara ☎ 0471/226 6501, ⊛ www.somatheeram.org. *Somatheeram* established the model for countless ayurvedic health resorts, packaging high-quality herbal therapies with accommodation in traditional-style Keralan houses fitted with a/c and other mod cons. When you're not being doused with medicinal oils, you can relax in a range of rooms – from budget stone cottages with thatched roofs and shared bathrooms to luxurious two-bedroomed wood *tharavadukal* sporting antique doors and pillared verandas – all stacked on terraces overlooking the beach. Sister concern *Manaltheeram* (☎ 0471/226 6222, ⊛ www.manaltheeram.com), next door, offers more of the same, plus a pool (open for guests of *Somatheeram*). Doubles $150–325. ❾

**Travancore Heritage** Chowara ☎ 0471/226 7828, ⓦ www.thetravancoreheritage.com. The centrepiece of this extravagant complex is a splendid 150-year-old mansion (serving now as the hotel reception), fronted by a kidney-shaped pool and sun terrace. Below it are set sixty relocated antique bungalows, some boasting alfresco garden bathrooms and their own plunge pools. At beach level, reached via a lift, there's a rather less inspiring modern block on two storeys, also with a big pool in front. $130–300. ❾

### Poovar

🏃 **Friday's Place** ☎ 0044/1428 741764 (March–Oct) or 0091/9744 161636 (Nov–Feb), ⓦ www.fridaysplacekerala.com. One of Kerala's more eccentric homestays: five beautifully made wood and thatch "Crusoe Cottages", set in an acre of palm and acacia gardens deep in the backwaters. Each has its own veranda, solar electricity supply, comfy beds and attractive hand-loom textile decor. There's also the option of the double-storey Tsunami House – a quirky, romantic Noah's Ark of a hideaway with stunning treetop views. *Friday's Place* is well cut off from the mainland (the river's not so much nearby as actually flowing through the plot via a network of little canals), but British-Sri Lankan owners Mark and Sujeewa are sociable hosts, offering fine organic south Indian cuisine, yoga tuition, engaging guided tours of the area and use of a 20cm telescope for stargazing. Doubles $200. ❾

**Isola di Cocco** ☎ 0471/221 0008, ⓦ www .isoladicocco.com. Another "heritage resort", offering a/c rooms, antique Keralan cottages and suites spread over thirty acres, but with the distinction of being surrounded on all sides by water. Facilities include a big pool, billiards room and library. US$175–200. ❾

# Padmanabhapuram Palace

Although now officially in Tamil Nadu, **PADMANABHAPURAM**, 63km southeast of Thiruvananthapuram, was the capital of Travancore between 1550 and 1750, and maintains its historic links with Kerala, from where it is still administered. For anyone with even a minor interest in Keralan architecture, the small **Padmanabhapuram Palace** (Tues–Sun 9am–1pm & 2–4.30pm; Rs50 [Rs20], cameras Rs20), whose design represents the high point of regional building, is an irresistible attraction – though as ever it's worth trying to avoid weekends, when the complex is overrun with bus parties.

Set in neat, gravelled grounds against a backdrop of steep-sided hills, the palace's predominantly wooden exterior displays a perfect combination of clean lines and gentle angles, the sloping tiled roofs of its buildings broken by triangular projecting gables that enclose delicately carved screens. In the **entrance hall** (a veranda), a brass oil lamp hangs from an ornate teak, rosewood and mahogany ceiling and is carved with ninety different lotus flowers. Beautifully ornamented, the revolving lamp inexplicably keeps the position in which it is left, seeming to defy gravity. The raja rested from the summer heat on the cool, polished-granite bed in the corner. On the wall hangs a collection of *onamvillu* (ceremonial bows) decorated with images of Padmanabha – the reclining form of Vishnu – which local chieftains would present to the raja during the Onam festival.

Directly above the entrance hall, on the first floor, the **mantrasala** (council chamber) is gently illuminated by light that filters through panes of coloured mica. Water filled with herbs was put into the boxed bench seats along the front wall as a natural air-cooling system. The highly polished black floor is made from a now-lost technique using burnt coconut, sticky sugar-cane extract, egg whites, lime and sand.

The oldest part of the complex is the **Ekandamandapam**, or "lonely place". Built in 1550, it was used for rituals for the goddess Durga and typically employed elaborate floor paintings known as *kalam ezhuttu*. A loose ring attached to a column is a *tour de force* of the carpenter's art: both ring and column are carved from a single piece of jackwood. Nearby is a *nalukettu*, a four-sided courtyard found in many Keralan houses, open to the sky and surrounded by a pillared walkway. A trapdoor once served as the entrance to a secret passageway leading to another palace, since destroyed.

The Pandya-style stone-columned **dance hall** stands directly in front of a shrine to the goddess of learning, Saraswati. The women of the royal household had to watch performances through screens on the side, and the staff through holes in the wall from the gallery above. Typical of old country houses, steep, wooden ladder-like steps, ending in trapdoors, connect the floors. Belgian mirrors and Tanjore miniatures of Krishna adorn the chamber, forming part of the **women's quarters**, where a swing hangs on plaited iron ropes, while a four-poster bed, made from sixteen kinds of medicinal wood, dominates the **raja's bedroom**. Its elaborate carvings depict a mass of vegetation, human figures, birds and, as the central motif, the snake symbol of medicine, associated with the Greek physician deity Asclepius. The **murals** for which the palace is famous – alive with detail, colour, graceful form and religious fervour – adorn the walls of the **meditation room** directly above the bedroom, which was used by the raja and the heirs apparent. Unfortunately, this is now closed to preserve the murals, which have already been damaged by generations of hands trailing along the walls. You can also see a **dining hall** intended for the free feeding of up to two thousand brahmins, and a 38kg stone which, it is said, every new recruit to the raja's army had to raise above his head 101 times.

### Practicalities

Frequent **buses** run to Padmanabhapuram from Thiruvananthapuram's Thampanoor station; hop on any service heading south towards Nagercoil or Kanyakumari and get off at **Thakkaly** (sometimes written Thuckalai). You can flag the same buses down from the side of the highway at Kovalam Junction (3km inland from the beaches). Heading back, two express buses leave Thakkaly at 2.30pm and 3.30pm for Thiruvananthapuram vai Kovalam Junction.

The small stalls inside the outer walls of the palace are the best place to get **snacks** and **drinks**, as the area around the bus station is noisy and dirty.

# North of Thiruvananthapuram

When it gets too hot at sea level, **Ponmudi** and the **Peppara Wildlife Sanctuary**, just northeast of Thiruvananthapuram, make a refreshing overnight break: in a couple of hours you can be strolling in the cool air through rubber and cardamom plantations and endless slopes of green tea bushes. Alternatively, the richly forested **Agasthya Hills** lie 25km northeast of the capital. Accessible as a day-trip, they form a beautiful backdrop to the **Neyyar Dam**, on the banks of which stands the world-famous **Sivananda yoga centre**. Just before you turn off to the Agasthya Hills, it's well worth pausing to visit **Koikkal Kottaram palace** at Nedumangad – as fine an example of traditional Keralan architecture as you'll find anywhere in the state, with the added attraction of an excellent little museum devoted to local archeology, history and coinage.

## Nedumangad and Koikkal Kottaram

The stately palace of **Koikkal Kottaram** (Tues–Sun 10am–5pm; Rs3, camera Rs10), 18km northeast of Thiruvananthapuram, sits on the outskirts of **Nedumangad**, a busy market town near the turning to the Neyyar Dam and Agasthya Hills. Built for Umyamma Rani, a local queen who reigned from 1677 until 1684, the palace sees few visitors, yet it represents one of the high points of regional architecture, retaining all its distinctive features: a bowed, triangular-gabled roof made of terracotta tiles, intricately carved teak accents, cool stone floors and dark rooms that open onto a private central courtyard for the ladies. The Archaeological Survey of India maintains the building, providing obligatory guides to show you around the small **museum** – currently the subject of a police investigation after many of its most valuable exhibits were pilfered.

The **ground-floor** rooms contain what remains of the vast coin collection – formerly one of India's finest, but now sadly depleted after years of pilfering. Other rooms around the courtyard contain Keralan household and farming implements dating from the eighteenth and nineteenth centuries, as well as three ornamental palanquins for carrying the royal ladies. **Upstairs**, the make-up and costumes for *kathakali*, *ottamthullal* and *theyyem* dance performances are displayed on ferocious-looking models, and there is a finely carved *kettuvialaku* (platform) for the goddess Durga, which is carried around town during local spring festivities.

### Practicalities

Regular **buses** run to Nedumangad from Thiruvananthapuram's Thampanoor stand, taking around 45 minutes. If you want to refuel before heading back or onwards to the hills, try the air-conditioned *Ponmudi* **restaurant** on the ground floor of the swish *Hotel Surya* on Surya Road, back towards town from the palace on your left, which serves sumptuous Keralan meals at lunch time (Rs120) in addition to a full multi-cuisine menu.

## Neyyar Dam and the Agasthya Hills

The jagged, forested **Agasthya Hills** form a verdant backdrop to the **Neyyar Dam**, which interrupts the flow of three major rivers to form a large reservoir. Standing on its banks is the world-famous **Sivananda Yoga Vedanta Dhanwantari Ashram**, one of the country's leading yoga centres. Among locals, however, the spot is better known as a picnic destination: streams of bus parties pour through on weekends to stroll around the ornamental gardens at the water's edge, dotted with garishly painted plaster images of gods and heroes. You can take a KTDC boat to an island in the reservoir where a tiny **safari park**

---

### The Flying Guru

Located amid the hills and tropical forests of the **Neyyar Dam**, 28km east of Thiruvananthapuram, the **Sivananda Yoga Vedanta Dhanwantari** (ⓦ www.sivananda.org) was founded by Swami Sivananda – dubbed the "Flying Guru" because he used to pilot light aircraft over war-stricken areas of the world, scattering flowers and leaflets calling for peace – as a centre for meditation, yoga and traditional Keralan martial arts and medicine. Sivananda was a renowned exponent of Advaitya Vedanta, the philosophy of non-duality, as espoused by the Upanishads and promoted later by Shankara in the eleventh century (for more on which, see p.283).

Aside from training teachers in advanced raja and hatha yoga, the ashram offers **introductory courses** for beginners. These comprise four hours of intensive tuition per day (starting at 5.30am), with lectures. During the course, you have to stay at the ashram and comply with a regime that some Western students find fairly strict (no sex, drugs, rock'n'roll or smoking, a pure-veg diet and early morning starts), as well as join in Hindu devotional worship. Some people have also noted strained relations with the local villagers, with whom ashramites are discouraged from mixing. For more details, contact the ashram itself (ⓣ0471/227 3093, ⓔyogaindia@sivananda.org).

holds a pride of seven rare Asian lions. Elephant rides are also on offer at a camp on the lakeside (accessible by boat or road); get here before 10am to help bathe the animals. Crocodile-sightings are guaranteed, too, thanks to the presence of a **Crocodile Breeding Park** near the interpretation centre (though it's a pretty miserable facility, with the reptiles crammed into small concrete enclosures).

With a little more time, you could also take a **trek** or **jeep trip** into the surrounding mountains. **Kurisumala** (literally, "Mount of the Cross"), the distinctive, three-peaked massif to the east of Neyyar Dam, is the focus of a frenzied Christian pilgrimage in March, when thousands climb to the crucifix on the highest summit, Neruka (900m). Starting outside the market town of **Panchamoodu**, 12km away from Neyyar Dam, the ascent is relentlessly steep and dusty, and takes around 2–3hr; allow five for the round-trip, and start early to avoid the afternoon heat. You can also reach the top of the massif by jeep (Rs450 for a maximum five people). A rough track begins at the village of **Arukani**, over the border in Tamil Nadu, winding up to the lowest of the three summits, **Kalimala**, site of a small Hindu temple, from where a path follows the ridge up to Neruka peak. You get spectacular views from the top down across the coastal plain, and back along the watershed of the mountains.

The most striking of the peaks visible from Kurisumala is the angular **Agasthya Malai** to the southeast, a mountain legendary in Kerala as the source of rare plants used in ayurveda medicine. Again, the summit may be reached via an ancient pilgrimage track, but the trek is a more serious undertaking than the ascent of Kurisumala, taking three days for the round trip to the top and back. Permits must be obtained in advance from the Forest Department Headquarters in Vazhuthakad, Thiruvananthapuram; these cost Rs6000 for a maximum of five people, and include the services of two obligatory guides. Food, porters and tents (also available through the Forest Department) have to be arranged separately. The pay-off for all this palaver is the chance to experience some of the most spectacular mountain scenery in south India, as well as plentiful wildlife sightings: the forested slopes of Agasthya Malai are grazed by wild elephant (including a few rare pygmy elephants), gaur, leopard and lion-tailed macaques.

### Practicalities

Neyyar Dam is accessible by hourly buses from Thiruvananthapuram's Thampanoor stand. The most appealing **accommodation** in the area – a perfect base for mountain-trekking and trips into the nearby Peppara sanctuary – is the delightful *Bio Veda* resort (☎9645 864754, ⓦwww.bioveda.in; ❻), a reasonably priced, beautifully situated guesthouse and ayurveda centre perched on a hillside overlooking the lake, just below a Kali temple. Wonderful views extend across the Ghats from its seven wooden, palm-thatched bungalows, with pillared verandas opening on to a well-kept garden. They offer quality ayurveda treatments and run an excellent little restaurant (open to non-residents) serving healthy local specialities. The owners are also immensely knowledgeable about the area, and can help arrange treks and wildlife safaris in both the nearby hills and Peppara sanctuary.

## Ponmudi and Peppara Wildlife Sanctuary

Located 1066m above sea level, the hill station of **PONMUDI** lies in a tea-growing region, 60km northeast of Thiruvananthapuram, on the top of a hill commanding breathtaking views out across the range as far as the sea. Apart from the views, the main incentive to come up here is to explore the 53 square kilometres of forest set aside as the **Peppara Wildlife Sanctuary**, which protects elephants, *sambar*, lion-tailed macaques, leopards and other wildlife. Although Peppara is open all year, the main season is from January until May. Although the park can get hectic on weekends, when it's swamped by noisy bus parties of picnicking locals, things quieten down considerably in the week.

The beautiful drive up, via the small towns of Nedumangad and Vithura, runs along very narrow roads past areca nut, clove, rubber and cashew plantations, with first the River Kavakulam and then the River Kallar close at hand. The bridge at **Kallar Junction** marks the start of the real climb. Twenty-two hairpin bends (numbered at the roadside) lead slowly up, starting in the foothills, heading past great outcrops of black rock and thick clumps of bamboo (*iramula*), then through the Kallar teak forest. Finally you wind into the tea plantations; the temperature is noticeably cooler and, once out of the forest, the views across the hills and the plains below become truly spectacular – on a clear day you can see as far as the coast. There really is very little to do up here, but the high ridges and tea estates make good rambling country.

### Practicalities

Six daily **buses** run from Thiruvananthapuram to Ponmudi, via Vithura, the first at 5.30am and the last at 3.30pm. The nearest **tourist office** is currently in Thiruvananthapuram, where information on Ponmudi is readily available. The *Government Guesthouse* (☎0472/289 0230; ❷–❸) has 24 rooms and seven cottages, all with bathrooms and hot water. Simple, inexpensive meals have to be ordered a couple of hours in advance; otherwise the cold drinks and snack shop is open daily until 4pm, or you can walk down the road to the teashop on the bend (400m from the hotel). The main building, which originally belonged to the Raja of Travancore, has lost any charm it may once have possessed, but the views across the hills and misty valleys from the terrace make up for it. Weekends get lively (to say the least), thanks to the beer parlour (daily 10am–6pm).

If your budget can stretch to it, the best place to sidestep Ponmudi's noisy day-trippers, and make the most of its beautiful woodland, is ⚜ *Duke's Forest Lodge* (☎0472/285 9273, ⓦnikkisnest.com/dukesforest; ❾) at Anapara, 51km from Thiruvananthapuram. Situated on the edge of a 130-acre rubber plantation, this family-run **resort** has five beautiful "pool villas", designed in traditional Keralan style with steeply slanted, tiled roofs and deep verandas set in landscaped gardens. Each stands on stone pillars, and spiral staircases wind from the upper floors to secluded jacuzzi terraces below, screened by roll-down cane blinds. There's also a big, sunny main pool, and a restaurant area in front of which recitals of music, dance and ritual theatre (including *theyyem*) are held. High-season rates are $170 for the pool villas and $135 for the far less nice standard rooms.

# Varkala and around

Devout Hindus have for hundreds, and possibly thousands, of years travelled to **VARKALA**, 54km north up the coast from Thiruvananthapuram, to immerse ashes of recently deceased relatives in the surf. Against a backdrop of superb, burnt-clay coloured cliffs, the ancient rituals are still performed daily on **Papanasam beach**, despite the presence just a stone's throw away of a fully fledged tourist resort, focused around the northern end of the bay.

The dramatic location, coupled with comparatively low-key development, makes Varkala a much more appealing place to spend a beach holiday than

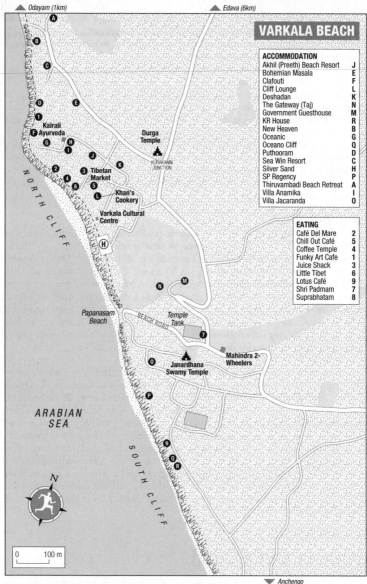

**VARKALA BEACH**

**ACCOMMODATION**

| | |
|---|---|
| Akhil (Preeth) Beach Resort | J |
| Bohemian Masala | E |
| Clafouti | F |
| Cliff Lounge | L |
| Deshadan | K |
| The Gateway (Taj) | N |
| Government Guesthouse | M |
| KR House | R |
| New Heaven | B |
| Oceanic | G |
| Oceano Cliff | Q |
| Puthooram | D |
| Sea Win Resort | C |
| Silver Sand | H |
| SP Regency | P |
| Thiruvambadi Beach Retreat | A |
| Villa Anamika | I |
| Villa Jacaranda | O |

**EATING**

| | |
|---|---|
| Café Del Mare | 2 |
| Chill Out Café | 5 |
| Coffee Temple | 4 |
| Funky Art Cafe | 1 |
| Juice Shack | 3 |
| Little Tibet | 6 |
| Lotus Café | 9 |
| Shri Padmam | 7 |
| Suprabhatam | 8 |

Kairali Ayurveda

Durga Temple

KURAKANNI JUNCTION

Tibetan Market

Khan's Cookery

Varkala Cultural Centre

NORTH CLIFF

Papanasam Beach

BEACH ROAD

Temple Tank

Mahindra 2-Wheelers

Janardhana Swamy Temple

ARABIAN SEA

SOUTH CLIFF

N

0    100 m

▼ Anchengo

Kovalam. Tightly crammed along the rim of crumbling North Cliff, its row of restaurants and small hotels stares out across a vast sweep of ocean – a view that can seem almost transcendental after sunset, when a myriad tiny fishing boats light up their lanterns.

Although dominated by long-staying, young backpackers, the demographic here is fairly mixed, with plenty of young families and 50-somethings sharing the sands. And if the numbers start to feel overwhelming, you can always retreat

# Playing gods

To experience Keralan ritual theatre in its authentic context – against a backdrop of coconut-oil lamps in a temple courtyard – is the closest you can come to time travel. Rigidly codified in ancient texts, some theatrical forms still regularly staged in the region have been enacted in the same settings and in exactly the same way for thousands of years. For worshippers, the performances bring the realm of the gods to earth. For travellers, they offer a vivid glimpse of the strange, archaic "otherness" that still underlies modern life in the state.

Kochi cultural centre ▲

Kerala Kalamandalam, Cheruthuruthy ▼

Kathakali performer ▼

# Epic theatre

The adventures of god-heroes and their demonic adversaries – as told in epics such as the Mahabharata and Ramayana – are the most common subjects of kathakali story-plays. Whether goodies, baddies, superheroes with special powers, or their female consorts, each of the four main character types wears instantly recognizable, and equally outlandish, costumes. Ridge-like masks of rice paper, decorative headgear set with red and green stones, and voluminous skirts and jewellery adorn the "green" (*pacha*) heroes. Audiences, however, tend to most enjoy the antics of the villainous, lustful, greedy and violent "knife" (*katti*) anti-heroes, with their fangs and red-and-black faces. *Kathakali* originated in the temples patronized by the region's rulers in the sixteenth and seventeenth centuries, when its core repertoire and complicated lexicon of gestures were fixed in writing. These cornerstone texts still form the basis of the arduous ten-year training young actors have to endure, starting at the tender age of eight.

*Kathakali*, however, was merely a modern elaboration of much older ritual theatre forms traditionally performed as offerings for temple deities. Quite when and where these first arose is a matter of conjecture, but some – such as kudiyattam – are referred to in Sanskrit texts dating back more than two thousand years. Regularly performed at various temples around the state, *kudiyattam* is thought to be the world's oldest surviving theatre form. In the countryside, meanwhile, it was more common for the villagers to see their favourite epics enacted by shadow or stick puppets. Like their full-sized cousins, these plays in miniature would span a week or more of nocturnal sessions in the local temple. No more than a handful of puppeteer families remain active today.

# Spirit possession

As well as the formal types of ritual theatre sponsored by the upper castes and nobility, Kerala also has its own **grass-roots forms**, deriving from traditions with ancient roots. Known in northern Kerala as **theyyem**, they're held for all kinds of reasons: to celebrate the safe return of a son from the Gulf, the construction of a new house or as part of a temple feast. And they come in an amazing number of different shapes and sizes, each with its own distinctive make-up, costume and outlandish masks.

In villages around Kannur (Cannanore) in the north, some *theyyem* performers don huge headdresses made of crimson-painted papier-mâché, metal studwork and tassles, framing meticulously painted faces and bodies loaded with jewellery. Flickering in the firelight, such apparitions seem from another realm – precisely the effect intended. For unlike in *kathakali* and *kudiyattam*, where the actors are seen as mere representations of the gods, in *theyyem* the bodies of performers are believed to be possessed by the deities themselves. As the god or goddess moves among the crowd, its spirit glares through the performer's bloodshot eyes, animating his every move and gesture.

It's hard to convey the electric mix of terror and adoration such visions invoke among onlookers. Despite having been outlawed, age-old **caste restrictions** are still often upheld in more conservative rural parts of Kerala, barring those at the lower end of the caste hierarchy from access to the region's most revered Tantric shrines – which only adds to the intensity of these local rituals. Whether staged for a small family-sponsored puja or a full-on temple festival with thousands in attendance, *theyyem* are always supercharged events.

▲ Initiation of a *theyyem* performer

▼ Muchilot Bhagwati *theyyem*

▼ *Theyyem* Gulikan, putting on mask

*Theyyem* performers waiting for devotees ▲

*Kathakali* artists putting on make up ▼

*Theyyem* ritual ▼

# Finding ritual theatre

Truncated, simplified versions of ritual theatre forms are staged at tourist shows in resorts and cities all over Kerala – especially in Fort Cochin and Ernakulam – but they're no replacement for the real thing.

Temple festivals (*utsavam*) are where you'll most often find proper all-night **kathakali**. Recitals generally start around 10pm and run until dawn, when audiences are treated to the final, dramatic disembowelling of the demon, followed by a restorative cup of chai at the temple gates. In Thiruvananthapuram, the **Margi School** (see p.89) lays on monthly shows of both *kathakali* and the more rarely performed *kudiyattam*. North of Kochi, visit the **Kalamandalam Academy** at Cheruthuruthy (see p.206), Kerala's foremost performing arts college, to watch classes of students being put through their paces; the academy also hosts top-drawer shows in its traditional-style auditorium.

Tracking down **theyyem** involves a bit more commitment. Set aside at least a week and base yourself in the town of **Kannur** (**Cannanore**; see p.247), where most guesthouse owners will be able to point you in the right direction.

Check the following sources to find out what's on, and where, during your trip.

▶▶ Ⓦ**http://english.manorama online.com** Forthcoming festivals are previewed in the online English edition of the state's bestselling daily.

▶▶ Ⓦ**www.theyyamcalendar.com** A detailed rundown of north Kerala's *theyyem* scene.

▶▶ **The Village Astrologer** Glossy handout, available free from the Tourist Desk in Kochi (see p.170), listing all the major festivals held around the state in any given month.

▶▶ Ⓦ**www.keralatourism.org /festivalcalendar** The most exhaustive database on Keralan festivals, which you can search by month and/or by region.

further north, to **Odayam** and **Edava**, where a series of smaller, quieter beaches offers a more chilled scene. In the opposite direction, the famous **Anathavalam elephant farm** at **Puthenkulam** is a must for pachyderm lovers.

## Arrival and information

Varkala beach lies 4km west of Varkala town, which is grouped around a busy market roundabout. The town's mainline railway station – Varkala-Sivagiri – is served by express and passenger **trains** from Thiruvananthapuram, Kollam and most other Keralan towns, and stands 500m north of this central junction. While some **buses** from Thiruvananthapuram's Thampanoor stand, and from Kollam to the north, continue on to within walking distance of the beach and clifftop area, most terminate in Varkala village, where you'll have to pick up an auto-rickshaw for the remaining five-minute ride (Rs50–60) to the seashore.

If you can't get a direct bus to Varkala, take any "superfast" or "limited stop" bus running along the main NH-47 highway to **Kallamballam**, 15km east, from where slower local mini-buses (Rs15), auto-rickshaws (Rs100–120) and taxis (Rs175–200) can transport you to the beach.

## Accommodation

Varkala offers a wide selection of **accommodation**. The hotels up on North Cliff are most people's first choice, with more inspiring views than those lining the road to the beach, but there are some even better options on quieter South Cliff if you don't mind being away from the thick of things. Auto-rickshaws from the railway station and village tank go as far as the helipad or round the back to North Cliff; South Cliff is also accessible by road. For options further north up the coast, see "Accommodation north of Varkala" on p.120.

### Budget

**Government Guesthouse** Cliff Rd ☎0470/260 2227, ⓦwww.keralatourism.org. Five minutes' walk north of the temple, on the hillside immediately above the *Taj* hotel, this former maharaja's holiday palace has been converted into a guesthouse for visiting bigwigs, though it also opens its doors to tourists. The two en-suite rooms in the original building are enormous and fantastic value. The others (all with good sized bathrooms) occupy a 1980s block in the same grounds and are much less inspiring – you'll need a good mosquito net, and expect lots of creepy-crawlies. They've had problems over the years with peeping toms and thieves, too. Basic meals available on request. ❶–❷

**KR House** South Cliff ☎0470/260 6400, ☎9349 741998. A real gem of a budget place – at a plum spot on South Cliff, with clean, modern, light, airy rooms, comfy mattresses, spotless bathrooms, and balconies overlooking a narrow garden running to the cliff edge, from where a flight of rock-cut steps drop steeply down to the beach. Well away from the bustle of North Cliff, it's quiet, and run with great efficiency by the kindly Mr Ramchandran. ❷–❹

**New Heaven** North Cliff ☎0470/215 6388 or ☎9846 074818, ⓦwww.newheavenbeachresort .com. Neither new nor indeed heavenly, but well scrubbed, with decent-sized rooms and sea-facing common verandas, just a stone's throw from the shoreline. There's a popular yoga centre on the rooftop. ❹

**Oceanic** North Cliff ☎0470/302 1330 or ☎9846 096912, ⓔoceanicresidence@yahoo.co.in. Very pleasant rooms, with flowering climbers trailing from its balconies, close to the clifftop. Among the better-run, better-value budget options close to the strip. ❹

**Silver Sand** North Cliff ☎9846 826144 or ☎9846 478432. This budget guesthouse, 200m back from the cliff edge behind the *Funky Art Café*, offers unbeatable value: its eight marble-clad, simply furnished rooms are large and comfortable for the price, with thick mattresses and doors opening to a sociable common veranda. It's invariably full, so book ahead. ❹

### Mid-range

**Akhil (Preeth) Beach Resort** North Clifftop area, off Cliff Rd ☎0470/260 0942, ⓦwww.preeth beachresort.com. Large, well-maintained two-star complex set 5min back from the cliff in a shady palm garden. Grouped around a kidney-shaped pool and sun terrace, its accommodation ranges from no-frills, marble-lined economy rooms to spacious a/c cottages with generous verandas and cane furniture. An additional attraction is the top-notch "Prana" ayurveda clinic – one of the few in Varkala with a fully qualified doctor. ❹–❼

**Bohemian Masala** Thiruvambadi, North Varkala ☎9287 215567 or ☎9567 441286, ⓦwww.thebohemianmasala.com. A chic hippie haven of 12 ethnic thatched huts moulded from mud, herbs and other natural materials according to ancient Hindu precepts, in a gorgeous garden full of trees, birds and butterflies. The interiors are a bit gloomy, but cool and beautifully styled using Indian handicrafts. They come in two categories: "Cosmic" (standard), and more spacious "Universe" – the latter boasting luxury bamboo beds and enough room to do yoga. Only a few minutes' walk from the clifftop, but tranquil. Diversions include a funky earth-floored restaurant and in-house ayurveda massages. ❻

**Clafouti** North Cliff ☎0470/2601414, ⓦwww .clafoutiresort.com. Congenial little "heritage beach resort" set right on the clifftop, offering non-a/c standards (Rs1500) in a little block to the rear and more spacious mock-Keralan a/c cottages (Rs2500) with tiny verandas and thatched tops – the two-storey #101 and #102 are good for families. Rates include breakfast. ❺–❻

**Cliff Lounge** North Cliff ☎9895 633896, ⓦwww .clifflounge.com. The nicest mid-range place on North Cliff, set back a short way behind the strip, but with uninterrupted sea views from its spacious double-bedded rooms. All have breezy balconies, and are pleasantly decorated with arty touches from your Keralan-German hosts, Sajeer and Elizabeth. Count on Rs1000 extra for a/c. ❺–❻

**Deshadan** North Cliff ☎9846 031005, ⓦwww .deshadan.com. The smartest and most efficiently run of Varkala's small-scale resort complexes. Centred on a great little swimming pool, its twelve individually themed rooms ("Asam", "Rajasthan", "Malabar", etc) are tastefully styled, with hand-painted furniture from around India and earthy, ethnic colour schemes. A pair of two-bedroomed cottages in the garden suit families well. And there's a quality ayurveda centre on site. ❼–❾

**Oceano Cliff** South Cliff ☎0470/309 4978, ⓦwww.oceanogate.com. If the first thing you want to see when you open your eyes in the morning is a spectacular view of the sparkling briney, book a sea-facing suite at the *Oceano Cliff*. Set on the highest stretch of secluded South Cliff, they're light, cool, stylish and good value. Those to

the rear don't have the views, but they're offered at bargain rates (if you don't opt for a/c). Meals are served in little thatched gazebos on the cliff edge, but the *pièce de résistance* here is the yoga platform, which hangs in an airy void high above the sands. Private steps lead to the beach via a plunge pool. ❺–❻

**Puthooram** North Cliff ☎0470/320 2007 or ☎9895 232209. Snug chalet-cottages made entirely of varnished wood, most with traditional Keralan railings, hanging oil lamps and thatched roofs, opening onto a trim little garden right on the cliff edge. Published rates are high, but you can usually haggle hefty discounts later in the day. Courteous management, and a quality on-site ayurveda centre ("Santhigiri"), as well as an internet café and well-stocked store. ❺–❻

**Sea Win Resort** Thiruvambadi, North Varkala ☎0470/260 1084 or ☎9747 902191. One of several swanky modern buildings to have sprung up recently at the end of the cliff on the back of Saudi riyals. The colour schemes are a bit offbeat, but the rooms themselves are enormous, with quality double and twin beds, fridges, a spacious common veranda on one side and large private sitouts on the other where you can crash out on cane furniture and watch the sea. Very good value. ❺

**SP Regency** South Cliff ☎0470/260 1432 or ☎9895 016446, ⓦwww.websiteaddress.com. It's worth booking a room in this smart, modern guest-house, close to the Janardhana temple in the South Cliff area, for the roof terrace alone, which has uninterrupted views of the sea through the palm tops. The rooms are pleasant and breezy; some have sea-facing balconies, but the pick of the bunch is no. 3, which opens onto a lovely rear garden running to the cliff edge. ❺–❻

**Thiruvambadi Beach Retreat** Thiruvambadi, North Varkala ☎0470/260 1028 or ☎9895 120299, ⓦwww.thiruvambadihotel.com. This idiosyncratic, family-run guesthouse at the far (quiet) end of the cliff has fifteen rooms, the best of them split-level a/c suites boasting big, sea-facing balconies and over-the-top Mughal-kitsch decor (cusped Islamic arches and elaborately carved wooden doors). There's a sizeable pool in the garden, a small German Bakery café, a billiards table, and on-site ayurveda. All in all, good value, though noise and fumes from the nearby prawn processing plant (under construction at the time of writing) may prove a disincentive. ❺

**Villa Anamika** North Cliff ☎0470/260 0095, ⓦwww.villaanamika.com. A welcoming homestay, 200m from the cliff, run by Keralan artist Shobhana (aka "Chicku") and her German husband Frank. Their five variously priced rooms are all light, airy, cool and attractively furnished, with block-printed bedspreads and paintings by the hostess. Guests get the run of a beautiful rear garden, and breakfasts feature home-made German bread and jams. ⑤

### Luxury

**The Gateway (Taj)** Cliff Rd ☎0470/260 3000, ⓦwww.tajhotels.com. Not the most alluring of the *Taj* group's five-stars (the architecture owes more to the costas than Kerala) but the most luxurious option in Varkala: thirty plush a/c rooms and suites (sea- or garden-facing), in three different categories, opening onto private balconies and lawns,

with direct access to a large curvi-form pool. Tariffs ($175–225) include breakfast and dinner buffets in the *Cape Comorin* restaurant. ⑨

🏃 **Villa Jacaranda** Temple Road West, South Cliff ☎0470/261 0296, ⓦwww .villa-jacaranda.biz. Bijou little guesthouse nestled amid the leafy lanes of the quiet South Cliff area, near the temple. Run by a refugee from the London rat race, it's small (with only four rooms) but perfectly formed, with relaxing sea-blue and mauve colour schemes, cool wooden furniture, crisp white sheets, a fragrant garden and lily pond. Go for room 4 if it's vacant, which has expansive sea views from its own private terrace. ⑧

## The beaches and village

Known in Malayalam as Papa Nashini ("sin destroyer"), Varkala's beautiful white-sand **Papanasam Beach** has long been associated with ancestor worship. Devotees come here after praying at the ancient **Janardhana Swamy Temple**, reached by following the stepped path up the hill from the crossroads in the village centre, to bring the ashes of departed relatives for their "final rest". Non-Hindus are not permitted to enter the inner sanctum of the shrine, but you can peep over the perimeter walls from the encircling path – a pleasant stroll in the morning, when the temple elephant is led around the lanes on her exercise walk.

Backed by sheer red laterite cliffs, the coastline is imposingly scenic and the **beach** relatively relaxing – although its religious associations do ensure that attitudes to public nudity (especially female) are markedly less liberal than other coastal resorts in India. Western sun-worshippers are thus supposed to keep to the northern end of the beach (away from the main puja area reserved for the funerary rites) where they are serviced by a nonstop parade of local "hallo-pineapple-coconut?" vendors. Whistle-happy lifeguards ensure the safety of swimmers by

▲ Varkala beach

enforcing the no-swim zones beyond the flags: be warned that the undercurrent is often strong, claiming lives every year. **Dolphins** are often seen swimming quite close to the coast, and, if you're lucky, you may be able to swim with them by arranging a ride with a fishing boat. Sea otters can also occasionally be spotted playing on the cliffs by the sea.

Few of Varkala's Hindu pilgrims make it as far as the **North Cliff area**, the focus of a well-established tourist scene that's grown steadily over the past fifteen years. Bamboo and palm-thatch cafés, restaurants and souvenir shops jostle for space close to the edge of the mighty escarpments, which plunge vertically to the beach below in a dramatic arc. Several steep flights of steps cut into the rock provide short cuts from the sand, and you can also get there via the gentler path that starts from the beachfront, or along the metalled road winding its way up from the village.

## Nanoo Swami

Varkala is inextricably linked in the popular Indian imagination with the philosopher, poet and social reformer **Sri Narayana Guru**, who founded an ashram – the famous **Sivagiri Mutt** – on a hilltop near the town. Pilgrims travel from all over the Subcontinent to pay their respects at his *samadhi*, where the guru's remains are enshrined, and at the Sri Sarada Saraswati temple he founded on the site. Both Gandhi and the Bengali poet and thinker Tagore came here during the sage's lifetime, claiming the great man's teachings had influenced their own political and religious ideas.

Born into an *ezhava* (low-caste) family near Thiruvananthapuram in 1854, "Nanoo Swami", as he became known to his devotees, followed a well-trodden route to sainthood, leaving his family while still in his twenties to seek enlightenment amid the hills, forests, remote beaches and temples of southern India. This itinerant *sannyasi* phase lasted five years, during which he not only studied yoga under a renowned guru, Ayyavu Swami, but also grew increasingly troubled by the treatment of low-caste communities in his homeland. Kerala was (and remains to a great extent) one of the regions of the country where caste divisions were most rigidly upheld: Untouchables were not allowed in any temples, and had to keep a distance of at least 27m from brahmins. Until 1914, women from the very lowest castes were not permitted to wear sari tops, or educate their children, and no low-caste person could legally travel on any roads.

The great watershed in the swami's life came in 1888, at his cave hermitage in **Arrivippuram**, on the Neyyar River in south Kerala, where he had begun to attract a band of acolytes and admirers. On the night of Shivratri, while bathing in the river, he pulled a rock from the water and with it consecrated a Shiva temple – held to be a heinous crime by brahmins, who considered *prathishta* (the act of installing a temple deity) the exclusive right of high-caste priests.

Nanoo Swami's heresy electrified his followers, and over the coming years, dozens more Shiva temples were opened in south India, welcoming all regardless of caste. Later, the Shiva idols would be replaced by mirrors, intending to demonstrate to worshippers that "God lay inside every person". The religious rebellion eventually coalesced into a much broader social movement that, with support from other great reformers of the day, would result in the gradual removal of caste bars.

From 1904 until the end of his life in 1928, the guru based himself and the SNDP (the organization he founded for the promulgation of his "One Caste, One Religion, One God" philosophy), at a 20-acre site on **Sivagiri** hill, 3km inland from Varkala beach. In keeping with his inclusive ideas, this is one of just a few holy places in Kerala that anybody can visit. Its centrepiece is a three-tiered, circular, cream- and red-painted tower, which stands on high ground above the sage's former residence, where an exhibition of his few personal possessions is displayed. For the full story, go to ⓦ www.sivagiri.org.

Heading in the opposite direction, **South Cliff beach** is the place to make for if you want to sidestep the tourist scene. Parts of it almost disappear at high tide, and there are some nasty hidden rocks below the waterline to keep an eye out for, but the atmosphere here is wonderfully tranquil, especially around sunset when the rest of the village's tourist population is downing cocktails up at North Cliff. You can walk there easily from the main beachfront; or ride to the remote southern end of the beach via the back lane running past South Cliff's hotels and guesthouses.

### Yoga and ayurveda

Countless private **ayurveda centres** and **yoga schools** have opened in Varkala to take advantage of the salubrious location and constant turnover through the winter months of well-off foreigners. As in Kovalam, many non-qualified practitioners have jumped on the bandwagon, so it's wise to look around, and get other travellers' recommendations before booking a treatment. Two clinics that stand out are *Kairali* (℡0470/329 4660, ⓦwww.kairalivaidhyamadomvarkala.com), near the *Silver Star* guesthouse behind the *Funky Art Café*, and *Prana*, in the *Akhil (Preeth) Beach Resort* (℡0470/260 0942). For **yoga**, one recommended teacher is Vasu, who works from a *shala* at the north end of the clifftop, behind *Papaya* restaurant. You can pick up medicinal oils and other health-oriented produce, such as herbs and handmade soaps, as well as books on yoga, meditation and massage, at the Prakrithi Stores on the clifftop.

### Culture shows

The **Varkala Cultural Centre** (℡0470/608793), behind the *Sunrise* restaurant on North Clifftop, holds daily **kathakali** and **bharatanatyam** dance performances (make-up 5–6.45pm; performance 6.45–8.15pm; Rs150). Using live musicians instead of a recorded soundtrack, the show provides a pleasant and authentic enough introduction to the two types of dance, especially if you're not going to make it to Kochi (see p.185). For anyone with a more serious interest in the classical arts, the centre also offers short courses on *kathakali* make-up and dance, *bharatanatyam*, devotional song (*bhajan*) and Carnatic percussion (*mridamgan*). In addition, the *Funky Art Café* hosts free recitals of **Indian classical music**, with tabla, sitar and vocals, from 7.30pm most days.

## Eating, drinking and nightlife

Seafood lovers will enjoy Varkala's clifftop **café-restaurants**, which specialize in locally caught seer fish, shark, marlin, kingfish and jumbo prawns, baked in a tandoori, masala-fried or simmered Keralan-style in spicy coconut-based gravies. You'll also find plenty of Italian, Thai and Mexican items on offer – but don't expect them to taste much like the real thing. Most places are staffed by young Nepali cooks who tend to be liberal with the old "taste maker" (MSG) but not so hot on hygiene (upset tummies are all too common in Varkala). Prices are high by Keralan standards, and service painfully slow when the season is in full swing, but the superb location more than compensates. Although alcohol is available in just about all the clifftop places, due to Varkala's religious importance **beer** tends to be served in discreet teapots.

Once the restaurants finish serving, **nightlife** is generally laidback. After 10pm, a druggy scene takes over at cafés such as the *Funky Art* and nearby *Rock 'n' Roll*, and the *Chill Out Café* further down the clifftop, which all host low-key parties through the season, advertised by flyers.

Café del Mare North Cliff. The most professionally run place to eat on North Cliff, with a proper Italian coffee machine and polite, uniformed service. It offers the usual jack-of-all-trades menu, but they can actually cook everything on it. Made with imported cheeses, the Italian dishes are especially good (try the baked aubergine lasagne) and there are also plenty of light bites and healthy salads. Pricey, with most mains Rs200–300, but you get what you pay for.

Chill Out Café North Cliff. Nicely set-up hippie hideaway, with lounge platforms and bolsters in a quiet palm garden just back from the cliff. It functions as an all-day café-restaurant but really comes alive after sunset, and has a lighter vibe than the *Funky Art*.

Coffee Temple North Cliff. Hot contender (along with *Café del Mar*) for the crown of "Best Coffee in Varkala". The premises are poky, the Brit expat service a bit random, and the cakes uninspiring German-bakery fare, but the mugs of brown stuff they dish up here are truly scrumptious, earning the *Coffee Temple* a loyal following among the resort's caffeine-heads.

Juice Shack North Cliff. Fresh juices churned out by the larger-than-life, resplendently bearded Umesh and his team. They also do a range of healthy snacks, and host popular buffets (Rs250) on Wed & Sat (buy your ticket in advance).

Little Tibet North Cliff. Decorated with cheerful multicoloured prayer flags and Buddhist *thangkas*, this large, bamboo and palm-thatch place, which catches the breezes at a prime cliff-edge location, whips up Mexican and Italian specialities, but most people come for the tasty Tibetan *momo* dumplings and *thukpa* soup (Rs100). Very friendly service and great views if you get a front-side table.

Lotus Café South Cliff. If you want to see what the North Cliff area was like 15 or more years ago, head south to this German-run restaurant, which enjoys arguably the best position of any in Varkala. After a sundowner on the cliff edge, accompanied by a serene Indian classical soundtrack, you can order flavoursome Keralan and vegetarian north Indian dishes, or the day's specials from a good-value, three-course set menu (Rs400 per head); and there's delicious home-made ice cream for dessert.

Shri Padmam Temple Junction. This dingy-looking café on the temple crossroads serves freshly made, cheap and tasty south Indian veg food (including Rs35 "meals" at lunchtime). You can walk through the front dining room to a large rear terrace affording prime views of the tank – particularly atmospheric at breakfast time. Check prices in advance as they tend to charge what they think they can get away with.

Suprabhatam Varkala village, 4km east of the beach. The cheapest and best pure-veg joint in Varkala, situated just off the main circle in a dining hall lined with coir mats and grubby pink walls. Their dosas and other fried snacks aren't up to much, but the lunchtime "unlimited" rice-plate "meals" (noon–3pm; Rs30), featuring the usual *thoran*, *avial*, dhal, *rasam*, buttermilk, curd, *papad* and red or white rice, pull in streams of locals and foreigners alike.

## Listings

Banks and ATMs There are numerous places to change money on North Cliff: City Tours and Travels, in front of the *Hilltop Beach Resort*, exchange currency and travellers' cheques, and offer advances on visa cards for a small commission. The nearest ATMs are at the banks up in Varkala village, just off the crossroads.

Cell phones Parvathy Digital Studio in Varkala village, 100m from the main circle down the road towards the train station on your right, do re-charges for all the major networks.

Cookery classes Learn how to make delicious north Indian and Keralan dishes with local chef, Sajeer, at Khan's Cookery Classes, held daily in a spruce little kitchen behind the *Chill Out Café* on North Cliff. Rates are Rs500/600 for veg/non-veg; book ahead on ☏9895 633896.

Internet centres in Varkala charge Rs40/hr for broadband surfing; connections are usually slow.

Motorcycles Kinetic 100cc scooters are available for rent everywhere in Varkala for around Rs300–350 per day (Rs400–500 for an Enfield), but if you're after something dependable, start your hunt at the Mahindra2Wheelers (Mon–Sat 9.30am–5pm; ☏9846 701975), near Temple Junction, whose vehicles are kept in top condition by owner Srikumar. Also worth a call are Wheels of South India, a business of no fixed abode that works up in North Cliff – just give Anbu a ring on his cell phone (☏9847 080412 or ☏9387 974698) and he'll drop a bike to your door. The nearest petrol pump is in Varkala town – 300m north of the main circle, on the left side of Station Rd as you head towards the railway station.

## South of Varkala: Anchengo Fort

Hemmed in by a poor Christian fishing settlement, the bleached, sloping walls of **Anchengo Fort**, 9km south of Varkala, rise neglected and forlorn behind the village beach, enclosing a half-hearted garden and a couple of rusty old cannons. You wouldn't know it from the building today, but the bastion played a pivotal role in the development of colonial power in India. In 1684, faced with the Zamorin of Calicut's reluctance to grant trading rights to Europeans, the East India Company obtained permission from the Rani of Attingal to site a "factory", or trading post, on a sandy beach near Varkala. Fortified walls were erected a decade later, and it wasn't long before Anchengo started to flourish as a spice port, second only to Bombay. Indeed, it might well have overtaken its sibling had not a dispute broken out: irritated by the colonial traders' manipulation of pepper prices, an irregular Indian force from the surrounding area massacred a column of 140 British troops and merchants as they marched to present annual tribute gifts to the Rani of Attingal in 1721. Anchengo Fort was besieged but held out for six months until reinforcements arrived from Tellicherry. The British were handsomely compensated, with a grant from the rani to the East India Company of a full monopoly over the region's lucrative pepper trade, as well as permission to build factories – the seed of what would later become the British Raj.

## North of Varkala: Odayam, Edava and Puthenkulam

**North of Varkala** the shoreline is a lot less densely populated, though more ostentatiously wealthy, with many large houses dotted around its hinterland of leafy lanes and palm groves. You can comfortably walk the 2km from the north end of Varkala cliff to **ODAYAM**, a mixed Hindu and Muslim village where a cluster of modest guesthouses has sprung up to service the small black-sand beach. Beyond, a paved walkway winds for another three or four kilometres over low cliffs to the next settlement, **EDAVA**, a busier place cut through by the main train line, whose fringes hold a couple of idyllic, empty coves and more low-key accommodation (reviewed on p.120). Shimmering north from there, one vast, unbroken, white-sand beach arcs almost to the horizon, backed by a lagoon and totally empty save for the odd fishing boat.

### Anathavalam elephant farm

A deservedly popular day-trip destination in this area – or a possible stopover on the journey to or from Kollam – is the **Anathavalam elephant farm** near the village of **Puthenkulam** (daily 8am–5pm; Rs100; ☎9847 144946), 16km north of Varkala. Owner Shaji keeps twenty animals – the largest private collection of tuskers in Kerala. They work the festival circuit in the winter, and rest here under the palm canopy during the wet months (rather than toil in timber yards, like most other domestic elephants in the off-season). One of the most famous, and majestic, of the farm's residents is giant Ananthapadmanabhan, winner of the prestigious 2009 "Gajaraja Pattnam" competition (Kerala's pachyderm beauty pageant). At 310m he's officially the tallest elephant in the state – though you're unlikely to see him from December to March, when he is in great demand as a deity-carrier in major festivals. The same is true of Shaji's number-one show-stealer, youngster Shivan, whose birth here in 2007 made national headlines. It's extremely rare for an elephant to be born in captivity, and his appearance brought tens of thousands of admirers to the farm. Visitors are welcome to help bathe and feed the animals; for an extra Rs150 you can also go for a short ride.

Puthenkulam lies 5km from Paravur, the next market town north of Edava on the coast. Take any KSRTC bus running from Varkala to Kollam, get off at **Parippally**, then catch an auto from there. If visiting in winter, especially, it's a good idea to call ahead (you'll need the help of a Malayalam speaker) to check that not all the elephants are away on festival duties.

If you're in this area around the end of February or early March, check the dates of the spectacular **Parippally Gajamela**, hosted by Kodimoottil Sri Bhagavathi (Badrakali) Temple festival in Paravur. The culmination of the ten-day event is a procession of no less than fifty tuskers, including some of Shaji's stars. The full crew, illuminated by burning firebrands, lines up after dark on the street outside the temple to be regaled by a massive drum orchestra (*chenda melam*) – one of the most spectacular events in Kerala's religious calendar.

### Accommodation north of Varkala

If you're happy to watch the bright lights of Varkala's clifftop from a distance, the coast further north has a lot to recommend it, offering better-value **accommodation** and access to a wild and windy shoreline where tourism has made little impact.

**Asin Momo** Street 8, Edava ☎9895 094112, ⊛asinmomo.com. Simple but superbly situated budget homestay run by a welcoming young couple, Shaiju and Jesini. It's nestled under the palms moments away from one of the loveliest, remotest stretches of coast north of Varkala. The rooms are very small and basic, but attached, and scooter hire, wi-fi and home-cooked meals are available. ❸

**Blue Water** Near Parambil temple, Odayam ☎9446 848534, ⊛www.bluewaterstay.com. A nicely set up, welcoming option in Odayam, comprising nine varnished palmwood chalets with tiled roofs – not all that spacious, but comfortably furnished, with cute little touches such as floating flowers in terracotta pots, cane blinds and silk throws on the beds – and they all have sea views. The open-sided restaurant, overlooking the waves at the bottom of a terraced plot, is also the best place to eat and drink hereabouts. ❼

**The First Place** Odayam ☎0470/299 2090 or ☎9746 983783, ⊛www.thefirstplace-odayam .com. Eco-friendly, Swedish-run guesthouse on the bluff overlooking the beach, with its own shady garden. The rooms aren't large, but they're nicely done – freshly painted with little wooden shelves, glossy red-oxide floors and mozzie nets. One of them serves as a classroom for Swedish kids, making this a particularly commendable option for young families. ❺

**Fragrant Nature** 18km north of Varkala at Nedun-golam, near Paravur ☎0474/252 4000, ⊛www .fragrantnature.com. Luxury resort on a secluded backwater midway between Varkala and Kollam. Its flagship options are the "Premium Lake View Villas" ($200), which have high-pitched roofs and wooden

decks overlooking a peaceful lagoon. Styled in earthy colours using natural materials, they're private and relaxing, and altogether more appealing than the more recently added "Lakeside" chalets ($150). A large curvi-form room, multi-cuisine restaurant and wellness spa are added attractions. Tariffs include a sunset cruise on a rice barge. ❾

**Kadaltheeram** Edava ☎0470/266 4218 or ☎9947 776787, ⊛www.kadaltheeram.com. Small but well-run ayurveda resort in neo-Keralan style, next to a lovely little cove that's deserted most of the time. All three types of room are neat, clean and spacious, with a/c and good-sized balconies looking over the hotel's well-tended gardens to the sea – though some have better views than others (if it's free, book #107). ❽

**Kattil Beach Resort** Odayam ☎0470/266 2226 or ☎9895 582740, ⊛www.kattilbeachresort.com. The best-value lower-mid-range option in this area, offering a choice of 14 en-suite rooms in three different wings, all on high ground above the beach, with pleasant views from private or common verandas. The ones in the block called *Sona* are the pick of the crop, looking through the palm groves to the nearby stream gulley and beach. ❺

**Munna** Edava ☎9895 528150 or ☎9846 689912. This no-frills budget guesthouse, situated on a palm-shaded terrace that's open to the sea breezes on one side, is the northernmost mark of tourism in the Varkala area, and an absolute steal, with rooms from only Rs500. They're very basic, but those on the upper floor share a common veranda looking straight out to sea. If you're happy with simple amenities and can sort out transport (Edava beach is a bit cut off), you'll probably end up staying for weeks. ❸

**Pink Aana** Odayam ☏ 9895 056543, ⓦ www.pinkaana.at. Easily the best-value place to stay in Odayam, behind the beach with uninterrupted ocean views from just four large, thatched bamboo huts. They're cool, well spaced and nicely furnished (with thick mattresses and sizeable bathrooms), and reasonably priced considering they're so near the sand. Kids' beds available on request. **⑤**

᠎᠎᠎

᠎᠎᠎

# Kollam (Quilon)

Sandwiched between the sea and Ashtamudi ("eight inlets") Lake, **KOLLAM** (pronounced "Koillam", and previously known as Quilon) was for centuries the focal point of the Malabar's spice trade. Phoenicians, Arabs, Greeks, Romans and Chinese all dispatched ships to the city, which was praised in the memoirs of travellers from Ibn Khurdadhibh in the ninth century to Duarte Barbossa in the sixteenth, before the rise of Calicut and Cochin eclipsed the port. These days, it's a workaday market town and busy transport hub for the southern backwater region, with surprisingly few vestiges of its former prominence. Lots of travellers overnight here, however, en route to or from Alleppey on the excursion boats that leave each morning from its lakeside ferry jetty. To kill time in the evening, your best bet is a stroll through the town's traditional **bazaar**, with its old wooden houses and narrow backstreets lined by coir warehouses, rice stores and cashew traders. A short auto-rickshaw ride south of the centre, Kollam's **beach** provides a welcome escape if the heat and traffic of the centre get too much.

## Arrival and information

Kollam's busy mainline **railway station** lies east of the clocktower that marks the centre of town. Numerous daily trains run from Ernakulam and Thiruvananthapuram and beyond. The KSRTC **bus stand** is across town, near the boat jetty on Ashtamudi Lake. The **District Tourism Promotion Council** (DTPC) has a tourist office nearby (daily 9am–6pm; ☏0474/274 5625, ⓦwww.dtpckollam.com) at the **boat jetty** on Ashtamudi Lake, where you can book tickets for the daily tourist backwater cruises (see below). The local **Alappuzha Tourism Development Council** office (ATDC; daily 7am–9pm; ☏0474/276 7440, ⓦwww.atdcalleppey.com), on the opposite side of the road, offers comparable services.

Useful **facilities** such as exchange bureaux, ATMs and internet outlets can be found in the smart Bishop Jerome Nagar shopping mall, just south of the main road between the jetty and the clocktower. The efficient ICICI bank also has a dependable ATM, next to the *Vaidya* hotel; and there's another convenient, cheap

---

### Backwater cruises from Kollam

DTPC and ATDC run popular **cruises from Kollam to Alappuzha** (Rs300) on alternate days, departing at 10.30am and taking eight hours, with stops for lunch and tea. Tickets for both can be bought on the day from the tourist offices at the boat jetty on Ashtamudi Lake, and at some of the hotels. In addition, the same companies offer exclusive overnight *kettu vallam* cruises, and DTPC also runs half-day canal trips to nearby **Monroe Island** (daily 9am–1pm & 2–6.30pm; Rs500), as well as guided village tours taking in coir-makers, boat-builders and bird-nesting sites.

Such cruises are a real money-spinner for the local tourist offices, but you may find that you get a far better impression of backwater life by hopping between villages on the very cheap **local ferries**, tickets for which are sold on the boats themselves. Consult either DTPC or ATDC for timetables and route information.

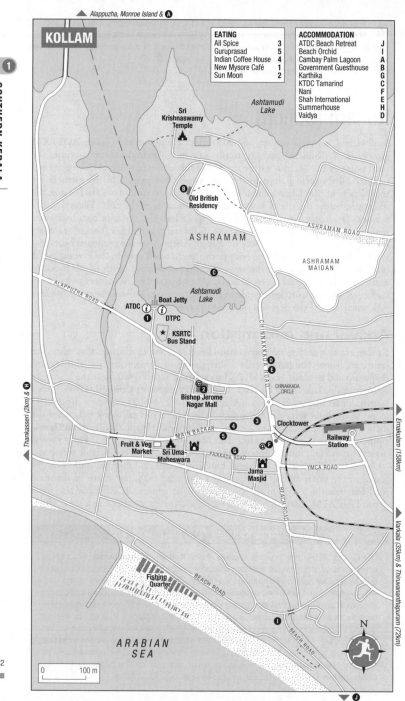

KOLLAM

Alappuzha, Monroe Island & Ⓐ

**EATING**
All Spice    3
Guruprasad    5
Indian Coffee House    4
New Mysore Café    1
Sun Moon    2

**ACCOMMODATION**
ATDC Beach Retreat    J
Beach Orchid    I
Cambay Palm Lagoon    A
Government Guesthouse    B
Karthika    G
KTDC Tamarind    C
Nani    F
Shah International    E
Summerhouse    H
Vaidya    D

*Ashtamudi Lake*

Sri Krishnaswamy Temple

Ⓑ Old British Residency

ASHRAMAM

ASHRAMAM ROAD

ASHRAMAM MAIDAN

ALAPPUZHA ROAD

Ⓒ

*Ashtamudi Lake*

Boat Jetty

ATDC ⓘ ⓘ
●1 DTPC

★ KSRTC Bus Stand

CHINNAKKARA ROAD

Ⓓ
Ⓔ

CHINNAKKADA CIRCLE

@●2
Bishop Jerome Nagar Mall

●4
●5 ●3 Clocktower

MAIN BAZAAR

Railway Station

Fruit & Veg Market
Sri Uma-Maheswara

PAIKKADA ROAD

Ⓖ @Ⓕ

YMCA ROAD

Jama Masjid

BEACH ROAD

Thankasseri (2km) & Ⓗ

Ernakulam (158km)

Varkala (35km) & Thiruvananthapuram (72km)

Fishing Quarter

BEACH ROAD

BEACH ROAD

Ⓘ

BEACH ROAD

N

ARABIAN SEA

0    100 m

▼ Ⓙ

internet place, Cyber.com, just south of the clocktower on the first floor of Yeskay Towers, charging just Rs30/hr.

**Moving on,** you can book express **buses** (every 15min or so) for Kochi (3hr) via Alappuzha (2hr) and for Thiruvananthapuram (1hr 45min); as ever, the express services are much better than the "limited stop" buses. Note that most Thiruvananthapuram-bound **trains** do not stop in Varkala.

## Accommodation

Kollam holds several new **business-grade hotels** offering good value in the mid and upper ranges, but very little of note at the budget end of the scale, other than the charismatic *Government Guesthouse*, on Ashtamudi Lake, which can't be booked in advance.

### Budget

**Government Guesthouse** Ashtamudi Lake, 2km northeast of town ☎0474/274 3620. Sleeping in this grand 250-year-old building, the former British Residency (see p.124), feels like overnighting in a museum. Full of original furniture and fixtures, the rooms are gigantic for the price (go for an a/c one on the first floor if it's offered) but, as with most government guesthouses, you'll have to try for a vacancy on spec as they rarely accept advance bookings – though do phone ahead to see if it's open (the place was closed for renovation at the time of writing). Breakfast and dinner available. ❶–❷

**Karthika** Near the Jama Masjid mosque ☎0474/275 1831. Large, popular budget hotel in a central location offering a range of acceptably clean, plain rooms (some a/c) ranged around a courtyard that centres, rather unexpectedly, on three huge nude figures. ❷–❸

**Shah International** Chinnakkada Rd ☎0474/274 2362, ⓦwww.hotelshahinternational.com. Fifteen years ago this used to be one of the top hotels in the area, but it's become terribly run-down of late and is only worth considering as a fallback economy option – the non-a/c "executives" (Rs750) are a lot more spacious and spruce than the turquoise-walled, lodge-style "budget" rooms (only Rs450). ❷–❹

### Mid-range

**ATDC Beach Retreat** 3km south of centre ☎0474/276 3793, ⓦwww.kollambeachretreat.com. Typical government-run place with smudged walls and average-sized rooms (some a/c), situated directly across the road from the beach, and good value considering its location. It's also quiet in the evenings, has a rooftop restaurant with sea views, and an untypically enthusiastic and helpful young staff. Station pick-up (Rs75) on request. ❸–❹

**KTDC Tamarind** Ashramam ☎0474/274 5538, ⓦwww.ktdc.com. This government hotel, facing the town from the shore of the lake, enjoys an unrivalled location and has just had a major face-lift. Even so, it's already started to look a bit grubby and can't compete with the *Nani* and *Vaidya* for price. Forget about the non-a/c rooms – they face southwest and are like ovens by late afternoon. Facilities include a small restaurant (best avoided) and beer parlour. ❺

**Nani** Opposite the clocktower ☎0474/275 1141, ⓦwww.hotelnani.com. The town's most stylish hotel, in a quirky, red-brick, Keralan-gabled tower block close to the railway station. At only Rs1200 for non-a/c or Rs1900 for a/c, its beautifully furnished standard rooms are the real bargain, though you might want the additional space of the "executive" room if there are two of you. Their lobby features beaten-copper murals by local artist, Sri Namboothiri. ❺–❼

**Summerhouse** Thirumallawaram and Thankasseri ☎0474/279 4518, ☎9895 662839, ✉contactsummerhouse@hotmail.com. See map on p.138. Run by the amiable Mr Shashi, this trio of suburban homestays offers simple, characterful accommodation on the northwestern edge of town near, or next to, the sea. Pick of the bunch is "No. 3", a cosy wood cabin with only three rooms (Rs600 per day; book them all for privacy), opening onto a wonderful veranda enfolded by palm trees, slap on the sea wall. "No. 1" is an older structure, also next to the waves, but more spartan. "No. 2", a former family house 5min walk from the shore in a leafy residential area, is large enough for a group and has its own garden. ❹

**Vaidya** Residency Rd, Chinnakkada ☎0474/274 8432, ⓦwww.hotelvaidyakollam.com. If you're just passing through and want somewhere clean and comfortable to crash in for a night, and aren't fussy about the view, give this business-oriented place on the north side of town a try. It's ugly from the outside, and the rooms have no balconies, zero outlook and even less character, but they're huge for the price, and gleaming. The standard ones (confusingly referred to as "deluxe") are the best value. ⑥–⑦

### Luxury

**Beach Orchid** Kollam Beach ☎0474/276 9999, Ⓦwww.thebeachorchidhotel.com. Panoramic views of the beach are the big selling point of Kollam's seaside five-star. Both the "deluxe" (Rs7600) and "premium" (Rs8700) have them – the only difference being the angle. You don't get a lot of space for the price, and service isn't great, but there's a

rooftop pool, and an infinity pool at lobby level, as well as a multi-cuisine restaurant, modest spa and gym; and any kids in your group will love the glass-sided elevator. ⑨

**Cambay Palm Lagoon** Vellimon West ☎0474/254 8974, Ⓦwww.thecambay.com. See map on p.138. Plush rooms, traditional cottages, environmental tents, mud houses, houseboats and floating cottages, set in a lush six-acre plot on Ashtamudi Lake, 18km from town. The complex includes a pool, plus a swimming enclosure in the lake itself; and quality ayurveda treatment facilities are available. They can also arrange bike, boat and fishing trips in the surrounding backwaters. Rs7000–9000. ⑨

## The Town

The one monument worth going out of your way to see in Kollam is the former **British Residency**, a magnificent 250-year-old mansion on the shores of the lake, now used as a *Government Guesthouse* (see p.123). Overlooking the balding expanse of the old maidan (parade ground) it's one of just a handful of monuments surviving from the early days of the Raj, and perfectly epitomizes the openness to indigenous influences that characterized the era, with typically Keralan gabled roofs surmounting British pillared verandas. Inside, palatial rooms retain their original early Georgian furniture, giant Chinese pickle jars and floor-to-ceiling shuttered windows, while the walls sport antique East India Company lithographs of Wellesley storming "Seringapatnam". Much of the structure is literally falling apart, but you're welcome to visit: there are no set hours – just turn up and ask the manager if you can have a look around.

A couple of kilometres southwest of the centre, on the seaward side of town, the district of **Thankasseri** holds fading remnants of still earlier eras, when the bay it overlooked would have been filled with ships. This is where Ibn Battuta, writing in the 1330s, saw massive Chinese junks being filled with pepper, as dozens more stood by in the bay. Encircling the modern, red-and-white-striped lighthouse are the partly collapsed walls of an early sixteenth-century **Portuguese fort**, while the **Church of St Thomas**, now a pile of rubble inside, may well have been one in which St Francis Xavier (see p.286) attended Mass during his evangelical mission to the Malabar coast in the 1540s. Other buildings in the area surviving from the Portuguese period include the **Church of Infant Jesus**, and the chapel attached to the **Bishop of Quilon's palace** – both five minutes' walk north of the old fort. Throughout the British period, Thankasseri was a primarily Anglo-Indian district, but after Independence most of its elegant old bungalows were sold off as residents emigrated to the UK and Canada. Many now lie empty and in states of evocative dereliction, languishing in overgrown gardens.

East of Thankasseri lies one of the town's two main **fishing quarters**, lined by hundreds of painted boats (the other is south of the centre). They're scattered over what must, four or five centuries ago, have been Kollam's fabled harbour. As ever, if you walk on the beach, remember it's used as a public toilet in the mornings.

## Eating

With the exception of *Summerhouse*, all of the hotels, resorts and guesthouses listed above provide meals, but if you'd prefer to eat out, try one of the following **restaurants** in the centre of town.

All Spice Near the main bazaar. This determinedly Western, brightly lit fast-food joint, above a bakery, is where the town's middle classes come for family evenings out, and where foreign tourists come to get away from Indian food. The a/c certainly hits the spot, but the burgers, pizzas and fried chicken turn out to be less appealing than the north Indian and Chinese dishes (Rs125–175).

Guruprasad Main bazaar. Cramped and sweaty, but wonderfully old-school "meals" on the market's main street: blue-and-cream walls, framed ancestral photos and Hindu devotional art provide the typical backdrop for pukka pure-veg rice plates and udipi-style snacks.

Indian Coffee House Main bazaar. Typical ICH fare – limp dosas, oily biriyanis, toast, omelettes, pot-chai and filter coffee – served on regulation chipped china by waiters wearing pleated pugris, at the regulation rock-bottom rates. It's worth eating here for the dining hall alone – a real period piece.

New Mysore Café Boat jetty, opposite KSRTC bus stand. This is the most popular of the "meals" joints clustered around the bus stand and boat jetty area, serving delicious "all-you-can-eat" rice plates for just Rs30 at lunchtime, then the usual udipi snacks through the rest of the day. A convenient option if you've time to kill before catching onward transport.

Sun Moon Top Floor, Bishop Jerome Nagar Mall ℡ 0474/301 3000. Traditional Keralan cooking – karimeen pollichathu (white fish steamed in banana leaf) and masala-fried calamari, as well as Continental dishes and a big multi-cuisine buffet – served in a blissfully cool, a/c rooftop restaurant, against a backdrop of carved stone temple brackets and woodwork. The food's the best in town, and so are the panoramic views. Count on Rs300 for three courses.

# Alappuzha (Alleppey) and around

Roughly midway between Kollam (85km south) and Kochi (64km north), **ALAPPUZHA** once ranked among the wealthiest ports along the Malabar coast, acting as a clearing house for spices, coffee, tea, cashews, coir and other produce shipped from the backwaters. Unlike its rivals elsewhere in the region, however, the town – known in colonial times, and still commonly referred to, as "Alleppey" – didn't see its heyday until the mid-1800s, by which time the main canal scything through its heart, linking the waterways with the Arabian Sea, was lined with factories and warehouses. Alappuzha prospered to such an extent that the successful British traders who had settled here during the Raj were loath to leave at Independence. A sizeable community of expats remained after 1947, but their luck ran out ten years later, when the newly elected communist government clamped down on private businesses and they were forced to return to Britain.

With its trading history and interconnecting **canals**, tourist literature is fond of referring to Alappuzha as the "Venice of the East". Don't expect too much of a resemblance, though: cut through by the main national highway, the busy centre is as ramshackle and chaotic as any mid-sized Keralan town, although it does boast some quiet and leafy suburbs sporting rows of old colonial-era wharfs and bungalows.

The town is still a major hub in the coir industry, which accounts for much of the water-borne traffic chugging to and from the nearby lakes. However, the big bucks these days are being made from **houseboat cruises**. Close on six hundred kettu vallam barges operate in the Kuttanad area – 480 of them out of Alappuzha itself. The resulting congestion has proved a major challenge for the ecosystem of the backwaters (see p.139). However, it is possible to explore the area ethically, and Alappuzha provides plenty of scope for backwater trips on more environmentally friendly man-powered punts or canoes, as well as offering some of the state's best-value accommodation – much of it in characterful **homestays**.

## Arrival and information

The KSRTC **bus stand**, served by regular buses to and from Kollam, Kottayam, Thiruvananthapuram, Ernakulam and most other major Keralan towns, stands at

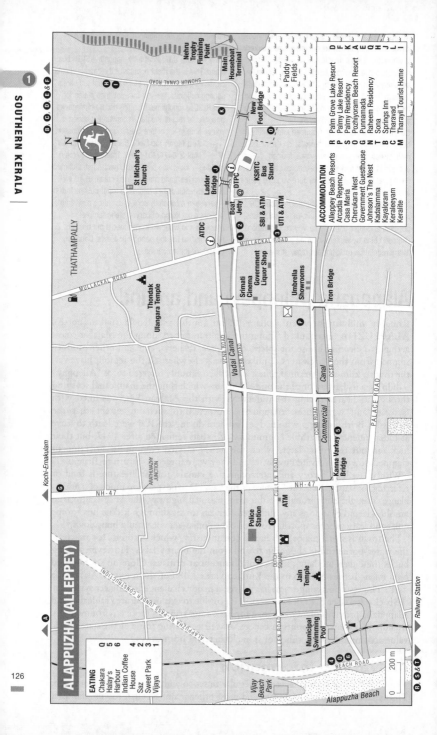

# ALAPPUZHA (ALLEPPEY)

**EATING**

| | |
|---|---|
| Chakara | Q |
| Halay's | 5 |
| Harbour | 6 |
| Indian Coffee House | 4 |
| Saz | 2 |
| Sweet Park | 3 |
| Vijaya | 1 |

**ACCOMMODATION**

| | |
|---|---|
| Alleppey Beach Resorts | R |
| Arcadia Regency | P |
| Casa Maria | S |
| Cherukara Nest | O |
| Government Guesthouse | N |
| Johnson's The Nest | G |
| Kadalamma | T |
| Kayaloram | B |
| Keraleeyam | C |
| Keralite | M |
| Palm Grove Lake Resort | D |
| Palmy Lake Resort | F |
| Palmy Residency | K |
| Pozhiyoram Beach Resort | A |
| Punnamada | Q |
| Raheem Residency | E |
| Sona | H |
| Springs Inn | J |
| Tharavad | L |
| Tharayil Tourist Home | I |

Nehru Trophy Finishing Point

Main Houseboat Terminal

SHOMUN CANAL ROAD

Paddy Fields

New Foot Bridge

St Michael's Church

Ladder Bridge

Boat Jetty

SBI & ATM

KSRTC Bus Stand

@ DTPC

UTI & ATM

ATDC

MULLACKAL ROAD

Srimati Cinema

Government Liquor Shop

Umbrella Showrooms

Iron Bridge

THATHAMPALLY

Thondak Ulangara Temple

MULLACKAL ROAD

VCNB ROAD

Vadai Canal

VCSB ROAD

Canal

CCSB ROAD

Kochi–Ernakulam

ARATHUNJORY JUNCTION

NH-47

CCNB ROAD

Commercial Canal

Kanna Varkey Bridge

PALACE ROAD

CULLEN ROAD

ATM

NH-47

Police Station

DUTCH SQUARE

Jain Temple

Municipal Swimming Pool

ALAPPUZHA BY-PASS (UNDER CONSTRUCTION)

BEACH ROAD

CULLEN ROAD

Vijay Beach Park

Alappuzha Beach

Railway Station

R, S & T

0    200 m

N

the northeast edge of town. Close to its north exit, the main boat jetty on **Vadai Canal** is where the daily tourist ferry to and from Kollam, and local boat connections with Kottayam, arrive and depart. The **railway station**, on the main Thiruvananthapuram–Ernakulam line, lies 3km southwest across town, on the far side of Alappuzha's main waterway, **Commercial Canal**.

The town has several rival **tourist departments**, all of them eager to offer advice and book you onto their respective houseboat tours. The most conveniently situated – at the jetty itself on VCSB (Vadai Canal South Bank) Road – are the DTPC **tourist reception centre** (daily 9am–5pm; ☎0477/225 1796) and adjacent Kerala Tourism office (Mon–Sat 10am–5pm; ☎0477/226 0722, ⓦwww.keralatourism.org). On the opposite side of the canal on the corner of Mullackal and Vadai Canal North Bank (VCNB) Road, ATDC's main information office (daily 8am–8pm; ☎0477/224 346 or "Shambhu" ☎9895 010833, ⓦwww.atdcalleppey.com) is more tucked away, on the second floor of the Municipal Shopping Complex. Both ATDC and DTPC sell tickets for their ferries, backwater cruises and charter boats, and can help you fathom the intricacies of local ferry timetables. Note that many of the houseboat booking agencies dotted around town call themselves "tourist information offices" – but they're nothing of the kind, and are there solely with the purpose of finding clients for their cruises.

You can **change money** at the efficient UTI bank at the far east end of Cullen Road, just off Mullackal Road (Mon–Sat 9.30am–4.30pm). Both it and the State Bank of India opposite have reliable ATMs. **Internet** access is widely available for Rs30–40 per hour, with several outlets along the road facing the boat jetty; Mailbox, on VCSB Road, five minutes' walk west of Mullackal Road, boasts the town's fastest connection.

## Accommodation

The choice of **places to stay** in the town centre is fairly uninspiring, but there are some great possibilities in all brackets if you are willing to travel to the outskirts and pay a little more. In the suburb of **Thathampally**, on the fringes of the Punnamada Lake, a string of ultra-luxurious resorts soak up the tour group and honeymoon custom in campuses of reassembled Keralan wooden houses on the water's edge. Further afield, the **backwaters** also harbour plenty of delightful homestays (reviewed on p.143).

Nearly everywhere, whatever its bracket, has some kind of tie-in with a houseboat operator: good-natured encouragement rather then hard-sell tactics tends to be the order of the day, but you may be able to negotiate a reduction on your room tariff if you do end up booking a backwater trip. Whenever you come, and wherever you chose to stay, brace yourself for clouds of **mosquitoes**.

All the hotels listed below are marked on, or arrowed off, the main Alappuzha map opposite; places further out of town also appear on the Kuttanad backwaters map (p.138), and the Alappuzha and Kumarakom area map (p.144).

### Budget

**Cherukara Nest** 9/774 Cherukara Buildings ☎0477/225 1509, ☎9947 059628. Nineteenth-century "heritage" home, run by the welcoming Mr Tony John and his wife Cecilia, on a quiet canal road just a short walk around the corner from the KSRTC bus stand. The cheaper two of his three rooms are light with high ceilings; the one to the rear, in a converted teak-lined granary, is gloomier but possesses more Keralan character.

Breakfast is served in an old courtyard under a huge mango tree. Eco-friendly houseboat cruises are a sideline. ❹–❺

**Government Guesthouse** NH-47 ☎0477/224 6504. Basically set up for the benefit of visiting officials, but they'll accommodate tourists if there are vacancies (though you'll probably have to call in person on the day). Ranged on two floors above a central courtyard, the rooms are plain and a touch institutional, but fantastic for the price

## Exploring the backwaters

To travel around the **Kuttanad backwaters** by boat is the main reason visitors come to Kerala, and with good reason. Chugging along the region's waterways reclined on the observation deck of a traditional rice barge is among the most pleasurable experiences India has to offer – though it doesn't come cheap, and may not live up to expectations if you fall into the clutches of a cowboy outfit. For those with limited time or money, cheaper day cruises are also on offer. And there are always local ferries.

### Kettu vallam (houseboats)

Whoever dreamed up the idea of showing tourists around the backwaters in old rice barges, or kettu vallam (literally "boat with knots"), could never have imagined that two decades on, five hundred or more of them would be chugging around Kuttanad waterways. These houseboats, made of dark, oiled jackwood with canopies of plaited palm thatch and coir, are big business, and almost every mid- and upmarket hotel, guesthouse and "heritage homestay" seems to have one. Some 480 work out of Alappuzha alone, the flashiest fitted with glass-sided a/c rooms, silk cushions on their teak sun decks, giant plasma-screen TVs and satellite dishes, imported wine in their fridges and jacuzzis that bubble away through the night. One grand juggernaut (called the *Vaikundan*, based near Amma's ashram in Kollam district) holds ten separate bedrooms and won't slip its lines for less than Rs100,000 ($2200). At the opposite end of the scale are rough-and-ready transport barges with gut-thumping diesel engines, cramped, smelly bedrooms and minimal washing facilities.

What you end up **paying** for your cruise will depend on a number of variables: the size and quality of the boat and its fittings; the number and standard of the bedrooms; and, crucially, the time of year. Rates double over Christmas and New Year, and halve off-season during the monsoons. In practice, however, Rs6000–15,000 is the usual bracket for a trip on a two-bedroom, a/c boat with a proper bathroom, including three meals, in early December or mid-January. The cruise should last a minimum of 22 hours, though don't expect to spend all of that on the move: running times are carefully calculated to spare gas. From sunset onwards you'll be moored at a riverbank, probably on the outskirts of the town where the trip started.

You can save quite a lot of cash, and be doing the fragile ecosystem a big favour, by opting for a **more environmentally friendly** punted *kettu vallam*. This was how rice barges were traditionally propelled, and though it means you travel at a more leisurely pace, the experience is silent (great for wildlife spotting) and altogether more relaxing.

Houseboat operators work out of Kollam, Karunaganapali and Kumbakonam, but by far the highest concentration is in Alappuzha, where you'll find the lowest prices – but also the worst congestion on more scenic routes. Spend a day shopping around for a deal and get it fixed on paper before setting off.

### Houseboat booking tips

- Avoid the main houseboat terminal in Alappuzha, where you'll be pounced on by dozens of aggressive touts as soon as you arrive.
- Fix the precise route with your operator in advance: make sure it avoids long stretches of Vembanad Lake (which can be monotonous), and includes narrow (more interesting) waterways as well as the wider channels and rivers.
- Ask your operator to specify the exact running time (it should be at least noon until sunset).
- Locate the site of your night halt – try for somewhere quiet rather than in a busy village or on the outskirts of Alappuzha.
- Ensure there's an English-speaking crew-member on board.
- Check the number of hours the a/c will be switched on (generally 9pm–7am); if

you're cruising in mid-Feb onwards you'll probably need it to get a good night's sleep.

- Make sure the food the operator intends to provide is to your taste, and that there'll be beer on board if you want it.
- Always give the boat you're going on a thorough look beforehand, making sure the bedroom, toilet and kitchen, in particular, are clean and in good order.
- Withhold a final payment until the end of the cruise in case of arguments.
- Don't forget to tip the crew if you're happy with their service.

### Recommended houseboat operators

The following firms are all based in Alappuzha – which is closer to the most interesting backwater districts and thus preferable as a departure point to Kumarakom, on Vembanand Lake, or Kollam, a day's journey to the south.

**Cherukara** 9/774 Cherukara Bldgs ℡0477/225 1509, or ℡9947 059628. Tony John's is one of the few firms running cruises on old-style punted boats. Solid, eco-friendly budget choice.

**Lakes and Lagoon** Punnamada Jetty ℡0477/223 6181, Ⓦwww.lakeslagoons.com. The largest operator, and one of the most dependable, with two-dozen boats of various sizes (including a magnificent honeymoon double-decker), staffed by uniformed, well-drilled crews. Not the cheapest outfit in Alappuzha, but you're guaranteed top service and conditions – or your money back if you're not happy.

**Marvel Cruise** Akkarakalam House, Mullackal Rd ℡0477/266 4341 or ℡9847 054884, Ⓦwww.marvelcruise.com. High-end trips on particularly lovely boats, with interiors decorated using natural materials.

**The Nest** Houseboat Lalbagh, Convent Square ℡0477/2245825 or ℡9961 466399, Ⓦwww.johnsonskerala.com. "No Cutting Corners!" is the motto of this friendly lower mid-range outfit, based at a backpackers' guesthouse in Alappuzha.

**River Goddess Houseboats** UK ℡01726/844 867, India ℡9847 846441, Ⓦwww .rivergoddesshouseboats.com. Part British-run, this outfit offers excellent value in the Rs5000–6000 bracket, where standards vary greatly in Alappuzha. Their boats are tastefully styled, with antique Keralan doors, hand-embroidered bedspreads, lotus-sculpted beds and larger-than-average windows; and the staff courteous and efficient. Reservations can be made over the phone or via email in the UK.

### Village tours and canoes

Quite apart from their significant environmental impact, most houseboats are too wide to squeeze into the narrower inlets connecting small villages. To reach these more idyllic, remote areas, therefore, you'll need to charter a **punted canoe** (see p.132). The slower pace means less distance gets covered, but the experience of being so close to the water, and those who live on it, tends to be correspondingly more rewarding. Individual guides have their own favourite itineraries. You'll also find more formal "village tours" advertised across the Kuttanad area, tying together trips to watch coir makers, rice farmers and boat builders in action with the opportunity to dine in a traditional Keralan village setting.

### Local ferries

*Kettu vallam* may offer the most comfortable way of cruising the backwaters, but you'll get a much more vivid experience of what life is actually like in the region by jumping on one of the **local ferries** that serve its towns and villages. Particularly recommended is the 29km trip from Alappuzha to Kottayam (dep 7.30am, 9.35am, 11.30am & 5.15pm; 2hr 30min; Rs10), which winds across open lagoons and narrow canals, through coconut groves and islands; arrive early to get a good place with uninterrupted views.

*(Contd.)*

## Exploring the backwaters *(contd.)*

There are numerous other local routes that you can jump on and off, though working your way through the complexities of the timetables and Malayalam name scan be difficult without the help of the tourist office. Good places to aim for from Alappuzha include Neerettupuram, Kidangara and Champakulam; all three are served by regular daily ferries, but you may have to change boats once or twice along the way, killing time in local cafés and toddy shops (all of which adds to the fun, of course). Services are outlined on the State Water Transport Department's website (W www.swtd.gov.in), but always check in advance that your chosen ferry is running – timetables are being scaled back each year as the road network is extended.

### ATDC/DTPC tours and cruises

The most popular excursion of all in the Kuttanad region is the full-day journey between **Kollam and Alappuzha**. All sorts of private hustlers offer their services, but the principal boats are run on alternate days by the Alleppey Tourism Development Co-op (**ATDC**) and the District Tourism Promotion Council (**DTPC**) – see p.127 for contact details. The double-decker boats leave from both Kollam and Alappuzha daily, departing at 10.30am (10am check-in); tickets cost Rs300 and can be bought in advance or on the day at the ATDC/DTPC counters, other agents and some hotels. Both companies make three stops during the eight-hour journey, including one for lunch, and another at the Mata Amritanandamayi Math at Amritapuri (see p.140), around three hours north of Kollam.

Although it is by far the main backwater route, many tourists find Alappuzha–Kollam too long, with crowded decks and intense sun. There's also something faintly embarrassing about being cooped up with a crowd of fellow tourists, madly photographing any signs of life on the water or canal banks, while gangs of kids scamper alongside the boat screaming "one pen, one pen". One alternative is to charter a four- or six-seater **motorboat** through DTPC and ATDC (around Rs300/hr). Slower, more cumbersome double-decker **country boats** are also available for hire from Rs250/hr.

---

(Rs250 non-a/c or Rs520 for much nicer a/c), with big, clean bathrooms. ❶–❸

**Johnson's The Nest** Lalbagh, Cullen Rd, 2km west of the centre T 0477/224 5825 or T 9961 466399, W www.johnsonskerala.com. Friendly, sociable homestay on a quiet suburban street, popular mainly with young backpackers. Its five individually themed en-suite rooms are large, with Barbie-pink mosquito nets, and most have funky little sitouts fitted with cane swings. Money exchange, laundry and meals available – and they offer enjoyable day-trips to a quiet beach north of Alappuzha. ❷–❹

**Keralite** Vadakekalam House, north of Dutch Square T 0477/224 3569 or T 9847 073405, E alice_thomas2150@hotmail.com. Opening onto a broad sand courtyard filled with pot plants, the heart of this delightful 100-year-old house is a high-ceilinged salon where hostess Alice Thomas serves traditional Syrian-Christian meals under the watchful eye of ancestral portraits. Comfortable antique beds furnish the guest rooms, which have lots of period atmosphere; the only

catch is that some lack en-suite bathrooms – hence the bargain rates. No sign, so phone for entry. ❹

**Palmy Lake Resort** Thathampally, 2km north of boat jetty T 0477/223 5938, T 9447 667888, W www.palmyresort.com. Spacious, neatly painted red-tiled "cottages" (a/c and non-a/c), grouped behind a modern family home on the northeastern limits of town. Despite the name, it isn't actually on the lake, but offers exceptional value for money. You get loads of space for the price: all rooms have private pillared verandas opening onto a restful garden. Owners Biggi and Mercy Matthews are smiling hosts, providing delicious home-cooked Keralan meals. Phone ahead for free pick-up. Internet access available. ❹

**Palmy Residency** Off VCNB Rd, near main houseboat terminal T 0477/223 5938, T 9447 667888, W www.palmyresort.com. Up a sidestreet 2-minutes' walk from Main Canal, this well-run guesthouse (an offshoot of the excellent *Palmy Lake Resort*) is situated in a quiet neighbourhood. It has six rooms in total – the cheaper ones are great no-frills options, with mozzie nets and attached bathrooms; an extra Rs250 buys you more space and a TV. Unbeatable value in the budget bracket. ❷

**Springs Inn** VCNB Rd ☎9847 750000. Three simple en-suite rooms with white walls, wood ceilings and red-oxide tiled floors, fronted by a shady veranda. A bit boxed in by the neighbouring block, and not as well maintained as it might be, but conveniently placed for the boat jetty. Tariffs include breakfast. ❸

**Tharayil Tourist Home** Shornur Canal Rd, Thathampally ☎0477/223 3543 or ☎9447 505524, ⊛www.tharayiltouristhome.com. In a 1990s building on the edge of town, this modest, family-run guesthouse soaks up most of the overspill from nearby *Sona* (see below). It has ten simple a/c and non-a/c rooms; they're spacious, brightly coloured, well ventilated and nicely furnished with comfy modern beds and individual balconies. A row of four recently added a/c "cottages" outside are fancier but not such good value. ❸–❺

## Mid-range

**Alleppey Beach Resorts** Beach Rd ☎0477/226 3408, ⊛www.thealleppeybeachresorts.com. See map on p.138. Eccentric, slightly Fawlty-Towers-esque hotel offering beachside rooms opening onto common verandas with great sea views. They're huge (the non-a/c "deluxe" on the first floor are vast) and a bit overpriced, but many will consider the relaxing, breezy location worth the extra. Moreover, the food is great. ❻–❼

**Arcadia Regency** Near the Iron Bridge ☎0477/223 0414, ⊛www.arcadiaregency.com. Hardly the most sympathetic addition to the town's historic centre in recent years, but this gleaming, multistorey tower block offers good-value three-star accommodation, a multi-cuisine restaurant and splendid rooftop pool, right in the thick of things. ❺–❼

**Casa Maria** Beach Rd ☎0477/223 0771, ⊛www.casamariabeachresort.com. Modern Keralan-style building just back from the beach; its deluxe a/c rooms on the first floor lack outside space, but the three non-a/c options on the ground floor open onto walled lawns from marble verandas (no sea views). A pleasant, comfortable location close to the beach and away from the bustle of the town centre, through its rates are ambitious. ❻

**Kadalamma** ESI Junction, Beach Rd ☎0477/223 8676, ☎9605 925457, ⊛www.kadalamma.com. Two-storey purple-and-white building rising

unexpectedly from the midst of the fishing quarter at the far south end of the beach. The a/c rooms are small and basic for the price, but impeccably clean; one has a private balcony; the others share a sea-facing veranda. ❻

**Palm Grove Lake Resort** Punnamada Kayal, 3.5km north of boat jetty ☎0477/223 5004, ☎9446 430434, ⊛www.palmgrovelakeresort.com. Near where the canal meets Punnamada Lake, this relaxed resort actually overlooks the water – a perfect, tranquil spot from which to watch the snake boat races. Shaded by areca and coconut palms, its pretty cottages have gabled tile roofs, private outdoor showers and sitouts opening onto the garden. *Palm Grove* isn't in the same league as the luxury places up the lane, but is a lot more affordable. ❺–❻

**Pozhiyoram Beach Resort** JRY Rd, 5km north of Alappuzha town ☎0477/325 6238, ☎9387 827235, ⊛www.pozhiyorambeachresort.com. See map on p.138. Only a 10min drive up the coast road, but a world away from the racket of Alappuzha town, on the edge of a small lagoon and white-sand beach. Accommodation comprises four simple "beach view" rooms, with sea-facing sitouts right next to the sand, and more comfortable, pricier "Kerala cottages" further back in the palm grove, sporting gabled roofs and little verandas. Traditional Kuttanad meals are served in a little restaurant overlooking the waterfront, featuring seafood straight off the nearby fishing boats. ❺–❼

**Sona** Shornur Canal Rd, Thathampally ☎0477/223 5211, ⊛www.sonahome.com. Elegant old Keralan home, with a graceful gabled roof, set back from the road to the lake. The four rooms in the original house, run by an elderly owner who loves to share his knowledge of the town and its backwaters, are far more attractive (and cheaper) than the three new ones in the garden. Among the least expensive heritage homestays within easy reach of the jetty. ❹–❺

**Tharavad** West of Police Station ☎0477/224 4599 or ☎9349 440408, ⊛www.tharavadheritageresort.com. Few of Alappuzha's heritage properties retain as pukka a feel as this former doctor's mansion, which rests in the shade of an old mango tree on the quiet, west side of town. Entered via a typically colonial-era veranda, its interior holds polished eggshell and teak floors, carved rosewood furniture and antique bell-metal curios collected by successive generations. The differently priced rooms (ranging from singles to family suites) are all large and well aired, the only concessions to the modern era being their bathrooms. Meals available. ❺–❻

## Luxury

**Kayaloram** Punnamada Kayal ℡0477/236 4480, Ⓦwww.kayaloram.com. See map on p.144. Twelve antique Keralan wood *tharavadukal*, complete with luxurious interiors and private "open-to-sky" bathrooms, dotted around an immaculate palm garden running right to the lakeside. The location is sublime, offering uninterrupted views across the water, and there's a good-sized pool and open-sided restaurant if you tire of relaxing on your own terrace. *Kayaloram* claims to have been the first resort to make use of relocated period houses, and it's still one of the most congenial of its type. Rates include boat transfer from the Nehru Trophy jetty. From $250. ❾

**Keraleeyam** Nehru Trophy Rd, Thathampally ℡0477/223 1468, Ⓦwww.keraleeyam.com. See map on p.144. This small-scale backwater resort, run by a famous ayurveda outfit, is centred on one of most beautiful period houses in the Alappuzha area, facing the Punnamada canal close to where it runs into the lake, near the start of the snake boat race. Capped with a picture-postcard twin-gabled roof, the old building has a few rooms; the palm-leaf huts in the garden, which open straight onto the water's edge and are perfectly placed to watch the houseboats chug past, are much better value. ❽

**Punnamada** 4km north, on Punnamada Lake ℡0477/223 3690, Ⓦwww.punnamada.com. See map on p.144. Large, formulaic five-star resort, sprawling over landscaped gardens and more than 1km of its own exclusive water frontage. The rooms come in four categories, the nicest of them "lake-facing" and double-storey "duplex villas", which both have their own private alfresco showers and pebble gardens. $175–265. ❾

**Raheem Residency** Beach Rd ℡0477/223 9767, Ⓦwww.raheemresidency.com. The glossiest of Alappuzha's heritage hotels occupies a grand 140-year-old mansion on the beachfront. Sumptuously restored from near dereliction by its Indian-Irish owners, the building encloses half-a-dozen spacious, richly furnished a/c rooms, equipped with carved four-posters (some of which you need a step to climb into) and original wood and glass window shutters. For outside lounging space, you've a gorgeous swimming pool, hammocks on a roof terrace and a breezy open-sided restaurant. $200–250. ❾

# The Town

Alappuzha tends to be eclipsed by the backwaters that unfold from its eastern flank, but it's worth setting aside an afternoon to sample the town's own idiosyncratic charms. Thanks to recent efforts by the local council to clean up the canals, some of the older side streets, with their colonial-era factories and warehouses, are a lot more salubrious than they used to be. The best way of **getting around** them is to rent a bicycle. There's usually someone in front of the DTPC tourist office with a couple of rattly old Heros to spare: if not, ask inside and they'll help you find one.

Because of the intense traffic pouring through it, you're more likely to want to browse the main bazaar, **Mullackal Road**, on foot. It's crammed with a typically Keralan assortment of shops, from gold jewellery emporia to bell metal, spices and fishing hardware suppliers. Beyond its southern side (on the north bank of the canal) is another quintessentially south Indian sight: a row of snazzy a/c **umbrella showrooms**, stocking every conceivable colour and size of brolly, from smart monsoon-grade varieties with lacquered handles to the faintly ridiculous plastic parasols backwater canoeists strap on their heads.

You might well want to invest in a sunshade for trips out to **Alappuzha's lakes**: Punnamada and, further north, Vembanad. Reaching them from town is most straightforward by water. For short cruises, it's possible to charter diesel-powered **motorboats** (Rs250/hr) or more sedate, twin-decked **country boats** (Rs300/hr) from ATDC/DTPC. Better still, dispense with engines altogether and opt for a guided **village tour** in a hand-paddled canoe. Aside from being more "green", these allow you to penetrate narrow waterways beyond the range of the other tourist boats. DTPC offer their own punted tours, carrying two people for Rs150/hr. A highly recommended private operator who's been ferrying tourists around Alappuzha's off-track backwaters for years is Mr K.D. Prasenan (℡9388 844712), based at the *Palm Grove Lake Resort* on the

Punnamada Kayal, 3.5km north of the boat jetty (see p.131). In a slender 10m boat, he offers five- and nine-hour trips (Rs1500/2500 respectively, for two people) via routes connecting the Holy Padma River and Punnamada Lake. A less expensive alternative, charging Rs150–200/hr for comparable trips, is Mr Joseph on ☏9446 584905.

### Alappuzha beach
In the opposite direction, on the west side of town, you pass through Alappuzha's formerly affluent, colonial-era suburbs, which gradually open out as you approach the town **beach**. Although unsuitable for swimming and sunbathing, the wide, gleaming white sands stretch out of sight in both directions and provide a welcome blast of fresh air. A British-built **pier** extends a kilometre into the surf from its centre. Dating from 1862, the jetty once supported three separate railway lines that fanned out to wharfs around the town. These days, however, its stark silhouette receives scant attention, except during Kerala Tourism's annual **beach festival** in late December, when it serves as a surreal backdrop for various cultural events and a procession of fifty caparisoned elephants.

### The Nehru Trophy snake boat race
Alappuzha really comes alive on the second Saturday of August, in the middle of the monsoon, when it serves as the venue for one of Kerala's major spectacles – the **Nehru Trophy snake boat race**. This event, first held in 1952, is based on the traditional Keralan enthusiasm for racing magnificently decorated longboats, with raised rears designed to resemble the hood of a cobra. Each boat carries 25 singers, while between 100 and 130 enthusiastic oarsmen power the craft along, all rowing to the rhythmic *vanchipattu* ("song of the boatman"). There are a number of prize categories, including one for the women's race; sixteen boats compete for each prize in knock-out rounds. Similar races can be seen at Aranmula (p.153), and at Champakulam, 16km by ferry from Alappuzha (p.140). The ATDC information office (see p.127) can tell you the dates of these other events, which change every year.

## Snake boat racing

Of all the craft native to the Kuttanad backwaters, none is more majestic than the mighty **snake boats** – *chundan vallam* – raced each year in around a dozen different locations at the start of the Onam harvest festival. Up to 130 rowers crew these slender, 70m-long vessels, which are distinguished by their graceful cobra-shaped sterns and beautiful brass studwork. The striking design evolved five centuries ago after a local ruler ordered a warship to be built that could absorb the recoil of a cannon. Nowadays, the position of the big gun on the firing platform is occupied by two drummers whose job it is to beat out the rhythm for the oarsmen to follow, aided by a choir of 25, whose job it is to drive the crew on with rhythmic *vanchipattu*, or boat songs. The strongest rowers sit at the front to set the pace, while the vessel is steered by six helmsmen at the rear.

Intense competition surrounds the **annual races**. Numerous religious rituals are also performed, and the oarsmen eat a special, strength-building diet, alternated with fasts; they also have to abstain from alcohol in the run-up to races – no mean feat for your average toddy-swilling Kuttanadi villager. Alappuzha's Nehru Trophy is the main meet of the year, but similar, more traditional, races are held on waterways across the Kuttanad region for the duration of the monsoons – the main ones at Champakulam (see p.140) and Aranmula (see p.153), further south.

## Moving on from Alappuzha

As Alappuzha isn't on the main railway network, but on a branch line, the choice of **trains** servicing the town is limited. There are, however, train connections to Thiruvananthapuram and Kollam in the south, and to Kochi/Ernakulam, Thrissur, Palakkad and other points in the north. **Bus** connections are adequate, especially to Kochi/Ernakulam, where there is a greater choice of trains to northern destinations. Although buses travel to Kollam, **boats** offers a more scenic, leisurely way of getting there. Regular ferry services connect Alappuzha to Kottayam, from where you can catch buses to Periyar, as well as several destinations along the coastal highway.

### By bus

The filthy KSRTC bus stand, on the east side of town and a minute's walk from the boat jetty, is served by regular buses to **Kollam** (2hr), **Kottayam** (1hr 30min), **Thiruvananthapuram** (3hr–3hr 30min) and **Kochi/Ernakulam** (1hr 30min). For Fort Cochin, catch any of the fast Ernakulam services along the main highway and get down at **Thoppumpady** (7km south of the city), from where local buses run the rest of the way.

### By boat

Tourist boats travel regularly to **Kollam**, with the ATDC and DTPC boats operating a similar schedule, departing at 10.30am and arriving in Kollam at 6.30pm. From the jetty just outside the KSRTC bus stand, much cheaper local **ferries** travel to **Kottayam** (service P380; 2hr 30min; Rs10, with four departures between 7.30am and 5.15pm), and a constellation of satellite villages in the backwaters. Regular services run to Champakulam, where you pick up less frequent boats to Neerettupuram and Kidangara, and back to Alappuzha again. This round route ranks among Kuttanad's classic trips, but you'll need some help from one or other of the tourist offices to make sense of the timetables.

### By train

As the backwaters prevent trains from continuing directly south beyond Alappuzha, only a few major daily services and a handful of passenger trains depart from the railway station, 3km southwest of the jetty. For points further north along the coast, take the Jan Shatabdi Express and change at Ernakulam, as the afternoon Alleppey–Cannanore Express (#6307), which runs as far as **Kozhikode** and **Kannur**, arrives at those destinations rather late at night. It is, however, a good service if you only intend to travel as far as Thrissur.

The following trains are recommended as the **fastest** and/or **most convenient** from Alappuzha.

### Recommended trains from Alappuzha

| Destination | Name | Number | Frequency | Departs | Total time |
|---|---|---|---|---|---|
| Ernakulam/ | Jan Shatabdi Exp. | #2076 | daily | 8.15am | 1hr |
| Kochi | *Alleppey–Chennai Exp. | #6042 | daily | 4.05pm | 1hr 15min |
| Thiruvananthapuram | Ernakulam–Trivandrum Exp. | #6341 | daily | 7am | 2hr 45min |
| | Jan Shatabdi Exp. | #2075 | daily | 6.20pm | 2hr 35min |
| Thrissur | *Alleppey–Chennai Exp. | #6042 | daily | 4.05pm | 3hr |

* This train also travels to Irinjalakuda and Palakkad.

# Eating

In addition to the **restaurants** listed below, most of Alappuzha's homestays and guesthouses provide meals for guests, usually delicious, home-cooked Keralan food that's tailored for sensitive Western tastes. Many of them also serve cold beers, albeit discreetly, in little china pots. For **take-outs**, you can join the scrum that forms each evening outside the government "beverages" shop, just off Mullackal Road in the main bazaar.

**Chakara** *Raheem Residency*, Beach Rd ☎ 0477/223 0767. "Chakara" means "bumper catch of fish" in Malayalam, and the accent in this, Alappuzha's classiest restaurant, is firmly on seafood, with specialities ranging from local-style fish curry (their signature dish) to seer fish simmered in flavoursome *moilee* coconut gravy, and crunchy masala-fried prawns to calamari – all fresh off the boats and prepared with minimal oil. They also have plenty of tempting, healthy Continental alternatives, courteously served on a raised terrace looking across the beach. Count on Rs750 for a fixed four-course menu; or a bit more à la carte.

**Halay's** CCSB Rd. Proper Keralan-Muslim restaurant that's been an Alleppey institution for generations. Much of its old-world character disappeared in a recent face-lift, but the food's as delicious as ever. Nearly everyone comes for their blow-out chicken biriyanis (Rs100), which you eat with the legendary house date pickle. It's also good for spicy lamb curries or a range of light Conti-nental meals, snacks and sandwiches, dished up in a dining hall with bare laterite walls under an old-style tiled roof. For dessert, there's fruit salad with ice cream and coconut. Most mains are under Rs150.

**Harbour** Beach Rd. All the food served in this gleaming little seafront restaurant is prepared in the kitchens of the swanky *Raheem Residency* next door, so quality and freshness are assured. You can order grilled prawns, Alappuzha-style chicken curry, Kuttanadi fish, chilli chicken or a range of light Conti-nental meals, snacks and sandwiches, dished up in a dining hall with bare laterite walls under an old-style tiled roof. For dessert, there's fruit salad with ice cream and coconut. Most mains are under Rs150.

**Indian Coffee House** Beach Rd. The usual smudged cotton uniforms and insipid *ICH* menu of *udipi* snacks and rice-based meals, but under a traditional pagoda-shaped shelter on the beach-front. The food may not be up to much, but the coffee is OK and the location pleasantly breezy in the afternoons.

**Saz** VCSB Rd, near Ladder Bridge. This no-frills non-veg place on Vadai Canal does a roaring trade at lunchtime with its fish-curry rice-plate "meals" (Rs40), while in the evenings half the tourist population of Alappuzha pours in for the succulent flame-grilled barbecue and tandoori chicken, served at a brisk pace by black-tie waiters. They also have a full-on kebab counter outside, and offer a range of typical Kuttanadi "specials", chalked on a board on the wall. It's a bit grubby, but hygienic enough and cheap, with most mains Rs100–150.

**Sweet Park** Next to UTI Bank, just off Mullackal Rd. The perfect pit stop in the main bazaar, serving freshly baked macaroons, chilli and cashew cookies, samosas, veg cutlets and flaky prawn patties, with hot coffees and teas, in an open-sided café overlooking one of the main crossroads in the market area.

**Vijaya** Boat Jetty Rd. Great little veg- and non-veg Keralan café serving tasty, freshly prepared thalis (Rs40) at lunchtime, and *udipi* snacks and biriyanis the rest of the day, served in neat white china bowls. It's cheap and popular, and much cleaner than the competition.

# North of Alappuzha

It's almost impossible to discern the northern limits of Alappuzha, as the town's fringes segue into a densely populated wedge of coconut country tapering all the way up to Kochi. To the west, contiguous fishing settlements cluster behind a long, unbroken white-sand beach, where a string of resorts revolves around **Mararikulam**, half an hour's drive up the coast. To the east, the main north-south corridor is bounded by the shores of tranquil Vembanad Lake – the site of several more luxury resorts, including some of Kerala's most gorgeous boutique hideaways.

## Marari and Arthungal

Tourist development between Alappuzha and Kochi is focused primarily on the fishing village of **MARARIKULAM** and its adjacent beach, nestled under the palm trees to the west of NH-47 and the railway line. For the time being, locals far outnumber visitors along this peaceful stretch of coast, and if you can afford the generally high tariffs, Marari's resorts and homestays offer tempting stopovers on the journey to or from the Keralan capital (Ernakulam airport lies less than a couple of hours' drive north on NH-47).

The one noteworthy sight in the area is **St Andrew's Forane Church** (popularly known as **St Sebastian's**) at **ARTHUNGAL**, 4km north of Mararikulam. Catholics who have recovered from serious illness or accidents make a pilgrimage here, hobbling on their knees from the altar to the beach via a path lined with crosses and candle stands. Curiously, it's also a popular stop on the Sabarimala trail (see p.162), and during the season hundreds of Hindu men in black *lunghis* pour through to pay their respects. Behind the main nineteenth-century Gothic church a much older chapel built in the 1590s by Portuguese Jesuits stands virtually forgotten. The best time to visit Arthungal is on Sunday evenings (around sunset), when a congregation of hundreds spills in to the main square for Mass.

## Mararikulam accommodation.

The following are marked on the **Kuttanad Backwaters** map on p.138.

**Arakal Heritage** Mararikulam-North, 3km north of *Marari Beach Resort* ☎0478/286 5545, ☎9847 268661, ⓦwww.arakal.com. A beachside hideaway with heaps of authentic Keralan village atmosphere. Dotted around a sandy plot close to the sea, its five 200-year-old houses come complete with beautiful gabled roofs, traditional railings and original antique furniture. All have shady verandas and hidden outdoor bathrooms – "Mango" even has a tree growing through the middle of it. Hosts Abi and Mini can help arrange bicycle, elephant and boat rides in the area, as well as cookery lessons and ayurveda treatments. From Rs5000 (plus Rs500 for a/c). ❽

**Arapakal Beach Villa** Marari Beach ☎9947 440334. Part-time auto-rickshaw driver Dominic runs this pair of simple en-suite rooms (with or without a/c), a stone's throw from the beachfront behind *Beach Symphony*. They're nothing to write home about, but clean enough, and the cheapest option in the village. ❺

**Beach Symphony** Marari Beach ☎0477/224 3535, ☎9744 297123, ⓦwww.abeachsymphony.com. Kerala has very few attractive small houses to rent as close to the beach as this desirable boutique place run by Belgian couple, Jan and Christel. The traditional architecture of the relocated wooden dwellings is as beautiful as the location, amid the palms of a busy fishing community. From their verandas, cusped arches and lathe-turned pillars frame views through the trees to the sea, while the interiors are a dreamy mix of natural, warm colours, traditional furniture and modern designer fittings. Rates include the run of a private walled pool. From Rs10,000 (US$220 per night), or higher over Christmas and New Year, tariffs are top whack, but you'll still have to book well in advance. ❾

**Heritage Haven** Mararikulam ☎0478/286 5270, ☎9447 414841, ⓦwww.theheritage haven.com. Less than 10 min from the beach, this is a great little mid-range heritage homestay, offering just two rooms in a 200-year-old twin-gabled *nalukettu* raised on pillars in a sandy compound. Smiling hosts Anil and Archana live next door. Rates include breakfast, served on a sand-floored, colonnaded terrace under the building itself. ❺–❻

**Marari Beach Resort** Mararikulam ☎0478/286 3801, ⓦwww.cghearth.com. Large, slick resort complex run by the eco-conscious *CGH* chain, and popular mainly with 50- or 60-something couples from northern Europe. Its 26 acres of leafy gardens, filled with tropical trees, hold an orderly village of whitewashed, palm-thatched villas, each with a low raised veranda and walled alfresco bathroom; the pricier ones also have plunge pools. Ringed by high, barbed-wire walls and a cordon of zealous security guards, it all feels very detached from its setting: most guests come primarily to lounge by the poolside or beach, though *CGH* also lay on culture shows, ayurveda spa treatments, guided nature walks and auto-rickshaw trips to nearby sights. US$375–782. ❾

**OG's** Mararikulam ☎9388 66666. A superbly situated place, right on the sand, with fishermen fixing nets and sorting their catch virtually on your doorstep. They offer two types of rooms: "cottages" (basically chalets in unattractive concrete blocks), or much prettier, primrose-painted "bungalows" further down, which share a pillared veranda. Standards of service, food and maintenance are a bit patchy, and the rates ambitious (Rs6000–7600 per night), but you can't beat the location. ❾

**Pollethai** Mararikulam ☎0484/301 1711, ⓦwww .cghearth.com. Run by the *CGH* chain. This smaller version of the nearby *Marari* consists of smart, widely spaced villas scattered around a grassy coconut grove interlaced by canals that you cross on little wooden bridges. It's very close to the beach, and very good value for the level of comfort, though lacks character. **7**

## Muhamma

Some of Kerala's most bijou resorts occupy prime spots on the western shores of **Vembanad Lake** – a vast, 200-square-kilometre expanse of shimmering lagoon that reaches its widest point at the village of **MUHAMMA**, a major centre for coir production. You can get there either on NH-47, turning off at **Kanjikudi**, or via a more scenic back road closer to the lakeshore. Dilapidated local ferries also run hourly up Vembanad's western bank from Alappuzha (5.45am–8.15pm), heading due east from there to Kumarakom. This was the route being followed by the ill-fated State Water Transport Department ferry A-53 when it ran aground in the middle of the lake early in the morning on January 27, 2002. Heavily overloaded with candidates for the annual government service exams, the 100-seater vessel capsized, drowning 29 people, before local sand miners and mussel-gatherers could pull survivors to safety.

### Accommodation and eating

**Accommodation** around Muhamma is exclusively upscale and expensive, and more formal than the homestays on offer around Alappuzha. Everywhere listed below offers quality **food**, but for a change of vibe, try the rough-and-ready seafood joint, *Vaidyarudde Kadda* (literally, "Vaidyar's shop"), at **Kayyipurram Junction** in Muhamma. A traditional, ramshackle, and rather grubby-looking Keralan tea shack, it doesn't even have a signboard (you'll have to ask a local to find it) but is famous in the area for its fiery fish curries (four varieties), and spectacular mussels, crab, prawns and fish steaks – prepared in pure Kerala style, with a glass of fresh buttermilk (*moru*) to round things off. This is where the chefs from nearby resorts come to eat, not least because the dishes cost between five and ten times less than in their own restaurants – and are twice as tasty. All the places below are shown on the Alappuzha and Kumarakom area **map** on p.144.

**Casa del Fauno** Muhamma ℡0478/286 0862, ⓦ www.malabarhouse.com. If Fellini had ever made a film in Kerala, its set might have looked like this dream villa on the shores of Vembanad Lake. The fusion architecture, given a face-lift by the *Malabar House* chain, blends polished marble and fragments of old Tamil stone sculpture to stunning effect (you approach the house via a mock acropolis of temple brackets), and the guest rooms are light, cool and exquisitely furnished. Gourmet meals are served alfresco in a secluded inner courtyard, on shabby-chic granite tables. And there's a suitably lovely pool in the garden. US$225–275. **7**

**Kovilakam** Muhamma ℡0478/286125, ⓦ www .kovilakam.com. Small campus of five traditional-style chalet rooms in a converted *tharavad*, with majestic tiled roofs, red-oxide floors and pillared verandas that catch the breezes from the lake. The modern interiors aren't as characterful, but offer international-standard comfort, while the open-sided multi-cuisine restaurant makes the most of the location. And (at around Rs4500) rates are low for this area. **8**

**Lemon Tree** Jana Sakthi Rd, Muhamma ℡0478/286 1970, ⓦ www.lemontreehotels.com. Imposing five-star luxury resort right on the lakeshore, conceived in grand Dutch colonial style. All 27 a/c rooms boast uninterrupted views across the water, as does the stylish infinity pool. Facilities include an über-luxurious *kettu vallam* with its own jacuzzi, and floating deck where guests are encouraged to join sunrise yoga sessions. Rooms, which increase in price the higher up the building you go, start at $430. **9**

**Privacy at Sanctuary Bay** Muhamma ℡0484/221 6666, ⓦ www.malabarhouse .com. Run by the *Malabar House* boutique hotel people from Fort Cochin, these two exquisite period properties are the ultimate Vembanad bolt holes. One's a three-room waterfront bungalow, with pillared veranda facing across the lake; the other, set back just behind it, is a relocated backwater cottage holding two self-contained rooms (rented out separately), divided by a central hallway. Both share a large pool set in lawned gardens. And the interiors, are as photogenic as the location. US$340–500 per night for the bungalow; US$200–300 per room for the cottage. **9**

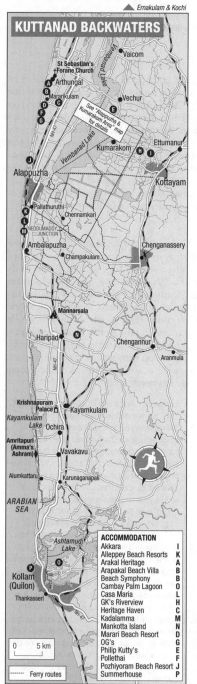

KUTTANAD BACKWATERS

Ernakulam & Kochi

Vaicom

St Sebastian's
+Forane Church
Arthungal
Mararikulam
Vechur
See "Alappuzha & Kumarakom Area" map for details
Kumarakom
Ettumanur
Alappuzha
Kottayam
Pallathuruthi
Chennamkari
NEDDUMADDY JUNCTION
Ambalapuzha
Champakulam
Chenganassery
Mannarsala
Haripad
Chengannur
Aranmula
Krishnapuram Palace
Kayamkulam
Kayamkulam Lake
Ochira
Amritapuri (Amma's Ashram)
Vavakavu
Alumkattaru
Karunaganapali
ARABIAN SEA
Ashtamudi Lake
Kollam (Quilon)
Thankasseri

**ACCOMMODATION**

| | |
|---|---|
| Akkara | I |
| Alleppey Beach Resorts | K |
| Arakal Heritage | A |
| Arapakal Beach Villa | B |
| Beach Symphony | B |
| Cambay Palm Lagoon | O |
| Casa Maria | L |
| GK's Riverview | H |
| Heritage Haven | C |
| Kadalamma | M |
| Mankotta Island | N |
| Marari Beach Resort | D |
| OG's | G |
| Philip Kutty's | E |
| Pollethai | F |
| Pozhiyoram Beach Resort | J |
| Summerhouse | P |

0    5 km

------ Ferry routes

Varkala & Thiruvananthapuram ▼

138

# The Kuttanad backwaters

A labyrinth of interlocking canals, rivulets and lakes, the backwater area stretching 75km from Kollam in the south to Kochi in the north is known as **Kuttanad**. Lines of sand bars and long, thin islands, formed by the action of waves and tides along the coastline, account for this region's unique geography. By impeding the outflow of four major rivers – the Pampa, Meenachil, Achankovil and Manimala – these natural dams have given rise to a crazy-patchwork of inland lagoons where fresh and salt water mingles. Massive swathes have been reclaimed in recent centuries to supply Kerala's burgeoning population with rice, vegetables and fruit, but water still dominates every aspect of life for the estimated two million inhabitants of Kuttanad.

The region's bucolic way of life – deployed to great effect as a backdrop in films such as Shaji Karun's *Piravi* and in Arundhati Roy's novel, *The God of Small Things* – has long fascinated visitors. And the ever-entrepreneurial Keralans were quick to spot its potential as a visitor destination – particularly after it was discovered that foreigners and wealthy tourists from India's cities were prepared to pay vast sums in local terms to explore the area aboard converted **rice barges**, or *kettu vallam*. Since its inception in the early 1990s, the houseboat tour industry has grown exponentially in both size and sophistication, reshaping not just the economy of Kuttanad, but the actual appearance of its waterways.

*Kettu vallam* and other tourist vessels now account for the bulk of traffic plying the canals and rivers east and south of Alappuzha – Kuttanad's principal gateway. However, once you press beyond the wider, more congested channels around the town itself, you enter a world on which tourism has made negligible impact.

Views constantly change as you navigate the narrow canals, enclosed by dense tunnels of vegetation, to enter wide, open expanses of rice paddy fringed by ranks of coconut palms. Homes, farms, churches, mosques and temples can be glimpsed among the trees, and every so often you might catch the blue flash of a kingfisher, the green of a parakeet, a cormorant perched on a log with its wings outstretched, or a Pallas fishing eagle flapping lazily along in search of prey.

Villages and farmsteads occupy even the tiniest islets, with some families living on pockets of land barely large enough for a simple house, yard and boat. They bathe and wash their clothes – and buffaloes, too, muddy from ploughing the fields – at the water's edge. Traditional country vessels glide past you, powered by gondolier-like boatmen with long poles, the water often lapping perilously close to their rims. Fishermen work from tiny dugout canoes, while massive Chinese nets dangle over the banks.

Poles sticking out of the water indicate dangerous shallows. Here and there, basic drawbridges can be raised on ropes, but major bridges are few and far between; most people still rely on boatmen to ferry them across the water to connect with roads and bus services, resulting in a constant crisscrossing of the waters from dawn until dusk.

This perpetual activity provides more than enough interest for travellers chugging around Kuttanad in a *kettu vallam*. But houseboat cruises can knock a hole in even

## A fragile ecosystem

With a population four times denser than other coastal zones of southwest India, the Kuttanad backwaters may seem irrepressibly fertile, but such abundance is underpinned by a delicate environmental balance – one whose equilibrium has come under mounting pressure over the past fifty years from **farming** and **tourism**.

The big shift in Kuttanad's ecology started back in the 1840s, when famine in southern India led to calls for large-scale land reclamation schemes on Kerala's lagoons. By building enclosures of dikes, or bunds, and pumping out the water from inside them, new fields could be created at roughly 2–3m below sea level. The process accelerated in the twentieth century, when giant **Blocks** were formed around the southern reaches of Vembanad Lake (the largest of them, 1500-acre **R Block**, to the east of Alappuzha).

Until this time, Kuttanadi rice fields had only been harvested once every two years. But under pressure to intensify production, the government in the 1940s and 1950s constructed a system of spillways and barrages to flush out the yearly monsoon floodwaters, while preventing the entry of saline sea water, thus enabling farmers to plant not just one, but two annual crops.

It also, however, had a number of unforeseen consequences – notably the spread of **African moss**, also known as **water hyacinth** (*Eichhornia crassipes*) – a free-floating, and extremely invasive, aquatic plant originally native to South America. With its pretty pink flowers and glossy green leaves, the hyacinth may look attractive, but it is actually a menace, starving underwater life of light. Formerly, the natural in-flow of sea water used to keep it under control, but after the barrages were built the plant became rampant, further stimulated by all the fertilizer running off rice fields.

Fishing, for centuries an important industry in Kuttanad, has been decimated as a result. And **tourism** is now adding to the problem, as the film of oil from motorized ferries and houseboats spreads through the waters, killing yet more fish, which has in turn led to a reduction of over fifty percent in the number of bird species found in the region. Some of the houseboat companies are trying to lessen the impact of visitors by introducing more eco-friendly vessels, but so far there has been relatively little appetite for the slower, smaller and less luxurious barges, while the overall amount of diesel-powered traffic on the waterways has rocketed.

the most flexible of budgets, and you'll probably find yourself looking for less expensive ways to extend your explorations of the area. One is to base yourself in Alappuzha, or a homestay out in the backwaters themselves (reviews of the best of these appear on p.143), making day-trips out to villages such as **Champakulam**, venue for one of the big **snake boat races** that are a unique feature of this region (see p.133). You'll have to rely on more humdrum road transport, however, to reach **Mannarsala**, where a Namboodiri priestess presides over an ancient forest shrine devoted to snake worship. But excursion boats and local ferries run to within striking distance of **Amritapuri**, where a more contemporary religious cult has taken root around the charismatic guru, Amma. Her candy-coloured ashram in the backwaters attracts devotees from across the globe, although its architecture can't hold a candle to the elegant lines and symmetry of the medieval royal palace at nearby **Kayamkulam**, where a wonderful set of traditional Keralan murals are the highlight of a small but fascinating museum.

## Champakulam

**CHAMPAKULAM**, 14km southeast of Alappuzha, is home to the **Church of St Mary's**, erected in 1579 by the Portuguese on the remains of a chapel believed to have been one of the seven founded by St Thomas the Apostle. Now a centre of Syrian-Christian worship, the church boasts an extravagantly decorated Rococo interior, dripping with gold leaf and elaborate murals – some fusing elements of Hindu and Christian iconography. It rises from the bank of a broad river where each year, in the Hindu month of Midhunam (June–July), the Champakulam boat race attracts large crowds. The village's own crew recently won the big Nehru Trophy race three years in succession, and the magnificent 40m-long **snake boat** they competed in is stored at a shed on the outskirts, ten minutes' walk from St Mary's. Head to the riverbank behind the church, turn right and follow the lane for 400m past the bazaar and boat jetty until you reach a stepped footbridge; instead of crossing it, keep going straight on until the next bridge and cross that, following the path as it skirts some houses, by which time you'll have the boat in your sights. If you get lost, ask for the *vallam* and someone will wave you in the right direction.

Champakulam is connected to Alappuzha by regular **ferries** (every 30min; 30min), and there are also more regular **buses** from the KSRTC stand. Reviews of **accommodation** in the village and surrounding area appear on pp.143–145.

## Mannarsala

The curved sterns of Kerala's traditional racing boats are said to imitate the unfurled hood of a cobra, and at **MANNARSALA**, near the village of **Haripad**, 25km south of Alappuzha on NH-47, 30,000 carved stones of rearing snakes were inspired by the same form. Dusted in turmeric and vermillion powder, they litter a leafy forest glade attached to the state's principal **Nagaraja temple**, dedicated to the "God of Serpents". Uniquely in Kerala, the shrine is officiated over by an elderly female Namboodiri priestess, "Valliamma", who leads processions and pujas from her adjacent house each morning (around 8am) and evening (6–7.30pm). It is particularly popular with childless couples: on Sundays, many come to propitiate the deity with offerings of turmeric and salt, holding a bell-metal urn (*uruli*) upside down if they've just made their petition, or carrying it right-side up if their wish has been fulfilled.

## Amritapuri: the Mata Amritanandamayi Math

The **Mata Amritanandamayi ("MA") Math**, or Amritapuri as it's more familiarly known, is the home ashram of Kerala's most famous living spiritual figure,

## The hugging saint

On Sept 27, 2003, an extraordinary birthday celebration was staged at Kochi's Jawaharlal Nehru Stadium. Around a half a million people from 91 countries turned up for the party, among them the Indian president and deputy prime minister. The queue of well-wishers spiralled out of the ground and across the city. At the head of it, embracing each one in turn, stood a small, round, 50-year-old Keralan woman wrapped in a white sari with a big smile on her face.

**Mata Amritanandamayi** ("Mother of Immortal Bliss") – or just plain "Amma" ("Mum") to her devotees – is one of India's all-time spiritual megastars. To call her a guru would be both an understatement and distortion, for although Amma does occasionally speak to her followers, she's regarded less as a teacher than an "embodiment of pure, selfless Love" – which she imparts primarily, and most famously, through the simple act of a hug.

Born in 1953 to a low-caste fishing family, "Sudhamani", as she was first called, showed signs of being special from an early age. While still a child she would spend hours in deep meditation, composing emotionally charged *bhajans* to Krishna, having strange visions and caring for elderly or sick neighbours. After her 21st birthday she left her family to escape an unwanted arranged marriage and made a vow of celibacy. Gradually, devotees began to gather around her; in May 1981, a small ashram was founded in the Kuttanad backwaters, in her home village of Parayakadavu. Thereafter, Amma's fame rapidly spread far beyond Kerala, inspiring a mass following in Europe and the States. In the process, her ashram, the **Mata Amritanandamayi ("MA") Math**, expanded into a huge complex of sugary-pink skyscrapers, with a permanent population of 1800 and a transient one of many times more.

When she's not receiving visitors at home, Amma is out on the road, taking her trademark embrace on tour to the organization's 33 centres worldwide. Over the past few decades it's been estimated that she's hugged a staggering 30 million individuals, which explains why her rate has sped up from one to five people per minute in recent years. Yet most of those who experience an Amma hug claim to be filled with a vivid, powerful feeling of love, as if she's somehow managed to tap into their own emotional core. "Her presence heals," declared Deepak Chopra, one of many high-profile fans, among whom number CEOs of some of the world's most successful multinationals.

The years of hugging, backed up by some well-focused marketing and merchandising in the US and Europe, have made Amma and her aides very wealthy indeed. No one can say for sure how much money the MA trust turns over, but the ashram spends vast sums on charitable works: hospitals, free food programmes, schools, medical camps, grants for poor students, pensions for widows, and 25,000 new homes for the needy each year, all receive generous funding by the *Math*. Amma's most public donation, however, was her pledge of $25 million to help tsunami victims in 2004. The district in which her ashram is located was badly hit by the Boxing Day waves, and the MA trust was quick to respond, providing disaster relief in Kerala, Tamil Nadu and the Andaman Islands.

Her much publicized generosity has seen a massive upsurge in Amma's popularity of late. You'll see her photograph beaming from roadside hoardings, taxi dashboards and hotel receptions all over Kerala, especially in the backwaters area. But Amma has her detractors, too, principally among Kerala's Christian and Muslim minorities, who accuse her of peddling a form of Hinduism with links to right-wing political groups.

Whether such claims are based on communal paranoia or actual fact, it's undeniable that Amma, who lives a modest existence in a one-bedroom flat in her ashram, has created an effective form of wealth redistribution, channelling huge amounts of cash from her wealthy supporters to the needy across India.

"Amma". It stands in the village of **VALLIKKAVU**, 9km southwest of Kayam-kulam – a striking vision of pink tower blocks, capped with concrete domed cupolas, rising incongruously above the palm canopy on a sliver of land between the sea and the backwaters. Thousands of visitors and residents may be here at any given time, but numbers swell considerably when Amma herself is in residence – January to April and August to mid-November are the best times to catch her.

Amma offers her famous **hugs** to visitors during *darshan* sessions (Wed–Fri from noon, Sat & Sun from 10am). After 5pm, *bhajans*, or devotional songs, precede a more formal Bhava *darshan* ritual, in which Amma dons the garb of Krishna and Devi (Goddess) and removes successive layers to reveal "a glimpse of the Divine beneath". Quite how this squares with Amma's repeated assertions that she does not wish to be seen as a Goddess is a matter that frequently gets debated in the Indian media, but it's a popular event for her devotees. Other more low-key activities visitors are welcome to attend include various ceremonial chants, meditation sessions, spiritual discussions and scripture classes facilitated by senior ashramites throughout the day and evening.

For those wishing to stay, **accommodation** is available in simple rooms (visitors are expected to put in a couple of hours' voluntary service). Free vegetarian meals are served three times daily. A few house rules apply: celibacy, modest dress and soft speech are mandatory; and drugs, alcohol and non-vegetarian food are forbidden.

The tourist excursion boats plying the main canal between Kollam and Alappuzha all make a brief stop at a jetty close to the ashram. You can also travel there by road on any of the buses running along NH-47; get down at Amritapuri junction, where minibuses and auto-rickshaws run the 4km from the main road to the ashram.

## Kayamkulam

**KAYAMKULAM**, midway between Kollam and Alappuzha on the main highway, was once the centre of its own small kingdom, which after a battle in 1746 came under the control of Travancore's king, Marthanda Varma. In the eighteenth century, the area was famous for its spices, particularly pepper and cinnamon. The French Renaissance social reformer and traveller Abbé Reynal claimed that the Dutch exported some two million pounds of pepper each year, one fifth of it from Kayamkulam. At this time, the kingdom was also known for the skill of its army, made up of 15,000 Nair (Kerala's martial caste). These days, NH-47's endless through traffic dominates the town's ailing economy, together with the local backwater coir and fishing industries. One vestige of Kayamkulam's former glory, however, survives.

Set in a tranquil garden on the outskirts of town, just off the main highway, the eighteenth-century **Krishnapuram Palace** (Tues–Sat 10am–4.30pm; Rs5, camera Rs15) is imbued with Keralan grace, constructed largely of wood with gabled roofs and rooms opening out onto shady internal courtyards. Inside, a small museum displays coins, puja ceremony utensils and oil lamps, some of which are arranged in an arc known as a *prabhu*, placed behind a temple deity to provide a halo of light. Fine miniature *panchaloha* ("five-metal" bronze alloy, with gold as one ingredient) figures include the water god Varuna, several Vishnus and a minuscule worshipping devotee. Small stone columns carved with serpent deities were recovered from local houses.

The prize exhibit, however, is a huge **mural** of the classical Keralan school, in muted ochre-reds and blue-greens, which covers more than fourteen square metres. It depicts **Gajendra Moksha** – the salvation of Gajendra, king of the elephants. In the tenth-century Sanskrit *Bhagavata Purana*, the story is told of a Pandyan king, Indrayumna, a devotee of Vishnu cursed by the sage Agasthya to be born again as an elephant. One day, while sporting with his wives at the edge of a lake, his leg was seized by a crocodile whose grip was so tight that Gajendra was held captive for years. Finally, in desperation, the elephant called upon his chosen deity Vishnu, who immediately appeared, riding his celestial bird-man vehicle, Garuda, and destroyed the crocodile. The centre of the painting is dominated by a dynamic portrayal of Garuda about to land, with huge spread wings and a facial expression denoting *raudra* (fury), in stark contrast to the compassionate features of the multi-armed Vishnu. Smaller figures of Gajendra in mid-trumpet, and of his assailant, are shown to the right. As with all paintings in the Keralan style, every centimetre is packed with detail. Bearded sages, animals, mythical beasts and forest plants surround the main figures. The outer edges are decorated with floriate borders, which at the bottom form a separate triptych-like panel showing Balakrishna, the child Krishna, attended by adoring women.

All **buses** travelling along NH-47 between Alappuzha and Kollam stop on the roadside at Kayamkulam, a short five-minute walk from the palace.

## Backwaters accommodation

Some of Kerala's most alluring accommodation lies hidden away in the backwaters around Aluppuzha, most of it in resplendently gabled **ancestral houses**, where you can while away hot afternoons watching river traffic from the comfort of a shady veranda. These places will also give you a much keener sense of daily life in Kuttanad than you gain from a houseboat. Hosts often arrange canoe or fishing trips along canals unreachable by larger vessels, and serve typical local cuisine. All of the guesthouses and homestays reviewed below – apart from *Mankotta Island* and *Olavipe* – appear on the "Alappuzha and Kumarakom area" map on p.144. Other recommended accommodation on the fringes of Kuttanad includes *Akkara*, in Ayemenem near Kottayam (see p.149); *Green Lagoon*, just south of Ernakulam/ Kochi (see p.175); and *GK's*, outside Kumarakom (see p.151).

**Akkarakalam Memoirs** Chennamkary ☎0477/276 2345, ⓦwww.akkarakalam memoirs.com. One of the few bona fide heritage hotels in the backwaters (as opposed to homestays), in a resplendent, recently converted Syrian-Christian mansion overlooking the Pamba River. You can get there by boat or car (follow the main Alappuzha–Kottayam highway for 11km as far as Pooppaly Junction, turn left and keep going for 2km until you run out of road). Rooms are offered in the old house, with its carved four-posters and oxide floors, or in more modern garden cottages. Great value considering the level of comfort, and the rates include a sunset cruise, use of a rowing boat, bicycles, night fishing tours and guided walks around the area. ⑥–⑦

**Bamboostix** Thayyil Kayal, Vembanad Lake ☎9995 821015 or ☎9995 821014, ⓦwww.istay .in. Australian-owned backpackers' lodge, close to Alappuzha as the crow flies but only accessible by water. Set on a narrow strip of land facing Vembanad Lake on one side and on the other by a similarly vast spread of rice paddy, it consists of a row of lofty bamboo and cement structures interconnected by flying metal walkways, with raised lounge platforms shaded by giant palm-thatch canopies. Accommodation is in 4- and 6-bed dorms (Rs550/650 per bed, or Rs1050/1150 full board). You're totally cut off from village life here (from any kind of life, in fact) but the location is superb. Phone ahead for their Rs50 launch transfer. ❸

**Chakkalayil** Champakulam ☎9847 323875 or ☎9288 185975, ⓦwww .chackalayil.com. Kuttanad mansions don't come much grander than this early eighteenth-century, Portuguese-style residence on the Pamba River. On the outskirts of the area's largest village, it's been beautifully restored, with whitewashed, wooden-floored rooms opening onto a colonnaded veranda on the first storey, and a traditional Syrian-Christian dwelling on the ground floor, where the family still live. Superb heritage accommodation, with a genuine historic patina, at homestay rates. ❻

**Emerald Isle** Kanjooparambil–Manimalathara ☎0477/270 3899 or ☎9447 077555, ⓦwww .emeraldislekerala.com. The real deal: an authentic, 150-year-old *tharavad*, still occupied by the owners in its original location deep in the backwaters, sandwiched between a river and acres of rice paddy.

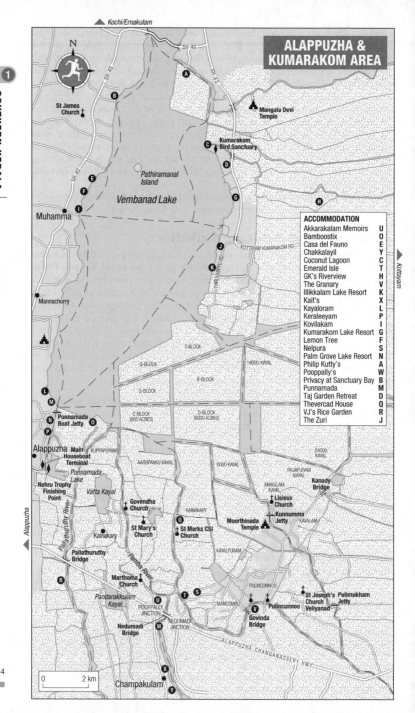

Kochi/Ernakulam

N

SH-40

SH-42

**ALAPPUZHA &
KUMARAKOM AREA**

St James
Church

Mangala Devi
Temple

Kumarakom
Bird Sanctuary

Pathiramanal
Island

Vembanad Lake

Muhamma

KOTTAYAM KUMARAKOM RD

Kottayam

**ACCOMMODATION**

| | |
|---|---|
| Akkarakalam Memoirs | U |
| Bamboostix | O |
| Casa del Fauno | E |
| Chakkalayil | Y |
| Coconut Lagoon | C |
| Emerald Isle | T |
| GK's Riverview | H |
| The Granary | V |
| Illikkalam Lake Resort | K |
| Kait's | X |
| Kayaloram | L |
| Keraleeyam | P |
| Kovilakam | I |
| Kumarakom Lake Resort | G |
| Lemon Tree | F |
| Nelpura | S |
| Palm Grove Lake Resort | N |
| Philip Kutty's | A |
| Pooppally's | W |
| Privacy at Sanctuary Bay | B |
| Punnamada | M |
| Taj Garden Retreat | D |
| Thevercad House | Q |
| VJ's Rice Garden | R |
| The Zuri | J |

Mannachorry

T-BLOCK

Q-BLOCK

14000-KAYAL

R-BLOCK

S-BLOCK

C-BLOCK
(800 ACRES)

D-BLOCK
(6000 ACRES)

Punnamada
Boat Jetty

Alappuzha    Main
Houseboat
Terminal

KUPPAPURAM

AARUPANKU KAYAL

8000-KAYAL

24000
KAYAL

RAJAPURAM
KAYAL

Kanady
Bridge

Nehru Trophy
Finishing
Point

Punnamada
Lake

Vatta Kayal

MANGLAM
KAYAL

Lisieux
Church

Govendha
Church

KAINAKARY

Kainakary

Alappuzha

St Mary's
Church

St Marks CSI
Church

Moorthinada
Temple

KAVALAM

Kunnumma
Jetty

Pamba River

KAYALPURAM

Pallathuruthy River

Pallathuruthy
Bridge

Marthoma
Church

PULINCUNNOO

St Joseph's
Church

Pulimukham
Jetty

Pandarakkulam
Kayal

POOPPALLY
JUNCTION

MANCOMBU

Pulincunnoo

Veliyanad

Nedumadi
Bridge

NEDUMADI
JUNCTION

Govinda
Bridge

ALAPPUZHA CHANGANASSERY HWY

0    2 km

Champakulam

Under an exquisite traditional Kuttanadi roof, four teak rooms have been converted for use by guests, with antique doors, lustrous carved-wood furniture and private outdoor bathrooms. The only downside is that they host noisy tour groups on weekends. To get there, head down the Kottayam highway from Alappuzha for 13km to Neddumaddy junction, turn left and keep going until you hit the backwater, where boatman Babu will be waiting with his dugout. Tariffs (Rs5000–6800) include all meals. ❽

**The Granary** Pulinkkunnu ☎0484/402 8308 or ☎9895 709403. Small, modern resort hotel on the banks of the Mancombu River, near one of Kuttanad's larger villages. Rooms come in an antique "heritage" wing facing the river (but with no views over the water and quite dark inside), or in a (much nicer) laterite block whose upper floor has private balconies to the rear looking across a sea of rice fields – great at sunset. ❼–❽

**Kait's** Champakulam ☎0477/273 6223 or ☎9447 249184, ⊛www.kaitshome.com. Lovely little mid-priced homestay right on the river bank, with just four rooms divided between two blocks, both facing the river in a garden patrolled by pet ducks. Fronted by pillared verandas, they're spacious and cool, with wood-panelled walls and high ceilings. There's also an option in the main house – a typical Kuttanadi bedroom featuring its own private alfresco bathroom. Meals are served in a delightful gazebo jutting over the river. Recommended for young families. ❺

**Mankotta Island** 8km east of Haripad ☎0477/221 2245 or ☎9447 113445, ✉mankotta@gmail.com. One of the oldest, and most atmospheric, backwater homestays, on an ochre-walled working farm surrounded by water and coconut trees. Retired naval captain Jai Chacko and his wife Laila are enthusiastic hosts (Chacko loves to regale guests with the clarinet of an evening). Meals are prepared in old-style clay pots on a wood fire, and the rooms – with high ceilings, Bakelite switches and teak furniture – have oodles of old-world Kuttanadi character, though they're not as well set up as some. Doubles from Rs8000, full board. ❾

**Nelpura** Edayady House, Mancombu ☎0477/220 2336 or ☎9447 473432, ⊛www.nelpura.com. Buried away up a narrow feeder canal off the Pamba River, near Mancombu village, *Nelpura* comprises a beautiful antique, three-bedroomed teak *nalukettu* house set in a neat garden beside a family home. Hosts Chacko and Salimma – university professor and chemistry teacher respectively – work during the week so guests are largely left to their own devices. There's precious little to do out here but unwind and wander the riverside paths. Rates (Rs5500 for a/c) include meals and pick-up by country boat. ❽

**Olavipe** Thekkanatt Parayil, Olavipe, Poochakkal ☎0478/252 2255, ⊛www .olavipe.com. *Olavipe*, roughly midway between Kochi/Ernakulam and Alappuzha, ranks among Kerala's old-established heritage homestays, and is still one of the very best. Set amid lush tropical greenery on a working organic farm, the Parayil family's mansion was built in 1890, and nothing much has changed since – save a few hundred more photos of relatives on the walls. The four guest rooms are spacious, with huge four-poster beds and original tiled floors. The food is traditional Keralan, cooked with ingredients straight off the farm, or from local producers and fishermen, and the surrounding lanes are perfect for leisurely ambles or cycle rides. ❽

**Pooppally's** Ponga, Pooppally, on the Pamba River ☎0477/276 2034 or ☎9343 575080, ⊛www.pooppallys.com. Everest legend, Sir Edmund Hillary, numbers among past visitors to this exceptionally pretty and hospitable homestay, hosted by Dr Joseph Pooppally and family. The old ancestral mansion is a typically Syrian-Christian home with double-gabled roof and guest rooms in twin wings opening on to a central courtyard garden next to the river. They're not overly large, but have delightful wood-pillared verandas. If it's free, splash out on the romantic, 200-year-old *nalukettu*, which sits on stilts above a pond in the back garden (though it does lie within range of distant traffic noise). *Pooppally's* is accessible by ferry or road (via Pooppally Junction, 11km southeast of Alappuzha). ❼

**Thevercad House** Kainakary ☎0477/272 4263 or ☎9447 347416. A relative newcomer that promises to be among the best-value, most authentic homestays in the area. It only holds a couple of rooms, both converted from a superb antique granary, complete with original wood architecture and fixtures intact, and river-facing verandas. Meals are served around a long, ancient table with warm hosts the Thomas family. ❻

**VJ's Rice Garden** Pallathurthy, 6km from Alappuzha ☎0477/270 2566 or ☎91944 611 8931, ⊛www.ricegardenkerala.com. If you'd like to be marooned in the backwaters but can't afford any of the heritage properties, give this quirky little guesthouse a try. Its rooms – a couple of simply furnished doubles and a larger "bamboo cottage" – hold less appeal than the romantic location, on a slither of riverbank backed by rice fields. You can reach it by boat, or by taking an auto-rickshaw along the Kottayam road for 5km as far as Pallathurthy Bridge (with a KTDC hotel below it); cross over to the other side and turn immediately right, keeping to the footpath along the bank for another 1km, where you'll be met by a boatman who'll paddle you across. ❹

# Kottayam

Lying roughly midway between the coast and the mountains, **KOTTAYAM,** 37km northeast of Alappuzha, is the largest town abutting the backwater region, with a population of around 65,000. For foreign visitors, it's a handy stopover on the long haul to and from the mountains, or as a springboard for nearby Kumarakom and Vembanad Lake. But among Keralaites, the town is synonymous with **money**, both old and new. The many **rubber plantations** around Kottayam, first introduced by British missionaries in the 1820s, have for more than a century formed the bedrock of a booming local economy, most of it controlled by landed **Syrian Christians**, for whom Kottayam is something of a heartland. Younger sons and their families not in line for a slice of the estate have tended for generations to leave home and seek their fortunes abroad, and signs of the resulting remittance wealth are everywhere, from adverts for foreign banks to the huge hoardings erected by gold merchants.

Aside from rubber and its famously well-educated workforce (this was the first town in India to achieve 100 percent literacy), Kottayam's other main export is the state's number-one newspaper, the *Malayala Manorama*, which is the largest of five dailies edited in the town. Boasting a readership of 1.5 million, the *Manorama* (literally "Entertainer") has been in circulation since 1890 and has had a chequered history. Fearing the rise of its Christian-minority backers, the Raja of Travancore once closed the paper down, and its owners have been embroiled in several major financial controversies since, most recently in 2006 after the collapse of a banking firm with which the *Manorama* was connected. These days, however, it's going stronger than ever: check out the English edition at Ⓦ www.manoramaonline.com.

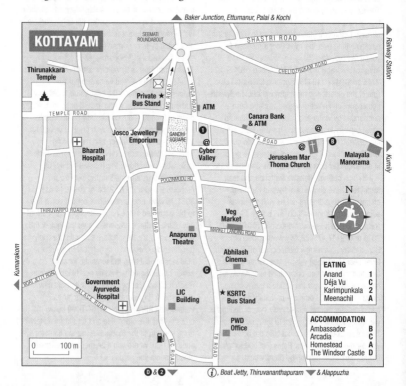

# Arrival and information

Kottayam's KSRTC **bus stand**, 500m south of the centre on TB Road (not to be confused with the private stand for local buses on MC Road), is an important stop on routes to and from major towns in south India. Four of the frequent buses to Kumily/Periyar (3–4hr) continue daily on to Madurai in Tamil Nadu (7hr), and there are regular services to Thiruvananthapuram, Kollam and Ernakulam. The **railway station**, 2km north of the centre, sees a constant flow of traffic between Thiruvananthapuram and points north, while **ferries** from Alappuzha and elsewhere dock at the weed-clogged jetty, 2km south of town.

DTPC maintain a tiny **tourist office** at the jetty (daily 9am–5pm; ☎0481/256 0479). The best place to **change money** is the Canara Bank on KK Rd, which also has one of several **ATMs** around the main square. **Internet** facilities are available at Intimacy (Rs30/hr), also on KK Road, just north of the KSRTC bus stand.

# Accommodation

**Accommodation** in Kottayam is very limited for a town of its size. Those travellers who do pause here tend to do so in one of the resorts or homestays in the surrounding area (see p.151 for Kumarakom, or p.149 for a review of *Akkara*, a particularly nice guesthouse in nearby Aymenem), although the following places in the town centre are fine for a night.

**Ambassador** KK Rd ☎0481/256 3293. Solid, old-fashioned economy place on the northeast side of town that's worn around the edges but well scrubbed. A/c costs only Rs75 extra, but the air coolers are noisy. ❷–❹

**Arcadia** TB Rd ☎0481/256 9999, ⓦwww .arcadiahotels.net. The town's top hotel, occupying its tallest building – a towering, white, angular monster block just south of the centre. Its rooms look much nicer from the inside, however, and are very good value (especially the "standard doubles"); there's also a fantastic rooftop pool on the 14th floor, as well as a restaurant (*Déja Vu*, see below) and bar (*Fahrenheit*). ❻–❼

**Homestead** KK Rd ☎0481/256 0467. The best mid-price option: "your key to a soft pillow" goes their slogan, though the beds in the economy rooms are rock hard and it's well worth shelling out an additional Rs130 for a "deluxe" with more space, better furniture and thicker mattresses. ❸–❻

**The Windsor Castle** MC Rd ☎0481/236 3637. Swanky lakeside resort, set in 20 acres of landscaped tropical gardens on the southern outskirts of town. Facilities include large outdoor pool and ayurveda spa. ❼–❽

# The Town

There is little to see in town itself, but Kottayam's long history of Syrian-Christian settlement is reflected by the presence of two thirteenth-century churches on a hill 5km northwest of the centre, just north off the main Kumarakom corridor road, and easily reachable by rickshaw. Two eighth-century Nestorian stone crosses with Palavi and Syriac inscriptions, on either side of the elaborately decorated altar of the **Valliapalli** ("big") church, are among the earliest solid traces of Christianity in India (9am–1pm & 2–5pm; if the gates are locked, ask at the first house on the left as you descend the nearby steps towards the river). The visitors' book contains entries from as far back as the 1890s, including one by the Ethiopian king, Haile Selassie, and a British viceroy. The barrel-vaulted apse of the nearby **Cheriapalli** ("small") church (9am–1pm & 2–5pm) is covered with lively paintings, thought to have been executed by a Portuguese artist in the early sixteenth century. Caretaker George, who works from the adjacent church office, gives an engaging guided tour, with explanations of the fabulously hybrid iconography enlivening the building's facade. His services are nominally free, but tips, which all go towards maintaining the church, are very welcome.

▲ Cheriapalli church

## Eating

Kottayam may not be a particularly alluring destination in itself, but it has a handful of decent **places to eat**.

**Anand** *Anand Lodge*, KK Rd, just off the main square. If you want a delicious, freshly cooked pure-veg thali, look no further. Of its two adjacent wings, the a/c family hall is the more relaxing – the meals only cost Rs10 more and it's cool inside. In addition to traditional "keep-it-coming" rice plates (Rs40) with three or four vegetables, *rasam*, butter-milk and all the trimmings, they also do excellent *udipi* snacks, including embarrassingly large paper-roast dosas over 1m in length.

**Déja Vu** *Arcadia* hotel,TB Rd. Glass-sided restaurant on the 14th floor of a business-oriented three-star. In a smart dining hall with polished marble floors, starched white napkins and wonderful panoramic views over the town, you can order from an exhaustive multi-cuisine menu (north and south Indian, Continental and Chinese); most mains Rs100–75. Their buffet breakfasts, featuring rich Syrian-Christian-style egg curry and *parotta*, are also worth travelling for.

**Karimpunkala** 6km south on the MC Rd, at Nattakom-Palam. This rough-and-ready place, which you'll need to catch an auto-rickshaw or taxi to reach if you don't have your own transport, doubles as a *toddy* shop, but is legendary in Kottayam for its village-style seafood dishes, such as *karimeen pollichathu* (spiced pearlspot steamed in a banana leaf), *kakairachi* (oysters), served with proper *kappa* (tapioca) or moreish, crusty-edged *appam*. Count on Rs150–250 for the works, or more if you order the other house speciality, king prawns.

**Meenachil** *Homestead* hotel, KK Rd. Quality non-veg Keralan food – Kuttanadi chicken curry, *karimeen pollichathu* – plus Punjabi-style tandoori and Chinese duck dishes, served in a popular little hotel restaurant close to the centre. It's a/c, the service is speedy and the rates restrained (with most mains Rs75–100). They also do set Keralan "meals" (Rs45 for veg; Rs58 non-veg).

# Around Kottayam

Some of Kerala's most attractive backwater scenery lies within easy reach of Kottayam. The mainly Syrian-Christian village of **Ayemenem**, on a spectacular bend in the Meenachil River just north of town, provided the setting for Arundhati Roy's Booker-Prize-winning novel, *The God of Small Things*; it also holds one of this area's most atmospheric homestays. More conventionally luxurious resorts line the shore of Vembanad Lake to the west, where the **Kumarakom Bird Sanctuary** and rice barge trips on the lagoon attract a steady stream of foreign and Indian tourists over the winter. The Mahadeva temple at **Ettumanur**, a short way north of town, is known to devotees as the home of a dangerous and wrathful Shiva and to art lovers as a sublime example of temple architecture, adorned with woodcarvings and murals (some of which, for once, are viewable by non-Hindus). Frescoes of a very different kind, dating from the eighteenth century, adorn one of the region's oldest churches at **Palai**, a fifteen-minute drive northeast of Ettumanur. South, towards Thiruvananthapuram, **Aranmula** is worth a visit to see *kannadi* metal mirrors being made by local artisans; it also has a Krishna temple that organizes a ritual "non-competitive" boat race.

## Ayemenem

Spread around a sweeping meander in the Meenachil River, 5km north of Kottayam, is the village of **AYEMENEM**, where novelist Arundhati Roy grew up, and which served as a setting for her Booker-Prize-winning novel, **The God of Small Things**. Fans sometimes venture up here in search of **real-life landmarks** featured the novel, and there are plenty of them. One of the easiest to identify is the main "Ayemenem house", actually an amalgam of two properties: Puliyampallil House and Shanti House, at the end of a path leading from the Reverand Rao Bahadur John Kuriyan School at Ayemenem Junction. "Paradise Pickles" was a barely disguised version of the real family business, "Palat Pickles", which is still run by Arundhati's Anglophile uncle Isaac (the "Chacko" of the novel), complete with the same slogan: "Emperor in the Realm of Taste". The "History House" of British planter and ghost "Kari Saippu" also exists – though not in Ayemenem. It was inspired by the old residence of missionary Henry Baker, later converted into a luxury five-star hotel by the *Taj Group* (see p.152).

A perfect place to soak up the atmosphere evoked so memorably by the novel is the **homestay** ⚘ *Akkara*, in the hamlet of Mariathuruthu, on the southern edge of Ayemenem (☏0481/251 6951, ☏9447 716951, ⓦwww.akkara.in). Just a fifteen-minute drive out of town, it's an ancestral Syrian-Christian homestead sitting proudly on the riverbank – an idyllic, typically Keralan building, with traditional gabled architecture and interiors that can't have changed much in forty years. Hostess Mrs Shanta Kurian provides warm hospitality and fragrant local cuisine, prepared on a wood fire in her ancient, smoke-blackened kitchen. Phone ahead for directions; access is by road or dugout canoe.

## Kumarakom

**KUMARAKOM**, 10km west of Kottayam, is spread over a cluster of islands on Vembanad Lake, surrounded by a tangle of lush tropical waterways and low-lying paddy fields. It was here that the British missionary **Henry Baker** chose to reclaim land to make a small rubber and fruit farm in the 1820s, which was subsequently expanded by his descendants into a full-blown plantation. After Independence, the estate and its main house were ceded to the government, who designated the core area abutting the lakeside as a nature reserve. Due to its easy accessibility by road from Kottayam, this has since become the focus of a boom in backwater tourism, with a row of large **luxury resorts** lined up along the water's edge. Baker, meanwhile, became immortalized as the "Kari Saippu" (Black Sahib) of Arundhati Roy's *The God of Small Things* (see p.150), while his house, featured as the ghostly "History House" in the novel, has been converted into a luxury hotel (see p.152).

## Arundhati Roy

In 1997, the sleepy village of Ayemenem, near Kottayam, suddenly found itself the subject of intense international media attention after a novel set in it, *The God of Small Things*, won the Booker Prize for fiction. Its Kerala-raised author, **Arundhati Roy**, who'd grown up in Ayemenem and whose family still lived in the area, became the first Indian woman ever to bag the award. *The God of Small Things* went on to sell more than six million copies worldwide, earning its author considerable acclaim and no small fortune.

In language that is by turns hauntingly poetic, playful and incantatory, *The God of Small Things* recounts the tragic turn of events surrounding the visit of an English girl, Sophie Moll, to the home of her twin cousins, Esther and Rahel, in the backwaters of Kerala.

While the sad events at the heart of the book derive from the novelist's imagination, the setting closely mirrors the circumstances of her own life. Like the twins, Arundhati Roy was born in the northeastern hill region of India to an alcoholic Bengali tea-planter father and young Keralan Christian mother (later the well-known social activist and educator, Mary Roy) who fled her violent marriage to settle in the family homestead back in Kottayam. There, in the shadow of their mother's perceived shame, her children led a slightly feral life, "on the edge of the community", as Arundhati later described it. "I didn't have a caste, and I didn't have a class, and I had no religion, no traditional blinkers, no traditional lenses on my spectacles, which are very hard to shrug off. I sometimes think I was perhaps the only girl in India whose mother said, 'Whatever you do, don't get married'."

When she was only 16, Arundhati left home and travelled to **Delhi**, where she lived in a squatter's colony on the margins of the city, infamously scraping a living by selling empty beer bottles. After a spell in the capital's school of architecture, she disregarded her mother's advice and did get married, to the (now internationally famous) architect Gerard de Cunha. The couple bummed around Goa for a while hawking home-made cakes on the beaches to tourists, but the marriage ended after only three years.

A couple of movie and drama scripts (including one with second husband, director Pradeep Krishen) were the first unpromising steps of her **literary career**. But it wasn't until Arundhati wrote a much-publicized condemnation of the film *Bandit Queen*, whose makers she attacked for distorting the facts of its heroine, Phoolan Devi's life, that she gained public notoriety. In the wake of the ensuing controversy, Roy retreated out of the public eye and, while working part-time as an aerobics instructor at home in Delhi, began writing what would, five years later, see the light of day as *The God of Small Things*.

Since its publication in 1996, the novel has caused some controversy back in Kerala. Communist politicians, including a former chief minister and the veteran leader E.M.S. Namboodiripad, publicly objected to its unflattering portrayal of party officials; and lawyers horrified by the cross-caste sexual content tried to get the book banned on the grounds that it was "obscene" and likely to "deprave the minds of readers". Roy, meanwhile, has devoted much of her time and money to **campaigning** on issues such as the Narmada dam scheme, India's nuclear arms race, globalization and the American-led "War on Terror". She still lives with husband Pradeep in Delhi, but is a frequent visitor to the Kottayam district, where her mother is the head teacher of the experimental Pallidoodam (formerly "Corpus Christi") School.

Kumarakom can be reached quite easily by bus (every 20–30min) from Kottayam, 15km to the east. The best time to visit the **Bird Sanctuary** (daily dawn–dusk; Rs45), occupying the westernmost island of Baker's former estate, is between November and March, when it serves as a winter home for many migratory birds, some from as far away as Siberia. Species include the darter or snake bird, little cormorant, night heron, golden-backed woodpecker, crow pheasant, white-breasted water hen and tree pie. Dawn is the quietest and best time for viewing. Although the island is quite small, a guide is useful; you can arrange one through any of the hotels.

Birds, or representations of them, feature prominently in the area's most bizarre visitor attraction, the **Bay Island Driftwood Museum** (daily 10am–6pm; Rs50; Ⓦ www.bay-island-museum.com), just off the main road on the outskirts of Kumarakom. While out on rambles along the shoreline of the distant Andaman Islands, schoolteacher Raji Punnoose used to collect lumps of driftwood, twisted and worn into shapes resembling animals, birds, fish and people. Once finishing touches had been applied with a chisel and varnish, these were shipped home to form the basis of a curious exhibition. Raji guides visitors through the highlights with a breathless commentary that's as idiosyncratic and entertaining as the pieces themselves. Allow at least an hour for the full tour.

## Accommodation

With a couple of exceptions, Kumarakom's **resort complexes** are resolutely upscale and exclusive, screened by the waters of Vembanad Lake on one side and by high walls and uniformed gurkhas on the other. However, smaller, authentic **homestays** are also starting to mushroom in the backwaters and rubber plantations further from the lakeside, the majority of them in landed Syrian-Christian households. See also *Akkara* in our account of Ayemenem, on p.149. All of the places featured below are marked on the "Alappuzha and Kumarakom Area" map on p.144.

**Coconut Lagoon** Kumarakom ☎0481/252 4491, Ⓦ www.cghearth.com. The original, and still the most stylish of the grand-scale luxury resorts in this area, reached by boat from Kavaratikara jetty, just north of the *Taj* (see p.152). The launch glides right into the heart of the complex: a miniature village of red-tiled "heritage bungalows" grouped around a transplanted 1860s mansion on the lakeshore. Although fitted with mod cons, the rooms have a traditional feel, with old wood, open-roofed bathrooms and some antique fixtures. A beautiful ayurveda centre, *kalari* pit and butterfly garden complete the picture. $230–435 in season. ⑨

**GK's Riverview** Thekkakarayil, Kottaparambil, near Pulikkuttssery, 4km by water from Kumarakom ☎0481/259 7527, ☎9447 197527, Ⓦwww .gkhomestay-kumarakom.com. Award-winning homestay, buried deep in the watery wilds between Kottayam and Kumarakom. The accommodation comprises four comfortable guest rooms in a separate block behind a family home, overlooking paddy fields. There's a garden and hammocks to lounge in, and husband-and-wife hosts George and Dai take you out in a canoe to look at the local snake boat and other sights. Delicious home-cooked food is also available. Phone ahead from Kottayam to be picked up (free if you stay two or more nights). Rates include full board. ⑥

**Illikkalam Lake Resort** Karottukayal, Kumarakom ☎0481/0252 3282, Ⓦ www.kumarakomtourism .org. A nice little mid-priced option: eight simple, spacious chalets (a/c or non-a/c) right on the waterside with waves lapping against the garden walls. Each has its own lake-facing sitout (with great views), and extra room to the rear side for children. The owner, a lawyer from Kottayam, stays on site, but this is more anonymous than a homestay, which some will prefer; meals available. ⑥–⑦

**Kumarakom Lake Resort** Kumarakom ☎0481/252 4900, Ⓦwww.klresort.com. One of India's top spa resorts, built on a similarly opulent scale to *Coconut Lagoon*, with relocated "heritage villas" ranged around a huge pool and network of canals, right on the lakeside – though it feels very artificial. $275–900. ⑨

**Philip Kutty's** Pallivathukal, near Ambika Market, Vechoor, 20km northwest of Kottayam ☎04829/276529, ☎9895 075130, Ⓦwww.philipkuttysfarm.com. Luxury homestay on a working island farm, 40min drive from Kottayam in the remote backwaters of Vembanad Lake. Five beautifully furnished villas, built in traditional style with whitewashed walls, tiled roofs, antique doors and open-plan interiors, offer private hideaways set back from the main farmhouse looking across the backwater. Owner Anu, mother-in-law Aniamma and children create a welcoming family atmosphere, leading cookery classes and walking tours of the 50-acre plot where nutmeg, bananas, cocoa and pepper are grown organically. $230–280 in season, including all meals. ❾

**Taj Garden Retreat** Kumarakom ☎ 0481/252 4377, ⓦ www.tajhotels.com. The Baker family's Edwardian mansion – the "History House" of Arundhati Roy's *The God of Small Things* – is the nucleus of this five-star resort. Its old wooden floors, high ceilings and verandas have been extensively refurbished but retain much period character,

though the plush a/c villas and cottages dotted around the grounds, with their pool and private lagoon, possess much less charm. From around $350. ❾

**The Zuri** Karottukayal, Kumarakom ☎ 0481/252 7272, ⓦ www.thezurihotels/kumarakom.com. Newest of the mega-resorts in this area, on a sprawling 18-acre site. Most of the villas overlook a central lagoon, and there's an award-winning spa, complete with sabai stone therapists and ayurveda treatment wing. Starting at around $400, rates are top-whack, even by Kumarakom's standards. ❾

## Ettumanur

The magnificent Mahadeva temple at **ETTUMANUR**, 12km north of Kottayam on the road to Ernakulam, features a circular shrine, fine woodcarving and one of the earliest and most celebrated of Keralan **murals**. The deity is Shiva in one of his most terrible aspects, described as *vaddikasula vada*, "one who takes his dues with interest" and is "difficult to please". His predominant mood is *raudra* (fury). Although the shrine is open only to Hindus, foreigners can see the sixteenth-century courtyard murals, which may be photographed after obtaining a camera ticket (Rs20, video Rs50) from the counter on the left of the main entrance gateway (the priests may try to charge you considerably more, but if you insist on seeing a printed tariff will drop the price to the official one).

The murals are spread over two 4m panels flanking the rear side of the main doorway. The most spectacular depicts Nataraja – Shiva – executing a cosmic *tandava* dance, trampling evil underfoot in the form of a demon. Swathed in cobras, he stands on one leg in a wheel of gold, with his matted locks fanning out amid a mass of flowers and snakes, while devotees gather round. Musical accompaniment is provided by Krishna on flute, three-headed Brahma on cymbals and, playing the ancient sacred Keralan *mizhavu* drum, Shiva's special rhythm expert Nandikesvara. Another noteworthy feature of the Ettumanur temple is its *valia vilakku*, a giant oil lamp at the entrance to the main shrine. Fed by constant streams of sesame oil donated by worshippers, it is supposed to have remained lit for more than 450 years.

Ettumanur's ten-day **annual festival** (Feb/March) reflects the wealth of the temple, with elaborate celebrations including music. On the most important days, the eighth and tenth, priests bring out the temple's golden elephants – seven large specimens, each fashioned from 95kg of gold, and a smaller one half the weight – which were presented in the eighteenth century by Marthanda Varma, the Raja of Travancore.

## Palai

**PALAI**, a small market town 30km northeast of Kottayam, is home to the **Church of St Thomas**, renowned for its beautiful eighteenth-century **frescoes**. Buses from Kottayam and Kochi pull in frequently at the KSRTC **bus stand** next to the bell tower in the centre of town. From here, the church is a 2km walk or autorickshaw ride east along the main road and over a small bridge; turn right into a lane that leads to St Thomas's.

Rebuilt several times (most recently in the eighteenth century), the church has a Portuguese-style white ornamental facade, with a squat spire and nave. Inside, a bizarre spiral pulpit carved from a single piece of teak stands under ceilings richly painted with gold leaf. The *pièce de résistance*, however, lies hidden behind the altar – you'll need to ask the resident caretaker for a candle. Extraordinarily well preserved in the darkness, a wall of exquisite frescoes rendered in earthy vegetable pigments depicts the life of St Thomas and Jesus as the Lamb of God.

The larger, more modern **church** alongside was built in 1981. A finger-bone relic of St Thomas is kept here and brought out for public viewing once a year on the Feast of the Magi (mid-October).

## Aranmula

The ancient Hindu temple at **ARANMULA**, 30km south of Kottayam, is dedicated to Parthasarathy, the divine name under which Krishna acted as Arjuna's charioteer during the bloody Kurekshetra war (recorded in the *Mahabharata*). About 1800 years old, the shrine is a major site on the Vaishnavite pilgrimage trail in Kerala, and, as Vishnu is represented here in the form of Annadanaprabhu ("One Who Gives Food"), it is said that no pilgrim worshipping at it will go hungry. Each year, towards the end of the Onam harvest festival (Aug/Sept), a **Snake Boat Regatta** is celebrated as part of the temple rituals, and crowds line the banks of the Pampa River to cheer on the thrusting longboats.

Aranmula is also known for manufacturing extraordinary *kannadi* **metal mirrors**, produced using the "lost wax" technique with an alloy of copper, silver, brass, white lead and bronze. Once a prerequisite of royal households, these ornamental mirrors are now exceedingly rare; only seven master craftsmen and their families still make them. The most modest models cost around Rs750, while custom-made mirrors can sell for Rs50,000. All of the village's artisans welcome visitors at their workshops, dotted around Aranmula's outskirts, where they'll talk you through the various stages of the manufacture process (there's no pressure to buy the items). The easiest way to arrange a visit is through one of the showrooms in the village centre, such as the Gopalakrishnan family's Viswasarathy Handicrafts Centre (℡9495 438067), on the right-angle bend before the main market area.

# Periyar and around

One of the largest national parks in India, the **Periyar Wildlife Sanctuary** occupies 777 square kilometres of the Cardamom Hills region of the Western Ghats. The majority of its visitors come in the hope of seeing **wild elephants** – or even a rare glimpse of a **tiger** – grazing the shores of the reservoir at the heart of the reserve. Safari boats daily ferry hundreds of day-trippers around this sprawling, labyrinthine lake, where **sightings** are **most likely** at the height of the dry season in April and May. However, for the rest of the year, wildlife is less abundant here than you might expect given Periyar's overwhelming popularity.

Just a few hours by road from the Keralan coastal cities, and Madurai in Tamil Nadu, it ranks among India's busiest reserves, attracting thousands of visitors over busy holiday periods. The park's ageing infrastructure, however, has struggled to cope with the recent upsurge in numbers. Just how overburdened facilities had become was brought into stark relief in September 2009 when an overloaded excursion boat capsized on the lake, killing 45 tourists. Since the so-called **Thekkady Disaster**, strict restrictions have been imposed on how many passengers the boats can hold, but the lake safari experience hasn't improved any; most foreign visitors leave disappointed, not merely with the park, but also its heavily commercialized surroundings and apparent paucity of wildlife.

That said, if you're prepared to trek into the forest, or splash out on luxury accommodation close to the core zone, Periyar can still be worth a stay. Elephant, *sambar*, Malabar giant squirrel, gaur, stripe-necked mongoose and wild boar are still commonly spotted in areas deeper into the park, and birdlife is prolific. Another selling point is Periyar's much-vaunted **eco-tourism** initiative. Instead of earning their livelihoods through poaching and illegal sandalwood extraction, local Manna people are these days employed by the Forest Department to protect vulnerable parts of the sanctuary. Schemes such as "Border Hiking", "Tiger Trail" and "Jungle Patrol" tours, in which visitors accompany the tribal wardens on their duties, both serve to promote community welfare and generate income for conservation work.

In addition, the area around Periyar holds plenty of engaging day-trip destinations, such as **spice plantations** and an **elephant camp**, as well as lots of scope for **trekking** in the surrounding hills and forest. It's also a lot cooler up here than down on the more humid coast, and many foreign visitors are glad of the break from the heat.

### Getting to Periyar

The base for exploring Periyar is the village of **Kumily**, 1km or so north of the main park entrance (known as **Thekkady**). The road that winds up through the undulating hills from Ernakulam and Kottayam makes for a slow drive but provides wonderful views across the Ghats. The route is dotted with churches and roadside shrines to St Francis, St George and the Virgin Mary – a charming Keralan blend of ancient and modern. Once you've climbed through the rubber-tree plantations into Idukki District, the mountains become truly spectacular, and the wide-floored valleys are carpeted with lush tea and cardamom plantations.

**Buses** from Kottayam (every 30min; 4hr), Ernakulam (8–10 daily; 6hr) and Madurai in Tamil Nadu (at least hourly; 5hr 30min) pull in to the scruffy bus stand east of Kumily's bazaar. **Auto-rickshaws** will run you from the bus stand to the visitor centre inside the park for around Rs50, stopping at the entrance at Thekkady for you to pay the fee. The gates close at 6pm, after which you will have to show proof of an accommodation booking before they will let you in. For the KTDC *Lake Palace* (see p.161), the last boat is officially at 4pm, though the hotel can arrange transport for guests as long as the light lasts.

---

#### Serene stopover

If your budget can stretch to it, a memorable place to pause on the long journey from the coast to the Periyar Wildlife Sanctuary is **Serenity at Kanam Estate**, 20km east of Kottayam on the Kumily–Periyar (KK) Rd, near Payikad, Vazhoor (☎0481/245 6353, ⓦwww.malabarescapes.com; ❽). This stylish boutique hotel, part of the German-run *Malabar House* boutique chain, is situated on a hilltop deep in a belt of rubber plantations and spice gardens. The dreamy old 1920s bungalow at its heart holds six rooms ($350 per double), designed in eclectic style blending antique chic with original modern art; all have sitouts or verandas. Facilities include a gym, yoga *shala*, ayurveda spa, mountain bikes and pool surrounded by rubber plants and cocoa trees. Guests are also invited to spend a day with the resident elephant, Lakshmi.

## Kumily

As beds inside the sanctuary are in short supply, most visitors stay in nearby **KUMILY**, a scruffy hill town centred on a busy roadside bazaar. In recent years, hotels and Kashmiri handicrafts emporia have spread south from the market area to within a stone's throw of the park, and tourism now rivals the spice trade as the area's main source of income. That said, you'll still see plenty of little shops selling local herbs, essential oils and cooking spices, while in the busy **cardamom sorting yard** behind the *Spice Village* resort, rows of Manna women sift through heaps of fragrant green pods using heart-shaped baskets.

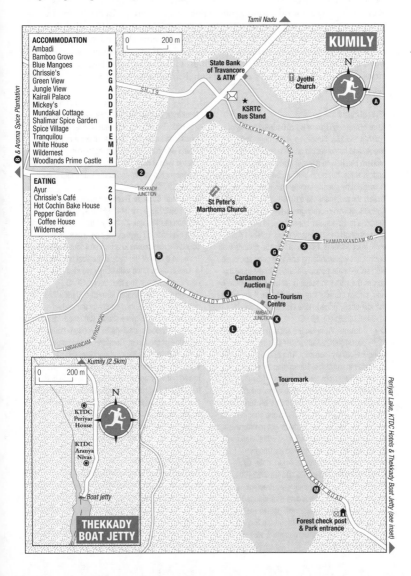

To book any of the Periyar Tiger Reserve's deservedly popular **eco-tourism tours** (see p.160), you'll have to walk down the Thekkady Road to the **Eco-Tourism Centre** on Ambadi Junction (daily 9am–8pm, last tickets sold at 7.30pm; ☎04869/224571) – or better still, book in advance.

Both the State Bank of Travancore, near the bus stand, and the Thekkady Bankers in the main bazaar can **change currency and travellers' cheques**; there's an ATM at the former. **Internet** facilities are available around Thekkady Junction for about Rs40 per hour.

## Accommodation

Kumily has **accommodation** to suit all pockets, offering particularly good value in lower price brackets, thanks to the recent proliferation of small homestay guesthouses on the fringes of the village. At the opposite end of the scale are some truly gorgeous colonial-era hideaways deep in the mountains which you'll need a car and driver to reach, but which provide atmospheric bases for explorations of less visited corners of the High Range. For accommodation in the sanctuary, see p.161.

### Budget

**Blue Mangoes** Bypass Rd ☎04869/224603 or ☎9744 995253. Simple en-suite rooms (with sitouts and balconies) in an impeccably clean modern block, with a larger family "cottage". Rock-bottom rates, but good bedding and a quiet location. Owner Bobby speaks excellent English. ❷–❸

**Green View** Bypass Rd ☎04869/211015, ☎9447 432008, ⓦwww.sureshgreenview.com. One of Kumily's most popular homestays, in a newish house just off the Thekkady Road. Offers 17 differently priced rooms, from basic Rs350 options with bucket hot water to large en-suite ones equipped with solar-heated showers and balconies looking across the valley to Kurusmalai mountain. A lovely rear garden attracts lots of wild birds. If it's full, try the identically priced *Rose Garden* next door (☎04869/223146). ❸–❺

🏃 **Jungle View** On the eastern edge of town ☎04869/223582, ☎9446 136407, ejungleview8@yahoo.com. The best-value budget homestay in Kumily, a 10min plod (or short auto-rickshaw ride) from the bus stand – literally on the Tamil Nadu–Kerala border. The clean, bright, attached bedrooms are all comfortably furnished; those on the upper storey are larger, opening onto a deep, marble-floored veranda just metres away from jungle. Nocturnal wildlife-spotting walks into the adjacent forest are offered for free by welcoming host, Mr Ramachandran. ❹–❺

**Kairali Palace** Bypass Rd ☎04869/224604, ☎9895 187789. Outstandingly attractive homestay in a fusion building that blends traditional and modern styles, with gabled roofs, and wooden railings wrapped around the airy first-floor terrace. Its en-suite rooms are well furnished for the price. ❹

**Mickey's** Bypass Rd ☎04869/222196, ☎9447 284160. One of the oldest guesthouses in Kumily, whose smiling owner, Sujata, offers a range of rooms and cottages, all with balconies or sitouts littered with relaxing cane furniture. The more expensive are larger and come with more outside space. ❸–❹

**Mundakal Cottage** Thamarakandam Rd ☎04869/223317, ☎9447 980924. Philip and Mariyamma Mundakal's budget travellers' homestay, up a side lane off Bypass Rd, comprises six squeaky-clean rooms in a peaceful spot well away from the bustle of the bazaar, the best of them inside a newish block fitted with comfy wooden beds, quality mattresses and tiled floors. ❸–❹

**Tranquilou** Thamarakandam Rd ☎04869/223269, ☎9447 612149. Sunny south-facing budget rooms, or shadier, more snugly furnished "deluxe" ones with wooden ceilings, in a modern house on the edge of the forest. Comforts include piped hot water and cane swings for lounging. ❸–❹

**White House** Thekkady Rd ☎04869/222987. A mixed but very good-value bag of bamboo huts, treehouses and rooms, handily placed for the park gates and run in a welcoming fashion by owner Mrs Lily Joseph. The best are her two rear-side doubles, whose balconies have lovely green views into the sanctuary. ❷–❸

### Mid-range

**Ambadi** Ambadi Junction, Thekkady Rd ☎04869/222193, ⓦwww.hotelambadi.com. Wood and red bricks dominate the architecture of this hotel, packed higgledy-piggledy onto the side of the road to the park. It offers three categories of rooms, all excellent value and with lots of Keralan character. Best are the "duplexes", which have beds on mezzanine floors and balconies sporting old-style pillars overlooking woodland. The location's busy during the day, but quiet in the evenings. ⑤–⑥

**Bamboo Grove** ☎04869/224571, ⊛www .periyartigerreserve.org. Part of the Forest Department's Eco-Tourism project, this eco-lodge between Kumily bazaar and the park gates offers spacious en-suite huts made of renewable, natural materials, serviced by staff drawn from local *adivasi* minorities. The location isn't nearly as inspiring as the brochure shots suggest, but rates do include breakfast, jungle treks and boat trips, making this a good all-in deal. ⑤

**Chrissie's** Bypass Rd ☎04869/224155, ☎9447 601304, ⊛www.chrissies.in. Smart four-storey hotel below the bazaar, run by expats Chrissie (from the UK) and Adel (from Egypt). It's pricier than most homestays in the area, but you get more privacy and better views, and relaxing, homely interiors featuring throws in warm colours, beds carved from local wood and watercolours of Dorset hanging on the walls. There's also a great yoga *shala* on the rooftop, and popular little café-restaurant on the ground floor (see p.159 for review). ⑤–⑥

🏃 **Wildernest** Thekkady Rd ☎04869/224030, ⊛www.wildernest-kerala.com. *Wildernest*'s ten quirkily designed rooms are the most appealing option in this bracket, despite their proximity to the main road. With high, slanted ceilings, red oxide floors and white walls, they're more like little maisonettes: wood staircases wind up to terraces overlooking the central courtyard, and French windows open onto secluded, private gardens. Rates include generous breakfasts. ⑦

**Woodlands Prime Castle** Thekkady Rd ☎04869/223469, ⊛www.thekkady.com /primecastle. Large, efficiently managed mid-scale hotel with a striking Chinese-pagoda-style roof, close to the bazaar. It holds differently priced options on three storeys, varying in size but all immaculately clean; some have rear balconies as well as front verandas. A dependable option if you prefer the anonymity of a hotel to a homestay. ⑤–⑥

## Luxury

**Green Mansions** Gavi ☎04869/224571. Deep in the tropical forest lining the state border, this remote, Forest Department-run eco-lodge stands on a low hillock overlooking Gavi Lake. Its bungalow accommodation, reached via a bone-jarring 30km jeep ride from Kumily, is simple, bordering on institutional, but perfectly comfortable and well placed for jungle trekking and wildlife-spotting trips. Tariffs (from Rs4000/person) include obligatory full board. Book through the Eco-Tourism Centre in Kumily. ⑦

🏃 **Shalimar Spice Garden** Murikaddy, 6km from Kumily ☎04869/222132, ⊛www .shalimarkerala.net. Teak huts in traditional Keralan style, on the edge of an old cardamom and pepper estate, with elephant-grass roofs, whitewashed walls, chic interiors and verandas looking straight onto forest. Facilities include a beautiful ayurveda centre, outdoor pool set amid the trees and an open-sided restaurant where you can fine dine off rough-hewn granite tables. $200–380. ⑨

**Spice Village** Thekkady Rd ☎04869/222514, ⊛www.cghearth.com. Part of the green-conscious *CGH* chain, this campus of mock-tribal huts is the first choice of most luxury tour groups. Its wooden thatched cottages ($300–475) are dotted around substantial landscaped gardens planted with spices and flowering trees. There's also a smart restaurant, a pool, and special wildlife resource centre where guests can attend daily lectures on Periyar's flora and fauna. ⑨

### Plantation visits and excursions

As well as the attraction of the wildlife sanctuary, **spice plantation tours** are offered by almost every hotel and tourist agency in Kumily. Unfortunately, many places have become heavily commercialized, so it's worth shopping around. The only certified organic spice garden in the area, and a particularly enjoyable one to visit, is the Aroma at Chelimada, a short walk west of Kumily on the Kottayam road; for more details, contact the owner, Mr Sebastian ("Baby"), on his mobile phone ☎9495 367837. Most of the plantations charge around Rs300–500 per person for a three-hour tour with guide and vehicle.

A popular excursion for families is to **Elephant Junction** (daily 9am–6pm; ☎04869/320474; Rs350), on the outskirts of Kumily just off the Murikkady road, where you can enjoy elephant rides, help with feeding and washing sessions in the river, and watch timber-dragging demonstrations. In addition, most winters see at least one baby tusker added to the resident herd – a child-friendly photo opportunity.

## Trekking

The windy, grassy ridgetops and forests around Kumily and Periyar afford many fine **trekking** possibilities, with superb views over the High Range, weather permitting. Ex-park wardens and other local people made redundant by the recent Eco-Tourism initiative (which reserved jobs for Manna tribal people) offer their services as guides through guesthouses, hotels and restaurants, and it can be worth employing someone for a day or more to show you the paths to the best viewpoints; check out their letters of recommendation and follow up tips from fellow visitors.

One route that's especially rewarding is the three-hour hike up **Kurusamalai**, the prominent peak towering to the northwest of Kumily, whose summit is crowned with a Holy Cross. As the summit falls within the boundaries of the national park, you're only permitted to hike to it under the auspices of the Eco-Tourism programme, who market the route as their "Cloud Walk" (Rs300). Contact their office at Ambadi Junction for more details.

## Other activities

Although hilly, this area is also good **cycling** territory; you can rent **bicycles** from several stalls in the market, and for heavier-going trips into the mountains, Touromark (☏04869/224332, ⓦwww.touromark.com), midway between Kumily and Thekkady, have imported 21-speed **mountain bikes** for rent. They also offer guided tours, ranging from four-hour/fifteen-kilometre hacks through local spice gardens, coffee plantations and woodlands to longer expeditions, such as the three-night/four-day ride across the Cardamom Hills from Periyar to Munnar.

From the Eco-Tourism Centre at Ambadi Junction, the Forest Department runs **village tours** (6–9am & 2.30–6.30pm; Rs750) to a remote tribal settlement on the Tamil Nadu side of the mountains bordering Periyar. You're transported 10km by taxi to the start of the route, which is covered by **bullock cart** and **coracle** through a variety of different habitats and farmland. Profits go to the development of the local community.

▲ Bullock cart, Kumily

## Eating

You're more likely to take meals at your guesthouse or hotel than eat out in Kumily, but for a change of scene the following are the best options within walking distance of the **bazaar**.

**Ayur** West side of the main bazaar. Quality south Indian thali "meals" (Rs75), freshly made each day and served on banana leaves from a buffet. It's more hygienic (and less manic) than the competition further down the main street. *Ginger*, upstairs, is a swisher a/c alternative offering an exhaustive Indian-Chinese-Continental menu.

**Chrissie's Café** Bypass Rd. This relaxing expat-run café, on the ground floor of *Chrissie's* hotel, pulls in a steady stream of foreigners throughout the day and evening for its delicious pizzas (Rs150–200), made with Kodai mozzarella; check out the specials board. They also do healthy breakfasts of muesli with fresh fruit, crunchy cereal, toast with home-made bread and cakes, with proper coffee. Count on Rs300 per head.

**Hot Cochin Bake House** Main bazaar. The best of a pretty unimpressive batch of "meals" places on the east side of the main street, close to the bus stand. Most people come at lunchtime for the tasty fish curry thali, with optional avioli (pearlspot) masala fry, served on china plates instead of the usual tin trays or leaves.

**Pepper Garden Coffee House** Thamarakandam Rd. In a garden filled with cardamom bushes behind a prettily painted blue-and-green house, a former park guide and his wife whip up tempting travellers' breakfasts (date and raisin pancakes, porridge with jungle honey, fresh coffee and Nilgiri tea), in addition to home-cooked lunches of veg fried rice, curry and dhal, using mostly local organic produce. Mains Rs35–100.

**Wildernest** Thekkaday Rd. Filling Continental buffet breakfasts (fruit, juices, cereals, eggs, toast, peanut butter, home-made jams and freshly ground coffee; Rs130) served on polished wooden tables in the ground-floor café of a stylish small hotel. In the afternoons they also do tea and cakes (including a particularly delicious, very British warm plum cake).

# The sanctuary

Centred on a vast artificial **lake** created by the British in 1895 to supply water to the drier parts of neighbouring Tamil Nadu, the **Periyar Wildlife Sanctuary** lies at altitudes of between 900m and 1800m, and is correspondingly cool: temperatures range from 15°C to 30°C. The royal family of Travancore, anxious to preserve its favourite hunting grounds from the encroachment of tea plantations, declared it a forest reserve, and built the Edapalayam Lake Palace to accommodate their guests in 1899. It expanded as a wildlife reserve in 1933, and joined **Project Tiger** in 1979.

Seventy percent of the protected area, which is divided into core, buffer and tourist zones, is covered with evergreen and semi-evergreen forest. The **tourist zone** – logically enough, the part accessible to casual visitors – surrounds the lake, and consists mostly of semi-evergreen and deciduous woodland interspersed with grassland, both on hilltops and in the valleys. Although excursions on the lake (either by diesel-powered launch or paddle-powered bamboo raft) are the standard ways to experience the park, you can get much more out of a visit by **walking** with a local guide in a small group away from the crowd. However, avoid the period immediately after the monsoons, when **leeches** make hiking virtually impossible. The **best time to visit** is from December until April, when the dry weather draws animals from the forest to drink at the lakeside.

The **entrance fee**, payable at the park entrance on the Kumily–Thekkady road, is Rs300 for foreigners (Rs100 for Indians). However, if you're staying at one of KTDC's places inside the sanctuary you can enter for free.

## Boat trips

By far the best option for wildlife-viewing from the lake is to sign up for one of the Forest Department's excellent **bamboo rafting trips**, which start with a short hike from the boat jetty at 8am and return at 5pm, with a minimum of three hours spent on the water. The rafts carry four or five people and, because they're paddled rather than motor-driven, can approach the lakeshore in silence, allowing you to get closer to the grazing animals and birds. Tickets cost Rs1000 per person and may be booked in advance from the Eco-Tourism Centre on Ambadi Junction. Note that during busy periods places sell out quickly so reserve as far ahead as possible.

As for the **boat tours**, though they are considerably less expensive it's quite a hassle to book yourself on one, and the trips themselves can come as a disappointment. It's unusual to see many animals – engine noise and the presence of dozens of other people make sure of that. To maximize your chances of sighting elephants, wild boar or *sambar* grazing by the water's edge, take the 7.30am service (for which you'll need to wear warm clothing in winter). Your best bets are those run by the **Forest Department** (7.30am, 11.30am, 1pm & 4pm; Rs40). Their boats are smaller and shabbier than the KTDC vessels, but can get closer to the banks (and thus the wildlife) – more importantly, they are the only ones with upper decks (seats on the lower decks are a waste of time). Note, however, that since the 2009 disaster, when 45 tourists died after one of these launches tipped over, only twenty people are permitted to travel on the upper decks. Tickets sell out very fast, so you'll need to be at the lakeside at least two hours before the scheduled departure time (or ninety minutes if you aim to get the 7.30am boat). The sales counters are located just above the main **visitor centre** (daily 6am–6pm; T04869/222027), next to the boat jetty. The Forest Department will issue two seats per person. You'll also need to fill in an indemnity form before boarding, and once on board life jackets must be worn at all times. The least satisfying option is to take one of KTDC's official **boat trips** (daily 7.30am, 9.30am, 11.30am, 2pm & 4pm; 1hr; Rs150), which use large launches with noisy engines; they also only have one deck. As with the Forest Department boats, tickets need to be bought two hours in advance from the sales counter by the jetty; KTDC allocates just one seat per person.

### Walks and treks

Although you can – leeches permitting – trek freely around the fringes of Periyar, access to the sanctuary itself on foot is strictly controlled by the Forest Department. Their community-based eco-tourism programme offers a variety of structured **walking tours**, ranging from short rambles to three-day expeditions, all guided by local Manna tribal wardens. Tickets should be booked in advance from the Eco-Tourism Centre on Ambadi Junction, where you can also pick up brochures and leaflets on the trips.

The **Nature Walk** (7am, 11am & 2pm; Rs100, maximum 5 people) is among the least demanding options, covering 4–5km of level evergreen and moist deciduous forest. Groups are led by a guide who identifies trees, plants and wildlife. You can also do a similar walk at night: the **Jungle Patrol** (7–10pm & 10pm–1am; Rs500) is loaded with atmosphere and the sounds of the forest, though you probably won't get to see much more than the odd pair of eyes picked out in a torch beam. For scenery, a better option is the full-day **Border Hiking** tour (8am–5pm; Rs750), which takes you into grassland and thick jungle at altitudes of between 900m and 1300m. The **Periyar Tiger Trail** (Rs3000–5000) is one for committed trekkers. Guided by former poachers, the itinerary lasts one night and two days, or two nights and three days. Armed guards equipped with walkie-talkies accompany the group, trekking through 35km of hill country, thick forest and grassland to top wildlife-spotting sites in the Periyar Sanctuary, sleeping outdoors in tent camps and eating vegetarian food prepared on kerosene stoves and open fires.

## Accommodation and eating in the sanctuary

For the *Lake Palace*, *Periyar House* and the *Aranya Nivas* you should book in advance at the KTDC offices in Thiruvananthapuram or Ernakulam – essential if you plan to come on a weekend, a public holiday, or during **peak season** (Dec–March), when rooms are often in short supply.

**Forest Department Jungle Inn** 3km east of Kumily at Kokkara, off the Mangaladevi Temple road. An hour's walk (3km) into the park, this simple "forest cottage" sits in a glade frequented by langur monkeys and giant tree squirrels. It's cramped and overpriced, though the location is serene and does allow you to be in position early for the wildlife. Tariffs include half-board; check-out 9am. Book through the Eco-Tourism Centre at Ambadi Junction ⑥

**KTDC Aranya Nivas** Near the boat jetty, Thekkady ☎04869/222282, ⓦ www.ktdc.com. Plusher than *Periyar House*, this former colonial manor has some huge rooms ($125–170), a restaurant, bar, garden and shabby pool – with plenty of marauding wild monkeys to keep you entertained – though as with all government places it's poorly managed. ⑧–⑨

**KTDC Lake Palace** Across the lake from the visitor centre ☎04869/222023, ⓦ www.ktdc.com.

The sanctuary's most luxurious and peaceful hotel, with six suites in a converted maharaja's game lodge surrounded by forest. Wonderful views extend from the old-fashioned rooms and lawns – this has to be one of the few places in India where you stand a chance of spotting tiger and wild elephant while sipping tea on your own veranda – though this being a government-run hotel, don't expect the same standards of service and comfort you'd get for comparable tariffs elsewhere: full-board costs an eye-watering $500 per double room (or $650 for the suite). ⑨

**KTDC Periyar House** Midway between the park gates and the boat jetty, Thekkady ☎04869/222026, ⓦ www.ktdc.com. Close to the lake, and cheaper than the other places in the park, but shambolic and invariably full of noisy groups. Best avoided. ⑥–⑦

# The Cardamom Hills

Periyar and Kumily are convenient springboards from which to explore Kerala's beautiful **Cardamom Hills**. Guides will approach you at Thekkady with offers of trips by jeep; if you can get a group together, these can be good value. Among the more popular destinations is the **Mangaladevi Temple**, 14km east. The rough road to this ancient ruin deep in the forest is sometimes closed due to flood damage, but when it is open the round trip takes about five hours. With a guide, you can also reach remote waterfalls and mountain viewpoints offering panoramic views of the Tamil Nadu plains. Rates vary according to the season, but expect to pay around Rs600–700 for a jeep-taxi, and an additional Rs200 for a guide. An easy day-trip by bus (or as part of a local plantation tour) from Kumily, the grand viewpoint of **Chellarcovil** is right on the edge of the mountains, with the endless green plains of Tamil Nadu falling away below. To get here, take a bus or jeep to the village of Anakkara, 15km north of Kumily, and jump on a rickshaw for the last 4km through the paddy fields to Chellarkovil; hang onto your driver if you don't want to walk back to the bus.

### Sabarimala

The other possible day-trip from Kumily, though one that should not be undertaken lightly (or, according to Hindu lore, by pre-menopausal women), is to the Sri Ayappa forest shrine at **Sabarimala** (see p.162). This remote and sacred site can be reached in a long day-trip, but you should leave with a pack of provisions, as much water as you can carry and plenty of warm clothes in case you get stranded. Though you can get there by jeep-taxi (see below), given the very real risks involved with missing the last jeep back to Kumily (the mountaintop is prime elephant and tiger country), it's advisable to get a group together and **rent a 4WD** for the day (about Rs1200–1400 including waiting time).

## The Ayappa cult

During December and January, Kerala is packed with huge crowds of men wearing black *dhotis*; you'll see them milling about train stations, driving in overcrowded and gaily decorated jeeps and cooking a quick meal on the roadside by their tour bus. They are all pilgrims on their way to the Sri Ayappa forest temple (also known as Hariharaputra or Shasta) at **Sabarimala**, in the Western Ghats, around 200km from both Thiruvananthapuram and Kochi. The **Ayappa devotees** can seem disconcertingly ebullient, chanting "*Swamiyee Sharanam Ayappan*" ("Give us protection, god Ayappa") in a lusty call-and-response style reminiscent of English football fans.

Ayappa – the offspring of a union between Shiva and Mohini, Vishnu's beautiful female form – is primarily a Keralan deity, but his appeal has spread phenomenally in the last thirty years across south India, to the extent that this is said to be **the largest pilgrimage in the world**, with as many as 40–50 million devotees each year. Pilgrims are required to remain celibate, abstain from intoxicants, and keep to a strict vegetarian diet for 41 days before setting out on the four-day walk through the forest from the village of **Erumeli** (61km, as the crow flies, northwest) to the shrine at Sabarimala. Less-keen devotees take the bus to the village of Pampa, and join the 5km queue. When they arrive at the modern temple complex, pilgrims who have performed the necessary penances may ascend the famous eighteen **gold steps** to the inner shrine. There they worship the deity, throwing donations down a chute that opens onto a subterranean conveyor belt, where the money is counted and bagged.

The pilgrimage reaches a climax during the festival of **Makara Sankranti**, when massive crowds congregate at Sabarimala. On January 14, 1999, 51 devotees were buried alive when part of a hill crumbled under the crush of a stampede. The devotees had gathered at dusk to catch a glimpse of the final sunset of *makara jyoti* ("celestial light") on the distant hill of Ponnambalamedu.

Although **males** of any age and even of any religion can take part in the pilgrimage, **females** between the ages of 9 and 50 are barred.

If that is not an option, hop onto one of the **jeep-taxis** that wait outside Kumily bus stand to transport pilgrims to the less frequented of Sabarimala's two main access points, a windswept mountaintop 13km above the temple (2hr; Rs75/person if the jeep is carrying ten passengers). Peeling off the main Kumily–Kottayam road at **Vandiperiyar**, the route takes you through tea estates to the start of an appallingly rutted forest track. After a long and spectacular climb, this emerges at a grass-covered plateau where the jeeps stop. You proceed on foot, following a well-worn path through superb old-growth jungle, complete with hanging creepers and monkeys crashing through the high canopy, to the temple complex at the foot of the valley – a surreal spread of concrete sheds and walkways in the middle of the jungle. Allow at least two hours for the descent, and an hour or two more for the climb back up to the roadhead – the cars wait till sunset. The alternative route from Kumily to Sabarimala involves a jeep ride on a forest road to **Uppupara** (42km), with a final walk of 6km through undulating country.

# 2

# Central Kerala

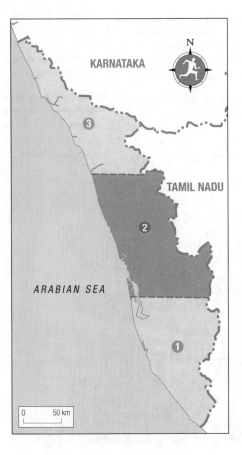

CHAPTER 2 # Highlights

* **Fort Cochin** No better-preserved crop of early colonial monuments survive in Asia than those lining Fort Cochin's sixteenth- and seventeenth-century backstreets. See p.176

* **Athirappally** Kerala's most spectacular waterfalls, best viewed from the romantic treehouse at the adjacent boutique hotel. See p.191

* **The Bharani festival** Join the drunken revellers who gather in March to sing bawdy songs and listen to sword-wielding oracles at the shrine of Kurumba Bhagavati at Kodungallur – an intense Tantric ritual, even by Keralan standards. See p.203

* **Parambikulam** A model wildlife reserve, where elephant and bison roam high on a spur of the Western Ghats. Quieter than Periyar, and with some great budget accommodation. See p.211

* **Tea bungalow stays, Munnar** Enjoy the sublime views of the High Range from an old British-era tea planters' bungalow. See p.218

▲ Kochi

# Central Kerala

T he plains of **central Kerala**, stretching from coastal backwaters to the mountains inland, and north as far as the mighty Krishna temple at Guruvayur, once formed the heartland of the princely state of **Kochi**, whose rulers traced their lineage back to the Chera kings. Its capital, the port of **Muziris**, ranked among the wealthiest in the ancient world, attracting streams of ships from Egypt, Greece, Rome, Persia, China and the Arabian peninsula. When a massive flood destroyed the harbour in 1341, the court moved south to **Cochin** (modern-day Kochi), on the mouth of the Periyar River, and the new docks soon became the focus of the rapidly expanding trade with Europe: first the Portuguese, and later the Dutch and British, left their mark on a city already awash with foreign influences, leaving an enduringly cosmopolitan legacy.

In the city's colonial district, **Fort Cochin**, Lusitanian churches, Dutch mansions and stately Raj-era bungalows rise from a waterfront lined with red-tiled *godown* warehouses. Despite the crowds and commercialism surrounding its monuments, the old quarter holds enough atmosphere to warrant a stay of at least a couple of days. Once you've admired the church where Vasco da Gama was buried and watched the Chinese fishing nets in action on the promenade, there's isn't a great deal to see, but funky little cafés and courtyard restaurants offer inspirational spots to catch up on some leisurely postcard writing, and there are possible side trips to waterfalls, backwater villages, a bird sanctuary and elephant training camp.

After the unhurried pace of life in the fort, the brightly lit malls and hectic traffic of its big-city counterpart across the water, **Ernakulam**, can come as a shock. Epitomizing the prosperous modern face of the state, Ernakulam is central Kerala's business capital and main transport hub and, as such, impossible to avoid – though its twenty-first-century shopping and swanky restaurants may tempt you onto a ferry if you've been buried deep in the backwaters for a couple of weeks.

Whether in heritage hotels in Fort Cochin or somewhere less touristy in the modern city, Kochi's plentiful **accommodation** makes it a convenient base from which to explore the wealth of **traditional Keralan culture** surviving in districts further afield. Temple festivals, featuring drum orchestras, elephant processions and ritual theatre, are common throughout the region during the winter, although the most splendid of all – the famous **Puram** at **Thrissur** – takes place in the stifling heat of April/May. You'll have to pass through Thrissur, an hour or two's train ride north, to reach **Guruvayur**, one of south India's most revered Hindu pilgrimage centres, where an elephant sanctuary stands as a popular sideshow to the religious intensity of the main Krishna temple. Thrissur is also the springboard for **Cheruthuruthy**, home of the world-renowned Kalaman- dalam academy of Keralan performing arts, where you can watch young students of *kathakali*, *kudiyattam* and *mohiniyattam* being put through their paces.

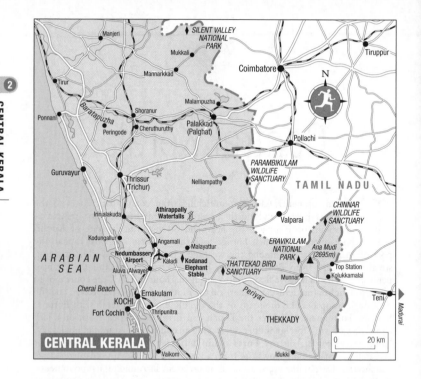

Inland, the greenery becomes more intense and the skies bluer and clearer as you head from the humid, waterlogged paddy and rubber forests of the plains towards the **Western Ghats**. Rising to well over 2500m, the wooded mountains dividing Kerala from Tamil Nadu offer optimal conditions for tea and coffee cultivation, as the British were quick to discover. Vast swathes of virgin teak forest were clear-felled in the late nineteenth century to make way for plantations, and the hillsides of central Kerala's **High Range** still support a giant patchwork of tea estates, interspersed with fragrant coffee and cardamom groves. One of the best introductions to the unique ambience of the tea-growing region is the hill station of **Munnar**, four hours by road east of Kochi. Around the town, some of south India's highest plantations carpet the lower flanks of spectacular peaks such as Ana Mudi (2695m), whose grassy uplands make ideal trekking terrain, and hold a couple of excellent **wildlife sanctuaries** populated by wild elephants and the delightfully gregarious mountain goat, the Nilgiri tahr.

Further north, the town of **Palakkad**, strategically sited on the main highway through the hills, acts as the transport hub for an even more pristine wilderness area, the **Parambikulam Wildlife Sanctuary**, which offers one of the most satisfying nature-based experiences of any park in India. Another off-track destination accessible from Palakkad is the tiny hill station of **Nelliampathy**, the approach to which yields superb views across the central Keralan plains.

### Some history

For more than two thousand years, central Kerala's prosperity has rested on the maritime trade passing through its ports. Spices grown on the forested hillsides of the interior originally drove this lucrative commerce, which lured traders from as far afield as Greece and Rome to the quaysides of **Muziris**, whose precise location archeologists continue to debate, but which must have lain somewhere close to modern Kodungallur, 38km north of modern Kochi. In *Periplus Maris Erythraei* ("Voyage Around the Erythraean Sea"), an anonymous Alexandrian text written on papyrus in the first century AD, it is recorded that the Romans sailed here with holds full of "flowered robes, eye-liner…mica and wine", returning laden with "spices, monkeys, tigers and elephants". **Pepper**, however, was always the prime commodity. Pliny the Elder (23–73 AD) famously complained that trade in the coveted "Malabar Gold" was draining the imperial coffers of silver – a claim backed up by the hoards of Roman coins that have come to light over the years in central Kerala. It was via Muziris that local tradition asserts **St Thomas the Apostle** introduced Christianity to the Subcontinent in 52 AD and where India's first major influx of Jewish refugees settled following the destruction of the second temple in Jerusalem.

After the decline of Rome, **Arab merchants** used their exceptional navigational skills to monopolize the spice trade. They well understood the power of central Kerala's heavy laterite-laden river silt to calm the surf that blocked most other south Indian ports through the monsoons. But build-up of sand also cause catastrophe, as in 1341 AD, when a wave of river mud flowed seaward and blocked the harbour mouth of Muziris.

Half a century later, the local rulers and their merchants decamped to the only tributary of the Periyar River still open to the sea, establishing a new capital at Cochin in 1405. **Vasco da Gama**, whose appearance off the Keralan coast in 1498 was to change the world map for ever, was the first European to spot its potential, and in 1503 the **Portuguese**, by exploiting the raja of Cochin's longstanding rivalry with the Zamorin of Calicut, obtained permission to erect a fortified trade post on a headland to the west, which was christened "Fort Manuel" – the forerunner of Fort Cochin. Several bloody encounters with Calicut followed as the Portuguese fought to break the Arab hold over the spice trade – the Zamorin lost 32,000 troops in a single encounter in 1504. But over time the Portuguese lost out to the superior naval strength and organizational powers of the **Dutch** who, in alliance with Calicut, took control of Cochin in 1613. They in turn were ousted by Raja Marthanda Varma of Travancore after the Battle of Colachen in 1741, after which the **British** gradually asserted control of the area and its sea trade.

A massive upgrade of the port in the 1920s saw Cochin emerge as the most dependable and richest harbour in south India. After Independence, however, its fortunes declined sharply. Economic stagnation set in and lasted until the liberalizing economic reforms of the 1990s. Since 2000, the service sector has boomed in central Kerala. Kochi now prides itself on being a major centre of gold trading, IT, health care, shipbuilding and spices, as well as **tourism**, which has transformed the formerly dilapidated, forlorn streets of Fort Cochin into one of India's busiest visitor attractions.

# Kochi

Forming a jigsaw puzzle of islands, promontories and inlets between the Arabian Sea and backwaters, **KOCHI** (Cochin) is Kerala's second-largest city, and its principal port and commercial hub. It's smaller than Thiruvananthapuram, but holds more of a big-city feel than the capital, with high-rise tower blocks looming over the waterfront, constant maritime traffic chugging through the port, and a

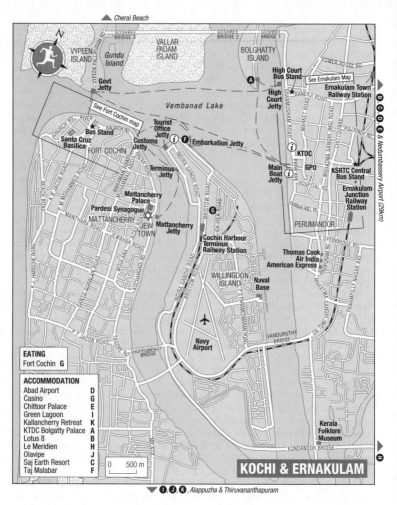

▲ Cherai Beach

**EATING**
Fort Cochin   **G**

**ACCOMMODATION**
| | |
|---|---|
| Abad Airport | **D** |
| Casino | **G** |
| Chittoor Palace | **E** |
| Green Lagoon | **I** |
| Kallancherry Retreat | **K** |
| KTDC Bolgatty Palace | **A** |
| Lotus 8 | **B** |
| Le Meridien | **H** |
| Olavipe | **J** |
| Saj Earth Resort | **C** |
| Taj Malabar | **F** |

0    500 m

**KOCHI & ERNAKULAM**

▼ **I**, **J**, **K**, Alappuzha & Thiruvananthapuram

modern, neon-lit centre, **Ernakulam**. Reached by a network of dilapidated passenger ferries and bridges, the old peninsular districts of **Mattancherry** and **Fort Cochin**, across the harbour, formed the focus of colonial trade until Independence, and now serve as Kerala's chief tourist enclave.

Most travellers arriving in Kerala do so at **Nedumbassery**, the huge new international airport on the distant outskirts, 29km northeast, and few rush straight off. With their photogenic mix of architectural styles, Fort Cochin's pretty backstreets, filled with two- and three-hundred-year-old merchants' houses, are an irresistible attraction. Memorable places to stay, eat and drink stand on virtually every corner – though the quarter's overwhelming popularity with high-spending foreigners has compromised its essentially relaxed, traditional feel in recent years.

Kochi also provides plenty of tourist-friendly introductions to **Keralan ritual arts** – among them the splendid **Kerala Folklore Museum**, on the southern edge of the city, with its extraordinary collection of artefacts from around south India. Top-notch **kathakali** performances feature alongside processions of elephants and drum troupes in the many annual *utsavam* festivals held in the area every October or November, the largest of them at **Thripunitra**, a 12km auto-rickshaw or bus ride southeast of Ernakulam.

### Some history

Kochi sprang into being after the silting up of Muziris harbour forced the royal family to move here in 1405. The name probably derives from *kocchazhi*, meaning the new, or small, harbour. **European** involvement in the rapid expansion of the town was characterized by constant blockades and clashes, as the Portuguese, Dutch and British competed to control the port and its lucrative spice trade. In the 1920s, the British expanded the port to accommodate modern ocean-going ships, and Willingdon Island, between Ernakulam and Fort Cochin, was created by extensive dredging.

These days, with a population of 1.54 million (if you include the greater metropolitan area), it's by far Kerala's fastest-growing city, and its most prosperous. The teeming industrial belt at Eloor, 17km north, and phalanx of skyscrapers springing up along Marine Drive bear witness to the boom Kochi has been enjoying since 2000. Other conspicuous symbols of the new prosperity, underpinned by a thriving IT sector and rapidly expanding port, include a crop of vast gold emporia and the construction of a ritzy new **yacht marina** (the first in India).

# Arrival and local transport

Kochi's modern, efficient **international airport** (ⓦwww.cochinairport.com) is at Nedumbassery, near Alwaye (Aluva), some 29km north of Ernakulam. A pre-paid taxi into town costs around Rs400 and takes an hour or so, traffic permitting. If you'd prefer to be met from your flight with an a/c car, call Mr Haris of Ashik Taxis on ⓣ9288 157145 or ⓣ9656 798481. Modern, comfortable a/c **airbuses** also cover the route hourly, running to Fort Cochin for Rs70. There are two main **railway stations**, Ernakulam Junction, near the centre, and Ernakulam Town, 2km further north. No trains run to Fort Cochin or Mattancherry, while the Cochin Harbour Terminus, on Willingdon Island, serves the island's luxury hotels.

## Kochi by ferry

Half the fun of a trip to Kochi is using the cheap local ferries, which depart from the various jetties marked on the map opposite. A pamphlet giving exact ferry times is available from the ticket hatches by the jetties and from the helpful Tourist Desk at the Main Boat Jetty in Ernakulam.

**Ernakulam to Fort Cochin** From Ernakulam (Main Jetty) to Fort Cochin (Customs Jetty). Every 20–55min; 5.55am–9.30pm; 15min.

**Ernakulam to Bolghatty Island** From Ernakulam (High Court Jetty). Six daily; 6.30am–9pm; 10min. There are also launches (only for guests of the KTDC Bolgatty Palace hotel).

**Ernakulam to Mattancherry** From Ernakulam (Main Jetty) via Fort Cochin (Customs Jetty) and Willingdon Island (Terminus Jetty) to Mattancherry (Mattancherry Jetty). Every 1hr 30min; 5am–5.45pm.

**Ernakulam to Vypeen** From Ernakulam (Main Jetty). This service has two routes: one via Willingdon Island (Embarkation Jetty; 25min), and a faster, direct one to Vypeen (Government Jetty; 15min). Every 30min–1hr; 7am–9.30pm.

**Fort Cochin to Vypeen** From Fort Cochin (Government Jetty) to Vypeen (Government Jetty). Every 10min; 6.30am–9pm; 10min.

**Willingdon Island to Fort Cochin** From Willingdon Island (Tourist Office Jetty) to Fort Cochin (Customs Jetty). Every 30min; 6.30am–6.15pm; 10min.

The KSRTC **central bus stand** (☎0484/237 2033), beside the rail line east of MG Road and north of Ernakulam Junction, is for state-run long-distance services. There are also two stands for private services: the **Kaloor stand** (rural destinations to the south and east) is across the bridge from Ernakulam Town railway station on the Alwaye Road; while the **High Court stand** (buses to Kumily, for Periyar Wildlife Reserve, and north to Thrissur, Guruvayur and Kodungallur) is opposite the High Court ferry jetty. The **Fort Cochin bus terminus** serves tourist buses and local services to Ernakulam.

**Auto-rickshaws** are plentiful and reliable in Ernakulam, where there's a pre-paid stand outside the railway station, but expect to pay well over the odds across the water in Mattancherry and Fort Cochin. Kochi's excellent **ferry system** (see p.169) provides a relaxing way to get around. **Bicycles** can be rented from many of the hotels and guesthouses in Fort Cochin. See "Listings" on p.188 for details of **motorcycle rental**.

For details of **moving on** from Ernakulam/Kochi, see p.188.

## Information and tours

**India Tourism**'s main office, providing reliable information and qualified guides, is on Willingdon Island (Mon–Fri 9am–5.30pm, Sat 9am–noon; ☎0484/266 8352, Ⓦwww.india-tourism.com), between the *Taj Malabar Hotel* and Tourist Office Jetty; they also have a desk at the airport. KTDC's **reception centre**, on Shanmugham Road, Ernakulam (daily 8am–7pm; ☎0484/235 3234, Ⓦwww .ktdc.com), reserves accommodation in their hotel chain and organizes sightseeing and backwater tours (see below); they too have a counter at the airport.

For general advice, the two most convenient sources are the **Kerala Department of Tourism's** office next to the Government Jetty in Fort Cochin (Mon–Sat 10.15am–5pm; no phone, Ⓦwww.keralatourism.com), and the tiny, independently run **Tourist Desk** (daily 8am–6.30pm; ☎0484/237 1761, Ⓔtouristdesk @satyam.net.in), which has counters at the Main Boat Jetty terminal in Ernakulam, and on Tower Road, Fort Cochin (same hours; ☎0484/221 6129). Both hand out maps of the town and backwaters, but you'll probably find the Tourist Desk more helpful when it comes to checking ferry and bus times. Publishing monthly guides to what's on in and around the city (ask for the free *Village Astrologer*), the Tourist Desk is also *the* place to obtain information on ritual theatre and temple festival dates.

### Tours and harbour cruises

KTDC's half-day **Kochi boat cruise** (daily 9am–12.30pm & 2–5.30pm; Rs100) is a good way to orient yourself, but doesn't stop for long in Mattancherry or Fort Cochin, so give it a miss unless you're pushed for time. Departing from the Sealord Jetty on Shanmugham Road, Ernakulam, it calls at Willingdon Island, the synagogue, Mattancherry Dutch Palace, St Francis Church, the Chinese fishing nets and Bolghatty Island. Book at the **KTDC reception centre** on Shanmugham Road (see above). In addition, most of the five-stars fronting the harbour, including *Brunton Boatyard* and the *Taj Malabar*, offer sunset cruises for guests. For details of boat trips into the backwaters south of the city, see p.189.

Day excursions from Cochin, covered on pp.189–192, are most easily tackled by **taxi**: a dependable firm, both for short trips and further afield, is Ashik Taxis (see p.169).

## Accommodation

Most foreign visitors opt to stay in **Fort Cochin**, which, with its uncongested backstreets and charming colonial-era architecture, holds considerably more appeal than the mayhem of modern Ernakulam. Dozens of period buildings have been turned over to heritage hotels and homestays in recent years. There are, however, drawbacks: rates are grossly inflated over busy periods (particularly Christmas and New Year), and there is a disconcertingly high concentration of tourists. **Ernakulam** may lack historic ambience, but it's far more convenient for travel connections, and offers lots of choice in all categories and far better value; however, its hotels do tend to fill up early in the day, so book well in advance – particularly if you're planning to be here on a weekend, when vacancies are like gold dust.

There are several luxury hotels on the islands of Kochi Harbour – **Bolghatty** and **Willingdon** – and a couple of new business-class hotels out at the **airport**. You might also consider a few exceptionally appealing heritage hotel options – including the splendid *Chittoor Palace* and über-chic *Green Lagoon* – **around the outskirts**.

Places to stay in Ernakulam and Fort Cochin are marked on their respective **maps** (p.182 & p.177); the others, including those on Willingdon and Bolghatty islands, appear on the main Kochi and Ernakulam map (p.168).

## Ernakulam

### Budget

**Biju's Tourist Home** Corner of Cannonshed and Market rds ☎0484/238 1881, ⓦwww .bijustouristhome.com. The pick of the budget bunch: a friendly, efficiently run block just a 2min walk from the boat jetty, with thirty spotless, well-aired and generous rooms ranged over four storeys. It has its own clean water supply and offers a cheap same-day laundry service. All in all, unbeatable value – though the *Maple Regency* and *Saas Tower* are snapping at its heels. Telephone reservations accepted. ④–⑤

**Maple Regency** XL/1511 Cannonshed Rd ☎0484/235 5156 or ☎237 1711, ⓔmaple regency@airtelmail.in. The best of the few rock-bottom options in the streets immediately east of the Main Boat Jetty, with 30 cheap, clean, non-a/c rooms close to the city centre. To the rear of the main building, the owners recently converted a couple of old ancestral bungalows, dating from 1891, into pleasant chalet-style "cottages", with red-tiled floors, wood ceilings and long pillared verandas. They're boxed in by the surrounding tower blocks, but excellent value nonetheless, and possess a lot more charm than anything else in this price bracket. Free internet (for guests) in the lobby. ②

**Park View Residency** Cannonshed Rd ☎0484/236 2945. The cheapest rooms in the city, and well scrubbed, with only a few smudges on the walls (though the bathrooms can be fusty). A bargain all the same, with rooms for less than Rs300. ①–②

**Saas Tower** Cannonshed Rd ☎0484/236 5319, ⓦwww.saastower.com. Since its refit, this tower block hotel, with 72 well-furnished rooms, has begun to rival nearby *Biju's* for quality and price at the upper end of the budget category. Singles from Rs300, and also some a/c options. ③–⑤

### Mid-range

**Government Guesthouse** Shanmugham Rd ☎0484/236 0502. The maharaja of Kerala's great-value *Government Guesthouse*, in a shiny eight-storey tower overlooking the harbour. Centred on a vast atrium lobby, with acres of brass hand rails and polished marble, its rooms offer comfort comparable to a four-star business-class hotel, only at amazingly low rates (Rs1500 per double, and they do single occupancy). Advance reservation, as with all Kerala state guesthouses, can be hit-and-miss, with priority given to government officials; if they have any free, ask for a sea-facing room at the top of the building. ⑤

**Grand** MG Rd ☎0484/238 2061, ⓦwww .grandhotelkerala.com. This is the most classically glamorous place to stay in central Ernakulam. Spread over three floors of a 1960s building, its relaxing a/c rooms are done out in retro-colonial style, with varnished wood floors and split-cane blinds. Surprisingly low tariffs given the level of comfort and location. ⑥–⑦

**Metropolitan** Chavar Rd ☎0484/237 5285, ⓦwww.metropolitancochin.com. Small, good-value business three-star close to Ernakulam Junction station – well placed for late-night arrivals and early-morning departures – with the usual multi-cuisine restaurant, 24hr coffee shop and bar. It's worth forking out an extra Rs400 for the much nicer "superior" or "deluxe" options. ⑥–⑦

**Sealord** Shanmugham Rd ☎0484/238 2472, ⓦwww.sealordhotels.com. The high-rise *Sealord*, near the High Court Jetty, has been an institution in the city for four decades and, with its handsome new interiors, offers excellent value for money. Their "deluxe" rooms are much better maintained than the "standard" ones (ask for the top floor), and there's a rooftop terrace restaurant and bar. ⑥–⑦

Travancore Court Warriam Rd ☎0484/235 1120, ⓦwww.travancorecourt.com. Modern, international-standard high-rise hotel close to the station. It's popular with visiting tour groups thanks to its competitive rates and facilities, which include a splendid rooftop pool and wooden sun deck. It's also famous locally for being owned by Malayali screen legend, Mohanlal. ❼–❽

Yuvarani Residency Jos Junction, MG Rd ☎0484/237 7040, ⓦwww.yuvaraniresidency .com. Comfortable, central and well-managed three-star with a choice of carpeted or tiled rooms – and especially good showers. The popular Keralan seafood restaurant hosts live music recitals daily (except Tues), and there's a bar and a coffee shop. ❺–❻

### Luxury

Avenue Regent 39/2206 MG Rd ☎0484/237 7977, ⓦwww.avenueregent.com. Slick, central four-star, close to the railway station and main shopping area, with a couple of restaurants, 24hr coffee shop and bar. Expect only the highest standards, as this place doubles as a well-respected hotel-management training college. From Rs7000. ❾

Le Meridien Maradu ☎0484/270 5777, ⓦwww .starwoodhotels.com (See "Kochi and Ernakulam" map, p.168). Luxury five-star on the southern outskirts of the city centre, popular mainly with business clients, flight crews and tour groups. In addition to 223 rooms overlooking the backwaters, the complex holds glitzy shopping arcades, an ayurveda spa and a wide choice of food and drinks outlets. Charmless by comparison with places across the water, but efficient and offering compet-itive rates online, from Rs5000. ❾

Taj Gateway Shanmugham Rd ☎0484/237 1471, ⓦwww.tajhotels.com. Ernakulam's most estab-lished business hotel, in a prime location overlooking the harbour, with all the usual *Taj Group* five-star trimmings, but small rooms for the price and not a particularly nice pool. $120–300. ❾

## Fort Cochin

### Budget

🏃 Adam's Old Inn 1/430 Burgher St ☎0484/221 8870, ⓦwww.adamsoldinn .com. Since its recent makeover, *Adam's* has estab-lished itself as the best of the budget options in the Fort district, with well-scrubbed little en-suite rooms opening on to a central corridor – only the "deluxe" one to the rear has a terrace. There's a helpful travel agent on the ground floor. ❷–❸

Elite Princess St ☎0484/221 5733. Several floors of basic, but clean and inexpensive, non-a/c rooms

(plus a few a/c options), stacked around a central gallery. It's a bit humid inside, but the rooms and landings are repainted annually, and the bathrooms are well scrubbed. ❷–❸

Orion 926 KL Bernard Rd ☎0484/321 9312, 9895 524797, ⓔmail@orionhomestay.com. Impec-cable little guesthouse on the quiet south side of town. Avoid rooms in the red-tiled family home, which get uncomfortably hot, in favour of one in the new multistorey block across the road: these are great value, with comfy beds, little balconies, wi-fi, and a/c for an additional Rs400. ❹

Oy's Burgher St ☎9947 594903, ⓦoys.co.in. Pleasant, clean and friendly backpackers' hideaway, with just three cosy rooms, just down the lane from *Kashi Arts*. Barred windows look onto a little raised terrace and there's a hip little travellers' café on the ground floor. ❸–❹

Santa Cruz Peter Celli St ☎0484/221 6250, ☎9847 518598. Half of the rooms in this small guesthouse behind St Francis' Church have windows opening onto an enclosed corridor, but the others are well ventilated – and they're all impec-cably clean, neatly tiled and freshly painted throughout, with new beds. A/c for an extra Rs600. Good value. ❷–❸

Sonnetta Residency 1/387 Princess St ☎0484/221 5744, ☎9895 543555, ⓔmail @sonnettaresidency.com. This small guesthouse opposite *The Old Courtyard* has to be one of the cleanest places to stay in Kerala: the surfaces are gleaming, bed linen boil-washed and bathrooms polished. It lacks character, and has no outside sitting space, but is efficiently run and provides a secure, convenient base, with some of the cheapest a/c rooms in the district. ❹–❺

Spencer Home 1/298 Parade Rd ☎0484/221 5049. Warm-toned wood pillars and gleaming ceramic-tiled floors line the verandas fronting this Portuguese-era house's eleven immaculate rooms, which open onto a painstakingly kept garden. Peaceful and good value for the area. A/c Rs500 extra. ❹

### Mid-range

Ballard Bungalow River Rd ☎0484/221 5854, ⓦwww.cochinballard.com. Eighteenth-century Dutch mansion, later used as the residence of the British Collector of Cochin, now converted into a good-value mid-range hotel run by the local Diocese. With their garish 1980s-style bedroom furniture, the ecclesiastical owners haven't quite grasped the heritage concept, but the original wood floors have come through the renovation unscathed and the place retains plenty of period atmosphere. Friendly, helpful staff. ❻–❼

**Bernard Bungalow** 1/297 Parade Rd ☎0484/221 6162, ☎9847 427999, ⓦwww.bernardbungalow .com. Half-a-dozen large, airy en-suite rooms, some with lovely new teak floors, in a 300-year-old Dutch house run by a welcoming couple. Despite some heavy-handed renovation, lots of historic atmosphere remains, and the accommodation is comfortable for the price. ⑥–⑦

**Chiramel Residency** 1/296 Lilly St ☎0484/221 7310, ⓦwww.chiramelhomestay.com. A great seventeenth-century heritage homestay, with welcoming owners and five lofty and carefully restored non-a/c rooms set around a fancily furnished communal sitting room. All have big wooden beds, teak floors and modern bathrooms. ⑤–⑥

**Delight** Ridsdale Rd, opposite the parade ground ☎0484/221 7658, ☎9846 121421, ⓦwww .delightfulhomestay.com. Occupying an annexe tacked onto a splendid 300-year-old Portuguese mansion, David and Flowery's homestay holds seven spacious, comfortable and well-aired rooms, all equipped with new bathrooms and quiet ceiling fans; some open onto a lovely courtyard garden; another has a long veranda overlooking the parade ground; and there's a high-ceilinged salon with original teak floors to lounge in. Breakfast available. ⑤–⑦

**Fort House** 2/6A Calvathy Rd ☎0484/221 7103, ⓦwww.forthousecochin.com. Stylishly simple rooms ranged along the sides of a sandy courtyard littered with pot plants and votive terracotta statues, cooled by breezes blowing straight off the waterfront. Those in the much preferable original block (rooms 1–6) have white walls and red-oxide floors, comfy king-sized beds with lathe-turned legs, and good showers in their chic little wet-room bathrooms – though the a/c units can be noisy. Avoid the older budget block on the west side, which is a rip-off. Rates include breakfast, and there's a good waterside restaurant on site (see p.186). ⑥–⑦

**Kapithan Inn** 1/931 KL Bernard Rd ☎0484/221 6560, ⓦwww.kapithaninn.com. Scrupulously clean, very nicely furnished rooms in a friendly homestay behind Santa Cruz Basilica, with four smarter, larger a/c cottages to the rear (large enough for families). Bargain rates for the level of comfort. ③–⑥

**Leelu** Queiros St ☎0484/221 5377, ☎9846 055377, ⓦwww.leeluhomestay.com. A very welcoming little homestay, tucked away down a quiet lane in a former family home that's been completely modernized. Its cheerfully decorated guest rooms are spacious, with squashy mattresses, huge bathrooms and optional a/c

(Rs500 extra). Landlady Mrs Leelu Roy also offers popular daily cookery classes (non-guests welcome). Especially recommended for women travellers. ⑤–⑥

**Napier House** Napier Lane, off Napier St ☎0484/221 5715, ☎9567 761263, ⓦwww .napierhouse.com. Relaxing, low-key guesthouse in a 120-year-old Dutch house. The interiors have been done in a somewhat anodyne Western style, but they're comfortable and some have bathtubs. The one outstanding room is the suite, which has preserved its original teak floorboards and opens onto a private balcony overlooking the street. Breakfast (included in the rate) is served on a pleasant common terrace. ⑥–⑧

**The Old Courtyard** 1/371–2 Princess St ☎0484/221 6302, ⓦwww.oldcourtyard .com. A gem of a heritage hotel, whose eight rooms flank a photogenic seventeenth-century courtyard framed by elegant Portuguese arches and bands of original *azulejo* tiles. For once the decor and antique furnishings (including romantic four-posters) are in keeping with the building – though some may find them dark and lacking modern refinements. Rooms on the upper storey are less disturbed by noise from the courtyard restaurant (see p.187). ⑧–⑨

**Raintree** 1/618 Peter Celli St ☎0484/325 1489, ☎9847 029000, ⓦwww.fortcochin.com. Five outstandingly smart rooms furnished in modern style (two of them with tiny balconies) in a cosy guesthouse that's within easy walking distance of the sights, but still tucked away. The really nice thing about this place is its plant-filled roof terrace, which has panoramic views over the Basilica and the old Portuguese and Dutch houses of the neigh-bourhood. ⑥

**Secret Garden** 11/745 Bishop Garden Lane 2, near Pattalam Market ☎9895 581489, ⓦwww.secretgarden.in. Buried in a maze of narrow back lanes, this is a hidden gem of a heritage guesthouse, run by Icelandic architect, Thóra Guðmundsdóttir. The four white-walled rooms, which have high wooden ceilings, hand-carved beds and traditional terracotta-tiled floors, all open on to balconies fronting an exotic garden with a good-size pool. Only a stone's throw from the heart of Fort Cochin, but tranquil and relaxing, and more luxurious than many starred hotels. Rates (Rs5500–6000 in high season) include (optional) morning yoga, and use of the house computer, books and bicycles. ⑧

**Walton's Homestay** 1/39 Princess St ☎0484/221 5309, ☎9249 721935, ⓦwww.waltonshomestay.com. Among Cochin's most characterful homestays, run by philosopher and local historian Mr Christopher Edward Walton, in a centuries-old Dutch house. The rooms, many of which open onto a delightful rear garden busy with birdlife, come in three categories and have all been beautifully renovated, with modern bathrooms, solar-powered hot water and comfy beds; all have the option of a/c (Rs400 extra). Facilities include a book-swap library and in-house yoga classes; breakfast (included in tariff) is served on a communal terrace. ⑤–⑥

## Luxury

**Brunton Boatyard** Bellar Rd, next to Fort Cochin Government Boat Jetty ☎0484/221 8221, ⓦwww .cghearth.com. The fort's grandest hotel, built on the site of an eighteenth-century boatyard. The architecture and furnishings set out to replicate the feel of the British era, with antique *punkah* fans dangling from the lobby ceiling, portraits of old worthies and Dutch charts on the walls, and a billiards table set against Keralan carved wood and whitewash. Two types of room are offered, both overlooking the harbour (you get sea views from your bathtub in the deluxe sea-facing) – everything in them is painstakingly in period, down to the Bakelite switches and high beds. Facilities include three speciality restaurants (see p.186), an ayurveda centre and a spectacular, granite-lined garden pool, right on the harbourside. $335–445. ⑨

**Koder House** Tower Rd ☎0484/221 8485, ⓦwww.koderhouse.com. One of the Fort's newest boutique hotels, in a converted 200-year-old house that originally belonged to a prominent Jewish merchant (poets, painters and visiting dignitaries used to attend the Koder family's legendary Sabbath suppers in the early 1900s). The imposing red, double-fronted facade is less alluring than its interiors, with their long, dark wood floors, original art and antique furniture. Six sumptuous suites are on offer, from around $375; there's a restaurant and ayurvedic spa. ⑨

**Malabar House** 1/268 Parade Rd ☎0484/221 6666, ⓦwww.malabarhouse.com. Fort Cochin's original and most stylish boutique hotel is set in a historic eighteenth-century mansion at the bottom of the parade ground. Decorated with antiques and contemporary Keralan art, the interiors are a hip mix of traditional charm and European chic, centred on a serene temple-style courtyard pool. You've a choice between deluxe rooms on the ground floor, or more spacious roof garden suites. Tariffs ($340–450) include a sumptuous buffet breakfast. ⑨

🏃 **The Old Harbour** 1/328, Tower Rd ☎0484/221 8006 or ☎9847 029000, ⓦwww.oldharbourhotel.com. This 300-year-old

former Portuguese hospice, later occupied by a firm of British tea brokers, was recently restored under the direction of German architect Karl Damschen (of *Brunton Boatyard* and *Surya Samudra* fame). A storehouse of graceful Lusitanian arches, lathe-turned wood pillars and teak floors, it now accommodates one of Kerala's top heritage hotels, in a prime location near the Chinese fishing nets. The thirteen individually styled rooms either have private balconies facing an internal courtyard or open onto the garden and large pool, and there are also a handful of separate "cottages" in the grounds, each with "open-to-sky" bathrooms and verandas. Rs7500–14,600 ($165–320). ⑨

**The Old Lighthouse Bristow** Beach Rd ☎0484/305 0102, ⓦwww.oldlighthousehotel.com. This is the most hip – and expensive – of Fort Cochin's boutique places, featuring ultramodern interiors that contrast sharply with the 1920s property, former home of the British port architect, Sir Robert Bristow. Striking antique sculptures adorn the walkways, which look across a rear terrace to the harbour mouth. You can choose between six garden-view rooms (Rs17,500/$385), three more spacious deluxe suites in the main house (Rs23,000/$500), or two super-luxurious villas (Rs29,000/$640). There's a spa, pool, cool lounge bar and terrace restaurant. ⑨

**Tea Bungalow** 1/1901 PM Mohammed Rd, Kunnumpuram ☎0484/301 9200 or ☎9388 719678, ⓦwww.teabungalow.in. Elegant, ochre-coloured residence – formerly a coir trader's office, later occupied by the Brooke Bond tea company – set in a delightful garden with a great pool. The rooms, named after different trading ports, are handsome, with polished hardwood floors and high pitched roofs, and there's a coffee lounge and restaurant. From Rs12,000 ($265) in season. ⑨

🏃 **The Tower House** 1/320-321 Tower Rd ☎0484/221 6960, ⓦwww.neemranahotels .com. The wonderful, French-run *Neemrana* chain do heritage hotels better than anyone else in India, and this latest venture of theirs – which describes itself as a "Non-Hotel Hotel" – doesn't disappoint. The location, in a graceful period house opposite the Chinese fishing nets, is perfect, and the airy interiors scrupulously in period. Antique prints and wood sculptures adorn the vast, airy, wood-floored suites, whose net-curtained galleries overlook the square, and there's a secluded pool in the white-walled garden. Don't expect the slick service of other places in this bracket, nor Fort Cochin's usual exorbitant rates – doubles Rs5000–8000 ($110–175). ⑧–⑨

**Trinity House** Ridsdale Rd, parade ground ☎0484/221 6666, ⓦwww.malabarhouse.com.

The last word in heritage-boutique chic: three contemporary designer apartments, occupying the old headquarters of the Dutch East India Company. An offshoot of the *Malabar House* across the road, its three exclusive suites ("red", "blue" and "yellow") share a living room and communal mezzanine area, and would thus better suit a family or group, though at $220–420 apiece, a block booking doesn't come cheap. 9

## Willingdon and Bolghatty islands

**Casino** Willingdon Island, 2km from Navy Airport, close to Cochin Harbour Terminus railway station ⓣ0484/266 8221, ⓦwww.cghearth.com. The first venture of the now-extensive CGH Earth chain, but utterly characterless and shut in by the grey docks. With its courtyard pool, ayurveda spa and shops, it's popular primarily with tour groups and thus often booked up. The *Casino's* one unrivalled plus is its *Fort Cochin* restaurant, the best seafood joint in town. $115. 9

**KTDC Bolgatty Palace** Bolghatty Island ⓣ0484/275 0500, ⓦwww.ktdc.com. Occupying a property originally built by the Dutch in 1744, and which later served as the home of the British Resident, this graceful old mansion on a peaceful island on the north side of the harbour was one of Kerala's first proper heritage hotels. These days, though, it's well outshone by the competition and showing signs of age, with standards of service and maintenance lagging well behind the rest of the pack – both in the uncharismatic new wing, and its heritage sibling, where the rooms are fabulously overpriced ($375 per night). That said, the location is idyllic and the garden pool a wonderful place to relax. Since the opening of a new bridge just to the north you no longer have to travel there by boat, though the hotel launch remains in operation, dropping guests at the High Court Jetty. Book online; and come armed with plenty of mozzie repellent. $150–375. 8–9

**Taj Malabar** Willingdon Island, by Tourist Office Jetty ⓣ0484/266 6811, ⓦwww.tajhotels.com. Pink-orange tower block in a superb location on the tip of the island with sweeping views of the bay; the old "heritage" wing, waterfront gardens and pool have been extensively refurbished, and the whole place has oodles of *Taj* style and quality. Their "sea view" rooms are big, but the "standard" ones are quite small for the price. $300–375. 9

## Near the airport

**Abad Airport** Opposite Nedumbassery Airport ⓣ484/261 0411, ⓦwww.abadhotels.com. A dependable, good-value transit option, this smart business-grade hotel next to the airport only charges Rs3500–4000 for its 56 a/c rooms. Efficient, clean and convenient, though there's no pool. 7

**Lotus 8** Opposite Nedumbassery Airport ⓣ0484/261 0640, ⓦwww.lotus8hotels.com. Gleaming tinted-glass and concrete tower block directly opposite the main terminal. The rooms are just what you'd expect from an international-standard business hotel, with king-sized beds, separate living-room areas and direct internet access, but the real selling point is that they take bookings for less than 24hr (Rs980 for 5hr/Rs1550 for 8hr/Rs4000 for 24hr), making this a great option if you're in transit and only need a room for a short while. Rates include breakfast. 8

**Saj Earth Resort** Saj Junction, Nedumbassery Airport ⓣ0484/261 0356, ⓦwww.sajhotels.com. Lavish Kerala-themed resort close to the airport comprising island cottages in traditional style, with artisanal carved wood railings and screens, focused on a large swimming pool; some have their own private jacuzzis and plunge pools. You enter through a spectacular reception structure designed to resemble a temple, and are whisked from there to the chalets in electric golf buggies. The multi-cuisine restaurant's enclosed in a glass-sided atrium, and has an open kitchen. Rs7000–14,000 ($150–300). 9

## The outskirts

**Chittoor Palace** 29km north of Kochi ⓣ0484/243 1380 or ⓣ9895 353720, ⓦwww.chittoorpalace.com. This 300-year-old royal palace, used by the local raja when attending festivals at the nearby Krishna temple, has been exquisitely restored to host one of India's most elegant heritage hotels. It sits on the riverside, amid stately lawns and tamarind trees – a traditional Keralan mansion of red-tiled roofs, elaborately carved eaves and pillared verandas. Inside, the three rooms are vast, retaining their original rosewood beds and swing chairs. Host Suresh, a descendant of the palace's original owners, is on hand to welcome guests. The food is wonderful Namboodiri vegetarian, so no alcohol. Trips in the palace's private boat are complimentary. $350 per double. 9

**Green Lagoon** Vethila Thuruthu, Eramaloor, 20km south ⓣ0478/645 1811, ⓦwww.green-lagoon.com. Uniformed butlers carrying temple umbrellas greet your arrival by boat at *Green Lagoon*, one of Kerala's most exclusive luxury hideaways. Located on a lush islet in the backwaters, just 45mins' drive south of the city, it's the utopian brainchild of retired professor and aesthete, Klaus Schleusener. Accommodation comes in the form of three serene little villas, built around exquisite 200-year-old *nalukettu* houses overlooking private pools by the waterside. You get your own ayurvedic massage room and the use of a secluded garden, and the food's as inspirational as the setting – though such luxury doesn't come cheap (from around Rs35,000/$790 per villa in season). ⑨

**Kallancherry Retreat** Kumbalanghi village, 24km south of Ernakulam ℡0484/224 0564 or ℡9847 446683. Charming little family homestay, a world away from the crowded streets of Fort Cochin, set under palm trees on the banks of a huge lagoon just half-an-hour's ride out of town. The en-suite rooms are squeaky clean and have balconies. You can get there by auto-rickshaw; phone ahead for directions. The owners also run engaging village tours in the area. ⑤

🏃 **Olavipe** Thekkanatt Parayil, Olavipe, Poochakkal, midway between Kochi and Alleppey ℡0478/252 2255 or ℡9847 047013, ⊛www.olavipe.com. One of Kerala's most atmospheric heritage homestays – the ancestral seat of landed Syrian Christian family, the Parayils, set on a large backwater estate between Kochi and Alleppey. Dating from around the turn of the last century, the mansion is in classic Kuttanadi style, with exotic gable-ended roofs framed by slender palm trees, and oil portraits of sombre-faced forebears on the walls. The rooms are lovely, and the Parayils generous hosts, presiding over leisurely meals around the dynastic dining table. Doubles from Rs10,000 ($220); children under 5 free. ⑨

# Old Kochi

**Old Kochi**, the thumb-shaped peninsula whose northern tip presides over the entrance to the city's harbour, formed the focus of European trading activities from the sixteenth century onwards. With high-rise development restricted to Ernakulam across the water, its twin districts of **Fort Cochin**, in the west, and **Mattancherry**, on the headland's eastern side, have preserved an extraordinary wealth of early-colonial architecture, spanning the Portuguese, Dutch and British eras – a crop unparalleled in India. Approaching by ferry, the waterfront, with its sloping red-tiled roofs and ranks of peeling, pastel-coloured *godowns* (warehouses), offers a view that can have changed little in centuries.

Closer up, however, Old Kochi's historic patina has started to show some ugly cracks. The spice trade that fuelled the town's original rise is still very much in evidence: scores of shops lining the narrow streets of Mattancherry enjoy a brisk turnover of Malabari cardamom, chillies, turmeric and ginger, while the famous Pepper Exchange has boomed since it went online a couple of years back. But since the late 1990s, an extraordinary rise in visitor numbers has had a major impact on the town. Thousands of free-spending foreign tourists pour through daily during the winter, and with no planning or preservation authority to take control, the resulting rash of new building threatens to destroy the very atmosphere people come here to experience. Whereas old Portuguese arches and Dutch wood verandas used to dominate the streets of Fort Cochin, now garish signboards and the glass fronts of air-conditioned Kashmiri handicraft emporia are more likely to draw the eye. That said, tourism has also brought some benefits to the area, inspiring renovation work to buildings that would otherwise have been left to rot. Quite a few splendid old mansions across the town have been restored to accommodate high-end **heritage hotels**, where you can savour the 300-year-old architecture from the comfort of an antique four-poster or courtyard plunge pool.

## Fort Cochin

The district where tourism has made its most discernible impact is **Fort Cochin**, the grid of venerable old streets at the northwest tip of the peninsula, where the Portuguese erected their first walled citadel, Fort Immanuel. Only a few fragments of the former battlements remain, crumbling into the sea beside Cochin's iconic Chinese fishing nets. But dozens of other evocative Lusitanian,

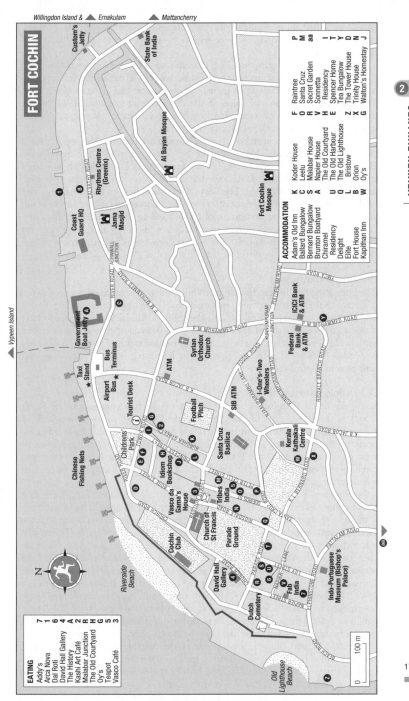

## FORT COCHIN

Willingdon Island & ▲ Ernakulam    ▲ Mattancherry

Vypeen Island

N

Riverside Beach

Old Lighthouse Beach

0    100 m

**EATING**
| | |
|---|---|
| Addy's | 7 |
| Arca Nova | 1 |
| Dal Roti | 6 |
| David Hall Gallery | 4 |
| The History | A |
| Kashi Art Café | 2 |
| Malabar Junction | R |
| The Old Courtyard | H |
| Oy's | G |
| Teapot | 5 |
| Vasco Café | 3 |

**ACCOMMODATION**
| | | | | |
|---|---|---|---|---|
| Adam's Old Inn | P | Koder House | K | Raintree | F |
| Ballard Bungalow | M | Leelu | C | Santa Cruz | O |
| Bernard Bungalow | aa | Malabar House | S | Secret Garden | R |
| Brunton Boatyard | | Napier House | A | Sonnetta | V |
| Chiramel | | The Old Courtyard | U | Residency | I |
| Residency | I | The Old Harbour | Q | Spencer Home | H |
| Delight | T | The Old Lighthouse | L | Tea Bungalow | E |
| Elite | Y | Bristow | Z | The Tower House | Z |
| Fort House | D | Orion | B | Trinity House | X |
| Kapithan Inn | J | Oy's | W | Walton's Homestay | G |

Custom's Jetty

State Bank of India

Coast Guard HQ

Rhythms Centre (Greenix)

Jama Masjid

Al Bayan Mosque

Fort Cochin Mosque

Government Boat Jetty

Taxi Stand

Bus Terminus

Airport Bus

Tourist Desk

Children's Park

Chinese Fishing Nets

Syrian Orthodox Church

ATM

Football Pitch

SIB ATM

Santa Cruz Basilica

Kerala Kathakali Centre

ICICI Bank & ATM

Federal Bank & ATM

I-One's-Two Wheelers

Idiom Bookshop

Vasco da Gama's House

Tribes India

Church of St Francis

Parade Ground

Cochin Club

David Hall Gallery

Fab India

Dutch Cemetery

Indo-Portuguese Museum (Bishop's Palace)

Dutch and British monuments survive, ranging from stately tea brokers' bungalows to Bishops' palaces, spice traders' mansions and the gabled facade of the oldest church in Asia.

A good way to get to grips with Fort Cochin's many-layered history is to pick up the free **walking-tour maps** produced by both Kerala Tourism and the privately run Tourist Desk, available from their respective offices and counters (see p.170). The routes lead you around some of the district's more significant landmarks, including the early eighteenth-century Dutch Cemetery, Vasco da Gama's supposed house and several merchants' residences.

Fort Cochin also has a small but active **arts scene** based around the popular *Kashi Art Café* (daily 8.30am–7.30pm) on Burgher Street (see p.187) and new **David Hall Gallery** on the Parade Ground (daily 11am–7pm). For **kathakali** and other traditional forms of ritual dance and drama, you've a choice of venues staging daily tourist shows (see p.185). The Fort's pair of **beaches**, on the northwest edge of the peninsula, are certainly not places you'd wish to swim from or sunbathe on, with slicks of dubiously coloured pollution washing over them periodically – although Riverside Beach (the northernmost of the two) is a good spot for viewing the Chinese fishing nets. The nearest decent seaside destination is Cherai Beach, 25km north (see p.190).

### Chinese fishing nets

The huge, elegant **Chinese fishing nets** lining the northern shore of Fort Cochin add grace to the waterfront view, and are probably the single most familiar photographic image of Kerala. Traders from the court of Kublai Khan are said to have introduced them to the Malabar region. Known in Malayalam as *cheena vala*, they can also be seen throughout the backwaters further south. The nets, which are suspended from arced poles and operated by levers and weights, require at least four men to control them.

### St Francis Church and around

South of the Chinese fishing nets on Church Road (the continuation of River Road) is the large, typically English **Parade Ground**, where generations of colonial troops were drilled in the merciless heat, and on which local lads now brush up their cricketing skills after school. In a handsome period building on its western side stands the David Hall Gallery & Café (daily 11am–7pm), where you can browse contemporary Indian art and enjoy high tea in a lovely rear garden (for a review, see p.186).

Overlooking it is the **Church of St Francis** (daily 8.30am–6.30pm), the first built by Europeans in India. Its exact age is not known, though the stone structure is thought to date back to the early sixteenth century; the land was a gift of the local raja, and the title deeds, written on palm leaf, are still kept inside. The facade, meanwhile, with its multi-curved sides, became the model for most Christian churches in India. Vasco da Gama was buried here in 1524, but his body was later removed to Portugal. Under the Dutch, the church was renovated and became Protestant in 1663, then Anglican with the advent of the British in 1795; since 1949 it has been attached to the Church of south India. Inside, various tombstone inscriptions have been placed in the walls, the earliest of which is from 1562. One hangover from British days is the continued use of *punkahs*, large swinging cloth fans on frames suspended above the congregation, operated by a *punkah-wallah*.

East of St Francis Church, the interior of the twentieth-century **Santa Cruz Basilica** will delight fans of a colourful, gaudy Indo-Romano-Rococo style. The building, from 1887, was constructed on the site of a much older Portuguese church demolished by the British a century earlier.

## The Indo-Portuguese Museum

At the southern end of Ridsdale Road, the grand Bishop's Palace of 1557 has been converted into the **Indo-Portuguese Museum** (Tues–Sun 9am–1pm & 2–6pm; Rs25 [Rs10]), displaying an assortment of mostly nineteenth-century Catholic relics, altarpieces and other religious paraphernalia, along with a wonderful old East India Company map, dated 1829. Some minimal ruins of the fort's foundations can be seen in the basement.

## Mattancherry

**Mattancherry**, the old district of red-tiled riverfront wharfs and pastel-coloured houses occupying the northeastern tip of the headland, was once the colonial capital's main market area – the epicentre of the Malabar's spice trade, and home to its wealthiest Jewish and Jain merchants. Like Fort Cochin, its once grand buildings have lapsed into advanced states of disrepair, with most of their original owners working overseas. When Mattancherry's Jews emigrated en masse to Israel in the 1940s, their furniture and other non-portable heirlooms ended up in the **antique shops** for which the area is now renowned – though these days genuine pieces are few and far between. Kashmiris have taken over the majority of them, selling handicrafts and curios at inflated prices to the tour groups and cruise-ship visitors who stream through daily during the winter.

The sight at the top of most visitors' itineraries is **Mattancherry Palace** (Sat–Thurs 10am–5pm; Rs2), on the roadside a short walk from the Mattancherry Jetty, 1km or so southeast of Fort Cochin. Known locally as the Dutch Palace, the two-storey building was actually erected by the Portuguese, as a gift to the Raja of Cochin, Vira Keralavarma (1537–61) – though the Dutch did add to the complex. While its squat exterior is not particularly striking, the interior is captivating, with **murals** that are among the finest examples of Kerala's underrated school of painting. Friezes illustrating stories from the Ramayana, on the first floor, date from the sixteenth century. Packed with detail and gloriously rich colour, the style is never strictly naturalistic; the treatment of facial features is pared down to the simplest of lines for the mouths and characteristically aquiline noses. Downstairs, the women's bedchamber holds several less complex paintings, possibly dating from the 1700s. One shows Shiva dallying with Vishnu's female form, the enchantress Mohini; a second portrays Krishna holding aloft Mount Govardhana; another features a reclining Krishna surrounded by *gopis*, or cowgirls. His languid pose belies the activity of his six hands and two feet, intimately caressing adoring admirers. While the paintings are undoubtedly the highlight of the palace, the collection also includes interesting Dutch maps of old Cochin, coronation robes belonging to past maharajas, royal palanquins, weapons and furniture. Without permission from the Archaeological Survey of India, **photography** is strictly prohibited.

A few hundred metres west of the palace, on Gujarati Road, lies the peaceful **Jain temple**, boasting a pair of airy marble sanctuaries with some delicate carving. The serene atmosphere is broken daily at noon when one devotee rings a bell loudly to announce the feeding of the local pigeons. At this point the courtyard turns into a mini-Trafalgar Square, and anyone around is encouraged to help dish out grain to the hungry birds.

## Jew Town

The history of **Jewish settlement** in Cochin dates back to the early 1500s. After an attack on their principal town, Cranganore (Shingly), by the Arab navy of Calicut, a wave of refugees sought a safe haven here under protection from the Raja of Cochin. These settlers, some of whom were descended from Jews that had lived on the Malabar coast for at least a thousand years, were soon joined by paler-skinned Sephardic Jews fleeing persecution in Spain and Portugal. The so-called Pardesi (literally "foreign"), or "White" Jews, received a warm welcome from the older-established Malabari, or "Black" Jews. But the two groups would remain socially separate, with the newcomers choosing only to marry among themselves to preserve the purity of their sub-culture (and paler skin colour).

The Pardesis' sophisticated knowledge of European commerce stood them in good stead over the coming decades, as the colonial pepper trade boomed. Vast fortunes were accrued by families such as the Koders, and prominent members of the community rose to become trusted advisors of the raja. A testament to the strength of this royal patronage is the siting of the **Pardesi Synagogue** (Sun–Fri 10am–noon & 3–5pm; Rs2), on a plot of land directly behind the palace in Mattancherry. It was built in 1524, while the Jews of Cochin were closely allied to the Dutch – an allegiance for which they would pay dearly a century later when rival power, the Portuguese, sacked the city and burned the synagogue to the ground. The replacement building on the same site, erected only two years after the attack in 1664, has become Cochin's most famous monument. Foreign visitors

## A Jewish apartheid

Thanks to their prominence on the local tourist trail, the Pardesis are often regarded as the only Jews in Cochin. But a second, less conspicuous, Jewish community also survives across the water in Ernakulam – the Malabari or **"Black" Jews**. For centuries, the two have lived resolutely apart, and often at loggerheads, divided not merely by the colour of their skin, but by a long history of oppression, jealousy, resentment and conflict.

The schism hinges on the Pardesis' long-held claim that they, and not their darker-skinned rivals, are the true descendants of **Joseph Rabban**, founding father of the oldest recorded Jewish settlement at Cranganore (modern Kodungallur; see p.203). The fact that the White, predominantly Sephardic, Pardesis arrived in Kerala at least five hundred years after Rabban and his followers seems to have been overlooked. Nevertheless, it was this version of events – along with assertions that the Malabaris were not originally Jews at all, but descended from converted slaves – which the Pardesis successfully propagated through their superior influence at court and among colonial traders.

Over the centuries, the divide been the two groups evolved into something close to apartheid. Contrary to Jewish law, Black Cochini Jews were forbidden from marrying Pardesis, and burying their dead in the same cemeteries; Malabaris were not permitted to hold circumcision or marriage ceremonies in White synagogues, nor even worship inside – they were instead obliged to sit on a terrace outside.

Resentment boiled over into rebellion in the nineteenth century, when the Black Jews founded their own synagogues in Fort Cochin. Despite interventions by no less than the Chief Rabbi of Jerusalem, however, the Pardesis would not relent, and eventually a campaign of Gandhian-style passive resistance was launched by Black lawyer **AB Salem** in the 1940s. One by one, Salem and his comrades managed to break down the old restrictions and prejudices, regularly attending services in the Pardesi synagogue, until finally, in 1950, a young couple of mixed Black and White heritage tackled the greatest taboo of all and married – the groom was AB's son, Balfour, and his bride, Seema ("Baby"), from the illustrious Pardesi clan, the Koders.

Since then, mass emigration has drained both communities, but this seems to have forced the two closer together. Out of necessity, they nowadays share a single Kosher butcher, and men from the Malabari side are required to make up a quorum for the few services still held in the Pardesi synagogue.

The full story of the feud and its legacy can be read in Edna Fernandes' engagingly written *The Last Jews of Kerala* (2008; see p.311).

pour year-round down the narrow street leading to it (dominated these days by Kashmiri shopkeepers selling fake antiques and bric-a-brac) for a glimpse of the last surviving members of the Pardesi community. Following the post-Independence exodus to Israel, only ten, mostly elderly, White Jews reside in the enclave, the sole youngster among them Yaheh Hallegua, the ticket-seller at the synagogue, who enjoys the dubious distinction of being the last female Pardesi of childbearing age. Notoriously frosty with visitors, Yaheh has long resisted attempts by community elders to marry her off to one of her cousins, and now spends her days refusing requests to have her photo taken.

The richly decorated **interior**, floored with individually painted willow-pattern tiles from Canton, recalls the abundance of bygone eras, with Venetian and Belgian crystal chandeliers of many and various sizes and shapes suspended from the ceiling. In the front of the main prayer hall, a silk curtain hides the Ark and its seven sacred Torah Scrolls, each capped with solid gold crowns encrusted with diamonds, rubies and emeralds – two of them gifts from the rajas of Cochin and Travancore. Also locked away in the Ark is the controversial thousand-year-old copper-plate inscription commemorating the gift of land to Jewish leader, Joseph Rabban, by Raja Bhaskara Ravi Varma – a relic which the Malabari Jews claim should by rights be theirs.

Just around the corner from the synagogue at the heart of Jew Town, the **Kochi International Pepper Exchange** once housed a noisy trading floor, packed with dealers shouting the latest prices and clinching deals by means of arcane sign language. Recently, however, the market was superseded by the India Pepper and Spice Trade Association (IPSTA) and converted to online trading (Ⓦ www.ipsta .com), since when the building has seen fewer sacks of actual pepper pass through its doors than do the majority of spice shops further north in the main bazaar, where trucks and handcarts loaded with jute sacks of the Malabar's "black gold" routinely block the narrow lanes.

## Ernakulam and south of the centre

**ERNAKULAM** presents the modern face of Kerala, with more of a big-city feel than Thiruvananthapuram – despite the fact it's marginally smaller. Other than the contemporary art on display at the small **Durbar Hall Art Gallery** (daily 11am–7pm; free) on Durbar Hall Road, and the remarkable **Folklore Museum** (see p.183) on the southern outskirts, there's little in the way of sights. If you spend any time here, it'll probably be to eat at one of Ernakulam's famous Keralan **restaurants**, or to drool at the glittering gold emporia springing up everywhere.

Running in parallel with the seafront, roughly 500m inland, **Mahatma Gandhi (MG) Road** is its main thoroughfare, where you'll find some of the largest textile stores, jewellery shops and hotels. Prime leisure destinations for the city's well-heeled middle classes are the massive **shopping malls**, 7km north of the centre around Edapally Junction. Spread over six storeys, the **Oberon** (daily 10am–10pm; Ⓦ www.oberonmall.com) used to be the high temple of modern Keralan consumerism until it was usurped by the colossal **LuLu Mall** (daily 10am–10pm; Ⓦ www .luluindia.com), a 16-acre complex with a seven-screen multiplex, 18 food outlets and parking for 3000 cars – said to be the largest air-conditioned shopping complex in Asia.

More traditional forms of entertainment take centre stage at the eight-day annual **festival** (Jan/Feb) at the Shiva temple, on Durbar Hall Road, where you can watch elephant processions and *panchavadyam* (drum and trumpet groups) performing out in the street. The festival usually includes night-time recitals of **kathakali**, during which the temple is decorated with an amazing array of electric lights.

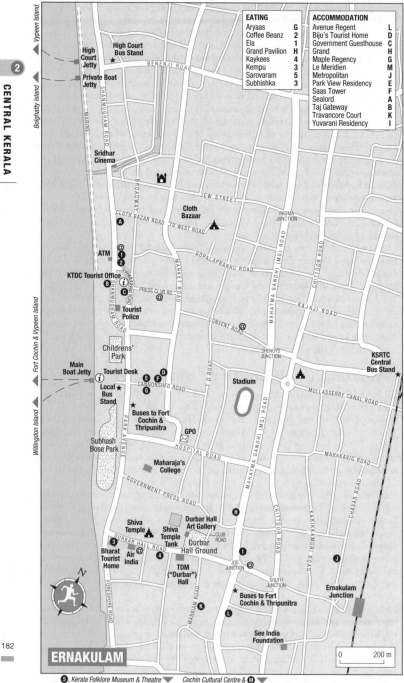

Vypeen Island

Bolghatty Island

Fort Cochin & Vypeen Island

Willingdon Island

**High Court Jetty**

**Private Boat Jetty**

**High Court Bus Stand**

BENERJI ROAD

**Sridhar Cinema**

MARINE DRIVE

SHANMUGHAM ROAD

BROADWAY

CLOTH BAZAR ROAD

JEW STREET

**Cloth Bazaar**

TD WEST ROAD

PADMA JUNCTION

GOPALAPRABHU ROAD

**ATM**

**KTDC Tourist Office**

**Tourist Police**

PRESS CLUB RD

MARKET ROAD

CONVENT ROAD

SHENOYS JUNCTION

**Childrens' Park**

**Main Boat Jetty**

**Tourist Desk**

**Local Bus Stand**

**Buses to Fort Cochin & Thripunitra**

CANNONSHED ROAD

TD ROAD

**Stadium**

**KSRTC Central Bus Stand**

MULLASSERRY CANAL ROAD

MAHATMA GANDHI (MG) ROAD

RAJAJI ROAD

CHITTOOR ROAD

**GPO**

HOSPITAL ROAD

**Subhash Bose Park**

PARK AVENUE

**Maharaja's College**

GOVERNMENT PRESS ROAD

MAHAKAVIG ROAD

**Shiva Temple**

**Shiva Temple Tank**

DURBAR HALL ROAD

**Durbar Hall Art Gallery**

CLUB ROAD

**Durbar Hall Ground**

**Bharat Tourist Home**

**Air India**

**TDM ("Durbar") Hall**

JOS JUNCTION

SOUTH JUNCTION

CHITTOOR ROAD

KARIKKAMURI ROAD

CHAVAR ROAD

**Ernakulam Junction**

WARRIAM ROAD

**Buses to Fort Cochin & Thripunitra**

**See India Foundation**

FORESHORE ROAD

N

**ERNAKULAM**

0        200 m

| EATING | |
|---|---|
| Aryaas | G |
| Coffee Beanz | 2 |
| Ela | 1 |
| Grand Pavilion | H |
| Kaykees | 4 |
| Kempu | 3 |
| Sarovaram | 5 |
| Subhishka | 3 |

| ACCOMMODATION | |
|---|---|
| Avenue Regent | L |
| Biju's Tourist Home | D |
| Government Guesthouse | C |
| Grand | H |
| Maple Regency | G |
| Le Meridien | M |
| Metropolitan | J |
| Park View Residency | E |
| Saas Tower | F |
| Sealord | A |
| Taj Gateway | B |
| Travancore Court | K |
| Yuvarani Residency | I |

Ernakulam Town Station (500m) & Nedumbassery Airport (29km)

Kerala Folklore Museum & Theatre        Cochin Cultural Centre & **M**

## Kerala Folklore Museum

The city's one outstanding visitor attraction after Fort Cochin is the **Kerala Folklore Museum** (daily 9.30am–7pm, ☎0484/266 5452; Rs200), on the distant southeast fringes of Ernakulam. Don't be put off by the long trip across town, nor the dismal location beside the main north–south highway. Housed in a multistorey laterite building encrusted with traditional wood- and tile-work, the collection of antiques displayed here is astonishing. Its owner, a local antique dealer, spent decades squirrelling away his best finds from around southern India, and there are literally thousands of them, ranging from dance drama masks and costumes, to ritual paraphernalia, musical instruments, pieces of temple architecture, Thanjavur paintings, cooking utensils, portraits and ancestral photographs. There are no priceless treasures, as such, but the exhibition provides an unrivalled window on the region's traditional material culture; you could literally spend an hour scrutinizing any single corner of the building. Its crowning glory is an exquisitely decorated **theatre** on the top floor, where evening performances of *kathakali* and *theyyem* are given against a backdrop of swirling Keralan temple murals and dark wooden pillars (see p.185).

Auto-rickshaws charge around Rs60–75 for the trip out to the museum from the Main Boat Jetty in Ernakulam – ask for Theyvara (aka "Shantinagar") Junction, or Kundulur Bridge. To really make the most of your trip, combine it with a sumptuous Keralan vegetarian meal at the nearby *Sarovaram* restaurant, just up the highway (see p.186).

## ENS Kalari

The village of **Netoor**, 10km southeast of the centre, is home to the ENS Kalari school of **kalarippayat** (☎0484/270 0810, ✉enskalari@eth.net), one of the leading centres of the Keralan martial art form (see p.89). The well-organized centre, established in 1954, is unusual in that it blends both the northern and the southern systems of *kalarippayat*. Twice-daily training sessions start at 4am; visitors are welcome to attend demonstrations (6–7pm) and the open session on Sundays (3–7pm). Alternatively, you can enrol on one of their *kalarippayat* certificate courses, which run from one week to one year and are tailored to the needs of the student. The centre also offers lessons in the unique **Uzhichil massage** – a treatment derived from ayurvedic medicine, designed as a cure to *kalari*-related injuries, which concentrates on the lymph glands to improve tone and circulation. To get to the school take a bus from the KSRTC or the Kaloor bus stands to the Netoor INTUC bus stand, and walk down the road for half a kilometre; the school is opposite the Mahadevar Temple.

# Eating

Until recently, the quintessential Kochi dining experience was buying a fish straight out of the **Chinese fishing nets** in the Fort, then having it grilled at one of the stalls nearby. Alas, the authorities recently closed the stalls down, and these days foreign tourists tend to congregate at the pavement joints along the nearby **Tower Road**, drinking warm beer disguised in tea pots to circumvent local liquor licensing laws. The food served in these cafés, however, is notoriously unhygienic, regularly causing stomach upsets.

As with everything in Fort Cochin, upmarket **restaurants** tend to be pricier, and more atmospheric, than those across the water in **Ernakulam**; but it is in Ernakulam that you'll find some of the finest regional cooking in south India. For a definitive Keralan banana leaf meal, try *Subhishka* or *Sarovaram*. Remember, if you're dining a boat-ride away from your hotel, to familiarize yourself with the ferry timetables (see box, p.169).

Unless otherwise stated, restaurants under the "Ernakulam" and "Fort Cochin" headings are marked on their relevant maps (see p.177 & opposite).

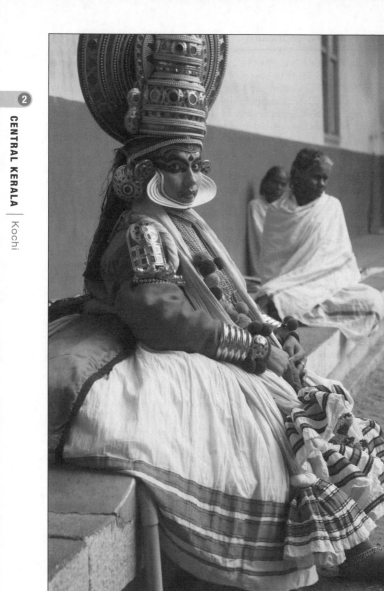

▲ *Kathakali* performer

### Ernakulam

**Aryaas** Ground Floor, *Maple Regency*, Cannonshed Rd. Popular, clean and well-run little *udipi* joint just east of the Main Boat Jetty. A much more salubrious place to eat dosas, *vadas*, and other south Indian bites than the gloomy *Indian Coffee House* down the road, and it's very cheap.

**Coffee Beanz** Shanmugham Rd. Trendy a/c cappuccino bar, patronized mainly by well-heeled students from the local management college shrieking into their mobiles over a full-on MTV soundtrack. The din notwithstanding, it's a good spot to beat the heat and grab a quick meal (burgers, fries, grilled sandwiches, dosas, fish

## Kathakali in Kochi

Kochi is the only city in the state where you are guaranteed the chance to see live **kathakali**, Kerala's unique form of ritualized theatre (see pp.296–298). Whether in its authentic setting, in temple festivals held during the winter, or at the shorter tourist-oriented shows that take place year-round, these mesmerizing dance dramas – depicting the struggles of gods and demons – are an unmissable feature of Kochi's cultural life.

Five venues in the city currently hold daily shows, each preceded by an introductory talk at around 6.30pm. You can watch the dancers being made up if you arrive an hour or so beforehand, and keen photographers should turn up well before the start to ensure a front-row seat. Tickets, costing Rs100–150, can be bought at the door.

Most visitors only attend one performance, but you'll gain a much better sense of what *kathakali* is all about if you take in at least a couple. The next step is an all-night recital at a temple festival, or one of the performances given by the top-notch Ernakulam Kathakali Club, which stages night-long plays by Kerala's leading actors once each month, either at the TDM Hall in Ernakulam or at the Ernakulathappan Hall in the city's main Shiva temple. For programme details phone ☎0484/236 9357, or drop in at the Tourist Desk at the Main Boat Jetty, Ernakulam (see p.170). The principal venues are listed below.

**Dr Devan's Kathakali** See India Foundation, Kalathiparambil Cross Rd, near Ernakulam Junction railway station ☎0484/236 6471. The oldest-established tourist show in the city, introduced by the inimitable Dr Devan, who starts the show with a lengthy discourse on Indian philosophy and mythology. 6.45–8pm (make-up at 6pm).

**Folklore Museum** Bypass Rd, southeastern edge of Ernakulam. The most atmospheric venue – an a/c theatre decorated with wonderful Keralan murals and traditional wooden architecture – though it's quite pricey (Rs350), and a long trek across town if you're staying in Fort Cochin. Try to combine a performance with a tour of the museum downstairs (see p.183), and maybe a meal at nearby *Sarovaram* (see p.186). Taxis charge Rs60–75 from central Ernakulam.

**Kairali Kathakali** River Rd, opposite *Brunton Boatyard Hotel*, Fort Cochin. The smallest, and most intimate, venue, in an old-fashioned hessian-roofed structure. Show daily 6–7.30pm; make-up starts at 5pm. And there's a Carnatic music programme from 9pm.

**Kerala Kathakali Centre** Bernard Master Lane, near Santa Cruz Basilica, just off KB Jacob Rd, Fort Cochin ☎0484/221 7552. Popular performances from 6–7.30pm (make-up from 5pm) in a dedicated a/c theatre by a company of graduates of the renowned Kalamandalam academy. You usually get to see three characters, and the music is live. In addition, they do *kalarippayat* demonstrations (4–5pm), and live Carnatic music from 8.30pm.

**Rhythms Theatre (Greenix)** opposite *Fort House*, Fort Cochin. Costing Rs450, this is the priciest show, but combines excerpts from *kathakali* plays with displays of *mohiniyattam* dance, *kalarippayat* martial art and, on Sundays, *theyyem*, set against a combination of live and prerecorded music. Performances aren't of the highest standard, but the evening is more likely to appeal to kids, as costumes and acts change in quick succession.

curries, *appam* and samosas). The coffee's freshly ground and delicious, though the service is far less snappy than the fast-food uniforms.

**Ela** Shanmugham Rd. Great value, air-conditioned Keralan speciality place where nothing costs more than Rs100. The vibe is upbeat and trendy, but the non-veg food's very trad: *meen pollichathu*,

deliciously rich Syrian-Christian vegetable stew, lamb-coconut curry and light, spongy *appams* to soak it all up. Lots of old-style desserts, too, including *payasam* and moreish banana fritters.

**Grand Pavilion** MG Rd ☎0484/238 2061. An Ernakulam institution, famous for its gourmet Keralan dishes, especially the *karimeen* pollichathu with appam, which draws crowds on Sun evenings. They also do a huge range of Far Eastern, north Indian and Continental options, served on white tablecloths by a legion of brisk waiters wearing black ties and waistcoats. The prices are restrained, too: count on Rs500–600 for three courses. Reservations recommended.

**Kaykees** Durbar Hall Rd. The city's most famous Muslim restaurant (pronounced "Kai-ka's") has two branches: an old-style place over in Mattancherry, and this much more salubrious, modern dining hall in the heart of the downtown area, with an a/c section on the first floor. They've recently added all kinds of items to the menu, but everyone comes for the Malabari biriyanis (veg, chicken or mutton), served with Kaykees' mellow palm-date pickle and Arabian tea. It gets packed at lunchtime, and there are always long queues on Sundays. Pay for your meal token in advance.

**Kempu** Bharat Tourist Home, Durbar Hall Rd. This relaxed coffee shop on the ground floor of BTH is a great place to chill between bursts of shopping on nearby MG Rd. The decor of terracotta murals, thick stone floors and dark Keralan wood is soothing, and the south Indian bites, prepared in an open kitchen, dependably good. Try their bonda – spicy vegetable and peanut balls, served with coconut-and green-chilli chatni that's so thick you have to spread it with a knife.

**Sarovaram** Bypass Rd, Kudunnur. People travel from all across the city for Sarovaram's famous veg sadyas (Rs90), served on banana leaves in a typical Laurie Baker building, with exposed bricks and stone floors. The food outstrips even Subhishka/BTH (see below) and the atmosphere is much more Keralan, though it's a long trek across town – maybe combine a meal here with a trip to the nearby Folklore Museum (see p.183), and expect to have to queue for 10min or so on weekends.

**Subhishka** Ground Floor, Bharat Tourist Home, Durbar Hall Rd. Delicious Keralan veg food in this popular city-centre hotel restaurant (usually just referred to as BTH). They're pricier than average (Rs80, unlimited), and the contemporary decor and muzak are incongruous, but the cooking is painstakingly traditional – and it's a great place for crowd-watching. If you can, come on a Sunday when everyone dons their best saris and shirts for the big family meal.

## Fort Cochin and Willingdon Island

**Addy's** 1/286 Elphinstone Rd. Ramshackle, atmospheric and friendly, this family-run place near the Indo-Portuguese Museum occupies the ground floor of a late eighteenth-century Dutch house. You can enjoy homely Keralan dishes in a dining room with peeling pink plaster walls; most tempting are the local seafood specialities steamed in banana leaves or pan-fried over a low flame on a proper thava griddle iron. Try the squid chootu porachathu, grilled seer fish with garlic and black pepper sauce, or chicken moillee. Most mains Rs250–350.

**Arca Nova** Fort House Hotel, 2/6A Calvathy Rd. One of the fort's hidden gems: carefully prepared Keralan specialities – including delicious karimeen pollichathu or a grilled fish steak – served on a romantic, candle-lit jetty jutting into the harbour. The food is consistently good, and not too pricey (most mains Rs250–300), and the location's perfect for watching the ships chugging in and out of the docks.

**Dal Roti** 1/293 Lilly St. In the short time it's been open, Dal Roti has become the first choice among Fort Cochin's hungry travellers, both Indian and Western – despite the generally grubby state of its walls, erratic service and shortage of tables. You'll know why as soon as you taste their signature kati rolls – deliciously flaky wraps filled with egg, chicken or vegetables – or good-value combo thalis (Rs170 for the works). The food is authentic north Indian fare, inspired by the village cooking of UP, Madhya Pradesh, Orissa and Punjab – hence full of smoky, spicy flavours you don't get to enjoy that often in Kerala. And the prices are as refreshingly honest as the cooking.

**David Hall Gallery** Parade Ground. A peaceful art gallery garden café serving proper coffee, cake and light meals, such as grilled tuna and salad, at reasonable prices. Occasional live music and dance from the Lakshadweep and Laccadive Islands.

**Fort Cochin** Casino Hotel, Willingdon Island; see map on p.168. Widely regarded to be the city's finest seafood restaurant, the Casino's flagship Fort Cochin has no printed menu, as such. You just pick your king prawns, snapper, pomfret, squid, mullet or seer fish – all straight off the boat that morning – and watch it steamed in banana leaves, baked, pan-fried or grilled to perfection by the resident chefs. Decor is faux-traditional, in earthy Keralan colours. Count on Rs1500 per head, more if you order lobster.

**The History** Brunton Boatyard, Bellar Rd, next to Fort Cochin Government Boat Jetty. Brunton's chefs have delved into the culinary traditions of Fort Cochin to devise the History's eclectic menu. Served on a breezy raised terrace looking across the water to Vypeen Island, favourites include the Anglo-Indian "First-Class Railway Lamb Curry", "Fernandes roast pork" and Arab-inflected fish in tahini sauce. Count on Rs1000–1200 for three courses, or more if you hit the wine list.

**Kashi Art Café** Burgher St. Chichi art gallery café, patronized almost exclusively by Westerners, and with a menu to match. Fragrant, freshly ground espresso is the big draw, along with the *Kashi's* famous house cakes (their chocolate gateau is legendary among travellers), but they also do a selection of light meals and savoury snacks all day: check out the specials board.

**Malabar Junction** *Malabar House* hotel, 1/268 Parade Rd ☎0484/221 6666, ⊛www .malabarhouse.com. Gourmet fusion cuisine, made from market-fresh ingredients and served on a chic garden dining terrace in one of Kerala's most stylish hotels. Their signature dish is the seafood platter (Rs1200), featuring juicy local lobster, tiger prawns, calamari and choice cuts of fish from the lagoon, but they offer a range of more sensibly priced Italian and south Indian alternatives, both veg and non-veg (Rs350–600).

**The Old Courtyard** 1/371–2 Princess St. Few places capture the feel of old-world Cochin as vividly as this courtyard restaurant, where candle-lit tables are laid out beneath Portuguese vaulted arches. The food is as fine as the location (hallmark dishes include baked seafood spaghetti and fish grilled with coriander butter) – and the *patronne-chef* is a dessert wizard.

Frequent live Carnatic music 7.30–9pm. It's also a pleasant spot for breakfast, with a wide choice of local and Western options. Most dinner mains Rs325–350.

**Oy's** Burgher St. Chilled little café, popular mainly with young backpackers, where you can enjoy travellers' breakfasts and inexpensive north and south Indian dishes, including tasty fish *moillee*, seated on low-slung sofas under the gaze of Bob Marley posters. The staff are friendly and the vibe laidback.

**Teapot** Peter Celli St. With its massive collection of teapots from around the world, shabby-chic colour-washed wood floors, tea-chest tables and funky little mezzanine floor, this backstreet tearoom has been giving the *Kashi* some much-needed competition over the past few seasons. Quality teas and coffees are its mainstay, but there's also a selection of light meals and delicious home-made cakes on offer (including a stupendous Death by Chocolate).

**Vasco Café** Bastion St. Tiny budget travellers' breakfast joint in the heart of the tourist enclave, with relaxing wood tables and a huge bell-metal bowl in its barred window. The food – toasties, omelettes, muesli, fruit salad with curd, pancakes, juices and the like – is prepared to order, tasty and inexpensive.

## Listings

**Airlines, domestic** Air India, Durbar Hall Rd ☎0484/237 1141, airport ☎0484/261 0041; Go Air, c/o UAE Travel Services, Chettupuzha Towers, PT Usha Rd Junction ☎0484/235 5522; Jet Airways/ JetLite, 39/4158 Elmar Square Bldg, MG Rd ☎0484/235 9212, airport ☎261 0037; Kingfisher Airlines, K.B. Oxford Business Center, 39/4013, Free Kandath Rd, MG Rd ☎0484/235 1144; Paramount Airways, airport ☎0484/261 0404.

**Airlines, international** Air India, Collis Estate, MG Rd ☎0484/238 1874, airport ☎0484/261 0070; Air India Express, Collis Estate, MG Rd ☎0484/238 1885, airport ☎0484/261 0050; Emirates, Plot No. 696-A, opposite Wyte Fort Hotel, NH-47 Bypass, Maradu ☎0484/408 4444, airport ☎0484/261 1194; Gulf Air, Room 201, *Travancore Court Hotel*, Warriam Rd, 1 800/221122, airport ☎0484/261 1346; Kuwait Airways, Room 35, International Terminal, Nedumbassery Airport ☎0484/261 0251; Qatar Airways, *Hotel Le Meridien*, Mezzanine Floor, Maradu ☎0484/261 1305; SriLankan Airlines, 70–71 DD Vyapar Bhavan, K.P. Vallon Rd, Kadavanthara, Ernakulam ☎0484/232 0372, airport ☎0484/261 1313.

**Ayurveda** Reputable ayurveda centres (for revitalizing spa therapies, not medical treatment) include

Agasthyatheeram, Peter Celli St, Fort Cochin, and the Cochin Ayurveda Centre in the *Fort House Hotel*, Calvathy Rd. All of the upscale hotels in the city also have spas.

**Banks** Branches on MG Rd in Ernakulam include: South Indian Bank (SIB), UTI, ANZ Grindlays; State Bank of India (which also has a branch opposite the KTDC Tourist Reception Centre); and Andhra Bank. To exchange travellers' cheques, the best place is Thomas Cook (Mon–Sat 9.30am–6pm), near the Air India Building at Palal Towers, MG Rd; they also have a branch at the airport. ATMs can be found all over the centre of Ernakulam. In Fort Cochin, the Canara Bank has an ATM on Kanumpuram Junction. The Wilson Info Centre and Destinations, both on Princess St (daily 9am–9pm) change cash and travellers' cheques at rates slightly higher than Thomas Cook, but are much more conveniently located.

**Bookshops** The two branches of Idiom (opposite the Dutch Palace, Jew Town, Mattancherry; and on Bastion St near Princess St, Fort Cochin) are wonderful places to browse for books on travel, Indian and Keralan culture, flora and fauna, religion and art; they also have an excellent range of fiction.

Cinemas The multiplex at LuLu Mall (⊛www
.luluindia.com), 7km north of the centre (see p.181),
hosts regular screenings of English-language movies
as well as Malluwood and Bollywood releases.
Sridhar Theatre (☎0484/235 2529), Shanmugham
Rd, near the *Sealord* hotel, also shows English-
language movies daily; check the *Indian Express* or
*Hindu* (Kerala edition) to find out what's on.
Dentist The Emmanuel Dental Centre, Noble
Square, Kadavanthara (☎0484/220 7544, ⊛www
.cosmeticdentalcentre.com) is an international-
standard practice that does routine dental procedures as well as more advanced cosmetic work.
Hospitals The 600-bed Medical Trust Hospital on
MG Rd (☎0484/235 8001, ⊛www.medical
trusthospital.com) is one of the state's most

advanced private hospitals and has a 24hr
casualty unit and ambulance service. Also recommended is the Ernakulam Medical Centre, NH
Bypass, Paalarivattom (☎0484/280 7101,
⊛www.emccochin.com).
Internet access There are plenty of small internet
places around Fort Cochin, charging Rs40/hr or
thereabouts. In Ernakulam, convenient options
include Net Park on Convent Rd and Mathsons on
Durbar Hall Rd (both Rs30/hr).
Motorcycle rental I-One's-Two Wheelers, at
1/946-A Njaliparambu (the lane opposite the
entrance to the Kerala Kathakali Centre, near the
Basilica in Fort Cochin), has Enfields for rent, as
well as a few automatic Honda Activas. You'll
need to leave your passport as security. Contact

## Moving on from Kochi/Ernakulam

### By air

The **international airport** (☎484/261 0113, ⊛www.cochinairport.com) at Nedumbassery, near Alwaye (aka Aluva), is 30km north of Ernakulam and serves as Kerala's
main gateway to and from the Gulf. A full list of domestic airlines, and the destinations they fly to from Nedumbassery, appears on p.187. Snazzy new a/c airport
buses run from the terminus in Fort Cochin (7.25am, 8am, 9.45am,11.30am, noon,
1.55pm, 3.30pm, 4pm & 6.05pm; 1hr 30min; Rs70).

### By bus

**Buses** leave Ernakulam's KSRTC Central bus stand for virtually every town in Kerala;
most, but not all, are bookable in advance at the bus station.

### By train

Kochi lies on Kerala's main broad-gauge line and sees frequent **trains** down the
coast to Thiruvananthapuram via Kottayam, Kollam and Varkala and north to
Thrissur. Although most **long-distance express** and mail trains depart from
Ernakulam Junction, a couple of key services leave from Ernakulam Town. To
confuse matters further, a few also start at Cochin Harbour station, so be sure to
check the departure point when you book your ticket. The main reservation office,
good for trains leaving all three stations, is at Ernakulam Junction. For details of how
to buy tickets online, see p.25.

The trains listed below are recommended as the fastest and/or most convenient
services from Kochi. If you're heading to Alappuzha for the backwater trip to Kollam,
take the bus, as the only train that can get you there in time invariably arrives late.

### Recommended trains from Kochi/Ernakulam

| Destination | Name | Number | Station | Frequency | Departs | Total time |
|---|---|---|---|---|---|---|
| Kozhikode (Calicut) | Netravati Express | #6346 | EJ | daily | 4.05pm | 5hr |
| Thiruvanan-thapuram | Parasuram Express | #6350 | ET | daily | 1.30pm | 5hr |
| Varkala | Parasuram Express | #6350 | ET | daily | 1.30pm | 3hr 50min |

EJ = Ernakulam Junction
ET = Ernakulam Town

Ivan Joseph ☎ 9847 155306, ⓦ www.rentabike cochin.com.

**Music shops** Music World, MKV Building, near Shenoy's Theatre on MG Rd, is Kochi's answer to a music superstore, with Western pop, classical, compilations, world music and Indian *filmi* music. Sound of Melody, DH Rd, near the Ernakulam Junction station, has a good selection of traditional south Indian and contemporary Western music.

**Musical instruments** Manuel Industries, Banerji Rd, Kacheripady Junction, is the best for Indian classical and Western instruments. For traditional Keralan drums, ask at Thripunitra bazaar (see below).

**Police** The city's tourist police have a counter at Ernakulam Junction railway station. There is also a counter next to the KTDC Tourist Office at the southern end of Shanmugham Rd.

**Post office** The GPO is on Hospital Rd, not far from the Main Jetty; the city's poste restante is at the post office behind St Francis Church in Fort Cochin.

**Taxis** Ashik Taxis ☎ 9288 157145 or ☎ 9656 798481 cover the entire state, and offer day-trip excursions at fair prices.

**Tour and travel agents** For air tickets, Kapithan Air Travel and Tours at 1/430 Burgher St in Fort Cochin (on the ground floor of *Adam's Old Inn*) is the Fort's only IATA-bonded agent. Wild Kerala Tours, at VI/480 KVA Bldgs on Bazaar Rd, Mattancherry (☎ 0484/309 9520, ☎ 9846 162157, ⓦ www.wildkeralatours.com), is recommended for wildlife and adventure safaris to some of Kerala's wildest corners, guided by local experts. The Tourist Desk at the Main Jetty in Ernakulam (☎ 0484/237 1761) and Tower Rd in Fort Cochin runs elephant-spotting tours to Wayanad and beach stays in its own guesthouses around Kannur (see p.170).

# Around Kochi

Enough day-trip destinations lie within easy reach of the capital to keep you here for weeks. Topping most visitors' lists are the enjoyable tours of small **backwater villages** to the south, where you can get a taste of rural life from a motorboat or canoe, and where the island of **Kallancherry** holds an award-winning community tourism project.

A bus or auto-rickshaw ride out of town, **Thripunitra** is the site a former royal palace and museum, while an hour's ride across the harbour and north up the coast from Fort Cochin brings you to a 3km stretch of sand known as **Cherai** – the nearest decent beach to the city. Further afield, at **Kodanad** there's an **elephant camp** where you can help bathe baby elephants in the river, and some spectacular waterfalls at **Athirapally**, a couple of hours' drive further northeast. And if you're heading inland towards Munnar, **Thattekkad**, Kerala's number-one bird sanctuary, has a batch of appealing guesthouses and camps nestling on the banks of the Periyar River, and makes an ideal spot to break the long journey into the hills. A commendable **taxi** firm for day-trips out of Kochi is Ashik Taxis (see p.169).

## Backwater trips

Coir-production, rope-making, toddy-tapping, fishing and crab-farming are the main sources of income in the backwater villages south of Kochi. Easily reachable via the national highway, they're scattered over an expanse of huge lagoons and canals, flowing west behind a near continuous beach. KTDC day-trips offer a leisurely and affordable way to explore the area, but they're not as well done as those run by the **Tourist Desk** (daily 8.30am–6.30pm; Rs550; bookable from their counters in Fort Cochin and the Main Boat Jetty in Ernakulam). The cost includes hotel pick-up, transfer to the departure point near **Vaikom**, 30km south, a morning cruise (in a motorized boat) on the open backwaters, a village tour, a Keralan lunch buffet on board the *kettu vallam* and an afternoon trip through narrow waterways in a much smaller punted canoe.

It's also worth considering the trip out to **KUMBALANGHI** village – an award-winning community-based tourism project where proceeds are shared among the villagers. You start the tour with an auto-rickshaw drive to the city limits, where you're transferred to a country boat for the punted 20- to 30-minute crossing to Kumbalanghi itself, on **Kallancherry Island**. Guided visits around the settlement and its various industries are followed by lunch next to the lagoon, where you can try your hand at fishing with a proper Chinese net (a great photo opportunity). The tour costs Rs1000, including a quality buffet lunch under a gazebo next to the water, and all transport to and from your hotel or guesthouse. To book, phone Biju Joseph on ☏0484/224 0329 or ☏9388 975508; full details appear at ⓦwww.kumbalanghivillagetours.com. Kumbalanghi, beautifully situated on the waterfront, is a great place to watch the sun set. Should you be tempted to stay, ask about **accommodation** at the pleasant *Kallanchery Retreat* homestay (see p.176).

## Thripunitra

**THRIPUNITRA**, an outlying suburb of Ernakulam 14km south of the city centre, is worth a visit for its dilapidated colonial-style **Hill Palace** (Tues–Sun 9am–5pm; Rs10), now an eclectic museum. The royal family of Cochin at one time maintained around forty palaces – this one was confiscated by the state government after Independence, and has slipped into dusty decline over the past couple of decades. You can get there by auto-rickshaw in around twenty minutes, or more slowly by bus from the bus stand just south of Jos Junction on MG Road.

One of the museum's finest exhibits is an early seventeenth-century wooden *mandapa* (hall) removed from a temple in Pathanamthitta, featuring excellent carvings of themes from the Ramayana, including the coronation of the monkey king Sugriva. Of interest too are the silver filigree jewel boxes, gold and silver ornaments, and ritual objects associated with grand ceremonies. The **epigraphy gallery** contains an eighth-century Jewish Torah, and Keralan stone and copperplate inscriptions. Sculpture, ornaments and weapons in the **bronze gallery** include a *kingini katti* knife, whose decorative bells belie the fact that it was used for beheading, and a body-shaped cage in which condemned prisoners would be hanged while birds pecked them to death. Providing the place isn't crowded with noisy school groups, you could check out the nearby **deer park**; there are peaceful spots to picnic beneath the cashew trees in the garden behind the palace.

Performances of theatre, classical music and dance, including consecutive all-night **kathakali** performances, are held over a period of eight days during the annual **Vrishikolsavam** festival (Oct/Nov) at the **Sri Purnathrayisa Temple** on the way to the palace. Inside the temple compound, both in the morning and at night, massed drum orchestras perform *chenda melam* in procession with fifteen caparisoned elephants. After dark, the outside walls of the sanctuary are covered with thousands of tiny oil lamps. The temple is normally closed to non-Hindus, but admittance to appropriately dressed visitors is usually allowed at this time.

## Cherai Beach

The closest beach to Kochi worth the effort of getting to is **Cherai**, 25km north on Vypeen Island. A 3km strip of golden sand and thumping surf, it's sandwiched on a narrow strip of land between the sea and a very pretty backwater area of glassy lagoons. Chunky granite sea defences prevent the waves from engulfing the ribbon of fishing villages that subsist along this strip. Nowhere, however, is the sand more than a few metres wide at high tide, and the undertow can get quite strong. Even so, Cherai seems to be gaining in popularity each year, and a row of small, overpriced resorts and guesthouses has sprung up to accommodate the trickle of mainly foreign travellers who find there way up here from Fort Cochin.

To get to Cherai, you can either jump on the car ferry (*jangar*) across to Vypeen Island from the jetty next to *Brunton Boatyard* in Fort Cochin, then transfer onto the hourly bus waiting on the other side, or catch one of the more frequent buses from opposite the High Court Jetty in Ernakulam. Alternatively, hire a scooter (see p.168) and ride up – in which case, a preferable route to the main road is the more picturesque coastal lane hugging the sea wall; you can pick this up by turning west (left) down a bumpy back road at **Nayarambalam**, 1km north of **Narakkal**, or via any of the lanes peeling left further on.

## Accommodation

Cherai's **accommodation** costs a little over the odds, reflecting its proximity to Fort Cochin, but you can haggle down the rates if trade is slack.

**Brighton Beach House** 3/783 Palli Fort, 2km north of Cherai ☎0484/310 7661, ⓦwww .brightonbeachhouse.org. Fairly basic en-suite rooms (some a/c) opening on to a yard right next to the sea wall, a 5min drive north of the main beachfront. Meals and sundowners are served in a small gazebo-cum-sun terrace, raised to overlook the sand, which is particularly narrow here. ⑤–⑥

**Cherai Beach Resort** ☎0484/241 6949, ⓦwww .cheraibeachresorts.com. A convoluted campus of 45 differently priced mini-villas, squeezed onto a leafy, green plot bounded on one side by the shore road and on the other by backwaters. Its bumf claims the resort "has been ranked as the ultimate quiet destination in the world" but the place feels a bit cramped when it's at full tilt, and the only useable band of beach opposite is very slim indeed. ⑦–⑨

**Ocean Breath** ☎9847 635206, ⓦwww .beachandbackwater.com. The best-value budget

option in Cherai, and the one with most Keralan atmosphere. No sea views (it's set back across the road from the sea wall) but the rooms are pleasant, with high, traditional Keralan ceilings and carved gables, shiny ceramic floors and small sitouts. ④

**Sealine** Beach Rd, Cherai ☎0484/241 8055, ⓦwww.sealinebeachresort.com. With no-frills a/c and non-a/c rooms costing from Rs4600/3450 respectively in season, this is Cherai's most overpriced option, but the only one with rooms actually opening onto the beach. Guests get to use a row of sunloungers on a level strip of sand bang in front of the property, and there's a breezy open-sided restaurant on the top floor. ⑦–⑧

**Veterans** 3km north of Cherai beachfront ☎0484/248 0785 or ☎9747 864584. Half a dozen very simple budget rooms in a friendly homestay on the roadside. Those on the first floor have sea views. ④

## Athirappally Waterfalls

Set against a backdrop of the densely forested Sholayar Hills, the waterfalls at **ATHIRAPPALLY**, 50km northeast of Kochi, are the most spectacular in Kerala. Streams of day-trippers travel up here by coach on weekends to watch the Chalakudy River plunge 24m down vertical, brown-granite cliffs – stopping at one or other of the massive water amusement parks en route.

The main tourist path down to the foot of the falls starts at a car park on the roadside. Once you've reached the bottom you can join the groups of locals posing for photos with the dramatic curtain of white water and spray frothing behind. Other paths head downriver through the trees, but it's virtually impossible to escape noisy coach groups here at the weekend.

### Getting to Athirappally

Athirappally makes an ideal staging post on the journey to or from Parambikulam (see p.211), or you can travel up from the capital in an easy day-trip by taxi (Rs1000–1500 round-trip), in which case take the short cut via **Kalady** and the airport, which reduces the journey by 30km. By bus, first pick up any service running northwards on NH-47 from the KSRTC central stand to **Chalakudy**, and change there onto one of the hourly services continuing east to the falls. En route you pass a Forest Check Post and pay the **entrance fee** (Rs30 [Rs15]).

## Accommodation

The only **accommodation** in the area that actually boasts a view of the falls is the stylish *Rainforest* boutique hotel (T0480/278 4071, Wwww.rainforest.in; ●), just below the road, where India's answer to Brangelina – Abhiskekh Buchchan and Aishwariya Rai – famously spent two months during a Bollywood shoot. Designed in mellow natural stone and palm wood, its split-level rooms are gorgeous, with layouts that ingeniously preserve your privacy and big windows looking straight across the valley. If you're travelling with someone special, splash out on the "Celestial" suite (from around Rs16,000/$360 in season), where you can savour the views from the comfort of a candle-lit jacuzzi or – for the ultimate honeymoon experience – their secluded treehouse (Rs11,250/$250), whose bed has an uninterrupted, totally exclusive view of the waterfalls. There's also an overflow pool in the garden, and a lawn terrace restaurant serving tea, home-baked cake or full-scale meals. A friendly slender loris regularly puts in an appearance here at supper time.

Other **places to stay** punctuate the road lower down the valley, but they're uniformally grungy and/or overpriced. If you're desperate, the *Bethania Resorts* (T0480/276 9666 or T9747 012225; ●–●), set back from the river 1km down the hill from *Rainforest*, is the best value of the bunch, with clean, chintzy rooms that have little entrance halls but not much outside space to speak of. Simple Keralan and Chinese meals are available.

## Kodanad

A day-trip from Kochi guaranteed to please children and animal lovers is the ride 52km northeast to **KODANAD**, on the banks of the Periyar River, where a former **elephant training camp**, or *kraal*, provides refuge for a handful of rescued domestic pachyderms. The current population comprises three adults and four charming youngsters. Get here by 8.30am and you can accompany them and their *mahouts* to the river to help bathe and scrub the animals down. To do that you'll need to arrange a taxi (around Rs1000 for the round trip; there are no buses) and leave by 6am. Admission to the camp is free, although the *mahouts* will appreciate a tip. To make a full day of it, combine a visit to Kodanad with Athirappally Waterfalls, another forty minutes or so north.

The best option if you want to **stay** in the area is the *Riverfront Resort* at nearby Kurichilakode (T9846 305986, Wwww.riverfrontresort.net; ●), 1km away from the elephant *kraal*, which offers attractively furnished, traditional-style cottages on the riverbank, as well as a bamboo treehouse. The rates are good value considering the pleasant location and facilities, and include breakfast. Evening meals are available on request.

## Thattekkad Bird Sanctuary

Kerala's best bird sanctuary, **THATTEKKAD** (daily 9am–5pm; Rs20), 58km east of Kochi, occupies a 25-square-kilometre wedge of former rubber plantation between two branches of the Periyar River. Lying just off the highway to Munnar, it offers a tranquil stopover on the journey from the mountains and the coast. When the world-renowned ornithologist Salim Ali visited the site in the 1930s, he described it as the "richest bird habitat in peninsular India". Since then much of the area's forest has been felled, but what remains gives you some idea of the phenomenal **avian diversity** that once characterized the Keralan lowlands. A total of 275 species have been sighted here, most of them endemics. On an average day, visitors can expect to see between eighty and one hundred, including rarities such as the crimson-throated barbet, grey-headed fishing eagle and Malabar grey hornbill; early morning, between 6am and 7.30am, is the best time for birdwatching. Larger animals, from flying lizards to elephants, also put in occasional appearances.

## Getting to Thattekkad

NH-49 runs to within 15km of Thattekkad; the turning off the main road is at the town of **Kothamangalam**, connected by infrequent buses to Ernakulam (55km; 2hr) and Munnar (120km; 3hr 30min). If you find yourself faced with a long wait for a service, catch one of the more frequent buses to **Muvattupuzha**, to the southwest, and change there. Once you're in Kothamangalam, you shouldn't have any problem finding a local bus for the remaining half-hour to the sanctuary. The nearest railway station is inconveniently situated 48km away at Aluva.

Private boat operators may also be on hand to ferry birders to the sanctuary and day-trippers to Boothathanketu Lake further upriver – though at the time of writing, services were suspended following a spate of accidents, including the deaths of 15 schoolchildren and their teacher in February 2007, when the boat they were travelling in capsized. If and when trips on the river resume, whether by boat or canoe, make sure to wear a lifejacket at all times.

## Accommodation

With the exception of the *Hornbill Inspection Bungalow*, **accommodation** within range of Thattekkad tends to be pitched at well-heeled foreign birdwatchers, set on plantations or close to the riverside for early safari departures. The only place to stay inside the sanctuary itself is a three-storey, double-bedded **watchtower** on stilts (**④**) surrounded by a panoramic open window and, at ground level, an electric (solar-powered) fence to keep out the elephants. You can book it through the Assistant Wildlife Warden in Kothamangalam (see the review below of *Hornbill Inspection Bungalow* for contact details).

**Hornbill Camp** Book through *Kalypso Eco Lodges and Camps*, G-307 Panampilly Nagar, Kochi ☎0484/209 2280, ⓦwww.thehornbill camp.com. Luxury camp, at a beautiful site slap on the banks of the Periyar River opposite the sanctuary. Each of the tents is furnished with comfy twin beds, a toilet and wash basin; shower facilities are in a common block. Home-cooked Keralan meals are served in a high thatched gazebo, and as well as arranging birding tours they also lay on free kayaking, cycling and spice plantation trips. From Rs4500 per day, full board. **⑧**

**Hornbill Inspection Bungalow** Book through the Assistant Wildlife Warden, Nyayapilly PO, Kotha-mangalam ☎0485/258 8302. No-frills government inspection bungalow close to the sanctuary gates, with simple, attached double rooms. It's a bit cheerless, and decidedly overpriced (Rs1200 per person), but still cheaper than the alternatives this close to the reserve. It's popular, so book as far in advance as possible. **⑤**

**Mundackal Estate** Pindimana PO, Kothamangalam ☎0485/257 0717, ☎9388 620399, ⓦwww .mundackalhomestay.com. Very welcoming homestay in the Western-style home of welcoming local aristos Jose and Daisy Mundackal, on their working rubber, coconut and pepper plantation. It's within easy range of the sanctuary and Kothamangalam bus stand, 7km southwest. The Keralan–Christian cooking gets rave reviews (Daisy runs courses by prior arrangement). Doubles Rs7500–8500. **⑨**

**Periyar River Lodge** Book through 31/1027-A Friends Ave, Vyttila Kochin ☎0484/220 7173, ☎9447 707173, ⓦwww.periyarriverlodge.com. This handsome teak-built lodge sits on the riverbank next to the Thattekkad Sanctuary, centred on a traditional *nalukettu* sunken courtyard. A spacious lounge separates its two en-suite bedrooms, also wood-lined and tastefully furnished, and the entire building is surrounded by a veranda on which you can enjoy river views from a cane swing chair. Rates (Rs3500 per double or Rs6000 for the whole house) include full board. **⑦**

# Thrissur

**THRISSUR** (Trichur), a bustling market hub and temple town roughly midway between Kochi (74km south) and Palakkad (79km northeast) on NH-47, is a convenient base for exploring the cultural riches of central Kerala. Close to the Palghat (Palakkad) Gap – an opening in the natural border made by the Western Ghat mountains – it presided over the main trade route into the region from Tamil Nadu and Karnataka. For years the town was the capital of Cochin State, controlled at various times by both the Zamorin of Kozhikode and Tipu Sultan of Mysore.

Modern Thrissur dates from the eighteenth century, when Raja Rama Varma, the ruler of Travancore, developed the town centre, laying out roads and establishing markets with which Christian merchants were invited to trade. Although a Hindu himself, the raja helped further ensure the welfare of the Christian communities by establishing enclaves for them to the east and south. The spire of Kerala's largest church, **Our Lady of Dolores**, dominates the roofscape to this day, but it's to pay their respects at the mighty **Vadukkunnathan** temple, at the centre of the huge open maidan in the middle of town, that most Hindu visitors travel to

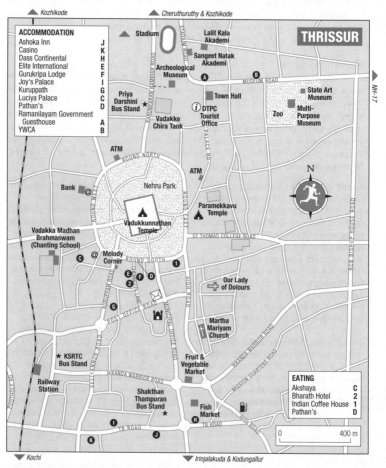

Thrissur – hundreds of thousands of them during the fierce heat of May, when the shrine plays host to Kerala's most extravagant, noisy and sumptuous *utsavam* festival, **Puram**.

## Arrival and information

The principal point of orientation in Thrissur is the **Round**, a road (subdivided into North, South, East and West) that circles the Vadukkunnathan Temple complex maidan in the town centre. On the main line to Chennai and other points in neighbouring Tamil Nadu, and with good connections to Kochi and Thiruvananthapuram, the **railway station** is 1km southwest, opposite the **KSRTC long-distance bus stand**. **Priya Darshini bus stand** (also known as "North", "Shoranur" and "Wadakkancheri" stand), close to Round North, serves Shoranur (for the Kalamandalam academy). The **Shakthan Thampuran bus stand**, on TB Road, around 1km from Round South, serves local destinations south such as Irinjalakuda, Kodungallur and Guruvayur.

The DTPC **tourist office** (Mon–Sat 10am–5pm; ☎0487/232 0800) is on Palace Road, opposite the Town Hall (five minutes' walk from Round East). Run by volunteers, its primary purpose is to promote the Puram elephant festival, but staff also give out maps of Thrissur. The best place to **change money** and travellers' cheques is the UTI Bank in the City Centre Shopping building (Mon–Fri 9.30am–3.30pm, Sat 9.30am–1.30pm) on Round West. The UAE Exchange & Financial Services (Mon–Sat 9.30am–6pm, Sun 9.30am–1.30pm) in the basement of the *Casino Hotel* building also changes currency and travellers' cheques. Both of the above, and a dozen or so other banks around the centre, have ATMs. The **main post office** is on the southern edge of town, just off Round South. **Internet** facilities are available at Hugues Net on the top floor of the City Centre Shopping building and SS Consultants next to the *Luciya Palace* hotel; rates are around Rs30/hr.

## Accommodation

Thrissur has plenty of competitively priced mid-scale **hotels**, but only a couple of decent budget places – the best of them the splendid *Ramanilayam Government Guesthouse*. Almost everywhere follows a 24hr checkout policy. If you're planning to be here during **Puram**, book well in advance and bear in mind that room rates soar – some of the more upmarket hotels, and those overlooking the Round, charge up to ten times their usual prices.

**Ashoka Inn** TB Rd ☎0487/244 4333, ⓦwww .ashokainn.co.in. Best value among the business-oriented three-stars in the bus stand district, in a spanking new, glass-sided tower block with spacious, impeccably clean rooms. ❺
**Casino** TB Rd ☎0487/242 4699, ⓦwww .casinotels.com. Sprawling three-star near the railway station that was the poshest place in town when it was built in the 1980s, but is now a bit frayed around the edges. Rooms in the original ("standard") block are best avoided, but the newly furnished "executive" ones are good value (Rs2300); those on the "privilege" floor are even more plush. There's a multi-cuisine restaurant, cocktail bar, lawn and kiddies' park, foreign exchange (residents only) – but no pool. ❺–❽

**Dass Continental** TB Rd ☎0487/244 6222, ⓦwww.dasscontinental.com. An anodyne, but perfectly serviceable, a/c business hotel close the bus stand – the best fallback if nearby *Ashoka* is full. ❺
**Elite International** Chembottil Lane, off Round South ☎0487/242 1033, ⓔmail@hoteleliteinter national.com. Pronounced "Ee-light", this massive gun-metal-grey tower block in the centre of town has rooms opening onto corridors, some with balconies overlooking the green. They're huge for the price, but dowdy. Rates include breakfast. ❸–❹
**Gurukripa Lodge** Chembottil Lane ☎0487/242 1895. Run with great efficiency by the venerable Mr Venugopal, the *Gurukripa*, just off Round South, offers a variety of simple en-suite rooms (including

several great-value singles) ranged around a long inner courtyard. Some a/c. ❶–❷

**Joy's Palace** TB Rd ☎0487/242 0199, ⓦwww .joyshotels.com. Opened in 2007, this is the nearest thing central Thrissur has to a five-star. The exterior is hilariously kitsch: each window in the ten-storey block is lit with randomly flashing coloured bulbs. Two kinds of room on offer: the "executives" have twin beds; and the "deluxe" have doubles and bathubs. The views from the upper floors are fantastic. Good value. ❻–❼

🦅 **Kuruppath** Mannadiara Lane, off Kuruppam Rd ☎9495 260000, ⓦwww.paithrukam .com. An impeccably restored heritage bungalow,

## Puram

Thrissur is best known to outsiders as the venue for Kerala's biggest annual festival, **Puram**, which takes place on one day in the Hindu month of Medam (April–May; ask at a tourist office or check online for the exact date). Inaugurated by Shaktan Tampuran, the Raja of Cochin, between 1789 and 1803, the event is the culmination of eight days of festivities spread over nine different temples to mark obeisance to Lord Shiva, at the peak of the summer's heat. Like *utsavam* festivals across Kerala, it involves the stock ingredients of caparisoned elephants, *panchavadyam* orchestras and firework displays, but on a scale, and performed with an intensity, unmatched by any other.

Puram's grand stage is the long, wide path leading to the southern entrance of the Vadukkunnathan Temple on the Round. Shortly after dawn, a sea of onlookers gathers here to watch the first phase of the 36-hour marathon – the **kudammattom**, or "Divine Durbar" – in which two majestic elephant processions, representing the Tiruvambadi and Paramekkavu temples of Thrissur, advance towards each other down the walkway, like armies on a medieval battlefield, preceded by ranks of drummers and musicians.

Both sides present thirteen tuskers sumptuously decorated with gold caparisons (**nettippattom**), each ridden by three young brahmins clutching objects symbolizing royalty: silver-handled whisks of yak hair, circular peacock-feather fans and colourful silk umbrellas fringed with silver pendants. At the centre of the opposing lines, the principal elephant carries an image of the temple's presiding deity. Swaying gently, the elephants stand still much of the time, ears flapping, seemingly oblivious to the crowds and huge orchestra that plays in front of them, competing to create the most noise and greatest spectacle.

When the music reaches its peak around sunset, the two groups set off towards different districts of town, Naickanal and Manikandanal. This signals the start of a spectacular **firework display** that begins with a series of deafening explosions and lasts through the night, with the teams once again trying to outdo each other to put on the most impressive show. Finally, in the afternoon of the second day, the elephant processions reconvene at the sacred courtyard inside the main temple, the Sri Moolasthanam, for a big farewell showdown, after which the deities are carried home to their respective temples on top of lone tuskers, leaving the crowd to discuss the relative merits of the teams, their elephants and firework extravaganzas.

If you venture to Thrissur for Puram, be prepared for packed buses and trains, and book accommodation well in advance. As is usual for *utsavam* festivals, many men use the event as an excuse to get hopelessly drunk. Women are thus advised to dress conservatively and only to go to the morning *kudammattom* session, or to watch with a group of Indian women – and at all times avoid the area immediately in front of the drummers, where the "rhythm madmen" congregate.

Note that **similar events** take place around the region throughout the year – many of them in the cooler winter months. A particularly fine example – featuring no less than 46 tuskers – is **Chembuthra Puram**, held in the nearby village of **Chembuthra**, 13km north of Thrissur, in late January or early February. In late March, **Arattupuzha Puram**, held at a temple maidan 14km out of town, boasts an even bigger line-up of 61 elephants.

cowering amid the high-rise tower blocks in the heart of town, only a stone's throw from Round South. Filled with dark wood and antique tiles, the interiors are light, wellaired, cool and amazingly peaceful considering the location, while the master bedroom on the first floor has a gigantic bathroom. There's also a covered veranda upstairs with a huge chess set where you can lounge in the evenings. Rates include meals. **⑦**

**Luciya Palace** Marar Rd ☎0487/242 4731, ⓦwww.hotelluciyapalace.comhotmail.com. An uninspiring mid-range option, though well maintained, efficiently run and decent value, and with a secluded rear garden. Don't be fooled by the large forecourt, which gives the impression it's much grander than it actually is. **④–⑤**

**Pathan's** Round South ☎0487/242 5620, ⓦwww .pathasresidentialhotel.com. Budget place on the Round holding only twenty rooms, all with larger than average bathrooms and generous outside

sitting space. The deluxe rooms are worn, but the a/c ones are smarter, bigger, better kept and afford grandstand views over the Round. Minimum two-night stay during Puram, when prices rise tenfold (though you're allowed to cram four people in for the price). **②–④**

**Ramanilayam Government Guesthouse** Palace Rd ☎0471/233 2016. Star-hotel comfort at economy lodge rates, in palatial suites with balconies, or smaller doubles (some a/c), set in manicured gardens on the northeast side of town near the zoo and museum. As with all *Government Guesthouses*, officials get priority (even at the last minute), which can make a mockery of advance bookings. **②–③**

**YWCA** Museum Rd ☎0487/232 2528. Women-only hostel opposite the town zoo and museum, popular mainly with long-staying students (both young and not so young). Its clean en-suite doubles (non-a/c) are a bargain. **②**

# The Town

Life in Thrissur revolves, quite literally, around the parched circle of grass in the dead centre known as **the Round**. The main sights all lie within walking distance of this hectic hub, but getting to and from them on foot in the heat can be a trial without an auto-rickshaw ride or two to help you along.

### Vadukkunnathan Temple

In the middle of the Round, the **Vadukkunnathan Temple** comprises a walled complex of fifteen shrines, dating from the twelfth century or earlier, the principal of which is dedicated to Shiva. Visitors lucky enough to be permitted inside (admission is reserved for Hindus only) enter a grassy compound that's surprisingly quiet and spacious, with a striking apsidal shrine dedicated to Ayappan (see p.162), decorated with some of the state's finest medieval murals. Once an essential ingredient of the temple's cultural life, but now under-used and neglected, the long, sloping-roofed **kuttambalam theatre** (also closed to non-Hindus), with carved panels and lathe-turned wooden pillars, serves as a venue for the ancient Sanskrit performance forms of *chakyar kuttu* and *kudiyattam* (see p.298).

### Vadakka Madham Brahmaswam

It has been speculated that some of the verses from the Rig Veda intoned by Namboodiri priests in the shrines of the Vadukkunnathan temple may be three or more thousand years old. The task of memorizing the ancient *slokas* – a dying art in the cyber era – begins at a tender age, and over at the **Vadakka Madham Brahmaswam** (daily 7.30am–2.30pm; free), five minutes' walk west of the temple off MG Rd, you can observe the process in action. Brahmin boys as young as eight attend **chanting** classes at this staunchly traditional Vedic *madham* – a typically Keralan complex of low-slung tiled roofs and halls with slatted wooden sides, sited next to an old stepped bathing tank. Wearing traditional white *mundu*, sacred threads and ash marks on their skin, the students sit cross-legged on little mats while they repeat verses modelled for them by their gurus – a scene that has changed little over twelve centuries, since brahmin traditions first permeated the region under patronage of the Kulasekharas. Chanting begins each morning at 5.45am sharp. Visitors are welcome from 7.30am onwards, but you should telephone in advance (T 0487/244 0877 or 244 6126) to ensure classes will be held on the day of your proposed visit, and that one of the staff will be available to show you around; donations towards the *madham*'s activities are welcome. Further details of the VMB Trust's activities are published online at W www.brahmaswammadham.org.

## Basilica of Our Lady of Dolours

Dating from 1929, the Indo-Gothic **Basilica of Our Lady of Dolours** (Puthan Pally in Malayalam) dominates the town's skyline southeast of the Round, thanks to its gigantic 79m belfry – allegedly the largest church tower in Asia. Visitors are welcome to scale the mighty edifice (Tues–Fri 10am–1pm & 2–6pm, Sat & Sun 10am–1pm & 2–7.30pm; Rs15), either via a lift or 350-step staircase, the latter enlivened by artwork depicting the life of Jesus in stained glass, woodcarving and garish frescoes. From the top, superb views extend across the palm forest surrounding Thrissur to the foothills of the distant Ghats. It's worth timing your visit to coincide with evening Mass, memorable for its haunting Malayali hymns and liturgies.

## The museums and art academies

Thrissur's museums are typical government-run affairs: dusty, half empty and poorly labelled, but worth a look if you've time to kill. The best of the bunch – not least for the splendid Keralan architecture of the former palace it's housed in – is the **Archeological Museum** (Tues–Sun 9.30am–1pm & 2–4.30pm; Rs10), opposite the Priya Darshini bus stand, a five-minute walk north of the Round. Former residence of the Cochin royal family, the 200-year-old Shaktan Thampuran Palace is beautifully decorated with intricate wood- and tile-work. Exhibits include fifteenth- and eighteenth-century hero stones, a fearsome selection of beheading axes, and a massive iron-studded treasury box still in its original place (presumably because no one has ever managed to shift its 1500kg dead weight). The real highlight, however, is the royal *palliyara*, or bedchamber, boasting a traditional carved wood four-poster and vibrant ceramic tiles. Visits wind up at the **Heritage Garden**, where you can cool off in the shade next to a delightful lily pond, with exotic birds and butterflies flitting through the greenery.

You'll need a sense of humour to get much from a visit to the gloomy **Multi-Purpose Museum** (Tues–Sun 9am–6.30pm; Rs8), ten minutes' walk from the Round in the northeast of town. Home to an odd assortment of skeletons, stuffed animals, pickled lizards, weapons and random dance costumes, it includes what must rank among the world's dullest exhibitions: a room devoted entirely to mud and silt, all painstakingly labelled ("greyish silt"; "light brown silt"; "grey mud with sand", and so on). In the same complex, the **State Art Museum** (same hours; admission by same ticket) is only slightly more engaging, though it does house one genuine treasure: a thirteenth-century solid silver cobra headdress that would once have adorned a life-sized temple deity. Next door, the **zoo** (same hours; same ticket) is a predictably depressing experience.

It's worth finding out if anything's on at the **Sangeet Natak Akademi** (T 0487/233 2134, W www.sangeetnatak.org) on Stadium Road, whose large auditorium hosts occasional music and dance concerts as well as contemporary Keralan theatre. Around the corner stands the **Lalit Kala Akademi** (Mon–Fri 11am–7pm; T 0487/233 3773, W www.lalitkala.gov.in) where contemporary *adivasi* (tribal) art is exhibited in a light, cool building designed by British architect, Laurie Baker.

## The tiger dance

Kerala's colourful Onam harvest festival, held in August/September, is celebrated with particular gusto in Thrissur, where the highlight of the festivities is the fabulously weird *Pulikali*, or **tiger dance**. Up to one thousand participants descend on the town for the event, in which troupes of masked men, their bodies adorned with elaborate tiger patterns, strut, stalk and wiggle their away around the Round – a spectacle as eccentric as any in this part of the world where outlandish costumes are a speciality.

*Pulikali* is thought to have been introduced to the region two hundred years ago by Muslim sepoys stationed here under the British. The East India Company native troops used to dress up as tigers to celebrate Muhurram and, true to form, the locals were quick to pick up on the custom, taking it to new extremes. Masks depicting the tigers' teeth, tongue and beard were added, along with tails, and belts and anklets of jingling bells, and – inevitably – massed ranks of traditional *chenda melam* drummers hammering away at full tilt.

Today, large troupes, or *sangam*, compete on the fourth day of Onam to present the most fabulous body paintings and choreographed routines. The teams are already well inebriated by the time they mass at the Ganapati (Ganesh) shrine in front of the Vadukkunnathan Temple for a propitious coconut-cracking session. This is when the dancing proper starts: performers with prominent bellies are particularly popular, shaking their midriffs (painted with striking tiger faces) for the amusement of the crowds.

Foreigners are welcome to join in, though if you're tempted, be warned the whole caper can be an ordeal. Dancers have to submit to a full body shave in the pre-dawn darkness before a heavy coat of oil-based undercoat is first applied, over which the tiger design is painted – a process taking five to seven hours. The dancing itself, in the intense heat and humidity of the late monsoon, lasts for two or three hours, the oil paint adding an asphyxiating, sweat-proof layer over the performers' skin. Despite such discomforts, *Pulikali* is growing in popularity, with bigger and more elaborately costumed *sangam* taking part. Quite what the whole event reveals about the Malayali psyche is a subject of amused debate in the local press.

▲ *Pulikali* tiger dance

## Shopping

Thrissur is a good place to pick up Keralan **crafts**, and its main shopping area is on the Round. On Round West, the **Kerala State Handicraft Emporium** stocks the usual carved wooden-elephant-type souvenirs, and, on the ground floor, a high-kitsch Aladdin's Cave of nodding dogs, Jesus clocks, Mecca table ornaments and parabolic nail-and-string art. **Melody Corner**, in the small arcade-mall at the top of Kuruppam Road, just off Round South, holds the widest selection of Indian music in the area, from compilations of Hindi and Malayalam film songs to obscure recordings of *sopana sangeet* recitals and local *panchavadyam* and *chenda melam* orchestras (see p.293).

Kuruppam Road, which leads south towards the railway station from the western end of Round South, is one of the best spots in Kerala to buy **bell-metal** products, particularly oil lamps made in the village of Nadavaramba, near Irinjalakuda (see p.202). The friendly **Nadavaramba Krishna & Sons** is a good place to start browsing. In the same area you'll also find stalls selling paraphernalia for Ayappan devotees, such as regulation black *mundus*, strings of sacred *rudraksha* beads and brass ritual implements.

## Eating and drinking

There are plenty of dependable places to eat in Thrissur, with many hotels and busy "meals" joints lining the Round. From 8.30pm onwards, you can also join the auto-rickshaw-wallahs, hospital visitors, itinerant mendicants, Ayappa devotees and student revellers who congregate at the popular **thattukada** hot food market on the corner of Round South and Round East, opposite the Medical College Hospital. The rustic Keralan cooking – omelettes, dosas, *parottas*, *iddiappam*, bean curries and egg masala – is always freshly prepared, delicious and unbelievably cheap.

**Akshaya** *Luciya Palace*, Marar Rd, just off the southwest corner of the Round. Hotel restaurant where black-tie waiters serve quality Keralan meals at lunchtime (Rs90) in a blissfully cold a/c dining hall. From 7.30pm you can order from an exhaustive multi-cuisine menu, sitting outside in a pleasant garden illuminated by fairy lights. Beer is permitted with meals.

**Bharath Hotel** Chembottil Lane, 50m down the road from the *Elite Hotel*. Thrissur's top pure-veg place, packed from 7.30am onwards. The food is unfailingly fresh and delicious. Try their tangy curd-*vada*, crammed with a hundred different flavours, or traditional lunchtime thali (Rs35), the queues for which stretch down the street on weekends, and be sure to leave room for

the *ada*, a mix of sugar cane, coconut and rice steamed in a banana leaf (which tastes discon-certingly like old-fashioned British treacle pudding).

**Indian Coffee House** Round South. The usual cheap and popular *ICH* range of south Indian snacks, as well as strong chai and weak coffee, served by waiters whose serious demeanour is undermined by their old-school ice-cream fan turbans and curry-stained tunics.

**Pathans** Round South. Much dingier than the *Bharath*, but with an equally devoted following. Its lunchtime meals (Rs45) are as good as any in the district, and they also do the full range of *udipi* standards, as well as some tasty Sri Lankan specialities.

# Around Thrissur

If Thrissur is the crucible of central Kerala's cultural and political life, then its hinterland serves as its main storehouse, dotted with towns and villages where both contemporary party politics and ancient art traditions are pursued with great enthusiasm, despite the disruptive impact on local life of mass out-migration. Countless **festivals**, at their peak in January and February, enable visitors to catch *kathakali* dance-drama and *kudiyattam*, the world's oldest surviving theatre form. **Nattika beach**, meanwhile, just over half an hour's drive southwest of Thrissur, is a great place simply to relax, with some of the most pleasant seaside accommodation in the region.

At **Irinjalakuda**, an important temple town thirty minutes by bus from Thrissur, one of the region's most acclaimed acting families hosts an annual festival devoted to **kudiyattam**; old-style crafts are also a feature of life here, and at the neighbouring village of **Nadavaramba** you can watch bell-metal oil lamps being made using the labour-intensive lost-wax technique. Nearby **Kodungallur**, site of the former port of Muziris, holds no traces of its historical role in the international spice trade, but does host one of Kerala's most outlandish and dramatic Tantric rituals, the **Bharani festival**, in which low-caste villagers cavort drunkenly around the local temple singing obscene songs for the Goddess. The pilgrimage scene at **Guruvayur**, Kerala's most important Krishna shrine, is more sober, but no less fervent. Foreign visitors aren't able to enter the main temple here, but the precinct around it buzzes with ritual activity; Guruvayur is also worth a visit for a stroll around the famous **Punnathur Kotta** elephant camp.

## Nattika

A little more than thirty minutes' drive southwest of Thrissur, **NATTIKA** village stands at the centre of a vast sandy beach, backed by stands of coconut palms and scattered fishing settlements. This idyllic location looms large in the popular imagination as the setting for Ramu Kariat's hit movie, *Chemmeen*, which bagged the President's Gold Medal for Cinema in 1965 and went on to become one of the best-loved Malayali films of all time. It told the story of love, betrayal and loss in a typical fishing community; Keralans of a certain age can still hum the hit songs from the movie. Other than the occasional crump of dynamite from the trawlers offshore, little has changed here since the film was shot, though the appearance under the palms of a handful of **luxury resorts** looks likely to alter the complexion of the village over the coming years.

The largest, and newest, of the complexes is the *Nattika Beach Resort* (℡0487/240 4182, Ⓦwww.thenattikabeach.com; ⑨), a campus of widely spaced laterite cottages, each fronted by a broad veranda and elegant wood pillars salvaged from antique Tamil mansions. Spread across a huge plot right behind the beach, the attractively furnished rooms come in three different sizes, all with naturally cool *ramacham* fibre ceilings, teak beds and clay-tiled floors; the priciest, sea-facing options also have lovely open-to-sky bathrooms. There's a large restaurant, and yoga area, but no pool. Next door, the much shabbier *Thalikulam* (℡0487/239 7239 or ℡9633 302111, Ⓦwww.thalikulambeachresorts.com; ❻–❼) enjoys a comparable beachside position, but is altogether less enticing, comprising chalets with Keralan-style roofs grouped around a murky green *faux* temple tank. Finally, a five-minute walk south lies the *Kaddpuram* (℡0487/239 7588, Ⓦwww.kadappurambeachresorts.com; ⑨), an eco-friendly, *Green Leaf* ayurveda resort popular mainly with German tourists. Its ten bamboo-and-coconut-leaf cottages sit under a shady palm grove crisscrossed by narrow tidal canals, surrounded by pot plants and borders of aromatic herbs. The beach is only 200m away. Rates start at around $150 for a double, including all meals and ayurveda treatments, but there's a minimum stay of two weeks.

## Irinjalakuda

The village of **IRINJALAKUDA**, 20km south of Thrissur, is the site of the unique **Koodal Manikiyam Temple**, dedicated to Bharata, the brother of Rama. Alas, the usual bar on non-Hindus means that few foreigners ever get to see the superbly elegant tiled *kuttambalam* **theatre** inside the main courtyard, which is renowned for its excellent acoustics. But you can peer at it through the bars to the left of the main gateway. On the low stage inside the building, enclosed by painted wooden columns and friezes of female dancers, stand two large copper *mizhavu* drums for use in the Sanskrit drama **kudiyattam** (see p.298), permanently installed in wooden frames into which a drummer climbs to play. The drama for which they provided music is still regarded as a holy ritual, and traditionally the instrument was only played by members of a special caste, the Nambyars.

One of Kerala's lesser known, but most archaic, ritual theatre forms, *kudiyattam* was on the verge of extinction two decades ago, when a family from Irinjalakuda embarked on reviving it, along with other still more obscure forms such as *nangia-rkoothu* (female mono-acting), shadow and puppet theatre. At their home ten minutes' walk east of the temple, Sri Gopal Venu, Nirmala Paniker and their daughter Kapila run a small centre for the documentation of Kerala's ritual arts, **Natana Kairali**. Casual visitors aren't encouraged to call, however, except during the centre's annual ten-day **festival** in January, when the family performs a full cycle of *kudiyattam* plays – a rare chance for non-Hindus to experience the form, which is usually only staged in the confines of closed temples. Schedules are posted at Kapila's homepage, Ⓦ virali.org.

While you're in the area, it's worth hunting out a pair of impressively large **metalware** shops, Alenghadens (AKP) and CKK Vessels, on the main street. Both sell the full range of traditional bell-metal vessels and lamps, as made at nearby Nadavaramba, along with a bewildering array of other objects, both religious and secular.

Irinjalakuda is best reached by **bus** from the Shakthan Thampuran stand in Thrissur rather than by train, as the railway station is an inconvenient 8km east of town. For a **meal**, the authentic local choice is the pure-veg *Hotel Woodlands*, diagonally opposite the bus stand on Temple Road, which does superb Rs30 lunchtime thalis and *udipi* snacks through the afternoon and evening. The Lakshmi Bakery, next door, has a pleasant mezzanine floor where you can order cooling milkshakes and Keralan-style biscuits. If you find yourself here during the Natana Kairali

## Nadavaramba bell-metal oil lamps

Keralan nights are made more enchanting by the use of oil lamps, which you'll see hanging from verandas and standing in front of house entrances throughout the state. The most common type, seen everywhere, is a slim, freestanding metal column topped by a spike that rises from a circular receptacle for coconut oil, with cloth or banana-plant fibre wicks. Every classical theatre performance keeps a large lamp burning centre-stage all night. The special atmosphere of temples is also enhanced by innumerable lamps, some hanging from chains; others, multi-tiered *deepa stambham*, stand metres high.

The village of **Nadavaramba**, 5km from Irinjalakuda on the Kodungallur road, is an important centre for the manufacture of oil lamps and large cooking vessels, known as *uruli* and *varppu*. Bell-metal alloys are made from copper and tin, and give a sonorous chime when struck. One of the best places to buy is the Bellwicks Handicrafts Cooperative (℡0480/282 5147, ℮bellwickskerala@yahoo.co.in), just north of Nadavaramba Church on the roadside, where you can watch the various stages of the casting process, from the making of sand and wax moulds to the pouring of molten metal, labour-intensive filing and polishing. The largest independent manufacturer in Kerala, Bellwicks produces an array of bell-metal utensils: fourteen different kinds of lamp, ayurvedic treatment utensils, cooking vessels of every conceivable size and temple decorations. Prices depend on the weight of the object, starting at Rs800 per kilogram.

festival and need to stay, head for the *Kallada Regency*, behind the Municipal Town Hall (☎0480/283 2601, ⓦwww.kallada.com; ④), whose generous rooms are clean and very good value, with large balconies and a/c for only Rs300 extra. The hotel restaurant also does a popular lunchtime Keralan veg buffet for Rs100, served on china instead of tin plates, in a blissfully cool a/c dining hall.

# Kodungallur

Virtually an island surrounded by backwaters and the sea, **KODUNGALLUR** (Cranganore), 35km south of Thrissur, has been identified as the site of the ancient cities of **Vanji** (one-time capital of the Chera kingdom), and **Muziris**, described in the first century AD by the Roman traveller Pliny as *"primum emporium Indiae"*, the most important trading post in India. The silting up of the harbour in 1341, however, led to its rapid decline and today the former city has disappeared almost without trace – only the odd pottery shard or Roman coins unearthed by farmers hint at its former significance. That said, a handful of minor monuments still stand and make a worthwhile detour if you're travelling through the area.

## Cheraman Juma Masjid

One of the few surviving monuments from early-medieval Muziris is the modest **Cheraman Juma Masjid** (ⓦwww.cheramanmosque.com), 1.5km south of modern Kodungallur centre on NH-17. Thought to be the oldest mosque in India, it was founded in 629AD by **Cheraman Perumal**, the legendary Keralan king who converted to Islam, abdicated and emigrated to Mecca. Unfortunately, due to weather damage, the building originally sited here has been entirely reconstructed, and the facade, at least, is now rather mundane, with concrete minarets. The wooden interior, however, remains largely intact, with a large Keralan oil lamp in the centre and a splendid lathe-turned, lacquered pulpit. Visitors are welcome to look around if prayers are not in progress; make yourself known to Mr Saraf, the secretary, who sits in an empty "museum" next door.

## Thiruvanchikkulam Mahadeva Temple

Less than 500m south from the Cheraman Juma Masjid, past a bend in the main highway (NH-17), a wide avenue leads past tall lamps to the **Thiruvanchikkulam Mahadeva Temple**, dedicated to Lord Shiva. Located in a peaceful setting with a backdrop of tall coconut trees, it's a fine example of traditional Keralan temple architecture. Non-Hindus are permitted inside the main courtyard, but not the shrine itself. Start by walking around the perimeter wall, which will take you to the temple's majestic east gateway, with its sloping roof and carvings of elephants, gods and goddesses. Inside the enclosure itself, a porch with carvings dedicated to the heroes of the great Hindu epic, the Ramayana, marks the furthest point non-Hindus are allowed.

## Kurumba Bhagavati Temple

On a large piece of open ground at the centre of Kodungallur, the **Kurumba Bhagavati Temple** is infamous in Kerala as the site of an extraordinary annual event that many upper-caste residents would prefer didn't happen at all. The **Bharani festival**, held during the Malayalam month of Meenom (March/April), attracts several thousand devotees, both male and female, mainly from low-caste communities previously excluded from the temple. Their devotions consist in part of drinking copious amounts of alcohol and taking to the streets to sing Bharani *pattu*, sexually explicit songs about, and addressed to, the goddess Bhagavati, which are considered obscene and highly offensive by many other Keralans. On Kavuthindal, the first day, the pilgrims run en masse around the perimeters of the temple three times at breakneck speed, beating its walls with sticks. Until the mid-1950s, chickens were sacrificed in front of the shrine; today, a simple red cloth symbolizes the bloody ritual.

The event also attracts a couple of thousand long-haired **sorcerer-oracles** (*velichapadus*, literally "light bearers"), the majority of them female, from goddess temples across central Kerala. Dressed in scarlet robes and heavy waist belts strung with brass bells, they carry special 1.5m-long swords with lethal, sickle-shaped ends. As the festival progresses, the *velichapadus*, and their weapons, take on a more central role. Delirious from lack of food and sleep, crowds form around them as, one by one, the shamans lapse into frenzied trance-dances which culminate with them slicing open the tops of their heads with their swords. Blood is offered as a symbol of their devotion to the goddess before the swords are temporarily handed over to a Nair temple manager (the brahmin priests having fled the shrine for the duration).

Thousands of cane-wielding police descend for the final, craziest day of the festival, when the *velichapadus* are ceremonially given back their swords. Whirling them triumphantly around their heads, they leap and scream their way through one final, day-long dance marathon, watched by crowds dangling from the trees and compound walls. Its final cadence is the emergence, from a secret side door in the temple, of an elderly, rather frail member of the royal family who climbs a podium to raise a silk umbrella, symbolizing the reassertion of his sovereignty. This sparks off one last, frantic burst from the *velichapadus*, who race around the temple, swords aloft, before dispersing. The shrine, by now a chaos of turmeric powder, broken coconuts and leaves, is then ritually cleansed, and normality restored.

### Mar Thoma Pontifical Shrine

The **Mar Thoma Pontifical Shrine**, fronted by a crescent of Neoclassical colonnades at Azhikode (pronounced "Arikode") Jetty, marks the place where the Apostle Thomas is said to have arrived in India in 52 AD. Situated on the watery outskirts of Kodungallur, it's a tranquil spot with a promenade and stalls selling religious paraphernalia, but hardly warrants a trip unless you're desperate to see the shard of the saint's wrist-bone enshrined within the church (daily 9am–6pm). Frequent buses from Kodungallur stop at Azhikode Jetty, at the end of the promenade past the fishing boats.

## Guruvayur

Kerala's most important Krishna shrine is the temple of **GURUVAYUR** (3am–1pm & 4.30–10pm; closed to non-Hindus), 19km northwest of Thrissur, which attracts a constant flow of devotees year round. Second only in popularity to Lord Ayappa at Sabarimala (see p.162), its presiding deity, **Guruvayurappan**, has inspired numerous paeans from Keralan poets, most notably Narayana Bhattatiri, who wrote the *Narayaniyam* in the sixteenth century, when the temple, whose origins are legendary, seems to have first risen to prominence. Guruvayur is one of the richest temples in Kerala and is constantly awash with **pilgrims**, dressed in their best white and gold-trim clothes. Newlywed couples also come here en masse to have their weddings blessed – on average, seventy of them each day, or as many as 300 on auspicious occasions, when the whole process takes on the appearance of a production line.

The **market** outside the temple is noisy and intense, with stalls full of glitter and trinkets and a palpable air of excitement, particularly when events inside spill out into the streets. A temple committee stall outside the main gates auctions off the donations, including bell-metal lamps, received at the shrine – according to superstition, if you buy any of these items they must be returned to the temple as gifts.

Of the temple's 24 annual **festivals**, the most important are **Ekadashi** and **Ulsavam**. The eighteen days of Ekadashi, in the month of Virchikam (Nov/Dec), are marked by processions of caparisoned elephants outside the temple, while the exterior of the building is decorated with the tiny flames of innumerable oil lamps from sunset onwards. Performances staged in front of the temple (check dates with a KTDC office) attract the cream of south Indian classical music artists. During Ulsavam, in the month of Kumbham (Feb/March), Tantric rituals are conducted inside, an **elephant race** is run outside on the first day, and elephant processions take place during the ensuing six days. On the ninth day, the Palivetta, or "hunt" occurs; the deity, mounted on an elephant, circumnavigates the temple accompanied by men dressed as animals, representing human weaknesses such as greed and anger, and are vanquished by the god. The next night sees the image of the god taken out for ritual immersion in the temple tank; devotees greet the procession with oil lamps and throw rice. It is considered highly auspicious to bathe in the tank at the same time as the god.

When not involved in races and arcane temple rituals, Guruvayur's tuskers are chained at the **Punnathur Kotta Elephant Camp** (daily 8am–6pm; Rs5, cameras Rs25), 4km north of town. Some 67 elephants, aged from 8 to 95, live here, munching for most of the day on specially imported piles of fodder and cared for by their three personal *mahouts*, who wash and scrub them several times a week in the sanctuary pond. The elephants are well cared for by Keralan standards, but many foreign animal lovers find the spectacle of these large animals hobbled in less than ideal conditions unsettling. The animals are considered the personal possessions of Lord Guruvayur, given to the temple by wealthy donors from as far afield as Bihar and Assam. All of them – apart from the most elderly, who are allowed an honourable retirement – are gainfully employed appearing at temple festivals. The standard daily charge is Rs5000 per elephant, but the prettiest pachyderms are often the subject of heated auctions, with rival villages bidding up to Rs200,000 for a single animal. As with domestic elephants everywhere, only approach an animal if a *mahout* allows you, as they can be unpredictable and dangerous.

▲ Elephant and *mahout*

## Practicalities

Buses from Thrissur (40min) arrive at the KSRTC **bus stand** on the west side of Guruvayur, five minutes' walk from the temple. The **railway station** is on the opposite side of town. Of the many clean and respectable **places to stay**, *Sopanam Heritage*, 500m west of the station on the main street leading to the temple (☎0487/255 5244, ⊛www.sopanamguruvayoor.com; ❹–❻), offers 72 smart, a/c rooms on five storeys. Their a/c multi-cuisine **restaurants** – *Agarsala* (veg) and *Rasoi* (non-veg) – are the swankiest in town. Otherwise, the town is crammed with strict veg restaurants, and there's an *Indian Coffee House* on the southern side of East Nada Street.

# Nila

Although sadly depleted these days by sand-mining and large-scale dams inland, the mighty **Bharatapuzha** (pronounced "bharatapura") – commonly referred as to the **Nila** – is the greatest of the rivers flowing west across the Keralan coastal plains. Countless **sacred sites**, including several major temples, punctuate its banks, which have over the centuries spawned an exceptionally large number of acclaimed Malayali poets, astronomers, holy men, musicians and *kathakali* performers.

A constellation of small villages clustered around large expanses of paddy fields that spill from the river's bleached, dusty banks, the area remains among the most traditional in the state – and is thus often difficult for outsiders to penetrate. But you can gain a taste of the arcane art forms that have evolved in the region at the **Kalamandalam Academy** in **Cheruthuruthy** – Kerala's principal college for ritual theatre, dance and arts. Deep in a lush rice-growing belt, Poonmully Mana in the village of **Peringode** is another crucible of ancient Keralan tradition, where a small heritage centre occupies the ancestral home of the late Aram Thampuran – a legend in the fields of martial arts and Sanskrit poetry. Thampuran was also a renowned ayurveda doctor, and the healing methods he adhered to are still practised at a small treatment centre in a converted wing of his former palace.

The banks of the Nila are also something of a homeland for a community of traditional bards called **Pulluvars**, who used to be a common sight in the rural villages of this area, but are slowly fading away as the age-old farming way of life along the river declines. Connected with snake worship, the Pulluvars traditionally perform songs and trance dances in temples, sacred wood groves (*kavu*) and low-caste homes, playing *veenas* made from bamboo and coconut shells, and instruments called *kutam* – a Keralan equivalent of the tea-chest bass fashioned from a clay pot, calf skin, long stick and piece of string. As an outsider, your chances of coming across a Pulluvar performance are slim. However, *Blue Yonder* (⊛www.theblueyonder.com) organize recitals for visitors as part of a broader initiative to raise awareness of the environmental threats to the Nila and the unique culture it supports.

### Cheruthuruthy

Some 32km north of Thrissur, and an easy day-trip, the village of **CHERUTHURUTHY** is internationally famous as the home of **Kerala Kalamandalam**, the state's flagship training school for indigenous performing arts. The academy was founded in 1927 by the revered Keralan poet Vallathol (1878–1957). At first patronized by the Raja of Cochin, it has since benefited from funding from both state and national governments, and has been instrumental in the large-scale revival of interest in *kathakali* and other unique Keralan art forms. Despite conservative opposition, the college has always followed an open-door recruitment policy, based on artistic merit rather than religious affiliation, which produces "scheduled caste" Muslim and Christian graduates along with the usual Hindu castes – something that was once unimaginable.

All comers are welcome to attend performances of *kathakali*, *kudiyattam* and *mohiniyattam* performed in the school's wonderful **theatre**, which replicates the style of the wooden, sloping-roofed traditional *kuttambalam* auditoria found in Keralan temples. You can also sit in on classes, watch demonstrations of mural-painting and mask-making, and see exhibitions of costumes by signing up for the fascinating **"day with the masters"** cultural programme (Mon–Sat 9.30am–1.30pm; $20 including lunch; book in advance ℡04884/262305, ℮info@kalamandalam.com). Try to time your visit to coincide with the annual, week-long **Thauryathrikam festival** in January. Held at the *kuttambalam* auditorium and at Kalamandalam's original riverside campus amongst the trees, the free event presents all the art forms taught at the academy. A short walk past the old school building leads to a small but exquisite **Shiva temple** in classic Keralan style. The exterior is lit by candles during the early evening puja, a particularly rewarding time to visit.

A handful of foreigners also come to the Kalamandalam academy to **study**: one-month introductions, three- to six-month intensives, and full vocational training from four to six years are all offered. You can apply from abroad (℡04884/262418, ℗www.kalamandalam.org), but it's best to visit first, as the training is rigorous, to say the least. Note that photography is not allowed anywhere in the Kalamandalam without a **photography permit**, which costs Rs500 (for ten images only). The cost of the "day with the masters" tour includes the photo fee.

### Practicalities

**Buses** heading to Shoranur from Thrissur's Priya Darshini (aka "Wadakkancheri") stand pass through Cheruthuruthy; the nearest mainline **railway station** is Shoranur Junction, 3km south, served by express trains to and from Mangalore, Chennai and Kochi.

Cheruthuruthy's **accommodation** is limited. For a touch of a/c luxury, head for the *River Retreat Heritage Ayurvedic Resort* (℡04884/262244; ℗www.riverretreat .in; ❻–❽), 2km from Kalamandalam. The former palace of the Raja of Cochin, the three-star heritage hotel and ayurvedic spa occupies an idyllic position on Palace Road on the banks of the Nila. Despite some heavy-handed renovation work, its rooms are elegantly furnished with fine teak furniture; some have private terraces facing the river. In the lawned garden, a crystalline pool, partly shaded by coconut palms, also looks across to the river. Other than at the resort, the only places to **eat** in Cheruthuruthy are simple *dhabas* in the centre of the village, including the vegetarian *Mahatma*.

### Peringode

**PERINGODE**, a small rice-farming village 14km northeast of Guruvayur, is the ancestral seat of one of Kerala's most powerful Namboodiri brahmin dynasties, the Poonmullis. Renowned as patrons of the arts and healing sciences, the family used to stage famous recitals by the region's most illustrious performers at their mansion, or *mana*, on the village outskirts. The previous dynastic head, **Aram Thampuran**, was also an acclaimed ayurvedic doctor and Sanskrit scholar, as well as a poet and *kalarippayat* martial artist. The old *mana* where he and his family lived until his death collapsed a few years back and has been dismantled, but its bachelor wing, where unmarried male members of the family resided, has been exquisitely restored for use as an ayurveda centre, *Ayurveda Mana* (℡0466/2370 660 or ℡9846 045696, ℗www.ayurvedamana.com; around $175 per day, ❾). Rates include all consultations, medicines, treatments, food and accommodation – not bad when you compare that with far less authentic places elsewhere in the state. Faithfully conforming to Aram Thampuran's methods, the treatments are of the highest order: locally picked herbs are prepared fresh each morning in bubbling bell-metal *urulis* to make the internal medicines and massage oils. But it's also for the wonderfully traditional atmosphere of the place that patients come. Swathed in greenery, the centre is next to an elegant, tile-roofed Rama temple which, for once, non-Hindus are permitted to enter. Patients can also watch local *kalarippayat* students being put through their paces at the adjacent earth-floored *kalari* pit, and to view the Poonmulli's antique *kathakali* costumes and palm-leaf manuscripts.

Regular buses run to nearby **Pattambi**, 6km northeast, from Thrissur, Guruvayur and Shoranur. If you're travelling by taxi, phone ahead for directions as the *mana* is difficult to find.

# Palakkad and around

The only sizeable breach in the mighty wall of mountains marching 1200km down the western flank of peninsular India is the **Palakkad Gap**. Invading armies, traders and migrants have poured through this 40km rupture in the Western Ghats for thousands of years, as underlined by the discovery by British road builders in the nineteenth century of a hoard of Roman coins dating from the reigns of Augustus and Tiberius. It remains a key transport corridor today, connecting the city of Coimbatore in Tamil Nadu with the west coast.

When Hyder Ali and Tipu Sultan's armies streamed through to annexe Kerala in the sixteenth and seventeenth centuries, **Palakkad** (Palghat) was the town they chose to erect a fortress to control traffic through the mountains. The pock-marks of British cannonfire still scar the citadel's dark-brown laterite walls in places, but the town barely warrants a stopover unless it happens to coincide with the annual **Car Festival** at nearby **Kalpathy**, when huge, excited crowds gather to haul three giant wooden chariots through the main street of a pictur-esque old brahmin colony.

If you're passing through, it'll probably be en route to one of the heritage homestays and ayurvedic resorts scattered around Palakkad's well-watered hinter-land, or to pick up transport to the little-visited hill station of **Nelliampathy** to the south. For a close encounter with the region's forest creatures, you should set aside a few days for **Parambikulam**, a remote reserve high on the Nelliampathy plateau, which can only be approached from the Tamil Nadu side of the range.

## Palakkad

An obvious overnight halt on the journey between central Kerala and the plains of Tamil Nadu is **PALAKKAD** (Palghat), 79km up NH-47 from Thrissur. Set against a distant backdrop of saw-toothed peaks and dark cliffs of brown laterite, the town is the hub of a major rice- and vegetable-growing area, as well as site of Kerala's best-preserved **fort** (daily 8am–6pm; free), built by Haider Ali of Mysore in 1766. The stronghold, with its imposing stone ramparts and weed-filled moat, witnessed a bloody skirmish when the British stormed it on behalf of their ally, the Zamorin of Calicut. These days, it's besieged every weekend by streams of local school groups and picnickers. Just outside the citadel, **Vatika Gardens** are another favourite family destination (daily 11am–8pm; Rs5), second only in popularity to the **amusement park** at **Malampuzha**, 10km north (daily 11am–9pm; Rs100 includes all rides), renowned locally for its cable car or "ropeway" and fantasy rock garden created by the artist Nek Chand of Chandigarh fame.

## Arrival and information

Palakkad is well connected to the rest of Kerala, and most of the express trains passing through stop at the mainline **railway station**, 6km northeast of the centre. The KSRTC **bus stand** is right in the middle of town. DTPC's **tourist office**, at Fort Maidan (Mon–Sat 9.30am–5pm; ☏0491/253 8996), is a good source of advice on local festivals and cultural events. The *Indraprastha* and the *Fort Palace* hotels offer residents-only foreign exchange facilities, and you can also **change money** and travellers' cheques at the State Bank of India, next to the *Indraprastha*, where there's also a 24hr ATM.

## Accommodation in and around Palakkad

Palakkad's small but adequate crop of **hotels** is pitched primarily at business clients passing through. Further afield, a handful of more upscale, foreigner-oriented heritage **homestays** and ayurveda **spas** are desirable destinations in their own right, with lots of traditional Keralan character and potential for trips into the less-frequented rural corners of the state.

**Fort Palace** 1km from bus stand on West Fort Rd ☏0491/253 4621, ✸www.fortpalace.com. Opposite the fort, this efficient mid-range hotel, built in mock-citadel style complete with crenellations, offers a choice of polished, very good-value a/c and non-a/c rooms, all en suite. Brace yourself for a rowdy vibe on Saturday nights, when the bar downstairs hosts noisy, male-dominated discos. ❹–❺

**Indraprastha** English Church Rd ☏0491/253 4641, ✸www.hotelindraprastha.com. Well-managed, though rather dowdy, place that's the best fallback if you can't get a room at the *Fort Palace*, with spacious, centrally a/c rooms (often block-booked by visiting government honchos, so reserve in advance). Its greatest asset is the excellent 24hr vegetarian coffee shop next to the main entrance (see p.210), built in traditional Keralan style. ❹–❺

**ITL Residency** Press Club Rd ☏0491/252 5262, ✉itlresidency@gmail.com. Well-scrubbed, functional lower-mid-range option in a quiet location overlooking a leafy disused railway line. The white-painted rooms are fresh and clean, and bathrooms immaculate. ❸–❺

🏃 **Kalari Kovilakom** 20km south of Palakkad at Kollengode ☏04923/263737, ✸www.kalarikovilakom.com. It's impossible to imagine a more exquisite place to receive ayurvedic treatments than *Kalari Kovilakom*. The eco-conscious CGH chain spent three years renovating this eighteenth-century palace, former residence of the Vengunad dynasty, and the result is as spectacular as the mountain backdrop. Guests are encouraged not to leave the premises during their stay, which is no great chore as the whole place, set in substantial grounds, is an architectural feast: colonnaded walkways lead to open *nalukettu* court-yards, hidden bathing pools and wood-lined interiors, lit by louvred windows and slatted

screens. The food served in the strictly vegetarian restaurant is tailored to fit individual treatment regimes; alcohol and tobacco are forbidden. Prices start at a hefty $6750 for one for a minimum 14-day stay, with discounts for two sharing. ❾

**Kandath Tharavad** Thenkurussi ☏04922/284124 or ☏9349 904124, ✸www.tharavad.info. Idyllic heritage homestay, in a 200-year-old ancestral seat set on the edge of a sleepy village 10km south of Palakkad. Surrounded by rice paddy, the mansion's most striking feature is the raised, colonnaded *puruthalum* veranda at the front, whose bulbous pillars are capped by carvings of elephants, snakes and dragons. Host Mr Bhagwaldas and his offspring, the fifth and sixth generations to live here, offer six simply furnished guest rooms, and activities ranging from guided birding and trekking to bullock-cart and cycle rides, cookery classes and even toddy-tapping trips. From Rs7600 (full-board). ❾

**KPM Regency** Press Club Rd ☏0491/253 4601, ✸www.kpmregency.com. Serviceable three-star in the town centre with pleasant a/c deluxe rooms, along with cheaper and far less appealing "executive" options on the lower ground floor, which are little bigger than the beds within them. ❸–❺

🏃 **Sradha** Anuragam Farm, Mechira, Muthala-mada ☏04923/275682 or ☏9496 235275, ✸www.myspace.com/sradharetreat. A wild-card option, for spiritually inclined budget travellers with a sense of adventure. Nestled at the foot of the mighty Nelliampathy escarpment, basic accommo-dation is offered on a working organic farm in a truly bucolic, timeless setting. Guests are encour-aged to pitch in with simple farm work (though it's not obligatory) and host Suman, a passionate Krishmurti devotee, can point you in the direction of spectacular local treks. Rates include vegetarian Keralan meals. ❸–❹

### Eating

The best place for high-quality, **vegetarian** *udipi* food, and traditional Keralan rice meals at lunch, is the *Hotel Indraprastha*'s coffee shop, where you you can tuck into crisp dosas served on banana leaves in a scrupulously clean, octagonal dining hall with louvred sides. Thalis cost Rs40–70, and the restaurant opens early for *iddli-vada* breakfasts. For **non-veg** food, the *Fort Palace*'s smart restaurant, *Caryota*, offers an exhaustive multi-cuisine menu – the Chinese dishes are particularly popular. Reserve if you want to eat on a Sunday evening, when the place gets packed out with local families. In dry weather you can eat alfresco in the garden.

## Kalpathy

Driven out of the Chola temple towns of neighbouring Tamil Nadu by Muslim invaders in the fourteenth century, waves of brahmin priests and their families started settling in Kerala under protection of the region's rulers. Some eighteen colonies – or *agraharam* – were founded in all, the largest of them 3km north of Palakkad at **KALPATHY**. Creeping urbanization and a four-lane bypass nowadays threaten to engulf the old settlement, but its way of life remains astonishingly remote from the mainstream of Keralan life. Lined up along a broad bazaar, terraces of low, red-tiled houses are fronted by pillared verandas where Namboodiri priests and students, bare-chested save for their sacred threads, relax between rounds of rituals in the two large Shiva temples located at opposite ends of the main street. Education, with a strong emphasis on the chanting of ancient vedic texts, has always been central to the community, and Kalpathy has produced more than its share of famous scholars over the years, as well as high-ranking civil servants and – unusually for Kerala – Carnatic singers (a legacy of the old Tamil influence).

Among Malayalis, however, the *agraharam* is known primarily for its annual festival, **Kalpathy Ratholsavam**, held over a week towards the end of Aippasi (mid-Nov; check ⓦ www.keralatourism.org for dates), when boisterous, inebriated crowds descend on the village to help haul giant chariots, or *raths*, down Kalpathy's main street. Festooned in coconuts, flowers, leaves and lavishly embossed window surrounds, the wooden colossi support huge towers draped in colourful cotton and brocade covers, on which the temple deities are enshrined as they're dragged between the temples. Excited teams jostle for the honour of pulling the ropes – women and girls on the right, boys and men on the left – while ranks of *chenda melam* drummers lead the procession. Foreigners are warmly welcomed at the festival, but non-Hindus are not permitted to enter the temples. The easiest way to **get to Kalpathy** from Palakkad is by auto-rickshaw. **Eating** options are limited to traditional, strictly vegetarian "meals" places.

## Nelliampathy

A popular escape from the heat in this area is the ramshackle hill settlement of **NELLIAMPATHY**, 75km south of Palakkad. Surrounded by teak forests and estates where tea, coffee, cardamom and oranges grow in profusion, the hill station certainly makes a refreshing change from the sweltering plains below. Unfortunately, however, reluctance on the part of the Keralan government to unlock Nelliampathy's tourist potential means there's a marked shortage of decent accommodation. Rather than staying the night, visitors tend to travel up for the day, taking jeep rides and short walks to viewpoints; proper paths into the surrounding hills are few and far between, and trekking permits impossible to obtain. That said, Nelliampathy, spread over undulating terrain at an altitude of a little above 1500m, is set amid some magnificent scenery, and the journey to get there, winding up a succession of spurs above the Pothundi Dam and reservoir, ranks among the most spectacular in the state.

Hourly KSRTC **buses** run to Nelliampathy from Palakkad (from 5.45am), although you'll probably get there more quickly by jumping on one of the more frequent services from Palakkad town bus stand to **Nemara**, from where shared jeeps (Rs500) cover the onward 26km leg. Nemara is also the jumping-off point for services east into Tamil Nadu from Thrissur. After the spectacular climb, buses terminate at Nelliampathy's **Kaikatty** crossroads, where a fleet of local **jeeps** wait to ferry arrivals to their guesthouses. Prices depend on the number of people and whim of the driver; expect to pay around Rs20–30/km.

Signboards advertise **accommodation** in several guesthouses and plantation stays in the area, but the only one worth considering is the excellent-value ℀ *Ciscilia Heritage*, on the Ranimedu Estate, 6km from Kaikatty (☎04923/206283 or ☎9447 033560, ⓦwww.cisciliaheritage.com; ❹–❺). Set amid dense shola forest, it's reached via a long, bone-jarring ride up a plantation track (phone ahead when you reach Kaiketty to summon the hotel jeep). You can sleep in teak-lined wooden huts with solar-powered hot water, overlooking tea gardens, or in smaller, cheaper rooms in a red-brick block opening onto an inner courtyard. Meals are served in a small, open-sided restaurant against a cacophony of exotic animal noises. Enclosed on all sides by trees, it's a superb setting for birdwatching. Trekking is not generally on the menu, but staff can show you to a nearby viewpoint, from where no one will stop you following unmarked trails up the exposed ridges encircling the plateau (though bear in mind if you do venture up the mountain that sudden, and extreme, changes in weather are common, and that the steep terrain may be lethal in poor visibility). As a fallback, you could always try the government-run *ITL Resort* down in Kaikatty (☎04923/246357; ❺) – a characterless, but clean, motel-style place on the roadside with large rooms opening onto lawns, and a restaurant serving indifferent Keralan meals. It's invariably booked out by boozy groups of men on weekends but during the week usually has vacancies.

## Parambikulam

With Periyar over-commercialized and overcrowded these days, and rapidly falling out of favour with foreign visitors, **PARAMBIKULAM**, immediately south of the Palakkad Gap in an isolated valley sandwiched between the Nelliampathy plateau and Anamalai range in Tamil Nadu, is fast becoming the park of choice for most serious wildlife enthusiasts in Kerala. Smaller, more remote and less frequented than Periyar, it is buffered on all sides by exceptionally well-protected forest, ensuring superlative biodiversity. Some 39 species of mammals are present here – including elephant, bison (*gaur*), panther, Nilgiri langur, lion-tailed macaque, tahr, sloth bear and the rare Travancore flying squirrel – as well as 268 species of birds (134 of which are classed as rare) and 124 different types of butterfly.

The **scenery** is varied and extremely picturesque, too. Ringed by peaks ranging from around 1000m to just under 1500m, the valley holds large tracts of evergreen tropical forest and mixed deciduous woodland, interspersed with grassy marshes, or *vayals*, kept moist by dozens of mountain streams and three major reservoirs. The whole basin tilts northwards, with the water draining through a rupture in the high ground where the Chalakkudy River plunges down to the plains near Palakkad.

What really sets Parambikulam apart, though, is the opportunity to actually get close to nature (a rarity in Indian wildlife reserves these days). A superb choice of treks and **activities** deepens your appreciation of this uniquely beautiful habitat, and the go-ahead Forest Department Wildlife Warden and his team have also devised some memorable **accommodation** options where you're right in the thick of things.

## Park practicalities

**Parambikulam** (daily 7am–6pm; Rs100 [Rs10], plus Rs30 with your own vehicle; Ⓦwww.parambikulam.org) lies 95km from the nearest railhead at Palakkad, but to reach it you have to loop around the north of the Anamalai range by road, approaching from the town of **Pollachi**, 35km northeast. If bringing your own car, book an entry slot at least thirty minutes in advance through the main Eco Care Centre at Anappady (☎04253/245025). **Buses** cover the route twice daily, leaving Pollachi at 6.15am and 3.15pm, and returning at 8.45am and 5.35pm.

The park has 150 **beds**, which may be booked by phone or in person at the Anappady office. The excellent website shows the various options available, from **treetop huts** (Rs2500–4000 for two per night) to a well-equipped **jungle tent camp**, with comfortable beds and en-suite bathrooms (Rs3500–4000), and – the *pièce de résistance* – a secluded **"nest"** on the island of Veettikunnu (Rs5000). All of the above rates include meals.

## Park activities

**Activities** on the so-called Tribal Eco-Development programme should be booked in advance through the park office. Rates are quoted for a maximum number of participants; a minimum rate also applies, which is usually only thirty percent less (even if you're alone) – so it's a good idea to get a group together to minimize costs. The tariffs cover the services of an armed ranger and guides, who accompany you throughout the trips. Guides are drawn from the four minority communities who inhabit the park, ensuring it's in their interests to preserve rather than poach the wildlife – a scheme that's proved hugely successful. Options range from family-friendly soft **treks** lasting an hour (Rs600 for a maximum of five) to more strenuous full-day hill hikes. You can also sign up for two-day **jungle expeditions** following the route of the old State timber tramway (Rs6000 for five, including meals and camping). Another memorable way to get deep into the Parambikulam forest is the **Full Moon Census** (only offered over the five nights of the full moon; Rs5000 for maximum of five), where you're taken to a treetop platform overlooking a marsh area known as the "Tigers' Dining Table", loaned a pair of binoculars and data sheet, and invited to record wildlife sightings through the night. Full details of this, and all the varied and wonderful initiatives at Parambikulam, are set out on the superb website.

# Munnar and the High Range

The hill tract of central Kerala – known as **the High Range** – starts roughly 50km inland from Ernakulam, where the paddy fields, lakes and backwaters of the coastal strip blister up into low, rolling ridges carpeted in rubber plantations. Thick forests of huge buttressed-root trees and liana creepers line the river valleys as you gain height, with the profile of the high peaks rising steeply on the horizon. Roughly 100km from the coast, the Ghats are the southernmost extension of a vast range stretching 1200km down the southwest seaboard of India. In Kerala, they reach their dramatic climax at **Ana Mudi** (2695m), the peninsula's highest mountain, before rippling into the sea just short of Kanyakumari.

Dividing the humid, tropical climes of the Keralan coast from the drier, boulder-studded Tamil plains, the interior mountains form a wall that breaks up the rain-laden **monsoon** clouds as they blow eastwards off the Arabian Sea in early June, forcing them to deposit 3-4m of moisture in less than six months (in some areas, the figure can rise to nearly 9m). This vast rainfall then drains back through the forests cloaking the range's western flank, and on to the densely populated backwaters. Around sea level, the woodlands, dominated by 30m-tall teak trees, are perennially moist, sticky, hot and green. Higher up, cooler and wetter montane rainforest takes over, ceding eventually to stunted deciduous trees and open expanses of savannah grassland.

The Ghats provide some of the planet's richest **ecosystems**: 4000 of the 15,000 or so plant species present in India grow in the southern portion – 1800 of them are endemic, and 1600 can't be seen anywhere else. Seven large mammals, including elephant, tiger, leopard, and bison, also survive here, along with around 300 types of bird. Recently, giant dam projects have threatened this extraordinary biodiversity, not least the dam on the Parambikulam River in Palakkad district, which is the largest in India, and one of the ten biggest dams in the world. But a much more devastating blow to the forest came towards the end of the nineteenth century, when the British clear-felled millions of acres for **tea plantations**. Despite the downturn in world consumption, Kerala's estates, the majority of them owned by the Indian multinational Tata, continue to churn out quantities of "CTC" ("crushed, torn and curled") tea powder for the voracious domestic market, and the central portion of the mountains is still dominated by neatly cropped tea gardens. The centre of the industry is **Munnar**, from whose riverside bazaar you can walk through vast hillsides wrapped in tea bushes and dotted with cosy British-era bungalows to reach the grasslands cloaking some of the Ghats' highest peaks. A couple of wildlife sanctuaries around the town protect some of the area's rarest flora and fauna, most notably the **Nilgiri tahr**, an unusually placid mountain goat, as well as wild elephants that trudge with characteristic insouciance through the forests lining the state border.

## Munnar

**MUNNAR**, 130km east of Kochi and 110km north of the Periyar Wildlife Sanctuary, is the centre of Kerala's principal tea-growing region. A scruffy agglomeration of corrugated-iron-roofed cottages and tea factories, its centre on the valley floor fails to live up to its tourist-office billing as a "hill station", but there's plenty to enthuse about in the surrounding mountains, whose lower slopes are carpeted with lush tea gardens and dotted with quaint old colonial bungalows. Above them, the grassy ridges and crags of the High Range offer superlative trekking routes, many of which can be tackled in day-trips from the town.

It's easy to see why the pioneering Scottish planters who developed this hidden valley in the 1870s and 1880s felt so at home here. At an altitude of around 1600m, Munnar enjoys a refreshing climate, with crisp mornings and sunny blue skies in the winter – though as with all of Kerala, torrential rains descend during the monsoons. When the mists clear, the mountain summits form a wild backdrop to the carefully manicured tea plantations below.

Munnar's greenery and cool air draw streams of well-heeled honeymooners and weekenders from the metropolitan cities of south India. However, increasing numbers of foreign travellers are stopping here for a few days too, enticed by the superbly scenic bus ride from Periyar, which takes you across the high ridges and lush tropical forests of the Cardamom Hills, or for the equally spectacular climb across the Ghats from Madurai in Tamil Nadu. Recent seasons have also seen the

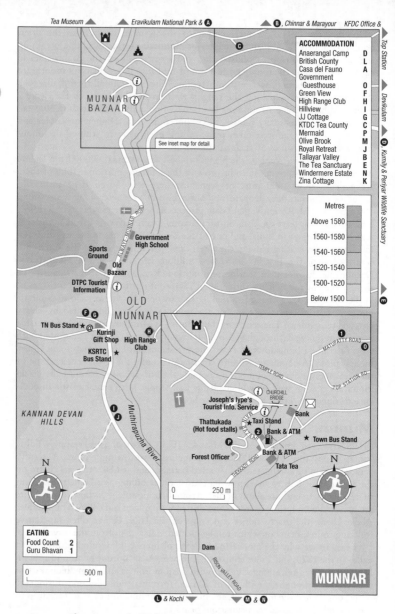

MUNNAR

ACCOMMODATION

| | |
|---|---|
| Anaerangal Camp | D |
| British County | L |
| Casa del Fauno | A |
| Government Guesthouse | O |
| Green View | F |
| High Range Club | H |
| Hillview | I |
| JJ Cottage | G |
| KTDC Tea County | C |
| Mermaid | P |
| Olive Brook | M |
| Royal Retreat | J |
| Tallayar Valley | B |
| The Tea Sanctuary | E |
| Windermere Estate | N |
| Zina Cottage | K |

| Metres | |
|---|---|
| Above 1580 | |
| 1560-1580 | |
| 1540-1560 | |
| 1520-1540 | |
| 1500-1520 | |
| Below 1500 | |

EATING

| | |
|---|---|
| Food Count | 2 |
| Guru Bhavan | 1 |

emergence of some wonderful **heritage** and **homestay accommodation**, some of it in restored British bungalows, where you can sip High Range tea on lawns against vistas of rolling estates and mountains.

### Arrival and information

Munnar can be reached by **bus** from Kochi, Kottayam and Kumily. State-run and private services all pull into the town bus stand in the modern main bazaar, near

214

CENTRAL KERALA | Munnar and the High Range

the river confluence and Tata headquarters; state ones continue through town, terminating at the bus stands nearly 3km south. For most hotels you should ask to be dropped off at **Old Munnar**, 2km south of the centre, near the ineffectual DTPC **tourist office** (daily 8.30am–7pm; ☏04865/231516). A better source of **information** on transport, accommodation and day-trips, including to Eravikulam, is the helpful **Joseph Iype**, who runs the **Tourist Information Service** (no set hours; ☏04865/231136 or ☏9447 190954) from a small office in the main bazaar. Immortalized in Dervla Murphy's *On a Shoestring to Coorg*, this self-appointed tourist officer has useful **maps** and newspaper articles, and can arrange **transport** for excursions. A few metres north is the **Munnar Tourist Information Centre** (daily 10am–8pm; ☏04865/230552), a government-sponsored body whose primary concern appears to be to promote its own guided tour, a whistlestop affair designed mainly for Indian tourists (daily 9am–5pm; Rs300). For booking **Forest Department treks**, you'll need to visit the Kerala Forest Department Corporation (KFDC) office (☏04865/230332). You can **change money** at the State Bank of Travancore, the State Bank of India or at numerous ATMs. **Internet** access is available from a couple of places around town, including Alpha Computer Centre (Rs50/hr), next to the Tamil Nadu bus stand.

## Accommodation

Munnar's **accommodation** costs significantly more than elsewhere in the High Range region, reflecting the town's popularity with middle-class tourists from the big cities. It possesses a couple of wonderfully genteel Raj-era places to stay, redolent of the Empire in its twilight days, while further afield in the hills around Munnar, the tea plantations and cardamom groves harbour several beautiful **heritage bungalows** and homestays overlooking some of the most magnificent mountain scenery in south India. See also the box on p.218 for further listings of places to stay in this area.

### Budget

**Green View** Sri Parvati Amman Kovil St, near the KSRTC bus stand ☏04865/230189 or ☏9447 825447. Clean and friendly budget guesthouse on the valley floor, down a side road just off the main drag, with rooms of various sizes – the best of them, #402, is a tiny double on the rooftop that has big windows and hill views. Pitched squarely at foreign backpackers, it's run by an enthusiastic, competent young crew who do a sideline in guided day treks (see p.219). ❷–❹

**JJ Cottage** Sri Parvati Amman Kovil St, near the KSRTC bus stand ☏04865/230104. Next door to *Green View*, and very much in the same mould, though it's been open longer, charges higher rates and tends to get booked up earlier in the day. Like its neighbour, the nicest of its clean, differently sized rooms is the one at the top (frontside), which has wood-panelled walls, fine views and 1960s-style, boudoir-chic curtains. A warm family welcome is guaranteed. ❸–❹

**Zina Cottage** Kad ☏04865/230349 or ☏9447 190954. British-era stone bungalow, nestled amid tea gardens high on the hillside above Munnar. Its flower-filled front terrace has magnificent views

across the town to Ana Mudi, and host Joseph Iype (see above) will fill you in on local walks over flasks of hot tea in his sitting room. The rooms themselves lack outlook and are basic and gloomy, and you'll probably need a pile of blankets at night, but all have their own entrances and bathrooms. This is somewhere you'd stay less for the creature comforts than for the atmosphere, and it has plenty of it. ❹

### Mid-range

**British County** ET City Road, Anachal, 12km from Munnar ☏0484/236 9811 or ☏9744 128761. On a ridge enjoying a vast valley view, this new property run by the Tourist Desk in Kochi has just four simply furnished rooms. They're clean and comfortable enough, but the real attraction here is sitting on the terrace, where there's nothing to disturb you other than the sounds of the birds and wind in the trees. Cook Ranjit rustles up tasty Indian food; rates cover full board. ❺

**Government Guesthouse** Matupatty Rd ☏04865/230385. On the far side of the river, around the hillside from the main bazaar, this former British bungalow stands in its own grounds

②

looking across the valley. It has just six rooms, lined up in an annexe just above the main reception and dining room area. They're large and dowdy, and lack outside space, but have big bathrooms. Meals by arrangement. ④

**High Range Club** Kanan Devan Hills Rd ☎04865/230253, ⓦwww.highrangeclub munnar.com. This old Raj-era club, founded by local British planters in 1909, must have been a nightmare of stuffiness and racism in its heyday. But now the faded colonial ambience, with turbaned bearers politely greeting guests in lounges filled with 1940s furniture and moth-eaten hunting trophies, feels undeniably quaint. Knock back a *chota-peg* of gin in the (men-only) bar, play billiards and tennis, enjoy a round of golf on the nine-hole course, or just laze with a book on the immaculate lawns. The club's guest wing holds three kinds of rooms and cottages, varying in size and comfort. Rates include obligatory full board. ⑥–⑦

**Hillview** Kanan Devan Hills Rd ☎04865/230567 or ☎9447 740883, ⓦhillviewmunnar.com. A big red block on the southern edge of town, it's not much to look at from the outside, but the interiors boast stripped wood floors and traditional carved wall panels. Some rooms are much darker than others. A dependable mid-range choice, despite its rough edges. ⑥

**Olive Brook** PO Box 62, Pothamedu ☎04865/230588, ⓦwww.olivebrookmunnar.com. Delightfully old-fashioned homestay, run by a schoolteacher, in the thick of a cardamom estate on a hillside overlooking the southern end of Munnar. Five rooms are spread over two blocks, all with wonderful views, and the home-cooked food is excellent. Rates include full board, cookery classes, trekking, evening barbecues and campfires. ⑦–⑧

**Royal Retreat** Kanan Devan Hills Rd ☎04865/230240, ⓦwww.royalretreat.co.in. Pleasant, efficiently run motel on the roadside at the south end of town. Go for one of its "super-deluxe" rooms if there are any free: they're south-facing, have brick fireplaces and cane

furniture, and are fronted by a cheerful little flower garden. ⑤–⑦

## Luxury

**Anaerangal Camp** Suryanelli, 25km east of Munnar on the Periyar road ☎0484/209 2280 or 401 2700, ⓦwww.munnarcamps.com. Half a dozen spacious luxury tents, fitted with quality beds and bathrooms, facing a magnificent panorama of mountain peaks, lake and forest. Delicious Keralan food, prepared at kitchens on site, is included in the rate (Rs4500/double), along with lakeside trekking, cycle rides, plantation visits and an evening camp fire. An inspiring location and friendly service from staff drawn from the local community. ⑧

**Casa del Fauno** Peak Gardens, Chinnakanal, 25km east of Munnar on the Periyar road ☎0484/304 8769 or ☎9895 766444, ⓦwww .casadelfauno.in. This glossily restored former tea bungalow, run by the *Casa del Fauno* boutique people from Muhamma (see p.137), boasts spectacular views and light, varnished wood interiors, with designer furniture and top-class service. French windows open on to well-kept lawns, where you can dine on the finest locally sourced food. Doubles from around $300 in season. ⑨

**KTDC Tea County** Off Matupatty Rd ☎04865/230460, ⓦwww.ktdc.com. The poshest address in Munnar town is a rather anodyne, government-run "four-star deluxe" resort offering a range of luxurious chalet-style rooms and suites ($155–255) stacked along a hilltop. There's a good multi-cuisine restaurant and beer parlour. ⑨

**Windermere Estate** PO Box 21, Pothamedu ☎04865/230512, ⓦwww.windermere munnar.com. Alpine-style chalet lodges, perched high on a hilltop above the town in cardamom and tea groves, with glorious views over the Chithirapuram Valley. Accommodation is offered in a converted farmhouse, plantation home and various garden cottages, all beautifully furnished and decorated with natural wood and stone and warm-coloured textiles. ⑨

## The Town

Clustered around the confluence of three mountain streams, Munnar town is a typical hill bazaar of haphazard buildings and congested market streets, which you'll probably want to escape at the first opportunity. The one sight of note is the **Tea Museum** (Tues–Sun 9am–4pm; Rs50), on Nallathany Road 2km northwest of the centre, which houses various pieces of old machinery and photos of the area's tea industry, from the 1880s pioneers to the modern Tata tea conglomerate. The social hub of the colonial period, and an important cultural icon in Munnar, the famous **High Range Club** is perched on a balcony overlooking the river on the southeastern edge of town. Indians were only officially permitted to enter the premises as recently as 1948, but these days non-members of any race are welcome to visit the typically Raj-era building for a round of golf, or to enjoy a gin and tonic served on the lawns by liveried retainers. The clock seems to have stopped ticking somewhere in the late 1940s at the men-only bar, whose walls are hung with rows of hunting trophies and topees. Aside from the ban on women in the bar, stiff-upper-lipped dress codes apply: no T-shirts or sandals, and after 7pm on Saturdays, men are required to don a dinner jacket and tie. You can also **stay** here on a full-board basis (see above).

### Eating
If your hotel, homestay or guesthouse package doesn't include meals, your best option will either be one of the popular local places reviewed below, or the **thattukada** (hot food stall market) just south of the main bazaar, opposite the taxi stand. This place gets into its stride around 7.30pm and runs through the night, serving delicious, piping-hot Keralan food – dosas, *parottas*, *iddiappam*, green-bean curry, egg masala – ladled onto tin plates and eaten on rough wooden tables in the street. As with all *thattukadas*, taxi drivers and single Malayali men working away from home make up most of the clientele, and the food is homely and cheap (you'd be hard pushed to spend Rs30).

**Food Count** Ground Floor of the *Munnar Inn*, main bazaar. Shiny, glassed-in café serving samosas, veg cutlets, sandwiches and light meals. The most hygienic option down in the main bazaar.
**Guru Bhavan** Matupatty Rd, Ikka Nagar. The most dependable of Munnar's local south Indian "meals" joints. It's a 10min plod north of the main bazaar, but worth the walk, with a daily changing menu of delicious Keralan vegetarian dishes, in addition to hot *parottas*, stupendously crunchy paper dosas and other *udipi* snacks. Recommended for local breakfasts, too.

## Around Munnar
Several of the summits towering above Munnar can be reached on day treks through the tea gardens, and buses wind their way up to the aptly named **Top Station**, a hamlet famed for its views and meadows of **Neelakurunji plants**, and

▲ Around Munnar

## Tea bungalows around Munnar

The pros and cons of the British rule are a subject of ongoing debate in India, but one thing's for certain: the old burrasahibs who pioneered the tea industry knew how to site a house. Scattered across the hillsides of the High Range around Munnar are dozens of former planters' bungalows with views to die for. Carpets of lush tea and coffee groves unfold from their prettily laid-out flower gardens, framed by a backdrop of high volcanic peaks. And at typical altitudes of around 1300–2250m, with streams babbling past and shady forest a stone's throw away, the bungalows enjoy climates as uplifting as the landscapes they survey. Little wonder that many of their inhabitants were reluctant to pack up and leave in 1947.

Having served as staff quarters and store houses for nearly half a century, many of the old planters' bungalows have recently seen a new lease of life as heritage guesthouses, where those able to afford their five-star prices can savour the distinctive atmosphere of the High Range in a style little changed since the Raj. Three companies manage the bulk of the properties available. All of them are located on working tea holdings owned, or previously owned, by Tata. However, only those on the Tallayar Valley Estate (℡04865/257314 or ℡9495 447748, ⓦwww.teabungalows .com; ⓞ), 20km out of Munnar on the road to Chinnar, give you a real taste of the tea business – thanks to its little-publicized "Make Your Own Tea" programme (see opposite). Of the estate's five bungalows, by far the nicest is *Tallayar Valley*, a three-bedroom, British-built place with spacious wood-floored rooms and plenty of pleasant short walks in the area to waterfalls and picnic spots. Rates (Rs6500–7250) are for full board, and include the services of an English-speaking manager.

More luxurious, offering slick service and fine interiors, are the bungalows run by the Kochi-based **CGH** hotel chain (ⓦwww.cghearth.com; ⓞ), of which *Mattupetty*, just off the Munnar–Top Station road, is the best set up. CGH also run a couple of more remote alternatives that will suit anyone really looking to get away from it all. One is *Kadalar*, in the valley just below the Eravikulam Wildlife Sanctuary, around 12km out of town. The other is *Silent Valley* (no connection with the national park of the same name north of Palakkad), which is a less appealing property in itself, but one ideally situated for long walks.

The third company running tea bungalow stays is the **Tea Sanctuary** (℡04865/230141, ⓦwww.theteasanctuary.com; ⓞ), which manages four properties scattered across the Kanan Devan Hill Plantations Company's 240-square-kilometre estate. The houses themselves are beautiful, and possess a dash more old-world feel than the competition, but they're rather poorly serviced, with elderly, non-English-speaking staff the norm (a fact reflected in the much lower rates). Pick of the bunch are *Kannimalai*, 7km out of Munnar off the Chinnar road, which boasts a wonderful view of Rajmalai, Kerala's second-highest mountain, and *Chockanad East*, 4km beyond the High Range Club at the head of a pretty side valley. Rates are a reasonable Rs4000 per double room, including breakfast; evening meals cost Rs250 extra.

Finally, a word of warning: the future of many of the bungalows on Tata Tea land (including those run by *CGH* and the *Tea Sanctuary*, but not *Tallayar*) was at the time of writing in some doubt due to a long-standing dispute between Tata and the Keralan government. The case is rumbling through the courts and may take some years to conclude, but in the meantime the bungalows remain open. Ask the companies for the latest update when you book.

to the more distant nature sanctuaries of Eravikulam and Chinnar, where you can spot Nilgiri tahr, elephant and many other wild animals. To reach the most remote attractions, however, you might want to hire a taxi for the day (easily done through your hotel, Joseph Iype [see p.215], or at the stand in the bazaar); rates are a standard Rs7–8/km.

## Tea plantation visits

The High Range is littered with working tea factories, but the only one open to visitors lies on the **Tallayar Valley Estate** (℡04865/257314 or ℡9495 447748, Ⓦwww.teabungalows.com), 20km out of Munnar on the road to Chinnar. Their "Make Your Own Tea" programme is a great – and affordable – way to experience life on a working plantation. It starts at around 9am (confirm timings when you book) with a walk around the tea gardens to pluck leaves, which you then take down to the factory for processing. Six or seven hours later, your own personal batch of tea, made with the very leaves you picked yourself, is delivered hot from the presses. While you're waiting, you can go for easy walks around the estate, visit the main factory and enjoy lunch on the lawns in front of an old British bungalow. The day costs Rs1250 per head, though you'll have to arrange transport to and from Tallayar Valley yourself.

## Walks and treks

Given the stupendous scenery rearing on all sides of Munnar, the **hiking** scene is surprisingly undeveloped. Joseph Iype at his office in the bazaar (see p.215) can suggest routes for rambles around nearby tea estates, but for anything more ambitious, it makes sense to use the services of a guide. The owner of Munnar's **Green View** guesthouse (see p.215) and his team of enthusiastic young guides (Ⓦwww.munnartrekking.com) can lead you on interesting local trails; rates range from Rs400–500 per person for soft treks to Rs500–800 for longer, more challenging outings, transport to and from the trailheads included.

The **Kerala Forest Development Corporation** (KFDC; Ⓦwww.keralafdc .org) also runs guided treks around Munnar, ranging from the one-day walk up Silent Valley (no relation to the national park of the same name north of Palakkad; depart 8am, return 5pm; Rs300) to longer routes involving nights under canvas (Rs1000–3000 per head, including meals and camping). You also have to budget for travel to and from the trailhead, which can also be arranged through KFDC. These walks are extremely popular and sell out quickly, so make bookings as far in advance as possible through KFDC's office in Munnar (℡04865/230332). The more upscale **Kestrel Adventures** also offer good day treks and camps, as well as cycling tours and guided wildlife trips. Contact them via their office near the *KTDC Hill Resort* (℡9447 031040, Ⓦwww .kestreladventures.com).

## Top Station and Kolukkumalai

One of the most popular excursions from Munnar is the 34km climb through some of the Subcontinent's highest tea estates to **TOP STATION**, a tiny hamlet on the Kerala–Tamil Nadu border which, at 1600m, is the highest point on the interstate road. Pack ponies still labour up the endless switchbacks to the site, which takes its name from the old aerial **ropeway** that used to connect it with the valley floor, the ruins of which can still be seen in places. Apart from the marvellous views over the Tamil plains, Top Station is renowned for the very rare **Neelakurunji plant** (*Strobilatanthes*), which grows in profusion on the mountainsides but only flowers once every twelve years, when huge crowds climb up here to admire the cascades of violet blossom spilling down the slopes (the next flowering is due in Oct/Nov 2018). Top Station is accessible by **bus** from Munnar (10 daily from 5.30am; 1hr 30min), and jeep-taxis do the round trip for Rs1000. To catch the best views, try to arrive before the mist builds up at 9am.

Top Station sees streams of visitors in season, but you can sidestep the crowds completely, and see even more awesome scenery, at the remote **Kolukkumalai**

**estate**, 23km out of Munnar. At an altitude of 2400m, it's officially India's highest tea plantation, producing leaves prized for their delicate flavour. The only way to reach it is by jeep, via the **Chinnakkanal Suryanelly Estate**. An old bridleway drops down the east flank of the mountain from here to the Tamil plains, visible in the distance – a popular local trekking route.

### Eravikulam National Park and Chinnar Wildlife Sanctuary

Encompassing 100 square kilometres of moist evergreen forest and grassy hilltops in the Western Ghats, the **Eravikulam National Park** (daily 7am–6pm; Rs220 [Rs40]; ⓦwww.eravikulam.org), 13km northeast of Munnar, is the last stronghold of one of the world's rarest mountain goats, the **Nilgiri tahr**. Its innate friendliness made the tahr pathetically easy prey during the hunting frenzy of the colonial era. On a break in his campaign against Tipu Sultan in the late 1790s, the future Duke of Wellington reported that his soldiers were able to shoot the unsuspecting goats as they wandered through his camp. By Independence the tahr was virtually extinct; today, however, numbers are healthy, and the animals have regained their tameness, largely thanks to the efforts of the American biologist Clifford Rice, who studied them here in the early 1980s. Unable to get close enough to observe the creatures properly, Rice followed the advice of locals and lured them with salt, and soon entire herds were congregating around his camp. You're almost guaranteed sightings of tahr from the minute you enter the park gates, reached by shuttle bus. From there, you can walk a further 1500m up a winding single-track road before the rangers turn you around, but expect to do so in the company of hundreds of other tourists on weekends – a rather hollow experience.

Although it borders Eravikulam, the **Chinnar Wildlife Sanctuary** (daily 6am–7pm; Rs100 [Rs10]; ⓦwww.chinnar.org) is far less visited, not least because its entrance lies a two-hour drive from Munnar along 58km of winding mountain roads. The reserve, in the rain shadow of the High Range and thus much drier than its neighbour, is one of the best spots in the state for birdwatching, with 225 species recorded to date. But the real star attractions are the resident **grizzled giant squirrels**, who scamper in healthy numbers around the thorny scrub here, and the near-mythical "**white bison of Manjampatti**", thought to be an albino Indian gaur. Supported **treks** through the reserve are run by the excellent Wild Kerala Tour Company (ⓣ0484/236 9121, ⓦwww .wildkeralatours.com), based in Kochi.

To reach Chinnar you have to pass through the small bazaar town of **MARAYOOR**, 42km east of Munnar, where it's worth stopping to admire Kerala's only wild **sandalwood forest**. The 92-square-kilometre reserve, a couple of kilometres out of town, holds an estimated 60,000 trees, whose wood currently sells for $1000–1500 per kilo on the international market. Wardens are on hand to shepherd visitors around the heavily protected zone which, despite its high fences and the death in 2004 of arch-smuggler Veerapan, continues to haemorrhage illegally felled sandalwood; they'll also show you **prehistoric rock-art** sites for which this area is famous. A collection of stone-capped **burial chambers**, known locally as the Munniozens, litter the land around the old Thenkasinathan Temple at the hamlet of **Kovilkadavu**, on the banks of the River Pambar.

# Northern Kerala

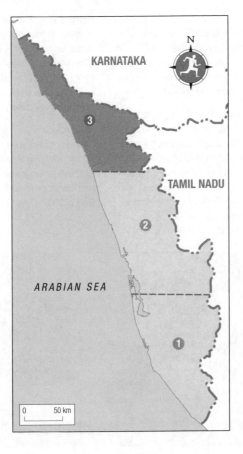

CHAPTER 3  # Highlights

✳ **Kuttichira mosques** A collection of beautiful wooden mosques, built between 700 and 1100 years ago in distinctive Malabari style. The last vestiges of Kozhikode's golden age as a spice port. See p.229

✳ **Moppila food** Enjoy one of the most hybrid, delicious regional cuisines of the south, a legacy of Arab influence in the region. See p.231

✳ **Wayanad** Trek through dense rainforest, past waterfalls and remote Hindu temples, to the green summits of the Western Ghats in one of Kerala's most beautiful mountain regions, where wild elephant sightings are almost guaranteed. See p.235

✳ **Theyyem** Otherworldly spirit possession rituals, involving elaborate masks, make-up and costumes, take place throughout the region between November and March. See p.251

✳ **Ezhara** The prettiest in a string of four exquisite beaches south of Kannur (Cannanore), where you can kick back at a handful of low-key, beautifully located guesthouses. See p.250

✳ **Valiyaparamba** Explore the "northern backwaters" – a less touristy alternative to Kuttanad – on a *kettu vallam* rice barge or local ferry. See p.253

▲ *Theyyem*

# Northern Kerala

orthern Kerala, where the state tapers into the hilly coastal belt of Karnataka, lies more than 600km from the capital, Thiruvananthapuram, and in many respects feels like a region apart. From the thirteenth century, its dominant rulers, the **zamorins of Calicut** and the **Kolathiri rajas** of neighbouring Cannanore (modern-day Kannur), formed their own distinct centre of gravity, beyond the reach of distant Travancore. International commerce flourished in the ports of what came to be known as the "Malabar coast", visited by ships from as far afield as China, Africa and the Middle East. Still grown in the hinterland, pungent "Malabari black" pepper was the commodity most came in search of, along with cardamom, cinnamon, timber and printed "calico" cotton (named after its principal source, the *chaliyan* weavers' workshops of Calicut). Tax raked off this trade filled the coffers of the Malabar's kings with unprecedented wealth, giving rise to one of South Asia's most refined and sophisticated societies.

Over time, **Calicut** (or "**Kozhikode**" as it's now officially called) emerged as the undisputed capital of northern Kerala, its trade monopolized by a class of Arab merchants, the Koyas, whose business acumen, political nous and treasuries proved invaluable to successive zamorins. Under the umbrella of their tolerant reign, **Islam** – spread through intermarriage between the local population and Arab merchant families, and the voluntary conversion of disenfranchised lower-caste Hindus – flourished as it never quite did anywhere else in Kerala, developing its own hybrid style of architecture and cuisine. All but a handful of the old wooden mosques of the Malabar have now been replaced by contemporary Mecca-style *masjids*, but the Muslim community – known as **Moppilas** – retain a distinctive presence in northern Kerala, and particularly in Kozhikode (Calicut) city itself, whose economy owes its current buoyancy to the flow of remittance riyals and dinars posted home each month by Malayalis working in the Gulf. Kozhikode's lack of sights – not to mention its heavily congested and polluted centre – have long acted as disincentives to tourism, but its outlying districts hold some of the region's finest old Moppila mosques, and around the busy markets of the centre are dotted many excellent restaurants, old-fashioned cafés and *halwa* shops, where you can sample the Malabar's famously spicy cuisine.

Moppila influence peters out as you head inland towards the mountains, where adivasi tribal people form the most conspicuous minority in a region still extensively covered in rainforest. The prospect of glimpsing the grassy uplands of the Western Ghats' watershed peaks tempts streams of travellers up to **Wayanad**, one of Kerala's most scenic hill districts. A scattering of upmarket eco-resorts nestle under the canopy, providing accommodation in luxury treehouses or romantic

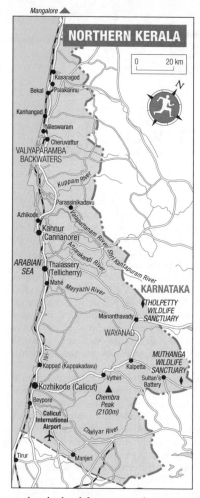

**NORTHERN KERALA**

0    20 km

teak *tharavadukal*, with views over coffee plantations from their verandas. Wild elephant and gaur still inhabit the surrounding forest and are the star attractions of the **Wayanad National Park**, divided into two separate portions: **Muthanga** and **Tholpetty**.

On the coast, the former colonial trading ports of **Mahé** and **Thalassery (Tellicherry)**, dominated by salt-worn bastions and bustling little harbours, serve as stepping stones on the long haul up to **Kannur (Cannanore)**, the centre of a district renowned for the extraordinary masked spirit possession dances known as **theyyem**. Each of these four hundred or so rituals has its own elaborate set of traditional costumes and mythological associations, harking back thousands of years to an era before brahmanical Hinduism spread to the fringes of peninsular India.

**Beyond Kannur**, you enter a still-more traditional corner of the state, well off the tourist trail, where traditional inshore fishing and rice cultivation (along with remittance money) dominate the local economy. Edged by stands of palm and casuarina trees, deserted beaches and sandbars line a shoreline broken only by occasional river mouths and hidden lagoons. The largest **backwater** area in the far north centres on the island of **Valiyaparamba**, which you can explore by local ferry or rice-barge cruise boat, from a far-flung jetty outside the town of **Nileswaram** on the main coastal highway. Few travellers make it as far as **Bekal Fort**, the most northerly and impressive of Kerala's coastal strongholds, but those who do are rewarded with a stupendous panorama of empty golden sand and palm forest. Another convenient staging post if you're heading further up the coast is **Kasaragod**, near the Karnatakan border, where a solitary homestay, at an island *tharavad* surrounded by backwaters, provides a window on a fast-disappearing world.

The **climate** this far north is a little different from further south, particularly in December and January, when humidity levels drop right back and the nights are frequently cool enough at sea level to require a thick blanket.

## Some history

Prior to the rise of colonial Cochin in the sixteenth century, Kozhikode's rulers, the **zamorins**, were the dominant force along the Malabar coast. It was to their court that Vasco da Gama first appealed for permission to trade in 1498, and their eventual demise enabled the Dutch and British to flex their imperial muscles in the region.

Kozhikode's emergence as a major port began in the twelfth century, after the decline of the Kulasekhara empire. The seat of the Polatiri dynasty, it was conquered by the **Eradis** of the Nediyiruppu kingdom to the east. The Eradis shifted their capital to the newly acquired seaport and set about constructing a large fortified palace, or *koyil kotta* – whence "Kozhikode" (later corrupted by the British into "Calicut"). The new kingdom was named **Nediyiruppu Swaroopam** and its rulers the "samuris", or "zamorins". Ibn Battuta, the Chinese-Muslim traveller Ma Huan and Nicolo de Conti were among the many foreigners who applauded the town's splendid buildings and tolerant regime in the fourteenth and fifteenth centuries. By declaring it a free port and espousing a liberal attitude to other religions, the Hindu zamorins were able to entice whole communities of Chinese and Arab merchants to their capital. Ultimately, it was the Arabs who would triumph in the struggle for control of the Malabar's spice trade. Arab ships, horses, arms and soldiers formed the backbone of successive zamorins' military campaigns in the region, which by the eve of da Gama's arrival had seen Calicut's territory extend from Cochin in the south to Cannanore, the domain of the Kolathiri rajas, in the north.

At the height of its power, Calicut was one of Asia's most prosperous and cultured cities. As well as powerful warlords, the zamorins were passionate sponsors of the arts, particularly literature. The magnificence of their court impressed Vasco da Gama's **Portuguese** delegation when it limped into the city after discovering the sea route around the Cape of Good Hope in 1498. The Zamorin was less enthralled by the lacklustre gifts offered by the European visitors, which some historians have suggested explains his refusal to grant requests from the Lusitanian navigator to site a trading post on the Malabar. The real root of the cool welcome was, however, probably the influence over the Zamorin of his close Arab advisors, who were quick to recognize the threat to their monopoly posed by the sudden appearance of the vehemently anti-Muslim "Franks".

The **second Portuguese expedition**, under Pedro Alvarez Cabral in 1501, succeeded in levering trade concessions from the Calicut court. But in the course of the visit, relations with the city's Arab merchants degenerated badly, unleashing a series of violent attacks and counterattacks that would leave an indelible mark on the history of the Malabar. There were many bloody encounters between the Zamorin and the Portuguese, who pursued their commercial ambitions on the Malabar by allying with Calicut's enemies, principally Cochin. Clashes, blockades and battles between the two rumbled on through the first decade of the sixteenth century. A treaty granting full trading rights and annual tribute to the Portuguese finally settled matters a decade later, but not before the Zamorin's palace had been reduced to ruins and the city set ablaze.

Over the coming centuries, Calicut's influence steadily waned as its traditional enemies, the houses of Cochin and Kolathiri, gained the upper hand. Meanwhile, the **French East India Company** and its British counterpart fought for supremacy on the northern Malabar, establishing outposts at **Mahé** and **Tellicherry** respectively, from where they exported pepper, cardamom, cinnamon, timber and calico cotton. With the defeat of Tipu Sultan in the Mysore wars of the late seventeenth century, the region finally became absorbed into the Raj's **Madras Presidency** in 1800. Civil disturbances directed by the region's Muslim Moppilas at their Hindu landlords (or Janmis) saw riots, killings and the desecration of temples erupt throughout northern Kerala between 1836 and 1856. The roots of the so-called **Moppila Riots** continue to be debated, but almost certainly lay in the consequences of ill-thought-out British tax reforms.

A second, more carefully orchestrated, Muslim uprising exploded in 1921, and this time directly targeted symbols of British authority. Dubbed the **Malabar Rebellion**, it later took the form of communal attacks on Hindus, before being brutally suppressed. The most infamous episode of the rebellion, whose ringleaders were rounded up and shot and followers imprisoned or deported to the Andaman Islands, was when 61 Moppila prisoners suffocated to death while being transported by train across the Ghats. The so-called "**Black Hole of Podanar**" left a legacy of enduring hatred in the Malabar region, playing a key part in the formation of the "Muslim League", which since Independence has held the balance of power in this fifty-percent Muslim region.

**Emigration** has been the prime shaping force of life in northern Kerala over recent decades. Hundreds of thousands of mostly Muslim Malabaris now work in the Gulf states, and the impact of the money they send home is more evident in the north than anywhere else in the state.

# Kozhikode (Calicut)

Formerly one of Asia's most prosperous trading capitals, the coastal city of **KOZHIKODE** (Calicut) occupies an extremely important place in Keralan legend and history. It was close to here, in 1498, that Vasco da Gama first set foot in India. When he and his fellow sailors were received at the court of the Zamorin, they were surprised to find themselves in the midst of a sophisticated, cosmopolitan metropolis already inhabited by Jewish, Arab and Chinese merchants, as well as Christians who'd been here since the time of St Thomas. Gem dealers and gold shops lined the bazaars en route to the splendid royal palace whose halls were hung with gold and silk brocade.

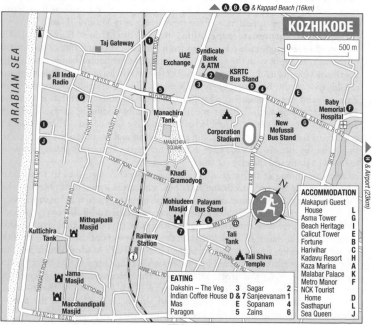

Nowadays, with the exception of a crop of handsome **Moppila mosques** and *tharavadukal* (mansions), precious few remnants survive of the city's illustrious past, and the few foreigners that do find their way here tend to be breaking longer journeys to somewhere else. Even so, it's a strikingly upbeat, prosperous and orderly place by Indian standards, riding high on a tide of remittance cheques from the Gulf and expanding rapidly in all directions (most conspicuously upwards).

## Arrival and information

The **railway station** (℡0495/270 1234), close to the centre of town, is served by coastal expresses, slower passenger trains, and superfast trains between Thiruvananthapuram, Kochi and all stations north on the Konkan Railway. There are three **bus stands**. All government-run services from destinations outside the city pull in at the **KSRTC bus stand** on Mavoor Road (aka Indira Gandhi – or IG – Road). Private long-distance – mainly overnight – buses stop at the **New Mofussil private stand**, 500m away on the other side of Mavoor Road – there's a row of agents for booking tickets on these along MM Ali Road. The **Palayam bus stand**, off MM Ali Road, serves the city and immediate area.

Kozhikode's **airport** (ⓦwww.calicutairport.com), at Karippur, 23km southeast, is the least efficient in the state. Primarily a gateway for heavily laden emigrant workers flying to and from the Gulf, its baggage claim and entry formalities can take hours if you're arriving from Dubai or Doha, but flights from domestic destinations, including Kochi and Mumbai, tend to clear more quickly. Pre-paid Ambassador taxis into the city centre, bookable from the hatch next to the exit, cost Rs500. Contact details for airlines and travel agents are listed on p.233.

KTDC's **tourist information** booth (officially daily 9am–7.30pm; ℡0495/270 0097) at the railway station has information on travel connections and sites around Kozhikode, but opening hours are erratic.

## Accommodation

**Hotels** in Kozhikode are plentiful, except at the bottom end of the range; this is one city where travellers on tighter budgets might be tempted to upgrade. Most establishments operate 24hr checkouts; because of the amount of traffic to and from the airport, the better-value ones rarely have vacancies at short notice so **reserve** well ahead. See also our listings for nearby **Kappad Beach** (p.233) and **Beypore** (p.234).

### Budget

**NCK Tourist Home** Mavoor/IG Rd ℡0495/272 3530. An enormous, lime-green-painted budget lodge slap in the city centre. Set back from the main road, it's marginally quieter and cleaner than the competition, and there's a bustling *Indian Coffee House* on the ground floor. Frequently booked up by wedding parties on weekends, so reserve ahead. Limited a/c available for Rs800. ①–②
**Sasthapuri** MM Ali Rd ℡0495/272 3281, ⓦwww .sasthapuri.com. Compact lodge on four storeys, close to the Palayam bus stand and market, and the only commendable budget place on the south side of the centre. Its wood-panelled rooms come at various rates, with or without a/c, and are well maintained, though cramped. Internet access available. ②–④

### Mid-range

**Alakapuri Guest House** Chinthavalappu Junction, MM Ali Rd, near the Palayam bus stand ℡0495/272 3451. Opening onto a large central garden, the rooms in this popular place range from old-fashioned, spartan, non-a/c doubles to more spacious "cottages" with polished wood chairs, pillared sitouts and sofas. All of them are neatly painted and clean; a/c costs an additional Rs300, and single rates are available. In the evening, you can eat on the lawn, or in their cavernous dining hall under the watchful gaze of a giant plaster elephant. ④–⑤
**Asma Tower** Mavoor/IG Rd ℡0495/408 8000, ⓦwww.asmatower.com. Sleek business-class hotel in the centre. With their colour schemes of muted greys and browns, rendered in wood and

polished steel, the a/c rooms are stylish, relaxing and well screened from the traffic noise below. The extra Rs500 for the pricier "executive" buys you more space – recommended for couples. ⑥

🏃 **Beach Heritage** Beach Rd, 2km west of the centre ☎0495/276 2055, ⓦwww.beach heritage.com. Dating from 1890, the premises of the colonial-era Malabar English Club, with its closely cropped lawns and high-pitched tiled roofs, now house a delightful heritage hotel retaining plenty of period feel. It's the kind of place where you'd expect to see Somerset Maugham sipping a gin sling on the veranda – which indeed he did; Chester Bowles and Jawaharlal Nehru also stayed here in the 1950s. There are just six rooms, all with discreet a/c units, balconies or private patios, split-cane blinds, paddle fans, and mod cons such as TVs and CD players. Those on the upper floor are larger and have the best sea views. Good value. ⑥

**Calicut Tower** Markaz Complex, off Mavoor/IG Rd ☎0495/272 3202, ⓔcalicuttower@yahoo.com. This 90-room tower block, tucked away down a quiet side street off the main drag and popular mainly with visiting Gulf Arabs, offers by far the best value in Kozhikode's lower-mid-range bracket. Impeccably clean, with shiny tiled floors and well-scrubbed bathrooms, its "standard a/c" rooms (only Rs200 pricier than the stuffier non-a/c options) are huge for the price, while the stylish "deluxe a/c" ones have a more contemporary look, new a/c units, balconies and flat-screen TVs. Strictly no alcohol. Ask for a room on the cooler north side of the block. ④–⑤

**Fortune** Kannur Rd, 3km north of the centre ☎0495/276 8888, ⓦwww.fortunehotels.in. Long the favoured option among visiting businessmen, but nowadays well undercut by the *Asma Tower*. Rooms come in two categories: "deluxe" are a bit bigger with kingsize beds. There's a pool on a raised terrace at palm level, multi-cuisine and Keralan speciality restaurants, a health club, gym and internet access in the lobby. ⑦

🏃 **Kaza Marina** Elathur, 10km north ☎0495/246 2162. This large wood-and-brick property sits right next to the waves, on the fringe of a residential area half an hour's drive north of the city – a perfect overnight pit stop if you're travelling with your own transport between Cochin and the far north of Kerala. The best of its three rooms has a huge balcony offering unimpeded sea views; the other two are smaller and more sparsely furnished, but impeccably clean and comfortable. Hosts Rudi and Sarli are in the background should you need anything. Home-cooked meals are available on request (Rs200–300). ⑤

**Malabar Palace** Manuelsons Junction ☎0495/272 1511, ⓦwww.malabarpalacecalicut.com. Faded

four-star in the city centre, ranged over six storeys. Avoid the gloomy, poorly aired "standard" rooms, in favour of the much nicer "executive" options on the sixth floor – furnished with luxurious beds, thick burgundy carpets and polished-wood writing desks. Those to the rear have great views over the palm forest to the east. Rates include buffet breakfast. ⑥–⑦

**Metro Manor** Opposite Baby Memorial Hospital, Mini Bypass Rd ☎0495/272 5811, ⓦwww .themetromanorcalicut.com. This gleaming, triangular hotel in the centre hasn't been open long, but if prices and standards are maintained it'll offer unbeatable value in the mid-range bracket. Rooms aren't especially large, though they are smartly furnished, stylish and comfortable. The non-a/c doubles are a steal at only Rs850. ④–⑤

**Sea Queen** Beach Rd ☎0495/236 6604, ⓦwww .seaqueenhotel.com. Bright yellow-and-blue brick building, next to a lorry park on the seafront, entirely refurbished a few years back. The pleasant, spacious a/c rooms are good value, especially the sea-facing "a/c-deluxe" (no. 213). The non-a/c rooms are fusty and not nearly as nice. Breakfast, served alfresco on the rooftop, is included in the rates. ⑤

## Luxury

🏃 **Harivihar** 4km north of the centre in the residential suburb of Bilathikulam ☎0495/276 5865, ⓦwww.harivihar.com. Ancestral home of the Kadathanadu royal family, converted into a particularly desirable heritage homestay. Set in beautiful gardens landscaped with lawns, herb beds, lotus ponds and an original laterite-lined bathing tank (which guests are welcome to use), the mansion is a model of traditional Keralan refinement: whitewashed, high-ceilinged rooms filled with antique furniture open onto pillared walkways inside. Distractions include short courses in yoga, astrology, cookery and Indian mythology, and treatments at their top-grade *Green Leaf*-accredited ayurvedic centre. ⑧

**Kadavu Resort** 15km southeast on NH-17, near the airport ☎0483/283 0023, ⓦwww.kadavuresorts .com. As five-stars go, this sprawling 120-room complex near the airport is exceptionally pleasant. Overlooking a sweeping bend on the Chaliyar, its nicest rooms are the "deluxe" and "superior" chalets, which have fabulous views over the river and surrounding palm forest from deep, shady balconies. The more recently built "standard" rooms in the Keralan-style main block (from Rs7000) have less character, but more mod cons. Elsewhere, there's a big lagoon-shaped pool, outdoor amphitheatre, restaurant, and beautifully situated ayurveda centre where you can bliss out gazing over the tree tops. ⑨

# The City

Named after the huge square water tank (*chira*) next to it, the large maidan of balding grass comprising **Manachira Square**, in the heart of the city, was the site of the zamorins' palace courtyard. Hardly a trace remains of the medieval city laid out around it, which followed a Hindu grid formula based on a sacred diagram containing the image of the cosmic man, Purusha. The axis and energy centre of the diagram was dictated by the position of the ancient **Tali Shiva temple** (closed to non-Hindus), just south of MM Ali Road, which survives to this day. Everything, and everybody, had a place in the grid. The district around the port in the northwest was reserved for foreigners: the Chinese community lived in and around Chinese Street (now Silk Street) and the Portuguese, Dutch and British later occupied the area. Keralan Muslims (Moppilas) lived in the southwest – as they do to this day. The northeast of the city was a commercial quarter, while the southeast housed the Tali temple, royal palace and fort; all but a couple of the military *kalaris* (martial art gymnasiums) that stood around the perimeter have gone.

## Kozhikode beach and Palayam market

Locals enjoy strolling along the **city beach**, 3km west of the centre, in the late afternoon and early evening – especially on weekends. Although not suitable for swimming, it's a relaxing place, where you can munch on freshly roasted peanuts and spicy fried mussels while scanning the sea for dolphins. With its straggling line of casuarina trees, the northern end, near the lighthouse and the All India Radio mast, is where most people head for, but there's a breezy paved esplanade further south, starting near the *Beach Heritage* hotel. Note that after dark auto-rickshaws can be thin on the ground.

Another good place for a wander – if you can get there during the coolest, busiest time of day, from 7am to 9am – is the fresh produce market in **Palayam**, next to the Palayam bus stand. Spilling into the backstreets around the **Mohiudeen Masjid**, it's a typically hectic north Keralan fruit and veg bazaar, with porters scurrying around balancing impossibly heavy loads of bananas, breadfruit, coconuts and watermelons on their heads.

## Kuttichira/Thekkepuram

In pre-colonial times, the Malabar's maritime trade lay largely under the control of a class of wealthy Moppila merchants, originally descended from Arabian and Middle Eastern immigrants to whom successive zamorins, in return for the weapons and horses they supplied to their armies, afforded protection. Tucked away in the Muslim quarter of the city, a cluster of traditional wooden **mosques** are the sole surviving monuments from this golden age. Unlike most of their counterparts elsewhere in the state – and in spite of repeated Portuguese attacks in the fifteenth and sixteenth centuries – they have retained their multi-tiered roofs, distinguished by gracefully angled teak beams, slatted screens and typically Keralan carved gables. Few foreigners ever set eyes on them, but Kozhikode's Moppila mosques rank among some of the most handsome antique buildings in southern India.

The three most impressive specimens lie off a back road running north–south through the **Kuttichira** quarter – also known as **Thekkepuram** – 2km southwest of the maidan (auto-rickshaw-wallahs know how to find it). Uniquely in the city, the district has preserved many of its elegant 200- and 300-year-old *tharavadukal* residences, belonging to descendants of prominent Muslim families known as Koyas who, in the time of the zamorins, were responsible for administering trade through the port. With their grand *padippura* entrance porches, long verandas and high-pitched roofs, the mansions are redolent of the influence the Koyas once wielded.

Non-Muslims are generally not allowed inside the mosques, but no one will mind you walking around them or admiring the carvings in their entranceways. Start at the 1100-year-old **Macchandipalli Masjid**, at the southern end of the lane leading from Francis Road to Kuttichira tank, whose ceilings are covered in crudely painted stucco and intricate Koranic script. An engraved stone inside, inscribed both in old Malayalam and Arabic, recounts the history of the thirteenth-century zamorins, providing a valuable chronology for the region's historians.

A couple of hundred metres further north, the **Jama Masjid**'s main prayer hall, large enough for a congregation of twelve hundred worshippers, dates from the eleventh century and holds another elaborately carved ceiling. The most magnificent of this trio of mosques, however, is the **Mithqalpalli** (aka **Jama'atpalli** or **Miskal Palli**) **Masjid**, at the northern end of the lane, overlooking the the 400-year-old Kuttichira bathing tank. Resting on 24 wooden pillars, its four-tier roof and turquoise exterior were built over 700 years ago by a Yemeni merchant named Nakhuda Miska. A marble plaque recalls the attack, on January 3, 1510, during which Portuguese raiders set fire to the building – a charred remnant of what the memorial stone ruefully describes as the "misdeed" is visible on the southwest edge of the third storey. For more on the neighbourhood, ask for a leaflet at the *tharavad* adjoining the northeast wall; owner, retired librarian Mr P.K.M. Koya, is a mine of information about the area.

## The Pazhassi Rajah and Krishnamenon Museum and Art Gallery

The **Pazhassi Rajah and Krishnamenon Museum** (Tues–Sun 9am–4.30pm; Rs10) and **Art Gallery** (10am–5pm; free) stand together 5km north of the centre on East Hill, fringed by palm groves and lawns that provide a breezy, shaded escape from the heat of the day. Copies of murals, coins, bronzes and models of the umbrella-shaped stone megalithic remains peculiar to Kerala dominate the museum's collection, while the gallery displays works by Indian artists and memorabilia associated with the left-wing Keralan politician V.K. Krishnamenon. The building itself, named after the martyred local leader of the 1805 revolt against the East India Company, originally served as the residence of colonial Calicut's British Collector. In the Moppila uprising of 1921, it was the scene of a brutal murder when four of the revolt's ringleaders killed the local magistrate, H.V. Connolly.

## CVN Kalari

Calicut district is renowned for its **kalarippayat** gymnasiums, the most illustrious of which, **CVN Kalari Sangan** (☎0495/276 9114, ⊛www.cvnkalarikerala.com), stands in the suburb of Nadakkavu, 2km north of the city centre. Established over fifty years ago by the father of the current Master, the centre enjoys an international reputation, with members regularly performing in Europe, the Middle and Far East. CVN Kalari's great claim to fame, however, is that it choreographed the combat scenes for the film *The Myth*, starring martial-arts supremo Jackie Chan. Visitors are welcome to watch demonstrations and lessons (Rs100; see CVN website), though you'll have to get up at the crack of dawn to catch the more worthwhile of the two daily training sessions, held from 6am to 9am; evening sessions are for beginners and children. The centre also offers full-blown shows featuring the full gamut of weapons, leaps and moves (Rs3000–4000), plus three- and six-month residential courses for those interested in learning the basics of the martial art along with the rudiments of *marma chikitsa*, the specialist ayurveda massage technique used by *kalari* practitioners.

▲ *Kalarippayat* in action

## Shopping

What Kozhikode lacks in monuments it more than makes up for in **shops** – a consequence of the vast number of Gulf riyals and dinars flowing through the city. You cannot fail to be dazzled by the wealth of gold jewellery emporia lining Mavoor/IG Rd, full of women spending lavishly ahead of family weddings. The government-run **Khadi Gramodyog**, behind the *KTDC Malabar Mansion* on VM Basheer Rd, is a great source of discounted handloom cotton and silk, as well as the usual array of carved-wood elephants, sandalwood Hindu deities, incense, herbal soaps and forest honey. At the entrance to the compound, look out too for the Mriganayanee Emporium, where you can pick up block-printed and batik bedsheets, and brocaded Maheshwari silk saris from the central Indian state of Madhya Pradesh.

**Palayam Road**, the market area running east from the end of MM Ali Road, is where you'll find the widest selection of **bell-metal lamps** and traditional Keralan door furniture. More colourful still are the Malabari-style **halwa** shops dotted around the city – there's a particularly vibrant row grouped next to the *Cool Bakery*, at the southwest end of Mavoor/IG Road. Nearby, in the **Markaz Complex** mall, around the *Calicut Tower Hotel*, look out for miniature **dhows**, replicas of those still made at Beypore, which you can pick up cheaply in the Muslim perfumeries, along with traditional Arab *ooud* fragrances sold from rows of pretty crystal bottles. Finally, DC Books, on the ground floor of the *Asma Tower* hotel, at the east end of Mavoor/IG Road, is a good English-language **bookstore**.

## Eating

Kozhikode is famous for its **Moppila cuisine**, which has its roots in the culinary traditions of the city's former Arab traders. Fragrant chicken biriyanis and seafood curries with distinctive Malabari spices crop up on most non-veg menus, but to sample the definitive versions you should aim to have a least one meal in *Paragon*,

*Sagar* or *Zain's* (or preferably all three). **Mussels** are also big news here; deep-fried in their shells in crunchy, spicy millet coatings, they're served everywhere during the season, from October to December (during the rest of the year they'll have been imported and won't be as fresh). Finally, no Kozhikode feast is considered complete without a serving of the city's legendary **halwa**: a sticky Malabari sweet made from rice flour, coconut, *jaggery* (sugar cane) and ghee. It comes in a dazzling variety of Day-Glo colours and flavours. An old favourite place to sample it on the south side of town is the Grand (aka *Nandhinee Sweets*) on MM Ali Rd, just down from the Palayam Bus Stand. Up on Mavoor/IG Rd, *Cool Bakery* and the adjacent *Aishwarya* have even more impressive displays.

**Dakshin – The Veg** Mavoor/IG Rd. Nearby *Sopanam* gets busier, but the pure veg *udipi* food served here on heavy black marble tables is a notch more refined and tasty. In addition to the usual south Indian snacks, they dish up unlimited thali meals at lunchtime, with a choice of white or (healthier) "raw" local rice. Go for a table on the ground floor, where it's worth enduring the "self-service" system to watch the dosa-flipping in the open kitchen.

**Indian Coffee House** Behind the *Imperial Lodge*, Kallai Rd, near Palayam Bus Stand. Cleaner than average outlet of the popular *ICH* chain, with waiters in regulation starched white tunics and *pagris*. Open from 7am to 11pm, it's especially popular for its lunchtime rice meals (Rs80), and mountainous biriyanis. There's another branch in the *NCK Tourist Home* on Mavoor/IG Rd.

**Mas** First Floor of the *Calicut Tower* hotel, Markaz Complex. This friendly little restaurant, tucked away on a mezzanine above the lobby of a Muslim hotel, serves the usual range of north and south Indian dishes, but the Malabari specialities, which include fragrant kadai biriyanis (Rs70–100) baked and served in terracotta pots, are a much safer bet. The surroundings are a bit gloomy, but staff are courteous and prices low.

**Paragon** Off the Kannur Rd. A short auto-rickshaw ride from the maidan, *Paragon* has been a city institution since it opened in 1939. Don't be put off by the gloomy setting beneath a flyover: the Malabari cooking here is as good as you'll find anywhere. Seafood dishes are *the* speciality – especially fish tamarind, fish-mango curry, *pollichathu*, *moillee* – but there are dozens of alternatives (try the mild, coconutty chicken "stew" and potato *kombath*). Make sure to order *Paragon's* famously light *appam* and *parotta* combination, too. Opens 8am for breakfast. Most mains Rs90–125.

**Sagar** Mavoor/IG Rd. Another old favourite of Calicut's middle classes, now with two branches: one on the west side of Mavoor/IG Rd next to the KSRTC bus stand, the other at the east end near the flyover. Both are housed in distinctive laterite

buildings, with non-a/c on the ground floor, and brighter a/c "family" dining halls on the floors above. Ignore the generic north Indian-Chinese-multi-cuisine menu. Everyone comes for the Malabari dishes such as egg curry, fish korma and, best of all, the flavour-packed chicken *porichathu* – boneless chicken pieces marinated in ginger, garlic, green chillies and curry leaves, and then crisp fried. For vegetarians, their rice-plate meals (Rs45) are a real feast, featuring delicious pumpkin curries, *kuruma*, crumbled coconut and green chilli, and raw beetroot salad.

**Sanjeevanam** MN's Ave, near 4th Railway Gate, off PT Usha Rd. The perfect, pure-veg antidote to all those rich Malabari meals across town, *Sanjeevanam* specializes in healthy, additive-free, Satvic cooking. Their sumptuous lunchtime thali, "rajakeeam" (served noon–3pm; Rs110), is out of this world, featuring twenty or more items – including raw and partly steamed vegetables, five types of juice, red rice and honey – spread on a banana leaf. They also do lots of equally healthy Chinese and north Indian dishes, plus the full range of *udipi* snacks.

**Sopanam** Delma Complex, Mavoor/IG Rd. Cheapest and most popular of the pure-veg *udipi* joints along the city's main thoroughfare. It gets packed out from breakfast time for huge, crunchy dosas, *iddli-vada* plates and delicious coconut *kurma*, *kadala* and spicy mixed vegetable stew with *parotta*.

**Zain's** Convent Cross Rd. An unassuming, green-painted family house down a dingy lane in the west end of town is hardly what you'd expect the Holy Grail of Moppila cuisine to look like, but people travel from across the city to eat here. Dishes of the day, displayed in a glass cabinet, generally include a choice of biriyanis (fish, chicken or mutton; Rs80–100), various fiery seafood curries, and a range of *pathiris* – the definitive Malabari rice-flour bread, which can be steam-cooked and flavoured with fish, shallow-fried, dipped in egg or layered with coconut. Most mains Rs100–125.

## Listings

**Airlines** Air India/Air India Express, Eroth Centre (☎0483/271 5005); Jet Airways/JetLite, Kuthiravattom, Mavoor (☎0483/274 1189); Kingfisher Airlines (☎1-800/209-3030).

**Ambulance** Baby Memorial Hospital on Mavoor/IG Rd (0495/272 3272, 🌐www.babymhospital.org).

**Banks and exchange** The Union Bank of India and the State Bank of India, opposite each other on MM Ali Road, are two of many large branches with 24hr ATMs; there are several others dotted along Mavoor/IG Rd. With so much Gulf money floating around, you shouldn't have any difficulty changing currency, either. Try UAE Exchange on the ground floor of the *Hyson Heritage*, Bank Rd (Mon–Sat 9.30am–1.30pm & 2–6pm, Sun 9.30am–1.30pm), and Thomas Cook, opposite (same hours as UAE).

**Car rental** See "Travel Agents" below.

**Internet** Internet access is available throughout the city for around Rs40/hr: a cool, clean option is the *Suvidha*, on the south side of MM Ali Rd next to the Burma Metal Shop.

**Hospitals** Baby Memorial Hospital (see above) and the Malabar Institute of Medical Sciences (MIMS), Mini ByPass Rd (☎0495/274 4000, 🌐www .mimsindia.com) are two of the best equipped in south India.

**Photography** Galaxy Colour Lab, Sharara Plaza, Mavoor Rd, near the *Asma Tower* (☎0495/272 4996); recommended for passport photos and fast digital printing.

**Post office** Kannur Rd, just northeast of the Manachira Tank.

**Travel agents** PL Worldways, 17/1-S Seema Towers, Mavoor/IG Rd (☎0495/401 3092, 🌐www .plworldways.com).

# Around Kozhikode

A couple of minor attractions – one to the north of town, one to the south – offer welcome respite from the traffic of central Kozhikode. Both **Kappad Beach**, a long, empty stretch of sandy coast that's changed little since Vasco da Gama first stepped onto it in 1498, and **Beypore**, where you can watch seagoing ships being built from wood, are accessible by bus from the city – though you'll reach them faster if you can bear the ride by auto-rickshaw.

## Kappad

**KAPPAD BEACH** (aka Kappakadavu), a long stretch of golden sand and churning surf 16km north of Kozhikode, is where – on May 27, 1498 – Vasco da Gama and his 170-strong crew made their first landfall in India after discovering the sea route around the Cape of Good Hope. This momentous event in the history of the Subcontinent is commemorated by a small obelisk on the edge of the village. Historic associations aside, Kappad's refreshing breezes offer a pleasant escape from the mayhem of the city, and it's only a 45-minute journey away. An esplanade has been built to tempt strollers out from Kozhikode, but apart from on weekend evenings, the beach itself sees far more fishermen than paddlers.

### Practicalities

**Buses** leave from Kozhikode's Mofussil stand (platforms 8 or 9); you have to jump on one bound for Badagam, and get off at Pookkal, where local services and auto-rickshaws will take you the remaining 2km. There are just two **places to stay**. A couple of hundred metres inland under a dense canopy of areca and coconut palms, the *Pannu Tourist Home* (☎0496/268 8634; ❹) offers basic, quiet and clean en-suite rooms that share a common balcony looking into the trees. They're small for the price, and a little dingy, but atmospheric in the evenings. A signboard on the lane running behind the beach points the way. For more comfort, try the *Kappad Beach Resort* (☎0496/268 8777, 🌐www.renaissancekappadbeach.com; ❽), a short walk further north next to the car park. A former government place now run by the

Kochi-based Renaissance chain, it's right behind the sand and offers two types of room. Both enjoy sea views from deep balconies hung with bentwood cane swings, but only those on the upper floors actually overlook the beach. There's a pool, a multi-cuisine restaurant with garden terrace and a small ayurveda centre. Tariffs are on the steep side, it has to be said, but the location can't be beaten.

## ③ Beypore

The coastal village of **BEYPORE**, 11km south of Kozhikode at the mouth of the Chaliyar River, is famous throughout Kerala for its ancient **shipyard** – one of only three in India where ocean-going vessels are still handmade out of wood using traditional methods (the others are in Azhikkal, near Kannur – see p.251 – and Mandvi, in Gujarat). Known in Malayalam as *paikappal* and in Arabic as *uru*, the ships are almost identical to those that transported *Haj* pilgrims, horses and trade goods across the Arabian Sea and down the east coast of Africa. These days, the few that are built here each year tend to be sold to wealthy Gulf Arabs as pleasure dhows or floating casinos. At the time of writing, only one yard – Haji PI Ahamed Koya's – remained in business. Located on an island on the far side of the river, it's difficult to reach, but you are welcome to look around provided you call the company's Kozhikode offices at South Beach in advance (℡0495/270 4853, ⓦ woodendhow.com). Access is by boat from the fishing beach at **Chaliyar**, on the south bank of the river, which you reach via the **car ferry** from the slipway next to the port – itself a great curiosity, comprising three wooden fishing boats lashed together pontoon-style.

Hidden beneath giant palm-leaf covers, the dhows taking shape across the water are the last dinosaurs of a species whose documented origins date back at least a thousand years, and probably well before that. More astonishing than the industry's survival into the modern era, however, is the entire construction process, which can take anywhere from six months to two years. All calculations are carried in the head of the yardmaster, or *maistri*, while the work – in typically Keralan fashion – is done by hand using skills and tools handed down through generations. A compelling account of the construction process features in Tim Severin's 1983 travelogue, *The Sinbad Voyage* (see p.309).

The technical expertise of Beypore's shipwrights, or *khalasis*, was called upon under tragic circumstances on July 21, 2001, after a train bound for Chennai plunged off the nearby **Kadalundi Bridge** into the monsoon-swollen waters of the Chaliyar. Four carriages derailed and three were left dangling in the air, killing 64 people and injuring 300 more. The *khalasis* teamed up with navy divers to haul the wreckage from the river.

If you've time, have a stroll around the **port** (Rs1), where if you're lucky you might see several huge *urus* moored up awaiting cargoes, and the nearby **fishing harbour**, just north of the ferry jetty. Like all such places in Kerala, it's smelly and filthy, but a photographer's dream – especially between 3pm and 4pm when the day's catch is landed. Further west, the slender new **breakwater**, extending for 1km into the mouth of the Chaliyar, is the perfect venue for a sunset stroll.

Frequent **buses** run to Beypore from the Moffussil bus stand on Mavoor/IG Road (7.30am–7.30pm; 1hr). Rickshaws cover the same route for Rs120–150 – though you'll have to agree the fare as they won't use their meters over such a distance. There's nowhere to **eat** in the village beyond a handful of local tea stalls; mineral water and fruit, however, are available.

### Tasara Creative Weaving Centre

A worthwhile stop on your way to or from Beypore is the **Tasara Creative Weaving Centre**, in Beypore North, 7km south of the city, just off the main road. Rugs, bedspreads and wall hangings are hand-woven here in vibrant, contemporary designs that are refreshingly different from the traditional patterns found elsewhere in Kerala. Finely spun, non-violent silks (produced without killing the worm) are another speciality. Visitors can watch the weavers at work, view the **art gallery** (daily 9am–6pm; free) and buy the finished goods – prices range from $15 to $1000. You are also welcome to study handloom techniques, and try your hand at dyeing, batik and printing, under the tutelage of the welcoming Mr Vasudevan Balakrishnan and his family (T 0495/241 4832, W www.tasaraindia.com). Five-night "Weaver Bird" courses cost $275, or you can stay for a month as an "artist in residence" for $1100. Prices include all meals, and **accommodation** in a modern, simple guesthouse.

# Wayanad

The seven mountains encircling the hill district of **Wayanad**, 70km inland from Kozhikode at the southern limits of the Deccan, enfold some of the most dramatic scenery in all of south India. With landscapes varying from semi-tropical savannah to misty tea and coffee plantations, and steep slopes that rise through dense forest to distinctive, angular summits of exposed grassland, the region ranges over altitudes of between 750m and 2100m. Even at the base of the plateau, scattered with typically ramshackle Indian hill bazaars, it's noticeably cooler than down on the plains. Moreover, compared with the Cardamom Hills around Periyar and High Range district of Munnar, further south, Wayanad is relatively unfrequented by foreign tourists.

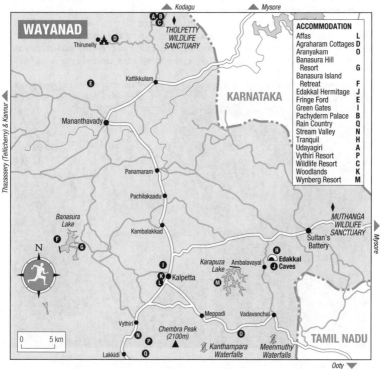

Inhabited since Neolithic times, Wayanad first came to the attention of the British when **Pazhassi Raja** and his guerrilla rebels mounted attacks from here during the so-called Pazhassi revolt of the 1890s. Four decades later, a gold rush spurred the construction of the first road across the mountains. Very little gold was ever mined, but the route quickened the pace of timber extraction and spread of tea plantations. Today, NH-17, following the course of the old British artery between Mysore and Kozhikode, is the source of a new income in the form of over-stressed dot-com executives and their families from Bangalore and Delhi. Numerous rejuvenation resorts, eco-hideaways and plantation stays have sprung up to service the screen-weary – some of them exquisitely situated on remote forest balconies, with panoramic views over the tea gardens and cardamom groves.

Even if you can't afford to stay in one of these bijou retreats, there are plenty of other reasons to venture up to Wayanad. Abutting the Tamil and Karnatakan borders, the twin reserves of **Muthanga** in the southeast, and **Tholpetty** in the north, collectively comprise the **Wayanad Wildlife Sanctuary** – part of the world-famous Nilgiri Biosphere and one of the best places in India to spot wild **elephant**, as well as numerous other mammals. Elsewhere, spectacular jungle waterfalls and high summits such as **Chembra Peak** (2100m) make perfect targets for day hikes, while the **Edakkal Caves** feature Neolithic rock-art amid breath-taking scenery. Most accommodation in the area is concentrated around **Kalpetta**, the district headquarters on the highway to Mysore and Ooty. The town and its satellite resorts make good springboards from which to discover the south of the region, but if you want to head into the remote northern jungles, consider basing yourself in one of the more isolated resorts around the market town of **Manan-thavady**, 27km northwest of Kalpetta.

**Getting to Wayanad** is an adventure in itself. From the plains east of Kozhikode, a beautiful but tortuous road climbs a series of nine hairpin bends up the Ghats through unspoiled forests, where macaques forage along the roadside, impervious to the groaning, diesel-belching trucks and buses going past. As the road arrives at the lip of the great plateau there are sweeping views back towards the coast, and

▲ Lion-tailed macaques in Wayanad

– fog permitting – you can glimpse the sea in the hazy distance. Travelling to the region from the north, you can follow a less frequented – but superbly scenic – back road running inland from Thalassery (Tellicherry), which scales the plateau just west of Mananthavady.

## Vythiri and Kalpetta

Approaching Wayanad from the west, via the busy Kozhikode–Mysore highway, the first settlement of any note you come to is **VYTHIRI**, a straggling ribbon development of shops and houses that serves the backcountry plantation villages spread over the hills to its north and south. Hidden from the road, several high-end hotels nestle in the surrounding jungle, among them the famous *Vythiri Resort* – one of the pioneers in this area of eco-tourism.

Budget travellers, however, will have to make do with one of the rather less enticing places crammed into the centre of the district's capital, **KALPETTA**, 11km down the highway from Vythiri. A hectic market hub straddling the main road, the town has little to recommend it except its central position and transport connections to points east, including the Muthanga Wildlife Sanctuary. The state **bus stand** in the centre of town has frequent services to Kozhikode (72km; 2hr) and Mananthavady (27km; 1hr). **Auto-rickshaws** and **jeeps** are available for local destinations. **Kerala Tourism**'s office (Mon–Sat 10am–5pm, closed second Sat of each month; ⓣ04936/204441) is in Kalpetta North, 1km from the bus stand, in a building sharing space with the local DTPC information desk. Helpful staff can assist with hiring **forest guides** (Rs500–600/day), and **jeeps** (Rs8–9/km plus the Rs100 vehicle entrance fee) for those going to the wildlife sanctuary independently. Note that all the Mysore buses also pass the entrance to Muthanga. Numerous small **internet** cafés are dotted around town, and there are plenty of 24-hour **ATMs**, as well as a UAE Foreign Exchange outlet.

### Accommodation and eating

**Accommodation** options in Vythiri and Kalpetta fall into two categories: beautiful resorts and plantation stays in far-flung locations in the surrounding hills; and more run-of-the-mill hotels, motels and lodges dotted along the main street in town. If you're just passing through and in search of a quick pit stop, *Swamy's Udipi*, on the ground floor of the *Affas* hotel at the south end of Kalpetta, serves the usual tasty south Indian snacks and rice-based meals. Don't be fooled by the name of the *Hotel New Palace*, just south of the bus stand – it's neither a hotel, nor new, nor remotely a palace, but a popular economy non-veg restaurant that fills up at lunchtime with locals shovelling down huge portions of chicken biriyanis and ghee rice; heavy, spicy, Malabari-style stews made with local quail (*kada*) are another speciality. A more hygienic option is the gleaming café (noon–3pm) on the ground floor of the *Woodlands Hotel*, just north of the bus stand, where you can order tasty Keralan chicken and fish curry meals (Rs60), fried rice, chapattis, and biriyanis from a daily changing menu. Everything is prepared fresh in an open kitchen; you can watch the street life through the picture windows as you dine.

**Affas** Kalpetta ⓣ04936/205185, ⓣ9447 234034, ⓦwww.hotelaffas.com. Multistorey budget motel in the centre of town. Its en-suite rooms are clean, and the town's best *udipi* joint sits on the ground floor, but book ahead on weekends when it gets swamped by visiting students. ❹

**Chandragiri** Main Rd, Kalpetta ⓣ04936/203049. The best cheapie in town, in a modern block in the centre, and the only place with beds under Rs600 that you'd want to sleep in. It has three kinds of room, varying in size from tiny to small, but they're well scrubbed and well aired. ❸–❹

**Green Gates** TB Rd, Kalpetta North ⓣ04936/202001, ⓦwww.greengateshotel.com. Modern three-star hotel, tucked away in its own lush grounds 300m north of the tourist office, offering a variety of rooms in the main multistorey block, or more private cottages to its rear. There's a pool, plenty of chill-out space in the gardens, and an ayurveda centre. The most comfortable option in Kalpetta, but not nearly as pleasant a location as the other resorts and homestays reviewed here. ⑥–⑧

**Rain Country** Lakkidi, 22km from Kalpetta ⊤04936/251 1997, ⊤9447 004369, ⓦwww .raincountryresort.com. A 3km track takes you from the main road to a secluded pocket of greenery overlooking the Lakkidi valley, where nine simply furnished, Keralan-style cottages with traditional gabled roofs are scattered over a clearing in the forest, centred on a spring-fed pond. Four of the chalets are beautifully reconstructed antique wooden *tharavadukal*, relocated from around the state and each housing two or three rooms, with semi-open-air bathrooms; the other five cottages have less character. Views are somewhat restricted by a natural balcony, but there are plenty of walks in the immediate surroundings – staff are happy to accompany you. ⑦–⑧

**Stream Valley** Vythiri, off NH-17 ⊤04936/205 5860, ⊤9847 502787, ⓦwww.streamvalley cottages.com. One of the few mid-scale options in this area, and a very pleasant one, comprising a handful of large, well-spaced chalets, some on stilts, set in extensive landscaped grounds. The most romantic space is a cosy treehouse looking across the valley (Rs3000), fitted with its own bathroom and windows. The staff are unfailingly helpful and serve delicious Keralan full board for Rs400. ⑥–⑦

**Vythiri Resort** booking at Kochi office ⊤0484/4055250, ⓦwww.vythiriresort .com. Set in a lovely seven-acre woodland plot with three boulder-strewn mountain streams flowing through it, *Vythiri* was the first forest resort in this area, and remains the benchmark. Accommodation comes in three forms: chalets with private verandas facing the stream and jungle (Rs6000/night); beautifully refurbished plantation workers' rooms, with stone-lined plunge pools (Rs6000); and spacious luxury houses with sunken jacuzzis, chic, earthy interiors and wooden decks (Rs10,000). They also have a couple of amazing treehouses (Rs12,000) nestled 45m off the ground under the forest canopy – you're winched up on counterweight-pulley lifts. Guided walks and early-morning yoga sessions number among the complimentary extras, and there's a pool, ayurveda centre, spa, and restaurant serving delicious south Indian buffets. Rates include half board. ⑧–⑨

**Woodlands** Kalpetta ⊤04936/202547, ⓦwww .thewoodlandshotel.com. Dependable place on the main drag at the north end of town. Its rooms are a little worn, but comfortable enough for a night and the staff are unfailingly courteous; there's secure parking, and separate veg and non-veg restaurants on the ground floor. ④–⑤

# Southern Wayanad

The lush green belt of rainforest, coffee plantations and tea estates forming the southern limits of Wayanad is overshadowed by the pyramidal form of **Chembra Peak**, at 2100m the highest point in the region. Any of the guesthouses and homestays clustered around its skirt tails can arrange guides to lead you to the top of the hill as well as transport to and from the **Muthanga Wildlife Sanctuary**, where sightings of wild elephants and Indian bison (gaur) are almost guaranteed. Closer to the main highway, the famous **Edakkal Caves** make another enjoyable day-trip – as long as you avoid weekends, when they get swamped by coachloads of boisterous locals. Crowds of noisy picnickers are also a feature of visits to the **Kanthampara waterfalls**, a beauty spot just down the road from Edakkal, but for those with the stamina for the steep trek to reach them, the nearby **Meenmuthy** falls are a wilder, more inspiring alternative.

## Chembra Peak

At 2100m, **Chembra Peak** is the highest point in the Wayanad region, dominating the landscape for many kilometres around. Carpeted on one side by soaring ridges and grassland and on the other by dense tropical forests, the massif can be tackled in around five to six hours (3–4 for the climb, 2–3 for the descent) – a stiff physical challenge given the heat and humidity, but one that's amply rewarded with a stupendous view over Wayanad and, on clear days, out to the distant coast. The springboard for the trek is the small town of **Meppadi**, 18km south of Kalpetta and reachable on southbound buses passing through the main KSRTC stand (30min). Permission has to be applied for in advance at the Forest Range Office, 1km west of Meppadi. The **permit** is free, but you have to pay Rs10 to access the trailhead, situated on the Chembra Tea Estate, 7km away along a paved road, and arrange for one of the two forest rangers to accompany you (Rs500). Auto-rickshaws will do the trip to the trailhead for about Rs100–150. The recommended start time is 6am and all necessary arrangements should ideally be made a couple of days in advance. Most homestays can help you with the necessary paperwork; alternatively, contact local District Tourism Promotion Council (DTPC) **guide** Sabu on his mobile phone, ☏9961 284874.

## Edakkal Caves

The **Edakkal Caves** (daily 9am–5pm; Rs10), a **prehistoric rock-art site** in the forests adjoining the Tamil border, are the region's most popular tourist attraction, drawing thousands of visitors up from the coastal cities on weekends. A natural cleft formed under two massive boulders, the cavern was discovered during a hunting expedition in 1894 by the Malabar Superintendent of police, Mr Fred Faucett, after his local tribal guides refused to approach the distinctive outcrop. On closer inspection, the rocks revealed a hidden chamber covered in enigmatic petroglyphs. Gouged with stone chisels by ancient hunter-gatherers, the oldest of them – comprising images of anthropomorphic figures, animals and birds – are thought to date from between 3000 BC and 1000 BC. Later marks include inscriptions in ancient Indian languages, probably made by Buddhist missionaries in the third century BC. Peacocks, an elephant, a dog wagging its tail, a wheeled cart and a figure of a man wearing a tall headdress may also be discerned amid the chaos of cross-hatchings and geometric shapes.

Edakkal is 37km east of Kalpetta. To get there by public transport, head for **Sultan's Battery**, 24km northeast, and change there to a bus bound for **Ambalavayal**, which passes the turning for Edakkal. Jeeps shuttle visitors from the road end to the ticket office, but the 800m climb is manageable on foot for anyone moderately fit. Ladders and some exposed scrambling have to be negotiated on the last leg up the cliff to the cave site itself – an ascent that can be treacherous at busy times. For this reason it's strongly recommended that you come first thing in the morning, by around 9am, before the crowds build up.

## Meenmuthy and Kanthampara waterfalls

Relatively few day-trippers ever make it to **Meenmuthy falls**, a spectacular cascade deep in the forest, 23km east of Kalpetta off the Ooty road. Buses from Meppadi pass through the village of **Vadavanchal**, where you can pick up an auto-rickshaw for the fifteen-minute run out to the start of an enjoyable 4km **walk**. The first 1500m involves an easy amble through picturesque coffee and tea plantations, but the remaining leg follows an exhilarating, and at times steep, jungle path requiring strong shoes, plenty of drinking water and, in damp conditions, a stick of some kind. Allow an hour for the descent and two or three times that for the climb back. Crashing down 300m of grey-black granite in three distinct phases, the falls themselves are a thrilling sight and well worth the trek.

A softer and more accessible – but less impressive – alternative to Meenmuthy is to visit the **Kanthampara waterfalls**, a popular local picnic spot 22km southeast of Kalpetta. Buses from Meppadi drop you at the turning, from where auto-rickshaws shuttle visitors to the car park at the head of the falls – although it's an easy and pleasant downhill stroll along tarmac, with fine views across coffee groves to the surrounding mountains. A footpath drops 250m from the car park to the falls themselves. At the bottom, you can also cross the river by means of three precarious-looking rope and bamboo footbridges to explore some beautiful forest on the far bank.

## Muthanga Wildlife Sanctuary

The southern portion of the Wayanad reserve, 40km east of Kalpetta, is known as the **Muthanga Wildlife Sanctuary** (daily 6–10am & 3–5pm; Rs110, camera Rs25). Like nearby Bandipur National Park, in neighbouring Karnataka, the park, with its dry deciduous forests, is noted for elephants and also shelters Indian bison (gaur), deer, wild boar, bear and tiger. **Trekking** in the sanctuary is only allowed during the morning slot; guides for the three-hour route charge Rs150. If you opt for the two-hour, 22km-long jeep trip, you'll also have to pay for a guide (Rs100) as well as the jeep rental (Rs300) and the vehicle's entry fee (Rs50).

The highway from Kalpetta to Mysore and Bandipur (via Sultan's Battery) crosses an important migratory corridor for elephants, which can frequently be seen plodding along the main road here. **Buses** bound for Mysore and Bengaluru run past the park gates, as do local services heading for Ponkuzhy.

## Accommodation

The forested slopes of Southern Wayanad harbour some of the loveliest **places to stay** in Kerala – if not in all southern India, though they're all well off the beaten track and require a taxi or jeep to reach. If you're not travelling with a car and driver who knows his way around, ask for advice on how to get to your chosen homestay when you book.

**Aranyakam** Valathur–Rippon, Meppadi ☎04936/280261, ☎9447 781203, ⊛www .aranyakam.com. Rooms in a handsome Keralan-style bungalow, with wood floors and verandas on both sides, the rear ones just a few metres from the coffee bushes. They're very simply furnished, and don't expect to be pampered – the staff are plantation workers who don't speak English, but everyone is eager to help, the traditional Malabari food is excellent and the location magnificent. Best options are the two huts that look across a spectacular wilderness of pristine forest and mountain. If coming by public transport, take the bus from Kalpetta to Vaduvanchal, get down at Rippon junction on the main Ooty road, then catch an auto-rickshaw for the last couple of kilometres (Rs30). Rates include all meals. ➏–➑

**Edakkal Hermitage** Near Edakkal Caves, Ambal-avayal ☎04936/221860, ⊛www.edakkal.com. Eight pleasantly furnished cottages, with old floor-boards and quality bathrooms, well spaced on small rock platforms overlooking the valley, with breathtaking views down to the plains. Pick of the bunch is "Chauvet", closely followed by "Lascaux". The candle-lit restaurant occupies a man-made cave. Rates are full board. ➐

**Tranquil** Kappamudi Estate, Kolaggappara ☎04936/220244, ☎9947 588507,

⊛www.tranquilresort.com. The crème de la crème of Wayanad's homestays, set amid 400 acres of rambling coffee, cardamom and vanilla plantations. Arrive in the late afternoon and you'll be whisked by jeep to the top of the estate for tea and samosas – and a view to die for. The planter's bungalow itself holds 8 comfy rooms (from $300), all opening on to a glorious veranda wrapped in manicured gardens, and there are two palatial treehouses ($400–425) perched above the void, as well as a large pool. The cooking's terrific, and the Dey family perfect hosts. Minimum two nights, but you'll want to stay longer. Rates are full board. ➒

**Wynberg** Kuzhivayal Estate, Thrikkaipetta, near Meppadi ☎04936/320620, ☎9847 846631, ⊛www.wynberg.in. A charmingly dishevelled little resort, hidden deep in the countryside, a twenty-minute ride off the highway beyond Karapuzha Lake. Rates are affordable, and the location, looking across an expanse of open paddy to a beautiful mountain, is wonderful. Smothered in coffee bushes, the accommodation ranges from mouldy tents to comfortable en-suite brick chalets. Best is the wonderful "deluxe treehouse" (Rs5000), which has oiled teak floors and a glorious view from its balcony. Rates are full board. ➏–➑

# Elephant madness

There exists in Malayalam a term for a kind of mania that Keralans succumb to en masse during the winter festival season: *anapraanth*, or "elephant madness". Various manifestations of this uniquely south Indian mentality occur, but the most pervasive is the tradition of parading elephants around temple precincts during festivities – or *utsavam* – accompanied by ear-splitting drum orchestras and firework displays. Tens of thousands turn up to adore the assembled tuskers, which are always caparisoned with gold headdresses (*nettippattom*).

Thrissur Puram ▲

Elephant transportation ▼

Festival parasols ▼

# Big stars

Around seven hundred elephants live in captivity in Kerala, ninety percent of them in the care of temples. The largest and best loved enjoy film-star status. One – a massive 3.2m-tall tusker called **Guruvayur Keshavan** who, before his death at the age of 72 in the 1970s, was adored for his exceptional intelligence and devotion to Krishna – has even had his skeleton, tusks, and a life-size effigy of him placed at the entrance to the famous **Guruvayur temple** for pilgrims to venerate. Temples actually compete to secure the services of the most beautiful animals, bidding often huge sums at auction for past winners of the prestigious annual **Gaja Raja** elephant beauty competition. Websites such as Ⓦwww.elephantstars.com keep fans in touch with their favourite performers, with enthusiasts animatedly comparing the lengths of different trunks, prominence of foreheads and the way they hold their heads.

However, the increasing popularity and scale of Keralan *utsavam* has placed the pachyderm population under considerable strain. Not only do processional elephants have to stand for hours enduring the barrage of drumming and fireworks, they also have to walk for up to twelve hours between venues, or be trundled over bumpy roads in the back of specially adapted Tata trucks. Moreover, to suppress must (an annual phase of sexual heat in which male elephants grow restless, oozing liquid from glands between their eyes and ears), their keepers, or *mahouts*, sometimes deprive them of water for two or three days at a stretch. Randy tuskers regularly crack under the strain and go on the rampage: an average of fifty people are trampled to death each year, and hundreds injured.

# A holy racket

Temple *utsavam* always follow a similar set structure. First off, the lead elephant, resplendently caparisoned in a golden *nettippattom*, carries the temple deity shield in procession around the temple courtyard, usually three times, accompanied by a small drum troupe. Then, the full team of tuskers lines up to be serenaded by the massed panchavadyam orchestra, comprising as many as 150 drummers playing traditional hard-skinned *chenda*. They stand in ranks before the animals, bare-chested in white cotton *mundu*, with a row of master performers at the front trying to outdo each other with their speed, stamina, improvisational skills and showmanship. Facing the *chenda* will be musicians playing long double-reed, oboe-like *kuzhals* and C-shaped *kompu* bell-metal trumpets. Over an extended period, the whole cacophony passes through four distinct phases, each twice as fast as the last, from a grand and graceful dead slow to a frenetic pace.

▲ *Panchavadyam* orchestra

▼ Puram

At the arrival of the fastest tempo, boys astride the elephants stand to perform elaborately choreographed routines with yak-tail fly whisks and giant peacock-feather fans. Sequined umbrellas are twirled in flashes of dazzling colour. Cymbals crash furiously, often raised above the head, and a chorus of trumpets, blasting in ragged unison, creates a sound that can have altered little in centuries.

All this is greeted by roars from the crowd: many people punch the air, while others are clearly *talam branthans*, rhythm "madmen", who follow every nuance of the structure, fuelled by copious quantities of alcohol. When the fastest speed is played out, the slowest tempo returns and the procession edges forward for the next cycle, the *mahouts* leading the elephants by the tusk.

▼ Elephant camp, Guruvayur

Ganesh and elephant at Guruvayur ▲

Kodanad ▼

Detail of *nettippattom* ▼

# 6 elephant hot spots

The granddaddy of all Kerala *utsavam* is the famous **Puram** in **Thrissur** (see p.196), but you'll encounter similar events almost everywhere between late November and March – the largest of which are listed below. Keep an eye out for huge posters and hoardings advertising forthcoming events on roadsides; a detailed festival calendar is also published daily in the *Malayala Manorama* newspaper, and online at Ⓦwww.kerala tourism.org/festivalcalendar. There are also a handful of camps, or *kraal*, where you can enjoy close encounters with domestic pachyderms.

▶▶ **Anathavalam** Famous elephant farm near the village of Puthenkulam, in southern Kerala, where elephants are trained for temple festivals. A baby was recently born here – one of the first recorded births in captivity. See p.119.

▶▶ **Arattupuzha Puram** (late March) The culmination of the annual festivities at Arattupuzha's Sri Ayappan temple, 14km from Thrissur, is a parade involving no less than 61 elephants.

▶▶ **Chembutra Puram** (late Jan/early Feb) Around 50 tuskers participate in the big *utsavam* at Chembutra, 13km from Thrissur.

▶▶ **Kodanad** This former elephant training camp on the banks of the Periyar River provides refuge for three adults and four delightful young calves; arrive early to help scrub them down. See p.192.

▶▶ **Parippally Gajamela** Kodimoottil Sri Bhagavathi (Badrakali) Temple in Paravur, southern Kerala, hosts a lamp-lit procession of fifty tuskers in late Feb/early March. See p.120.

▶▶ **Punnathur Kotta Elephant Camp**, Guruvayur. Some 67 elephants, donated by wealthy devotees of the nearby Krishna temple, are kept in this walled enclosure. Several of the largest participate in an annual elephant race, held around the temple in late Feb. See p.205.

# West Wayanad: Banasura

Tourism has only recently found its first foothold in the wild **west of Wayanad**, an area of soaring, green-topped mountains and shola forest centred around the man-made lake of **Banasura**. Dotted with tiny islets, the reservoir took shape in the late 1970s after the construction of India's largest earth dam – part of a massive, and highly controversial, hydel project to stem the Karamanathodu, a tributary of the Kabini River.

Seen in the early-morning light, with mist drifting between the dead trees protruding from its surface, the lake can be an impressive spectacle. But it's the awesome backdrop of peaks rising sheer from the water's edge that's the real show stealer. Named after the thousand-armed demon son of the god Bali, **Banasura mountain**, the culminating point of the massif, is the second-highest summit in the region after Chembra, at a height of 2073m. Trekking routes up it rise through a swathe of dense jungle where wild elephant graze in healthy numbers. Permission is required from the Forest Department to walk in the area, but it's a formality and easily arranged, along with local guides, by either of the hotels sited on the lakeshore.

## Accommodation

There are only two **places to stay** in this remote western corner of Wayanad. Both make the most of the stupendous mountain and lake views, but the less expensive *Banasura Island Retreat* is better placed for early-morning departures up the hill.

**Banasura Hill Resort** Vellamunda
☎04935/277900 or ☎9539 701354, ⊛www
.banasura.com. Set in 35 acres of greenery, this impressive eco-resort (formerly known as *Juggu's*) comprises 31 twin villas and suites in double-storey blocks, made entirely from rammed earth, red laterite, bamboo and coconut palm roots. The architecture is romantic, and views of the mountains magnificent, though the place has an air of formality somewhat at odds with the wild landscape. Doubles from Rs6000. ❺

**Banasura Island Retreat** Kuttiyamvayl
☎0496/227120, ⊛www.banasuraisland.com. One of the most remote properties in the region, set on a low hilltop overlooking Banasura reservoir. They offer standard rooms in an unsightly laterite block, or more appealing Keralan-style villas whose balconies make the most of the lake vista. Most people come for the superb trekking (from only Rs300), but it's a top spot for birdwatching too. ❼–❽

# North Wayanad

The teak forest takes over completely as you climb towards the northern limits of Wayanad, tracked by the savannah grass summits of the Brahmagiri massif. Some travellers use the potholed trunk road cutting north towards Mysore to reach the Nagarhole National Park or the Kodagu (Coorg) district in neighbouring Karnataka. But the majority of people who venture up here press no further north than the **Tholpetty Wildlife Sanctuary**, close to the state boundary, whose jungles shelter large herds of elephant. You'll see plenty of pachyderms at temple festivals down at sea level, but viewing them in the wild, foraging amid buttressed tree roots and stands of giant bamboo, with the cloud-swept summits of the Keralan border nosing above the forest canopy in the distance, is quite another thing. Some exceptionally fine hill walking is also to be had in this area, particularly in the imposing watershed ridges enfolding the **Sri Thirunelli temple**, a revered Hindu pilgrimage site set amid breathtaking scenery.

## Mananthavady

The main transport hub for the far north (although not somewhere you'd remotely wish to spend the night) is the scruffy little market town of **MANANTHAVADY**, connected by regular KSRTC buses to and from Kalpetta, 49km south (taxi jeeps also cover the one-hour trip for Rs600–750). It's famous throughout the state as the place where the rebel leader **Pazhassi Raja** – aka "the Lion of Kerala" (Kerala Simha) – met his end in 1805. A local chief who had made a stand against punitive British takes, Pazhassi fought a protracted guerrilla campaign against the East India Company, using the forested hills of northern Wayanad as a hideout. The defining moment of the decade-long insurgency was the ambush of an entire British Division camped at nearby Panamaram, in which 360 sepoys were slaughtered. The victory won the raja considerable admiration in India, but finally galvanized the Madras Presidency into dispatching a large force of troops from Tellicherry. After his two closest generals were decapitated and with the Company army closing in, Pazhassi Raja swallowed his diamond ring rather than submit to capture. At his cremation, the British accorded their old adversary a respectful 21-gun salute. A small **museum** (daily 9am–5pm), housing tribal weapons and memorabilia donated by families who sheltered Pazhassi Raja during his campaign, marks the site of the royal rebel's final resting place, on a low hill 1km east of the bus stand. It's seen an upsurge in visitor numbers since the 2009 release of a hit Malluwood movie on Pazhassi Raja, staring Malayali screen legend Mammooty.

## Tholpetty

Forming the northern sector of the Wayanad reserve, **Tholpetty Wildlife Sanctuary**, 25km northeast of Mananthavady, is one of the best parks in south India for sighting elephants, as well as bison, boar, *sambar*, spotted deer, macaques and Nilgiri langurs. Tigers also inhabit the reserve and their pug marks are commonly encountered along the muddy margins of forest trails, although you'd be lucky indeed to see any big cats in the flesh these days; decades of poaching have reduced the population to vestigial numbers. The Forest Department runs 24km **jeep safaris** (daily 7–9am & 3–5pm; 90min) from the park's main gates along a network of rutted tracks, passing through stands of old teak and bamboo groves, interspersed with boggy waterholes where watchtowers and observation huts have been erected. The cost depends on numbers – count on Rs250–300 per head, or better still, let the *Pachyderm Palace* make the arrangements for you if you're staying there. You can also join guided **treks** (daily 8am–1pm; Rs800 for up to four people), though the pace can be brisk, and stops few and far between.

**Taxis** charge Rs400 for the trip from Mananthavady to Tholpetty, and the frequent KSRTC **buses** to Kutta will drop you off at the sanctuary entrance. Buses back to Mananthavady run until 8.45pm.

## Thirunelli

One of Wayanad's most celebrated temples, Sri **Thirunelli**, lies in a remote part of the district 30km northwest of Mananthavady, reached via a bumpy back road winding west off the Kogadu road. Set amid an awesome amphitheatre of mountains draped in vegetation, the temple is an unusual mix of Keralan tiled roofs and north Indian-style pillared halls. It is dedicated to the god Vishnu and is considered to be a *tirtha*, or crossing, between the mundane world and the divine. Devout pilgrims bathe in the nearby **Papanasini stream**, 400m west of the main shrine, which is believed to absolve pilgrims of their worldly sins. Ritual offerings for the spirits of departed relatives are made at a sacred rock nearby, known as the Pinnapara, where cremated ashes are immersed. It is said that Lord Rama himself performed *pitru karma* here (a ritual plea Hindus make to their forebears to ensure a future free of impediments). Rajiv Gandhi's ashes were disposed of at this spot following his assassination by a Tamil suicide bomber in 1991. Behind the temple you can see the end of a small stone **aqueduct** resting on beautifully carved pillars – part of an ingenious system that brings spring water from the nearby mountains.

A dozen **buses** daily connect Mananthavady to Thirunelli; jeeps will run you out there for around Rs300.

## North Wayanad accommodation

**Agraharam Cottages** Near Sri Thirunelli temple, 30km north of Mananthavady ℡9605 005020 or ℡9605 005024, ⓦwww.agraharamcottages.com. A campus of tidy little chalets with red-tiled roofs and verandas, set amid neatly cropped lawns, is not what you expect to find in such a remote spot, but this is a welcoming place that makes a tranquil base for visiting the adajcent Sri Thirunelli temple, and for forays on foot into the surrounding woods and hills. The *appam* breakfasts and fish curry suppers are superb. ❼

**Fringe Ford** Cherrakarra, Mananthavady ℡9845 442224 or ℡9347 333122, ⓦwww.fringeford.com. Blissfully remote *Fringe Ford*, in the far northwest of Wayanad, takes the plantation stay experience to a new level. The low-slung 1950s bungalow isn't as pretty as some, but the location, at the head of a richly forested valley looking across the treetops to the high peaks of the Karnataka border, is sublime. As you lounge in your snug, chunkily furnished room, elephants and bison routinely plod past the window, and there are bonfires each evening on the terrace. Rates include fragrant Malabari-Andhran meals cooked on charcoal braziers, and the services of an enthusiastic young tribal guide, who leads treks to wildlife spots and viewpoints. From Rs7200 per double, including all meals. ❾

**Pachyderm Palace** Near the Tholpetty Forest Check Post; book through the Tourist Desk in Kochi on ℡0484/237 1761. Traditional Keralan bungalow with five simple rooms and garden hut on stilts rented on an all-inclusive basis. On arrival, many guests are surprised by how basic their room is for the price, but are invariably won over by the authentic Keralan cuisine and friendly welcome of host Mr Venu. Jeeps for wildlife drives can be arranged, along with guides for treks into the nearby Brahmagiri range. ❻

**Udayagiri** 3.5km from the Tholpetty Forest Check Post ℡04935/250945 or ℡9539 840303, ⓦwww.ayurvedayogavilla.com. On a coffee plantation high in the hills overlooking the Tholpetty reserve, these two Kerlalan-style chalets boast magnificent views from their traditional slatted verandas. The interiors are a touch chintzy, but the location can't be beaten – great for lazing or as a base for forest and plantation walks. Rates include all meals (vegetarian; no alcohol). ❻

**Wildlife Resort** 500m from the Tholpetty Forest Check Post ℡9656 566977 or ℡9744 770500, ⓦwww.wildliferesort.in. The most comfortable option within easy walking distance of the Tholpetty park gate. Its recently built laterite, red-tiled "cottages", set in steeply sloping gardens just off the main road, are bland, and a bit overpriced, but well furnished (with good mattresses) and with private sitouts. ❼

# The far north

A seemingly endless succession of near-deserted beaches, backed by palm-fringed lagoons and low, wooded hills spreads **north from Kozhikode**. This was one of the first parts of the Malabar to be targeted by early colonial prospectors, and wind-worn seventeenth- and eighteenth-century laterite forts punctuate the coast at regular intervals, dating from an era when the Portuguese, Dutch, British and various local rulers were vying for control of the pepper trade.

Typically Malabari fishing harbours, markets and Moppila mosques comprise the workaday charms of these former trading posts, the liveliest of them **Mahé**, an erstwhile French colony, and **Thalassery**, the first British garrison and port in the area. The main reason most tourists venture this far north, however, is to experience **theyyem**, the extraordinary masked spirit possession rituals staged in villages across the region between November and May. **Kannur**, another former colonial outpost, makes the most appealing base, with a wider choice of accommodation than anywhere else in the area, including some gorgeous beachside guesthouses.

Taxis are on hand for early-morning departures to the remote villages where the ceremonies are held, and to whisk visitors out to nearby **Parassinikadavu**, the only temple in Kerala hosting daily *theyyem*.

**Beyond Kannur**, sights become thinner on the ground as the coastal highway and rail line approach the Karnatakan border. In this conservative, predominantly Moppila corner of the state, the rambling ruins of **Bekal Fort** are the number-one weekend destination for locals, with laterite ramparts affording panoramic views of the gloriously empty beaches stretching away on both sides. To the south, the **Valiyaparamba backwaters** comprise a tangle of largely uninhabited creeks, islets and winding rivers served by a mere handful of houseboats and local ferries.

## Mahé

Clustered on a broad spit of land at the mouth of the Mayyazhi River, **MAHÉ**, 58km north of Kozhikode, became the French East India Company's first foothold on the northern Malabar coast in 1721. The British factors at nearby Tellicherry were dismayed by the appearance on their doorstep of their Gallic rivals, and encouraged the local rulers to resist the incursion. But the French dug in and – by means of the timely arrival in 1725 of Admiral de Padaillon and his fleet, and some clever political manoeuvring – managed to hold onto the fort they erected overlooking the river mouth.

Opinion is divided over whether the town was renamed after **Bertrand François Mahé La Bourdonnais** – the legendary naval commander who served under de Padaillon during the 1725 recapture of the fort and who later went on to play a vital role in the establishment of French interests in south India – or whether the commander added the name of the colony to his own in honour of the victory. Either way, it remained a French protectorate until 1954, since when the six-square-kilometre enclave has been administered as a Union Territory from France's principal former possession, Pondicherry (now Puducherry), on the opposite coast of India in Tamil Nadu.

Mahé's colonial past is visible in the tumbledown remains of a fort, a handful of nineteenth-century Gothic churches and administrative buildings, and a statue of Marianne, symbol of the French Republic, in a park on the waterfront. But the most conspicuous legacy of French rule are the distinctive *képis* (military caps) still worn by local policemen, and an overwhelming number of **liquor shops** – Mahé's Union Territory status means lower excise duties on booze and fuel than the rest of Kerala. As a consequence, bus-loads of brandy-swilling men tend to inundate the town on weekends. The busiest time of year, however, is the first fortnight of March when the area's temples stage exuberant *theyyem* ceremonies during the annual **Puthalam Festival**.

### The Town

Fringed on one side by dense palm groves and on the other by a white-sand beach (not safe for swimming), Mahé's most picturesque quarter fronts the river on the north side of town, where well-groomed public gardens line a waterside walkway from where you can watch the comings and goings of local boat traffic. Three-hour **dolphin-spotting trips** (daily 9am–6pm; Rs400) operate out of the government-run **Water Complex**, 1km or so upriver, just before the big railway bridge.

Barely discernible beneath its mantle of overgrowth, the ruined French East India Company's **St George's Fort** crowns a hillock on the north side of the river. The crumbling remains barely warrant the effort, but if you're determined, ask an auto-rickshaw to take you up to the TV relay station, from where one of the locals will lead you through a backyard to view the lone turret and fragment still standing.

En route, you could pay a visit to the **Malayala Kalagramam** (Mon–Fri 9.30am–4pm; ℡0490/223 2961), a renowned school of traditional performing arts 100m upriver from the town bridge. With prior permission from the Director, M.V. Devan – a nationally famous artist and critic – visitors are welcome to watch classes in dance, music, sculpture, mural painting, Malayali graphics and yoga.

### Practicalities

Mahé is easily reachable by regular **buses** from Kannur and Kozhikode via NH-17, although there's no bus stand as such – services pull up at various points along the main street, Church Road. The **railway station**, 1500m southeast of the centre, lies on the main line and is served by seventeen daily express trains in both directions. **Accommodation** options are limited, and most visitors end up staying in nearby Thalassery. The best-presented and most welcoming of an uninspiring bunch is *Zara Resorts* (℡0490/233 2503; ❹–❺), on Railway Station Road, midway between the station and town centre, which has a choice of rooms (some a/c) set in a laterite walled compound. There's a small family restaurant and an a/c bar on site. Cheaper fallbacks closer to the centre include the *Ashwathi Guest House* (℡0490/233 4475; ❸–❹), just off Maidan Road near the Syndicate Bank, which has basic non-a/c doubles, and the similarly plain *Hotel Arena*, around the corner on Maidan Road (℡0490/233 7084; ❸–❹), 200m from the beach and riverfront.

## Thalassery (Tellicherry)

**THALASSERY**, or "Tellicherry" as it was known in colonial times, was the lynchpin of early British trade in pepper, cardamom and timber in the northern Malabar, and the site of many a skirmish between the East India Company and its European rivals, not to mention their local Indian adversaries, the **Kolathiri** rajas.

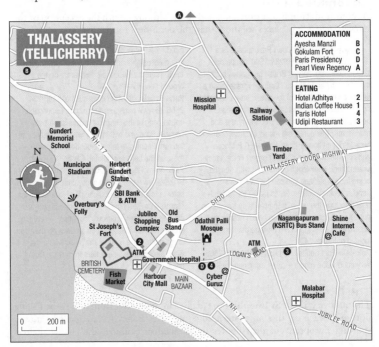

Built in 1708, the square **fort** erected by the British on a rocky bluff overlooking the waterfront still dominates the town. Its slanting ramparts witnessed particularly fierce action during the Mysore Wars at the end of the eighteenth century, and in the Pazhassi Revolt of the 1890s, when among the young defenders who distinguished themselves in battle was one Colonel Arthur Wellesley, the future Duke of Wellington. Aside from the old British stronghold, there's little here to warrant a detour, although the busy **fishing harbour** and an antique Moppila mosque – the stalwart **Odathil Palli Masjid** – hold plenty of local atmosphere. You could also enjoy traditional hospitality and famous regional cooking at the *Ayesha Manzil*, one of Kerala's top heritage **homestays**.

### Arrival and information

Thalassery is well connected by rail and road to Kozhikode and Kannur, and to most major towns in central and southern Kerala via the main Thiruvananthapuram–Mangalore line. Both the **railway station** and **Narangapuran bus stand**, where you'll be dropped if you arrive from Kozhikode or Kannur, lie on the east side of town, just over 1km northeast of the fort and beach. The usual welcoming committee of khaki-clad auto-rickshaw-wallahs is on hand at both to speed you down the hill, although you can walk to the fort and fishing harbour in around fifteen minutes.

There's a UAE Exchange (Mon–Sat 9.30am–6pm & 1.30–2pm, Sun 9.30am–1.30pm) in the Sahara Centre, opposite Alukkas jewellery shop on A.V.K. Nair Road, a short rickshaw-ride or walk from the new bus stand or fort. The HDFC Bank **ATM** is in the same building. Cyber Guyz (Rs30/hr), near the *Paris Presidency* on Logan's Road, offers **internet**.

### Accommodation

**Accommodation** is plentiful and good value, although, with the exception of the *Ayesha Manzil*, few places see more than the occasional tourist.

**Ayesha Manzil** Court Rd, opposite Sea View Park ☎0490/234 1590, ✉cpmoosa @rediffmail.com. Former British bungalow, built in the 1860s by an East India Company trader atop a hillock on the outskirts of town, and later converted by its present owners into a splendid heritage homestay. Filled with carved wood furniture and other family heirlooms, the rooms (all attached) are huge, airy and comfortable. Host Mr C.P. Moosa and his wife, Malabari cooking expert Faiza, enjoy sharing their knowledge of the area with guests: come for a week and you can follow Faiza's famous cookery course. Rates ($200 for two full-board) include the use of a temple-style swimming pool, free transfers to a hidden beach nearby and superb local cuisine, served on a garden terrace looking out to sea. ❾

**Gokulam Fort** Goods Shed Rd ☎0490/234 2666. Very good-value rooms – clean, spacious, well

aired – in a large pink, mock-Neoclassical building in a quiet neighbourhood on the northern fringes of town. There's a decent a/c restaurant on the ground floor. ❹–❺

**Paris Presidency** Off Logan's Rd ☎0490/234 2666, ⊛www.parispresidency.com. Dependable option bang in the centre of town just off busy Logan's Road and within easy walking distance of the fort. Rooms are large, though slightly worn – those at the back are quieter. ❸–❹

**Pearl View Regency** Kannur Rd ☎0490/232 6702, ⊛www.pearlviewregency.com. The smartest hotel in town and the first choice of local business clients, with 52 rooms – from enormous non-a/c doubles to equally spacious "cottages" – facing a grubby pool amid landscaped gardens on the edge of town. Ask for a room at the back, with a river view; the opposite side suffers from noise from the nearby highway. ❺

### The Town

The massive walls of **St Joseph's Fort** (daily 8am–6pm; free) lord it over the fishing port and beach on the far western edge of town. Entered via a gabled gateway sporting European guardian figures in Elizabethan clothing, the citadel shelters neatly kept gardens and a (disused) lighthouse. You can clamber over the ramparts for a view of the jetty below, but a better spot from which to appreciate the scale of the structure is the encircling path to the rear (follow the dirt trail running anti-clockwise around the fort from its main gateway, past St Joseph's Boys' School). In the old British cemetery behind stands the grave of Edward Brennan, an Englishman who was swept ashore after a shipwreck in the nineteenth century and liked the town so much he decided to stay. The school he eventually founded, Brennan College, now ranks among the Malabar's foremost educational institutions.

Ambles around the superb local **fish market**, down near the waterfront, occupy Thalassery's handful of foreign visitors in the mornings, and the fresh vegetable bazaar is another source of vivid local colour. The only monument of note here, however, is a striking two-hundred-year-old Moppila mosque known as the **Odathil Palli Masjid**, erected by a family of wealthy local merchants, the Keyis, on a former Dutch sugar-cane plot. A splendid specimen of hybrid Malabari style, it stands in a palm-filled, walled enclosure close to the old bus stand at the bottom of town, just off the busy junction behind the fishing harbour. Non-Muslims are barred from entering the prayer hall and adjacent graveyard, and photography is also strictly forbidden, but no one should mind you viewing the exterior, with its multi-tiered copper and tiled roofs, turquoise-painted slatted eaves and a gold-covered conical dome.

Thalassery has long been an important centre of **kalarippayat**, Kerala's own martial art (see p.89), and at the prestigious **CVN Kalari Kalarippayat** gymnasium in the suburb of Chirakava, 3km southeast of the fort near the Sri Rama Swami temple, you can (by prior arrangement) watch daily training sessions in a traditional earth-floored pit (dry season 6.30–9am; monsoons 4.30–9pm). Call Mr Devadas, the *kalari gurukkal* (master), on ☎0490/232 0030 the day before your intended visit. A small donation of Rs100–200 for the students is welcome.

## Eating

For authentic non-veg Moppila **food**, including Thalassery's famous biriyanis and freshly fried *kallmakaya* (mussels), try the rough-and-ready *Paris Hotel*, down a lane off Logan's Road. It's almost next door to the *Paris Presidency*, whose a/c dining hall is the poshest place to eat in the centre, serving north Indian, Chinese and Continental food from around Rs75–200. Traditional Keralan rice-plate meals are served at the *Hotel Adhitya* on Gundert Road, opposite the fort. The *Indian Coffee House* near the old bus stand is another popular, dependable veg option, as is the slightly smarter *Udipi* at the top of Logan's Road, not far from the bus stand, which serves the usual range of tasty south Indian snacks and meals.

# Kannur (Cannanore)

**KANNUR** (Cannanore), 92km north of Kozhikode, was for many centuries the capital of the Kolathiri rajas, who prospered from the thriving maritime spice trade through its port. India's first Portuguese Viceroy, Francisco de Almeida, took the stronghold in 1505, leaving in his wake an imposing triangular bastion, **St Agnelo's Fort**. This was annexed in the seventeenth century by the Dutch, who sold it for one *lakh* rupees a hundred or so years later to the Arakkal rajas, Kerala's only ruling Muslim dynasty. They in turn were ousted by General Abercrombie's East India Company troops, who besieged the citadel in 1790, forcing the Arakkals' female ruler, Ali Raja Beebi, to sign a treaty of dependency.

These days, the town is the largest in the northern Malabar region – a typically Keralan market and transport hub, jammed with giant gold emporia and silk shops, and seething with traffic. Land prices are booming ahead of the proposed

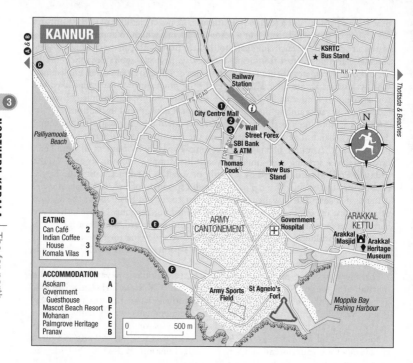

construction of an international airport, which will doubtless see more skyscrapers rise on the outskirts. Kannur's few sights can be slotted into a morning, but increasing numbers of travellers are using the beaches to the south as bases from which to venture into the hinterland in search of **theyyem** rituals.

### Arrival and information

Straddling the main coastal transport artery between Mangalore and Kochi/Thiruvananthapuram, Kannur is well connected by **bus** and **train** to most major towns and cities in Kerala, as well as Mangalore in Karnataka. Most local services, including those from Thalassery and other towns in Malabar, pull into the snazzy **New Bus Stand**, five minutes' walk southeast of the big and bustling **railway station**; long-distance Kerala state services arrive at the **KSRTC stand**, a short hop by auto-rickshaw north.

Most local auto-rickshaw-wallahs use their meters without prompting and no trip around town should cost you more than Rs25. White Ambassador **taxis** queue to the left of the main exit of the railway station The State Bank of India has an **ATM** opposite the main exit to the railway station, and another on Fort Road, where you'll also find a branch of Thomas Cook that **changes money**. Wall Street Forex, at the top of Fort Road, is the local Western Union agent and also changes currency and travellers' cheques.

Kerala Tourism have an **information counter** on the main concourse of the railway station (Mon–Sat 9am–4pm; ☎0497/270 3121) where you can find out about homestays and *theyyem* rituals. **Internet** is widely available; try the a/c Padinharakandy, 150m south of the pink City Centre mall on Fort Road. Inside the mall itself, **DC Books** is the place to buy reading material.

## Accommodation

Kannur's noisy and congested centre is packed with **hotels**, but it's a much better idea to head east across the cantonment district to the leafy suburb behind **Baby Beach**, or better still, further north to **Palliyamoola Beach** (a Rs50–75 ride away), where a string of more relaxing hotels, small resorts and homestays offers cooler, breezier accommodation close to the sea. Places on the beaches to the southeast are reviewed on p.251.

**Asokam** Palliyamoola Beach ☎ 0497/320 5265, ⓦ www.ayurvedaresort.co.in. Little cabin-style chalets (non-a/c), with tiled roofs, sitouts and rustling palms overhead, in a neat garden right behind the beach, or more substantial a/c rooms in a concrete house set further back. Ayurveda treatments on site, but you'll have to eat in town. ❺–❻

**Government Guesthouse** Cantonment area ☎ 0497/270 6426. Superb-value government-run place on a clifftop at the edge of Kannur, with large, simple a/c and non-a/c rooms whose huge balconies have uninterrupted sea views; it's primarily for visiting VIPs but usually has a few vacancies. As ever, advance booking can be a problem; ring ahead when you arrive. Inexpensive veg meals on request. ❷

**Mascot Beach Resort** 300m before Baby Beach ☎ 0497/270 8445, ⓦ www.mascotresort.com. Perched on the rocky shoreline, offering large a/c rooms and cottages with views across the cove to the lighthouse. Facilities include a grubby swimming pool, foreign exchange and a so-so restaurant – but no bar. ❺–❼

**Mohanan** Beach Rd, Palliyamoola ☎ 0497/274 4168 or ☎ 9895 879567. Welcoming homestay in a large, marble-lined house facing an empty stretch of beach to the north of town. The cheaper rooms to the rear are much less enticing than those with balconies looking straight out to

sea. Guests have the run of a lounge with TV; there's a friendly dog (Mitu), and great food available on request. ❺

**Palmgrove Heritage** Mill Rd, near *Government Guest house* ☎ 0497/270 3182, ⓦ www .palmgroveheritageretreat.com. Dating from the 1930s, this former palace once belonged to the last raja of Arikkal but now accommodates an offbeat little heritage hotel, with a choice of bargain rooms or threadbare suites in the old portion, and large, modern, good-value doubles (some a/c) in the two adjacent, multistorey blocks. There's secure parking, and meals are served on a rear-side lawn. ❸–❺

**Pranav** Beach Rd, Palliyamoola ☎ 0497/274 1148 or ☎ 9986 603756, ⓦ www .pranavbeachresort.in. A well-run little resort, in a lawned palm grove a stone's throw from the beach, which offers a wide range of accommodation, from attractive laterite cottages with a/c and pillared sitouts to smaller cabins made of palm wood. There are also some bargain rooms with shared toilets in a beautiful old *tharavad* – they're small and simply furnished, but have a huge traditional veranda with oodles of Keralan atmosphere. Manager "KP" is a gracious host, and cook Pushpa rustles up fabulous Malabari meals (included in the price). The owners also show guests around their nearby organic farm on request. ❸–❻

## The Town

Kannur town has two main centres of gravity: the area of busy streets and shops outside the railway and bus stations, where most travellers arrive; and **Moppila Bay**, 1km or so to the south, dominated by the fishing harbour and its adjacent citadel. Accessed through a gateway on its northern side, **St Agnelo's Fort** (daily 8am–6pm) remains in good condition and is worth visiting to scale the massive laterite ramparts, littered with British cannons, for views over the town's massive Norwegian-funded fishing anchorage. The splendid whitewashed building facing the beachfront below the fort – once the Raja and Bibi of Arrakal's palace – now houses the government-run **Arakkal Heritage Museum** (Mon–Sat 10am–6pm; Rs25), where documents, weapons, various pieces of 400-year-old rosewood furniture and other heirlooms relating to the family's history are displayed – though they're somewhat upstaged by the old building itself, with its high-beamed ceilings and original floorboards. Five times daily, the *muezzin* reverberates from the prayer tower of the former royal mosque, the **Arakkal Masjid**, immediately behind the museum (not open to visitors), next to which lies an ancient stepped laterite ablutions tank. Other remnants of the Arakkals' former palace survive in the heritage district to the rear, **Arakkal Kettu**, some of whose dilapidated, red-tiled *tharavadukal* are fronted by long, pillared verandas and intricately carved doors.

A gentle half-hour walk around the headland to the northwest of St Agnelo's fort brings you to quiet **Baby Beach**, behind the *Government Guesthouse* in the army's cantonment area (daily access 9am–5pm), where a leafy seaside promenade (Rs2) leads to a lighthouse (daily 3–5pm; Rs5), with fine views of the rocky coastlines and distant beaches. However, the most popular destination among locals for a stroll and splash in the surf is **Palliyamoola Beach**, a long stretch of white sand reachable in a ten-minute rickshaw ride from town. The crowds that congregate on the sands here on evenings and weekends can be sidestepped by walking further north, where a string of breezy guesthouses face a 4km stretch of empty golden sand and crashing surf, backed by a granite sea wall. Opinion is divided locally as to whether swimming is safe.

Extravagant costumes worn in *theyyem* and other lesser-known local art and ritual forms, including the Muslim dance style *oppana*, dominate the collection of the **Folklore Museum** (Mon–Sat 10.30am–12.30pm & 2.30–4.30pm; Rs10; ☎0497/277 8090), 5km north of Kannur town in the village of **Chirakkal**, just off NH-17. Housed in the 130-year-old *nalukettu* palace, the engaging collection also features masks and weapons used in Patayani rituals performed in local Bhadrakali temples, and displays of *todikkalam* murals. Facing the museum is a large, man-made tank, or *chira*, also built by the local ruling family, the Chirakkals. You can get to the museum by auto-rickshaw (Rs100–150); local buses also run (every 30min) from the Padanna Paalam bus stand on the northwest edge of Kannur town.

## Eating

Packed with commuters and travellers in transit, the best traditional *udipi* **restaurant** in town is the diminutive *Komala Vilas*, tucked away down a side street opposite the railway station exit, which serves the usual range of south Indian *iddli-vada* and *uppma* breakfasts, dosas and rice meals for next to nothing. There's also a good *Indian Coffee House* on Fort Rd, 50m south of the City Centre shopping mall. Just behind the same building, the trendier *Can Café* is a popular non-veg alternative, offering biriyanis as well as inexpensive Malabari chicken and fish curries. Like Kozhikode, Kannur is also famous for its **sweet shops**; local specialities sold in the many outlets dotted along Station Road include *kinnathappam* and *kalathappam* cakes, made with rice flour and *jaggery*.

## Around Kannur

The nocturnal *theyyem* rituals held in village temples **around Kannur** provide the main focus in this area, but there are plenty of other typically Malabari sights worthy of short day-trips. The best bases if you're planning to stay more than a night or two are the guesthouses nestled under the palms behind a string of empty **beaches** further southeast down the coast towards Thalassery. Peaceful and clean, the beaches are safe to swim from and totally undeveloped – for the time being. The construction of the new international airport will doubtless put an end to their serenity.

Local guesthouse-owners can point you toward **handloom weaving workshops** dotted around nearby villages – a legacy of the old calico cotton trade. One that's used to receiving visitors is the **Kanhirode Co-operative** (Mon–Sat 9am–3.30pm; ☎0497/285 7259), 13km northeast of Kannur on the main road to Mattanur, which employs around four hundred workers to make upholstery and curtain fabrics, plus material for luxury shirts and saris.

## Theyyem around Kannur

**Theyyem**, the dramatic spirit possession ceremonies held at village shrines throughout the northern Malabar region in the winter, rank among Kerala's most extraordinary spectacles. Over four hundred different manifestations of this arcane ritual exist in the area around Kannur, each one with its own distinctive costumes, make-up, music and atmosphere.

**Finding** *theyyem* can be a hit-and-miss affair, requiring time, patience and, because many of the ceremonies run through the night, stamina. The best sources of advice are the owners of local guesthouses, who will be able to consult the daily *Malayala Manorama* on your behalf: notices of forthcoming performances are listed at top left of page two. A **full rundown of temple festivals** in the area is also listed online at the exhaustive ⓦwww.theyyamcalendar.com. Anyone pushed for time might also consider a trip out to **Parassinikadavu** (see p.252), where a form of *theyyem* is staged daily.

Wherever you end up watching this uniquely Keralan phenomenon, bear in mind that for local people *theyyem* rituals are far more than mere theatre. *Theyyems* are considered actual manifestations of gods or goddesses, and their appearance in the ritual arena, in front of a rapt crowd, is an event of great **religious intensity** and significance. As a foreigner, you'll usually be welcome to attend, but should conduct yourself as you would on any other sacred occasion: dress respectfully, with legs, shoulders and arms covered (no shorts or knee-length skirts); never smoke or eat in the presence of the deity or around the temple or shrine; and refrain from drawing attention to yourself by talking loudly, moving around or pointing (if you turn up in a group, it can also be a good idea to disperse and blend in rather than stay bunched together).

*Theyyem* **ceremonies** always have one main coordinator (usually seated at a table); ask him where best to position yourself during the performance. Certain key areas exist where non-Hindus, in particular, will be less than welcome, and these might not be obvious to the uninitiated. The coordinator will also be able to tell you if it's OK to photograph the *theyyems* – it generally is, but flashes can be very distracting. If you have a digital camera, use high ISO settings instead.

Finally, try to stay until the end. As *theyyem* rituals invariably last all night, culminating at dawn, this isn't always easy, but it will demonstrate that you appreciate the religious importance of the event. Leaving a **donation** (Rs100–200) will also be much appreciated. For more **background**, see p.299 and the *Playing gods* colour section.

Another vestige of this coast's ancient seafaring heritage lies 10km up the coast at **Azhikkal**, where large ocean-going vessels are made from Malabari hardwood at the **Sulkha Shipyard** (☎04972/770195, ⓦsulkhashipyard.in). Casual visits are not encouraged, but if you have a special interest, the owner, Mr Abdul Hakeem, will show you around the premises. Mr Hakeem is the ninth generation of the Thalangara family to run this firm, which makes fishing trawlers, pleasure dhows and gigantic cargo *urus* for sale mainly to Gulf Arab sheikhs. While the latest computer-aided design technology is deployed at the planning stages, only centuries-old skills and materials are used in the construction of the ships taking shape under the yard's colossal corrugated-iron shelters.

### Accommodation

**Chera Rocks** 14km south of Kannur at Chera Kalle, Tayeechery ☎0490/234 3211 or ☎9446 610131, ⓦwww.cherarocks.com. If you're dreaming of a room where you can watch the moonlight on the waves from your bed and fall asleep to the sound of surf crashing through the coconut trees, then this place won't disappoint. Its "super deluxe", three-bedroom cottage is a pretty orange building huddled in a palm grove behind an idyllic beach, with a pitched tiled roof and long pillared veranda open to the sea. The less pricey "deluxe" rooms occupy a white house set back just behind it. Rates include full board and pick-up from Kannur railway station. ⑥–⑧

**Costa Malabari** 10km south of Kannur, near Thottada village, ⓦwww .costamalabari.com; book through the Tourist Desk, Main Jetty, Kochi (☎0484/237 1761). Take no notice of the name: there's nothing naff about these three traditional Keralan bungalows, set in cashew and coconut groves on the bluff above Thottada Beach. *Costa Malabari II* is the pick of the crop, perched on a clifftop where a flight of rickety wooden steps takes you down to the most glorious golden sand cove. The food is fantastic, too. Pick-up from Kannur by arrangement. ⑥–⑦

**Ezhara Beach House** House 7/347, near Ezhara Moppila School, Ezhara Kadappuram, Kuttikkagam ☎0497/283 5022, ☎9846 819941, ⓦwww .ezharabeachhouse.com. Tucked under the palms on the edge of a traditional Moppila quarter, close to a Muslim school and mosque, this old, blue-painted bungalow is a great place to experience village life at close quarters. It's just a stone's throw from the sand, within easy walking distance of long, empty beaches, and has a great first-floor

veranda where people lounge about, swapping stories with hosts Hyacinth and Georgio. The five rooms are snug, divided into two units, each with bathrooms, basic kitchens and outside space. ⑤

**Kannur Beach House** Thottada ☎9847 186330 or ☎9847 184535, ⓦwww .kannurbeachhouse.com. Descendants of high-ranking local Muslim families, Nazir and Rosie dropped out of the IT rat race to move from Singapore with their three children to start this gem of a guesthouse. It's hard not to feel envious: sandwiched on a slither of land between a river and the beach, the location is sublime and the rooms, with their antique wooden doors and windows, luminous interiors and lovely verandas, are perfect havens. Price includes meals of fragrant Malabari cooking served around a communal dining table. They run trips out to *theyyem* most evenings; you can recover afterwards with a splash along the adjacent backwater by canoe. ⑥

**Shoreline** Thottada Beach ☎9496 55444 or ☎9746 376680, ⓦwww.shorelinegarden.com. New property, bang on the beach with a river at the rear and rooms opening on to a sea-facing Keralan-style veranda. A non-English-speaking cook-cum-caretaker runs the place. ⑥

# North from Kannur

The only village in Kannur district where you can be guaranteed a glimpse of *theyyem* is **Parassinikadavu**, half an hour's drive north, where temple priests don elaborate costumes, dance and make offerings to the god Muthappan each morning and evening. With an early enough start, it's possible to catch the morning session and still have time to continue north to explore the little-visited **Valiyaparamba back-water** region. Local ferries criss-cross this fascinating necklace of lagoons, and there's even a company running rice-barge trips – though foreign tourists are few and far between.

To press on further north into Kasaragod district, you'll have to spend a night or two in one of the homestays or boutique retreats that have sprung up recently – the loveliest of them near the roadside town of **Nileshwaram**, at the head of the Valiya-paramba backwaters. Larger hotel complexes, pitched at wealthy holidaymakers from Bangaluru, are beginning to appear further north still around **Bekal Fort**, where you can walk along some impressive ramparts overlooking swathes of empty coast. **Kasaragod**, the last sizeable town before the border, is a predominantly Muslim enclave with its own distinct hybrid culture. A quirky river island homestay, well-preserved hill fort and remote lake temple are three reasons to pause there.

## Parassinikadavu

The **Parassini Madammpura** temple in the village of **PARASSINIKADAVU**, 20km north of Kannur beside the River Valapatanam, is visited in large numbers by Hindu pilgrims for its *theyyem* rituals (6.30–8.30am & 5.45–8.30pm). Elaborately dressed and accompanied by a traditional drum group, the resident priest, or *madayan*, becomes possessed by the temple's presiding deity – Lord Muthappan, Shiva, in the form of a *kiratha*, or hunter – and performs a series of complex offerings. The two-hour ceremony culminates when the priest/deity dances forward to bless individual members of the congregation – an extraordinary spectacle, even by Keralan standards.

Regular local **buses** leave Kannur for Parassinikadavu from around 7am, dropping passengers at the top of the village. If you want to get there in time for the dawn *theyyem*, however, you'll have to leave at around 5am, taking one of the Ambassador taxis that line up outside Kannur bus stand (around Rs600 round-trip); cars may also be arranged through most hotels. Alternatively, stay in the conveniently located *Thai Resort* (℡0497/278 4242; ❺), 80m from the temple. Shaded by coconut trees, seven binocular-shaped stone cottages with red roofs are dotted around a tiny garden and lily pond, with cool, comfortable a/c rooms. If you've come for the morning performance and have a few hours to spare afterwards, you could take a bus from Parassinikadavu to **Trichambaram temple**, a magnificent piece of traditional architecture dedicated to Krishna, with tiered clay roofs and slatted wooden walls. A smaller temple nearby, no more than a puja room surrounded by a moat, is devoted to Durga Devi. Buses take fifteen minutes, and drop you at a junction 800m from the temple complex.

Three kilometres before the temple stands a little **Snake Park** (daily 9am–6pm; Rs100), where kraits, vipers, cobras and – the star attraction – a couple of 5m-long **king cobras** are kept in less than ideal conditions.

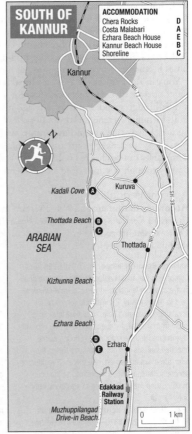

## Valiyaparamba and Nileshwaram

For the ultimate antidote to the traffic fumes and crowded streets of the Malabar's market towns and cities, press on 50km north of Kannur to one of the quietest stretches of coast in the state. Edged by a thin sliver of white sand and coconut trees, the **Valiyaparamba backwaters** – often misleadingly dubbed "the northern backwaters" – centre on a small, 30km delta fed by four rivers whose various bands and tributaries form a tangle of inland lakes, creeks and winding lagoons speckled with tiny islets. Kuttanad it most assuredly isn't: Valiyaparamba holds comparatively few permanent dwellings, and traffic on its waterways largely consists of country fishing boats. All the same, it makes a wonderful region for off-track explorations, not least because of the virtual absence of other tourists. At present, only one firm runs **houseboat cruises** in the area. Based on the northern edge of the backwaters area, Bekal Boat Stay (℡0467/228 2633, ⓦwww.bekalboatstay.com) has four canopied *kettu vallam* for hire, each one with bed space for a maximum of four. Prices start at Rs1500 for a 1hour cruise, or Rs7000–9500 for 24 hours, including meals. Shorter sunset and dinner trips are also available. Bekal Boat Stay works out of a small waterfront office at the **Kottappuram** boat jetty, where an amazing 300m **footbridge** – the longest of the kind in the state – crosses the backwater to the island of Acham Thuruthi. The jetty lies 2km south of **NILESHWARAM**, a busy hub on NH-17, which can be reached by any of the buses heading north on the highway, or by train via the coastal main line.

You can also explore the area on a **local ferry**. The State Water Transport Department operates five daily services (Rs9 for a 2hr 30min trip) around Valiyaparamba: a ride through wonderful lakes and lagoons, with panoramic views of the Ezhimala Hills forming a serene backdrop. Boats leave from **Ayitty Jetty**, an 8km minibus or auto-rickshaw ride east of **Payyannur**, which is 24km north of Kannur on NH-17 (served by passenger trains on the mainline railway and any northbound bus). Timetables can be checked online at Ⓦ www.swtd.gov.in, or by calling ☎ 0467/221 3566 – though you may need a Malayalam speaker to help you.

## Accommmodation

**Accommodation** around Nileshwaram includes two of the most fabulous places to stay in Kerala – the dreamy *Neeleshwar Hermitage*, and rather more idiosyncratic *Oyster Opera*, marooned in the nearby backwaters – with the *Valiyaparamba Retreat* for budget travellers.

**Nalanda Resort** Nileshwaram ☎ 0467/228 2662. Comprising five traditional-style cottages (a/c and non-a/c) set in landscaped gardens on a riverbank next to the highway, the *Nalanda* serves as the area's main watering hole, so expect late-night noise from the bar if you end up here. The rooms themselves, with terracotta-tiled floors, wood-panelled ceilings and little verandas facing the river, are clean and smart, and there's a restaurant serving local specialities in addition to the usual multi-cuisine menu. Consider as a fallback option only. ⑤–⑦

**Neeleshwar Hermitage** Nileshwaram ☎ 0467/228 8876–8, Ⓦ www.neeleshwar hermitage.com. This campus of sixteen gabled, palm-thatched cottages, tucked away behind a gloriously pristine stretch of beach just outside Nileshwaram, ranks among the most attractively set-up resorts in southern India. The rooms are a hip fusion of traditional Malabari and contemporary styles, featuring hand-crafted woodwork, private alfresco bathrooms and pebble gardens, with pillared verandas facing the water or lawned garden. You can enjoy expert ayurveda massages and outdoor yoga lessons, lounge by a lovely pool with a long ginger-and-mint drink, or tuck into fine

local seafood at their breezy beach shack. Lectures on Indian art and history provide evening entertainment. Doubles $420–500. ⑨

**Oyster Opera** Thekkedadu, Padanna Kadappuram ☎ 0467/227 6465 or ☎ 9447 176465, Ⓦ www.oysteropera.in. Go for the full Valiyaparamba monty with a night or two on a working mussel and fish farm, hidden deep in a patchwork of mangrove-fringed lagoons. Owner Mr G.S. Gul has built a cluster of laterite cottages on an islet facing the water; you can also sleep in a floating bamboo hut, with sea bass writhing centimetres below your mattress, or in a cosy casuarina treehouse. The seafood – literally hauled from the water fresh before every meal – couldn't be more succulent, and there's plenty of it. ⑦–⑧

**Valiyaparamba Retreat** Oriyara village, 15km north of Payyannur; book through the Tourist Desk, Main Jetty, Kochi (☎ 0484/237 1761). A cosy, attractively furnished four-bedroom house facing the backwater on the northern side of Valiyaparamba. Well placed for swimming, cruises and visits to *theyyem* rituals. Rates (Rs3000 per double) include full board. Regular buses run to Oriyara (30min) from the nearest railhead at Payyanur: get directions when booking with the Tourist Desk. ⑦

## Bekal

**BEKAL** is popular among Keralans as a weekend day-trip destination, with a **fort** (daily 8am–5pm; Rs100 [Rs5]) standing on a promontory between two long, classically beautiful palm-fringed **beaches**. Although this is one of the largest fortresses in Kerala and has been under the control of various powers including Vijayanagar, Tipu Sultan and the British, it's nothing to get excited about. Heat haze permitting, the bay views from the bastion are impressive enough, but the

▲ Bekal Fort

vast maidan inside the walls is a hot and dry wasteland – hardly deserving of the stiff admission fee. That said, it's an enjoyable place to people-watch, especially around late afternoon, when local families turn up for a stroll in their best clothes.

A short walk beyond the main entrance to the fort stands the *Bekal Resorts Development Corporation* (**BRDC**) **tourist office** (Mon–Sat 9.30am–5pm; ☏0944/779 3815), which can point you toward local *theyyem* performances. The nearest **accommodation** is the *Nirvana* (☏0467/227 2900, ⓦ www.nirvanabekal.com; ❼), a small resort of six laterite cottages clustered at the foot of the fort in a walled compound just a stone's throw away from the sea. Alternatively, head 7km inland to the *Gitanjali Heritage* (☏0467/223 4159 or ☏9447 469747, ⓦ www.gitanjaliheritage.com; $100/person full board, ❾), in Panayal village, where the Jaganth family run a welcoming little homestay in a 70-year-old ancestral home – a particularly good option if you're travelling with kids. The old house has three rather cramped and dark rooms, furnished in traditional Keralan style, with bent-cane chairs, wooden ceilings and slatted windows. The organic vegetable garden supplies the kitchen with fresh produce year round, and the family takes guests out to a local silk farm and *theyyem* rituals in the area. In expectation of increased tourist traffic from high-living Bangaloreans over the coming decades, a belt of ultra-luxurious, hermetically sealed five-stars has also started to take shape just up the coast from Bekal behind **Kappil Beach**. The largest is the *Lalit* (☏011/4444 7474, ⓦ www.thelalit.com; ❾), spread over 26 acres, with its own twisting lagoon, rejuvenation spa and spacious villas. The scale and opulence of the resort is astounding – not to say incongruous in this hard-core Muslim neighbourhood. Guests can relax in their own private jacuzzis, pampered by polo-shirted butlers; and there's a helipad for quick getaways. Rooms start at $500.

### Kasaragod and around

The traditional border between Kerala and the medieval kingdom of Tuluva was the **Chandragiri River**, and the town overlooking its mouth, **KASARAGOD**, still retains a distinctively different feel from coastal hubs further south. Predominantly Muslim, its inhabitants speak a unique dialect of Malayalam known as "Beary Bashe" (or "Byaris"), blending Arabic and Kanad words with the arcane grammar of Tulu, a Dravidian tongue spoken by people from the neighbouring

Dakshini Kannada region of southeast Karnataka. Shipbuilding was the basis of the town's former prosperity but has long since been superseded by emigration to the Gulf. Nearly every family has at least one relative working in Dubai, and the impact of the Dirham on Kasaragod's architecture, particularly its mosques, is plain to see.

A survivor from the town's earliest contact with the Arab world, and one that's miraculously escaped the attentions of the cement mixers, is the beautiful **Malik Deenar Jama Masjid**, a typically Malabari wooden building staring seawards from a low hillock in the **Thalangara** district of town, next to the mouth of the Chandragiri. The triple-storeyed structure, sporting multi-tiered roofs and elaborate wooden decoration, is said to have been founded in 738 AD by the Muslim missionary Malik Deenar, who first brought Islam to southwest India during the lifetime of the Prophet Muhammad. Thalangara is also famous for a particular kind of hat, the Thalangara *topi*, a white-cotton cap embellished with intricate embroidery which used to be a major export but is now only made by a couple of elderly craftsmen in the streets behind the mosque.

On the opposite, southern, side of the river from Thalangara, **Chandragiri fort** (daily sunrise to sunset) is a large seventeenth-century citadel giving fine views over the river mouth from its chunky laterite battlements. Built by the chieftain Sivappa Nayak of Bednore and later enlarged by Tipu Sultan, it can be reached by turning west off NH-17 at the roadside village of **Melparamba**, 3km south of Kasaragod, from where a narrow lane runs 1km to the citadel.

An architectural oddity 15km further up the highway from Kasaragod near the town of **Kumbla**, the **Ananthapuram temple** (daily 8am–6pm) is better known as the **Lake Temple** for being situated in the middle of a large, square water tank. The site, nestled amid an oasis of palms at the top of a parched laterite hill, stands in stark contrast to the barren plateau surrounding it. Pilgrims come to worship Lord Vishnu, made here not from metal or stone but an amalgam of herbs; the idol is even said to have replica internal organs. The shrine's other claim to fame is its resident crocodile – a sixty-something vegetarian called Babiya. You won't meet anyone who has actually seen it, but the friendly resident priests insist the croc lives in a little cave on the north corner of the tank. To reach the temple by **bus**, catch any service heading north on NH-17 and get down at Kumbla, where auto-rickshaws will take you the remaining 4km inland.

### Practicalities

Kasaragod's mainline railway station and KSRTC bus stand, both in the centre of town, are stops on all services heading north and south along the coast. For a quick bite, the old-fahioned *Arya Bhavan* **restaurant** on MG Rd, two minutes' walk from the bus stand, serves very good masala dosas, generous lunchtime thalis at and other *udipi* specialities throughout the day. Accommodation is uniformally unappealing, with the exception of one little homestay, the *Thrill Island Resort* (☎9447 403329, ⓦwww.thrillholidays.com; ❺) at Pilikunje, 1.5km south of town just off NH-17 (turn off the highway at the Bajaj showroom, just after the big road bridge). Don't be misled by the name: it's nothing like a resort, and is unlikely to thrill, except in the sense of its unexpected remoteness. Located on an island smothered with areca and coconut palms in the middle of a bend in the Chandragiri River, the homestay comprises three simple, newly built en-suite rooms, tacked onto the side of a century-old ancestral *tharavad* inhabited by an elderly family member and his retainers. After a twenty-minute trip in a punted canoe you finally reach the property which, although only just out of earshot of the highway bridge, inhabits a world apart. Rates include meals and guided walks (the place is teeming with birdlife). Come armed with a sense of adventure and a fully charged mobile phone (to summon the boatman when you wish to leave).

# Contexts

# Contexts

# History

T
he most radical upheavals in Indian history have always tended to emanate from the far northwest. The Khyber Pass, dividing the steppes of central Asia from the fertile Gangetic plains, served time and again as a gateway to invaders who transformed the societies they conquered with new religions, weapons, art forms, languages and sensibilities. These influences did, over the centuries, percolate southwards, crossing the Deccan plateau and the Vindhya mountains to reach the tropical tip of the peninsula. But they tended to do so slowly, by a process of gradual absorption rather than at the point of the sword.

Insulated by distance, the Dravidian culture that held sway in the distant region now known as Kerala evolved along its own distinct trajectory. What major changes did come invariably blew in from the ocean. For thousands of years, merchants, adventurers, religious refugees and colonizers crossed the Arabian Sea to trade in spices and settle on the so-called **"Malabar coast"**, giving rise to one of the most heterogeneous cultures in the ancient world. The ways of life they imported, however, over-layered an indigenous society with amazingly resilient roots – roots that can be traced back not just to the earliest phases of recorded history in India, but, in some cases, to the very beginnings of Asian civilization itself.

# Prehistory

Archeologists are still debating the chronology of the Keralan **Prehistoric** period. **Megalithic monuments** – dolmen burial chambers, cists, "umbrella" standing stones and rock-cut caves – litter the state, grouped mostly in the mountains. But they probably date from a much more recent era than their appearance suggests. Most, including the elaborately decorated **Edakkal Caves** in Wayanad (see p.239), could only have been made with the help of iron implements, which came comparitively late to the far south of the Subcontinent: around the middle of the second millennium BC.

It is, however, widely agreed that there were hunter-gatherers in southwest India long before the arrival of metal tools, and that their descendants are the aboriginal *adivasi* tribals who live to this day in the forested areas of the Western Ghats. The physical appearance of some of these tribes, such as the Kadar, Mutuvans and Iralis of Wayanad district, suggests Asian-Negrito origins. Quite how aboriginal travellers with primitive technologies were able to cross the Andaman Sea tens of thousands of years ago remains a matter of conjecture, but cross the ocean they did – genetic research on some of the indigenous peoples of the Andaman Islands, who share similar black skin and peppercorn hair, have shown ancestral connections with Papuan and aboriginal Japanese populations.

Metal, and knowledge of **rice cultivation**, were probably first imported into south India from the northwest, where the sophisticated civilization of the **Indus Valley** – the region straddling the present-day India–Pakistan border – was already well established by 3000 BC. Paleo-botanical studies have shown that a sharp rise in rainfall occurred around this time, which probably explains why farming was able to flourish and cities emerge. The inhabitants of **Harappa** and **Mohenjo Daro**, large urban centres which reached their peaks between 2300 and 1800 BC, were certainly experts in the management of water. Huge communal granaries stored the surplus grain that underpinned a flourishing foreign trade, and the existence of palaces and spacious houses shows that this was a highly stratified society, with its own script and formalized religion.

Current archeological thinking holds that prolonged drought, rather than invasions, caused the eventual decline of the Indus Valley civilization. Over time, as rainfall decreased and agricultural output dropped, the impoverished inhabitants of the Indus plains drifted south in search of more fertile land, taking their tools, language and beliefs with them.

## The Dravidians

Some historians have advanced this migration theory to account for the origins of the **Dravidians**, who are believed to have colonized the southwest of India around 1800 BC – the same time the Indus Valley civilization went into decline. The most compelling evidence that the Dravidians originated in the northwest – and were, in fact, descended from the peoples of the Indus Valley – is linguistic. Malayalam and Tamil – the principal modern languages of south India – have completely different roots from the main languages of the north, which derive from the Indo-Aryan group, brought to India by invaders from central Asia, and are based principally on Sanskrit. Over the years, some wild comparisons have been made between Dravidian and other Asian tongues (notably Japanese), but the only surviving Asian language with definite Dravidian antecedents is Brahui, spoken by the nomadic people of the Baluchistan uplands on the Iran–Pakistan border. This suggests that the Dravidians almost certainly came from the Baluchi grasslands in the fourth or third millennium BC, via the Indus Valley, where they developed the metalwork and farming techniques that subsequently allowed them to establish permanent settlements in the far south.

One Hindu myth often interpreted as some kind of transmission from this distant age is the story of **Parasurama**, the axe-wielding sixth incarnation of the

### The Rig Veda

Between 1800 and 1700 BC, after the disappearance of the Indus Valley cities, a wave of chariot-riding invaders, calling themselves the **Aryas** or **Aryans**, swept onto the Gangetic plains of northern India from the northwest. Most of what is known about these aggressive newcomers derives from an extraordinary body of literature called the **Rig Veda**, a vast compendium of 1028 hymns, epic chants, spells, songs and instructions for religious rituals composed between 1500 and 900 BC, and trans-mitted orally until they were set down in writing in the medieval era.

The Aryans' sacred scriptures contain a wealth of detail about their daily life, philo-sophical ideas and religious practices. Frequent references to Agni, the "God of Fire", and Indra, the "Fort Breaker", are indicative of violent encounters with the indigenous inhabitants of northern India, known as **Dasa** or **Dasyus**, literally "dark-skinned ones" or "slaves". They were "rich in cattle", knew how to work gold, built forts and towns and spoke a different language from the Aryans, who evidently disapproved of the fact they were also *sisna*-devi, "phallus worshippers". The *Rig Veda* implies a long spell of intermingling between the Aryans and Dasa, but over time the latter were swept aside as the invaders expanded eastwards in the middle of the second millennium BC. These conquests were facilitated by the Aryans' use of horse-drawn, spoke-wheeled **chariots**, an incomparably fast and effective way of crossing the dry plains.

By the dawn of the **Iron Age** early in the first millennium BC, the dominion of the Aryans, by now a loose confederacy of tribes who fought each other as much as their indigenous enemies, stretched south as far as the Vindhya Range and the rich soils of the Deccan Plateau. Beyond lay the wild unexplored territory of **Dakshinapatha**, "the Way South" – the route taken by the Dravidian peoples the Aryans had displaced.

God Vishnu. As a reward for defeating the Kshatriya warrior caste, it is said that Varuna, God of the Oceans, and Bhumidevi, Goddess of the Earth, granted Parasurama any land that could be encompassed by a throw of his axe from Kanyakumari, India's southernmost point. From the place where the axe fell, the waters receded and Parasurama Kshetra ("Parasurama's Country") was formed. The legend may well reflect the massive elevation of southwest India's seaboard that occurred sometime between 12,000 and 10,000 BC, and the intensive reclamation, drainage work and forest clearance carried out in its wake (*parasura* means "axe") by the first farmers of the Malabar coast.

## Early trade and the Ay Kingdom

The essentially agrarian economies of the Dravidians were, like their Harappan forerunners in the northwest, supplemented by trade in **luxury goods** such as shells, precious stones and pearls. Teak found in the third- and second-millennium BC ruins of the Mesopotamian city of Ur, in present-day Iraq, almost certainly came from the Malabar coast and both the ancient Egyptians and Phoenicians crossed the Arabian Sea to acquire sandalwood, pepper, cinnamon and other spices. In the Old Testament, King Solomon is said to have sent ships every three years to the port of Orphyr (thought to have been at Poovar, south of modern-day Kovalam) to buy silver, gold, ivory, monkeys and peacocks.

This maritime trade expanded steadily over the centuries, enabling the region's chiefs to extend their rule inland and create larger settlements away from the coast. Among the first dynasties to emerge as overlords in the region were the **Ay Kings**, whose domain stretched from the backwaters region of Kuttanad down to the tip of peninsular India, where they waged constant wars with the Pandya rulers of the Tamil lowlands to the east. Ancient Pandyan texts say their adversaries' lands, administered from their capital at Vizhinjam (see p.102), were "fertile and teemed with elephants". One of the Ay's most illustrious rulers, Antiran, was the first of many Keralan rajas to use the elephant as his royal emblem.

# The Sangam age: 00–500 AD

A huge storehouse of historical detail relating to the early kingdoms of Kerala has survived in a remarkable body of classical Tamil poetry known as the **Sangam**, composed between the first and third centuries AD in the literary academies (*sangam*) of Madurai, in modern-day Tamil Nadu. The texts, which were only rediscovered in the nineteenth century, refer to an era when the indigenous Dravidian culture of the deep south was being transformed by Sanskritic influences from the north. Nevertheless, they vividly demonstrate that some of the most distinctive characteristics of Keralan civilization – including yoga, Tantra, the cult of the god Murugan and goddess worship – were almost certainly indigenous to the south, and widespread well before the arrival of the Aryans.

The first five centuries of the Christian era, known to Indian historians as the **Sangam Age**, were dominated by a dynasty whose lineage would ripple in various incarnations across more than a thousand years of Keralan history: the **Cheras**. From their capital **Vanchimutur**, or **Vanchi**, in the watery lowlands of Kuttanad, these expansionist kings spread their rule east into the mountains and northwards up the Malabar coast. Their well-equipped armies comprised infantry, cavalry, chariots and elephant brigades, backed up by a formidable fleet of warships. Roads crisscrossed their territories, which were patrolled by a prototypical police force of watchmen.

Under the patronage of successive Chera kings and their regional tributaries, the arts also flourished, particularly poetry, dance and music, as did private property ownership, agriculture and herbal medicine. Although different classes existed, caste was nonexistent, and the status and freedoms accorded women were high.

As for **religious practices**, the people of ancient Kerala followed old Dravidian forms of worship, venerating totemic gods and spirits residing in trees, rivers, hills and other natural features. It is likely that *theyyem* and other similar rituals still practised in many parts of Kerala, and now absorbed into Brahminical Hindu mythology, are vestiges of these. Other more formal religions, however, are known to have coexisted with the indigenous Dravidian traditions. From the third century BC, India – with the exception of the unconquered south – was controlled by the **Mauryan empire**, whose state religions were first **Jainism** and, later, **Buddhism**. Evidence that both took root in Kerala survives in many Sangam texts and in the region's architectural heritage. Many Hindu temples seem to have been built over foundations of Jain or Buddhist monasteries, and sculpture fragments dating from Chera times are scattered across the region to this day. Only with the spread of Brahmanical Hinduism across the south from the seventh century onwards did these two great faiths go into decline; in modern Kerala they've since died out.

## The expansion of trade

The prosperity of the Sangam era under the Cheras – and cultural flowering that flowed from it – were stimulated not merely by the spoils of military conquest, but by a rapid growth in **maritime trade**, from which the kings raked handsome taxes. Only a few kilometres inland from the Chera capital, Vanchi, lay one of the richest ports in the ancient world, **Muziris**. As well as Phoenician and Arab merchants, the Cheras' harbour supplied fleets of **Roman** ships. After a century of relentless civil war, peace had returned to Rome by the middle of the first century BC, bringing with it renewed demand in the imperial capital for luxury goods such as pearls, spices, perfumes, precious stones and silk. Augustus's conquest of Egypt (opening up the Red Sea) and Hippalus's discovery that the monsoon winds would blow a ship across the Arabian Sea in forty days brought the means to supply this appetite within the Romans' grasp.

A vivid picture of the boom that ensued has survived in an extraordinary mariners' manual entitled the *Periplus of the Erythraean Sea*, written in the middle of the first century AD by an anonymous Alexandrian merchant-adventurer. Featuring meticulous descriptions of the trade, ports and capital cities of India's far south, it reveals that Muziris was the main trading point for valuable foreign goods – notably Chinese silk and oil from the Gangetic basin – and the principal warehouse for locally grown spices, including pepper, ginger, turmeric, cardamom and cinnamon. So great were the sums spent by the Romans on "Malabar gold" (as they nicknamed pepper), that the chronicler Pliny the Elder (23–73 AD) famously complained that trade was fast emptying the imperial coffers – a remark substantiated by the hoards of Roman coins that have come to light over the years in central Kerala. It was also through Muziris that **St Thomas the Apostle** reportedly brought Christianity to India after the Resurrection in 52 AD, and where the first major influx of **Jewish refugees** settled following the destruction of the temple in Jerusalem.

## The post-Sangam era

The stormy relations between the Cheras and the **Cholas** and **Pandyas**, across the mountains in Tamil Nadu, is a constant theme in Sangam literature. Throughout the first half of the first millennium AD, these rival powers were frequently at war with each other, or with the rulers of neighbouring Sri Lanka. Ultimately, however, they all seem to have succumbed to an enigmatic fourth dynasty, the **Kalabhras**, about whom the Sangam poems say very little other than that they were "bad kings" (*kaliarasar*). Later Buddhist texts suggest they were originally hill tribes who swept down from the Deccan Plateau to harass the inhabitants of the river valleys and coastal areas, and who later took up Jainism and Buddhism.

Whatever their origins, the arrival of the Kalabhras – coupled with the decline of trade with Rome and resulting demise of Muziris – brought an end to five or more centuries of Chera rule in the southwest of India, ushering in a kind of "**dark age**" in the far southwest of the peninsula. From around 500 AD onwards, the region was repeatedly overrun by armies from the east, principally the Chalukyas and Pallavas. Little detail has survived about the regional chiefdoms that must have existed under them in the former Chera homelands.

# The Brahminization of the south

The "long historical night", as Keralan historians characterize the turbulent period between the sixth and eighth centuries, drew to a close with a silent revolution brought about by the rise to prominence of the **brahmin** caste, descendants of the Aryans who had conquered the northern plains more than a thousand years before. No one is exactly sure when these paler-skinned priests started migrating south, but Sangam texts record that "Vedic sacrifices" were performed under the patronage of successive Chera rulers, and that brahmin quarters existed in major towns and ports from at least the third century BC. However, from the seventh century AD, the in-migration of Brahmins intensified, probably because they were encouraged to settle on lands newly conquered by kings from the Deccan, who were already adherents of Brahminical tradition.

Along with their Sanskrit verses, Vedic rituals and philosophies, the Brahmins introduced radically new concepts of social order to Kerala. Precisely how notions of **caste** permeated the more egalitarian society of the tropical southwest remains a matter of debate among social historians. But the most likely explanation is that by controlling the large tracts of land they were gifted, and through their role as spiritual and political advisors to local rulers, the Brahmins – or **Namboodiris**, as the uppermost strata of priests became known in Kerala – were able to impose the four-fold **Chaturvarnya** hierarchy which prevailed in their native north.

As the intermediaries between the people and their gods, the Brahmins occupied the topmost layer of this rigid system. Under them came the **Ambalavasis**, or temple servants, and the **Kshatriyas**, or "Warriors" – a position of high status which the Brahmins conferred on the ruling elite of Kerala in return for patronage. Unlike in northern India, there was no middle portion of the pyramid, as the positions of merchants, traders and shopkeepers (corresponding to the mid-ranking Vaishya castes of northern India) were dominated by Syrian-Christians, Muslims and Jews.

The **Nairs**, or martial caste, were technically near the bottom of the pile, employed in periods of peace as clerks and accountants by the nobility, though over time many prominent Nair families rose to become powerful landlords in their own right. Below them were manual labourers, field workers and servants, such as the **Tiyyas**, whose traditional role was the plucking of coconuts. At the base itself sat the so-called "polluting castes", the largest of which were the **ezhavas**, or landless farmers. Finally, there were also out-castes – "**slaves**" or "untouchables" – basically anyone who performed activities deemed highly polluting such as fishing, butchery, clothes washing, street sweeping or toilet emptying. Ideas of **ritual pollution** in Kerala developed to an extraordinary degree. Namboodiris, for example, had to perform purifying rites if they so much as set eyes on a member of a slave caste, or if their shadow touched a Nair. An *ezhava* had to keep forty paces behind a Nair; an untouchable sixty-six.

By the end of the eighth century AD, 32 separate brahmin settlements, or *gramam*, had sprung up in Kerala and the caste system was well entrenched. Vedic philosophies promulgated by the new priesthood formed the religious bedrock of the region's many chiefdoms and larger principalities. Alongside temples, Namboodiris controlled education, and exercised great influence over the local rulers.

## Bhakti and the poet-saints

One of the great driving forces behind the spread of Brahminical Hinduism across the south was **bhakti**, a popular religious movement that blossomed in Tamil Nadu and quickly spread west across the mountains into Kerala. A devotional form of Hinduism encouraging devotees to forge a personal relationship with a chosen god (*ishtadevata*), *bhakti* was an approach that would revolutionize Hindu practice in the region forever.

Its great champions were the **poet-saints** of Kerala and Tamil Nadu, who were often said to have "sung" the religions of Jainism and Buddhism out of south India. Although in practice a variety of deities were worshipped, the movement had two strands: the **Nayanmars**, devoted to Shiva, and the **Alvars**, faithful to Vishnu. Collections of their poetry, the greatest literary legacy of south India, remain popular today, and the poets themselves are almost deified, featuring in carvings in many temples. All the poems tell of the ecstatic response to intense experiences of divine favour, an emotion frequently described in terms of conjugal love, and expressed in verses of great tenderness and beauty. They stress selfless love between man and god, claiming that such love alone can lead to everlasting union with the divine. Devotees travelled the length and breadth of the south, singing, dancing and challenging opponents to public debates.

By emphasizing the importance of the individual's devotion to a particular god or goddess, *bhakti* inspired a massive upsurge in popular worship and, inevitably, a proliferation of shrines to accommodate worshippers. This process went hand in hand with the assimilation of important regional deities into the Hindu pantheon. In time, the same happened to lesser local gods and village deities, until innumerable cult centres across Kerala and beyond became bound in a complex web of interconnections. The institution of **pilgrimage**, linking local and distant deities, emerged as an essential element of Hinduism for the first time during the era of the poet-saints, and has remained an important unifying force in India ever since. It is no coincidence that some of the most defining texts of the *bhakti* movement are the *Mahatmyas*, oral chants intoned by Brahmins that elucidate the significance of individual temples and their relationship to other shrines.

## The Kulasekharas and Second Chera Empire: 800–1102 AD

Against this backdrop of mounting religious fervour, a lineage of Keralan chiefs descended from the old Chera kings emerged as the region's overlords. Under the **Kulasekharas**, Kerala experienced three centuries of unprecedented peace and prosperity, during which the Malayalam language and many of the ritual art forms that characterize the state today took shape. The founding father of the so-called **Second Chera Empire** was **Kulasekhara Varma** (ruled 800–820 AD) who, under the *nom de plume* of Kulasekhara Alwar, became one of only two Keralan poet-saints among the 75 immortalized in *bhakti* tradition. A Vaishnava (devotee of the god

Vishnu), he composed some of the most celebrated Sanskrit and Tamil songs ever written in praise of Rama and Krishna, verses still regularly sung in Keralan temples. His successor, the Shaivite (Shiva-worshipping) **Rajasekhara Varman** (ruled 820–844 AD), achieved sainthood under the name of Cheraman Perumal.

In the course of the Kulasekhara rule over the ninth and tenth centuries, the spice trade with China and the Arab world revived the fortunes of the Malabar harbours, and the dynasty's capital, **Mahodayapuram** – which some scholars think was established on the site of the ancient Chera port of Muziris, near present-day Kodungallur – became one of the wealthiest cities in south Asia. Profits from the pepper trade financed the construction of Kerala's first large-scale **temples**, including Padmanabhaswamy in Thiruvananthapuram. These, in turn, served as crucibles for ritual art forms such as *kudiyattam* and *mohiniyattam* dance, as well as classical music, mural painting and sculpture. Vedic colleges, or *salais*, attached to the shrines, meant Namboodiri boys could study philosophy, Sanskrit grammar, calligraphy, law and theology in libraries filled with thousands of palm-leaf manuscripts. Ayurvedic dispensaries also proliferated in the sacred precincts, staffed by Namboodiri-Brahmin families whose descendants still run hospitals and clinics across Kerala today.

## The Chera–Chola Wars

The Kulasekhara's "Golden Age" ground to an abrupt halt in 999 AD with the outbreak of war against the Tamil **Cholas**. The conflict, one of the bloodiest in Keralan history, would last for more than a century and leave a devastating legacy in the region. Temple building ceased almost overnight. *Salais* were converted into

### The Mamakam

The temple town of Thirunavaya, near the mouth of the Nila River, was once the venue for an extraordinary clan gathering, or **Mamakam**, in which the region's chiefs would assemble to elect an overlord, or *Keralaraja*. Held every twelve years, the event was an excuse for exuberant pageantry and a huge market to which traders would travel by boat from all over south India.

But at some point in the fifteenth century, it seems the honorific over-lordship was forcibly seized by the Zamorin of Calicut, unleashing a war with its rightful owners, the Valluvanad rajas. The Valluvanads never accepted the Zamorin's act of hubris, and instead of paying tribute at the twelve-yearly Mamakam used to dispatch a **suicide squad**, or **Chave-Pada**, sworn to fight to the death. Faced by unassailable opposition, the Chave-Padas, chosen from the ranks of the most highly trained Nair martial artists, would be ritually slaughtered in front of a huge crowd – though not, one imagines, without taking quite of few of the Zamorin's soldiers with them to their next incarnation.

The tradition lasted until 1695, when against the odds, a fifteen-year old Chave-Pada called Chandranath Panicker somehow managed to break through the cordon of bodyguards and take a swipe at the Zamorin, seated on his tented platform – an event recounted by Captain Alexander Hamilton in his *New Accounts of the East Indies* (1727). "The youth", says Hamilton, "got through the guard into the tent and made a stroke at His Majesty's head and had certainly despatched him, if a large brass lamp which was burning over his head had not marred the blow; but before he could make another he was killed by the (Zamorin's) guards". A re-enactment of the great Mamakams of yore was held in 1999 on the banks of the Nila, since when smaller events featuring marches and displays of *kalarippayat* have mushroomed along the course of the river during the winter; for details, ask at Kerala Tourism's information offices.

military academies and with the end of royal patronage the temple arts went into sharp decline. Generations of Keralan youths from the Nair caste – both men and women – were called up for compulsory training in a chain of *kalari* gymnasiums, where the martial art of **kalarippayat** (see p.89) was taught. Some went on to enlist in **Chave-Pada suicide squads**, whose bravery would eventually help turn the tide of the war.

Another consequence of the Chera–Chola conflict was a gradual increase in the power of the Namboodiris. Large areas of agricultural land were handed over as endowments by wealthy philanthropists to the temples – both to avoid the increased tax they generated, and to ensure their protection from pillage by the enemy (temple land was considered inviolable). But instead of ploughing the land revenues back into the war effort, the Namboodiris charged with their management often pocketed the profits. The upshot was the emergence of a new class of super-rich brahmin landlords, known as the **Janmis**, and a system of feudal exploitation that would not be overturned until the Communist era of the 1950s.

After nearly a century of conflict, the last Kulasekhara king, **Rama Varma Kulasekhara** (ruled 1090–1102 AD), rallied his army for a final push against the Cholas in the far south. Large sections of his forces transformed themselves into *Chave-Pada* brigades and managed to repulse the aggressors once and for all. The war eventually petered out, but not before Mahodayapuram had been burnt to the ground and its palaces destroyed. With the royal treasury exhausted, Rama Varma moved south to Quilon (modern Kollam) and the Kulasekhara era drew to a close.

# The age of the Naduvazhis

Over the three centuries of Kulasekhara rule, Kerala's regions – or *nadus* – were administered by viceroys with the title of **Naduvazhis**, who were responsible for the collection of taxes and recruitment of men to fight in the army. When the Second Chera empire declined at the end of the Chola wars, it was these regional chiefs who stepped into the power vacuum to assert their independence from the centre, giving rise to four distinct kingdoms, or *swaroopam*.

In the south, **Venad** encompassed the territory of the former Ay kings. Its chief port, **Quilon**, grew wealthy on the spice trade with Arabia and China, blossoming into a splendid city filled with temples, grand mansions and paved roads. Marco Polo was one of many foreigners dazzled by its splendour in the thirteenth century, when the harbour was crammed with vast, multi-decked Chinese junks. By this time, successive Venad kings had, in spite of waves of attacks by the Nayaks of Madurai, to the northeast, expanded their domain across the border into Tamil territory, and in 1312, **Ravi Varma Kulasekhara** (1299–1314) finally defeated the Pandyas, crowning himself the "Emperor of the South".

Further north, a lineage descended from the Cheras ruled much of central Kerala from what remained of the old capital, Mahodayapuram. Known as **Perumpadappu Swaroopam**, and later as the **Kingdom of Cochin**, it drew its wealth from trade through a harbour on the Periyar River, probably on, or close to, the site of ancient Muziris. But when floods swept a massive bar of silt across its entrance to the sea in 1341, the Cochin rajas were forced to relocate further south to a new site – the port that would eventually become Cochin.

The spice trade also enriched the Kolathiri rajas, who ruled the far north of Kerala – **Kolathunad** – from the fourteenth century onwards. They, however, were little more than tributaries of a much more powerful state to their immediate south. **Nediyiruppu Swaroopam** and its capital, **Kozhikode (Calicut)**, was the domain of the Eradi dynasty, whose kings called themselves the "samuris", later corrupted to "**zamorins**". By running its harbour as a free port, the zamorins encouraged communities of able Chinese and Arab merchants to settle. The Arabs, in particular, proved generous allies, donating ships, horses, arms and soldiers for military campaigns, and acting as wily advisors in political and economic matters. With their wealth and guile allied to the zamorins' military ambitions, Calicut had risen to become one of the world's most prosperous and sophisticated cities by the fifteenth century. As well as building splendid forts and palaces, the zamorins were passionate sponsors of the arts, particularly literature, holding an annual competition that attracted bards from across south India.

# The Portuguese and Dutch

With the Moors ousted from the Iberian peninsula and Christendom established in the North African port of Ceuta, the crusading **European superpowers** began to seek fresh pastures in which to exercise their proselytizing zeal. The Americas, recently discovered by Columbus, provided the Spanish with potentially rich pickings, while the rival Portuguese turned their sights towards the African Gold Coast and beyond. Their initial goal had been to spread Christianity and locate the mythical Christian ruler Prester John, whom the Portuguese hoped would aid them in their quest against Islam in Africa. Later, however, the lure of cheap silk, pearls and, above all, Malabari spices overshadowed other motives, particularly after Bartolemeu Dias rounded the Cape of Good Hope in 1488, making a route across the Indian Ocean at last seem within reach. If this route could be opened up, it would bypass the much slower trans-Asian caravan trail, threatening the old Venetian-Muslim monopoly on Indian luxury goods and providing direct access to the spice ports of the Malabar coast – all of which meant potentially vast profits for any nation able to maintain maritime dominance.

As a result, the Portuguese were quick to throw their Spanish rivals off the scent, informing them that the Cape lay a good ten degrees further south than it did. This ruse made the voyage around the tip of Africa seem a lot less viable as a short cut to the spice islands, and contributed in no small part to the **Treaty of Tordesillas** of 1494, in which the Spaniards relinquished any claims to territories east of a dividing line set at 370 leagues west of the Cape Verde Islands, off the coast of West Africa.

Once rights to the world's seas had been carved up between the two Iberian nations, the way was open for the Portuguese to capitalize on their earlier efforts along the rim of the Indian Ocean. Aside from Dias' pioneering expedition, several secret voyages, of whose existence historians have only recently learned from naval records, probed up the east coast of Africa.

## Vasco da Gama

By the close of the fifteenth century, the scene was thus set for the entry onto the world stage of **Vasco da Gama**, dispatched from Lisbon in July 1497 by the king of Portugal to find a sea route to the Indies. With the help of an expert Arab navigator, **Ibn' Masjid**, whom he hired at Malindi on the east coast of Africa to help him cross the Arabian Sea, da Gama and his fleet of three *caravelas* took just under ten months to reach Calicut. However, news of atrocities committed by the Portuguese en route had preceded their arrival, and the Zamorin, **Mana Vikrama**, briefly imprisoned da Gama before allowing him to fill his holds with pepper and leave – an insult the proud Portuguese admiral would never forget.

The cost of da Gama's expedition was recouped sixty times over by the profit from the spices it carried back to Lisbon, and barely a year elapsed before a fleet of 33 ships set sail to Calicut, under the command of **Pedro Àlvares Cabral**. Cabral was able to extract more concessions from the Zamorin than did his predecessor, gaining permission to site a warehouse outside the city. However, relations with local merchants quickly degenerated. Fearing (with some justification, as it turned out) that the Portuguese intended to usurp their monopoly over the Malabar's spice trade, Arab advisors to the Calicut king successfully lobbied against the Europeans. Cabral retaliated by rounding up Arab vessels standing off Calicut harbour and massacring their crews. On land, a mob stormed the Portuguese factory, putting all 53 of its inhabitants to the sword.

This last bloody episode was at the forefront of Vasco da Gama's mind when he returned in 1502. He waylaid a Muslim ship en route from Mecca and burned alive all seven hundred of its passengers and crew, then set about bombarding Calicut. While the cannonade rained down on the city's temples and houses, da Gama ordered the crews of a dozen or so trade ships anchored in the harbour to be rounded up. Before killing them, he had the prisoners' hands, ears and noses hacked off and the pieces sent ashore piled in a small boat. Leaving Calicut in flames, da Gama sailed south to **Cochin**, where a mixture of gifts and threats was enough to make the local raja fill his holds with pepper and cardamom at favourable prices. More pepper was purchased at Quilon from the rulers of Venad before the admiral began his return voyage, slipping past the waiting navy of the angry Zamorin.

Da Gama's tactics unleashed turmoil on the Malabar. Within months a major offensive was launched by the Zamorin to punish the raja of Cochin for his collusion. After some initial success, the invasion was forestalled by the monsoons. It then foundered completely after a Portuguese naval squadron sailed to Cochin's aid in September 1503. The grateful raja responded by granting the Portuguese permission to build a fort at the mouth of his capital's harbour: erected in 1504, **Fort Manuel** – the nucleus of Fort Cochin – would be the first ever colonial stronghold on the Indian coast. A second, and much more desperate attack was ordered by the Zamorin shortly after, involving 280 ships, 4000 sailors and 60,000 land troops. But after a five-month campaign, it too ended in failure: 19,000 infantrymen lost their lives in a single action trying to cross Cochin harbour, and a further 13,000 died of cholera during the siege.

A treaty was eventually signed between the Portuguese and Calicut in 1513, but not before the Zamorin's city had been reduced to rubble. Notwithstanding, maverick Muslim commanders from his navy – the **Kunjali Marakkars** – took up the fight and further hostilities rumbled through the 1520s until, finally, Vasco da Gama was brought back from retirement to resolve matters. His viceroyalty, however, was only to be short-lived. On December 24, 1524, da Gama died, probably from malaria, in Cochin's Fort Manuel, just three months after his third arrival on the Malabar.

## The rise of the Dutch

Over the coming decades, the Portuguese – based at their capital city, Goa, to the north – extended their trade along the Malabar by exploiting enmities between the region's rulers. At the same time, conflicts regularly erupted between them and the zamorins, while at sea, the Kunjali Marakkars were playing havoc with Portuguese shipping. The Kunjalis' naval supremacy enabled an expedient coalition between the Kolathiri raja and Zamorin of Calicut to take Fort St Agnelo at Cannanore in 1564, and Chaliyam seven years later – losses which marked the beginning of the end of Portuguese power on the Malabar.

It was the **Dutch**, however, who would bring an end to Lusitanian trade in Kerala. Determined not to allow its Roman Catholic rivals free reign in Asia, the Protestant Dutch East India Company – founded in 1592 – systematically took control of the international spice trade in the early seventeenth century, relieving the Portuguese of Quilon in 1598 and Colombo in 1663. An appeal from a prince of the Cochin royal family to intervene in a succession struggle gave them the excuse they needed to annexe the lynchpin of Portuguese operations, **Fort Cochin**, which they did after a fierce battle in 1663.

Yet Dutch supremacy on the Malabar – underpinned by their more manoeuvrable *fluyt* ships, which easily outsailed the more old-fashioned, ungainly *caravelas* from Lisbon – was to last for only a century. French and British trading posts started to pop up in the region soon after their triumph at Cochin, and their arms, munitions and military know-how enabled local rulers such as the rajas of Travancore to wage effective attacks against Dutch interests.

## Colonial influence

Ultimately, it was the Portuguese rather than the Dutch who would leave the most lasting legacy on the Malabar coast. Corruption and self-interest among colonial officials, and some gratuitous acts of cruelty, may have prevented them from establishing an effective system of government in the territories they acquired. But the Portuguese policy of holding the power of zamorins in check while reducing the status of the Cochin rajas to that of de facto vassals accelerated the rise of **minor principalities** elsewhere, and thus political disunity across the entire region. This, in turn, provoked constant wars and disrupted agriculture. Massacres and the repeated destruction of temples and mosques by the Portuguese further demoralized a civilian population already impoverished by deep economic recession – a result of the new foreign-imposed trade monopoly, which forced down the prices of local produce such as pepper and cloth.

In response, the Malabaris turned with renewed fervour to religion, especially the devotional **bhakti cults**. Writing in Malayalam, poet-scholars such as **Tunchat Ezhuthacan** and **Puntanam Namboodiri** did much to revive the mystical adoration of Vishnu in the region, in particular his incarnations as Rama and Krishna. It was during this era that Kerala's most revered Krishna shrines at Guruvayur and Ambalapuzha acquired the prominence they enjoy today.

At the same time, **Roman Catholicism**, spread by Jesuit missionaries in the sixteenth century, claimed around 60,000 converts, mostly from the oppressed lower castes of Hinduism. Churches founded during the Portuguese period continue to have a high profile in Kerala, particularly among fishing communities along the coast. Finally, the Portuguese also introduced numerous novelties which were enthusiastically adopted in the Malabar and whose use spread rapidly across the rest of the Subcontinent: gunpowder (which made the Nair soldiers and their *kalarippayat* martial arts redundant), tobacco, the practice of distilling coconut sap to make alcohol, cashew nuts (now one of Kerala's major exports), custard apples, pineapples, papaya and, not least, chilli peppers.

## Travancore and Marthanda Varma

From the highpoint of Ravi Varma Kulasekhara's reign as "Emperor of the South" in the early fourteenth century, Venad – which later became known as **"Thiruvitamkode"** (corrupted by the British to **Travancore**) – had steadily declined as a regional power, its domain whittled away to a narrow band in the far southwest. A succession of kings and regents struggled unsuccessfully to hold at bay the invading armies of both the **Nayaks of Madurai** and the **Vijayanagar rajas**, who descended at regular intervals to exact tribute. One of the largest attacks launched by the Vijayanagars, the last and most powerful Hindu empire to rule over south India, was in the 1540s, ostensibly to curb the proselytizing activities of Jesuit missionary, Francis Xavier. The emperors disliked the liberal stance of Thiruvita-mkode's rulers towards the spread of Christianity along the Malabar coast – less an act of tolerance from the Malabari kings than a placatory gesture towards the Portuguese, whose aggression was wreaking havoc in the Calicut region.

Instability in the far south was further compounded by conflicts with the high-ranking temple trustees (or Yogakkar) from the priestly Namboodiri caste who, in cahoots with the local Nair nobility, exercised increasing control over the kingdom's politics and finances. Over time, a mega-aristocracy emerged called the **Pillamar**, or "Eight Lords", who grew to pose a major threat to the authority of Travancore's rulers. The kingdom's coffers, meanwhile, were gradually emptying following the Dutch capture of its chief port, Quilon, in 1598.

Travancore would have to wait until the accession of **Marthanda Varma** in 1729 before it could regain its former glory. **Marthanda** (ruled 1729–58) made peace with the Nayaks of Madurai, and with financial support from them and the British East India Company, who by now ran a trading post out of his territory at Vizhinjam, managed to assemble a powerful army. Once he'd crushed the power of the Pillamar, Marthanda began advancing northwards. A succession of minor princedoms, including Quilon, were recaptured before the culmination of the campaign in 1754, when the Travancore army finally defeated the Dutch at **Colachen** – the first time an Asian army ever vanquished European forces in battle.

Marthanda Varma marked his military successes with an extraordinary gesture. On January 3, 1750, the raja went to the Padmanabhaswamy temple in Thiru-vananthapuram (Trivandrum), his new capital, and, in a lavish ritual, handed over ownership of his recently expanded kingdom to the tutelary deity enshrined inside it. The sacrifice – known as **Trippatidanam** – played a symbolic role in preventing future rebellions across Travancore territory: henceforth, any uprising against the state would also, in effect, be an act of sacrilege against the god Vishnu.

# The British

The **British East India Company**, formed two years before its Dutch counter-part in 1600, made its first tentative forays into the Malabar's spice trade in the early 1630s, while the Dutch were chipping away at Portugal's maritime empire. Permission to export pepper out of Cochin was granted by the Portuguese in 1636, and eight years later the raja of Travancore allowed the Company to erect a small factory at **Vizhinjam** (next to modern Kovalam), where spices and cloth could be stored awaiting annual shipment to London. It wasn't until 1690, however, that the first British fort appeared in the region. **Anchengo**, just south of Varkala, provided a perfectly placed stronghold from which to extend the Company's influence on the Malabar. But its presence – or, more accurately, the manipulation by its factors of the area's pepper prices – soon enraged the local Pillamar. In 1721, a series of violent clashes culminated in the massacre of 150 British troops, attacked while marching to present tribute to the Rani of Attingal (on whose lands Anchengo was sited). The rebels besieged the fort for six months, but were defeated by the eventual arrival of British reinforcements.

As compensation for the outrage, Attingal paid reparations and granted the Company a full monopoly over the local spice trade with, crucially, the power to fix prices – an agreement that was further consolidated by a fully fledged treaty with Marthanda Varma, the raja of Travancore. In return, the British offered military and financial support for Marthanda's campaign against the Pillamar and rival states further north. The Company, who came initially to pursue nothing more than "a peaceful trade", were thus drawn into regional conflicts between the Malabar's rulers – the thin edge of a long wedge that would, within a century and a half, see them overlords of the entire peninsula of India.

## Anglo-French conflict

In the northern Malabar, British trade, based at the newly constructed fort at **Tellicherry**, was hampered by the 1721 arrival of the **French** at **Mahé**, only a few kilometres to the south. Armed conflict between the two was expressly forbidden by their respective governments, but this didn't stop the factors from scheming with local chiefs to launch attacks against each other's forts – often with support from the companies' own troops. Remarkably, the uneasy standoff held firm throughout the War of the Austrian Succession in 1740, during which British and French armies and their respective local allies slogged it out on the plains of Tamil Nadu to the east. Twenty-one years later, however, after the eight-month siege of Pondicherry (the French capital in India) ended in victory for the British, Mahé fell to the East India Company.

## The Mysorean interlude: 1766–92

Following the fall of Pondicherry, the French were certainly down, but they were not yet quite out, thanks to the one remaining thorn in the side of British territorial ambitions in south India: the Muslim warlord **Haider Ali**. A former general of the maharaja of Mysore, Haider had usurped his master's throne in 1761 and within a short time managed to conquer virtually the entire southeast of the peninsula. The secret of his success lay in his readiness to learn from the Europeans, in particular the French, whose military tactics he emulated, and who provided him with officers to train his infantry.

To feed his voracious military machine Haider Ali needed a dependable flow of arms through the northern Malabar, at this time embroiled in regional conflicts between the Zamorin of Calicut and his neighbours, backed by the competing European powers. Haider saw in this political turmoil just the opportunity he needed to march across the Western Ghats and annexe Mahé. In the event, however, the smash-and-grab campaign would grind on for some 26 years and, ultimately, deliver the Malabar into the hands of the very enemy his military adventures were intended to expel from the Subcontinent.

The first **Mysore invasion** got under way in 1766. Ahead of a 16,000-strong army, bolstered by 8000 militiamen mustered by his Muslim ally Ali Raja of Cannanore, Haider Ali swarmed into northern Kerala. After taking a string of minor princedoms, he turned to Calicut, where he offered the Zamorin terms of surrender not even the richest king on the Malabar could afford. Having packed his family off to the hills for safety, the Zamorin blew up his palace and committed ritual self-immolation.

With Calicut subjugated and the monsoons about to break, Haider returned to his base across the mountains at Coimbatore, leaving his newly conquered territory under the stewardship of his ally Ali Raja and local Moppila leaders. When news spread of his departure, however, Nairs throughout the Malabar rose up to attack Mysorean garrisons, prompting Haider's swift return with reinforcements. This pattern was repeated several times over the following decade, until

Haider finally set his sights on the British fort at **Tellicherry**. Assisted by the Kolathiri rajas, Mysorean forces laid siege to the East India Company's stronghold for eighteen months, but the attack failed.

Mysore's defeat at Tellicherry and the demise of Haider, who died shortly after in 1782, turned the tide of the Mysorean invasions, inspiring further uprisings by the Nairs; and it took several major offensives in the region before Haider's son, **Tipu Sultan** – dubbed the "Tiger of Mysore" by his enemies – could reassert control. In the end, however, it was the declaration of war by Great Britain on Mysore rather than local rebellions that brought the episode to a definitive close. Led by Lord Wellesley and his brother Arthur (later the Duke of Wellington, of Waterloo fame), East India Company troops stormed the Mysorean capital, **Srirangapatnam**, in 1792. Tipu died defending a breach in his walls (a story that later inspired Wilkie Collins's novel, *The Moonstone*), and through the resulting treaty, the British found themselves masters not only of the Malabar, but of the whole of south India.

Besides ushering in East India Company rule, the Mysorean interlude had lasting **consequences** for the southwest. Agriculture had been decimated by the mass flight of peasants into the forests and hills to escape Mysorean atrocities; pepper cultivation was especially badly hit, leaving the region's trade in the doldrums. Even the monolithic Keralan caste system was severely shaken up: Haider and Tipu's Muslim troops had shown scant respect for the higher-caste Namboodiris, while the Nairs were all but wiped out in many areas as punishment for their repeated insurrections. Many Naduvazhi and Janmis landlords were also deprived of their estates, and administration of the region was taken on by a more centralized government.

## The Madras Presidency and Pazhassi Revolts

Following the victory at Srirangapatnam, the British consolidated their southern territory into a single unit, the **Madras Presidency**. It started life as a "hands-off" regime, with vast administrative districts on which colonial officers could make very little impact. But resentment at British rule bubbled up repeatedly, precipitating a series of bloody encounters on the Malabar in the late eighteenth and early nineteenth centuries.

The roots of the so-called **Pazhassi Revolts**, which troubled much of central and eastern Kerala between 1793 and 1805, lay in the imposition of harsh new taxes by the British on farmers in the Kottayam area. Marshalled by their ruler, **Raja Kerala Varma Pazhassi**, local people refused to pay taxes demanded by the colonial authorities. The Company responded by ordering its troops to occupy the Pazhassi palace, but the raja had by then already fled to the jungles of the Western Ghats where, for the next twelve years, he masterminded a guerrilla-style insurrection against British rule. Thousands of Nairs joined the rebellion, whose most infamous episode was the slaughter of 1100 Company troops as they crossed the Periyar Pass in 1797. The Pazhassi raja was eventually flushed out of his forest hideaway and shot dead in 1805, but another major rebellion erupted four years later – this time organized by the disgruntled former chief ministers of Travancore and Cochin. However, the two-pronged attack met with little success, serving merely to tighten the British grip on the Malabar's ruling houses.

Under the Madras Presidency, Kerala was divided into **three districts**. In the south and centre, Travancore and Cochin retained their traditional royal houses, but were administered by a British "Resident-Dewan" (effectively a prime minister) who maintained ultimate responsibility for revenue collection, law, order and the functions of state. From 1810 until 1819, the position of Dewan in both Travancore and Cochin was occupied by **Colonel** (later Major-General) **John**

**Munro**. During his tenure, significant steps forward were made in the fields of health and education. Hospitals, colleges and free schools were opened; slavery was abolished (the first step towards the abolition of "untouchability"); greater civic rights were accorded to members of disadvantaged castes; unjust taxes were repealed; and various land reforms initiated, enabling tenant farmers to lease land off feudal lords at fairer rates. The legal system was also remodelled along British lines, corruption stamped out in the civil service and a major programme of improvements to infrastructure begun. The reign of **Maharaja Swathi Thirunal** (ruled 1813–46) also saw a renaissance of the traditional arts, notably music – celebrated in the annual festival held in the grounds of his former palace in Thiruvananthapuram (see p.88).

In the north, the erstwhile kingdoms of the Calicut zamorins and Kolathiri and Ali rajas, run directly by the British as the district of Malabar, fared less well. Some progress was made in the areas of communication, social reform and education. But from 1836, civil unrest among the region's Muslims, the **Moppilas**, became a source of growing concern for the region's colonial rulers. Directed mainly at Hindu temples and upper-caste Janmis landlords, the riots were initially dismissed as mere "religious fanaticism", but after a special police force set up to deal with them failed to halt the disturbances, a judicial enquiry concluded that they were more probably the result of a failure in taxation policy. Unlike in the southern districts, where land reform had improved the lot of tenant farmers, in the Malabar the Moppilas enjoyed few rights and were subject to systematic exploitation by the Janmis. Laws were introduced to protect tenants from eviction, and improved employment opportunities under the colonial administration – in the army, on spice plantations and on the railways – further soothed Muslim anger. But the seeds of a deeper militancy had been sown, and would re-emerge to dog the British over the coming decades.

## The "Home Rule" movement

Across the north of the country, increasing discontent at British rule erupted in 1857 in the Uprising (or "Great Mutiny", as it was dubbed by the Raj). Although its shock waves never reached the far south, which was enjoying prosperity and civic improvements during the Pax Britannica, calls for freedom from colonial suzerainty grew over the next five decades, culminating in the Home Rule movement, which coalesced after World War I around the **Indian National Congress**. With the accession of Mohandas Gandhi to its leadership in 1920, the nationalist struggle found expression in the strategy of **swadeshi** ("self-sufficiency"), which called for a boycott of imported goods, in particular British textiles, and the revival of India's own production techniques. *Swadeshi* spread across southern India, and Congress committees were formed all over Travancore and Cochin. Up in the Malabar, however, opposition to British rule focused more on the **Khilafat movement**, a mainly Islamic political campaign protesting against the British government's treatment of the Ottoman Empire in the wake of World War I. Both Gandhi and his colleague, Khilafat leader Maulana Shaukat Ali (who would later split with Congress to co-found the pro-Partition Muslim League), visited the Malabar to lend their support to demonstrations.

The swelling ranks of the Khilafat in northern Kerala provoked a knee-jerk clampdown on political activity by the British. All public meetings were banned, Khilafat leaders were rounded up and imprisoned without trial, and mosques raided. This, in turn, triggered violent clashes between Moppilas and the Indian police, which eventually snowballed into a full-blown insurrection – the so-called **Malabar Rebellion** of 1921. Following a series of bloody riots, martial law was declared and extra troops drafted in, leading to many deaths on both sides. The defining episode of the revolt, still commemorated in the region on November 20 each year, was the **"Wagon Tragedy"**, in which 61 Moppila prisoners being transported by rail suffocated in a closed carriage.

## Caste agitation and the Temple Entry campaign

While violent disturbances wracked the Muslim-majority Malabar district in the first decades of the twentieth century, Gandhian principles of non-violent protest were being adopted to overturn some of the more egregious iniquities of the old Hindu caste order further south. Until the 1930s, caste in Kerala functioned as a kind of **apartheid**. Different laws and punishments applied to different groups (Brahmins, for example, were exempt from the death penalty), and age-old economic inequalities, fixed since the "Brahminization" of the far south of India a thousand years or more ago, were perpetuated through systems of education and land tenure.

Caste divisions were most stark in rural areas where, even at the end of the nineteenth century, a form of bonded **slavery** still prevailed. Landless peasants could be bought and sold by their Janmis. They were forbidden from owning milking cows, roofing their huts with clay tiles (only thatch was allowed) and using metal utensils. They were also obliged to pay punitive taxes for the right to carry umbrellas, ride in palanquins and, bizarrely, grow moustaches. Most insulting of all, though, was the ban on wearing sari blouses imposed on women: in more conservative districts, female members of some sub-castes were even expected to uncover their breasts if they passed within sight of a person of rank. It was this particularly offensive symbol of caste oppression that sparked Kerala's first explicitly anti-caste campaign, the so-called **"Breast Cloth Agitation"**. In defiance of local custom, women of the low-caste Shannar community in southern Travancore, recently converted to Christianity by Anglican missionaries, started wearing sari tops and shoulder scarves (*neryathu*), in the same way as brahmin women. This provoked attacks from upper-caste traditionalists but, in 1859, forced a proclamation from the government abolishing all caste dress restrictions in the state.

Fifty years later, state-wide movements against caste inequality began to take shape around leaders such as **Sri Narayana Guru** (see p.116), a Shaivite holy man from the low *ezhava* caste, who outraged Brahmins in Kerala by consecrating temples for his followers – hitherto an exclusive right of Namboodiri priests. The doors of Hindu shrines were at this time still firmly closed to all the lower castes; even the approach roads to them were strictly off-limits. In 1924, however, the **Vaikom Satyagraha**, a campaign of direct non-violent action supported in person by Gandhi, obliged the authorities at Vaikom temple near Cochin to open the roads around its shrine to all, irrespective of caste. This paved the way for the famous **Temple Entry Proclamation** of 1936, in which the maharaja of Travancore, before a huge crowd in the capital, announced that "henceforth there should be no restriction placed on any Hindu by birth or religion on entering and worshipping in temples" in his domain. Gandhi hailed the declaration as "a miracle of modern times".

## The Salt Satyagraha and Congress split

Meanwhile, in north India the *swadeshi* Independence movement was gathering momentum too. Gandhi's **"Salt Satyagraha"** – in which the Mahatma marched at the head of a mass demonstration to his native Gujarat to harvest salt in defiance of a British-imposed monopoly – inspired similar acts in Kerala. At Calicut beach in May 1930, thirty salt *satyagrahis* were wounded in police charges, leading to the arrest and imprisonment of all the region's Congress leaders.

To increase pressure on the British government, campaigns of civil disobedience intensified all over the country through the early 1930s. Boycotts of the courts, schools, colleges and shops selling foreign goods led to widespread arrests. But when Gandhi called a temporary halt to the boycott in 1934 it provoked a three-fold **split** in the Keralan Congress party. "Rightist" moderates who supported Gandhian principles were squeezed out of the leadership by "Leftist" radicals such as **E.M. Sankaram Namboodiripad** (aka "**E.M.S.**") and **P. Krishna Pillai**. In the Malabar, non-violence as a weapon in the fight for self rule was rejected outright by extremist Muslims who – once formed into the more militant **Muslim League** – had started to agitate for a separate Islamic state called Pakistan. By the time the British finally relinquished power to Congress on August 15, 1947, after feverish negotiations coordinated by Louis Mountbatten, India's last British Viceroy, the schisms that would dominate Keralan politics for decades had already become entrenched.

# Post-Independence

In comparison with the north, where Partition unleashed a mass exchange of populations and the massacre of hundreds of thousands, Indian Independence passed smoothly in Kerala. Travancore and Cochin were merged, while Malabar became part of Madras State. Nine years later, the States Reorganization Act of 1956 combined all three to form a single unit whose boundaries were drawn along linguistic lines, grouping together all the districts in the southwest where Malayalam was the majority language. In 1957, elections for the newly created **Legislative Assembly** returned a **Communist government** – one of the first in the world to be democratically elected – with E.M.S. Namboodiripad, now the head of Kerala's Communist party, as its Chief Minister.

Born into a Namboodiri-Brahmin family in Palakkad district in 1909, E.M.S. turned his back on his aristocratic roots to become the great ideologue of Keralan Communism. **Land reform** was top of the agenda in his self-styled "Liberation struggle" (*vimochana samaram*). But the "peaceful transition" to a better deal for the peasantry envisaged by E.M.S. was anything but: within a year, fierce resistance to his coalition's plans from landowners and the Church had descended into widespread riots, assassinations and famine. Kerala was teetering on the brink of total anarchy in 1959, when Prime Minister Jawaharlal Nehru intervened to impose **President's Rule** from New Delhi.

Fresh elections the following year voted a Congress-led coalition to power, but in 1967, E.M.S. and his party were back at the helm again – this time heading up a coalition dominated by a Communist party that had split into two rival factions: the Communist Party of India and the Communist Party of India (Marxist) – the CPI (I) and CPI (M). E.M.S. adopted a more restrained approach in his second term, causing a rift with the party's backers in Beijing, who labelled his tactics "parliamentary cretinism". But it proved much more fruitful, pushing through the radical **Land Reform Amendment Act**, by means of which Keralan tenants became virtual owners of the land they farmed. No family was allowed to possess more than eight hectares; the remainder was apportioned between those who traditionally worked it, benefiting around 1.5 million landless families.

# Kerala today

The past four decades of political life have seen innumerable twists and turns, as smaller parties jostle for power in larger coalitions dominated either by Congress or the Communists. Since the 1980s, the **Left Democratic Front** (LDF), led by the two Communist parties, has alternated with the **United Democratic Front** (UDF), led by the largest of five separate Congress factions. In common with the rest of India, each of these sub-groups tends to draw its support from a core community or caste, whose wider interests it is then expected to pursue when in government. Thus, the Congress represents mainly Christian and Nair groups, and the Communists the state's various lower castes, while the Indian Union Muslim League (IUML) is the party of north Kerala's Moppila population.

The region's ever-changing political landscape and the exploits of its flamboyant leaders provide the main topics of conversation in thousands of tea shops across the state each morning, where men gather to read the paper and engage in debate. If Kerala is one of the most religious places on earth, it's also one of the most political. Rarely a day passes without some strike or flag-waving demonstration paralyzing traffic in the capital.

## The "Kerala Model"

An exceptionally high **literacy** rate is one of the notable legacies of Communist rule, and the century or so of missionary schools and state-funded education that preceded it. Some 91 percent of Malayalis, including those from the poorest of backgrounds, read and write. Coupled with this are some impressive health and welfare statistics: a birth rate 40 percent lower than the national average; life expectancy at 74 and rising – comparable with the US; infant mortality at a mere 14 per 1000 (compared with 91 for most developing countries); and a gender balance of 1040:1000 in favour of women – about right by international standards, but well above the figure for India, where female infanticide is a growing trend.

In spite of its extraordinary achievements in the field of human development, however, Kerala has suffered severe **economic stagnation** since Independence – an unusual combination often dubbed "**the Kerala Model**" by economists. GDP and annual growth lag well below the national norm, largely because more than half of Malayalis live off small-scale farming. Investment levels are also comparatively low: potential employers tend to be wary of Kerala's politicized workforce, preferring to locate to states with more flexible labour laws. The result has been perennially high unemployment, and thus a spiralling budget deficit. The popular response to Kerala's economic lassitude since the 1970s has been a mass **exodus to the Gulf states**: some 25 percent of GDP derives from remittance cheques sent home by relatives from abroad, and in parts of the Muslim north the figure is far higher.

Much of the rest of the country suffered similar economic problems prior to the 1990s, but under Rajiv Gandhi and successive prime ministers, India has managed to liberalize its economy, attracting major foreign investment and turning around its balance of payments. The boom seemed to have passed Kerala by until a sudden upturn in the service sector in 2000 saw a new **prosperity** emerge in urban centres, spurred by rises in the prices of major cash crops such as rubber, spices and vanilla. The state's economy wobbled briefly in the wake of the 2008 global economic crisis, which saw unemployment spiral in Dubai and other Gulf states where Malayalis work in large numbers, but rallied the following year and by 2010 was booming again – notably in the IT sector.

## Gold Rush

Responsible for one-fifth of global consumption, India is the largest buyer of **gold** in the world – and Kerala alone accounts for a quarter of national sales. Nowhere else on the planet spends so much on the stuff per head of population. Huge hoardings showing beautiful, wheat-ish complexioned Malluwood stars and models loaded with lavish jewellery loom over every road intersection, and Keralan towns have the largest number of showrooms in the country (around 5000), many of them glittering multistorey tower blocks staffed with armies of snappily dressed salesmen and security guards. Some 4000 goldsmiths (*thattan*) work out of Thrissur alone, fashioning items to mark the major rites of passage in the Keralan lifecycle.

Gold – or *swarnam* – is traditionally given to infants at their naming ceremony, the *iruvathettu* (literally "28th" – the event is held on the 28th day after birth), when the child's grandfather whispers the baby's name in his or her ear. But it is for **weddings** that the credit cards are really flexed. Hindu, Muslim and Christian women are all given gold by their families ahead of the big day, whether *kasu mala*, made from overlapping coins, *palakka mala*, where familiar motifs are strung together with a round pendant in the centre, or the *nagapadda thali* (literally "serpent's hood"), favoured by women of the Nair caste, in which charms shaped like a cobra's head are woven into a choker.

Driven by the influx of Gulf remittances, coupled with a crash in the value of property in recent years, **gold prices** soared in Kerala from around Rs4000 per 8g sovereign (*pava*) in 2000 to a peak of Rs12,500 in 2008–9. Demand spikes each year on the third day of the Hindu month of Baisak (late April), which local merchants have successfully marketed as **Akshaya Trithiya** – said to be an especially auspicious time to splash out on precious metal. Close to 50 tonnes of gold are typically sold in Kerala on that day, causing a ten percent hike in prices.

So where does all the money for this frenzied buying come from? The short answer is gold itself. Interest rates on loans secured with gold are much lower than for other types of borrowing, so when a family needs to finance the purchase of wedding jewellery for a daughter, its female members put *their* wedding gold in a vault to raise the cash. So-called **gold loans**, of course, are also used to buy other goods, notably cars and new houses, and have played no small part in keeping the region's economy buoyant in the 2000s.

As the vast shopping malls rising on the outskirts of Erankulam and Thiruvananthapuram underline, middle-class Keralans have plenty of money to spend. The state accounts for only 3 percent of India's population, but currently consumes about 15 percent of the nation's total retail goods, and buys more **gold** per head of population than anywhere else in the country. Against this backdrop of growth, the government continues to haemorrhage millions of dollars annually in lost revenue due to strikes and corruption. Declining tax revenues are frequently blamed for the parlous condition of Kerala's ageing passenger ferries, which led to the **disaster** of 2002 when 29 travellers were drowned while crossing Vembanad Lake. Another 15 deaths followed the sinking of an excursion boat at Thattekkad Bird Sanctuary on the Periyar River in 2007. Then in September 2009, a Kerala Tourism Development Corporation boat capsized on Thekkady Lake, at the Periyar Wildlife Sanctuary, killing 39 tourists.

Since then, Kerala has made few national headlines – though a consortium of local business magnates created a media storm in 2010 when they successfully bid for the state's first Twenty20 cricket franchise.

# Religion

Kerala is one of the most intensely religious places on earth. Ritual permeates nearly every aspect of life, from the daily ceremonies conducted inside private homes to the large-scale festivals associated with every temple, mosque and church in the state. Hinduism, the predominant religion, has its own distinct style and traditions in Kerala, and an extraordinary feature of the region is the extent to which these have been soaked up by the more recent faiths of Islam and Christianity. You'll see examples everywhere: from garlands of marigolds adorning Madonna icons to the *chenda melam* drummers and Hindu temple elephants that appear at Muslim saints' day celebrations. The results are forms of worship in all religions that are as identifiably Keralan as they are representative of their own faith. Moreover, adherence to one creed in Kerala does not necessarily preclude a person's involvement in acts of worship staged by another. Several mosques and Christian churches feature on the Hindu Sabarimala pilgrimage circuit, and Christians and Muslims mingle easily among the crowds of enthusiastic devotees at elephant parades, *kathakali* recitals and *panchavadyam* orchestra performances held during Hindu temple festivals.

# Hinduism

Unlike Islam and Christianity, **Hinduism** has no orthodoxy. Rather, India's greatest faith – practised by a little under sixty percent of the state's population – is a loose agglomeration of thousands of different beliefs and practices which, over several millennia, have been bound into an overarching mythological framework. Involving a plethora of gods, goddesses, shrines, cults and customs, it nevertheless binds the nation together: pilgrims from all over India travel to Kerala to worship in the region's major temples, and Malayali Hindus venerate shrines as far away as the Himalayas. At the same time, there exist in Kerala forms of Hinduism that are unique to the southwest – a consequence of its geographical isolation. Hinduism as most people recognize it today derived largely from the traditions of the Aryans, who colonized northern India from around 1500 BC. Having absorbed many indigenous cults, these "Vedic" religious forms (the term derives from the Aryans' most sacred texts, the Vedas) gradually made their way southwards, finally arriving in Kerala in the middle of the eighth century AD, where they were spread by brahmin priests among the local Dravidian population.

Rather than wipe out the older Dravidian traditions it encountered, however, **Brahminical Hinduism** incorporated them into its own mythology. Thus the nature spirits worshipped in the far south three or more thousand years ago – trees, animals, features of the landscape and other elemental forces – re-emerge in the modern era as part of the Hindu pantheon. The nomenclature may have altered, but the essence of these ancient rites remains intact in a multitude of local religious traditions.

## Tantra and snake worship

One of the most pervasive of these forms is worship of the Mother Goddess, or **Mahadevi** – often referred to by the names of her many associated deities: Bhagawati, Badrakali and Ottakkali, among others. Hindus regard goddesses as repositories of divine female energy, or **shakti**, the power from which the visible world emanates, and which drives the universe forwards. In Kerala, more than

Whether in large temples or local shrines, integral to Hindu worship throughout Kerala are the **ritual arts** – sacred dramas such as *kathakali* or *kudiyattam* plays, *mohiniyattam* dances and *kalam ezhuttu* powder patterns, which are offered to the gods during important festivals. For details of some of these extraordinary traditions, most of which are unique to the region, see pp.288–300.

anywhere else in India, numerous so-called **Tantric** forms of goddess worship survive in which the object of ritual is to appropriate and channel *shakti* into one's own self – to attain magical powers, overcome illnesses, promote fertility or just to bring good luck. Tantra is often associated with transgressional acts of worship involving sex and blood sacrifice, but in Kerala it more often takes the form of spirit possession, where the body of a ritual specialist is inhabited by the deity invoked. This is the essence of *theyyem* – a particularly dynamic and theatrical ritual form still prevalent in northern Kerala (see p.251). It is also the animating principle of the famous **Bharani festival** of Kodungallur (see p.203), where long-haired, crimson-clad oracles beat themselves with swords, watched by a drunken crowd singing sexually explicit songs dedicated to the goddess Bhagawati. The Bharani festival, whose participants are drawn from the lower castes, vividly demonstrates another important feature of Tantricism as it exists in Kerala. Unlike temple-based Brahminical rituals, which are mediated by priests, Tantric practices are accessible to all, without distinction of caste or gender.

Another example of Tantricism is the popular tradition of **snake worship** – again, an aspect of pre-Vedic, non-Brahminical Hinduism that remains especially strong in the state. When the first settlers cleared the region's woodland to make fields for agriculture, they set aside small areas of virgin forest known as *kaavus* – "sacred groves" – where no flower was ever picked, plant disturbed or, most importantly, snakes harmed. Many of these centres of nature worship still exist across the state, often filled with roughly carved *naga* (cobra) stones dusted with propitious turmeric or vermillion powder. The largest and most famous of them is the one at Mannarsala, in Alappuzha district (see p.140), which is run by a lineage of female Namboodiri priestesses.

## Temples

Temple worship, as practised across the rest of India, came relatively late to Kerala. Only with the arrival of Brahminical Hinduism and the emergence of the devotional **bhakti** tradition during the Second Chera (Kulasekhara) empire in the ninth century AD (see p.264), did local rulers start to sponsor the building of large, permanent shrines. Made of wood, laterite and clay tiles, they're generally low-rise and low-key compared with those of neighbouring Tamil Nadu – sometimes indistinguishable from their surrounding structures save for the presence of a ceremonial brass flagstaff (*dwajastambha*). The complex is set out according to the traditional **pancha prakara** layout of five interlocking courtyards, next to which is a stepped water tank for ritual ablutions. At the centre of the temple, the deity and its accessory gods and goddesses are enshrined in an enclosed sanctum, called the *shreekovil*.

Temple ceremonies, or **pujas**, are conducted in the *shreekovil* in Sanskrit by Namboodiri-Brahmin **pujaris**, sometimes called shantis. The shantis tend the image of the deity in daily rituals that symbolically wake, bathe, feed and dress the god, and finish each day by preparing him or her for sleep. The most elaborate is the evening ritual, *aarti*, when lamps are lit, blessed in the sanctuary, and passed around devotees amid the clanging of drums, gongs and cymbals. Worshippers attend for a ritual glimpse (*darshan*) of the deity. They'll also leave personal offerings of flowers, coconuts and incense, in return for which the priests will hand them special food (usually sweets), which has been blessed as **prasad** by the deity and thus infused with its energy.

Communal worship is celebrated with *kirtan* or *bhajan*, the singing of hymns or verses in praise of Krishna taken from the Bhagavad Gita, or repetitive cries of "Jay Shankar!" ("Praise to Shiva"). In many villages, shrines to *devatas*, village deities who function as protectors and may bring disaster if neglected, are more important than temples.

## Popular Hindu gods and goddesses

The Hindu pantheon is presided over by three principal deities: **Vishnu** (the Preserver), **Brahma** (the Creator) and **Shiva** (the Destroyer). Most of the rest of the gods and goddesses commonly worshipped in Kerala are either incarnations of these three, or else of their consorts or offspring. There are also numerous regional cults following gods of local origin.

### Vishnu

The chief function of **Vishnu**, the "Preserver", is to keep the world in order. Blue-skinned and with four arms holding a conch, discus, lotus and mace, he is often either shaded by a serpent or resting on its coils, afloat on an ocean. He is usually seen alongside his steed, the half-man-half-eagle Garuda. Vaishnavites, distinguishable by two vertical lines on their foreheads, recognize Vishnu as the supreme lord, and believe that he has manifested himself on earth nine times. These incarnations, or **avatars**, have been as fish (Matsya), tortoise (Kurma), boar (Varaha), man-lion (Narsingh), dwarf (Vamana), axe-wielding brahmin (Parasuram), Rama, Krishna and Balaram (though some say that the Buddha is the ninth avatar). Vishnu's future descent to earth as Kalki, the saviour who will come to restore purity and destroy the wicked, is eagerly awaited.

The most important avatars are **Krishna** and Rama, star of the epic *Ramayana*. Krishna is the hero of the Bhagavad Gita, in which he proposes three routes to salvation (*moksha*): selfless action (*karmayoga*), knowledge (*jnana*) and devotion to the gods (*bhakti*). Krishna explains that *moksha* is attainable in this life, even without asceticism and renunciation. This appealed to all castes, as it denied the necessity of ritual and officiating brahmin priests, and evolved into the popular *bhakti* cult that legitimized love of God as a means to *moksha*. Through *bhakti*, Krishna's role was extended, and he assumed different faces (though some say that he is always blue). Most popularly he is the playful cowherd who seduces and dances with cowgirls (*gopis*), giving each the illusion that she is his only lover. At other times he is also pictured as a chubby, mischievous baby, known for his butter-stealing exploits, who inspires tender motherly love. A third popular version shows Krishna dancing and playing the flute.

In Kerala, Vishnu is worshipped most fervently in the form of Lord Krishna at **Guruvayur**, near Thrissur (see p.204). The main Krishna shrine in southern Kerala is at **Ambalappuza**, just south of Alappuzha in the backwaters.

### Brahma

Despite being the Creator god of Hinduism, **Brahma** has only a handful of temples dedicated to him in India. Two of these are in Kerala, at Thirunavaya and Kotakkal. In mythological art, Brahma is generally depicted as having four arms and four faces; his vehicle is a swan.

## Shiva

**Shaivism**, the cult of Shiva, was also inspired by *bhakti*, requiring selfless love from devotees in a quest for divine communion, but Shiva has never been incarnate on earth. He is presented in many different aspects, such as **Nataraja**, "Lord of the Dance", **Mahadev**, "Great God", and **Maheshvar**, "Divine Lord" and source of all knowledge. Though he does have several terrible forms, his role extends beyond that of destroyer, and he is revered as the source of the whole universe. Shiva is often depicted with four or five faces, draped with serpents, holding a trident and bearing a third eye in his forehead. In temples, he is identi-fied with the lingam, or phallic symbol, resting in the yoni, a representation of female sexuality. Whether as statue or lingam, Shiva is guarded by his bull steed, Nandi, and often accompanied by a consort, who assumes various forms and is looked upon as the vital energy (**shakti**) that empowers him. Their erotic exploits – a legacy of ancient Tantricism – were a favourite sculptural subject between the ninth and twelfth centuries AD.

Shiva is the object of popular veneration all over India; devotees are identifiable by the horizontal lines (between one and three) painted on their foreheads. In particular, Shaivite ascetics worship Shiva in the aspect of the terrible **Bhairav**. These ascetics renounce family and caste ties and perform extreme meditative and yogic practices. Many smoke ganga, Shiva's favourite herb; all see renunciation and realization of Shiva as the key to *moksha*. Some ascetic practices enter the realm of **Tantricism**, in which confrontation with all that is impure, such as alcohol, death and sex, is used to merge the sacred and the profane, and bring about the realiza-tion that Shiva is omnipresent.

## Mahadevi: the mother goddess

Female deities worshipped in Kerala are all manifestations of the supreme mother goddess, Mahadevi. She's most often venerated in her wrathful, destructive aspect as **Kali**, the "black one", but frequently appears as **Bhagawati** (the "fortunate" or "adorable"), Bhadrakali (the "virtuous" and "radiant"), or Durga. Other less common incarnations include Nagakali (Kali with a serpent), and the demoness Chamunda. As Shiva's consort, Parvati, or Uma, Mahadevi is remarkable for her beauty and fidelity. In whatever form, however, she incarnates *shakti*, the divine energy that animates the universe.

## Ayyappan

**Lord Ayyappan** is Kerala's most popular deity, the subject of a pilgrimage that for a couple of months each year sees the state swarming with millions of bare-chested male devotees dressed in black *lunghis* en route to his principal shrine, situated deep in the forests of the Western Ghats. Legend tells that he was born of a union between Shiva and Vishnu in his female form, Mohini, and as such symbolizes a synthesis of the two main strands in Brahmanical Hinduism ("Ayya" means Shiva and "Appan" means Vishnu). Another explanation for his current popularity is that his temples have always been open to members of all castes.

## Ganesh (Vingishwara)

The elephant-headed **Ganesh** (*Vingishwara* in Malayalam) is the first son of Shiva and Parvati. Tubby and smiling, he's invoked before every major undertaking (except funerals) and you'll see his image, seated on a throne or lotus, placed above temple gateways, in shops and in houses. In his four arms he holds a conch, a discus, a bowl of sweets (or club) and a water lily, and he is always attended by his vehicle, a rat. Credited with writing the Mahabharata as it was dictated by the sage Vyasa, Ganesh is regarded by many as the god of learning, success, prosperity and peace.

## Murugan

Pictured as a triumphant youth bedecked with flowers, **Murugan** (or Kartikeya, or Subramanyam) is the second son of Shiva and Parvati. The god of war, he has a huge following in neighbouring Tamil Nadu, where his cult probably predates the arrival of Brahminical Hinduism in the south by a couple of millennia. Murugan's symbols are the peacock (his sacred vehicle) and a bow; his battle standard bears the emblem of a rooster.

## Hanuman

India's great monkey god, **Hanuman** features in the Ramayana as Rama's chief aide in the fight against the demon king Lanka. He wields a mace and is the deity of acrobats and wrestlers, but is also seen as Rama and Sita's greatest devotee, and an author of Sanskrit grammar. As his representatives, monkeys find sanctuary in temples across southern India.

## Saraswati

The most beautiful Hindu goddess, **Saraswati**, the wife of Brahma – with her flawless milk-white complexion – sits or stands on a water lily or peacock, playing a lute, sitar or *vina*. A goddess of purification and fertility, she is also revered as the inventor of writing, and the goddess of eloquence and music.

## Lakshmi

The comely goddess **Lakshmi**, usually shown sitting or standing on a lotus flower, and sometimes called Padma (lotus), is the embodiment of loveliness, grace and charm, and the goddess of prosperity and wealth. Vishnu's consort, she appears in different aspects alongside each of his avatars; the most important are Sita, wife of Rama, and Radha, Krishna's favourite *gopi*. In many temples she is shown as one with Vishnu, in the form of Lakshmi Narayan.

## Practice

A Hindu has three aims in life: **dharma**, fulfilling one's duty to family and caste, and acquiring religious merit (*punya*) through right living; **artha**, the lawful making of wealth; and **karma**, desire and satisfaction. The primary concern of most Hindus is to reduce bad *karma* and acquire *punya*, by honest and charitable living within the restrictions imposed by caste and worship, in the hope of attaining a higher status in rebirth.

These goals are linked with the four traditional **stages in life**. According to ancient custom, the life of a high-class Hindu man progressed through these four distinct phases – *brahmachari* (celibate), as a child and student devoted to learning; *grhastha* (householder), providing for a family and raising sons; *vanaprashta* (forest dweller), a period of self-isolation and meditation; and finally, *sanyasi* (a renunciate) – renouncing all possessions to become a homeless ascetic, hoping to achieve the ultimate goal of *moksha*. However, in practice, few now follow this course and the *vanaprashta* is no more; in general, life is meant to progress along ordered lines from initiation (for high-caste Hindus) through to education, career and marriage. A small number of Malayalis who follow the ideal life, including some women, assume the final stage as *sanyasis*, saffron-clad sadhus who wander throughout India, begging for food and retreating to isolated caves, forests and hills to meditate. They are a common feature in most Indian towns, and many stay for long periods in particular temples. Some assume the life of a sadhu at an early age as a *chella* (pupil or disciple) to an older sadhu.

## Adi Shankara

Religious history in India tends to stress the transforming influence of northern, Brahminical traditions on the Dravidian south. But in the middle of the eighth century, at a time when Hinduism was splintering into dozens of different sects, a philosophical movement spread from Kerala that would unify the competing strands of the Subcontinent's most ancient religious tradition, and in the process save it from near-extinction.

The movement's core philosophy was that of **advaita** – literally "not-two"-ness – and its chief exponent was a brahmin guru called **Adi Shankara** (788–820 AD). The essence of his teaching, refined from ancient Vedic texts called the Upanishads, held that the soul (*atman*) was indivisible from the supreme creator being, Brahman. "Brahman is the only truth," he wrote. "The world is illusion and there is ultimately no difference between Brahman and individual self."

A precocious intellect from an early age, Shankara is said to have mastered Sanskrit, one of the world's most complex languages, while only three, and left home at eight in search of a guru. By the time he was sixteen, he'd written commentaries on the Upanishads, the Bhagavad Gita and other Vedic texts that would turn Hindu philosophy on its head. Travelling around India on foot, he engaged in debates with the greatest thinkers of the era and succeeded in convincing them of the truth of *advaita*.

Before his death at the age of 32, Shankara founded four major monasteries, or *mathas*, across India. These are still in existence today and stand as hubs on an extensive pilgrimage network that the guru did much to popularize in his lifetime. *Bhajans*, or devotional hymns, composed by him are also regularly sung in Hindu homes to this day.

Shankara's greatest legacy, however, lies in the emphasis he placed on meditation and the individual's quest for truth over Brahminical ritual. All the sects of modern Hinduism remain to some extent influenced by his philosophies, and many scholars have argued that without his rigorous collation of Vedantic thought, Hinduism itself might never have outlived the threat to its survival posed by state-sponsored Buddhism and Jainism in the first five hundred years AD.

Strict rules apply to the dharmic principles of **purity** and **pollution**, the most obvious of them requiring high-caste Hindus to limit their contact with potentially polluting lower castes. All bodily excretions are polluting. Above all else, **water** is the agent of purification, used in ablutions before prayer, and revered in all rivers, especially Ganga (the Ganges).

Each of the great stages in life – birth, **initiation**, marriage, death and cremation – are marked by fervent prayer, energetic celebration and feasting. The most significant event in a Hindu's life is **marriage**, which symbolizes ritual purity, and for women is so important that it takes the place of initiation. Feasting, dancing and singing among the bride and groom's families, usually lasting for a week or more before and after the marriage, are the norm all over Kerala. The actual marriage is consecrated when the couple walk seven times round a sacred fire, accompanied by sacred verses read by an officiating brahmin. Today, most Hindu marriages traditionally involve the parents, who negotiate the match; love marriages are increasingly common, especially in urban areas, but still tend to depend on parental consent and collusion. The age-old Malayali tradition of giving **dowry**, a gift of money, jewellery and goods from the bride's family to the groom's, is now officially illegal, but still widely demanded and invariably given, for fear that a daughter's welfare will be in jeopardy if it is withheld. Dowry is prevalent in both Hindu and Christian communities, and is as much practised by the upper and middle classes as it is by the poor, but for the latter it can represent an endless cycle of saving and debt with each new generation. Among more wealthy and cosmopolitan families, scooters, TVs and holidays are now the essential elements of a modern dowry. As it is a "gift", dowry is undeclared income, and the groom's family can place relentless pressure on the bride's family to continue providing "gifts" long after the wedding.

For Hindus, **death** is an essential process in an endless cycle of rebirth in the grand illusion (*maya*) until the individual attains enlightenment and freedom (*moksha*) from *samsara* (transmigration). Hindus cremate their dead, except for young children, whom they bury or cast into a river. The eldest son is entrusted to light the funeral pyre and the ashes are scattered, usually on a sacred river, or at sites on the coast associated with funerary rituals (the main one is Varkala Beach; see p.115). Death rites can be lengthy and complicated according to each Hindu community, and the role of the *purohit* (priest) is indispensable. Widows traditionally wear white.

# Islam

**Muslims** make up around a quarter of Kerala's population. They form a significant presence in almost every town, city and village, but especially in coastal parts of the north of the state, where they're known as **Moppilas** (also written as "Mapillas"). In most of India, Islam was spread by force during the Turkish and Mongol invasions of the medieval era, but in Kerala it took root peacefully, introduced by Arab traders who settled in the region from the eighth century AD onwards. Local Muslims played a pivotal role in the trade that underpinned the Kulasekhara empire, and the rise of Calicut in the fourteenth and fifteenth centuries. Moppila naval expertise, and their wealth, also placed them at the forefront of efforts to resist European colonialism, from the Portuguese to the British.

Despite the great differences in their religious beliefs, dress and dietary laws, Kerala's Hindus and Muslims coexisted harmoniously for over a thousand years. Only at the end of the nineteenth century, when taxes and exploitative land laws provoked clashes between the Moppilas and their Janmis landlords, did communal violence erupt. Recent decades have seen a worrying rise in communalism, mirroring a nationwide trend, but the violence has never approached the scale seen in parts of northern India.

More than anywhere else in the region, the Muslim districts of northern Kerala depend on **remittance money** sent by relatives working in the Persian Gulf. The mass out-migration to Saudi Arabia and the Gulf Arab states has not only increased prosperity among Keralan Muslims, but also had an impact on their religious practices. Over more than a thousand years, the Moppilas evolved an extraordinarily hybrid culture, evident in their dress, cuisine and architecture. Their mosques, sporting temple-like gables and slatted wood eaves, were heavily influenced by local Hindu style. Now, however, the Gulf phenomenon has injected a much more sober dye into the Moppila mix, and the old mosques have nearly all been torn down to be replaced by more modern, Mecca-style structures with domes and minarets.

## Origins and development of Islam

Islam, "submission to God", was founded by **Mohammed** (570–632 AD), who is regarded as the last in a succession of prophets and who transmitted God's final and perfected revelation to mankind through the writings of the divinely revealed "recitation", the **Koran**. The Koran is the authoritative scripture of Islam that sets down the tenets of Islamic belief: that there is one god, Allah (though he has 99 other names), and that Mohammed is his prophet. The birth of Islam is dated at 622 AD, when Mohammed and his followers, exiled from **Mecca**, made the *hijra*, or migration, north to Yathrib, later known as Medina, "City of the Prophet". The *hijra* marks the start of the Islamic lunar calendar; the Gregorian year 2010 corresponds roughly to the Muslim year 1431 AH (Anno Hijra).

From Medina, Mohammed ordered raids on caravans heading for Mecca, and led his community in battles against the Meccans, inspired by jihad, or "striving" on behalf of God and Islam. This concept of holy war was the driving force behind the incredible expansion of Islam – by 713 AD Muslims had settled as far west as Spain and as far east as the banks of the Indus. When **Mecca** surrendered peacefully to Mohammed in 630 AD, he cleared the sacred shrine, the Ka'ba, of idols, and proclaimed it the pilgrimage centre of Islam. Mohammed was succeeded as leader of the *umma*, the Islamic community, by Abu Bakr, the prophet's representative, or caliph, the first in a line of caliphs who led the orthodox community until the eleventh century AD. However, a schism soon emerged when the third caliph, Uthman, was assassinated by followers of Ali, Mohammed's son-in-law, in 656 AD. This new sect, calling themselves **Shi'as**, "partisans" of Ali, looked to Ali and his successors, infallible *imams*, as leaders of the *umma* until 878 AD, and thereafter replaced their religious authority with a body of scholars, the *ulema*.

By the second century after the *hijra* (ninth century AD), orthodox, or **Sunni**, Islam had assumed the form it takes today. A collection of traditions about the prophet, **Hadith**, became the source for ascertaining the *Sunna* (customs) of Mohammed. From the Koran and the Sunna, seven major **articles of belief** were laid down: belief in one God; in angels as his messengers; in prophets (including Jesus and Moses); in the Koran; in the doctrine of predestination by God; in the Day of Judgement; and in the bodily resurrection of all people on that day. Religious practice was also standardized under the Muslim law, *Sharia*, in the **Five Pillars of Islam**. The first "pillar" is the confession of faith, *shahada*, that "There is no god but God, and Mohammed is his messenger". The other four are: prayer (*salat*) five times daily, almsgiving (*zakat*), fasting (*saum*), especially during the month of Ramadan, and, if possible, pilgrimage (*Haj*) to Mecca, the ultimate goal of every practising Muslim.

# Christianity

When Vasco da Gama stepped ashore in Calicut in 1498, he was amazed to find the city already full of Christians – although somewhat less thrilled to discover that they were not Roman Catholics, but adherents to an obscure eastern Orthodox tradition. Today, Christians account for around 21 percent of the total population in Kerala, with a history dating back to the first century AD, some three centuries before the faith received official recognition in Europe.

No less than five main denominations exist, alongside a bewildering assortment of sects and sub-sects: **Nestorians** (confined mainly to Thrissur and Ernakulam), **Roman** or **Latin Catholics** (found throughout Kerala), the **Syrian Orthodox Church** (previously known as the Jacobite Syrians), **Marthoma Syrians** (a splinter group of the Syrian Orthodox Church) and the Anglican **Church of south India**.

## Some history

Local legend asserts that the **Apostle Thomas** ("Doubting Thomas") arrived in Kerala in 54 AD to convert itinerant Jewish traders living in the flourishing port of Muziris. Traditional accounts from Jews who later arrived there in 68 AD state that they encountered a community of Christians known as **Nazranis**, or "followers of the Nazarene" (Jesus). The Nazranis encountered little opposition to their religion from their Hindu hosts, and absorbed many indigenous practices into their worship.

There are numerous tales of the miracles performed by "**Mar Thoma**", as St Thomas is known in Malayalam. One tells of how he approached a group of Hindu Brahmins in Palur, who were trying to appease the gods by throwing water into the air; if the gods accepted the offerings, the droplets would hang above them. St Thomas also threw water in the air, which miraculously remained suspended, leading to the on-the-spot conversion of the assembled Brahmins to Christianity.

By oral tradition, the church he founded in India is the **oldest Christian denomination** in the world. Concrete documentary evidence of Christian activity in the Subcontinent, however, can only be traced back to the fourth century AD, when immigrant Syrian communities, belonging to seven tribes from Baghdad, Nineveh and Jerusalem under the leadership of the merchant **Knayi Thoma** (Thomas of Cana), were granted settlement rights along the Malabar coastline by royal charter. As they built Christian churches, the Syrians introduced architectural conventions from the Middle East, and so incorporated the nave and chancel with a gabled facade, which resulted in a distinctive style of Keralan church. They also adopted architectural traits from the Hindu-influenced Nazranis, retaining the *dwajastamba* (flag mast), the *kottupura* (gate house) and the *kurisuthara* (altar with a mounted cross).

A significant faction of the Syrian-Christian community, the **Nestorians** (after Nestorius, the patriarch of Constantinople) were the dominant Christian group in Kerala after the sixth century AD and at one stage had centres in various parts of India. However, the assertive spread of **Roman Catholicism**, led by the Jesuit missionary Francis Xavier out of Portuguese Goa in the sixteenth century, later reduced the Nestorians to a small community, which survives today mainly in Thrissur.

Kerala's early Christians followed a liturgy in the **Syriac language** (a dialect of Aramaic). Latin was introduced by missionaries who visited Kollam in the Middle Ages, and once the Portuguese appeared on the scene in the 1530s, a large community of **Roman** or **Latin Catholics** developed, particularly on the coast, and came under the jurisdiction of the pope. In the middle of the seventeenth century, with the ascendancy of the **Dutch**, part of the Church broke away from Rome, and local bishops were appointed through the offices of the Jacobite patriarch in Antioch.

The **British** initially took the attitude that the Subcontinent was a heathen and polytheistic civilization waiting to be proselytized. Their brand of Anglicanism particularly appealed to members of the lower castes and sub-castes, who converted en masse in some districts to form the **Church of south India**. At the same time, elements in the Syrian Church advocated the replacement of Syriac with the local language of Malayalam. The resultant schism led to the creation of the new **Marthoma Syrian Church**. Today, numerous large and popular churches, as well as roadside shrines known as *kurisupalli*, or "chapels of the cross", bear witness to the continuing strength of the Christian communities throughout the state. **Christmas** is an important festival in Kerala; during the weeks leading up to December 25, star-shaped lamps are put up outside shops and houses, illuminating the night and identifying followers of the faith.

## Practice

Christian practice in Kerala has, over the centuries, absorbed many elements of Hindu worship. **Festivals** are highly structured along "caste" lines and, like their Hindu brethren, some communities never eat beef or pork, which are considered to be polluting. In many churches across the state, you will see devotees offering the Hindu *arati* plate of coconut, sweets and rice, and women wearing a *tilak* dot on their forehead. Christians carry plates of food to the graves of their ancestors

## The Jews of Kerala

Until their mass departure to Israel in the 1950s, **Jews** formed a significant minority in Kerala for a thousand years or more, acting as prominent merchants and bankers to the region's rulers. Tradition holds that the first Jewish arrivals on the Malabar coast were fleeing the occupation of Jerusalem by Nebuchadnezzar in 587 BC. Another legend claims they came 1500 years previously as part of King Solomon's trading fleet. However, the first concrete evidence of their presence in the region dates from around 1000 AD, in the form of a couple of inscribed copper plates, now stored in the Pardesi Synagogue in Mattancherry, detailing the privileges granted to one Joseph Rabban by Raja Bhaskara Ravi Varma. According to the Tamil inscriptions, the ruler gave to Rabban and his community the village of Anjuvannan, near Cranganore, and all proceeds deriving from it, in perpetuity; he was also permitted to ride in a palanquin and carry a parasol – rights generally accorded to only the highest-ranking individuals in society.

Rabban's Jews, and the waves of other Jewish immigrants who seem to have travelled to the Malabar from across northern Africa, Egypt, Persia and the Middle East in the first millennium AD, became known as **Meyhuhassim** (literally "privileged") – or **"Black Jews"**. They were joined by Sephardic Jews fleeing the Spanish and Portuguese inquisitions in the sixteenth and seventeenth centuries, who later became known as the **"Pardesi"** (literally "foreign") – or **"White Jews"**. Both groups also had slaves who converted and were later freed to become the so-called **Meshuhararim** ("released"). These slaves formed the lowest-ranking group, the **"Brown Jews"**.

The largest settlements of Jews on the Malabar, including Anjuvannan, were around Kodungallur (Cranganore), near the ancient port of Muziris. However, persecution in the Portuguese era, when houses and synagogues were routinely destroyed and Jews packed off to the Inquisition's dungeons in Goa, led to mass migration to **Cochin**, where the local raja set aside a parcel of land for the Jews in 1567. The new Jewish community, centred on Mattancherry, still known as Jew Town, thrived under the more tolerant regimes of the Dutch and British; and by the end of the seventeenth century there were ten synagogues and around five hundred Jewish families in Cochin. Wealthy Jews, such as the Koders (whose splendid old mansion nowadays serves as one of the state's premier heritage hotels; see p.174), rose to occupy important positions of influence and authority. Today, only ten (mostly elderly) White Jews remain in Cochin (see p.181); the rest departed for Israel in the 1940s and 1950s. Other synagogues survive around the state, but the Pardesi (see p.180), despite having been destroyed by the Portuguese and rebuilt under the Dutch, remains the one in best condition and is still in use.

on the anniversary of their death, in much the same manner that a Hindu family will share a feast on such a day.

**Pilgrimage** is considered an integral part of faith, and Keralan Christians of all denominations tend to visit churches where there is a relic, such as a shard of finger bone alleged to have belonged to St Thomas. These relics are brought out on special feast days, and huge crowds will jostle to catch a sight of the tiny bit of yellowing bone lying in a casket.

Christians in Kerala have never adopted the practice of giving or receiving **dowry** on the occasion of marriage, although in an arrangement similar to Hindu practice, a Christian **marriage** tends to take place between members of the same denomination or sect. In most cases, the parents of the couple play a central role in the selection process, paying particular attention to the social status and education of the prospective bride or groom. If a woman becomes a **widow**, she is not socially ostracized as a Hindu woman would be, but is instead encouraged to remarry.

# The sacred arts

Since the beginning of Indian history, art and religion have been inextricably linked. Paid for by royal patrons, the finest expressions of human creativity – whether sculpture, painting, music, dance or drama – were always reserved for temples. Sometimes they were deployed for decorative effect, to intensify the act of worship. Other forms of art, notably dance and ritual drama, were conceived as acts of worship in themselves: ritualized performances that served both as offerings for the resident deities and as entertainment for the higher castes permitted to enter their shrines.

In Kerala, the great temples erected during the "golden age" of the Kulasekhara empire were where the region's trademark sacred arts were refined, over three or more centuries of **patronage** from kings, nobility and wealthy pilgrims. Later, between the sixteenth and eighteenth centuries, regional dynasties such as the zamorins of Calicut and rajas of Cochin acted as enthusiastic patrons of newer, emerging forms – including *kathakali* – which drew on the older traditions fostered in the temples.

Meanwhile, in the villages, lower-caste communities preserved their own **folk art forms** as rituals outside shrines. Stretching back to Kerala's distant Dravidian past, the roots of these in many cases predate not just the arrival of Europeans, but also Brahminical Hinduism itself. Kerala's localized, village-based, low-caste arts are the repositories of India's last thriving **Tantric** tradition, barely veiled by a cloak of Vedic mythology, and based around worship of the Mother goddess, Mahadevi. In contrast to the sacred arts of the great temples, the object of Tantric rituals was not to amuse or praise the deity, but manifest the god's power in a tangible form that worshippers could tap into.

Whether a frenzied Tantric *theyyem* dance at a shrine in the remote north of Kerala or a stately *kathakali* recital in one of the royal temples of Kochi, the region's sacred arts can provide unforgettable experiences – even if you don't have any grasp of their arcane symbolic languages. Drawing on traditions set down in writing more than two millennia ago, they hold the power to transport audiences in ways that defy cultural boundaries.

The rundown that follows is far from complete. Covering only the most common types of sacred art prevalent in Kerala, it sets out the bare bones of traditions that have innumerable variations, sub-branches and sects. One of the most rewarding pleasures of travelling around the state is discovering styles of dance, music and ritual theatre you've never heard of and could not possibly have imagined. Coming across them is largely a matter of chance, but you'll increase the odds by attending as many **festivals** – at as many different locations – as possible during your stay.

For more serious study, foreigners are welcome to visit the **academies** set up to preserve Kerala's performing and sacred arts in Thrissur (see p.197), Irinjalakuda (see p.202) and Cheruthuruthy (see p.206). Details of major **arts festivals** – such as Malabar Mahotsavam in Kozhikode and Nishagandi and Swathi Sangeetotsavam in Thiruvananthapuram – are given in Basics on pp.52–55, and in the relevant accounts throughout the Guide.

## Murals

One of the best-kept secrets of south Indian art are the unique **Keralan murals** found at Mattancherry Palace in old Kochi (see p.179) and at around sixty other locations in the state. Most are on the walls of functioning temples; they are not marketable, transportable, or indeed even seen by many non-Hindus. Few date from before the sixteenth century, though their origins may go back to the seventh century, probably influenced by the Pallava style of Tamil Nadu, but only traces in one tenth-century cave temple survive from the earliest period. Castaneda, a traveller who accompanied Vasco da Gama on the first Portuguese landing in India, described how he strayed into a temple, supposing it to be a church, and saw "monstrous-looking images with two-inch fangs" painted on the walls, causing one of the party to fall to his knees exclaiming, "if this be the devil, I worship God".

Technically classified as **fresco-secco**, Kerala murals employ vegetable and mineral colours, predominantly ochre reds and yellows, white and blue-green, and are coated with a protective sheen of pine resin and oil. Their ingenious design incorporates intense detail, portraying human and celestial figures with clarity and dynamism; subtle facial expressions are captured with the simplest of lines, while narrative elements are always bold and arresting. In common with all great Indian art, the murals possess a complex iconography and symbolism.

Non-Hindus can see fine examples in Kochi's Mattancherry Palace, Padmanabhapuram (see p.107), Ettumanur (see p.152) and Kayamkulam (see p.142). Visitors interested in how they are made should head for the Mural Painting Institute at Guruvayur (ⓦwww.guruvayurdevaswom.org). *Murals of Kerala*, by M.G. Shashi Bhooshan, serves as an excellent introduction.

Also worthy of mention are Kerala's **Christian murals** – the finest examples of which are preserved in the Church of St Thomas in Palai, near Kottayam in southern Kerala (see p.152).

# Temple sculpture

**Hindu sculpture** saw its finest flowering in the stone workshops of neighbouring Tamil Nadu, whose giant temples are encrusted with elaborate carvings and painted stucco figures. By comparison, Keralan shrines are more restrained, but they still contain some extraordinary stonework, principally in the form of carved pillars and doorways, but also the deities themselves, many of which are hewn from rare coloured granites or black basalt. Even if you are not able to enter the innermost confines of Hindu temples in the region, this sacred art can still be admired at a distance: from the courtyards, it's usually possible to peek inside the soot- and ghee-covered interior chambers, and at the colonnaded walkways surrounding the complexes.

All sacred sculpture in south India follows the strictest rules of iconography, originally set down in ancient canonical texts called the **Shilpa Shastras**. When it comes to creating images of gods and goddesses, measurement always begins with the proportions of the artist's own hand and the icon's resultant face-length as the basic unit. The overall scheme is allied to the equally scientific rules applied to classical music, specifically *tala* or rhythm. Human figures total eight face-lengths, eight being the most basic of rhythmic measures. Figures of deities are *nava-tala*, nine face-lengths.

Like their counterparts in medieval Europe, south Indian sculptors remained largely anonymous. Even though the most talented artists may have been known to their peers – in some rare cases earning renown in kingdoms at opposite ends of the Subcontinent – their names have become lost over time. An explanation often advanced for this is the *Shastras*' insistence that the personality of an individual artist must be suppressed in order for divine inspiration to flow freely.

Some fine examples of Hindu temple sculpture, most of them made in the stone-carving town of Mamallapuram in Tamil Nadu, are displayed in Kerala's top handicrafts shops, such as Natesan's in Thiruvananthapuram and around the antique emporia of Mattancherry. You'll also see some superb specimens in the lobbies of five-star hotels, where they're often placed amid pools of water and floating flowers.

# Kalam ezhuttu

The tradition of **kalam ezhuttu** (pronounced "kalam-*erroo*-too") – detailed and beautiful ritual drawings, in coloured powder, of deities and geometric patterns (mandalas) – is very much alive all over **Kerala**, although few visitors to the region even know of its existence. The designs usually cover an area of around thirty square metres, often outdoors and under a *pandal* – a temporary shelter made from bamboo and palm fronds. Each colour, made from rice flour, turmeric, ground leaves and burnt paddy husk, is painstakingly applied using the thumb and forefinger as a funnel. Three communities produce *kalams*: two come from the temple servant (Ambalavasi) castes, whose rituals are associated with the god Ayappan (see p.162) or the goddess Bhagavati; the third, the Pullavans, specialize in serpent worship. Icono-graphic designs emerge gradually from the initial grid lines and turn into startling figures, many of terrible aspect, with wide eyes and fangs. Noses and breasts are raised, giving the whole a three-dimensional effect. As part of the ritual, the signifi-cant moment when the powder is added for the iris or pupil, "opening" the eyes, may be accompanied by *chenda* drums and *elatalam* hand-cymbals.

Witnessing the often day-long **ritual** is an unforgettable experience. The effort expended by the artist is made all the more remarkable by the inevitable destruc-tion of the picture shortly after its completion; this truly ephemeral art cannot be divorced from its ritual context. In some cases, the image is destroyed by a fierce-looking *velichapadu* ("light-bringer"), a village oracle who can be recognized by shoulder-length hair, red *dhoti*, heavy brass anklets and the hooked sword he or she brandishes either while jumping up and down on the spot (a common sight), or marching purposefully about, controlling the spectators. At the end of the ritual, the powder, invested with divine power, is thrown over the crowd. *Kalam ezhuttu* rituals are not widely advertised; check at tourist offices.

# Music

India is most famous for its Hindustani music, as played in the north of the country by maestros such as Ravi Shankar and Ustad Bismillah Kahn, but the south has its own, very different – and considerably more ancient – classical form, known as **Carnatic**, which enjoys a huge following in Kerala. In addition, Kerala preserves a uniquely Malayali style of devotional song called Sopana *sangeetham*, developed in the region's temples as accompaniment for ritual dramas. These, and the immensely popular percussion of **chenda melam**, can still be heard at religious festivals all over the state during the winter.

## Carnatic music

The **Carnatic music** of south India might be labelled "classical", but it's nothing like classical music anywhere else in the world. Rather than being the domain of

You're most likely to hear top-notch Carnatic music in **Thiruvananthapuram**. The capital hosts two major annual classical festivals: **Swathi Sangeetotsavam**, held in the first or second week of January in the grounds of the Puttan Malika palace; and the **Nishagandi Festival**, staged a couple of weeks later at the open-air auditorium next to Kankakannu palace. See p.86 & p.88 for more details.

an urban elite, it's an explosion of colour, sound and popular Hindu worship – part of the warp and weft of the region's culture. The other major difference is that, lacking written notation, the form is learned by ear or – in the case of its highly sophisticated rhythmic system – taught by a marvellous, mathematical structure of "finger computing" which enables a percussionist to break down a complex *thaalam* (rhythmic cycle) into manageable units. You'll hear it performed outside temples and during major cultural festivals in Kerala, for which top artists from Tamil Nadu and other southern states travel to the region.

While devotional and religious in origin, Carnatic music is as much a vehicle for education and entertainment as for spiritual elevation. **Kritis**, a genre of Hindu hymn, are hummed and sung as people go about their daily business. Tuneful and easily recognizable, they hold a similar position in popular culture to the Christian hymn in Western societies.

In performance, Carnatic musicians will distil the essence of a *ragam* – the melody – into six to eight minutes. In part this is because a *kriti*, the base of many recitals, is a fixed composition without improvisation. Carnatic musicians' creativity lies in their ability to interpret a piece faithfully while shading and colouring the composition appropriately. The words of a *kriti* affect even non-vocal compositions: instrumentalists will colour their interpretations as if a vocalist were singing along; the unvoiced lyric determines where they place an accent, a pause or melodic splash. Improvisation has its place too, most noticeably in a sequence known as **ragam-thanam-pallavi**. This is a full-scale flowering of a Carnatic *ragam* and is every bit the equal of a Hindustani performance, although it is employed more sparingly, tending to be the centrepiece or climax of a Carnatic concert.

Whereas Carnatic music generally breaks down into three strands – temple music, temple dance-accompaniment, and music for private devotional observance – paying concert performances have somewhat blurred these distinctions. Concert-giving led to other changes, too, and **microphones** came into use during the 1930s. They lent soft-voiced instruments such as members of the *vina* family (see below) a new lease of life, and replaced full-tilt vocal power with greater subtlety. Nowadays, concerts will typically feature a named principal soloist (either vocal or instrumental) with melodic and rhythmic accompaniment and a *tanpura* or drone player. Percussionists of standing are often included in concert announcements and advertising as they are attractions in their own right. Female musicians involved in a principal role tend to be vocalists, *vina* players or violinists. Male musicians have access to a wider range of musical possibilities as well as outnumbering female principal soloists or accompanists by roughly three to one.

## Carnatic instruments

The **vina** (or *veena*) is the foremost Carnatic **stringed instrument**, the southern equivalent (and ancestor) of the sitar. A hollow wooden fingerboard with 24 frets is supported by two resonating gourds at each end. The *vina* has seven strings, four used for the melody and the other three for rhythm and drone. The **chitra vina** (or *gotuvadyam*) is an unfretted 21-string instrument with sets for rhythm and drone as well as sympathetic strings. It has a characteristically soft voice, which, before amplification, meant it was best suited to intimate surroundings.

As in the north, the transverse bamboo flute goes under the name of **bansuri** or **venu**, although it is typically shorter and higher in pitch than the Hindustani instrument. The **nadaswaram** is a piercing double-reed oboe-like instrument. It's longer and more deep-toned than the Hindustani *shehnai*, is associated with weddings, processions and temple ceremonies and is often paired with a drone. Besides its ceremonial functions – and it is perhaps best heard in the open air – it is sometimes employed in formal classical concert settings.

The Carnatic counterpart to the tabla is the **mridangam**, a double-headed, barrel-shaped drum made from a single block of jackwood. Both heads are constructed from layers of hide and can be tuned according to the *ragam* being performed. Other percussion instruments include the **tavil**, a folk-style barrel drum commonly found in ceremonial *nadaswaram* ensembles, and the **ghatam**, a clay pot tuned by firing. The latter is frequently found in south Indian ensembles and, unlikely as it may seem, in the hands of a top player can contribute some spectacular solos. The **morsing** (or *morching*) is a Jew's harp, often part of the accompanying ensemble, although it is frequently dropped when groups tour to save on the air fare. The **jalatarangam** (or *jalatarang*) is something of a curiosity: a melodic percussion instrument comprising a semicircle of water-filled porcelain bowls. It can create a sound of extraordinary beauty as the lead melody instrument in a typical Carnatic ensemble with violin, *mridangam* and *ghatam*.

From the nineteenth century, Carnatic music began to appropriate **Western instruments**, notably the violin and clarinet, and more recently the mandolin and saxophone. The violin is played sitting on the floor with its body against the upper chest and the scroll wedged against the ankle, leaving the left hand free to slide more freely up and down the strings. South India's child prodigy, **U. Srinivas**, popularized the mandolin as a Carnatic instrument. He is a very devout musician and his performances usually have a devotional ingredient.

The **saxophone** is another recent import, and its champion, Kadri Gopalnath, is one of south India's most popular musicians, with dozens of recordings to his credit. Gopalnath demonstrates Carnatic music's ability to be ancient and modern at the same time. When he plays the Carnatic *ragams*, the powerful sound of the saxophone echoes the ancient *nadaswaram*, but with a distinctively contemporary tone and attitude.

## Sopana and kathakali sangeetham

Whereas Carnatic music nowadays tends to be staged in concert halls, the context of Kerala's own classical vocal tradition, **Sopana sangeetham**, remains primarily the Hindu temple – specifically the steps leading to the central shrine. Sopana is always sung by a soloist, accompanied by the hour-glass-shaped *ettaka* drum, whose pitch can be shifted to shadow the vocals. The origins of the form are obscure. Thought to have started as the accompaniment to Tantric rituals, such as the making of *kalam ezhuttu* powder patterns for the goddess Kali (see p.281), it was later taken up by the **bhakti cult** – the distinctive structure of Sopana, which was supposed to reflect the ascent of devotees to ecstatic bliss, lent itself well to the intensely fervent atmosphere of Krishna worship, as popularized from the ninth century in temples such as Guruvayur, under patronage from the Kulasekhara rajas. During the cultural renaissance of the nineteenth century, however, Sopana was shunned by the salons of kings like Swati Thirunal – one of the great patrons of Carnatic music in the region – because it was deemed too "rustic".

Although you might not get a chance to hear Sopana performed in its authentic setting, you'll hear something pretty close to it sung during *kathakali* recitals. *Kathakali sangeetham* is similar to Sopana in terms of vocal technique, but it employs additional percussion of small cymbals (*kaimani*), gongs (*chengila*) and large, double-sided *chenda* drums. Here, the *ettaka* is deployed when female characters take the stage, its sing-song sound creating a feel that complements the drama.

The state's principal music colleges, where you can sit in on classes of *kathakali sangeetham* and Carnatic singing, are the Kerala Kalamandalam Academy at Cheruthuruthy (see p.206), and Sangeet Natak Akademi, Thrissur (see p.198).

## Chenda melam: Keralan ritual percussion

The noisiest, rowdiest and most intense phase of any Keralan temple festival is the one presided over by the local drum orchestra, or **chenda melam**, whose ear-shattering performances accompany the procession of the deity around the sacred precinct and into the shrine. As impressive for their mental arithmetic as percussion technique and showing enormous stamina in the intense heat, the musicians play an assortment of upright barrel drums (*chenda*) supported over the shoulder, bronze cymbals and wind instruments – the oboe-like *kuzhal* and the spectacular C-shaped brass trumpets (*kombu*), which emphasize and prolong the drum beating.

**Performances** invariably begin with an impressive "*ghrr*" and "*dhim*" produced on the drums. This is said to symbolize a lion's roar and was probably once performed in support of a lion hunt. After this mighty introduction, the drums drop the tempo and the music builds up like a pyramid, starting slowly with long musical cycles before working up to a short, fast, powerful climax. During the performance, an elephant, musicians and the crowd process round the temple precinct, until, after more than two hours, the excited crowd and sweating musicians celebrate the conclusion and follow the elephant and deity into the **inner temple**.

### Yesudas

You can't go anywhere in Kerala, not even the most remote backwaters, without hearing the honey-toned voice of Yesudas drifting out of a *chayakada* or toddy shop. For Malayalis the world over – as well as tens of millions of Tamils – his songs provide the soundtrack to everyday life as well as important rites of passage. From the instant a bus driver slots one of his albums into the dashboard cassette player, dozens of eyes will mist over, recalling loved ones in the Gulf, a scene from a forgotten Malluwood movie or memories of last Onam's *sadya* feast.

**Kattassery Joseph Yesudas** was born in 1940, the son of a poor Christian family in Kochi. His father, a singer-actor on the local stage, trained him in Carnatic vocals from the age of 3, but it wasn't until 1961 that the star had his first breakthrough as a playback artist in a Tamil film, singing four lines from a poem by his spiritual hero, Sri Narayana Guru. It's hard to imagine a more appropriate start to a career that would, in less than a decade, see him become a household name in India, performing songs from all the major faiths in more than twenty different Indian languages.

Narayana Guru's message of "One Caste, One Religion, One God" has always been particularly close to the heart of the vocalist. One of his best-loved hits is a track whose title translates as "I Will Pray at the Guruvayur Temple One Day" – an ironic reference to the fact that, as a Christian, Yesudas has never been permitted to enter Kerala's most hallowed Hindu shrine.

Yesudas's **devotional songs** to Lord Ayyappan blare from pilgrim coaches all over the state in January and February, and accompany millions of black-*mundu* wearing devotees on their way to and from Sabarimala each year – just a small part of a repertoire covering an estimated 30,000 recordings. In spite of his success, however, Kerala's highest-profile musician has remained as famous for his level-headedness and humility as his vocal talent, attributing his meteoric stardom to "Love of God".

The first stage broadly symbolizes the ordinary life of men, while the peak of the last stage shows the ideal human or divine aspect of reality. The music must please the god on top of the elephant and, of course, the assembled temple crowd. While the main beats are provided by hitting the underside of the *chenda*, the skilled solo *chenda* players create intricate patterns over the top. Different players may gather for each event, but they are capable of playing together perfectly with no rehearsal – the concept is more like a big jazz band than a European classical orchestra.

A **typical setup** for a medium-sized temple festival kicks off with a turn from the *panchavadyam* orchestra, comprising three types of drums, cymbals and the *kombu* trumpets. A conch is blown three times, symbolizing the holy syllable "Om", and the performance begins its first stage with a slow, 1792-beat rhythmic cycle. The cycles speed up and contract into 896, 448, 224 and 112 beats, ending with a 56-beat cycle. Fireworks, a large crowd and elephants trumpeting support the ecstatic climax.

For the evening, performances of *tayambaka*, *keli* and *kuzhal pattu* are announced. Each is a solo performing style, with players from the *chenda melam* and *panchavadyam* orchestras. *Tayambaka* is the main attraction, an improvised *chenda* solo played with a small ensemble of accompanying treble and bass *chenda* and cymbals. The other solo styles, *keli* (with a soloist on the *maddalam*, a horizontally slung barrel drum) and *kuzhal pattu* (oboe), precede the midnight performance of the last *chenda melam*.

# Dance

Among the most magical experiences a visitor to south India can have is to see one of the dances that play such an important part in the region's cultural life. India's most prevalent classical style, **bharatanatyam**, originated in the Chola temples of neighbouring Tamil Nadu and still fills concert arenas in cities today, as does the more uniquely Keralan form, **mohiniyattam**.

## The Natya Shastra

All forms of Indian dance share certain broad characteristics and can be traced back to principles enshrined in the **Natya Shastra**, a Sanskrit treatise on dramaturgy dating from the first century BC. The text covers every aspect of the origin and function of **natya**, the art of dance-drama, which combines music, stylized speech, dance and spectacle, and characterizes theatre throughout south Asia. The spread of this art form occurred during the centuries of cultural expansion from the second century BC to the eighth century AD, when south Indian kings sent trade missions, court dancers, priests and conquering armies all over the region. Even in countries that later embraced Buddhism or Islam, dances continue to show evidence of Indian forms, and Hindu gods and goddesses still feature, mixed with indigenous heroes and deities.

South Indian dance and dance-dramas are divided into two temperaments: **tandava**, which represents the fearful male energy of Shiva, and **lasya**, representing the grace of his wife Parvati. *Kathakali* is *tandava* and *bharatanatyam* is *lasya*, while some other forms combine the two elements. Equally, they include in differing degrees the three main components of classical dance: **nritta**, pure dance in which the music is reflected by decorative movements of the body; **natya**, which is the dramatic element of the dance and includes the portrayal of character; and **nritya**, the interpretive element, in which mood is portrayed through hand and facial gestures and the position of the feet and legs.

The term **abhinaya** describes the resources at the disposal of a performer in communicating the meaning of a dance; they include costume and make-up, speech and intonation, psychological understanding and, perhaps the most distinctive and complex element, the language of gestures. Stylized gestures are prescribed for every part of the body – there are seven movements for the eyebrows, six for the nose and six for the cheeks, for example – and they can take a performer years of intensive training to perfect. Once complete control of the body has been mastered, a performer will have a repertoire of several thousand meanings. In combination with other movements, a single hand gesture, with the fingers extended and the thumb bent for example, can be used to express heat, rain, a crowd, the night, a forest, a flight of birds or a house. Similarly, up to three characters can be played by a single performer by alternating facial expressions.

Despite frequent feats of technical brilliance, performers are rarely judged by their skill in executing a particular dance, but by their success in communicating certain specific emotions, or **bhava**, to the audience. This can only be measured by the quality of **rasa**, a mood or sentiment, one for each of the nine *bhavas*, which the audience experiences during a performance.

## Bharatanatyam

The best-known Indian classical dance style is **bharatanatyam**, a composite term made up of **bharata**, an acronym of "*bhava*" (expression), "*raga*" (melody) and "*tala*" (rhythm), and **natyam**, the Tamil word for "dance". It is a graceful form, rich in gesture, performed only by women. A popular subject for temple sculptures throughout south India (especially in Tamil Nadu), it originated in the dances of the **devadasis**, temple dancing girls. Usually "donated" to a temple by their parents, the young girls were formally "wedded" to the deity and spent the rest of their lives dancing or singing as part of their devotional duties in the great Tamil shrines. Later, however, the *devadasi* system became debased, and the dancers, who formerly enjoyed high status in Hindu society, became prostitutes controlled by the Brahmins, whom male visitors to the temple would pay for sexual services.

In the latter half of the nineteenth century, four brothers set themselves the task of saving the dance from extinction and pieced together a reconstruction of the form through study of the *Natya Shastra*, the images on temple friezes and information gleaned from former *devadasis*. Although the dance today is largely based on their findings, this was only the first step in its revival, as *bharatanatyam* continued to be confined to the temples and was danced almost exclusively by men – the only way, as the brothers saw it, of preventing its moral decline. Not until the 1930s, when **Rukmini Devi**, a member of the Theosophical Society, introduced the form to a wider middle-class audience, did *bharatanatyam* begin to achieve popularity as a secular art form.

As ward of the nineteenth-century British rebel **Annie Besant**, Devi had greater exposure to foreign arts than many women of her generation. She became interested in Western dance while accompanying her husband, George Arundale, former principal of the Theosophical Society's school in Adyar, Chennai, on lecture tours. Having studied under Pavlova, among others, in 1929, after witnessing a *bharatanatyam* performance, she dedicated her life to its revival. The dance school she founded at Adyar, now known as Kalakshetra, continues to develop some of the world's most accomplished exponents. In her determination to make the art form socially respectable, Devi eliminated all erotic elements and held authoritarian views about how *bharatanatyam* should be danced. Many ex-pupils have gone on to develop their own interpretations of the style, but the form continues to be seen as essentially spiritual. Its theme is invariably romantic love, with the dancer seen as a devotee separated from the object of her devotion. In this way, she dramatizes the idea of **sringara bhakti**, or worship through love.

As with other classical dance forms, training is rigorous. Performers are encouraged to dissolve their identity in the dance and become instruments for the expression of divine presence. Performances – which last about two hours and are divided into nine stages – are preceded by a *namaskaram*, a salutation to the gods, offered by the stage, musicians and audience; a floral offering is made to a statue of the presiding deity, which stands at the right of the stage. The pivotal part of the performance is **varnam**, which the preceding three phases (*alarippu*, *jatiswaram* and *sabdam*) build up to through *nritta* (pure dance based on rhythm), adding melody and then lyrics. In *varnam*, every aspect of the dancer's art is exercised through two sections, the first slow, alternating *abinhaya* with rhythmic syllables, and the second twice the pace of the first, alternating *abinhaya* with melodic syllables. In the following two phases (*padams* and *javalis*) the emphasis is on the expression of mood through mime, and in the penultimate phase, the *tillana*, the dancer reverts again to the pure rhythm which began the dance. A *mangalam*, or short prayer, marks the end of a performance.

## Mohiniyattam

A semi-classical form that originated in Kerala, **mohiniyattam**, like *bharatanatyam*, grew out of the temple dances of the *devadasis*. It, too, was revived through the efforts of enthusiastic individuals, first in the nineteenth century by Swati Thirunal, the raja of Travancore, and again in the 1930s, after a period of disrepute, by the poet Vallathol. *Mohiniyattam* ("the dance of the enchantress") takes its name from the mythological maiden **Mohini**, who evoked desire and had the ability to steal the heart of the onlooker. Usually a solo dance performed by women, it is dominated by the mood of *lasya*, with graceful movements distinguished by a rhythmic swaying of the body from side to side. The central theme is one of love and devotion to god, with Vishnu or Krishna appearing most frequently as the heroes. Dancers wear realistic make-up and the cream-white, gold-bordered Kasavu sari of Kerala. The music which accompanies the dancer is Sopanam-inflected Carnatic, with lyrics in Malayalam.

# Ritual theatre

Various forms of ritualized theatre have always been performed in Indian temples, both as visual sacrifices to the deities and as entertainment. If you're lucky enough to catch an authentic recital *in situ* during a temple festival you'll never forget it: the stamina of the performers and the spectacle of an audience sitting up all night to see the finale of a dance-drama at dawn is utterly remarkable.

## Kathakali

Here is the tradition of the trance dancers, here is the absolute demand of the subjugation of body to spirit, here is the realization of the cosmic transformation of human into divine.

Mrinalini Sarabhai, classical dancer

The image of a **kathakali** actor in a magnificent costume with extraordinary make-up and a huge gold crown has become Kerala's trademark. There are still many traditional performances, which take place on open ground outside a temple, beginning at 10pm and lasting until dawn, illuminated solely by the flickers of a large brass *nilavilakku* oil lamp centre stage. Virtually nothing about *kathakali* is naturalistic, because it depicts the world of gods and demons. Both male and female roles are played by men.

Standing at the back of the stage, two musicians play driving rhythms, one on a bronze gong, the other on heavy bell-metal cymbals; they also sing the dialogue. Actors appear and disappear from behind a handheld curtain and never utter a sound, save the odd strange cry. Learning the elaborate hand gestures, facial expressions and choreographed movements, as articulate and precise as any sign language, requires rigorous training that can begin at the age of eight and last ten years. At least two more drummers stand left of the stage; one plays the upright **chenda** with slender curved sticks, the other the **maddalam**, a horizontal barrel-shaped hand drum. When a female character is "speaking", the *chenda* is replaced by the hourglass-shaped **ettaka**, a "talking drum" on which melodies can be played. The drummers keep their eyes on the actors, whose every gesture is reinforced by their sound, from the gentlest embrace to the wildest sword fight.

Although it bears the unmistakeable influences of *kudiyattam* and indigenous folk rituals, *kathakali*, literally "story-play", is thought to have crystallized into a distinct theatre form during the seventeenth century. The plays are based on three major sources: the Mahabharata, the Ramayana and the Bhagavata Purana. While the stories are ostensibly about god-heroes such as Rama and Krishna, the most popular characters are those that give the most scope to the actors – the villainous, fanged, red-and-black-faced *katti* ("knife") anti-heroes. These types, such as the kings Ravana and Duryodhana, are dominated by lust, greed, envy and violence. David Bolland's handy paperback *Guide to Kathakali*, widely available in Kerala, gives invaluable scene-by-scene summaries of the most popular plays and explains in simple language a lot more besides.

When attending a performance, arrive early to get your bearings before it gets dark, even though the first play will not start much before 10pm. Members of the audience are welcome to visit the dressing room before and during the performance, to watch the **masks** and **make-up** being applied. The colour and design of these, which specialist artists take several hours to apply, signify the personality of each character.

The principal characters fall into the following seven **types**. **Pacca** ("green" and "pure") characters, painted bright green, are the noble heroes, including gods such as Rama and Krishna. **Katti** ("knife") are evil and clever characters such as Ravana. Often the most popular with the audience, they have green faces to signify their noble birth, with upturned moustaches and white mushroom knobs on the tips of their noses. **Chokannatadi** ("red beard") characters are power-drunk and vicious, and have black faces from the nostrils upwards, with blood-red beards. **Velupputadi** ("white beard") represents Hanuman, monkey son of the wind god and personal servant of Rama. He always wears a grey beard and furry coat, and has a black and red face and green nose. **Karupputadi** ("black beard") is a hunter or forest-dweller and carries a sword, bow and quiver. He has a coal-black face with a white flower on his nose. **Kari** ("black") characters, the ogresses and witches of the drama, have black faces, marked with white patterns, and huge breasts. **Minnukku** ("softly shaded") characters are women, Brahmins and sages. The women have pale yellow faces sprinkled with mica and the men wear orange *dhotis*.

Once the make-up is finished, the performers are helped into their costumes – elaborate wide skirts tied to the waist, towering headdresses and long silver talons fitted to the left hand. Women, Brahmins and sages are the only characters with a different style of dress: men wear orange, and the women wear saris and cover their heads. The transformation is completed with a final prayer before the performance begins.

Visitors new to *kathakali* may get bored during such long programmes, parts of which are very slow indeed. If you're at a village performance, you may not always find accommodation, so you can't leave during the night. Be prepared to sit on the ground for hours, and bring warm clothes. Half the fun is staying up all night to witness, just as the dawn light appears, the gruesome disembowelling of a villain or a demon *asura*.

For more on *kathakali*, see the *Playing gods* colour section.

## Kudiyattam

Three families of the Chakyar caste and a few outsiders perform the Sanskrit drama **kudiyattam**, the oldest continually performed theatre form in the world. Until recently, it was only staged inside temples, and then only in front of the uppermost castes. Visually, it is very similar to its offspring, *kathakali*, but its atmosphere is infinitely more archaic. The actors, eloquent in sign language and symbolic movement, speak in the bizarre, compelling intonation of the local Brahmins' Vedic chant, unchanged for more than two millennia.

A single act of a *kudiyattam* play can require ten full nights; the entire play forty. A great actor, in full command of the subtleties of gestural expression, can take half an hour to do such a simple thing as murder a demon, berate the audience, or simply describe a leaf falling to the ground. Unlike *kathakali*, *kudiyattam* includes comic characters and plays. The ubiquitous Vidushaka, narrator and clown, is something of a court jester, and traditionally has held the right to openly criticize the highest in the land without fear of retribution.

To the uninitiated, the costumes look like pared-down versions of those worn in *kathakali*, with mask-like make-up featuring rice-paper borders, heavy jewellery and pleated white skirts of starched fabric. Versions of just such outfits, including heavy gold headdresses, appear in ancient Indian murals, decorating the rock-cut caves of Ajanta in Maharashtra.

The ideal place to watch *kudiyattam* is at one of the purpose-built **kuttambalam** theatres in Keralan temples – beautiful works of art in their own right, with carved panels and lathe-turned wooden pillars. Entrance to them is often restricted to Hindus, but during festivals at major shrines in towns such as Thrissur, Irinjalakuda and Guruvayur non-Hindus may be allowed in during festivals (you'll increase your chances of admission if you're dressed correctly, in a white *mundu* or sari). Otherwise, you can always catch authentic performances by some of Kerala's top actors at the Margi School in Thiruvananthapuram (see p.89), which stages monthly shows. The Natana Kairali centre at Irinjalakuda (see p.202) also holds an annual *kudiyattam* festival in the first fortnight of January.

For real aficionados, nothing beats the 41-day ritual cycle of **Chakyar koothu**, a solo form of *kudiyattam*, staged in September and October in Thrissur's Vaddukannathan temple. While men and women percussionists of the Nambiyar caste create complex rhythms on the *elathalam* (cymbals) and the *mizhavu*, a large copper drum, the Chakyar stands on a platform wearing special headgear, starched white cloths bound around the waist and distinctive clown-like make-up. *Koothu* means "dance", but this is a bit of a misnomer as there's little body movement involved; rather, facial and hand expressions convey the narrative, which usually follows one of the Hindu epics, but with lots of comic asides criticizing contemporary events and personalities. The greatest exponent of *koothu* was **Mani Madhava Chakyar** (1889–1990), a Sanskrit scholar and ritual artist from

Kozhikode district, who was especially renowned for his mastery of *rasa-abhinaya* (enacting sentiment through facial expression) and *netrabhinaya* (beautiful eye movements). His wife, **P.K. Kunjimalu**, was one of Kerala's greatest exponents of *nagiarama*, an all-female form of *kudiyattam* (unlike in *kathakali*, women, not men, play women's roles).

## Ottamthullal

**Ottamthullal** is another form of solo mime, but one that's performed in less rarefied atmosphere than Chakyar *koothu*. Often dubbed the "poor man's *kathakali*", it's commonly staged in temple courtyards during festivals, where it serves as a kind of ritualized stand-up comedy. From atop small raised platforms, actors sing, dance and recite simple rhythmic verses in Malayalam (rather than the stylized Sanskrit of Chakyar *koothu*), swaying to and fro, accentuating their story with hand and arm movements. *Thullal* compositions were usually based on well-known Puranic stories, only incorporating asides that satirized local rulers, courtiers, Namboodiri-Brahmins and other prominent people. The costumes can be wonderfully elaborate, featuring gilded, mirror-inlaid crowns and breastplates with woollen tassels and matching epaulettes, colourful starched and pleated skirts, and striking face make-up.

The man credited with inventing the form was **Kunchan Nambiar** (1705–70), an eighteenth-century actor-poet who is said to have fallen asleep during a long performance of Chakyar *koothu* and dreamed of a simplified, more accessible (and humorous) version.

## Theyyem

The most visually exciting of all Kerala's ritual arts is a form of spirit possession practised in villages in the far north of Kerala around Kannur (Cannanore). Its name – **theyyem** (aka *theyyam* or *theyattam*) – derives from the Malayalam word for god, *deivam*. Unlike in *kathakali* and *kudiyattam*, where actors impersonate goddesses or gods, or characters from mythology, here the performers actually become the deity being invoked, acquiring their magical powers for the duration of the ceremony. These allow them to perform superhuman feats, such as rolling in hot ashes, remaining impervious to flames (while dressed in highly flammable palm-leaf cloaks), or dancing with a crown that rises to the height of a coconut tree. By watching the *theyyem* enact legends associated with his or her life, members of the audience believe they can partake of the magical powers – to cure illness, conceive a child or get lucky in a business venture.

Traditionally staged in small clearings (*kaavus*) attached to village shrines, *theyyem* rituals are always performed by members of the lowest castes; Namboodiri and other high-caste people may attend, but they do so to venerate the deity – a unique inversion of the normal social hierarchy. Each *theyyem* has its own distinctive **costume**, made of elaborate jewellery, body paints, intricate face make-up and, above all, gigantic headdresses (*mudi*) weighing many kilos.

Performances generally have three distinct phases: the *thottam*, where the dancer, wearing a small red headdress, recites a simple devotional song accompanied by the temple musicians; the *vellattam*, in which he runs through a series of more complicated rituals and slower, elegant poses; and the *mukhathezhuttu*, the main event, when he appears in full costume in front of the shrine. From this point until the end of the performance, which may last all night, the *theyyem* is manifest and empowered, dancing around the arena in graceful, rhythmic steps that grow quicker and more energetic as the night progresses, culminating in a frenzied outburst just before dawn, when the dancer may well be struck by a kind of spasm. The complicated series of moves takes up to a decade of training to acquire. From the age of 8 or 9, boys follow courses of *kalarippayat*, Kerala's martial art (see p.89), to build up the necessary strength. Performances are also usually preceded by a period of rigorous fasting.

Four hundred or more different forms of *theyyem* exist in the hinterland of Kannur. Most are manifestations of the Mother Goddess (Mahadeva) such as Bhadrakali or Bhagawati; others are spirit folk heroes and legendary characters from the epics. These days, they may be held for a family celebration or temple feast. But with each passing year, as younger generations of *theyyem* families move away from home or take up wage labour, performances are getting rarer and many of the *theyyems* danced a couple of decades ago have died out. The box, p.251 gives pointers that will help you track down the rituals around Kannur; see also the *Playing gods* colour insert.

Further south from Kannur, the area between Ernakulam and Kottayam in central Kerala is the heartland of another kind of Tantric ritual theatre form whose roots, like those of *theyyem*, stretch back to Dravidian times. **Mutiyettu** is based on re-enactments of mythic combats between the goddess Bhadrakali and the demon Darika. Again, they feature dazzling headdresses, costumes, and make-up, and usually a larger cast of performers than *theyyem*. Another interesting aspect of the rituals is that they're preceded by the making of large *kalam ezhuttu* powder paintings, which the actors later destroy by dancing over them.

## Puppetry

Traditional **shadow puppetry**, or *tholpabavakoothu*, is a dying art form based in the Palakkad district of central Kerala, where it is staged in temples. The deerskin puppets, representing over 130 different divine and mythological characters, are manipulated against a large, 12m-long screen of white cotton, back-lit by as many as 21 oil lamps. Musical accompaniment comes from *chenda* drums, with occasional blasts from a conch, whistle or pipe. Performances typically span a continuous period of between twelve and twenty-one nights and tell the story of the Ramayana, from the birth of Rama to his coronation – ostensibly for the benefit of the goddess Bhadrakali, who is believed to have missed Rama's big tussle with the demon Ravava because she was herself grappling with another devil, Darika. Bhadrakali's presence is symbolized by cloth drapes, removed from her shrine and suspended within view of the puppets.

The Natana Kairali centre in Irinjalakuda (see p.201) is the best place to watch Keralan **glove puppetry**, or *pavakathakali*. Its director, Gopal Venu, is one of the form's finest exponents. Like *tholpabavakoothu*, however, its traditional heartland is Palakkad district, where it is thought to have been introduced in the eighteenth century by itinerant puppeteers from Andhra Pradesh. Stories from the Mahabharata, Ramayana and Puranas provide the narratives for shows, which resemble *kudiyattam* and *kathakali* recitals in miniature: the puppets, carved from wood and decorated with gilded, jewel-inlaid headdresses, colourfully painted faces and elaborate cloth costumes, appear from behind an appliqué curtain, illuminated by flames from a sacred *nilavilakku* oil lamp. Only one sculptor, Ravi Gopalan Nair from Nedumangad near Thiruvananthapuram, still makes traditional *pavakathakali* puppets.

# Wildlife

A fast-growing population and the rapid spread of industries have inflicted pressures on the rural landscape of Kerala, but the region still supports a wealth of distinct flora and fauna. Walking on less frequented beaches or through the rice fields of the coastal plain, you'll encounter dozens of exotic birds, while the hill country of the interior supports an amazing variety of plants and trees. The majority of the peninsula's larger mammals keep to the dense woodland of the Western Ghat mountains, where a cluster of reserves affords them some protection from the hunters and loggers who have wrought such havoc on India's fragile forest regions over the past few decades.

# Flora

Something like 3500 species of flowering plants have been identified in Kerala, as well as countless lower orders of grasses, ferns and brackens. In the Western Ghats, it is common to find one hundred or more different types of tree in an area of just one hectare. Many species were introduced from Europe, South America, Southeast Asia and Australia, but there are also many indigenous varieties that thrive in the moist climate.

Along the coast, rice paddy and **coconut** plantations predominate, forming a near-continuous band of lush foliage. Spiky **spinifex** helps bind the shifting dunes behind the sandy beaches lining the coast, while **casuarina** trees stand as windbreaks where coconut palms have been felled.

In towns and villages, you'll encounter dozens of beautiful **flowering trees**. The Indian **laburnum**, or cassia, throws out masses of yellow flowers and long seed pods in late February before the monsoons. This is also the period when mango and Indian **coral trees** are in full bloom; both produce bundles of stunning red flowers.

One of the region's most distinctive trees, found in both coastal and hill areas, is the stately **banyan**, which propagates by sending out roots from its lower branches. The largest specimens spread out over an area of 200m. The banyan is revered by Hindus, and you'll often find small shrines at the foot of mature trees. The same is true of the **peepal**, which has distinctive spatula-shaped leaves. Temple courtyards often enclose large peepals, which usually have strips of auspicious red cloth hanging from their lower branches.

The Western Ghats harbour a wealth of flora, from flowering trees and plants to ferns and fungi. **Shola** forests, lush patches of moist evergreen woodland which carpet the deeper mountain valleys, exhibit some of the greatest biodiversity. Sheltered by a leafy canopy, which may rise to a height of 20m or more, buttressed roots and giant trunks tower above a luxuriant undergrowth of brambles, creepers and bracken, interspersed with brakes of bamboo. Common tree species include the kadam, sisso or martel, kharanj and teak, while rarer sandalwood thrives on the higher, drier plateaux in the mountains above Munnar. There are dozens of representatives of the fig family, too, as well as innumerable (and ecologically destructive) eucalyptus and rubber trees, planted as cash crops.

# Mammals

Although peninsular India boasts more than fifty species of wild mammals, visitors who stick to populated coastal areas are unlikely to spot anything more inspiring than a monkey or the occasional mongoose. Most of the larger animals have been hunted to the point of extinction; the few that remain roam the dense woodland lining the Western Ghats, in the sparsely populated forest zones of the **Nilgiri Biosphere Reserve**.

The largest Indian land mammal is, of course, the Asian **elephant**, stockier and with much smaller ears than its African cousin, though no less venerable. Travelling around Kerala, you'll regularly see elephants in temples and festivals, but for a glimpse of one in the wild, you'll have to venture into the mountains where, in spite of the huge reduction of their natural habitat, around 6500 still survive. Among the best places for sightings are Periyar (see p.153) and the twin reserves comprising the Wayanad Wildlife Sanctuary (see p.235). Today, wild elephants, which are included under the Endangered Species Protection Act, are under increasing threat from villagers: each adult animal eats roughly 200kg of vegetation and drinks 100l of water a day, and their search for sustenance inevitably brings them into conflict with rural communities.

Across the state, especially in the hill districts, local villagers displaced by wildlife reserves have often been responsible for the poaching that has reduced **tiger** populations to such fragile levels. These days, sightings in Kerala are very rare indeed, though several kinds of big cat survive. Among the most beautiful is the **leopard**, or panther (*Panthera panthus*). Prowling the thick forests of the Ghats, these elusive cats prey on monkeys and deer, and occasionally take domestic cattle and dogs from the fringes of villages. Their distinctive black spots make them notoriously difficult to see among the tropical foliage, although their mating call (reminiscent of a saw on wood) regularly pierces the night air in remote areas. The **leopard cat** (*Felis bengalensis*) is a miniature version of its namesake, and more common. Sporting a bushy tail and round spots on soft buff or grey fur, it is about the same size as a domestic cat and lives around villages, picking off chickens, birds and small mammals. Another cat with a penchant for poultry, and one which villagers occasionally keep as a pet if they can capture one, is the docile Indian **civet** (*Viverricual indica*), recognizable by its lithe body, striped tail, short legs and long pointed muzzle.

Wild cats share their territory with a range of other mammals unique to the Subcontinent. One you've a reasonable chance of seeing is the **gaur**, or Indian bison (*Bos gaurus*). These primeval-looking beasts, with their distinctive sleek black skin and knee-length white "socks", forage around bamboo thickets and shady woods. The bulls are particularly impressive, growing to an awesome height of 2m, with heavy curved horns and prominent humps.

With its long fur and white V-shaped "bib", the scruffy **sloth bear** (*Melursus ursinus*) – whose Tamil name (*bhalu*) inspired that of Rudyard Kipling's character Baloo in *The Jungle Book* – ranks among the weirder-looking inhabitants of the region's forests. Sadly, it's also very rare, thanks to its predilection for raiding sugar-cane plantations, which has brought it, like the elephant, into direct conflict with man. Sloth bears can occasionally be seen shuffling along woodland trails, but you're more likely to come across evidence of their foraging activities: trashed termite mounds and chewed-up ants' nests. The same is true of both the portly Indian **porcupine** (*Hystrix indica*), or *sal*, which you see a lot less often than the mounds of earth it digs up to get at insects and cashew or teak seedlings; and the **pangolin** (*Manis crassicaudata*), or *tiryo*, a kind of armour-plated anteater whose hard, grey overlapping scales protect it from predators.

Full-moon nights and the twilight hours of dusk and dawn are the times to look out for nocturnal animals such as the **slender loris** (*Loris tardigradus*). This shy creature, a distant cousin of the lemur, with bulging round eyes, furry body and pencil-thin limbs, grows to around 20cm in length and moves as if in slow motion, except when an insect flits to within striking distance. The **mongoose** *(Herpestes edwardsi)* is another animal sometimes kept as a pet to keep dwellings free of scorpions, mice, rats and other vermin. It will also readily take on snakes – you might see one writhing in a cloud of dust with king cobras during performances by snake-charmers. Late evening is also the best time for spotting **bats**. Kerala has four species, including the fulvous fruit bat (*Rousettus leshenaulti*), or *vagul* – so called because it gives off a scent resembling fermenting fruit juice; Dormer's bat (*Pipistrellus dormeri*); the very rare rufous horseshoe bat (*Rhinolophus rouxi*); and the Malay fox vampire bat (*Magaderma spasma*), which feeds off the blood of live cattle. **Flying foxes** (*Pteropus gigantus*), the largest of India's bats, are also present in healthy numbers. With a wingspan of more than 1m, they fly in cacophonous groups to feed in fruit orchards, sometimes falling foul of electricity cables on the way: frazzled flying foxes dangling from live cables are a common sight in the interior.

Other species to look out for in forest areas are the Indian **giant squirrel** (*Ratufa indica*), or *shenkaro*, which has a coat of black fur and red-orange lower parts. Two-and-a-half times larger than its European cousins, it lives in the canopy, leaping up to 20m between branches. The much smaller **three-striped squirrel** (*Funambulus palmarum*), or *khadi khar*, recognizable by the three black markings down its back, is also found in woodland. The five-striped **palm squirrel** (*Funambulus pennanti*) is a common sight all over the state, especially in municipal parks and villages.

Forest clearings and areas of open grassland are grazed by four species of deer. Widely regarded as the most beautiful is the **cheetal** (*Axis axis*), or spotted axis deer, which congregates in large groups around water holes and salt licks, occasionally wandering into villages to seek shelter from its predators. The plainer, buff-coloured **sambar** (*Cervus unicolor*) is also common, despite being affected by diseases spread by domestic cattle during the 1970s and 1980s. Two types of deer you're less likely to come across, but which also inhabit the border forests, are the **barking deer** (*Muntiacus muntjak*), whose call closely resembles that of a domestic dog, and the timid **mouse deer** (*Tragulus meminna*), a speckled-grey member of the *Tragulidae* family that is India's smallest deer, growing to a mere 30cm in height. Both of these are highly secretive and nocturnal; they are also the preferred snack of Kerala's smaller predators: the **striped hyena** (*Hyaena hyaena*), or *colo*, and **wild dog** (*Cuon alpinus*), which hunt in packs, and the more solitary **jackal** (*Canis aureus*).

A species of mountain goat endemic to the Western Ghats, whose last stronghold is the grassy uplands surrounding the tea-plantation town of Munnar in central Kerala (see p.213), is the delightful **Nilgiri tahr**. The tahr's famously inquisitive nature made it an easy target for hunters in colonial times: sportsmen could shoot them for supper without leaving their fireside chairs in camp. Numbers had plummeted by the 1940s, but are on the rise again thanks to the strict protection they're accorded in the Eravikulam National Park, just outside Munnar, where herds of tahr congregate a stone's throw from the main car park.

Long-beaked **dolphins** are regular visitors to the shallow waters of Kerala's more secluded bays and beaches. They are traditionally regarded as a pest by local villagers, who believe they eat scarce stocks of fish. However, this long-standing antipathy is gradually being eroded as local people realize the tourist-pulling potential of the dolphins.

Finally, no rundown of Keralan mammals would be complete without some mention of **monkeys**. The most common species is the mangy pink-bottomed **macaque** (*Macaca mulatta*), or *makad*, which hangs out anywhere scraps may be scavenged or snatched from unwary humans: temples and picnic spots are good places to watch them in action. The black-faced Hanuman **langur**, by contrast, is less audacious, retreating to the trees if threatened. It is much larger than the macaque, with pale grey fur and long limbs and tail. In forest areas, the langur's distinctive call is an effective early-warning system against big cats and other predators, which is why you often come across herds of cheetal grazing under trees inhabited by large colonies of langurs. Kerala is one of the last strongholds of the rare **lion-tailed macaque**. Only a few hundred of these distinctive primates survive in their native habitat of southwestern India, and the population in Kerala's parks is the most robust. Distinguished by their corona-style mane of blonde fur and amber-coloured eyes, lion-tailed macaques, sometimes called "wanderoos", have traditionally been hunted for their meat and fur by the indigenous tribes of the Western Ghats.

# Reptiles

**Reptiles** are well represented in the region, with more than forty species of snakes, lizards, turtles and crocodiles recorded. The best places to spot them are open, cultivated areas: paddy fields and village ponds provide abundant fresh water, nesting sites and prey (frogs, insects and small birds). Your hotel room, however, is where you are most likely to come across tropical India's most common reptile, the **gecko** (*Hemidactylus*), which clings to walls and ceilings with its widely splayed toes. Deceptively static most of the time, these small yellow-brown lizards will dash at lightning speed if you try to catch one, or if an unwary mosquito or fly scuttles within striking distance. The rarer **chameleon** (*Chamaeleonidae*) is more elusive, mainly because its constantly changing camouflage makes it virtually impossible to spot. They'll have no problem seeing you, though: independently moving eyes allow them to pinpoint approaching predators, while prey is slurped up with their fast-moving 40cm-long tongues. The other main lizard to look out for is the **Bengal monitor** (*Varanus bengalensis*). This giant brown-speckled reptile looks like it has escaped from *Jurassic Park*, growing to well over 1m in length. It used to be a common sight in coastal areas, basking on roads and rocks. However, monitors are often killed and eaten by villagers, and have become increasingly rare.

The monsoon period is when you're most likely to encounter **turtles**. Two varieties paddle around village ponds and wells while water is plentiful: the flap-shell (*Lissemys punctata*) and black-pond (*Melanochelys trijuga*) turtles, neither of which are endangered. Numbers of Olive Ridley marine turtles (*Lepidochely olivacea*), by contrast, have plummeted over the past few decades as a result of villagers raiding their nests when they crawl onto the beach to lay their eggs. This amazing natural spectacle occurs each year at a number of beaches in the region, notably Kolavippalam, near Kanhangad in the far north of the state.

An equally rare sight nowadays is the **crocodile** (*Crocodylidae*). Populations have dropped almost to the point of extinction, although the backwaters support vestigial colonies of saltwater crocs, which bask on mud flats and river rocks. Dubbed "salties", they occasionally take calves and goats, and will snap at the odd human if given half a chance. The more ominously named mugger crocodile, however, is harmless, inhabiting unfrequented freshwater streams and riversides.

## Snakes

Twenty-three species of snake are found in Kerala, ranging from the gigantic **Indian python** (*Python molurus*, or *har* in Konkani), a forest-dwelling constrictor that grows up to 6m in length, to the innocuous worm snake (*Typhlops braminus*), or *sulva*, which is tiny, completely blind and often mistaken for an earthworm.

The eight **venomous snakes** in the region include India's four most deadly species: the cobra, the krait, Russell's viper and the saw-scaled viper. Though these are relatively common in coastal and cultivated areas, even the most aggressive snake will slither off at the first sign of an approaching human. Nevertheless, 10,000 Indians die from snake bites each year, and if you cut across paddy fields or plan to do any hiking, it makes sense to familiarize yourself with the following four or five species, just in case; their bites nearly always prove fatal if not treated immediately with anti-venom serum – available at most clinics and hospitals.

Present in most parts of the state and an important character in Hindu mythology, the **Indian cobra** (*Naja naja*), or *naga*, is the most common of the venomous species. Wheat-brown or grey in colour, it is famed for the "hood" it unfurls when confronted and whose rear side usually bears the snake's characteristic spectacle markings. Its big brother, the **king cobra** *(Naja hannah)*, or *naga raja*, is rarely encountered. Inhabiting the remote forest regions along the Kerala–Karnataka border, this beautiful brown, yellow and black snake, which grows to a length of 4m or more, is very rare, although the itinerant snake-charmers who perform in markets occasionally keep one. Defanged, they rear up and "dance" when provoked by the handler, or are set against mongooses in ferocious (and often fatal) fights. The king cobra is also the only snake in the world known to make its own nest.

Distinguished by their steel-blue colour and faint white cross markings, **kraits** (*Bungarus coerulus*) are twice as deadly as the Indian cobra: even the bite of a newly hatched youngster is lethal. **Russell's viper** (*Vipera russelli*) is another one to watch out for. Identifiable by the three bands of elliptical markings that extend down its brown body, the Russell's hisses at its victims before darting at them and burying its centimetre-long fangs into their flesh. The other common venomous snake is the **saw-scaled viper** (*Echis carinatus*). Grey with an arrow-shaped mark on its triangular head, it hangs around in the cracks between stone walls, feeding on scorpions, lizards, frogs, rodents and smaller snakes. It also hisses when threatened, producing the sound by rubbing together serrated scales located on the side of its head. Finally, **sea snakes** (*Enhdrina schistosa*) are common in coastal areas and potentially deadly (with a bite said to be twenty times more venomous than a cobra's), although rarely encountered by swimmers, as they lurk only in deep water off the shore.

Harmless snakes are far more numerous than their killer cousins and frequently more attractive. The beautiful **golden tree snake** (*Chrysopelea ormata*), for example, sports an intricate geometric pattern of red, yellow and black markings, while the **green whip snake** (*Dryhopis nasutus*), or *sarpatol*, is a stunning parakeet-green. The ubiquitous **Indian rat snake**, often mistaken for a cobra, also has beautiful markings, although it leaves behind a foul stench of decomposing flesh. Other common non-venomous snakes include the wolf snake (*Lycodon aulicus*), or *kaidya*; the Russell sand boa (*Eryx conicus*), or *malun*; the kukri snake (*Oligodon taeniolatus*), or *pasko*; and the cat snake (*Boiga trigonata*), or *manjra*.

# Birds

You don't have to be an aficionado to enjoy Kerala's abundant **birdlife**. Breathtakingly beautiful birds regularly flash between the branches of trees or appear on overhead wires at the roadside. Three common species of **kingfisher** frequently crop up in the paddy fields and wetlands of the coastal plains, where they feed on small fish and tadpoles. With its enormous bill and pale green-blue wing feathers, the stork-billed kingfisher (*Perargopis capensis*) is the largest and most distinctive member of the family, although the white-throated kingfisher (*Halcyon smyrnensis*) – which has iridescent turquoise plumage and a coral-red bill – and the common kingfisher (*Alcedo althis*), identical to the one frequently spotted in northern Europe, are more alluring.

Other common and brightly coloured species include the green, blue and yellow **bee-eaters** (*Merops*), the stunning **golden oriole** (*Oriolus oriolus*), and the **Indian roller** (*Coracias bengalensis*), famous for its brilliant blue flight feathers and exuberant aerobatic mating displays. **Hoopoes** (*Upupa epops*), recognizable by their elegant black-and-white tipped crests, fawn plumage and distinctive "*hoo…po… po*" call, also flit around fields and villages, as do **purple sunbirds** (*Nectarina asiatica*) and several kinds of **bulbuls**, **babblers** and **drongos** (*Dicrurus*), including the fork-tailed **black drongo** (*Dicrurus macrocercus*) – which can often be seen perched on telegraph wires. If you're lucky, you may also glimpse the **Asian paradise flycatcher** (*Tersiphone paradisi*), which is widespread and among the region's most exquisite birds: males more than four years old sport a thick black crest and long silver white streamers, while the more often-seen females and young males are reddish-brown.

Paddy fields, ponds and saline mudflats usually teem with water birds. The most ubiquitous is the snowy white **cattle egret** (*Bubulcus ibis*), which can usually be seen wherever there are cows and buffalo, feeding off the grubs, insects and other parasites that live on them. The **great egret** (*Casmerodius albus*) is also pure white, although lankier and with a long yellow bill, while the **little egret** (*Egretta garzetta*) sports a short black bill. Look out too for the mud-brown Indian pond heron, or "**paddy bird**", India's most common heron. Distinguished by its pale green legs, speckled breast and hunched posture, it stands motionless for hours in water, waiting for fish or frogs.

The hunting technique of the beautiful **white-bellied sea eagle** (*Haliaetus leucogaster*), by contrast, is truly spectacular. Cruising 20 to 30m above the surface of the water, this black-and-white osprey stoops at high speed to snatch its prey – usually sea snakes and mackerel – from the waves with its fierce yellow talons. More common birds of prey such as the **brahminy kite** (*Haliastur indus*), identifiable by its white breast and chestnut head markings, and the **black kite** (*Milvus migrans*), a dark-brown bird with a fork tail, are widespread around towns and fishing villages, where they vie with raucous gangs of house **crows** (*Corvus splendens*) for scraps.

Other birds of prey to keep an eye open for, especially around open farmland, are the **white-eyed buzzard** (*Butastur teesa*), the **oriental honey buzzard** (*Pernis ptilorhyncus*), the **black-shouldered kite** (*Elanus caeruleus*) – famous for its blood-red eyes – and the **shikra** (*Accipiter badius*), which closely resembles the European sparrowhawk.

## Forest birds

The region's forests may have lost many of their larger animals, but they still offer exciting possibilities for birdwatchers. One species every enthusiast hopes to glimpse while in the woods is the magnificent **hornbill**. The Malabar grey hornbill (*Ocyceros griseus*), with its blue-brown plumage and long curved beak, is the most common, although the Indian pied hornbill (*Anthracoceros malabaricus*), distinguished by its white wing and tail tips and the pale patch on its face, often flies into villages in search of fruit and lizards. The magnificent great hornbill (*Buceros bicornis*), however, is more elusive, limited to the most dense forest areas, where it may occasionally be spotted flitting through the canopy. Growing to 130cm in length, it has a black-and-white striped body and wings, and a huge yellow beak with a long curved casque on top.

Several species of **woodpecker** also inhabit the interior forests, among them three types of flameback woodpecker: the common black-rumped flameback (*Dinopium bengalense*) has a wide range and also ventures into gardens and hotel

## Keralan wildlife sanctuaries and national parks

Kerala holds fourteen reserves set aside for the protection of wildlife, covering a little under five percent of the state's total surface area. Most are up in the Western Ghat range, which preserves the highest concentrations of biodiversity anywhere in peninsular India. The following are the best.

**Chinnar Wildlife Sanctuary** 58km from Munnar in the depths of the mountains. This reserve is much drier than neighbouring Eravikulam, but is a birding hot spot, with 225 species listed. It also hosts an enigmatic white bison. Best time to visit: Oct–March. See p.220.

**Eravikulam National Park** 13km northeast of Munnar, amid south India's highest peaks. Famous for its thriving population of Nilgiri tahr. Your best sightings will be on longer treks. Best time to visit: Nov–April. See p.220.

**Kumarakom Bird Sanctuary** On the eastern shores of Vembanad Lake, between Kottayam and Alappuzha, in the heart of the backwaters district of southern Kerala. Tourism has badly disrupted the peace and quiet of this famous reserve, but it's still a good site for spotting migrant birds during the winter. Best time to visit: Nov–March. See p.149.

**Parambikulam Wildlife Sanctuary**. This hidden valley, high on the Tamil Nadu–Kerala border above Palakkad, holds a stupendous list of species, and an equally impressive conservation management policy. Accommodation is provided in tents, treehouses and jungle camps. See p.211.

**Peppara Wildlife Sanctuary**. Amid the hills inland from Thiruvananthapuram, and the least rewarding of the state's nature reserves, though it does still hold breeding populations of lion-tailed macaques, as well as wild elephants. Best time to visit: Jan–April. See p.111.

**Periyar Wildlife Sanctuary**. A former maharaja's hunting reserve, centred on an artificial lake high in the Cardamom Hills. Occasional tiger sightings, but you're much more likely to spot an elephant. Well placed for trips into the mountains and tea plantations, with good accommodation, including remote jungle lodges which you have to trek to, though it's rather become a victim of its own popularity of late. Best time to visit: Oct–March. See p.153.

**Thattekkad Bird Sanctuary**. Kerala's top bird reserve, easily reachable between Munnar and Kochi. Spread along the banks of the Periyar River, its 25 square kilometres host 275 species, the majority of them endemics. Best time to visit: Nov–March. See p.192.

**Wayanad Wildlife Sanctuary**. Split into two separate reserves – Muthanga and Tholpetty – Wayanad encompasses some of the finest scenery in southern India, as well as Kerala's most imaginatively constructed eco-resorts. Most of the large fauna of the Western Ghats, and an amazing wealth of plant life, can be seen here – though tiger sightings are extremely rare. Best time to visit: Nov–March. See p.235.

grounds. A bird whose call is a regular feature of the Western Ghat forests, though you'll be lucky to catch a glimpse of one, is the wild ancestor of the domestic chicken – the **jungle fowl**. The grey or Sommerat's jungle fowl (*Gallus sonneratii*) has dark plumage scattered with yellow spots and streaks.

# Wildlife viewing

Although you can expect to come across many of the species listed above on the edge of towns and villages, a spell in one of Kerala's nature reserves (see p.307) offers the best chance of viewing wild animals and birds. These reserves are a far cry from the well-organized and well-maintained national parks you may be used to at home, although at the larger and more easily accessible wildlife reserves – such as Periyar and Eravikulam – a solid infrastructure exists to transport visitors around, whether by jeep or, in the case of the former, boat and bamboo rafts. Don't, however, expect to see much if you stick to these standard excursion vehicles laid on by the park authorities. Most of the rarer animals keep well away from noisy groups of trippers. Wherever possible, try to organize **walking safaris** with a reliable, approved guide in the forest. In Periyar, guides are recruited from the area's indigenous minorities – formerly responsible for most of the region's poaching – and possess a wealth of local knowledge.

# Books

For a region with such a long history of literacy and colonial rule, surprisingly few books have been written about Kerala in English. This neglect may well be reversed as the state's tourist boom gathers momentum, but in the meantime, most titles are either lavish coffee-table tomes with little substance or dry academic studies on economics, politics and the anthropology of sacred arts.

The titles listed below aim to appeal to a broader readership. While some are stocked by high-street bookshops in Western countries, those published in India tend only to be available in Kerala itself, or via online retailers. If you can wait until you get to Kochi, the wonderful **Idiom Bookshop** in Fort Cochin (see p.187) holds the best selection of literature on Kerala assembled in any one place – and at much lower prices than you'll pay for the same back home. Titles marked 🏃 are particularly recommended.

## History and travel

**Eric Axelson** *Vasco da Gama: the Diary of his Travels through African Waters 1497–1499*. An anonymous first-hand account of da Gama's voyage to Calicut, written by one of his crew, which was rediscovered in the nineteenth century after lying forgotten in the library of a Portuguese convent. It's framed by a detailed introduction by Axelson outlining the efforts of other explorers and mariners to reach India.

**Alexander Frater** *Chasing the Monsoon*. Frater's wet-season jaunt down the Malabar coast and across the Ganges plains took him through an India of muddy puddles and grey skies: an evocative account of the country as few visitors see it, and now something of a classic of the genre.

🏃 **John Keay** *India: a History*. In this, the most recent of his five consistently excellent books on India, Keay manages to coax a clear, impartial and highly readable narrative from five thousand years of fragmented events. The best single-volume history of India currently in print, though it focuses more on the north than the south.

**John Keay** *The Honourable East India Company*. In characteristically fluent style, Keay strikes the right balance between commentators who regard the East India Company as a rapacious institution with malevolent intentions, and those who present its acquisition of the Indian empire as an unintended, almost accidental process.

**William Logan** *Malabar Manual Vols I&II* (Asian Educational Services, India). Logan was the last British Collector of the Malabar, and his rambling account of the region under his charge, originally published in 1887, still serves as its major reference book. It's packed full of history, ethnography and background on religion and tradition that's still relevant today. Widely available in bookshops locally, but expensive abroad it comes in two hardback volumes.

**Tim Severin** *The Sinbad Voyage*. In 1979, mariner-historian Tim Severin recruited a team of master boat-builders from Beypore, near Calicut in north Kerala, then took them and a hold of Malabari timber across the Arabian Sea to Muscat. There they built a traditional Arab dhow and sailed it to China via India, recreating Sinbad's legendary voyage. You can't fail to be amazed by the skills of both the shipwrights and sailors described in this page-turner of a travelogue, which provides a riveting, fine-grain insight into the medieval maritime traditions that have shaped the modern day.

**A. Sreedhara Menon** *A Survey of Keralan History* (S. Viswanathan, India). A comprehensive survey of the region's past – from Prehistoric times to the present day – by Kerala's best-known historian. While much of it comprises dry, bare-bone lists of dynastic rulers and their achievements, Sreedhara Menon also draws on cultural, economic and social history. Not the easiest of reads, but the best general introduction currently available.

**Stark World** *Kerala* (Stark World, India). Not a pebble in the state is left unturned in this unbelievably thorough, 820-page guide. It's the size of a New York telephone directory and weighs far too much to be of practical use on holiday, but serves as an excellent reference guide, and is generously illustrated with top-quality colour photos.

**Sanjay Subrahmanyam** *The Career and Legend of Vasco da Gama*. Erudite biography of the great fifteenth-century Portuguese explorer, based on a mass of published and unpublished sources in Portuguese and other languages, which gets behind the self-made myth of da Gama. As well as putting his achievements in context, it provides a compelling account of the voyages themselves, including the violent episodes on the Malabar.

## Photography

🏃 **Raghubir Singh** *Kerala*. This wide-ranging selection of 87 colour images by India's most acclaimed photographer gives a rounded and vivid portrait of the state in the mid-1980s. Singh's genius lay in his ability to spot the telling detail amid swirls of Indian life; there are plenty of quirky moments here, as well as sumptuous set pieces from his famous National Geographic commission, when he turned his eye on Thrissur Puram and snake boat races to dramatic effect.

🏃 **Jonathan Watts & Laurent Aubert** *Kerala: Of Gods and Men* (Five Continents, Italy). A superb study of Kerala's sacred arts, assembled over five years of ethnographic trips to temples, village shrines and festivals across the state. Watts' colour images capture with particular vividness the intensity of *theyyem* from making-up to midnight firebrand-swinging.

## Literature

🏃 **Anita Nair (ed)** *Where the Rain is Born*. An eclectic anthology of essays, short stories, poems and extracts from published works (both in English and Malayalam) about Kerala. Arundhati Roy, Salman Rushdie, William Dalrymple and Alexander Frater number among the foreign contributors, and a string of local authors recall childhood memories and reflect on the changing face of the modern state. The perfect introduction to Kerala and its many complexities.

🏃 **Arundhati Roy** *The God of Small Things*. Haunting Booker Prize-winning novel about a well-to-do Syrian-Christian family caught between the snobberies of high-caste tradition, a colonial past and the diverse personal histories of its members. Seen through the eyes of two children, the assortment of scenes from backwater life are as memorable as the characters themselves, while the comical and finally tragic turn of events says as much about Indian history as the refrain that became the novel's catch-phrase: "things can change in a day".

**Salman Rushdie** *The Moor's Last Sigh*. Rushdie's Whitbread Prize-winning novel is a typically spleen-ridden portrait of India's paradoxes, telling the life story of Moraes Zogoiby, aka

"Moor" – the only son of an aristocratic family who leads a life of depravity in Bombay before becoming embroiled in a financial scandal in London. Its early chapters, set in Cochin, give a delightfully lurid evocation of the ancient port city, with its mixed Jewish and Portuguese legacies.

## Society

**Achamma Chandersekaran (ed)** *Daughters of Kerala*. An anthology of 25 short stories by Keralan women, written in direct, accessible prose that brims with insights into what it's like to be female in contemporary Kerala.

**Edna Fernandes** *The Last Jews of Kerala*. An affectionate portrait of Kochi's vestigial Jewish community, focusing on indivdual survivors rather than bare-bones history. The book caused some controversy for its coverage of the hitherto taboo subject of the feud between the "White" and "Black" Jews.

**Nathan Katz & Ellen S. Goldberg** *Kashrut, Caste and Kabbalah: the Religious Life of the Jews of Cochin* (Monohar, India). This candid examination of Kochi's remaining Jewish population comes from two anthropologists who lived, ate and worshipped with the community. It stresses the extent to which "Indian-ness" and "Jewishness" intermingle in this fast-disappearing culture.

**Edward Luce** *In Spite of the Gods*. "An unsentimental evaluation of contemporary India" is how this book bills itself, and there's no more authoritative, penetrating account of the current state of the nation in print. Written by the *Financial Times'* former South Asia correspondent, it's packed with sobering statistics and myth-busting facts that challenge common misconceptions about India, while managing to remain eminently readable.

**Susan Visvanathan** *The Christians of Kerala: History, Belief and Ritual among the Yakoba*. A great contextualizer for anyone with an interest in Syrian-Orthodox Christianity, written by a community insider who nevertheless retains an objective eye.

## The arts and religion

**Stuart H. Blackburn** *Inside the Drama House: Rama Stories and Shadow Puppetry in south India*. The disappearing traditions of Palakkad district's Tamil shadow puppeteers, whose epic, month-long performances require almost as much skill and stamina as Rama needed to kill the demon Ravana – the subject of their shows.

**Albrecht Frenz & Krishna Kumar Marar** *Wall Paintings in North Kerala: 1000 Years of Temple Art*. Popular, readable and richly illustrated introduction to Kerala's forgotten Hindu murals – the benchmark book on the subject, though it only covers the north of the state.

**Kannur Tourism** *Theyyem Guide* (DTPC, India). This illustrated booklet, available from information counters around Kannur district, provides one of the most practical rundowns of *theyyem* in print, listing locations, dates and descriptions of the four hundred or so rituals still in existence.

**Ramu Katakam & Joginder Singh** *Glimpses of Architecture in Kerala* (Rupa & Co., India). Beautifully photographed introduction to the architecture of Kerala, including many images of temple interiors, palaces and aristocratic residences off-limits to visitors.

**Mohan Khokar** *Traditions of Indian Classical Dance* (Clarion Books, India). Detailing the religious and social roots of Indian dance, this lavishly illustrated book, with sections on regional traditions, is an excellent introduction to the subject.

**Parsram Mangharam** *Raja Ravi Varma: the Painter Prince* (Bangalore, India). Reproductions of 76 of the Keralan artist's most famous works, drawn from museums and private collections all over the country, with a biography that describes Varma's travels around India in engaging detail.

**George Michell** *The Hindu Temple*. The definitive primer, introducing the significance and architectural development of Hindu temples.

**Amina Okada & Martine Chemans** *Sacred Walls of Kerala* (India Research Press). The latest and most scholarly work on Kerala's unique temple murals.

**Phillip B. Zarrilli** *When the Body Becomes All Eyes*. This paperback's catchy strap line is "Paradigms, Discourses and Practices of Power in Kalarippayat, a south Indian Martial Art", which perfectly conveys its rather turgid academic style, but there's no better overview of *kalari* in all its arcane, bewildering complexity.

**Phillip B. Zarrilli** *Kathakali Dance Drama: Where Gods and Demons Play*. Dating from the early 1990s, this scholarly overview sets the form in its social and historical context before outlining its arcane principles and training procedures. Four plays – set pieces from the traditional repertory – are also translated (with stage directions), and there's a collection of essays on *kathakali* in the modern era. The best all-round source, though – much like the drama form itself – hard going in places.

## Wildlife and the environment

**P.V. Bole & Yogini Vaghini** *Field Guide to the Common Trees of India*. A handy-sized, indispensable tome for serious tree-spotters.

🏃 **Grimmet & Inskipp** *Birds of Southern India*. The birders' bible, a beautifully organized, written and illustrated 240-page field guide listing every species known in south India.

**Insight Guides** *Indian Wildlife*. An excellent all-round introduction to India's wildlife, with scores of superb colour photographs, features on different animals and habitats and a thorough bibliography.

**Kamierczak & Van Perlo** *A Field Guide to the Birds of the Indian Subcontinent* (Pica/Helm, UK). Less popular than Grimmet and Inskipp's competing guide, but just as thorough, expertly drawn and well laid out, with every species named.

**S. Prater** *The Book of Indian Animals*. The most comprehensive single-volume reference book on the subject, although only available in India.

**Romulus Whitaker** *Common Indian Snakes*. A detailed and illustrated guide to the Subcontinent's snakes, with all the Keralan species included.

## Yoga

**B.K.S. Iyengar** *Yoga: the Path to Holistic Health*. The definitive guide to yoga by the world's leading teacher, and the only book of its kind recommended by practitioners from across the yoga spectrum. Some 1900 colour photos illustrate step-by-step instructions on how to achieve the postures, and there's a copious introduction giving the philosophical background and history. Too heavy to cart around India with you, but indispensable as a reference tool. A lighter (and much less expensive) version – fully endorsed by the great man, though modelled and written by three of his senior pupils – is *Yoga: the Iyengar Way*, by Silva, Mira and Shyan Mehta.

# Language

# Language

# Language

M alayalam, the official state language of Kerala, is spoken by an estimated 37 million people worldwide. It is closely related to Tamil, from which it diverged around the fifth century AD, but boasts its own script, recently boiled down from a bewildering 900 characters to a more keyboard-friendly 51 – including 16 vowels. Reflecting the region's complex cultural history, lots of Romance, Hebrew, Arabic, Portuguese, Dutch and English words have their place in the Malayali lexicon, although only four English words – teak, catamaran, coir and copra – have travelled in the opposite direction. The first Malayalam-English dictionary was written in 1872, by the German missionary Herman–Gundert (grandfather of the novelist Herman Hesse).

India's official national language, **Hindi**, has a place in Kerala, too, largely thanks to the increasing number of settlers from the north of the country and the popularity of Bollywood movies. However, the language of higher education, law and the quality press is English, which is so prevalent in the resorts that you can easily get by without a word of Malayalam. Even fluent English speakers, though, will be flattered if you attempt a few words of their native tongue.

## Malayalam words and phrases

The lists of words and phrases below are intended as an aid to meeting people and travelling independently around more off-the-beaten-track areas of the state, where English is less commonly spoken.

### Meeting and greeting

| | | | |
|---|---|---|---|
| Hello | Namaskaram | Good morning | Suprabhaatham |
| Yes | Aa | Good night | Shubha raathri |
| No | Illa | How do you do | Sugamano |
| Thank you (informal) | Nanni | How are you? | Engane? |
| Thank you (formal) | Uppakaarm | Fine (formal) | Sukhamayiriknu |
| I'm sorry (quick courtesy) | Kshemikkoo | Fine (informal) | Kozhappam illa |
| | | My name is Sam | Ente peru Sam |
| I am sorry (formal apology) | Ennodu kshamikkoo | What is your name? (formal) | Entha ningalude peru perenthaa? |
| Goodbye | Veendum kaanaam | | |

### ZH

In English transliterations of Malayalam, the letters "zh" refer to a reflex consonant that sounds somewhere between a "d" and an "r", only pronounced in a distinctively South Asian way, beginning with a flick of your tongue from the roof of your mouth (rather than your teeth). Ask a Malayali to say the word "Alappuzha" and you'll get the idea.

| | | | |
|---|---|---|---|
| What is your name? (informal) | Entha ningalude perenthaa? (or just enthaperi?) | I don't speak Malayalam | Enikku malayalam samsaarikkan ariyilla |
| I'm from England/ the USA/Australia | Njaan England'il/ USA'il/Australia'il | Welcome | Swagatham |
| I don't understand | Mansillayilla | Sit down | Irikku |
| Do you speak English? | Ningal Inglishu samsarikkumo? | Bye | Pinakamanku |

## Getting around

| | | | |
|---|---|---|---|
| Stop | Nilkkoo | Train | Tren |
| Next stop | Adutha stop | Bus | Bus |
| Let's go | Namukku pkaam | Where does this train/bus go to? | Engottanu ee tren/bus pokunnathu? |
| I want to get out/ down here | Eniku ivide eranganam | Where is the train/ bus to Kochi? | Evide annu Kochikkulla tren/ bus? |
| How far is...? | Etra duramanu...? | Does this train/bus stop in Kochi? | Ee tren/bus Kochi nirutthumo? |
| Is this water ok to drink? | Ei vellam kudikkan kollamo? | | |
| How much is a ticket to Kochi? | Kochikku ticket ethra rupayanu? | No parking | Ivide niruthan paadilla |
| | | Speed limit | Vega paridhi |
| One ticket to Kochi, please | Kochikku oru ticket venam? | | |

## Directions

| | | | |
|---|---|---|---|
| Left | Idathekku | Intersection | Koodicherunna sthalathu |
| Right | Valathekku | | |
| Straight ahead | Nere | North | Vadakku |
| Street | Theruvu | South | Thekku |
| Turn left | Idatthekku thiriyuka | East | Kizhakku |
| Turn right | Valatthekku thiriyuka | West | Padinjaru |
| Straight ahead | Nere povuka | Uphill | Kayattathil |
| Past | Kazhinhu | Downhill | Irakkathil |
| Before | Munpu | Which way to the bus stand? | Bus standilekku vazhiyethu? |

## Accommodation

| | | | |
|---|---|---|---|
| Do you have any rooms available? | Ivide oru muri ozhivundo? | Bigger | Valiyathu |
| | | Cleaner | Vrithiyullathu |
| How much is a room for one person/ two people? | Onno/rendo perkkulla murikku vaadeka ethra aanu? | Cheaper | Vila koranjathu |
| | | OK, I'll take it | Njan edukam |
| May I see the room first? | Aadyam muri kandote? | I will stay for one/ two night(s) | Njan onu/randu raatri thamassikkum |
| Bedsheets | Virippe | Please clean my room | Muri onnu vrithiyakkanam |
| Bathroom | Kulimuri | | |

## Time

| | | | |
|---|---|---|---|
| Now | Ippol | Tomorrow | Naale |
| Later | Pinne | Week | Azhcha |
| What is the time? | Samayam enthayi? | Month | Maasam |
| Morning | Ravile | Year | Varsham |
| Afternoon | Uchha | This week | Iyazhcha |
| Evening | Vaikunneram | Last week | Kazhinhayazhcha |
| Midnight | Paathi rathri | Next week | Adutha azhcha |
| Night | Rathri | Hour | Mankoor |
| Yesterday | Innale | Day | Divasam |
| Today | Innu | | |

## Days of the week

| | | | |
|---|---|---|---|
| Monday | Thingalazhcha | Friday | Velliyazhcha |
| Tuesday | Chovvazhcha | Saturday | Shaniyazhcha |
| Wednesday | Budhanazhcha | Sunday | Nhayarazcha |
| Thursday | Vyazhazhcha | | |

## Numbers

| | | | |
|---|---|---|---|
| half | Paadi | 19 | Pathombathuh |
| 1 | Onnu | 20 | Irupathuh |
| 2 | Randu | 21 | Irupathonnuh |
| 3 | Moonnu | 22 | Irupathirunduh |
| 4 | Naalu | 23 | Irupathimoonuh |
| 5 | Anju | 30 | Muppathuh |
| 6 | Aaru | 40 | Nalpathuh |
| 7 | Eezhu | 50 | Anpathuh |
| 8 | Ettu | 60 | Arupathuh |
| 9 | Onpath | 70 | Ezhupathuh |
| 10 | Pathh | 80 | Enpathuh |
| 11 | Pathinonuh | 90 | Thonnooru |
| 12 | Pantharunduh | 100 | Nooru |
| 13 | Pathimoonuh | 200 | Irunooru |
| 14 | Pathinaaluh | 300 | Munnooru |
| 15 | Pathinanjuh | 1000 | Aayiram |
| 16 | Pathinaaruh | 2000 | Randayiram |
| 17 | Pathinezhuh | One million | Pathu-laksham |
| 18 | Pathinettuh | One thousand million (one crore) | Nooru kodi |

Each of Kerala's many religious and caste communities have their own dishes and food terms, and a full glossary would be almost impossible to compile. The following list, however, covers most of what you regularly encounter on menu cards.

| | |
|---|---|
| **aadu nirachathu** | lamb with a rich stuffing of chicken and egg |
| **achar** | a type of sour pickle |
| **appam** | steamed pancake made from semi-fermented rice-flour, with speckled holes |
| **avial** | steamed root vegetables, coated in roughly ground coconut and yogurt – generally without oil |
| **avioli** | a kind of flatfish |
| **bagheri** | small aubergine |
| **biriyani** | rice baked in clay pots with saffron or turmeric, whole spices and meat, and often hard-boiled egg; a Muslim speciality of northern Kerala |
| **chakkal** | jackfruit |
| **chapatti** | unleavened bread made of wholewheat flour and baked on a round griddle-pan |
| **chatni** | a tangy paste, or chutney; in Kerala traditionally made from ground coconut and finely chopped fresh green chillis |
| **chena** | elephant yam |
| **chikoo** | a fruit that resembles a kiwi but tastes like a pear |
| **chop** | minced meat or vegetable surrounded by breaded mashed potato |
| **chota peg** | small measure used for spirits (whiskey, rum, etc) |
| **cutlet** | minced meat or vegetable fried in the form of a flat cake |
| **dhal** | spicy stew made with a base of lentils |
| **dosa** | rice pancake – should be crispy; when served with a filling it is called a masala dosa and when plain, a *sada* dosa |
| **elakka** | cardamom |
| **erachi olathu** | pieces of lamb simmered in ground fennel seeds and other spices until dry |
| **eshtew** | meat stew enriched with coconut, cinnamon, ginger, pepper and chillis, traditionally eaten in Kerala's Christian community |
| **ghee** | clarified butter sometimes used for festive cooking, and often drizzled over food before eating |
| **gram dhal** | dried chickpea dhal |
| **halwa** | sticky Keralan sweet made from rice flour, coconut, *jaggery* (sugar cane) and ghee, often brightly coloured |
| **iddiappam** | a kind of vermicelli made from finely ground rice |
| **iddli** | steamed rice cake, usually served with *sambar* |
| **iddli-vada-sambar** | light meal comprising one *vada* (lentil-flour doughnut), *iddli* and servings of *sambar* and chutney (*chatni*) |
| **inji thayyir** | pungent ginger-based condiments |
| **ishtew** | see *eshtew* |
| **jaggery** | unrefined sugar made from sugar cane |
| **jeera rice** | rice cooked with cumin seeds |
| **jeerakam** | cumin |
| **kada** | quail |
| **kadala** | a spicy mixture of chickpeas and onions |
| **kakairachi** | oysters |
| **kallmakaya** | mussels |
| **kallu** | toddy (alcohol made from fermented pure coconut sap) |

| | |
|---|---|
| kambalanga | bottle gourd (a vegetable similar to a cucumber) |
| kappa | tapioca, usually steamed or sautéed |
| kariyappila | leaves of the curry (a type of laurel) plant, a prime ingredient of savoury Keralan dishes (*karhipatta* in Hindi). |
| kariampu | cloves |
| karimeen | a river fish |
| karimeen pollichathu | river fish marinated in spices and steam-baked in a banana leaf |
| keema | minced meat (usually lamb or goat) |
| khichari | rice cooked with lentils in various ways, from plain to aromatic and spicy |
| kodampuli (kokum) | a kind of tamarind, used as a souring agent |
| kofta | balls of minced vegetables or meat in a curried sauce |
| kootu | maize flour and lentils cooked with plantain, elephant yam and snake gourd |
| kozhi curry | country chicken curry, traditionally eaten in Kerala's Christian community |
| kozhi kootu | spicy chicken and lentil curry |
| kurumulakku | pepper |
| malli | coriander seeds |
| malli illa | coriander leaf |
| manjal | turmeric |
| masala | any mixture of spices |
| meen moillee | fish curry simmered in coconut juice, green chillis, ginger and curry leaves |
| meen vattichathu | fish (usually mackerel or sardines) cooked in red curry sauce and soured with tamarind |
| methi | fenugreek |
| naan | white, leavened bread kneaded with yogurt and baked in a tandoor |
| nakkam | mango and lime pickles |
| olan | a type of stew, often made of lentils and cucumber |
| ozhikan | dhal and *sambar* served in little terracotta pots for pouring over rice |
| paan | a digestive and mild stimulant consisting of areca nut, lime, calcium and aniseed wrapped in a betel leaf and chewed; it is mildly addictive |
| pachadi | vegetables coated with curry leaves and mustard seeds |
| pachari | white rice |
| pachhakai | plantain |
| pachha mulaku | green chilli |
| padavalanga | snake gourd (a long, dark green vegetable) |
| palak | spinach |
| papad/papadam | crisp, thin cracker |
| paratha | north Indian wholewheat bread made with butter, rolled thin and griddle-fried; a little bit like a chewy pancake, sometimes stuffed with meat or vegetables |
| parotta | south Indian bread, made by griddle-frying a wheat-flour dough that's been partly fermented and wound into a coil |
| pathiri | rice-flour bread, a speciality of the Moppila communities of northern Kerala |
| patta | cinnamon    (*contd. overleaf*) |

| | |
|---|---|
| payasam | sweet rice and mung bean pudding, typically flavoured with cardamom. *Paal payasam* is made with rice and sugar; *parippu payasam* with mung beans and molasses; *pazham payasam* with pineapple and banana |
| pilau | see *pulau* |
| pollitchathu | steamed in a gravy of coconut milk, turmeric, chillis, ginger, garlic and shallots |
| pomfret | a flatfish, often stuffed with spicy paste or tandoori baked – tasty but with many bones |
| pulau | also known as *pilaf, pilau* or *pullao*, rice, gently spiced and pre-fried |
| puri | crispy, puffed-up, deep-fried wholewheat bread |
| puttu | cylinders of roughly pounded rice and coconut steamed together |
| puzhukkalari | red-streaked variety of Keralan rice with plump, separate grains |
| rasam | spicy pepper water often drunk to accompany "meals" |
| roti | loosely used term; often just another name for chapatti, though it should be thicker, chewier and may be baked in a tandoor |
| sadya | a traditional feast served at Onam (Hindu harvest festival) |
| sambar | soupy lentil and vegetable curry with asafoetida and tamarind; used as an accompaniment to *dosas, iddlis* and *vadas* |
| sherwarma | rotating kebab, usually made of chicken |
| sharkaravaratti | fried plantain chips smothered in *jaggery* |
| tarka | hot oil infused with mustard seeds and curry leaves |
| thaaravu | duck |
| thaaravu kootu | duck curry, traditionally eaten in Kerala's Christian community |
| thali | combination of dishes, chutneys, pickles and rice and bread served as a single meal on a banana leaf or stainless steel thali dish |
| thoran | vegetables coated in a paste made from fresh coconut and shallots |
| toddy | (*kallu* in Malayalam): Keralan "beer" – made from fermented coconut sap |
| udipi | type of strict vegetarian fast-food cooking named after the pilgrimage town in coastal Karnataka where it originated. The masala dosa is *udipi* cuisine's hallmark snack |
| unakka mulaku chuvanna | red chilli |
| upperi | fried plantain chips |
| uppma | popular breakfast cereal made from semolina, spices and nuts, and served with *sambar* |
| uttapam | thick rice pancake often cooked with onions |
| vada | also known as *vadai*, a doughnut-shaped deep-fried lentil cake, which usually has a hole in its centre |
| vattichathu | spicy casserole flavoured with chillis, turmeric, garlic, fenugreek, black pepper and shallots, and traditionally cooked in a clay skillet |
| vazhuthanaga | small aubergine |
| vellarika | cucumber |
| vindaloo | hot and spicy sauce of Portuguese-Goan origin, whose sour taste comes from a combination of garlic and vinegar |

## Eating out

| | | | |
|---|---|---|---|
| Breakfast | Prathal | Enough! | Padiya! |
| Lunch | Oonu | The menu please | Menu card kanikku |
| Supper | Athazham | The bill please | Billu taru |
| Excuse me, waiter? | Hallo/chetta | I'm a vegetarian | Njan sasyabhojiyaa |
| I've finished | Njan mathiyakkuvaa | Two beers, please | Randu beer tharoo |
| Delicious | Gambeeram | When is closing time? | Eppozha adakkunnathu? |
| Hot/cold | Chutulla/thanuppulla | | |
| Spicy | Erivulla | | |

## Shopping

| | | | |
|---|---|---|---|
| How much is this? | Ithu ethra vilayanu? | I don't want it | Enikyu athu venda |
| That's expensive | Athu villa koothuthalanu | You're cheating me | Ningal enne chadikyukayannalle |
| Less | Kurachu | OK, I'll take it | Sari, njan itheduthollam |
| More | Kooduthal | | |

## Emergencies and trouble

| | | | |
|---|---|---|---|
| Help! | Rakshikkoo! | I've lost my wallet | Ente purse nashtappettu |
| Leave me alone | Enne thaniye vidoo | I want to talk to a lawyer | Enikku oru kananam vakkeeline |
| Don't touch me! | Enne thodaruthu! | | |
| I'll call the police | Njaan policine vilikkum | Can I just pay a fine now? | Njan ippol oru fine adachotte? |
| Stop! Thief! | Nilkoo! kallan! | | |
| I need your help | Enikku ningalude sahaayam venam | I'm sick | Enikku sukhamilla |
| | | I need a doctor | Enikku doctorude sahaayam venam |
| It's an emergency | Ithu athhyaa vashyamaanu | | |
| | | Can I use your phone? | Njaan ningalude phone upayogichoote? |
| I'm lost | Njaan vazhithetti | | |
| I've lost my bag | Ente bag nashtappettu | Where is the toilet? | Toilet evideyaanu? |

# Glossary

**Acharya** Religious teacher.

**Adivasi** Official term for tribal person.

**Agarbati** Incense.

**Agraharam** *Namboodiri-Brahmin colony.*

**Ahimsa** Non-violence.

**Arak** Liquor distilled from rice or coconut.

**Arati** Evening temple puja of lights.

**Asana** Yogic seating posture; small mat used in prayer and meditation.

**Ashram** Centre for spiritual learning and religious practice.

**Ashtanga** Brand of yoga, founded by Sri Krishnamarcharya and his student, Sri Pattabhi Jois of Mysore, and popularized in the West by stars such as Madonna and Sting.

**Atman** Soul.

**Avatar** Reincarnation of Vishnu on earth, in human or animal form.

**Ayurveda** Ancient system of medicine employing herbs, minerals and massage.

**Azulejos** Portuguese-style blue-and-white ceramic tiles.

**Baksheesh** Tip, donation, alms, occasionally meaning a corrupt backhander.

**Bandh** General strike.

**Banyan** Vast fig tree, used traditionally as a meeting place, or to shade people while teaching or meditating.

**Banyain** Cotton vest.

**Batta** Tip.

**Bazaar** Commercial centre of town; market.

**Beedi** Tobacco rolled in a leaf; the "poor man's puff".

**Betel** Leaf chewed in *paan*, with the nut of the areca tree; loosely applies to the nut.

**Bhajan** Devotional song.

**Bhakti** Religious devotion expressed in a personalized or emotional relationship with the deity.

**Bharatanatyam** Classical Indian dance form that originated in the south of India.

**Bhawan** (also *bhavan*) Palace or residence.

**Brahmin** A member of the highest caste group, traditionally priests.

**Bundh** (also *bandh*) Literally "closed", which is why it also denotes a general strike.

**Burra-sahib** Colonial official, boss or a man of great importance.

**Calico** Printed cotton cloth, derived from the name of the city Kozhikode (Calicut).

**Cantonment** Area of town occupied by military quarters.

**Caparison** Decorative covering, or armour, worn by animal; see "nettippattom".

**Caste** Social status acquired at birth.

**Chappal** Sandals or flip-flops (thongs).

**Charas** Hashish.

**Chauri** Fly whisk, used in elephant processions.

**Chayakada** Tea shop.

**Chenda melam** Keralan drum orchestra.

**Chillum** Cylindrical clay or wood pipe for smoking *charas* or ganja.

**Chital** Spotted deer.

**Choli** Short, tight-fitting blouse worn with a sari.

**Chowkidar** Watchman, caretaker.

**Coir** Woven fibre from coconut husk.

**Cot** Bed.

**Crore** Ten million.

**Cupola** Small delicate dome.

**Dalit** "Oppressed", "out-caste"; the term is preferred by so-called "untouchables" as a description of their social position.

**Dargah** Muslim shrine.

**Darshan** Ritual viewing of a deity or saint.

**Devadasi** Temple dancer.

**Desi** Indian.

Devi Goddess.

Dewan Chief minister.

Dhaba Roadside food stall selling local dishes, mainly to truck drivers.

Dham Important religious site, or a theological college.

Dharamshala Rest house for pilgrims.

Dharma Sense of religious and social duty (Hindu).

Dhobi Laundry-man.

Dhurrie Woollen rug.

Dowry Payment or gift offered in marriage.

Dravidian Ancient culture of southern India.

Eve-teasing Sexual harassment of women, either physical or verbal.

Ezhavas One of the lower castes, now among the more upwardly mobile; 29 percent of Hindus in Kerala are *ezhavas*.

Filmi Bollywood soundtrack music – can also be applied to Bollywood-influenced clothing, etc.

Finial Capping motif on temple pinnacle.

Ganja Marijuana leaf (grass).

Gaur Indian bison.

Geiser Hot-water boiler.

Ghat Mountain, landing platform, or steps leading to water.

Godown Warehouse.

Gopi Young cattle-tending maidens who feature as Krishna's playmates and lovers in popular mythology.

Gopura Towered temple gateway.

Guru Teacher of religion, music, dance, astrology, etc.

Gurukkal Master of *kalarippayat* martial art.

Haj Muslim pilgrimage to Mecca.

Harijan Title – "Children of God" – given to "untouchables" by Gandhi.

Hartal Strike.

High ranges Name for the area of the Western Ghat mountains around Periyar and Munnar.

Illam Ancestral home of Namboodiri-Brahmin (upper, priestly-class family).

IMFL Indian-made foreign liquor.

Janmis Hindu landlord, usually member of brahmin caste.

Jati Caste, determined by family and occupation.

-ji Suffix added to names as a term of respect.

Kalam Painting; sometimes used as a shorter form of *kalam ezhuttu*

Kalam ezhuttu Elaborate floor painting.

Kalari See "kalarippayat", also a traditional Keralan gym.

Kalarippayat Keralan martial art.

Khalasi Muslim caste of labourers employed in shipyards.

Kannadi Keralan metal mirrors.

Kathakali Traditional Keralan dance-drama.

Kettu vallam Traditional Keralan rice boats, many of which are now used in the tourist trade.

Kettumaran Catamaran; log-raft.

Khadi Home-spun cotton; Gandhi's symbol of Indian self-sufficiency.

Kirtan Hymn.

Kshatriya The martial caste.

Kudiyattam Ancient Keralan form of ritual theatre – the forerunner of *kathakali*.

Kumkum Powder, used to draw a red mark on the forehead.

Kuttambalam Traditional Keralan temple theatre, where *kathakali* and other ritual dance drama was performed.

Lakh One hundred thousand.

Lathi Sturdy bamboo cane used by police for crowd control.

Lingam Phallic symbol in places of worship, representing the god Shiva.

Lunghi Male garment; long wrap-around cloth – north Indian term for a *mundu*.

Lusitanian Portuguese.

Maha- Common prefix meaning great or large.

Mahadeva Literally "great god", a common epithet for Shiva.

Mahadevi Literally "great goddess", a common epithet for Shiva's wife, Parvati.

Maharaja (*maharana, maharao*) King.

Maharani Queen.

**Mahatma** Great soul.

**Mahout** Elephant-driver or keeper.

**Maidan** Large open space or field.

**Malabar/Malabar coast** The northern coastal part of Kerala, although in times past used to designate the entire region.

**Malayalam** Official language of Kerala.

**Malayali** Keralan (speaker of Malayalam).

**Malluwood** Colloquial term for Malayali cinema.

**Mandala** Religious diagram.

**Mandir** Temple.

**Mantra** Sacred verse or word.

**Marg** Road.

**Masjid** Mosque.

**Math/Matha** Hindu or Jain monastery.

**Memsahib** Respectful address to European woman.

**Minaret** High slender tower, characteristic of mosques.

**Mohiniyattam** Keralan classical dance form performed by women.

**Montane** Highland areas below the tree line.

**Moppila** Keralan Muslim.

**Mridamgan** Drum used in Carnatic classical music.

**Mundu** Length of cotton worn as a sarong by men or women; in Kerala, it's traditionally off-white with a gold border.

**Mutt** Hindu or Jain monastery.

**Namboodiris** Highest caste of brahmins, traditionally employed as priests in temples.

**Nadumattam** Middle of Hindu household's central courtyard – a ritually auspicious point.

**Naga** Mythical serpent; cobra.

**Nairs** Kerala's martial caste (also Nayars).

**Nalukettu** Inner courtyard of a traditional Keralan house; also used to describe antique *tharavadukal* homesteads in which four halls open onto a central courtyard.

**Nangiarkoothu** An ancient theatre form of female mono-acting, associated with *kudiyattam*.

**Natak** Drama.

**Natya** Dance.

**Nettippattom** Golden headdress worn during festival parades by elephants.

**Nilavilakku** Bell-metal oil lamp.

**Nilgai** Blue bull.

**Nilgiris** "The Blue Hills" – Tamil name for the Western Ghats.

**Niwas** Building or house.

**Om** (or AUM) Symbol denoting the origin of all things, and ultimate divine essence, used in meditation by Hindus and Buddhists.

**Onam** Keralan harvest festival (Hindu).

**Ottamthullal** Costumed mono-acting; an irreverent, satirical kind of ritual theatre, performed by a green-faced jester figure wearing a gold headdress.

**Paikappal** Traditional ocean-going ship, in common use over the last millennium, now built in small numbers for the wealthy Gulf Arabs.

**Palanquin** Enclosed sedan chair, shouldered by four men.

**Pali** Original language of early Buddhist texts.

**Pali** Old mosque or church in Kerala.

**Panchakarma** Internal cleansing of the body used in ayurveda treatments.

**Panchaloha** An alloy of five metals – often called "bell metal" – used since ancient times in India to cast ritual and ayurveda utensils.

**Panchavadyam** Traditional Keralan orchestra, comprising five ("panch") different instruments, deployed for Hindu festivals.

**Panchayat** Village council.

**Pradakshina patha** Processional path circling a monument or sanctuary.

**Prakara** Enclosure or courtyard in a temple.

**Pranayama** Breath control, used in meditation.

**Prasad** Food blessed in temple sanctuaries and shared among devotees.

**Pugri** Literally "turban" – often tied with an ice-cream-wafer-shaped fan at the top by *Indian Coffee House* waiters.

**Puja** Worship.

**Pujari** Priest.

**Pukka** Correct and acceptable, in the very English sense of "proper".

**Purana** A genre of ancient Hindu texts, generally in Sanskrit.

**Puruthalum** Raised veranda at the front of a Hindu *tharavad* (ancestral house).

**Raga/Raag** Series of notes forming the basis of a melody.

**Raj** Rule; monarchy; in particular the period of British imperial rule 1857–1947.

**Raja** King.

**Ramayana** Much-loved Hindu epic recounting the story of Lord Rama, Prince of Ayodhya.

**Rangoli** Geometrical pattern of rice powder laid before houses and temples.

**Rath** Processional temple chariot.

**Sadhu** Hindu holy man with no caste or family ties.

**Sagar** Lake.

**Samadhi** Final enlightenment; a site of death or burial of a saint.

**Samsara** Cyclic process of death and rebirth.

**Sangam** Sacred confluence of two or more rivers; an academy.

**Sangeet** Music.

**Sannyasi** Homeless, possessionless ascetic (Hindu).

**Sari** Usual dress for Indian women: a length of cloth wound around the waist and draped over one shoulder.

**Satyagraha** Literally "grasping truth": movement that included Gandhi's campaign of non-violent protest.

**Scheduled castes** Official name for "untouchables".

**Shaivite** Hindu recognizing Shiva as the supreme god.

**Shala** Practice hall, usually in the form of an open-sided shelter, for yoga and meditation.

**Shastra** Treatise.

**Shloka** Verse from a Sanskrit text.

**Shola** High-altitude, stunted, evergreen forest, prevalent in the Western Ghats.

**Sri/Shri** Respectful prefix; another name for Lakshmi.

**Sudra** The lowest of the four castes or *varnas*; servant.

**Sutra** (*sutta*) Literally "thread": verse in Sanskrit and Pali texts.

**Swami** Title for a holy man; lord or master.

**Swaraj** "Self-rule"; synonym for Independence, coined by Gandhi.

**Swaroopam** Old Malayali word for kingdom.

**Tagore** Rabindranth Tagore (1861–1941): famous Bengali mystic-philosopher, artist, composer, novelist and cultural icon.

**Taluka** District.

**Tandoor** Clay oven.

**Tantra** Body of esoteric religious practices rooted in Dravidian forms of worship of the Mother Goddess, in which the power of the deity is invoked and internalized.

**Travancore** Former kingdom of southern Kerala whose capital was Thiruvananthapuram (Trivandrum).

**Tharavad/Tharavadukal** Ancestral Keralan aristocratic home – often made of teak, with gabled tiled roofs, and incorporating rice granaries.

**Thattukada** Literally "hot food" – street stalls selling freshly cooked Keralan cooking.

**Theyyem (also Theyyam/Theyyattam)** A kind of spirit-possession ritual, involving elaborate masked costumes, performed in northern Kerala.

**Thiruvathirakali** Folk dance performed by women at Onam.

**Topi** Pith helmet – now refers to any hat or cap.

**Union territory** Administrative division of India, ruled directly from New Delhi – unlike states, which are semi-autonomous. A status accorded former Portuguese and French colonies, including Goa and Pondicherry.

**Untouchables** Members of the lowest strata of society, formerly considered polluting to all higher castes.

**Uruli** Circular bell-metal or brass vessel, used for cooking and for displaying floating flowers.

**Utsavam** Hindu temple festival.

**Vahana** The "vehicle" of a deity; the bull Nandi is Shiva's *vahana*.

**Vallam** Boat.

**Valia vilakku** Giant oil lamp at the entrance to the main shrine of a Hindu temple.

**Vijayanagar** The last great Hindu empire to rule southern India (1336–1565), from its capital in the Deccan.

**Vedas** Sacred texts of early Hinduism.

**Wallah** Suffix implying occupation, eg *paan*-wallah, rickshaw-wallah.

**Yogi** *Sadhu* or priestly figure possessing occult powers gained through the practice of yoga (female: *yogini*).

**Zamorin** Title given to the former rulers of Calicut.

**Zenana** Enclosed portion of a Muslim house where the women would have lived in seclusion (*purdah*).

# Travel
# store

## Travel

**Andorra** The Pyrenees, Pyrenees & Andorra Map, Spain
**Antigua** The Caribbean
**Argentina** Argentina, Argentina Map, Buenos Aires, South America on a Budget
**Aruba** The Caribbean
**Australia** Australia, Australia Map, East Coast Australia, Melbourne, Sydney, Tasmania
**Austria** Austria, Europe on a Budget, Vienna
**Bahamas** The Bahamas, The Caribbean
**Barbados** Barbados DIR, The Caribbean
**Belgium** Belgium & Luxembourg, Bruges DIR, Brussels, Brussels Map, Europe on a Budget
**Belize** Belize, Central America on a Budget, Guatemala & Belize Map
**Benin** West Africa
**Bolivia** Bolivia, South America on a Budget
**Brazil** Brazil, Rio, South America on a Budget
**British Virgin Islands** The Caribbean
**Brunei** Malaysia, Singapore & Brunei [1 title], Southeast Asia on a Budget
**Bulgaria** Bulgaria, Europe on a Budget
**Burkina Faso** West Africa
**Cambodia** Cambodia, Southeast Asia on a Budget, Vietnam, Laos & Cambodia Map [1 Map]
**Cameroon** West Africa
**Canada** Canada, Pacific Northwest, Toronto, Toronto Map, Vancouver
**Cape Verde** West Africa
**Cayman Islands** The Caribbean
**Chile** Chile, Chile Map, South America on a Budget
**China** Beijing, China, Hong Kong & Macau, Hong Kong & Macau DIR, Shanghai
**Colombia** South America on a Budget
**Costa Rica** Central America on a Budget, Costa Rica, Costa Rica & Panama Map
**Croatia** Croatia, Croatia Map, Europe on a Budget
**Cuba** Cuba, Cuba Map, The Caribbean, Havana
**Cyprus** Cyprus, Cyprus Map
**Czech Republic** The Czech Republic, Czech & Slovak Republics, Europe on a Budget, Prague, Prague DIR, Prague Map
**Denmark** Copenhagen, Denmark, Europe on a Budget, Scandinavia
**Dominica** The Caribbean
**Dominican Republic** Dominican Republic, The Caribbean
**Ecuador** Ecuador, South America on a Budget
**Egypt** Egypt, Egypt Map
**El Salvador** Central America on a Budget
**England** Britain, Camping in Britain, Devon & Cornwall, Dorset, Hampshire and The Isle of Wight [1 title], England, Europe on a Budget, The Lake District, London, London DIR, London Map, London Mini Guide, Walks In London & Southeast England
**Estonia** The Baltic States, Europe on a Budget
**Fiji** Fiji
**Finland** Europe on a Budget, Finland, Scandinavia
**France** Brittany & Normandy, Corsica, Corsica Map, The Dordogne & the Lot, Europe on a Budget, France, France Map, Languedoc & Roussillon, The Loire, Paris, Paris DIR, Paris Map, Paris Mini Guide, Provence & the Côte d'Azur, The Pyrenees, Pyrenees & Andorra Map
**French Guiana** South America on a Budget
**Gambia** The Gambia, West Africa
**Germany** Berlin, Berlin Map, Europe on a Budget, Germany, Germany Map
**Ghana** West Africa
**Gibraltar** Spain
**Greece** Athens Map, Crete, Crete Map, Europe on a Budget, Greece, Greece Map, Greek Islands, Ionian Islands
**Guadeloupe** The Caribbean
**Guatemala** Central America on a Budget, Guatemala, Guatemala & Belize Map
**Guinea** West Africa
**Guinea-Bissau** West Africa
**Guyana** South America on a Budget
**Holland** see The Netherlands
**Honduras** Central America on a Budget
**Hungary** Budapest, Europe on a Budget, Hungary
**Iceland** Iceland, Iceland Map
**India** Goa, India, India Map, Kerala, Rajasthan, Delhi & Agra [1 title], South India, South India Map
**Indonesia** Bali & Lombok, Southeast Asia on a Budget
**Ireland** Dublin DIR, Dublin Map, Europe on a Budget, Ireland, Ireland Map
**Israel** Jerusalem
**Italy** Europe on a Budget, Florence DIR, Florence & Siena Map, Florence & the best of Tuscany, Italy, The Italian Lakes, Naples & the Amalfi Coast, Rome, Rome DIR, Rome Map, Sardinia, Sicily, Sicily Map, Tuscany & Umbria, Tuscany Map,
**Venice**, Venice DIR, Venice Map
**Jamaica** Jamaica, The Caribbean
**Japan** Japan, Tokyo
**Jordan** Jordan
**Kenya** Kenya, Kenya Map
**Korea** Korea
**Laos** Laos, Southeast Asia on a Budget, Vietnam, Laos & Cambodia Map [1 Map]
**Latvia** The Baltic States, Europe on a Budget
**Lithuania** The Baltic States, Europe on a Budget
**Luxembourg** Belgium & Luxembourg, Europe on a Budget
**Malaysia** Malaysia Map, Malaysia, Singapore & Brunei [1 title], Southeast Asia on a Budget
**Mali** West Africa
**Malta** Malta & Gozo DIR
**Martinique** The Caribbean
**Mauritania** West Africa
**Mexico** Baja California, Baja California, Cancún & Cozumel DIR, Mexico, Mexico Map, Yucatán, Yucatán Peninsula Map
**Monaco** France, Provence & the Côte d'Azur
**Montenegro** Montenegro
**Morocco** Europe on a Budget, Marrakesh DIR, Marrakesh Map, Morocco, Morocco Map,
**Nepal** Nepal
**Netherlands** Amsterdam, Amsterdam DIR, Amsterdam Map, Europe on a Budget, The Netherlands
**Netherlands Antilles** The Caribbean
**New Zealand** New Zealand, New Zealand Map

Available from all good bookstores

**Nicaragua** Central America on a Budget
**Niger** West Africa
**Nigeria** West Africa
**Norway** Europe on a Budget, Norway, Scandinavia
**Panama** Central America on a Budget, Costa Rica & Panama Map, Panama
**Paraguay** South America on a Budget
**Peru** Peru, Peru Map, South America on a Budget
**Philippines** The Philippines, Southeast Asia on a Budget,
**Poland** Europe on a Budget, Poland
**Portugal** Algarve DIR, The Algarve Map, Europe on a Budget, Lisbon DIR, Lisbon Map, Madeira DIR, Portugal, Portugal Map, Spain & Portugal Map
**Puerto Rico** The Caribbean, Puerto Rico
**Romania** Europe on a Budget, Romania
**Russia** Europe on a Budget, Moscow, St Petersburg
**St Kitts & Nevis** The Caribbean
**St Lucia** The Caribbean
**St Vincent & the Grenadines** The Caribbean
**Scotland** Britain, Camping in Britain, Edinburgh DIR, Europe on a Budget, Scotland, Scottish Highlands & Islands
**Senegal** West Africa
**Serbia Montenegro** Europe on a Budget
**Sierra Leone** West Africa
**Singapore** Malaysia, Singapore & Brunei [1 title], Singapore, Singapore DIR, Southeast Asia on a Budget
**Slovakia** Czech & Slovak Republics, Europe on a Budget
**Slovenia** Europe on a Budget, Slovenia
**South Africa** Cape Town & the Garden Route, South Africa, South Africa Map
**Spain** Andalucía, Andalucía Map, Barcelona, Barcelona DIR, Barcelona Map, Europe on a Budget, Ibiza & Formentera DIR, Gran Canaria DIR, Madrid DIR, Lanzarote & Fuerteventura DIR Madrid Map, Mallorca & Menorca, Mallorca DIR, Mallorca Map, The Pyrenees, Pyrenees & Andorra Map, Spain, Spain & Portugal Map, Tenerife & La Gomera DIR
**Sri Lanka** Sri Lanka, Sri Lanka Map
**Suriname** South America on a Budget
**Sweden** Europe on a Budget, Scandinavia, Sweden
**Switzerland** Europe on a Budget, Switzerland
**Taiwan** Taiwan
**Tanzania** Tanzania, Zanzibar
**Thailand** Bangkok, Southeast Asia on a Budget, Thailand, Thailand Map, Thailand Beaches & Islands
**Togo** West Africa
**Trinidad & Tobago** The Caribbean, Trinidad & Tobago
**Tunisia** Tunisia, Tunisia Map
**Turkey** Europe on a Budget, Istanbul, Turkey, Turkey Map
**Turks and Caicos Islands** The Bahamas, The Caribbean
**United Arab Emirates** Dubai DIR, Dubai & UAE Map [1 title]
**United Kingdom** Britain, Devon & Cornwall, Edinburgh DIR England, Europe on a Budget, The Lake District, London, London DIR, London Map, London Mini Guide, Scotland, Scottish Highlands

& Islands, Wales, Walks In London & Southeast England
**United States** Alaska, Boston, California, California Map, Chicago, Colorado, Florida, Florida Map, The Grand Canyon, Hawaii, Los Angeles, Los Angeles Map, Los Angeles and Southern California, Maui DIR, Miami & South Florida, New England, New England Map, New Orleans & Cajun Country, New Orleans DIR, New York City, NYC DIR, NYC Map, New York City Mini Guide, Oregon & Washington, Orlando & Walt Disney World® DIR, San Francisco, San Francisco DIR, San Francisco Map, Seattle, Southwest USA, USA, Washington DC, Yellowstone & the Grand Tetons National Park, Yosemite National Park
**Uruguay** South America on a Budget
**US Virgin Islands** The Bahamas, The Caribbean
**Venezuela** South America on a Budget
**Vietnam** Southeast Asia on a Budget, Vietnam, Vietnam, Laos & Cambodia Map [1 Map],
**Wales** Britain, Camping in Britain, Europe on a Budget, Wales
**First-Time Series** FT Africa, FT Around the World, FT Asia, FT Europe, FT Latin America
**Inspirational guides** Earthbound, Clean Breaks, Make the Most of Your Time on Earth, Ultimate Adventures, World Party
**Travel Specials** Camping in Britain, Travel with Babies & Young Children, Walks in London & SE England

For more information go to www.roughguides.com

# Be a houseguest in Gods Own Country

Kerala- the very name conjures verdant backwaters that ply houseboats, ayurvedic massages and plantations heavy with the aroma of spices. With Mahindra Homestays, experience its local flavour guided by your host and savour experiences that nobody else can offer.

Mahindra Homestays offers you the authentic experience of staying with a Kerala family in their home that has been selected for its comfort, cleanliness, safety and originality.

Ply the backwaters on a houseboat, explore a spice plantation, learn to cook a curry, watch a traditional martial art or dance performance, fish for lobster, trek to hidden waterfalls while you explore Gods Own Country. Mahindra Homestays is dedicated to providing you with comfortable, safe and enriching experience of 'The Real India'.

Visit www.mahindrahomestays.com
or call
**UK No.** 02031408422
**INDIA No.** 1800–425–2737
**for booking assistance.**

**Choose from the following destinations**
- Cochin • Alleppey • Thekkady • Munnar
- Wayanad • Kottayam • Kumarakoam
- Varkala • Trivandrum

**Types of homestays**
- Heritage Homes • Plantation Homes
- Modern Homes

**mahindra homestays**

STAY IN FAMILY HOMES – EXPERIENCE THE REAL INDIA

# www.roughguides.com

nformation on over 25,000 destinations around the world

- **Read** Rough Guides' trusted travel info
- **Access** exclusive articles from Rough Guides authors
- **Update** yourself on new books, maps, CDs and other products
- **Enter** our competitions and win travel prizes
- **Share** ideas, journals, photos & travel advice with other users
- **Earn** points every time you contribute to the Rough Guide community and get rewards

# Small print and

# Index

## A Rough Guide to Rough Guides

Published in 1982, the first Rough Guide – to Greece – was a student scheme that became a publishing phenomenon. Mark Ellingham, a recent graduate in English from Bristol University, had been travelling in Greece the previous summer and couldn't find the right guidebook. With a small group of friends he wrote his own guide, combining a highly contemporary, journalistic style with a thoroughly practical approach to travellers' needs.

The immediate success of the book spawned a series that rapidly covered dozens of destinations. And, in addition to impecunious backpackers, Rough Guides soon acquired a much broader and older readership that relished the guides' wit and inquisitiveness as much as their enthusiastic, critical approach and value-for-money ethos.

These days, Rough Guides include recommendations from shoestring to luxury and cover more than 200 destinations around the globe, including almost every country in the Americas and Europe, more than half of Africa and most of Asia and Australasia. Our ever-growing team of authors and photographers is spread all over the world, particularly in Europe, the US and Australia.

In the early 1990s, Rough Guides branched out of travel, with the publication of Rough Guides to World Music, Classical Music and the Internet. All three have become benchmark titles in their fields, spearheading the publication of a wide range of books under the Rough Guide name.

Including the travel series, Rough Guides now number more than 350 titles, covering: phrasebooks, waterproof maps, music guides from Opera to Heavy Metal, reference works as diverse as Conspiracy Theories and Shakespeare, and popular culture books from iPods to Poker. Rough Guides also produce a series of more than 120 World Music CDs in partnership with World Music Network.

Visit www.roughguides.com to see our latest publications.

# Rough Guide credits

**Text editor**: Samantha Cook
**Layout**: Umesh Aggarwal
**Cartography**: Animesh Pathak
**Picture editor**: Jess Carter
**Production**: Erika Pepe
**Proofreader**: Jan McCann
**Cover design**: Nicole Newman, Dan May, Chloë Roberts
**Photographer**: Tim Draper
**Editorial**: **London** Andy Turner, Keith Drew, Edward Aves, Alice Park, Lucy White, Jo Kirby, James Smart, Natasha Foges, Róisín Cameron, James Rice, Lara Kavanagh, Emma Beatson, Emma Gibbs, Kathryn Lane, Monica Woods, Mani Ramaswamy, Harry Wilson, Lucy Cowie, Alison Roberts, Eleanor Aldridge, Ian Blenkinsop, Joe Staines, Matthew Milton, Tracy Hopkins, Ruth Tidball; **Delhi** Madhavi Singh, Lubna Shaheen, Jalpreen Kaur Chhatwal
**Design & Pictures**: **London** Scott Stickland, Dan May, Diana Jarvis, Mark Thomas, Nicole Newman, Sarah Cummins, Emily Taylor; **Delhi** Ajay Verma, Jessica Subramanian, Ankur Guha, Pradeep Thapliyal, Sachin Tanwar, Anita Singh, Nikhil Agarwal, Sachin Gupta

**Production**: Rebecca Short, Liz Cherry, Louise Daly,
**Cartography**: **London** Ed Wright, Katie Lloyd-Jones; **Delhi** Rajesh Chhibber, Ashutosh Bharti, Rajesh Mishra, Jasbir Sandhu, Karobi Gogoi, Swati Handoo, Deshpal Dabas, Lokamata Sahu
**Online**: **London** Faye Hellon, Jeanette Angell, Fergus Day, Justine Bright, Clare Bryson, Aine Fearon, Adrian Low, Ezgi Celebi; **Delhi** Amit Verma, Rahul Kumar, Narender Kumar, Ravi Yadav, Debojit Borah, Rakesh Kumar, Ganesh Sharma, Shisir Basumatari
**Marketing & Publicity**: **London** Liz Statham, Jess Carter, Vivienne Watton, Anna Paynton, Rachel Sprackett, Laura Vipond; **New York** Katy Ball; **Delhi** Aman Arora
**Digital Travel Publisher**: Peter Buckley
**Reference Director**: Andrew Lockett
**Operations Assistant**: Becky Doyle
**Operations Manager**: Helen Atkinson
**Publishing Director (Travel)**: Clare Currie
**Commercial Manager**: Gino Magnotta
**Managing Director**: John Duhigg

# Publishing information

This second edition published November 2010 by
**Rough Guides Ltd**,
80 Strand, London WC2R 0RL
11, Community Centre, Panchsheel Park, New Delhi 110017, India
**Distributed by the Penguin Group**
Penguin Books Ltd,
80 Strand, London WC2R 0RL
Penguin Group (USA)
375 Hudson Street, NY 10014, USA
Penguin Group (Australia)
250 Camberwell Road, Camberwell, Victoria 3124, Australia
Penguin Group (NZ)
67 Apollo Drive, Mairangi Bay, Auckland 1310, New Zealand
This paperback edition published in Canada in 2010. Rough Guides is represented in Canada by Tourmaline Editions Inc., 662 King Street West, Suite 304, Toronto, Ontario, M5V 1M7
Cover concept by Peter Dyer.
Typeset in Bembo and Helvetica to an original design by Henry Iles.

Printed in Singapore
© David Abram, 2010
Maps © Rough Guides
No part of this book may be reproduced in any form without permission from the publisher except for the quotation of brief passages in reviews.
344pp includes index
A catalogue record for this book is available from the British Library
ISBN: 978-1-84836-541-4
The publishers and authors have done their best to ensure the accuracy and currency of all the information in **The Rough Guide to Kerala**, however, they can accept no responsibility for any loss, injury, or inconvenience sustained by any traveller as a result of information or advice contained in the guide.

1    3    5    7    9    8    6    4    2

# Help us update

We've gone to a lot of effort to ensure that the second edition of **The Rough Guide to Kerala** is accurate and up-to-date. However, things change – places get "discovered", opening hours are notoriously fickle, restaurants and rooms raise prices or lower standards. If you feel we've got it wrong or left something out, we'd like to know, and if you can remember the address, the price, the hours, the phone number, so much the better.

Please send your comments with the subject line "**Rough Guide Kerala Update**" to ©mail @roughguides.com. We'll credit all contributions and send a copy of the next edition (or any other Rough Guide if you prefer) for the very best emails.

Have your questions answered and tell others about your trip at ®www.roughguides.com

# Acknowledgements

**David**: Thank you first and foremost to PJ Sinna of Trans Indus and Aadi Kerala, without whose generosity and expertise this guide would be far less comprehensive than it is. Sinna steered me towards many lesser-known highlights across the state, generally smoothed my path (despite continual last-minute changes of itinerary) and answered interminable follow-up questions with great patience. Thanks also to my drivers, Manoj and Haris, for keeping me alive and on track over all those kilometres.

For their kind hospitality and conversation en route, thank you (from north to south) to: Mr Abdul Hakeem of the Sulkha Shipyard in Azikkal; Rosie and Nazir in Thottada; Mr and Mrs C & F Moosa, Thalassery; Victor, Rajini, Ajay and Nisha in Wayanad; Kapila Venu, Irinjalakuda; Sajeev Kurup of Ayurveda Mana; and, as ever, PJ Varghese at the Tourist Desk in Ernakulam. For providing help with transport and accommodation during my trip to the far south, thank you to Kerala Tourism. Fiona Jeffry of Neyyar Dam sent some great background and trekking tips for the area inland of Thiruvananthapuram. Andrew Lubran, touring the hills on his trusty Enfield, tied up some important loose ends in Munnar while I was laid up in Fort Cochin. Fellow Rough Guide wallah, Paul Gray, wrote some useful feedback on the previous edition which helped plug a few holes. And had it not been for the timely intervention of Mrs Amrit Singh, MD of Trans Indus, who helped speed up the beaurocratic cogs in which my visa was trapped, I may never have made it to Kerala at all.

In the UK, I was very fortunate to have veteran author-editor Sam Cook on board to see this book from its raggle-taggle first draft state to the sleek creature it is today. Sam had to cope with more than her fair share of authorial grumpiness over an overloaded couple of months, so thanks to her for doing such a splendid job, and to the other Rough Guide staff members who worked on this book. Animesh Pathak had to process some unusually detailed and complicated specs, and turned in some fine renditions of places that have never been mapped before. Jess Carter found some terrific new images to supplement the outstanding contributions of photographer Tim Draper.

Last, but by no means least, my biggest thank you goes to partner VM, who cared for our two small sons, Morgan (3) and Aeris (1), back home over a very cold winter while I was away researching in Kerala. Without her efforts none of this book could have been written.

# Readers' letters

Thank you to all those readers of the first edition of this guide who took the trouble to write to us with comments and suggestions (apologies to anyone whose name may be missing from this list, or misspelt):

Jonni Aromaa; Sam Athol-Murray; Barry Atkinson; Louise Attwood; Chris Baumann; Berl Peck; Peter Castro; Bill Clark; Malcolm Clark; Lydia Dawson; Ann Day; Hans Dieter Schmitt; Sonia Khan and John Hendry; Christine Foster; Stuart Graham and Beryl Jackson; Sharon "Shazbaz" Foxwell; John Kehoe; Judith and Bill Landles; Hannah McKerch ar; Zak Nields; Joe Norman; Robin Pritchard; GS Rajmohan; Adam Rowland; Pia Russo; Noori Siddiqui; Michelle Superle; David Trelawny-Ross; Geke van der A; Kathryn Barley; Bob Wiggins; Jackie Williams; Rev. Fr Ynte de Groot.

# Photo credits

### Introduction
Sunset on Kerala Backwaters © Michele Falzone/ Getty
Aranmula mural © Sepia/Alamy
*Kathakali* performer © Martin Harvey/Getty
Tea plantation © Jack Simon/Getty
Houseboat on the backwaters © Michele Falzone/Getty
*Pulikali*, or tiger dance © Stringer/India/Corbis
Fishermen, Kollam © Mitchell Kanashkevich/ Getty

### Things not to miss
**01** Snake boat race © Frédéric Soltan/Sygma/ Corbis
**02** Chinese fishing nets © Blaine Harrington III/ Corbis
**03** Treehouse, Wayanad © Dave Abram
**04** Malabari fish © Simon Reddy/Alamy
**05** Papanasam Beach © Dave Abram
**06** *Kalarippayat* © Remi Benali/Corbis
**07** Puram, Thrissur © Frans Lanting/Corbis
**08** A *kathakali* dancer © Asnar/Alamy
**09** Munnar © Bob Krist/Corbis
**10** Backwater cruises © Noble Images/Alamy
**11** Padmanabhapuram © Antographer/Alamy
**12** *Ayurveda* treatment © Yadid Levy/Alamy
**13** Langur, Parambikulam © Darkroom /Alamy
**14** *Sadya* © Simon Reddy/Alamy
**15** Kuttanadi homestay © Dave Abram

### Playing gods colour section
*Theyyem* performer © Stringer/India/Corbis
*Kathakali* at the Kochi Cultural Center © Bob Krist/Corbis
Boys practice at dawn in a dance class at the Kerala Kalamandalam © Stuart Freedman/ Corbis
Initiation of a young *theyyem* performer © Frédéric Soltan/Sygma/Corbis

Muchilot Bhagwatti *theyyem* © Mitchell Kanashkevich/Getty
*Theyyem* Gulikan putting on mask © Christophe Boisvieux/Corbis
*Theyyem* performers waiting for devotees © Mitchell Kanashkevich/Getty
*Kathakali* artists putting on make up © Mitchell Kanashkevich/Getty
*Theyyem* ritual, Kannur District © Mitchell Kanashkevich/Getty

### Elephant madness colour section
*Mahout* checking on his elephant during a temple festival ©Martin Harvey/Getty
Thrissur Puram © Manjunath Kiran/Corbis
Elephant transported on specially adapted truck © AadiKerala/Cochin
Colourfully decorated parasols © Manjunath Kiran/Corbis
Drummers and trumpeters © Lindsay Hebberd/ Corbis
Decorated elephants with parasols, Puram © SCPhotos/Alamy
*Mahouts* feed elephants at Punnathur Kotta Elephant Camp © AFP/Getty
Ganesh and elephant at Punnathur Kotta Elephant Camp © José Navarro/Alamy
Washing a baby elephant, Kodanad © Mel Longhurst/Getty
Detail of *nettippattom* on dressed elephant © Neil Emmerson/Getty

### Black and whites
**p.199** *Pulikali*, or tiger dance © Stringer/India/ Corbis
**p.236** Lion-tailed macaques © Frans Lanting/ Corbis

SMALL PRINT

# Index

Map entries are in colour.

INDEX